YUCATÁN

YUCA

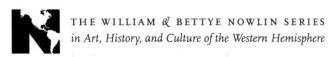
THE WILLIAM & BETTYE NOWLIN SERIES
in Art, History, and Culture of the Western Hemisphere

TÁN

RECIPES *FROM A* CULINARY EXPEDITION

David Sterling

UNIVERSITY OF TEXAS PRESS, AUSTIN

The publication of this book was made possible by the generous support of Ellen and Ed Randall in honor of Laura and Tom Bacon.

Copyright © 2014 by the University of Texas Press
All rights reserved
Printed in Singapore
First edition, 2014

Requests for permission to reproduce material
from this work should be sent to:
Permissions
University of Texas Press
P.O. Box 7819
Austin, TX 78713-7819
http://utpress.utexas.edu/index.php/rp-form

♾ The paper used in this book meets the minimum
requirements of ANSI/NISO Z39.48-1992 (R1997)
(Permanence of Paper).

LIBRARY OF CONGRESS
CATALOGING-IN-PUBLICATION DATA

Sterling, David, 1951–
    Yucatán : recipes from a culinary expedition /
by David Sterling. — First edition.
        pages   cm — (The William and Bettye Nowlin
series in art, history, and culture of the Western
Hemisphere)
    Includes bibliographical references and index.
    ISBN 978-0-292-73581-1 (hardbound : alk. paper)
1. Cooking—Yucatán Peninsula. 2. Maya cooking.
3. Yucatán Peninsula—Description and travel.
4. Yucatán Peninsula—Social life and customs.
5. Mayas—Social life and customs.
I. Title.
    TX716.Y83S74   2014
    641.59'7265—dc23   2013021911

doi:10.7560/735811

PHOTO AND DRAWING CREDITS

Cover photo by Eduardo Cervantes

The initials following photo and drawing
captions represent the following individuals:

AC = Andrés Martínez Canul
AH = Aurea Hernández
DK = David Katzenstein
DS = David Sterling
EC = Eduardo Cervantes
F&KS = Forest and Kim Starr
FPG = Fototeca Pedro Guerra
JC = Julien Capmeil
JFMT = Jorge Francisco Maury Tello
KO = Kevin Oke
MC = Mario Canul
MG = Marie Z. Gardner
MIPA = Manuel Isaias Pérez Alamilla
MM = Miguel A. Martínez de la Fuente
MR = Mark Randall
OM = Otto Monge
RW = Richard Westell

To the
proud
and
smiling
people of
Yucatán

CONTENTS

See page iv for photo and drawing credits.

ACKNOWLEDGMENTS

AT CHRISTMASTIME OF 2009, Diana Kennedy joined me for a special class at my Yucatecan cooking school, Los Dos. During her stay, we had the great pleasure of "*pueblear*-ing," as she called it—driving together from one pueblo to the next, sampling food along the way and talking endlessly about cuisine.

On one of our many jaunts, she pronounced, "David, you absolutely must do a cookbook on Yucatán! You really know the material!" Coming from Diana, it was quite a compliment indeed. I told her that I had approached a few agents with my outline, but all had rejected me, and all for the same reason: they opined that without a TV program or some other media vehicle, my book would be impossible to sell.

When I related this to Diana, she stomped her foot and uttered an expletive. "That's ****! I'm going to put you in contact with my publisher and encourage them to take on your project." The University of Texas Press was just putting the finishing touches on the English-language version of her magnum opus, *Oaxaca al Gusto*, and I was soon introduced to her editor, Casey Kittrell.

My first thanks, then, must go to Diana, without whom I would still be hoping to have a TV show and *then* a cookbook. Furthermore, without Diana's pioneering expeditions into the previously uncharted territory of Mexican cuisine, I would have needed much more than a TV show

to sell a book on what might be considered an obscure regional cuisine.

Casey is every writer's dream of an editor: patient, encouraging, responsive, sharp as a tack, and responsible for shaping my original manuscript from an orgiastic Roman banquet into what I hope is a more digestible buffet. I was also delighted to learn that he is quite a seasoned gastronome himself, which reassured me that the latest culinary trends would not be overlooked in the editing process. Thanks, too, to the University of Texas Press for taking on such an ambitious project from an untested author.

The research for the book was accomplished over the course of ten years. Three scholars affiliated with the Autonomous University of Yucatán were invaluable in the process: Jorge Francisco "Paco" Maury Tello—an archaeology postgrad specializing in Maya ceramics—led me to rare documents, faculty, and other scholarly resources to which I would never have had access otherwise. Carmen Salazar, MSc., from the Botany Department at the same university, helped me conduct the extensive research on Yucatecan ingredients that you will find in Part One, "The Yucatecan Market." I am also thankful for the assistance of linguist Asunción Quintal Pérez in providing me with the correct Mayan names of many dishes in this book.

Special recognition must be granted to my faithful assistant and "Guy Friday," Mario Canul, who performed ceaseless research and planning for my many trips through the peninsula, not to mention applying his suave liaison skills with sometimes secretive local cooks and vendors. He is also responsible for some excellent photography that appears in the book, and if that weren't enough, he is becoming quite a good sous chef, too.

The recipes I have included in this book accumulated and evolved over that same ten-year period. Dozens of Yucatecan and Maya cooks welcomed me into their kitchens—sometimes no more than a rustic shelter with a small wood fire on a dirt floor—to share their recipes with me. They deserve utmost praise, since their Yucatecan dishes recorded herein are about as real as it gets. All of these people are cited with their recipes in the text. In addition to acquiring recipes in this manner, I completed research into historical gastronomy resources, not least of which was a handful of vintage regional Yucatecan cookbooks, which I detail in the Introduction.

During recipe development, it was of vital importance to me to know that the recipes be achievable in home kitchens beyond Mexico. This led me to establish a casual network of avid nonprofessional cooks from coast to coast in the United States and Canada to test a random sampling of the recipes. Criteria had to do with availability of ingredients, clarity of instructions, variables like altitude and climate, and several others. These folks generously cooked, ate, and gave ample constructive criticism afterwards, leading to important insights into and modifications to my basic recipe approach. I thank my testers, listed in alphabetical order: Erin Blaesing-Miller, Grand Rapids, Michigan; Janet Boileau, Ottawa, Ontario; Mario Canul, Mérida, Yucatán; John Cheek, South Egremont, Massachusetts; Anne Holland, Hubbardton, Vermont; Elizabeth Holland, Egremont, Massachusetts; Ryan Keefe, with Emily Naegeli and Elizabeth Pinkham, Chicago, Illinois; María del Socorro Rodríguez Larrache, Mérida, Yucatán; Alexander and Jessica Lawrence, Chehalis, Washington; Carlene McGuire, Jones, Oklahoma; Nancy Packard, Seattle, Washington; Mark Randall, New York, New York; Kevin Rhoades and Carolyn Siegel, Denver, Colorado; Roxanne Rhoades, St. Louis, Missouri; Leigh Salge, San Anselmo, California; Patsy and Wayne Salge, Johnstown, Colorado; Mariela Silveira Rodríguez, Mérida, Yucatán; Donna Smith, Grand Rapids, Michigan; Leanna Staines, San Francisco, California, and Mérida, Yucatán; and Susan Zutz, Minneapolis, Minnesota.

Like any epic, a book of this scope has a cast and crew of thousands, it seems. Literally dozens of people contributed the photography and illustrations you will see, but I wish to highlight one special contributor: my dear friend and colleague Mark Randall. Mark has a gift for capturing the graphic essence of any scene, resulting in unique (and dare I say quirky) photographs that lend energy to this book. I also wish to thank Leslie Doyle Tingle, managing editor, and Kathy Bork, copy editor, both part of the UTP team who assumed the overwhelming task of scrutinizing and whittling until the finished manuscript was publication ready. Finally, word and image were brought together in the handsome graphic design by Derek George of the University of Texas Press.

Without indulging in the kind of maudlin speeches one hears on Oscar night, it would be impossible for me to enumerate all of the many ways in which my partner, Keith Heitke, facilitated this project. As so many writers say of spouses in their acknowledgments, "Thank you for your patience and tolerance of me during the stresses of being an author." Perhaps many writers in the throes of work can be monsters, but I must be the poster child. The concentration, obsessiveness, and single-mindedness required on a project of this scale (and by a first-time author, at that) are surely grounds for divorce. Keith weathered it all, calm as ever, and looked forward to the end result—namely, the food, which he always ate without complaint and frequently with gusto—leading me also to thank him for being a brilliant Royal Taster. Obsessed with flavors and fragrances, and picky in a good way, Keith made countless invaluable comments and critiques about dishes that came out of the Los Dos kitchen. I always anxiously awaited his pronouncement, hopefully, *Calificación*: 10 (Score: 10)—using the 10-point qualification system initiated by our caretaker, Gilberto Canul—and only with the mortification of the chef, never lower than *Calificación*: 8. And now we are all on a diet together.

Finally, a big ¡Gracias! to the many students who have shared a day or two with me at Los Dos. By now, literally thousands have flowed through our doors and left the house full, happy, and with the famous Los Dos apron. As is true for all student-teacher relationships, it remains to be seen who has learned more. Without a doubt, the questions students have asked me and the observations they have made during classes have taken me ever deeper into the endless exploration of the cuisine of Yucatán.

HOW TO USE THIS BOOK

L ONG BEFORE JULIE BLOGGED ABOUT JULIA, when I was sixteen years old, I cooked an anniversary dinner for my parents, working from Julia Child's *Mastering the Art of French Cooking* (both volumes). I remember that I made Suprêmes de Volaille as the main course, and Napoleons for dessert. My ambitious menu took me three days to prepare—and I had a ball! I have cooked many similarly elaborate meals over the years, requiring days of concentrated kitchen time, because nothing is more thrilling to me than an adventure in cooking.

"But," my students frequently ask me, "what do you eat on Tuesday nights in front of the TV?" Fast and easy is the ticket, and pasta and salad dishes are my fallback position.

I have written this book for the two cooks inside of me: the ardent explorer who wants to learn something new and stretch his culinary skills to the limit; and the time-crunched, multitasking businessperson who wants something quick and delicious. I believe that either one or both descriptions will suit most readers, and that there are recipes to satisfy both cooking approaches.

This book leads you on an expedition through Yucatán, collecting recipes from place to place. While recipes are not organized according to standard cookbook categories, coincidentally, the different sections align more or less neatly with traditional organizational niches, which I outline below. Or see the Index to Recipes by Category on page 547 to find recipes organized by category.

APPETIZERS, COCKTAIL PARTY FOOD, AND SNACKS

The sections titled *"Comida Callejera," "La Cantina,"* and *"La Chicharronería* contain dozens of recipes for casual entertaining. Most are quick and easy to prepare.

- **Calabacita frita:** Warm Sautéed Zucchini Dip, p. 276
- **Sikil p'aak:** Vegetable Dip of Toasted Squash Seeds, Roasted Tomatoes, and Chile, p. 285
- **Taquitos de castacán:** Pork Belly Confit Tacos, p. 212

QUICK ONE-POT SUPPERS

In the section titled *"La Cocina Económica"* you will find recipes from women who operate small restaurants in their homes. Most dishes at *cocinas económicas* are inexpensive and very quick and easy to assemble, usually cooked in a single pot or a large skillet. The recipes are easy to scale up for large families or for entertaining, or to scale down for just a few servings.

- **Albóndigas con yerbabuena:** Minted Meatballs in Broth, p. 258
- **Bistec a la cazuela:** Beef and Potatoes Stewed in Oregano and Black Pepper Sauce, p. 265
- **Picadillo en chilmole:** Mincemeat in Charred Chile Sauce, p. 254

SEAFOOD

Seafood of every kind has been central to the Yucatecan table since ancient Maya times. A bounty of recipes for fish and shellfish can be found in several sections of this book: Part Three, "Fertile Shores"; Part Four, "The People's Food"; and Part Five, "Campeche" and "Valladolid":

- **Calamares rellenos:** Breaded Fried Squid Stuffed with Shrimp and Longaniza, p. 306
- **Langosta con leche de coco:** Lobster Tails Poached in Sweet Coconut Milk, p. 182
- **Pescados blancos fritos con alcaparras:** Fried Fish with Capers, Olives, and Chiles in Vinaigrette, p. 401

FANCY DINNERS

In several sections of this book, particularly "Valladolid" (Part Five), you will find recipes that will impress, for which reason I suggest them as "fancy dinners." Some of these dishes are labor intensive, others less so, but for those that do require more time, the recipes explain plan-ahead steps to help you break down the work into manageable units.

- **Faisán en pipián rojo:** Pheasant in Red Squash-Seed Sauce, p. 98
- **Pato con glaseado al Xtabentún:** Duck Magrets in Honey–Anise Liqueur Glaze, p. 154
- **Pollo en Macalú:** Chicken Stewed in Spiced Wine, p. 404

FOR THE INTREPID COOK

The dishes presented in Part Two, "The Maya Heartland," are the oldest in the book, many dating to the pre-Columbian era. All of the dishes—especially the bean and vegetable dishes—are easy to prepare, but most take time and some vigilance at the stove. Foods that include *masa*—ground corn dough—are the real bugaboos, since the preparation of foods with *masa* will require a learning curve for most people. But since so many of the most typical Maya foods are based on *masa*—tamales and tortillas at the core—I encourage you to be brave and take the plunge into a world you may never have explored. A comprehensive overview of *masa* is provided on page 517:

- **Ibewahes:** Bean and Squash-Seed *Tamal*, p. 136
- **Pol'kanes:** Maize, Bean, and Squash-Seed Fritters, p. 111
- **Sopa de joroch':** Zucchini and Squash-Blossom Stew with Tiny Corn Pancakes, p. 124

VEGETARIAN DISHES

Historically, the Mayas have been omnivores, although animal proteins were and remain only an occasional pleasure. Naturally, then, a number of classic Maya dishes are vegetarian. Most of these recipes appear in Part Two, "The Maya Heartland." Today, most of the fat incorporated into these dishes is lard, but you may use good Spanish olive oil instead:

- **Chulibu'ul:** Maya "Succotash" of New Corn and Black-Eyed Peas, p. 117
- **Pipián de frijol:** Black Beans in Red Squash-Seed Sauce, p. 98
- **Toksel:** Toasted Ground Squash Seeds with Lima Beans, p. 113

BAKED GOODS

Bakery treats are such an important aspect of daily eating in Yucatán that I felt it important to devote an entire section to them. Most of the recipes can be found in Part Four, *"La Panadería,"* on page 190:

- **Conchas:** Sweet Breakfast Breads with Flavored Shell-Shaped Toppings, p. 202

- **Hojaldra de jamón y queso:** Sweet and Savory Ham and Cheese Pastry, p. 199
- **Pastel de queso de bola:** Vanilla Layer Cake with Edam Cheese Filling, p. 206

ICE CREAM, SORBETS, CHOCOLATE, AND SWEETS

Where would any regional cuisine be without desserts? Recipes for these are scattered throughout the book, but Part Four, "The People's Food," features a concentration of ice creams and sorbets. Chocolate lovers will want to visit Oxcutzcab in Part Six, "The Pueblos," and in the same chapter you will visit Tetiz, known for its artisanal production of meringues and many other sweet treats and candies:

- **Helado de crema morisca:** Guava, Maraschino Cherry, and Sherry Frozen Custard, p. 249
- **Buñuelos de yuca:** Honey-Drenched *Yuca* Fritters, p. 381
- **Esquimos:** Coconut Sorbet Ice Pops, p. 247

THE SECRET OF YUCATECAN COOKING

To those uninitiated in Yucatecan cooking, a quick review of the recipes in this book may give the impression that it is a highly elaborate cuisine, with an inordinate number of steps and processes required to fabricate a given dish. Certainly, for most of us, a single recipe herein may require the preparation of a few others in advance, as noted in the "To prepare ahead" section of many recipes. In fact, no real Yucatecan would bother with a complicated recipe, except perhaps for feast foods. But the Yucatecan cook enjoys an advantage that we don't: she has within arm's reach everything she needs to whip up a meal in short order. For example, the distinctive seasoning blends known as *recados* are on every pantry shelf or are easily acquired. Or, leftover foods are given a second life by repurposing them: a simple pot of beans or stew can be served to the family on one day, and transformed into a completely different dish on the next. So, for those of us who may be tempted by that second dish, we must go through the pains of preparing the first, too. If you spend some time preparing the key Pantry Staples a day or two in advance, many Yucatecan meals will come together in an hour or less.

Aside from unique ingredients and seasonings, special cooking techniques in Yucatán give foods their characteristic flavor. Learn how to roast chiles, toast spices, and smoke meats in the section titled "Basic Techniques" to give your foods a true taste of Yucatán.

PANTRY STAPLES

The Pantry Staples section (p. 494) provides all of the essential components you will need to assemble full Yucatecan meals. Following is an overview of the staples and a description of how each contributes to the whole:

- *Recados:* Sometimes called "the curries of Yucatán," *recados* are exotic seasoning blends that are used to flavor almost all of our savory dishes. In Yucatán, paste or powdered *recados* are sold by the bag in the central markets; three are available commercially outside Mexico, but most of them you will have to make yourself. Most take only a few minutes: grind a big batch and store in an airtight container.
- **Beans:** Plated meals in Yucatán would be naked without beans in one form or another. Further, they are often prepared as meals in themselves when cooked with meats or vegetables. All bean dishes freeze well, so you can always have some on hand.
- **Salsas:** The essential finishing touch to virtually every dish in Yucatán, salsas may range from mild chopped-vegetable combinations to fiery hot chile purées. All are quick and easy to make. Most last for several days in the refrigerator and others for several weeks in the freezer.
- **Lard:** Don't wince. Pork lard is an invaluable flavoring in cooking throughout Mexico, and as you read more of this book, you will learn that it is not the health demon it was once thought to be. Commercially available lard tends to be quite insipid; this section gives instructions for enriching lard for the recipes in this book.

BASIC TECHNIQUES

Many recipes in this book will refer you to the Basic Techniques section. Spend a few moments before you begin cooking to familiarize yourself with some of them:

- *Masa:* This indispensable dough made of ground corn is employed in everything from beverages and sauces to tamales, tortillas, and cocktail party appetizers. The traditional way of preparing it is easy but labor intensive, involving cooking dried corn, rinsing it, and then grinding it, for which reason shortcuts as well as resources for purchasing ready-made *masa* are offered. *Masa* freezes brilliantly such that it can easily be prepared or purchased in advance.

- **Making tortillas:** Tortillas are the sine qua non of all meals in Yucatán. Spend an hour or so practicing before you plan on serving them at a dinner party.
- **Forming, wrapping, and cooking tamales:** Most tamales in Yucatán are wrapped in banana leaves; a couple are wrapped in corn husks. Techniques for both are provided. Yucatecan methods for cooking tamales range from baking in an oven or underground pit to steaming. Detailed instructions for all are given.
- **Rice:** Along with beans, rice is an essential component of most Yucatecan meals. This section details the pilaf method—the standard cooking technique for rice throughout most of Mexico.
- **Charring/toasting and grinding:** Many recipes in Yucatán include chiles, tomatoes, or onions that have been charred on hot coals or directly over a flame; the next step is to crush and grind the ingredient before including it in the pot. These simple techniques are essential to the flavor and texture of our foods.
- **Working with chiles:** Tips for how to protect your hands and reduce the heat of both fresh and dried chiles are some of the techniques illustrated here.
- **Brining:** The ancient Mayas did not brine meats, but they did use salt to preserve them, giving me poetic license to employ this useful technique for improving the flavor and texture of meat and poultry.
- **Basic smoking techniques:** Many foods of Yucatán are grilled over a wood fire, baked in wood-burning ovens, or cooked in underground pits. This lends many of our dishes a distinctive smoky quality. In this section, I offer three easy smoking methods.

OTHER SECTIONS OF THIS BOOK

- **Part One, "The Yucatecan Market":** Working with a Yucatecan university–affiliated ethnobotanist, I have compiled a list of over seventy ingredients generally found in local markets, many of them indigenous to the region. Several will be unfamiliar to the outsider, and not all will be available elsewhere, although a steady march of imports is making inroads into U.S. and Canadian supermarkets. I provide the rarer varieties for informational value and, where necessary, suggest substitutes in the recipes.
- **Resources:** Except for one or two cases, a great majority of the ingredients and tools required for the preparation of the recipes in this book are now available north of the border. Your local Mexican grocer or even the "ethnic foods" sections of large supermarkets will stock many of these items; others are now widely available through online shopping. The Resources section tells you where to look.

A NOTE ON MEASUREMENTS

Measurements in this book are offered in four basic formats: (1) the way people shop, for example, "one medium onion"; (2) the U.S. Customary System; (3) the metric system; and, when appropriate, (4) cup measures for chopped foods (e.g., "½ cup chopped onion").

I chose this format for a few reasons. I overwhelmingly prefer the metric system. It is wonderfully precise, and also—once you get the hang of it—it is easy to divide or multiply (200 g chopped onion is far easier to scale up or down than ⅔ cup chopped onion). I also include metric measurements because this book may be used in countries where that is the standard. The U.S. Customary System is offered for readers in the United States. Finally, realizing that many home cooks enjoy cooking more when it's just a pinch of this or that, rather than being weighed down with precision, I also offer the "1 medium onion" approach. Hopefully, the variety of measurement formats will satisfy the needs of a wide range of cooking styles.

To avoid awkward numbers, I have taken a few liberties and rounded up or down for neatness. For volumes, I established 1 quart (4 cups) as equal to 1 liter (1000 ml), then divided into cups, half cups, and so on. In this way, while ½ cup of liquid is in truth 118.294 milliliters, in this book it is presented as 125 milliliters; one cup is 250 ml, and so on. For weight, I have done the same thing: in this book 1 kilo is equal to 2 pounds, then greater or lesser weights are calculated accordingly. These minor discrepancies will not affect the finished product.

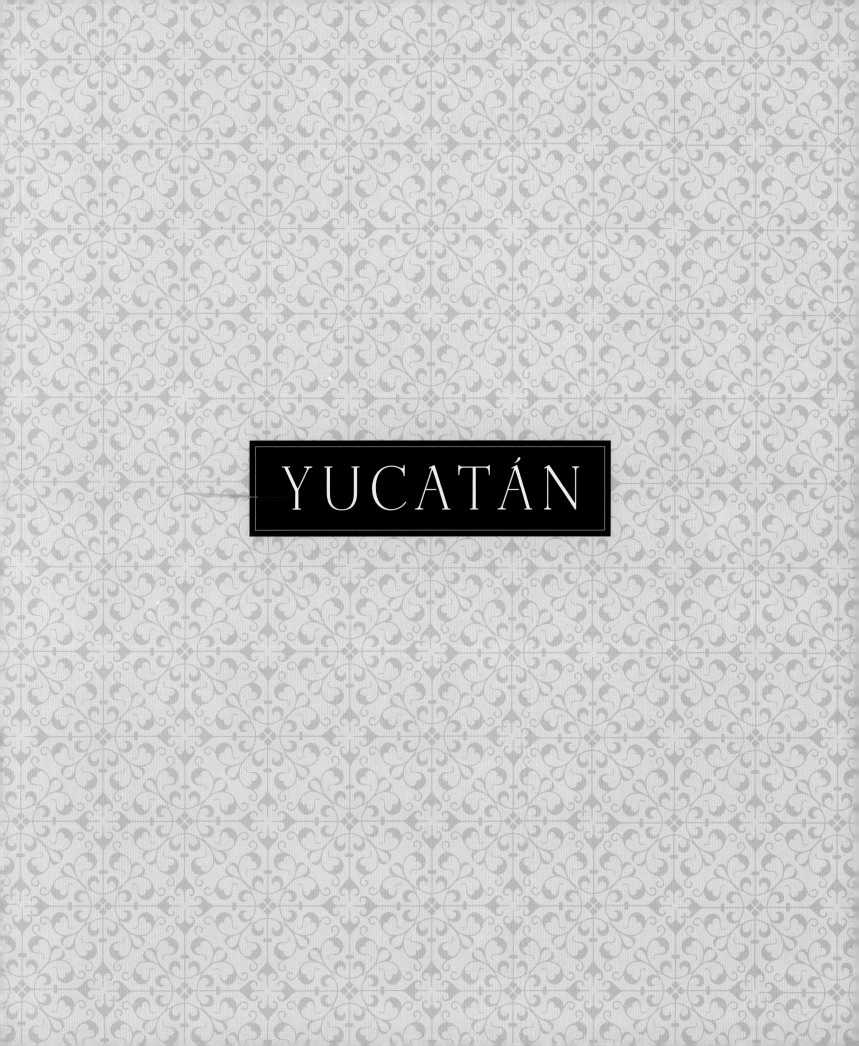

YUCATÁN

INTRODUCTION

¡EXPLORA YUCATÁN!

THIS IMPERATIVE UNDERSCORES the colorful photomontage that shrink-wraps the tour bus making its daily trawl through Mérida's steaming streets. I assume the lure to "explore Yucatán" has worked, because the behemoth double-decker is full. Sophisticated advertising strategies fueled by the deep pockets of the tourism industry weave fabulous fantasies of the adventures that can be yours in the land of the Mayas.

But long before Madison Avenue discovered the wealth to be made in the peninsula, a caravan of conquerors, explorers, archaeologists, missionaries, artists, and pirates heard the call to explore Yucatán and came here to leave their mark, make their fortunes, and—unbeknownst to them—burnish the sheen of the region's exoticism.

The adventurers keep arriving—most recently, those in the culinary arts. Pioneering researcher, writer, and cook Diana Kennedy first came to explore Yucatán in 1958 and has included in her masterly volumes many recipes from the region. In the 1980s, Rick Bayless followed suit and traversed the peninsula documenting some of Yucatán's best-known dishes. Even gourmet cooking magazines and television cooking programs have popularized Yucatecan dishes and ingredients, such as Sopa de lima and *achiote*.

As travel opportunities have increased, so has our hunger for the new and untried, and our wander- and salivary lusts lure us into new gastronomical territory. Increasingly, the gourmet cognoscenti are shattering the myth of

(opposite page) Los Dos kitchen, Mérida. [EC] *(above) The Maya city of Labná as painted by Frederick Catherwood, who traveled through the region in the 1840s.* [LIBRARY OF CONGRESS PRINTS AND PHOTOGRAPHS DIVISION]

1

the homogeneity of Mexican cuisine and boldly exploring its diversity: from Veracruz-style pork and fish dishes, to Oaxacan *moles* and the succulent *carnitas* of Michoacán—and now, the smoky pit barbecues, the citrus-based pickles, and the fiery chiles of Yucatán.

Yucatán: Recipes from a Culinary Expedition evolved as a way of sharing my own savory adventures with students at my cooking school, Los Dos, and with others who love food, travel, and learning. Through the medium of this book, we will travel from remote jungle towns where Mayas concoct centuries-old recipes with a few simple ingredients they grow themselves, to rich tidal estuaries in search of lobster, shrimp, and other aquatic creatures for a fisherman's cookout on a tranquil tropical beach. Descendants of Spain's original landed gentry will invite us into their private haciendas to share elegant recipes from the colonial era. We will hopscotch from pueblo to pueblo across the peninsula, nibbling everything along the way: street foods, the favorite Sunday stew at a family gathering, and the tiny plated dishes that are served gratis with your beer at the raucous *cantinas*.

And at each stop, we will learn recipes that are unique to the region, often updated for modern tastes and achievable in the home kitchen. With each new journey—and every bite—I will share with you an appetizing story, an anecdotal apéritif, a side dish of history, such that your culinary expedition through Yucatán will, hopefully, satiate your hunger while it whets your appetite for more eating adventures.

YUCATECAN CULTURE AND CUISINE

The first thing I make clear to my students when they arrive at Los Dos is that they are not in Mexico; they are in Yucatán. Our cuisine is Yucatecan, not Mexican. Hopefully, they are not terribly disappointed when they realize that we will not be making *mole* in class. Meals they later enjoy in local restaurants prove my point: menus are graphically—almost defiantly—divided between Yucatecan dishes and Mexican specialties.

While Yucatecan cuisine shares much with other regions of Mexico, there are just as many differences as similarities. The same could be said for all things cultural beyond the culinary. These facts are due to several physical realities and historical occurrences.

GEOGRAPHY, HISTORY, POLITICS

The Yucatán Peninsula is geographically isolated from the rest of the country. In fact, for at least a couple of decades after Europeans first landed in Mesoamerica, Yucatán was believed to be an island, and maps of the era depict it as such. In a certain way, the early cartographers were not too far off base: during an interglacial epoch, the peninsula was cut off from the mainland by the sea, resulting in the isolated evolution of several unique species, including the wild turkey of Yucatán, *Meleagris ocellata*. In the 1800s, it was easier for wealthy Yucatecans to travel to Cuba or Europe than to the interior of Mexico—a geographical reality that augmented a sense of psychosocial isolation.

History and politics have contributed to the isolation, too: for many years at different times, Yucatán claimed sovereignty as a republic wholly separate from Mexico, and many battles were fought to keep it so. This almost palpable ideological isolation from the rest of the country is perpetuated in the present day by Yucatecans themselves, some of whom retain a "good old days" mentality and would just as soon secede from the union—again.

It is risky and foolish to generalize about anything such as a regional psychology. Still, I must say that I have experienced more than a few situations in which native Yucatecans invested a fair amount of wind in distinguishing between "them" and "us"—"them" invariably being folks from the rest of Mexico.

This attitude extends to the table: even market vendors defend the battle lines. For example, cilantro comes in two forms—local or *chilango*. Here, *chilango* is a somewhat pejorative reference to anyone or anything from central Mexico. When the locally grown herb is not available, Yucatecan vendors will offer you the import, lowering their eyes and whispering apologetically, "Es chilango."

The upside of this consensual isolation is that native-born Yucatecans exhibit a profound pride of place that manifests itself in strong local cultural traditions. And these traditions are uniquely Yucatecan thanks to the valiant energies put forth in this ongoing social play of parsing "them" versus "us."

Gastronomically speaking, this hyperactive cultural separatism pays off in surprising and delicious ways. While

(opposite page) Map of Yucatán. Courtesy of Yucatán Today

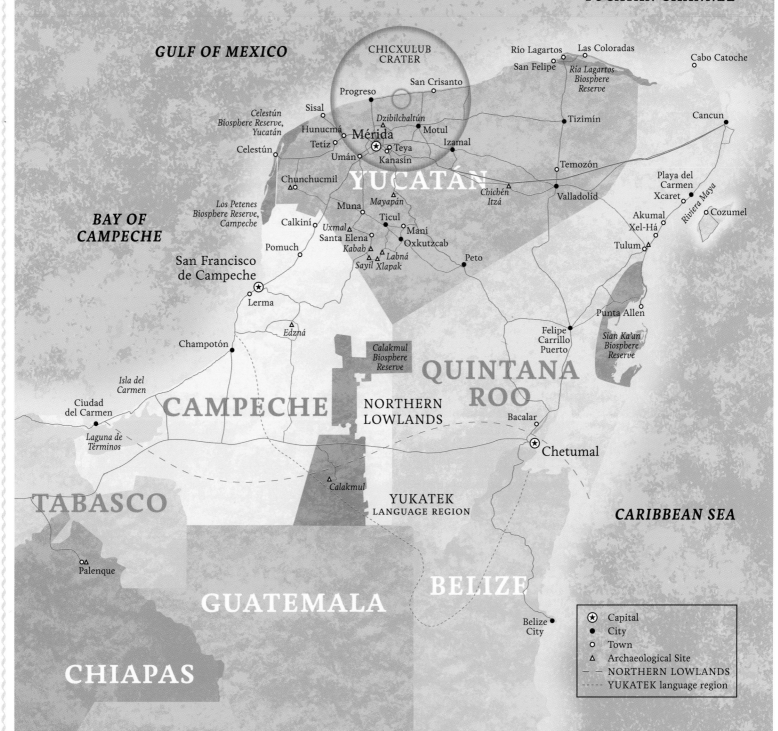

YUCATÁN CHANNEL

GULF OF MEXICO

CHICXULUB CRATER

Río Lagartos
Las Coloradas
San Felipe
Ría Lagartos Biosphere Reserve
Cabo Catoche

Celestún Biosphere Reserve, Yucatán

San Crisanto
Progreso
Sisal
Dzibilchaltún
Motul
Hunucmá
Mérida
Izamal
Teya
Tetíz
Kanasín
Umán

Tizimín

Cancun

Temozón

YUCATÁN

Chunchucmil

Chichén Itzá

Valladolid

Playa del Carmen
Xcaret

Riviera Maya

BAY OF CAMPECHE

Los Petenes Biosphere Reserve, Campeche

Muna
Mayapán
Ticul
Calkiní
Uxmal
Maní
Santa Elena
Oxkutzcab
Kabah
Labná
Pomuch
Sayil *Xlapak*

Peto

Akumal
Xel-Há

Cozumel

San Francisco de Campeche

Tulum

Lerma

Punta Allen

Edzná

Felipe Carrillo Puerto

Sian Ka'an Biosphere Reserve

Champotón

Calakmul Biosphere Reserve

QUINTANA ROO

Isla del Carmen

CAMPECHE

NORTHERN LOWLANDS

Bacalar

Ciudad del Carmen

Laguna de Términos

Chetumal

Calakmul

TABASCO

YUKATEK LANGUAGE REGION

CARIBBEAN SEA

Palenque

GUATEMALA

BELIZE

Belize City

CHIAPAS

⊛	Capital
●	City
○	Town
△	Archaeological Site
— —	NORTHERN LOWLANDS
⋯⋯	YUKATEK language region

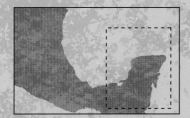

culinary fusions certainly happened in Yucatán (I am thinking of Pavo en escabeche: New World turkey stewed in Old World vinegar), it seems that, for all the reasons outlined above, many Yucatecans prefer to keep their boundaries well traced. In this way, most of the oldest dishes still retain their Mayan names, such as *sikil p'aak* (a paste or dip composed of tomatoes and squash seeds). *Pan árabe* (Arabic bread, or pita), on the other hand, carries a bona fide passport of foreign origin. With some exceptions, most of our delicious fusions happen at the moment of eating: a crispy, toasted Lebanese *pan árabe* dipped into the earthy Maya *sikil p'aak* is the perfect example, and something I encourage you to try when you visit Yucatán.

PRE-COLUMBIAN FOODS

We have some knowledge of the foods consumed by the ancient Mayas prior to the arrival of Europeans, thanks to the archaeological record. We know, for example, that squash was domesticated in southern Mexico as early as 4900 BCE. Corn and *yuca*, too, appear early in the peninsular fossil record, introduced before 3000 BCE. And as for Yucatán's much-prized wild turkey, some 70 percent of the identifiable bone content found in a trash heap of Mayapán—a Late Postclassic (thirteenth-century) Maya capital—were those of this native turkey species.

In fact, the list of pre-Columbian foods in Yucatán is mouthwateringly long. Fruits like guava and papaya; vegetables and root vegetables like *chaya* and jícama; lima beans; and the remarkable and now broadly distributed flavorings vanilla, allspice, *cacao*, and chile—all demonstrate wild populations in the lowland Maya area and have most likely been the subjects of some degree of agricultural manipulation by local human populations since at least 3400 BCE.

But how did the ancient Mayas combine these ingredients into dishes that surely pleased the palate as well as satisfied hunger? While we can decode some "recipes" in Mayan glyphs on food vessels and murals and in codices, we learn much more about the menu of the Mayas after Europeans arrived and began to document the dishes they saw and savored in this New World.

Not surprisingly, the written records of these recipes are largely preoccupied with the Mesoamerican staple—maize (*Zea mays*)—something never previously tasted by the Europeans, and something of obviously vital importance to their new hosts. A recipe for tamales is elaborated by Bartolomé de las Casas: "They had an abundance of maize bread, which was mixed with ground beans, as they make them. The beans are like lupines." While we are not certain exactly which local bean las Casas is referring to, it is evident in markets throughout Yucatán that the same technique of mixing beans with *masa* continues to the present day in tamales like Pimes (p. 106) and several others.

Corn found many gastronomical expressions beyond tamales. Fray Diego de Landa describes a popular Maya beverage: "They also toast the maize and then grind it and mix it with water into a very refreshing drink, putting into it a little Indian pepper or *cacao*." He may be combining a couple of beverages he remembered drinking: *atole de pinole* (*k'áaj sa'* in Mayan) features dried field corn that is toasted and ground, mixed with water, flavored with honey or salt, then cooked until thickened. And T'anchukwa' (*xtáan chukwa'*, p. 466) is a cooked maize porridge to which ground *cacao* is added. Both beverages are still prepared in Yucatán today.

PRE-COLUMBIAN COOKING METHODS

Las Casas, Landa, and other early gourmands also documented Maya cooking methods. One of the foremost of these was smoking. The Mayas used smoke as a preservative and, one presumes, as a flavoring for many foods, including corn, chiles, meat, and fish. Archaeological research and anthropological fieldwork demonstrate that the Mayas have traditionally cooked foods in underground ovens (*p'íib*) or on the *barbacoa* (a wooden rack placed above a fire and used for roasting or smoking, a method and word imported from the Antilles); they also steamed or boiled foods in pots, or simply placed them directly in the hot ashes of a fire—in short, all the cooking techniques still in use throughout Yucatán today.

CONTACT AND BEYOND

The Yucatecan table changed dramatically after European contact. On Columbus' first American voyage, a pantry full of foreign ingredients was introduced: garbanzos, olive oil, vinegar, black pepper and other spices, capers, raisins, olives, almonds. By the second and third voyages, more bounty had arrived: pigs, citrus trees, sugarcane. Gradually, each of these ingredients was absorbed into the local cuisine, and by now all have become indispensable in many Yucatecan recipes.

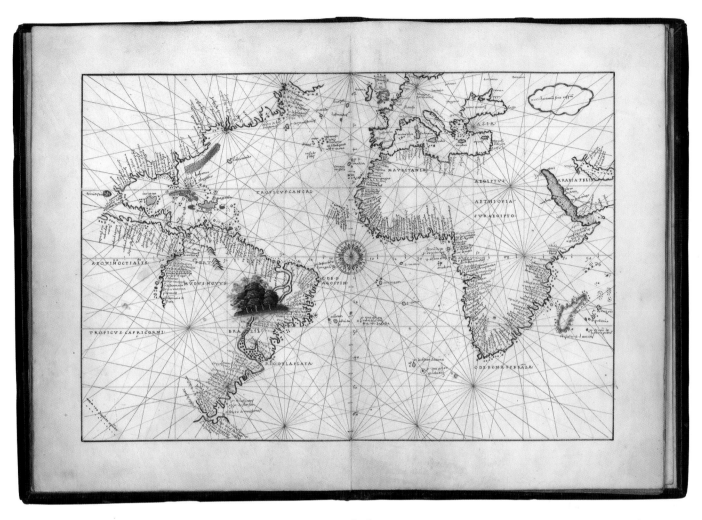

World map of 1544, by Battista Agnese, depicts "Iucatan" as an island. [LIBRARY OF CONGRESS GEOGRAPHY AND MAP DIVISION]

Not only ingredients but also culinary traditions arrived with the Europeans, each leaving its mark on Yucatecan cuisine. The Spanish and Portuguese brought the art of sausage making; the Spanish brought pickling techniques; the French introduced fine baking; and centuries later, the Lebanese brought spit-roasting. And new introductions continue: pancakes (*panqueques*) are popular breakfast fare; pizza and pasta are local favorites for the evening *cena*; and novel fusions like French crêpes filled with Mexican *cajeta* are offered as treats at the movies.

The recipes in this book reflect the panoramic history of the peninsula: from traditional Maya foods and later Spanish dishes, to up-to-the-minute culinary trends.

"YUCATÁN," "MAYAN," AND OTHER NOMENCLATURE

Given the peninsula's recent "discovery" in gourmet circles, menu items like "Yucatán Grilled Shrimp" or "Mayan Chicken Skewers" are appearing with flash-fire speed. The thoughtful diner might well ask not only what is "Mayan chicken" but also "Where or what is 'Yucatán'?"

To start, some grammatical clarification is in order. "Yucatán" is a proper noun, more specifically, a place name. "Yucatecan" is the accepted adjectival form in English to describe that which or one who hails from Yucatán. (Therefore, it makes as much grammatical sense to say "Yucatán Grilled Shrimp" as it does to say "France Pastry.")

Even some of my students confess they aren't exactly certain where it is they have landed when they visit Los Dos. Is Yucatán a state or a peninsula? Or is it a wholly separate province? Residents, too, sometimes display ambivalence regarding what "Yucatán" refers to and what exactly is "Yucatecan." Ask a native anywhere in the peninsula, "Are you Yucatecan or Mexican?" and he will likely answer, "I am Yucatecan." On the other hand, ask a young professional from Quintana Roo, "Are you Yucatecan?" and she will answer a resounding "No!" even though the state of Quintana Roo is located in the Yucatán Peninsula. But if you ask both of them, "Is Cochinita pibil a Mexican dish or a Yucatecan dish?" they will unhesitatingly respond "Yucatecan!" regardless of whether they enjoy this pulled pork classic in Quintana Roo or Campeche. State identities are recent glosses, but the identity of being Yucatecan seems to be primal.

So back to the questions: What is the place I refer to when I use the word "Yucatán"? And what layers of meaning are communicated by the term "Yucatecan"?

GEOGRAPHY AND IDENTITY

First, a brief history and geography lesson. The Mayas are the indigenous people of this region. The Mayan language is still spoken by 1.5 million people in Mexico, and Maya culture is vibrant. The area the ancient Mayas occupied was vast, including all of what is now considered the Yucatán Peninsula and extending south into several countries of Central America. Occupation of the region has been dated to around 9000 BCE. The Maya civilization grew to enormous importance throughout Mesoamerica, with impressive ceremonial centers and extensive trade networks. The civilization reached its peak between 300 and 900 CE, known as the Classic period, and gradually diminished in power and importance thereafter and up to the arrival of Europeans.

When the Spanish *conquistadores* landed in Mesoamerica, the soil on which they first set foot was in fact this Maya region. Three decades later, in 1544, a world map by Italian cartographer Battista Agnese perpetuated a common misunderstanding of the time: Yucatán was drawn as an enormous island between a sketchy North American coast and Cuba. The island encompassed all of what would eventually become the present-day states of Campeche, Yucatán, and Quintana Roo and even encroached into other Mexican states and northern Central America.

As the Spaniards learned the extent of this uncharted land, maps were redrawn. But "Yucatán" by the mid-1500s was still a vast terrain with no political divisions other than cities and pueblos and spread well beyond modern-day borders.

The concept of state identity in the Yucatán Peninsula is a relatively recent phenomenon. Campeche was long considered one of the political "departments" of Yucatán and did not achieve independent statehood until 1863. Quintana Roo changed from a federal territory to a state only in 1974. Therefore, the modern states of Yucatán, Quintana Roo, and Campeche were all formed by partitioning the earlier province of Yucatán, the boundaries of which had in turn been defined from the previously more amorphous place depicted on the Agnese map.

So to answer the question "What is 'Yucatán'?" we can answer that it is one of the thirty-one states in the Mexican union. It is also the name still used to describe a peninsula. Natives of the region sidestep the split personality of the word by specifying "the state of Yucatán" or "the Yucatán peninsula." I adopt the same strategy in this book, stipulating "Yucatán state" or "Yucatán Peninsula" as appropriate.

Beyond political history, geographical evolution, and even cultural identity, there are other criteria that guide us in our usage of the adjective "Yucatecan." Topography and language also come into play.

Because the zone that encompasses the entire reach of the ancient Mayas is so geographically extensive and geologically varied, modern anthropologists and archaeologists subdivide the zone into two distinct topographical areas: highlands and lowlands. The highlands are further subdivided into southern and northern highlands, and the lowlands into southern, central, and northern lowlands. Yucatán—whether that depicted in the Agnese map or in Google maps—corresponds to the northern lowlands.

Language groupings also help us pinpoint our terminologies. The Mayan language is actually a family comprising twenty-eight distinct languages, although linguists acknowledge their close relationship. One of these is known as Yukatek (or Yucatec), evolved from the earlier language called Yukatekan, which in turn evolved from a Proto-Mayan language. The range of the Yukatek language corresponds almost identically to the terrain of the northern lowlands—a terrain identified by its original inhabitants as *Ma'ya'ab* (Mayab).

For these reasons, the territory, culture, and cuisine we

shall explore in *Yucatán: Recipes from a Culinary Expedition* will be those that can be found in the northern lowlands in the region occupied by the Yukatek-speaking Mayas. I shall employ the adjectives "Yucatecan" or "*yucateco*" to describe the people and the cultural products of this entire region regardless of which modern state they may be from.

"MAYA" VERSUS "MAYAN"

"Mayan" is another hot-button word circulating in circles ranging from the culinary to the spiritual-holistic (e.g., "Mayan crystals"). In current archaeological and anthropological parlance, which has informed the terms I have used in this book, the word "Mayan" is reserved exclusively for the language, while "Maya" is used for everything else: the Maya race, Maya ceramics, Maya cuisine, even (saints help us) Maya crystals. "Mayas" is the proper plural for describing the people.

Second, and more important, the Mayas occupied a vast territory that included the Yucatán Peninsula but that also extended well beyond into parts of Central America. Therefore, the word "Maya" to describe a cuisine or a culture should never be used interchangeably with "Yucatecan." More specifically, "Yucatecan cuisine" might indeed include some Maya foods, but "Maya cuisine" is not necessarily Yucatecan.

"AUTHENTIC" VERSUS "TRUE"

After all this precision with regard to terminology, and historical and cultural accuracy, you might assume I am also a stickler for "authentic" recipes. But frankly, I don't believe in such a notion as "authenticity," at least as far as food is concerned. Everyone swaps recipes, and every cook adds her own *sazón*—or unique and flavorful touch. If you were a Yucatecan traveling to the United States for the first time and asked someone for an "authentic" meatloaf recipe, you would be bombarded by thousands of responses if not incredulous stares. There simply is no such thing. The same is true here: Pavo en escabeche (and every other dish in Yucatán) will certainly have some recognizable attributes from one version to the next—but I learned quickly that even the most devout traditional cooks here will approach each dish in slightly different ways. Finally, time changes everything—the *panucho* of today bears only a faint resemblance to its predecessor of the 1950s much less to its early-twentieth-century ancestor.

A recurring reference throughout this volume is to a 1910 cookbook entitled *La verdadera cocina regional* (True regional cuisine). The title became my watchcry as I wrote. What I have attempted to offer you here, then, is a *true*—if not *authentic*—taste of Yucatán. I have tried to get at the essence of each dish and therefore at times may exaggerate certain flavor profiles toward that end. Generally speaking, too, I take these liberties when historical sources give me at least a modicum of permission to do so. I offer my use of smoked bacon and dairy products as examples.

When asked, "What is the key flavor or ingredient indispensable to Yucatecan cooking?" my answer is invariably "Smoke." The cooking methods—even the utensils—used by my Yucatecan teachers all impart the ethereal essence of smoke to the cuisine. Foods are charred directly in the coals; pots are balanced atop wood fires, or, even if on the stovetop, the well-worn pot (often a couple of generations old) has acquired a patina of smoke and burnt fat that undeniably affects the flavor of foods. In addition, the region has a centuries-long history of smoking foods, and today, meat smoking has become a small industry in a handful of pueblos.

Hence my use of smoked bacon: a bit of it in some dishes adds a hint of that essential smokiness. And after all, my use of bacon may not be so far off base: a smattering of recipes from vintage regional cookbooks include *tocineta*—fat-striated, salt-cured pork belly that at times may have been smoked. Another example in my effort to impart smokiness to foods is my use of the chipotle chile—an almost heretical act to some Yucatecans since the chile is thought to be "too Mexican." But because the chipotle is smoked, it seems to me to be an appropriate occasional addition, too.

Finally, in some recipes I have suggested the use of dairy products—from thick Mexican *crema* to tangy *queso cotija*. Until the middle of the twentieth century and the broader availability of refrigeration in the peninsula, dairy did not have the culinary importance in Yucatán that it did in central Mexico, although several recipes from vintage regional cookbooks do specify it. I have chosen to employ it in dishes where it seems natural (for instance, in early-twentieth-century recipes in which French touches were increasingly embraced) and because today it is being more widely used as influences continue to arrive from beyond our borders.

Food keeps changing, and the cuisine of Yucatán is no exception. Thank heaven for that, or we might just fall asleep in our *frijoles*. The consumption of food is as basic as how we grow it or catch it, cook it, and eat it. But beyond those basics, the permutations are endless, based on locale, history, even customs and beliefs. If as a documentarian I have captured for you a *true* taste of Yucatán as it may have been in the past and as it is at this point in time, then I have accomplished something. Future generations will revisit that truth and change the definition of "true regional cuisine" yet again. The most important thing I have learned in my culinary expedition is that there is only one truth with regard to food, and I quote my dear friend and partner, Keith: "People keep eating."

¡Buen provecho!

HISTORICAL RECIPES

In addition to entering the kitchens of contemporary Yucatecan cooks to learn their culinary secrets, I also completed extensive research into historical resources while writing this book, not least of which were vintage regional cookbooks.

The oldest I found, titled *Prontuario de cocina para un diario regular* (Handbook for everyday cooking), was written in 1832 by doña María Ygnacia Aguirre of Mérida. It is a brief volume of only thirty-two pages, but is full of important historical tidbits regarding the cuisine of Yucatán at that time and contains recipes that most likely date to the mid-1700s and before—while Mexico was still a Spanish colony. It is fascinating to the culinary historian to see that even in those years dishes familiar to us were already present: Spanish *albóndigas*, fish in *escabeche*, and a handful of Maya tamales, to name a few.

Another marvelous discovery was *La verdadera cocina regional* (True regional cuisine), published in Valladolid in 1910 by Manuela Navarrete A. During my research, a new "Collector's Edition" of the book was fortuitously released, rescued and reprinted to the letter by Greisy G. Arjona Martín from a battered volume found on a shelf at the home of a friend. *La verdadera cocina regional* includes many classic dishes of the region's cuisine, most of them specific to Valladolid.

Still more recent is the comprehensive *Cocina yucateca* (Yucatecan cooking), by Lucrecia Ruz *vda.* de Baqueiro, originally published in 1944 by El Porvenir in Havana, Cuba. By this point, the repertoire of Yucatecan dishes is extensive—the book contains over 400 recipes—and up-to-date—cooks are instructed to purée foods in a blender (or if you don't have one, use your *molcajete*).

All of these cookbooks make a bow to locally available ingredients and indigenous recipes, but their upper-crust Spanish colonial timbre cannot be masked. Spanish imports such as wines from Málaga or Jerez are frequently on ingredient lists, as are many Old World spices such as black pepper that would have been expensive prestige items.

Prontuario de cocina para un diario regular was expanded and updated in 1896. The cookbook sets aside an entire section (although at the rear of the book) devoted to what might be called "fully formed" Yucatecan dishes—Mucbilpollo (p. 430), Mechado (p. 397), Cochinita pibil (p. 420), Papadzules (p. 280), and several others. It surprised me to learn that during this period—the rule of pro-French president Porfirio Díaz, the throes of the Caste War of Yucatán, and the eve of the Mexican Revolution—Yucatecan cuisine finally came of age and expressed its own unique identity and pride.

Many of the recipes found in these books are alive and well, prepared lovingly by *mamás* and *abuelas* for family and friends to the present day. Still others are less frequently found, but are fondly remembered by this or that older relative, and a handful are all but extinct. The vintage recipes I chose for inclusion in this book are a representative sampling, with an emphasis on those falling into disuse, since rescuing them seemed to me to be not only a fascinating but also an important task.

(opposite page) Baking class in Mérida, ca. 1900. [FPG]

1

The YUCATECAN
MARKET

TWO LIVE TURKEYS BOUND TOGETHER at the feet seem oddly tranquil as a squat, portly man lowers them onto the floor alongside cages filled with other doomed birds. Chickens, ducks, and guinea fowl squawk and chatter, competing in decibels with a tinny, impromptu band. A nearby table is piled high with bags of peanuts and crates of eggs hawked by a shaggy-headed boy of no more than twelve years of age. Stooped men and women with white hair and white clothes sell stacks of deep green five-pointed *chaya* leaves, bouquets of yellow squash blossoms, clusters of glistening red radishes, or bunches of aromatic sage-green medicinal herbs. Others sell assortments of earthy-smelling warm tamales, deftly dousing them with rich red sauces or mixtures of cabbage and chile, customers greedily gobbling them from their fingers. Does this description offer a view of the Maya market as it was 300 years ago? Or that of only yesterday? In truth, it could be either, and whether in the tranquil pueblos or in swelling metropolises, the scene is the same today.

FRUTERIA
"ALEX"
le ofrece: FRUTAS y VERDURAS FRESCAS DE PRIMERA CALIDAD...

Pozole vendors in the Mérida market. [MR]

BEFORE THE ARRIVAL OF EUROPEANS, the markets of Yucatán were brimming with the products of land and sea. Some scholars speculate that the Maya market would have had many times the quantity of food items that were available in Europe in 1492, largely because of the diversity of species in the tropics, coupled with a longer growing season.

The roster of ingredients changed considerably in the 500 years after European contact. Yet it is astonishing to read a list of the Mayas' precontact market goods and compare it to the list of today. I translate and paraphrase a Yucatecan historian, italicizing those items still present in contemporary markets: *cloth of both cotton and sisal*; *sisal cord*; *statues of deities*; *sleeveless and collarless shirts*; flint blades; *honey*; wax; *vanilla*; *copal resin*; chicle; *medicinal herbs*; *paper*; *chile*; *beans*; *vessels of wood, stone,* and *ceramic*; *stone mortars*; slaves; skins; exotic bird plumage; rubber balls for the sacred ball game; *salted fish*; and *salt*. Perhaps some things are best left off the shopping list.

The tiniest town still has its central market, with vendors and shoppers—all neighbors—living in proximity and attending the market daily. The larger urban zones of San Francisco de Campeche, Mérida, and Valladolid all boast impressive market structures and even compounds of multiple buildings that receive thousands of shoppers every day, the largest of these being in Mérida.

THE MAYA MARKET

Some of the most dramatic evidence for pre-Columbian markets in the Maya lowlands is a series of 18 murals discovered at the site of Calakmul in the state of Campeche. The illustrations and glyphs would all seem to depict a bustling marketplace where people are buying or selling everything from salt and tamales to polychrome pots, tobacco, and tools for auto-sacrifice. The North Plaza of Calakmul, where these murals were found, appears to have several of the physical characteristics of many marketplaces, specifically, a cluster of narrow structures running between two sidewalks, with two-sided rooms looking out to each sidewalk—resembling nothing so much as stalls for vendors. With their own gods and revered in society, Maya merchants constituted what we might think of as the middle class. One scene in the Calakmul murals shows a merchant selling maize gruel to a satisfied customer. The Classic Mayan hieroglyphs *aj ul* at upper left signify "maize gruel person."

The Maya market as depicted in murals at Calakmul. [AUREA HERNÁNDEZ AFTER CARRASCO VARGAS ET AL. 2009, FIG. 5]

PORTAL DE GRANOS The first formal market of colonial Mérida was constructed on the esplanade of the Ciudadela de San Benito, an old fortress built to defend the city from a threatened pirate attack. The original program, ordered in 1770, called for the construction of five massive *portales* (colonnades), only one of which was ever completed, the Portal de Granos. With its thirty-three arches along the front and two on the sides, the façade of Portal de Granos is still the widest in Mérida, measuring about 387 feet (117.84 m).

Stereoscopic postcard of the Mérida market, c. 1900. The colonnaded building at left is the Portal de Granos; other market buildings surround it. At rear is the Catedral de San Ildefonso, and in the middle ground is one of Yucatán's signature windmills, this one drawing water for the market's needs. [FPG]

MERCADO CENTRAL / LUCAS DE GÁLVEZ

To contend with Mérida's growing population, the market has been extended over the decades. One of the most popular of these extensions—Lucas de Gálvez—was inaugurated on Independence Day, 16 September 1887. In those early days, it had a thatched roof, three galleries with 553 stalls, and a windmill for drawing water. With a renovation inaugurated in 1949, today's market claims 156,000 square feet (14,500 m2), with almost 2,000 vendors selling everything from fruits, vegetables, kitchen equipment, and toys to tins for crematory remains and potions for "white magic." Many of the more than 100,000 daily visitors to the market pass through the colonial colonnade of Portal de Granos on their way to Lucas de Gálvez, which still stands at the intersection of Calles 67 and 54 (visible in the background). The market never sleeps: cleaning crews finish by 3:00 am, and the food stalls that served them through the night close, too, just as other merchants are arriving to start the next day of selling. From 5:00 am until about 8:00 am, some 8,000 people take shortcuts through the market on their way to work or school. Then, slowly, other merchants arrive, all the stalls open, and the market is bustling by 9:00 am. It is a rhythm that continues 7 days a week, 365 days a year, not even stopping to catch a breath at Christmas or New Year.

INDEX TO INGREDIENTS

[MR]

FRUITS AND VEGETABLES

There is a very large and fresh tree that the Indians call on; *it bears a fruit like largish small calabashes, soft and tasting like butter; it is fatty and of much substance and nourishment. It has a large kernel, a thin skin, and is eaten cut in slices like a melon, and with salt.*

—FRAY DIEGO DE LANDA, 1566

[MR]

AGUACATE

BOTANICAL / *Persea americana* Mill. / Family Lauraceae
ENGLISH / avocado
MAYAN / *on*

DESCRIPTION: Native to Mesoamerica, the avocado has been incorporated into countless dishes now found on the international table. The most consumed variety in Yucatán is a large, pear-shaped fruit about 6–7 inches (15–18 cm) in length, with thin, smooth, dark green skin. The flesh is soft with a pale green to yellow color lightening toward the center, where one large seed is located. The avocado was one of the earliest domesticated trees in the neotropics. In the Maya region, evidence of the consumption of varieties cultivated in family orchards since at least 3,400 years ago has been found.

The primary growing season for avocados in Yucatán is July–October, although they can be found year-round. The Hass avocado variety, patented in California in 1935, is available in supermarket chains, but is only rarely found in local markets.

CULINARY USES: The main consumption of avocado in Yucatán is sliced, as a plate garnish or as a topping for tacos. Its most famous use must surely be in the preparation of guacamole—a word derived from Náhuatl: *ahuacamolli* (*ahuacatl* = avocado + *molli* = sauce), recipe variants for which are almost infinite.

[MC]

[EC]

ANONA / ANONA COLORADA, ANONA ROJA, CORAZÓN

BOTANICAL / *Annona reticulata* L. / Family Annonaceae
ENGLISH / bullock's-heart, bull's-heart, custard apple
MAYAN / *óop, poox, ts'ulil poox*

DESCRIPTION: *Anona* acquired its English names because of both form and flavor: "bull's-heart" refers to its symmetrical heart shape, and "custard apple" describes the flesh's creamy color, smooth texture, and delicately sweet taste. The bulbous, lobed fruit, measuring about 3–6 inches (8–15 cm) wide, contains between fifty-five and seventy-five small seeds. Probably native to Guatemala and Belize, *anona* was distributed naturally throughout the Yucatán Peninsula and the Caribbean; it is now cultivated in the tropics globally. Growing season is December–March.

CULINARY USES: In Yucatán, the mature fruits of *anona* are consumed fresh. The pulp may be served with a bit of sugar, or it may be mashed to include in ice cream, sorbet, or *agua fresca*—refreshers made of water, puréed fruit, and sugar.

BONETE / CUAGUAYOTE, PAPAYA DE MONTAÑA

BOTANICAL / *Jacaratia mexicana* A.DC. / Family Caricaceae
ENGLISH / wild papaya
MAYAN / *k'úumche'*

DESCRIPTION: This space age–looking fruit—a relative of papaya—gets its Spanish name from its shape: "*bonete*" is the word for the ducal hat worn by nobles and high orders of the Catholic church. The fruits, which are 5–7 inches (13–18 cm) tall and 1½–2½ inches (4–6 cm) wide, are characterized by five vertical ribs or fins that flare out top to bottom. Native to broad swaths of southeastern Mexico and Central America, *bonete* is rarely planted; rather, the fruits are harvested from the wild in season, April–May. *Bonete* only occasionally appears in the markets, and its survival is considered to be threatened.

CULINARY USES: *Bonete* is consumed as a hand fruit and has a taste similar to papaya. Fray Diego de Landa reported that the Mayas resorted to eating the bark of the tree during times of famine after the conquest; other colonial chroniclers mention its consumption as a conserve "with a taste of citron" and as a beverage.

CAIMITO / CAINITO, ZAPOTE CAIMITO, CAYUMITO

BOTANICAL / *Chrysophyllum cainito* L. / Family Sapotaceae
ENGLISH / star apple
MAYAN / *chi keejil*

DESCRIPTION: When this fruit is sliced open across the width, the configuration of the flesh and seed cells radiates from the center like a star, giving *Chrysophyllum cainito* L. its English name. *Caimito* originated in Panama and arrived in Yucatán prior to European contact, probably even before the arrival of the first Mayas. Throughout the tropics, the tree is prized as an ornamental. The purplish fruit is spherical or ellipsoid, ranging in size from 2 to 6 inches (5–15 cm). The skin and rind are inedible, containing a bitter, milky latex. For this reason, the French call the fruit *pomme du lait* (milk apple). The season for *caimito* is April–June.

CULINARY USES: Fruits are consumed fresh. Never bite into a *caimito*; instead, you must slice it open, being careful not to allow any of the latex to touch the pulp. It can then be eaten with a spoon or the flesh scraped out to make *agua fresca*.

[MC]

[MC]

CALABAZA / CALABAZA LOCAL, CALABAZA DE PEPITA MENUDA

BOTANICAL / *Cucurbita moschata* Duch. ex Poir. / Family Cucurbitaceae
ENGLISH / winter squash, West Indian pumpkin, butternut squash, Cuban pumpkin
MAYAN / *k'úum*

DESCRIPTION: The genus *Cucurbita* originated in tropical America. It is composed of approximately twenty-seven species, nineteen of which are wild and six, domesticated; the center of diversity is Mesoamerica. *Cucurbita* has been cultivated for at least 4,000 years in the Yucatán Peninsula, where a great diversity exists and where it is still possible to find its wild ancestor. It continues as one of the most important species of all Mesoamerica since it forms part of a nutritionally complementary trio along with corn and beans. The fruits of this squash are varied, although the most common form seen in the markets is flattened with segmented ridges all the way around. The skin is very thin and dark green when young and small (2–6 in. / 5–15 cm in diameter), thick and yellow when it matures and enlarges (up to 12 in. / 30 cm in diameter). Young squash is harvested July–October, mature ones, November–December.

CULINARY USES: Young *Cucurbita moschata* is consumed in a variety of ways in Yucatán: it is a principal ingredient in Puchero (p. 350), or it might be cut into bite-sized pieces and added to a pot of cooked beans. Mature fruits have a special value in that they can serve two purposes: the small, brownish seeds (*pepita menuda* in Spanish; *sikil* in Mayan, p. 61) are extracted, toasted, ground, and used in a range of dishes; if the flesh of the mature fruit is not fed to livestock in the *solar*, or household garden, it may be covered in burnt-sugar syrup and baked in a *píib*.

[MR]

[MC]

CALABAZA DE PEPITA GRUESA / XCAITA, CALABAZA PIPIANA

BOTANICAL / *Cucurbita argyrosperma* Huber ssp.
argyrosperma / Family Cucurbitaceae
ENGLISH / cushaw
MAYAN / *(x) ka'*

DESCRIPTION: *Cucurbita argyrosperma* was domesticated in southern Mexico around 7,000 years ago. This squash is one of the first fruits harvested in the *milpa*, or crop field: young ones are gathered July–August, and mature ones, September–October. The spherical form of the species can reach a diameter of 8 inches (18 cm). The distinctive pattern of the outer skin features white and dark-green striations. The flesh, too, is whitish to pale yellow and almost translucent. The seeds of this species are valued as much or more than the flesh, such that the fruit itself is rarely found for sale in the markets. The seeds have a white body and, occasionally, a gray-green border and measure ½–1 inch in length (1.5–2.8 cm). Because *C. argyrosperma* grows and spreads rapidly, forming an effective weed control, it is often the first crop to be planted.

CULINARY USES: *C. argyrosperma* is consumed in Yucatán as a vegetable when it is very young, fried in lard and salted, or boiled in water with salt and Seville orange juice. Its flowers are chopped and fried with onion, mixed with scrambled eggs, or added to a soup called Sopa de joroch' (p. 124). As it matures, the flesh becomes very fibrous, such that it is undesirable as food for humans and is used instead as feed for pigs and barnyard fowl. However, the seeds of this species are particularly prized: they may be toasted, salted, and eaten whole, or shelled and ground to become the rich green sauce of Yucatán's famous Papadzules (p. 503).

CALABACITA / TSOLITA, CALABAZA ITALIANA, CALABACÍN

BOTANICAL / *Cucurbita pepo* L. /
Family Cucurbitaceae
ENGLISH / summer squash, zucchini
MAYAN / *ts'ol*

DESCRIPTION: *Cucurbita pepo* L. is the world's most extensively grown and polymorphous of the genus. Among its long list of cultivars are such diverse forms as the crookneck, acorn, and zucchini squashes, as well as the Halloween and pie pumpkins of the United States and Canada. In Yucatán, it is the least cultivated squash with the least diversity, with only one variety—zucchini—appearing in the markets, and then only infrequently. *C. pepo* is notable for being the oldest cultivated squash, and one of the oldest of all species to be domesticated in Mesoamerica, with archaeological remains dating to approximately 8750 BCE. The *calabacita* is a long, slender cylinder (4–6 in. / 10–15 cm in length) of a light green color with white streaks. The flesh is a pale yellow-green and has soft, edible seeds when the fruit is young. The plant flowers June–August; young fruits are harvested in August.

CULINARY USES: Young *calabacita* is used much like the *moschata* variety, appearing in soups and stews. Fruits, stems, and flowers are all consumed.

*Those which close the opening to the throat
of the netherworld are a* camote *and a* jícama.

—CHILAM BALAM DE CHUMAYEL, 1775–1800

[MIPA]

CAMOTE / BONIATO, BATATA

BOTANICAL / *Ipomoea batatas* (L.) Lam. / Family Convolvulaceae
ENGLISH / sweet potato
MAYAN / *iis*

DESCRIPTION: This starchy root vegetable has long played an important role in the life of the Mayas, both as a food and as a symbolic "lid" to the underworld. For this reason, in some places the root is harvested only at noon, because farmers consider it a less risky hour to open the passageway to darkness. In past times, children made a bracelet of thread painted indigo blue and hung from it the bone of an agouti, or paca (*jaleb* in Mayan, p. 88), a small burrowing animal, believing this to be a lucky charm to help them easily locate *camotes*. There are four principal varieties in Yucatán: "Cuban," white (*blanco*), purple, and yellow. The flesh of the first three is white, that of the last, yellow. Each variety, measuring 6–10 inches (15–25 cm) in length, has a slightly different texture and degree of sweetness.

The main season for *camote* is November–February, although it can usually be found year-round in the market because it can be stored for long periods.

CULINARY USES: *Camote blanco* is the most consumed of the four varieties in Yucatán. It is a common ingredient in Puchero (p. 350). It may be candied in sugar or honey. In rural Maya communities, it is still cooked in the *k'óoben*, or cooking hearth, nestled among the hot ashes, or it is cooked "buried" in the *píib* (p. 418). It is also combined with maize *masa* to make a special *atole*, or porridge. Sweetened *camote* is also used to fill Pastelitos (p. 201), the tiny Yucatecan empanadas dusted with powdered sugar.

CANISTÉ / MAMEY AMARILLO, ZAPOTE BORRACHO

BOTANICAL / *Pouteria campechiana* Baehni / Family Sapotaceae
ENGLISH / canistel, eggfruit, yellow sapote
MAYAN / *kaniste'*

DESCRIPTION: *Canisté* is native to the region stretching from southeast Mexico (including the Yucatán Peninsula) south to Panama. The skin and flesh are a pale yellow-orange color, and the fruit shape varies dramatically, from spherical to an elongated egg shape measuring 1½–2½ inches (4–6 cm) in length. The flesh is sweet and soft with a color and texture that many compare to a cooked egg yolk, explaining another of its English names. Although it is still occasionally cultivated in private orchards, it rarely appears in the markets. It fruits November–February.

CULINARY USES: Mature fruits are consumed fresh or puréed with milk to make a refreshing beverage. It is also used in pies similar to pumpkin pie, as well as cupcakes, pancakes, and preserves.

[F&KS]

They have a small tree with soft branches containing much sap, whose leaves they eat as a salad, tasting like cabbage and good with plenty of fat bacon. The Indians plant it wherever they make their homes, and then have the leaves for gathering the whole year.

—FRAY DIEGO DE LANDA, 1566

CHAYA / ÁRBOL ESPINACA, ESPINACA MAYA

BOTANICAL / *Cnidoscolus chayamansa* McVaugh /
Family Euphorbiaceae
ENGLISH / tree spinach
MAYAN / *chaay, chay, chaykeken*

[MC]

DESCRIPTION: *Chaya* has long been a staple of Yucatecan cuisine. Related to poinsettia, it is a bushy perennial that can grow up to 20 feet (6 m) in height. Its three- to five-lobed leaves resemble the maple leaf and can measure up to 12 inches (32 cm) long and 10–11 inches (30 cm) wide. *Chaya* has been cultivated since pre-Hispanic times and is still planted in family gardens or close to the house as an ornamental, making it easily accessible for daily use and to sell for subsistence income. There are several varieties of *chaya*, but the most common, *chayamansa*, cannot reproduce sexually; as a domesticated plant it must therefore be tended by human beings, propagated by means of cuttings. Among the Mayas of Yucatán and the Q'eqchi Mayas of Guatemala, *chaya* remains a significant part of the staple diet and is the main dietary source of green, leafy vegetables. Although found widely throughout the Maya world, the greatest variety of names for the plant and widest knowledge of its use are found in Yucatán, which points to the region as the area of origin and the place where *chaya* was ultimately domesticated. It is found year-round in the markets, but during the rainy months (June–November), it is more abundant, and the leaves are more tender.

CULINARY USES: The leaves of *chaya*, which taste something like kale or chard when cooked, are exceptionally high in protein, Vitamins A and C, niacin, riboflavin, thiamine, and carotene, as well as minerals such as calcium, iron, potassium, and phosphorus. In fact, its nutritional content is two- to threefold greater than that of most edible leafy green vegetables. *Chaya* should not be eaten raw: the leaves contain a high level of hydrocyanic acid and therefore can be toxic when consumed in quantity. However, just one minute of boiling destroys most of the acid. Further, *chaya* is covered with invisible microfibers that can be irritating to the skin; people with skin sensitivities should wear gloves when handling it. Because *chaya* is rather tough, the leaves should be plunged into boiling, salted water and simmered over moderately high heat for 20 minutes, drained, and chopped before being incorporated into a recipe. In Yucatán, there are many recipes that call for *chaya*, such as tamales (Dzotobilchay, p. 130), scrambled eggs, and even beverages. It is also sautéed with onions, garlic, and bell peppers to make a nourishing side dish, Chayas fritas (p. 129)—perhaps less nourishing but more delicious if we follow Landa's suggestion to use plenty of fat bacon.

CHAYOTE / CHAYOTERA

BOTANICAL / *Sechium edule* (Jacq.) Swartz /
Family Cucurbitaceae
ENGLISH / christophene, vegetable pear, mirliton,
chayote, alligator pear
MAYAN / *k'i'ix pach k'uum* (in disuse)

DESCRIPTION: A member of the squash family, chayote is unusual in that, rather than spreading along the ground, its vine must climb up a vertical surface. The fruit measures 3½–5 inches (9–12 cm) in length; it is pale green, and the flesh is watery and somewhat insipid, with a vaguely sweet taste. It has one large, soft edible seed in the center, which has a slight flavor of almonds. There are two varieties of chayote: a smallish one with a smooth skin, and a larger one covered with spines. Chayote is native to broad swathes of Mexico and Guatemala. It is harvested year-round in Yucatán.

CULINARY USES: When chayote is sliced in half lengthwise, it has the whimsical appearance of the sole of a shoe. Stuffed with meat, the dish is known as Chancletas, or "sandals" (p. 353). Chayote is a prime ingredient in the regional stew Puchero (p. 350).

CIRICOTE / SIRICOTE, ZIRICOTE

BOTANICAL / *Cordia dodecandra* A. DC. / Family Boraginaceae
ENGLISH / zericote (Belize)
MAYAN / *k'oopte*

DESCRIPTION: One of the most valuable and used trees of the peninsula—as much among the ancient Mayas as in contemporary times—*ciricote* is native to Yucatán and is now distributed throughout southern Mexico and into Guatemala and Belize. All parts of the tree are so valued that wild populations are badly deteriorated, and, unfortunately, it is now considered a vulnerable species. The robust tree is identifiable by its large, rounded leaves, which fall when the tree produces beautiful, bright orange flowers prior to fruiting. The fruit is the size of a small guava—about 1–1½ inches (3–4 cm) long—green when young and yellow when mature. Its time of greatest fruition is April–May, but when consumed green it can be harvested sooner.

CULINARY AND OTHER USES: The fruit of *ciricote* is somewhat insipid when raw, such that the greatest consumption of it is as a preserve in dark syrup: the popular *dulce de ciricote*. The stiff leaves of the tree are surprisingly rough, like fine sandpaper; they have been used since ancient times for washing pots and to clean and smooth gourd utensils. It is perhaps the wood that is the most coveted part of the *ciricote* tree: it is extremely hard with beautifully contrasting dark and light grain. Its durability and natural patterning make it a favored material for flooring and a top choice for furniture makers. It is also prized for its acoustic qualities as well as its beauty in the fabrication of guitars. The trees are frequently used as ornamental plants in parks and gardens.

[MC]

[MC]

CIRUELA / JOCOTE

BOTANICAL / *Spondias purpurea* L. / Family Anacardiaceae
ENGLISH / Spanish plum, hog plum, purple mombin
MAYAN / *abal*

DESCRIPTION: Although the translation of *ciruela* is "plum," the fruit bears no resemblance to the European plum, nor are they even related. In the same family as the mango, the *ciruela* is oval shaped and about 1–1½ inches (3–3.5 cm) in diameter. It has a large pit and little flesh. Depending on the variety, it turns yellow, orange, or red when it matures. *Ciruela* is a native of southern Mexico and Central America. In Yucatán, there is great diversity, with thirty-two varieties; each tree fruits at different times of year, but the major abundance occurs from May to September.

CULINARY USES: When mature, the *ciruela* is made into a beverage or included in sorbets. Just before maturity, the tart, almost sour taste of *ciruela* is enjoyed with a pinch of chile powder and salt. At this green stage, too, the sourness of the fruit is important in various Yucatecan dishes, such as Pipián rojo (p. 96) and Chilmole de frijol con puerco (p. 267). The pulp of the fruit is cooked and mixed with toasted, ground squash seeds to make a paste or dip called Sikil abal (p. 286).

COCO

BOTANICAL / *Cocos nucifera* L. / Family Arecaceae
ENGLISH / coconut
MAYAN / none

DESCRIPTION: The coconut is one of the most used plants in the world, and every part of it is employed. It produces a beverage, fiber, food, fuel, and even utensils. The origin of coconut is disputed, but it is generally agreed that it was naturally dispersed to tropical coasts around the world by means of the fruits floating and drifting on the seas. The edible part of the fruit measures about 4–6 inches (10–15 cm) in diameter. *Coco* is available year-round but is most plentiful March–May.

CULINARY USES: An impressive sight in the markets of Yucatán is the scores of burlap bags filled to overflowing with hairy coconuts. And always seated nearby will be a group of teenagers wielding machetes, hacking away at the hard exterior to expose the sweet meat inside. In Yucatán, the meat of coconut is consumed with a spritz of lime juice and a sprinkle of ground chile. Whole peeled coconuts are stacked on ice, a straw penetrating a small hole at the top and into the coconut water inside, sold as a refreshing drink. Throughout the peninsula, vendors carry wooden trays full of sweet treats made of coconut, like Cocadas (p. 165). Many desserts feature coconut, too, such as Pay de coco—Coconut Macaroon Pie—(p. 164) and Pastelitos—Fruit-Filled Crescent Pastries (p. 201).

[One palm] is a low, very spiny palm whose leaves are very short and thin, and serve no purpose; these bear great bunches of a round green fruit, of the size of pigeons' eggs. When the husk is removed there remains a very hard kernel, inside of which is a pit the size of a hazelnut, of good taste and useful in times of poor harvests.

—FRAY DIEGO DE LANDA, 1566

COCOYOL / COYOL

BOTANICAL / *Acrocomia aculeata* (Jacq.) Lodd.
ex Mart. / Family Arecaceae
ENGLISH / macaw palm, macauba palm, grugru palm
MAYAN / *tuk'*

DESCRIPTION: Many small, round fruits can be seen bobbing about in dark pools of sugar syrup in colorful plastic tubs in Yucatán's markets. Some of these may be *ciruela* or nance (see below); others will be *cocoyol*—a member of the coconut family. This is a favorite treat of Yucatecan children, a "fun food" on the order of jawbreakers. The nut of *cocoyol* has a thin coating of what seems somewhat like coconut meat covering an extremely hard shell. The whole nut goes into your mouth, and you chew and suck to get off all the sweet flesh, a process that can take hours or even days. Finally, when none of the meat is left, kids place the nut on a stone and use another stone to smash it open. Inside is the "very hard kernel" to which Landa refers and which indeed resembles a hazelnut but tastes like coconut—the prize for all that hard work of mastication. Fruits are spherical, 1–1½ inches (3–4 cm) in diameter. *Cocoyol* fruits October–January.

CULINARY AND OTHER USES: In addition to its being cooked in sugar syrup, *cocoyol* is used in a variety of traditional remedies in Yucatán, and the hard outer shell is carved into buttons, beads, and a variety of other personal items.

[MC]

[MR]

ELOTE

BOTANICAL / *Zea mays* L. / Family Poaceae
ENGLISH / corn, maize
MAYAN / *nal*

DESCRIPTION: One of the most vivid experiences of visiting the Yucatecan market is to breathe in the earthy aroma of steaming corn, the cobs plucked from battered pots, sprinkled with chile and lime juice. Other times, you will spot stacks of brown cobs: this is *píibinal*, or smoky corn that has been roasted underground in a *píib* (p. 418). *Zea mays* remains a cornerstone of Maya civilization as well as that of the greater part of the Americas—and in modern times, throughout the world. The fresh cob of *Zea mays* is called "*elote*" in Spanish, when the kernels are soft and milky; once fully matured and dried, the kernels are called "*maíz*." In Yucatán, several distinct varieties can be found, varying in the size of the cob (which ranges anywhere from 3 to 8 in. / 8–20 cm in length), the number of rows of kernels, the time to reach maturity, not to mention the color of the kernels: yellow, white, red, and blue, although in Yucatán the most common and popular to consume in its fresh state is *elote blanco* (white). While a considerable amount of *elote* that is sold in the market is "imported" (usually from other parts of Mexico), the Mayas continue planting their *milpas* in a tripartite cultivation system used for centuries—corn, beans, and squash. The principal harvest period of fresh *elote* is September-November, although it is available throughout the year.

CULINARY USES: *Elote* is a common street food seen everywhere in Mexico, and Yucatán is no exception, where you will hear vendors singing "¡Hay elotes!" (Corn on the cob here!) throughout the day. Fresh, steaming cobs are impaled on wooden sticks for eating convenience, enjoyed unadorned or with any number of condiments. *Elote* is also an important feature in many recipes of the Yucatecan table. Kernels sliced from the cobs are used in the preparation of many dishes of ancient Maya origin: tortillas or *tamales de maíz nuevo* for which the fresh, untreated corn is ground into *masa nueva*; *pan de elote*, rather like cornbread but using *masa nueva*; and the popular harvest dish, Chulibu'ul (p. 117)—a "succotash" of fresh beans, puréed corn kernels, and ground squash seeds. The whole cob, too, has its own special native recipes: *píibinal* is the cob baked underground mentioned above; *chaakbil nal* are simple boiled cobs; *póokbil nal* is the fresh cob roasted on a grill; and *kuxum nal* are the *píibinal* left to develop a mold—rather like the *huitlacoche* of central Mexico—then grilled.

[MR]

[MC]

GROSELLA / CIRUELA COSTEÑA, CUATELOLOTE, MANZANA ESTRELLA

BOTANICAL / *Phyllanthus acidus* (L.) Skeels /
Family Phyllantaceae
ENGLISH / Otaheite gooseberry, Malay gooseberry
MAYAN / *pay juul*

DESCRIPTION: This mouth-puckering berry is another favorite with Yucatecan children, who love to suck and chew the extremely sour fruit before spitting out the seed. The translation of *grosella* is "gooseberry" or "currant," both of which are related to each other, but in fact neither is related to *grosella*. *Grosella* is a pale yellow-green-to-white berry characterized by six to eight small ridges running vertically around the ½–¾-inch (1–2 cm) diameter fruit. In Yucatán, it appears in the market during its two seasons: April–May and August–September.

CULINARY USES: *Grosella* is sold in plastic bags accompanied by chile powder and salt and is eaten whole; it may also be cooked in sugar syrup and served as a compote.

GUANÁBANA / GUANABA, GRAVIOLA

BOTANICAL / *Annona muricata* L. / Family Annonaceae
ENGLISH / soursop
MAYAN / *tak' oop*

DESCRIPTION: *Guanábana* is sometimes referred to disparagingly as "the world's ugliest fruit." The bulbous, ovoid fruit measures 6–8 inches (15–20 cm) in length; it is bumpy, a splotchy gray-green color, and covered with sharp yet flexible spines that remind one of nothing so much as pimples. But once you cut it open and savor the fruit itself, all thoughts of its appearance fade away. The white flesh is creamy, sweet yet slightly acidic, and exotically perfumed, although the preponderance of black seeds requires patience while eating. *Guanábana* has apparently been cultivated in Yucatán for a very long time, since it is common to see it in family orchards; further, it has a name in Mayan, which is typical only for the oldest species. The tree fruits April–June.

CULINARY USES: Mature fruits are broken open and consumed fresh, either with the fingers or a spoon. Liquefied with water and sugar, it becomes the refreshing Agua fresca de guanábana (p. 226). It is also used in the preparation of a couple of delicious desserts: Sorbete de guanábana (p. 245) and Crema de guanábana (p. 384).

[MC]

GUAYA / HUAYA, HUAYO, GUAYA PAÍS, GUAYA CUBANA, MAMONCILLO

BOTANICAL / *Talisia olivaeformis* (Kunth) Radlk.
and *Melicoccus bijugatus* Jacq. / Family Sapindaceae
ENGLISH / honeyberry, genip
MAYAN / *wayum, uayam*

DESCRIPTION: This unusual fruit is considered by some home-owners to be a pest, since its fruits and leaves are abundant and fall to the ground, suffocating any other plant life below. But *guaya* is a children's favorite: they scale the tree, pluck down a cluster of the fruits, and while away the hours pinching off the skin and sucking out the sweet/sour flesh and juice. In the markets, *guaya* is sold much like grapes, still clinging to the stalk in bunches. Fruits are completely spherical, about 1 inch (3 cm) in diameter. The skin is olive green; inside, a hard seed is covered with a peach-colored, cottony pulp with a sweet yet acidic flavor and astringent aftertaste. There are two varieties of *guaya* found in Yucatán: *Talisia olivaeformis*, known as *guaya país*, is native to southern Mexico and appears to be associated with the Mayas, since its main concentration of growth is typically around the region's archaeological zones; an intro-duced variety, *Melicoccus bijugatus*, originated in northern South America and is known as *guaya cubana* or *mamoncillo*. *Guaya* is harvested June–September.

CULINARY USES: *Guaya* is only consumed fresh. The custom-ary way to eat it is to peel it, put the whole thing into your mouth, then move the fruit around in circles between teeth and tongue, gradually consuming the pulp. Local friends tell me that another popular way to consume *guaya* is to peel all the fruits, place the fleshy spheres in a bowl with a bit of lime juice and salt, and douse liberally with finely chopped chile habanero.

"Son, bring me a maiden of white and radiant calves; I want to raise up her petticoat to the thighs." "Thus it shall be, oh father. I have here that which you wish: a jícama. In peeling it you are lifting up its skirt."

—CHILAM BALAM DE CHUMAYEL, 1775–1800

GUAYABA / GUAYABO

BOTANICAL / *Psidium guajava* L. / Family Myrtaceae
ENGLISH / guava
MAYAN / *pichi', julu'*

DESCRIPTION: Guava is available much of the year in Yucatán, but most abundantly in December, when the air is filled with the smell of the fruit as it ripens on the tree, falls off, and ferments on the ground, emanating an exotic smell of floral decay. Native to southern Mexico into Central America, *guayaba* can have a variety of forms, sizes, and colors, but the most common in Yucatán is spherical, about 1½–2¼ inches (4–6 cm) in diameter, with a yellowish skin and pulp. Other varieties have rose-colored or white flesh. The skin is very thin, and the inside is characterized by a somewhat sandy flesh, like that of pears, and a cluster of seeds. The famous costume of Yucatecan men—the *guayabera*, which originated in Cuba—according to legend got its name from its large waist-level pockets, which were used for gathering *guayabas*.

CULINARY USES: Guavas are consumed fresh when fully ripened, or turned into preserves and sorbet as well as a refreshing drink. *Guayaba* is also the star ingredient of Helado de crema morisca (p. 249), an exotically flavored local ice cream. Guavas have one of the highest concentrations of Vitamin C of any fruit—three to five times more than oranges.

JÍCAMA

BOTANICAL / *Pachyrhizus erosus* (L.) Urb. / Family Fabaceae
ENGLISH / Mexican turnip, jicama, Mexican potato, yam bean
MAYAN / *chikam*

DESCRIPTION: The earthy brown, leathery skin of the jicama, when removed, reveals snow-white flesh beneath. Its crunchy, watery texture is refreshing in the tropical heat. Jicama can be seen year-round in the markets, bagged with mandarin wedges and dusted with red chile powder. The root of the jicama is the only edible part of the plant; when young, the flesh is juicy and lightly sweet, but as it matures it can become fibrous and floury. In Yucatán, there is a smaller version measuring about 4 inches (10 cm) with a thin, pale skin and sweet flavor. An even smaller variety, measuring only about 1 inch in diameter (2–3 cm), is harvested from October to December and is used to fill piñatas at Christmas. The jicama is mentioned in the *Chilam Balam de Chumayel* as one of the lids to the underworld, along with the *camote* (p. 25).

CULINARY USES: Besides being sold as a snack year-round, the mandarin orange/jicama combination known in Mayan as Xek ("hodgepodge," p. 228) becomes particularly important during autumn rites, known here as Hanal Pixán, or "feast of the spirits." Along with tamales, chocolate, and many other foods, the medley appears as an offering on altars to departed loved ones.

[MC]

[MC]

JITOMATE / TOMATE, TOMATE ROJO

BOTANICAL / *Solanum lycopersicum* L. / Family Solanaceae
ENGLISH / tomato
MAYAN / *p'ak, p'aak*

DESCRIPTION: The tomato is undoubtedly one of the most used fruits in the world. It is difficult to imagine many international dishes without it, although being a New World species, it did not arrive in Europe until the 1500s. The words "*jitomate*" and "tomato" derive from the Náhuatl "*xitomatl*," or "plump thing with a navel." In most of Mexico, the word "*jitomate*" is used to denote the red tomato while "*tomate*" refers to the green tomatillo (*Physalis philadelphica*). There have always been many varieties of tomato, and with modern hobbyist hybrids, today there are even more, varying according to size, shape, sweetness, acidity, number of seeds, and juiciness. There are several varieties available in Yucatán's markets—*bola* (spherical), *saladet* (Roma or plum), and *uva* (grape)—but the most common form found in the *milpa* and *solar* is round and flattened, about 3 inches (8 cm) in diameter, with pronounced segments, very juicy and more acid than other varieties. *Jitomate* is grown year-round.

CULINARY USES: Perhaps the most common use of tomato in Yucatán is in a cooked sauce—Tomate frito (p. 507)—poured onto a wide range of foods, including tamales. While this may not seem surprising in an age of bottled tomato sauces used on just about anything, in fact, predecessors of this Maya sauce date to the pre-Columbian era. Slices of fresh tomato appear as a garnish in *pibil* dishes (p. 418). Chopped, it is a component in fresh salsas like X'nipek (p. 512). And charred in the ashes of a fire, then mashed and mixed with chiles, it is called Chiltomate (p. 451)—the requisite accompaniment for Poc chuc (p. 448) and Longaniza asada (p. 482).

The Indians have not lost, but have gained much with the coming of the Spaniards, even in small matters. [For example], hens, pigeons, oranges, limas, citrons, grapes, pomegranates, figs.

—FRAY DIEGO DE LANDA, 1566

LIMA / LIMA DE CHICHI

BOTANICAL / *Citrus limetta* Risso / Family Rutaceae
ENGLISH / limetta, sweet lime
MAYAN / none

DESCRIPTION: One of the most revered and emulated dishes of Yucatán is the famous Sopa de lima (p. 341). I am always somewhat amused when I see chefs and writers from elsewhere translating this as "lime soup." (Even the translation of the Landa book uses the word "lime.") There is a marked distinction between the *lima* and the *limón*, or "lime." Tart yet not as sour as the Persian lime, the *lima* is noted for its delicate perfume. *Lima* is easy to identify in the market: almost a perfect sphere, its signature characteristic is the pronounced nipple at the bottom opposite the peduncle (stem end). The Yucatecan *lima* is quite unlike other varieties found in the rest of Mexico. It is smaller, with a diameter of only about 1½ inches (4 cm), and its taste is somewhat sweeter and more perfumed than that found elsewhere in the country. *Lima* trees produce fruit all year long, but most prolifically in December.

CULINARY USES: Elsewhere in Mexico, *lima* is consumed primarily as a hand fruit, rather than being used as an ingredient in the kitchen. In Yucatán, the soup mentioned above is popular, as is a refreshing *agua fresca* prepared with water and sugar, like lemonade. However, because the fruit is more expensive than other lime varieties, those are frequently substituted. In some restaurants and during certain seasons, Sopa de lima may be served with large round slices of lime—obviously not the petite *lima*—with a notable and disappointing difference in taste. Unfortunately, the fruit is not likely to be found beyond its growing zone, such that the only suitable substitute is lime.

[MC]

[MC]

[MC]

LIMÓN / LIMÓN CON SEMILLA, LIMÓN AGRIO, LIMÓN PAÍS, LIMÓN INDIO

BOTANICAL / *Citrus aurantifolia* Swingle / Family Rutaceae
ENGLISH / key lime, West Indian lime, bartender's lime, Mexican lime
MAYAN / none

DESCRIPTION: This citrus variety takes its English name, "key lime," thanks to an interesting story. Dr. Henry Perrine (1797–1840), who served as U.S. consul in Campeche in the 1830s, was an enthusiast of introducing tropical species into the United States. Shortly before his death in Florida at the hands of Seminole Indians, he brought specimens of this variety from Yucatán to plant where he had taken up residency, in Indian Key. The fruit of the Mexican, or key, lime is spherical and roughly 1–2 inches (2.5 cm–5 cm) in diameter. *Limón* is often seen in Yucatecan household gardens or *solares* (p. 126). The tree fruits year-round but produces more prolifically May–June and November–December.

CULINARY USES: It would be difficult to imagine Mexican cuisine without the lime. Everything from margaritas to ceviche makes ample use of its juice. Wedges of it are squeezed onto a feast of foods—from Tacos al pastor (p. 238) to Frijol con puerco (p. 262). Along with salt and powdered chile, it is the dressing for many "street foods" such as Esquites (p. 239) and *elotes* (p. 31). The peel is also used: its high pectin content makes it useful in making jellies; bits of it add a surprising tropical flavor to Merengues (p. 486).

LIMÓN PERSA / LIMÓN SIN SEMILLA, LIMÓN AGRIO

BOTANICAL / *Citrus latifolia* Tanaka / Family Rutaceae
ENGLISH / Persian lime, Bearss lime, Tahiti lime, lime
MAYAN / none

DESCRIPTION: Similar in flavor to the key lime, this variety is larger (2–2½ in. / 5–6 cm in length) and has an elongated body. The rind is a bit thicker and less aromatic. Small growers favor the Persian lime since the trees don't have thorns and the fruits don't have seeds—unlike other lime varieties. It produces year-round, but greatest yields are June–August, lowest, February–April.

CULINARY USES: The Persian lime is used in much the same way as the Mexican lime, but because it is larger and gives more juice, it is favored for *limonada*, limeade.

MAKAL / MALANGA

BOTANICAL / *Xanthosoma yucatanense* Engl. / Family Araceae
ENGLISH / elephant ear
MAYAN / *kukut makal*

DESCRIPTION: Tropical-plant hobbyists may not be aware that the lovely ornamental plant known in English as elephant ear has an edible root—more accurately, a corm—that has sustained the Mayas for centuries. Fray Diego de Landa mentions that it was very good to eat during times of famine. *Makal* is related to the Central American plant *yautia* or *cocoyam* (*Xanthosoma sagittifolium*), but the particular species consumed here grows only in Yucatán. Further, makal should not be confused with taro (*Colocasia esculenta*), the Old World cousin of the New World *makal*, which produces a plant and corm that are similar in appearance and are used in much the same way. Since it is a perennial, the roots can be extracted at any time for consumption. All plants in this group should be well cooked, since they contain calcium oxalate crystals, which can be very irritating.

CULINARY USES: Cooked roots are eaten with honey; additionally, the roots may be ground and combined with corn to make tortillas or *atole*. The small, starchy corm is also cooked in sugar syrup, like other candied fruits and vegetables (p. 414). Prior to the arrival of Europeans, who brought banana plants, the leaves of *makal* were used as wrappers for tamales, and in fact still are in remote regions. Care must be taken in this endeavor, however, since the sap from the plant can cause itching and skin inflammation.

[MC]

There is a very large tree that bears a large, longish fruit, and fat with a red meat, very fine to eat; it does not produce a flower, but only the fruit, at first very small and growing by degrees.

—FRAY DIEGO DE LANDA, 1566

[MC]

MAMEY / MAMEY COLORADO

BOTANICAL / *Pouteria sapota* (Jacq.) H.E. Moore & Stearn / Family Sapotaceae
ENGLISH / mamey sapote
MAYAN / *chakal ha'as*

DESCRIPTION: Mamey may be Yucatán's fruit mascot. It is a much-beloved shade tree; just about everyone has a couple in their yard. The fruit, too, is a favorite, with its intense coral-colored flesh and thick brown, fuzzy skin. Its football shape, ranging from 4 to 10 inches (10–25 cm) in length, is distinctive and attention getting. Vendors in the market stack large, pyramidal piles of them, some neatly sliced open in a wedge, tempting buyers with what appears to be a beautiful coral smile. Illustrated plaques throughout Mérida's *centro histórico* identify intersections—a tradition since colonial times, when many people were illiterate—and, not surprisingly, one intersection is branded with a whimsical engraving of the fruit. The taste of the creamy, sweet pulp is unique, reminding me of a cross between a peach and a cantaloupe. Inside is a single hard seed with an aroma of bitter almonds, which in the past was used to flavor Horchata (p. 437). Fruits take one year to mature and are harvested March–June.

CULINARY USES: Mamey is consumed fresh; slice open and eat as you would a mango. Alternatively, the flesh may be scooped out with a spoon. Mamey also appears as the main ingredient in a broad range of treats, from beverages and sorbets to gelatins and mousses.

MANGO

BOTANICAL / *Mangifera indica* L. / Family Anacardiaceae
ENGLISH / mango
MAYAN / none

DESCRIPTION: Mango is one of the most beloved tropical fruits in the world, so revered, in fact, that more than 1,000 varieties have been developed. Shapes and colors vary widely, but all feature a vaguely oval shape with a single, flat seed and fibrous but juicy flesh. The pulp is very fragrant owing to a high resin content. Varieties cultivated in Yucatán are the *anis*, which is small (2½ in. / 6 cm long); *indio*, which can be recognized by its curved and pronounced pointed end (4 in. / 10 cm long); and "*tommy*," or *petacón*, known for its large (5–6 in. / 12–15 cm long), roundish form, red skin, and aromatic pulp. Some varieties of mango are available year-round in Yucatán's markets, but the greatest abundance and the best local varieties are found April–September.

CULINARY USES: Mango is usually consumed when ripe and juicy, although many Yucatecans prefer it when still green, firm, and tart and eat it with powdered chile. It is also used in ice creams or sorbets and in fruit smoothies.

[MC]

[MC]

MARAÑÓN / ANACARDO, NUEZ DE LA INDIA

BOTANICAL / *Anacardium occidentale* L. / Family Anacardiaceae
ENGLISH / cashew apple, cashew
MAYAN / none

DESCRIPTION: Being a fan of cashews, I almost lost my composure the first time I saw a *marañón*—the fruit that produces them. *Marañones* hang down from the branches of an evergreen tree and look rather like postmodern pears from a distance, but up close you see that a kidney-shaped seed is growing on the outside of the fruit. The leathery outer shell of the seed contains cardol, an oily liquid that is highly caustic and can cause skin ulcers, which is why it is recommended to remove the seed and discard. Tempting as it may be to try to extract the cashew, leave it to the professionals, who have developed a method of roasting the seed in cylinders that collect the caustic but valuable cardol oil. They crack open the seed to release the nut and dry it. The *marañón* fruit measures about 3¼ inches (8 cm) in length, and the nut about ¾–1¾ inches (2–3 cm). *Marañón* is yellow-orange to red as it matures, with a peachy-floral fragrance. The juicy flesh has a sweet flavor and slight acidity and is quite astringent. *Marañón* is a native to northeast Brazil, but after the 1500s, it was dispersed throughout the tropics. In Yucatán, it is principally grown in Campeche, where it is harvested February–May.

CULINARY USES: Few people in Yucatán make (or care about) the connection between the cashew and the *marañón*, or cashew apple fruit. While there is a limited regional production of and market for organic cashews and cashew butter, they are expensive and remain inaccessible for the majority of the population. The fruits are another matter: when they arrive in the markets in late February, they quickly sell out. Demand is so high that bushels of fresh fruits are brought in daily during the season. Once the seeds are plucked off, *marañones* are eaten as a hand fruit or used to prepare *agua fresca*. In other places in the tropics, they may be used to produce liqueurs, sorbets, ice cream, and preserves, such as Conserva de marañón (p. 328), although in Yucatán those are only occasionally seen.

ÑAME

BOTANICAL / *Dioscorea alata* L. and *D. bulbifera* L. / Family Dioscoreaceae
ENGLISH / yam, winged or water yam, air potato
MAYAN / *aki' makal, xvolador*

DESCRIPTION: From India to Yucatán via the colonial era, yams are now cultivated in the peninsula in two forms; both plants feature an edible tuberous root measuring 2–4 inches (5–10 cm) in length that is consumed in a similar way to potatoes. In *D. bulbifera*, the roots grow all over the plant and are exposed to the air and are therefore known in some places as *papas voladoras* (flying potatoes) and in Yucatán simply as *volador*. *Ñame* is harvested October–March.

CULINARY USES: *Ñame* is cut up and added to soups and stews much like potatoes. In Quintana Roo, a dish is prepared called *ts'aaxa'akbil makal*—yams stewed in recado rojo. They are also cooked in pipián rojo, a thick stew of toasted, ground squash seeds. As with the majority of plants in this genus, *ñame* must be cooked to remove toxins.

NANCE / NANCEN, NANCHE / NANCE AGRIO, NANCE BLANCO

BOTANICAL / *Byrsonima crassifolia* (L.) Kunth and *Byrsonima bucidaefolia* Standley / Family Malpighiaceae

ENGLISH / murici, golden spoon, sour murici, nance

MAYAN / *chi', sakpaj*

DESCRIPTION: In Yucatán's markets, you cannot avoid noting scores of jars filled with tiny golden spheres suspended in clear liquid. This is *nance en almíbar*—murici in sugar syrup—a popular snack and dessert item throughout the region. Nance is also sold fresh, with lime and chile powder on the side to garnish. Similar to but not quite a cherry, it is a distant relative of acerola. The fruit is small—just ⅓–½ inch (1–1.5 cm) in diameter—with a bright yellow skin when ripe and whitish flesh. Nance is another of those fruits kids seem to love: it is bite-sized and "suckable," with a small seed inside that presents a challenge to extract with the tongue and teeth. The taste is sweet-sour and extremely astringent, making it unpleasant to some. Native to the tropical Maya lowlands and south into Central America, it is frequently cultivated in orchards and household gardens. *Nance agrio* (sometimes called *nance blanco*) is less common, appreciated in rural communities but rarely seen in cities. I have, however, spotted *nance agrio* in the market of Valladolid, packed in brine. It looks and tastes much like a green olive. Nance fruits in May and again in August–September. It plays an important role in the *Popol Vub*, the Postclassic sacred text of the Quiché Mayas, which states that the nance tree belonged to Lord Macaw, because the tree gave him fruits to eat. But the Hero Twins, Hunahpu and Xbalanque, who were set on conquering the vain Lord Macaw, attacked him one day while he was resting in a nance tree, distracted by the pleasure of eating the small, golden fruits.

CULINARY USES: When the fruits are still green and just before ripening, they are eaten with chile; when ripe, usually with no other flavoring. Nance is also made into a delicious locally produced liqueur.

[DS]

[MR]

NARANJA AGRIA / NARANJA AMARGA

BOTANICAL / *Citrus aurantium* L. / Family Rutaceae
ENGLISH / Seville orange, sour orange, bitter orange,
marmalade orange
MAYAN / *suuts pak'aal*

DESCRIPTION: *Naranja agria*, or "sour orange," is such an important ingredient in the cuisine of Yucatán that it is hard to believe it hasn't always been here. But, along with other citrus varieties, it is an Old World import, arriving with the Spanish in the 1500s. Well before that, the Moors brought the sour orange to Andalucía, and it became so prolific there that now it bears the English name Seville orange. The shape and size (3 in. / 8 cm in diameter) of the Seville orange are similar to those of sweet oranges, but the rind is thick, pimply, and bitter. The pulp is fibrous, with many seeds and an acidic juice low in sugar content. In other parts of Mexico, sour orange is used primarily as an ornamental tree, but in Yucatán the fruit is widely consumed, and almost every house has at least one of the trees, which fruit year-round.

CULINARY USES: The tart juice of *naranja agria* makes a refreshing beverage when mixed with water and sugar and served over ice, much like lemonade. It is used in a wide variety of Yucatecan salsas, such as X'nipek (p. 512) and Chile tamulado (p. 509). Wedges of *naranja agria* are served alongside meat dishes, such as Poc chuc (p. 448), so that the diner can squeeze on fresh juice to taste. A couple of local distilleries produce a liqueur from the juice, and it is an important component of Grand Marnier. Like the grapefruit, sour orange may interact negatively with some medications such as calcium channel blockers and statins. If you take any of these or similar drugs, consult with a physician before consuming it.

NARANJA DULCE / NARANJA CHINA

BOTANICAL / *Citrus sinensis* L. Osbeck /
Family Rutaceae
ENGLISH / sweet orange
MAYAN / *chujuk pak'aal*

DESCRIPTION: Yucatán is a major grower of the sweet orange for markets in Mexico. Although the fruits grown here are not very large (about 3¼ in. / 8 cm in diameter) or attractive, they are very juicy and sweet. Nevertheless, the importance of the sweet orange in Yucatán pales in comparison to that of the sour orange. Columbus brought the species to the New World on his second voyage in 1493. Like the Seville orange, sweet oranges are available all year long.

CULINARY USES: A colorful aspect of markets and street life in Yucatán is the *naranjeros*, vendors of sweet oranges. The tool of their trade is a peculiar apparatus, which, according to one historian, was invented in Yucatán for the purpose of peeling oranges. Reminiscent of an antique apple peeler, the device features a skewer that holds the orange in place while the vendor uses a crank to turn it; a blade moves from side to side, slicing off the peel in a spiral and resulting in a hilariously long curl of fragrant rind that piles up on floors and streets. Once peeled, the fruit is easy to pull open and eat in segments, often with salt and ground chile. Sweet orange was also a fashionable ingredient during the French-inspired Porfiriato in Valladolid in a variety of dishes like Pavo en naranja china (p. 402).

Another [tree], exceedingly beautiful and fresh, bears a fruit like large eggs; the Indians gather it green and ripen it in the ashes; when ripe it lasts well, is sweet and tastes like the yolk of an egg.

—FRAY DIEGO DE LANDA, 1566

PAPAYA

BOTANICAL / *Carica papaya* L. / Family Caricaceae
ENGLISH / papaya, papaw, pawpaw
MAYAN / *chich puut*

DESCRIPTION: In Yucatán, papaya is so hardy that it grows like a weed, spreading prolifically along highways and throughout forests. Native to the tropical Americas, papaya was probably domesticated in Yucatán and elsewhere in southern Mexico as well as in northern Central America. There are small varieties of papaya (3¼ in. / 8 cm in length), but it is generally quite a large fruit, with some specimens I have seen in Yucatán achieving sizes as large as a watermelon and measuring 12 inches (30 cm) long or more. The greatest differences among papayas are the color, ranging from yellowish to orange, and the flavor, from more sweet to less sweet. The center of papayas is hollow and spotted with multiple small spheres that feature a black, wrinkled external membrane protecting a liquid and the seed inside. Papaya fruits all year long.

CULINARY USES: Papaya is consumed widely throughout Mexico in a variety of forms, including sorbets and ice cream, jellies, or fresh off the tree. A popular dessert in Yucatán is Dulce de papaya (p. 414), frequently served at the end of the main meal of the day. Underripe papayas are cut into pieces, soaked in a solution of water and slaked lime (possibly a holdover of the ancient practice of ripening it in ashes to which Landa refers), then cooked in a syrup of burnt sugar or *piloncillo* (cone sugar), honey, and spices. In the cities it is accompanied by Edam cheese. In some coastal communities, such as San Crisanto (p. 162) and Santa Clara, small, wild papayas are cooked in a thick syrup until it is completely absorbed by the fruit, and then the papayas are filled with grated coconut.

[MC]

[MR]

[MC]

PEPINO KAT / CUAJILOTE

BOTANICAL / *Parmentiera aculeata* (Kunth) Seem. /
Family Bignoniaceae
ENGLISH / tree cucumber
MAYAN / *kat*

DESCRIPTION: Surely one of the more unusual looking ingredients to appear in Yucatán's markets, the *pepino kat* is a long (4–6 in. / 10–15 cm), ridged fruit, yellowish, with small nodes running along the peak of each ridge. Some scholars posit that what appear to be *cacao* pods held by monkeys or deities on certain vase paintings may in fact be *pepino kat*: the two have very similar forms and both grow from the trunks of trees rather than hang down from the branches. When young, the fruit is acidic, and when mature it sweetens pleasantly. *Pepino kat* is broadly distributed throughout lowland tropical Mexico. In Yucatán, it appears wild in forests as well as in family orchards and gardens. The tree fruits in the wet summer months.

CULINARY USES: According to noted anthropologist and food historian Sophie Coe, pre-Hispanic Mayas ate *pepino kat* with honey. Nowadays it may also be cooked in honey or sugar syrup, but its most common use is in Salpimentado (p. 352), a stew for which it is thickly sliced and added to the pot along with carrots, potatoes, plantain, and a variety of other meats and vegetables.

PIÑA

BOTANICAL / *Ananas commosus* (L.) Merr. /
Family Bromeliaceae
ENGLISH / pineapple
MAYAN / none

DESCRIPTION: Sophie D. Coe relates that pineapple was one of the fruits the Mayas bestowed on the Spanish when they landed on the shores of Yucatán. Pineapple is produced on a commercial scale in the peninsula, but it is also a favorite in family orchards. Sizes range from small (6 in. / 15 cm long) to large (10 in. / 25 cm). In this region, pineapple is harvested in summertime, although irrigation and imports make it available year-round.

CULINARY USES: Besides being consumed fresh, pineapple appears in Sorbete de piña (p. 246), and in sweets like Pastelitos (p. 201), little sugar-dusted empanadas filled with the fruit. In the streets of Mérida, it is sometimes possible to see vendors with carts bearing wooden barrels containing *tepache*, a lightly fermented pineapple beverage that originated in Mexico.

[DS]

[MC]

PIÑUELA / MALLA, PIÑUELILLA

BOTANICAL / *Bromelia pinguin* L. /
Family Bromeliaceae
ENGLISH / wild pineapple
MAYAN / *ch'am, ch'om*

DESCRIPTION: *Piñuela* is native to Yucatán, extending through tropical South America and the Caribbean. In the same family as pineapple, the *piñuela* is a small fruit that grows in a cluster at the center of the rosette leaf–form of a bromeliad. Like most bromeliads, the plant has a lifespan that extends only a short time after flowering. At the beginning of *Bromelia pinguin*'s final year, it produces a long stem displaying a burst of fuzzy red-orange flowers. A few months later, a cluster of 1½-inch (3.5 cm) elliptical berries ripens. The plant dies about one year after the start of fruiting. The sticky juice of the berries is quite acid, with a flavor reminiscent of pineapple or tamarind. In some areas, the plants are grouped in rows as a hedge; the spiny-toothed edges of the leaves serve as a barrier to entry of fields or property, which perhaps explains the Spanish nickname, *malla*, mesh or screen.

CULINARY USES: Maya women selling *piñuela* in Yucatán's markets collect the berries from the plants' natural habitat. They lightly roast them, pack them in small bags or plastic cups, and sell as a snack. *Piñuela* is eaten somewhat like a fig by tearing open the outer skin lengthwise and pushing the flesh upward and outward from the back. A quick scrape of the finger gets rid of the seeds. Then the flesh is chewed and the refreshing juice sucked.

PITAHAYA / PITAYA

BOTANICAL / *Hylocereus undatus* (Haw.) Britton & Rose /
Family Cactaceae
ENGLISH / dragonfruit, strawberry pear
MAYAN / *chakam*

DESCRIPTION: *Pitahaya* is the fruit of a trailing cactus that can be either terrestrial or epiphytic. It grows wild throughout Yucatán—snaking over walls from one neighbor's property to the other or scaling up forest trees. It is also cultivated, trained to climb on other orchard varietals or special structures. The fruit is a vibrant pink-to-red and features green-tipped points that actually are the vestigial sepals of the flower, appearing like scales and suggesting its English name of dragonfruit. The fruit measures about 5 inches (12 cm) in diameter, and the sweet flesh is translucent white with hundreds of minute black seeds. Native to the vast land of the Mayas stretching from Yucatán to the Pacific side of Guatemala, and farther south from El Salvador to Costa Rica, the *pitahaya* cactus yields fruit from August to September.

CULINARY USES: Mature *pitahayas* are sliced open and the pulp eaten with a spoon; it can also be frozen and consumed like a sorbet. In the market, a grayish-pink liquid with thousands of tiny black specks is the refreshing *agua fresca de pitahaya*— a beverage made by liquefying the fruit with water and sugar.

[MC]

PLÁTANO / PLÁTANO MACHO / PLÁTANO MANZANO

BOTANICAL / *Musa acuminata* Colla, *Musa balbisiana* Colla,
and *Musa sapientum* var. *champa* L. / Family Musaceae
ENGLISH / plantain, banana
MAYAN / *macho ja'as, xk'an manzano ja'as*

DESCRIPTION: There is such a great variety of banana hybrids
worldwide that the nomenclature in all languages, as well as
the scientific taxonomy, becomes labyrinthine and confusing.
In Spanish, using the root *plátano* to distinguish the general
species, followed by a descriptor to denote the particular variety, mitigates the problem. For example, *plátano macho* is the
Spanish term used for our word "plantain." Other descrip-
tors describing varieties available in Yucatán include *roatan*
(also known as Gros Michel or "Big Mike," from 7–10 in. /
18–25 cm), *tabasco* (6 in. / 15 cm), *dominico* (2¾ in. / 7 cm), and
morado (5¾ in. / 12 cm). Another Asia native that arrived in
Yucatán via Africa, *plátano* is available year-round.

CULINARY USES: The two banana varieties that predominate
in Yucatán are the *plátano macho* and the *plátano manzano*. The
former—a large variety measuring about 12 inches in length
by about 2 inches in width (30 cm × 5 cm)—which we know
as the plantain, is starchy and barely sweet. It is generally not
consumed fresh, but, rather, is cooked or fried. In Yucatán,
the plantain is used in many regional stews such as Puchero
de tres carnes (p. 350); it is also sautéed and served as a garnish
for dishes like Huevos motuleños (p. 454), or thinly sliced
and fried as a chip-type snack. The *manzano* (in some English-
speaking countries known as lady finger banana or apple
banana) is short and stubby, eaten like a regular banana, but
with a creamy texture and distinctive taste that evokes a flavor
blend of banana, strawberry, and apple. As important as the
banana fruits are in Yucatán, the leaves are, too, and perhaps
even more so. They form the wrapper for almost all of our
tamal varieties, and they protect many meat, poultry, and fish
dishes as they bake, grill, or roast, giving the foods inside an
earthy, herbaceous flavor.

[MC]

[MC]

SARAMUYO

BOTANICAL / *Annona squamosa* L. /
Family Annonaceae
ENGLISH / sugar apple, sweetsop
MAYAN / *ts'almuy*

DESCRIPTION: Not well known beyond the world's tropical belt, *saramuyo* is the most commonly cultivated neotropical fruit in family orchards throughout Yucatán. It has been consumed in the Yucatán Peninsula for at least 3,500 years. It is a heart-shaped fruit measuring 4–5 inches (10–12 cm) in length with many protuberances, giving it the appearance of a large, soft pinecone. It is characterized by sweet, juicy white pulp and a large quantity of black seeds. It is in season June–August.

CULINARY USES: Like other fruits in the Annonaceae family, *saramuyo* may be consumed fresh when it is ripe, liquefied to make a refreshing drink, or included in sorbet.

TOMATE / TOMATILLO, TOMATE DE CÁSCARA, TOMATE VERDE

BOTANICAL / *Physalis philadelphica* Lam. / Family Solanaceae
ENGLISH / husk tomato, tomatillo
MAYAN / none

DESCRIPTION: In Yucatán, the words "*tomate*" and "*jitomate*" are virtually interchangeable. In the rest of Mexico, however, "*jitomate*" is the word for the red tomato, and "*tomate*" refers to the species known in the United States as tomatillo. In Yucatán, we add an adjective to differentiate: *tomate verde* (green tomato). In pre-Columbian times in central Mexico, the green *tomate* was preferred above the red *jitomate*—possibly because the latter is more difficult to grow at Mexico's higher elevations. Conversely, *jitomate* grows brilliantly in Yucatán, but not the *tomate*, which means that any we consume must come from Mexico. Today in Mérida, there are only a couple of vendors in the large central market who stock *tomates*, and then only occasionally, although the larger supermarkets usually carry them to cater to their Mexican customers. Related to the gooseberry, the *tomate* is characterized by a papery outer husk that is removed before eating. Fruit sizes vary widely, from ⅜ to 2 inches (1–5 cm) in diameter. The flesh is peppered with dozens of tiny seeds, and the flavor is tart and acidic, making it a natural for many Mexican table salsas. *Tomate* is harvested year-round.

CULINARY USES: The *tomate* is not a feature of Yucatecan cooking. However, many Mexican dishes that include it are popular here, such as *chilaquiles verdes*, *enchiladas verdes*, and Chicharrón en salsa verde (p. 217). Further, in Yucatán the *tomate* occasionally substitutes for *ciruela* when the latter is not in season, since it adds an important tartness to dishes like Pipián rojo (p. 96).

[MC]

YUCA / MANDIOCA, GUACAMOTE

BOTANICAL / *Manihot esculenta* L. / Family Euphorbiaceae
ENGLISH / cassava, manioc
MAYAN / *ts'iin*

DESCRIPTION: Along with *makal* (p. 39), *camote* (p. 25), and jicama (p. 35), *yuca* has long been a source of nutrients as well as legend and lore for the Mayas. All of these vegetables except *camote* are honored with riddles in the *Chilam Balam de Chumayel*. As retold by Sophie D. Coe, "When asked to bring a bone of his father, buried for three years, the answer is for the youth to bring a manioc root baked in a *pib*." Not to be confused with the ornamental plant known as yucca (genus *Yucca*, family Asparagaceae), the *yuca* plant visible above ground is bushy with five- or seven-pointed leaves, often variegated. The edible tuber is elongated and can grow to be quite large, up to 3 feet (1 m) long and 4 inches (10 cm) in width. *Yuca* is covered with a thin, brown bark that is easily removed; the flesh inside is white and fibrous, with hundreds of wick-like strands aligned to form the root. In Yucatán, *yuca* is harvested primarily October–November.

CULINARY USES: As suggested by the *Chilam Balam* riddle above, one common way *yuca* was consumed (and still is occasionally) was roasted in a *píib*. Most commonly nowadays it is seen in the markets swimming in sugar or honey syrup and garnished with cloves and cinnamon sticks. Globally, the flour from ground *yuca* is converted into the popular pudding, tapioca. In Valladolid, Buñuelos—a kind of Spanish doughnut—are made of *yuca* instead of wheat flour (p. 381).

ZAPOTE / CHICOZAPOTE

BOTANICAL / *Manilkara zapota* (L.) P. Royen /
Family Sapotaceae
ENGLISH / sapodilla
MAYAN / *ya*

DESCRIPTION: This enormously useful tree produces not only a delicious fruit, but also a durable hardwood and a treat beloved worldwide: chicle, the resin that for decades was the basis of chewing gum. *Zapote* is one of the most abundant trees in Yucatán's forests, where it originated, with wild family members extending into Central America. In the colonial era, the Spanish took it to the Philippines and from there to all the tropical zones of the world. The round-to-oval fruit measures about 2–4 inches (5–10 cm) in diameter and has a very thin yet rough brown skin. The pulp is brownish, too, with 3–12 shiny black seeds. It has a very sweet but delicate flavor. Fruits are found in the markets twice a year: February–April and again October–December.

CULINARY AND OTHER USES: The Mayas so revered the *zapote* tree that carvings of it appear on the sarcophagus of Pakal, an important ruler in ancient Palenque. The fruit was widely consumed; it was even dried like prunes for times of scarcity. The wood of the tree is extremely durable and resistant to humidity and pests, making it a prime choice for lintels and other structural and decorative elements in ancient Maya royal cities. But perhaps the real story of *zapote* is the sticky white latex that the Mayas saw flowing out of the tree whenever the bark was damaged. They learned how to extract it by carving zigzag patterns that scaled the heights of the trunk and collecting the sap that slowly oozed out—a method used into the twentieth century. They also learned that chewing the resin refreshed the mouth, quenched thirst, and staved off hunger. Like many products of Yucatán, chicle was heavily traded throughout ancient Mesoamerica; the Aztecs craved it, and Spanish chroniclers commented on their use of it. While it was broadly chewed behind closed doors, it was considered that those who chewed chicle in public were prostitutes or homosexuals. A chance meeting between the son of Thomas Adams and Mexican president General Antonio López de Santa Ana, who offered him chicle, launched the history of the most consumed sweet treat in the world. The fruit of *zapote* is enjoyed in Yucatán in smoothies as well as in sorbets.

[MC]

ZAPOTE NEGRO / ZAPOTE PRIETO

BOTANICAL / *Diospyros digyna* Jacq. / Family Ebenaceae
ENGLISH / black persimmon, black sapote, chocolate pudding fruit
MAYAN / *ta'uch*

DESCRIPTION: There are several fruiting trees throughout Yucatán with very similar Spanish names, even though unrelated botanically. *Zapote negro*, for example, should not be confused with the unrelated mamey sapote (*Pouteria sapota*) or *chicozapote* (*Manilkara zapota*), from which chicle is extracted. However, all too often people use the names interchangeably, which can create considerable confusion. Like so many popular fruits in Yucatán, the *zapote negro* is native to the lowlands as well as the region of Central America that extends to northern Nicaragua. The fruit's appearance is unusual to say the least: it turns from a bright green to pitch black—even the pulp—just a day or two after harvesting. Its color is the obvious source of the Spanish descriptor (*negro* = black, *prieto* = dark skinned), and its frankly rotten appearance when ripe resulted in the Mayan word for the fruit: *ta'uch*, which, tactfully translated, means "mashed down excrement." Fruits measure 3–4 inches (8–10 cm) in diameter. The pulp of ripe fruits has anywhere from one to ten seeds about 1 inch (2.5 cm) in length, although some fruits are seedless; the color is very dark brown, almost black; the texture is soft and rather jelly-like; and the taste is mildly sweet. *Zapote negro* is available September–January. Beyond the growing zone, the fruits have never achieved popularity.

CULINARY USES: Puréed pulp of *zapote negro* can be eaten as is, or sweetened with sugar or honey and topped with cream or milk. It is also used to make a delicious sorbet and ice cream.

[MC]

[MC]

CACAHUATE / MANÍ

BOTANICAL / *Arachis hypogaea* L. / Family Fabaceae
ENGLISH / peanut
MAYAN / none

DESCRIPTION: Domesticated in Peru between 5,300 and 5,800 years ago, peanuts were distributed throughout the Americas by the Incas and were carried to Europe as well as to Asia and Africa by Spanish explorers. Today in Yucatán, peanuts are often cultivated in household gardens, or in the *paach pak'al*, a special growing section of the *milpa* (p. 99). This is generally small production, enough for family consumption or modest sales to the public. The Spanish name "cacahuate" derives from the Náhuatl word "*tlalcacahua-tl*," which translates to "*cacao* grain of the earth" (*tlal-li* = earth and *cacahua-tl* = grain of *cacao*, or, by extension, any small grain or seed), no doubt because the nut forms beneath the soil.

CULINARY USES: A familiar yet sadly disappearing sight on the streets of Yucatán is the men who carry slung around their shoulders a double canvas bag full of freshly roasted peanuts. Maya women hawk *palanquetas*—rather like peanut brittle, cooked with either sugar or honey, and formed into long rectangular bars. These same ladies may also sell *cacahuates garapiñados*, little crunchy balls of sugar with a peanut buried inside and a sprinkle of salt on the outside, sometimes tinted red or pink, something like our glazed peanuts. And the peanut makes for an unusual ingredient in the popular frozen treat, Sorbete de cacahuate (p. 244).

CACAO

BOTANICAL / *Theobroma cacao* L. / Family Malvaceae
ENGLISH / cacao, cocoa
MAYAN / *kawkaw*

DESCRIPTION: The great importance *cacao* has historically had throughout the Maya region is indisputable, as proven in archaeological remains of *cacao* nibs as well as traces of the chemicals caffeine and theobromine in chocolate vessels. Representations of the fruit frequently occur in paintings and ceramics. Its production into chocolate is well documented by colonial authors. Fray Diego de Landa narrates in his *Relación de las cosas de Yucatán* that the Mayas prepared a foamy beverage of corn and ground *cacao*, and another with cocoa butter and corn. Modern-day Maya ceremonies still often include *cacao*: *xtáan'ukul* is a dish prepared with maize *masa*, honey, *canela*, and *cacao* and is offered to God or Maya deities on various occasions. At the conclusion of Maya wedding ceremonies, each witness is paid ten *cacao* beans, and any extra is given to the father of the bride and the godfather—probably a vestige of pre-Columbian customs, when the beans were used as money. Although not native to Yucatán, *cacao* has long been cultivated here by the Mayas in *cenotes* and in certain silviculture situations. Read more about *cacao* on page 459.

CULINARY USES: In many markets in Yucatán you will see small, shiny black disks resting atop scraps of brown paper: this is *chocolate*—formed into convenient tablets by patting chocolate paste into a tortilla-like shape—the way *cacao* has been prepared for the chocolate beverage for hundreds of years. Nowadays, the disk will also include sugar and *canela*; simply dissolve the disk in water or milk and whisk to whip up a froth. Although water was the customary liquid for the chocolate beverage for millennia before the arrival of the Spaniards (who brought European cows), today it is more common to use milk. Hot or cold, the chocolate beverage is still a breakfast tradition, served with plain buttered bread, sweet breads, or special breads for certain holidays such as *pan de muertos* on Day of the Dead and *rosca de reyes* on 6 January, the Day of the Three Kings.

[MC]

ESPELÓN / CAUPÍ

BOTANICAL / *Vigna unguiculata* (L.) Walp. / Family Fabaceae
ENGLISH / black-eyed pea, cowpea
MAYAN / *xperoon, x'pelon*

DESCRIPTION: Stacks of dull green bean pods are seen throughout Yucatán's market, men and women seated to one side shelling them and depositing the beans into brightly colored tubs. These are Yucatán's popular *espelones* (locally spelled *x'pelones*, which I use throughout this book), or cowpeas. An African native, the black-eyed pea was introduced into the New World in the seventeenth century. Since it is drought resistant, it is well suited to the dry tropics of Yucatán, where it is planted among corn, squash, and other species in the *milpa*. The greatest harvest periods are September–November, but with irrigation it can yield small quantities year-round.

CULINARY USES: In spite of being an introduced species, the *espelón* has insinuated itself robustly in the cuisine of Yucatán, so much so that many people think it is a native bean. Occasionally sold dried, the most common way it is sold is freshly shelled out of the pod and packed in one-pound (500 g) bags. Since it is a fresh bean, it can be thoroughly cooked in about fifteen minutes. Its most popular use is mixed with *masa* and formed into tamales. One, Vaporcito de x'pelon (p. 107), is a tiny *tamal* studded with the dark beans. Another, Mucbilpollo (p. 430), is a giant festival *tamal* typical of Yucatán's Hanal Pixán commemorations. Another small *tamal* filled with *espelones* is cooked underground in a *píib* and is known in Mayan as *p'ich ich*, or "bird's eye." *Espelón* is also sometimes used instead of the common black bean for Frijol con puerco (p. 262).

[MC]

[MC]

[MC]

FRIJOL

BOTANICAL / *Phaseolus vulgaris* (L.) / Family Fabaceae
ENGLISH / beans
MAYAN / *bu'ul, xkoolibu'ul*

DESCRIPTION: The common bean is the second most important grain legume in all of Mexico, surpassed only by corn. It is a legume with one of the most diverse ranges of varieties, although in Yucatán the most frequently consumed is black. Native to both Mexico and Peru, the common bean probably arrived in Yucatán more than 5,000 years ago, along with other essential cultivars of the *milpa*—corn and squash—both of which it complements ecologically as well as nutritionally.

CULINARY USES: A plain pot of unadorned black beans is a common sight throughout Mexico. In most of the country, this is known as *frijoles de la olla* (pot beans), but in Yucatán it is called K'abax (p. 504), cooked only with a bit of salt and epazote. In many states of Mexico, the most common way to eat beans is accompanied only with tortillas and chile; but in Yucatán, they are eaten with a squeeze of lime juice and garnished with a mixture of chopped red onion and cilantro. One of the most representative dishes of Yucatecan cuisine is Frijol con puerco (p. 262)—always on the menu for Mondays—which consists of black pot beans cooked with pork leg or hock; it is typically served with white rice and a mixture of chopped red onion, radishes, cilantro, and citrus juice. Another typically Yucatecan bean dish is Frijol colado (p. 505), which features the pot beans puréed and strained. In Yucatán, cooks swear that adding a couple of sprigs of epazote during cooking eliminates the issue of flatulence once and for all.

IBES

BOTANICAL / *Phaseolus lunatus* L. / Family Fabaceae
ENGLISH / lima bean
MAYAN / *ib, iib*

DESCRIPTION: The *ib*, or common lima bean, is a Yucatecan native. *Ibes* are the fourth most important species in the Yucatecan *milpa*, along with common beans, corn, and squash. There are approximately twelve varieties of *ib*, the most typical being *sak ib* (white and flat), *mulición* (small, round, and white), and *chak ib* (red). In the Maya market, bags of *sak ib* are a common sight, whether dried or fresh. The most plentiful harvest of *ibes* occurs December–January, although irrigation technology has made them more consistently available.

CULINARY USES: *Ibes* are used in several Maya dishes: they are a basic component of the *milpa* dish Toksel (p. 113), comprised of toasted ground squash seeds and *ibes*. The most common use of Toksel is as a filling for tamales like Ibewahes (p. 136), or the Maya "fritter" known as Pol'kanes (p. 111). Because of their ready availability in Yucatán, *ibes* are often used instead of black beans for any number of bean dishes, such as Frijol blanco con puerco (p. 263), and puréed as Ibes colados, the de rigueur accompaniment for the spicy pork stew Lomitos de Valladolid (p. 394).

MAÍZ

BOTANICAL / *Zea mays* L. / Family Poaceae
ENGLISH / maize, corn
MAYAN / *ixiim*

DESCRIPTION: Maize is not merely the staple food of the peoples of Mexico, it also has played a protagonistic role in all aspects of the life of Mexicans since pre-Hispanic times. Among the Mayas of the Yucatán Peninsula, maize is considered a sacred food and is treated with great respect; it is often called "*gracia*" (grace). Maize and its multiple manifestations are symbols of the societies that have evolved in the Americas for more than 10,000 years. Maize was domesticated in Mesoamerica, although the exact center of domestication is still debated. One theory posits that it was actually domesticated in several centers independently. The date is calculated at around 8,000 years ago, when domesticated maize was first derived from a wild species known as *teocintle*. One of the most notable phenomena with regard to maize is its enormous diversity: there are around fifty-nine different races in Mexico alone, and when one takes into account the varieties now found globally, the number soars exponentially. Rural life in Yucatán revolves around maize—its planting, harvest, and conversion into food, not to mention its use in ceremonies, religion, and art. Read more about maize on page 108.

CULINARY USES: "*Maíz*" is the word applied to the dried kernel; "*elote*" is the word used to refer to fresh corn on the cob; "*mazorca*" refers to the cob itself. Many parts of the maize plant are used: the husks (*jolo'och* or *holoch* in Mayan) are occasionally used in Yucatán for wrapping tamales, although banana leaves are more common. The silk from cobs is used to make an infusion employed in traditional medicine; leaves and cobs are used in handcrafts; and the stripped cob is used as a combustible. Maize is transformed into a more flavorful and digestible substance through a process known as nixtamalization, which involves boiling dried maize in water mixed with *cal*—calcium hydroxide (p. 517). Once treated and softened in this way, it is ground into a thick dough known as *masa*. *Masa* then becomes the fundamental element of Mexican gastronomy, used for making tortillas, tamales, and even beverages. In Yucatecan cuisine, *masa* is often used as a thickener for meat or poultry stocks to create *k'óol* (p. 86), a kind of gravy or sauce served with many dishes.

PEPITA

BOTANICAL / *Cucurbita moschata* Duch. ex Poir.; *Cucurbita argyrosperma* Huber ssp. *argyrosperma* / Family Cucurbitaceae
ENGLISH / squash seeds
MAYAN / *sikil, xtoop*

DESCRIPTION: In Yucatán's markets, you will notice big burlap bags full of three main types of squash seeds: a small, pale brownish one that still has its shell; a larger one with a white shell; and a green one from the same seed as the larger one but with the white shell removed. The small seed is known as *pepita menuda* (*sikil* in Mayan) and comes from *C. moschata*; the other two are known as *pepita gruesa* (or *pepita verde* if the shell is removed; *xtoop* in Mayan) and come from the *C. argyrosperma*. While squash seeds are used occasionally in other parts of Mexico, in Yucatán they continue as a vital part of nutrition and cuisine and appear in many regional dishes.

CULINARY USES: The most commonly used seed in Yucatán is the *menuda* (*sikil*), which is toasted and ground—shell and all—and used to make dips like Sikil p'aak (p. 285), or as a filling for tamales or fritters like Pol'kanes (p. 111). The white *pepita gruesa* is toasted and salted and eaten as a snack. Once peeled, the green seed (*pepita verde*) is ground to make Mazapán de pepita (p. 385) or is cooked in sugar or honey to make brittle. The most hallowed use for *pepita verde* is to make the rich, green sauce for Papadzules (p. 280).

[MR]

Another fresh and beautiful tree also holds its leaves
without their falling, and bears a small fig they call ox.

—FRAY DIEGO DE LANDA, 1566

[COURTESY ARBORETUM ALAIN MEYRAT / UNIVERSIDAD NACIONAL AGRARIA, NICARAGUA]

RAMÓN / OJITE, CAPOMO

BOTANICAL / *Brosimum alicastrum* Sw. / Family Moraceae
ENGLISH / breadnut, Maya nut
MAYAN / *ox*

DESCRIPTION: Although *ramón* is not found in the market, it has an important history in the region. It is a large, leafy evergreen tree in the same family as fig and mulberry; it is naturally distributed throughout Mesoamerica, into Central America, and as far south as Brazil. In addition to having lush foliage that is used as fodder for horses and cattle, *ramón* produces a small yellow fruit—about 1–1¼ inches (2–3 cm) in diameter—inside of which is a thin layer of sweet pulp that forest animals love. At the core is a large edible seed that is highly nutritious. While scholars debate whether *ramón* was a staple or a famine food among the ancient Mayas, there is no disagreement that the *ramón* seed was consumed (whether by choice or out of desperation) in March and April, a season in which corn had yet to be planted but the *ramón* was giving fruit. *Ramón* is a quintessentially Maya foodstuff, legendary in its historical role and promising in its contemporary possibilities. Because of the ready availability of *ramón* and its impressive nutritional value, programs throughout the Maya region have been initiated to teach impoverished people their ancestors' primal knowledge about gathering the *ramón* nut and processing it into food.

CULINARY USES: In Quintana Roo, the fruits are cooked whole, then ground with salt and eaten with tortillas. Once the seed is cooked and ground into flour, it may also be mixed with maize *masa* for making tortillas. Groups promoting the commercialization of *ramón* to bolster income among rural Maya families have developed recipes that employ it as a substitute for coffee, or in the preparation of *buñuelos* and cakes. Highly nutritious, *ramón* is rich in dietary fiber, calcium, potassium, folic acid, iron, and zinc, and it contains Vitamins A, E, C, and B complex in addition to a high content of amino acids.

CHILES, SPICES, HERBS, AND OTHER FLAVORINGS

[MIPA]

ACHIOTE

BOTANICAL / *Bixa orellana* L. / Family Bixaceae
ENGLISH / annatto, lipstick tree, achiote
MAYAN / *kiwi'*

DESCRIPTION: The *Bixa orellana* tree produces a prickly pod inside of which are bright red seeds that have many uses. Through the centuries, *achiote* came to define many aspects of the Mayas' existence and is still a hallmark of their culture. When left to macerate in water, the seeds deteriorate into a vivid red paste that the Mayas employed as a paint for bodies, buildings, and manuscripts and as a dye for fabrics. The *achiote* (annatto) plant is a profusely fruiting shrub or small tree that grows 16½–33 feet (5–10 m) in height. The tree produces a delicate pink-to-white flower that eventually morphs into the heart-shaped prickly pod. Approximately fifty seeds grow inside each pod. The seeds are protected by a reddish covering, which is the source of the orange-yellow dye.

CULINARY USES: The primary use of *achiote* in preconquest times was as a colorant for the sacred chocolate beverage, a technique later borrowed by the Aztecs and, in turn, the conquering Spanish. They took both the seed and the technique back with them to the Old World, where the use of annatto to deepen the color of chocolate remained common until the seventeenth century. Commercially, it is used to color packaged foods such as cheeses and snack items. In Yucatán, *achiote* is fried in lard to stain the fat a bright yellow-orange, which is then added to *masa* to make colorful local tamales, or to rice to impart a color not unlike saffron. Its primary culinary use today is in the preparation of Recado rojo—a seasoning blend of *achiote*, oregano, salt, pepper, allspice, and cumin. This heady paste is diluted with Seville orange juice to create a marinade for meats and poultry, which are finally wrapped in banana leaves and baked in an underground oven, or *píib* (p. 418).

[MC]

CANELA

BOTANICAL / *Cinnamomum verum* J. Presl /
Family Lauraceae
ENGLISH / Ceylon cinnamon, Mexican cinnamon
MAYAN / none

DESCRIPTION: While the English and Spanish languages each have only one word for this popular flavoring, in fact there are two very distinct spices to which the words refer. "*Canela*" refers to *Cinnamomum verum*—"true cinnamon" in the Greek/Latin binomial, also known as Ceylon cinnamon—which comes from Sri Lanka (formerly Ceylon). The bark of the tree is thin and fragile, easily crumbled between your fingers, and has a light aromatic fragrance. This is the spice we use in Mexico, known elsewhere as Mexican cinnamon. By contrast, the "cinnamon" used in the United States is the species *Cinnamomum aromaticum*—also known as cassia cinnamon, considered to be the "poor relation" of Ceylon cinnamon; it features a thick, hard bark with a strong and pungent aroma. Interestingly, a native species with a similar fragrance and flavor is dispersed throughout the Caribbean and the Yucatán Peninsula; its botanical name is *Canella winterana*, known as "white cinnamon" in English, and it belongs to the Canellaceae family. Although colonial reports suggest that the leaves, bark, and even berries of *C. winterana* were regularly used in food and drink—especially since it was plentiful and cheaper than either cassia or Ceylon cinnamon—today, Ceylon cinnamon is the preferred spice in Yucatecan cuisine.

CULINARY USES: Whole sticks of *canela* are often seen peering out of tubs of sweet potatoes, pumpkin, or papaya swimming in dark-brown sugar syrup; it is also used whole in Puchero de tres carnes (p. 350). Ground *canela* is sprinkled on top of Horchata (p. 437), flan, or other desserts. It is a primary ingredient in several regional breads, such as Conchas (p. 202). Mexican cinnamon is now widely available, but lacking it you may substitute cassia cinnamon at half the specified quantity.

CHILES

BOTANICAL / *Capsicum annuum* L., *Capsicum chinense* Jacq. / Family Solanaceae
ENGLISH / chillies, chiles, chilies, chilis
MAYAN / *iik*

DESCRIPTION: Chile is the definitive Mexican condiment, and it is inconceivable for most Mexicans to eat a meal without it. Colonial chroniclers noted this fact: Bartolomé de las Casas wrote, "Without chile, [the Mexicans] do not believe that they are eating." There are five cultivated species and about twenty wild species. The most commonly consumed chile is *Capsicum annuum*, which was domesticated in Mexico sometime between 6,500 and 5,000 BCE. The center of domestication may have been in the Valley of Tehuacán, although recent scholarship suggests multiple centers of domestication, including the Yucatán Peninsula. There is a great diversity of expression in *Capsicum annuum*, many varieties of which are consumed only locally and others that are more broadly distributed. In Yucatán, the varieties most commonly consumed are x'catik, dulce, and ya'ax iik (also known as "chile país" when dried). More widely consumed *C. annuums* include jalapeño or cuaresmeño, serrano, ancho, pasilla, guajillo, and piquín, which in Yucatán is known as "max." But perhaps the most representative chile consumed in Yucatán is from another species, *Capsicum chinense*, specifically, the habanero, unquestionably the chile "mascot" of Yucatán.

Chile heat is measured in Scoville Heat Units. Wilbur Scoville was a U.S. scientist who, in the 1920s, systematically measured the quantity of capsaicin (the heat-producing chemical) found in a range of chiles. The chemical is measured in parts-per-million, with the highest mark being for 100 percent pure capsaicin at 16,000,000 Units.

CHILE HABANERO

ENGLISH / habanero, Scotch bonnet

SCOVILLE HEAT UNITS: 150,000–325,000 / Length: 1½–2 inches (4–5 cm)

At one time the hottest chile in the world, the habanero is so popular in Yucatán and so valued in world markets that a recent battle was waged over its nomenclature. Producers in the state of Yucatán registered a trademark for "Chile habanero de Yucatán." But farmers in Campeche and Quintana Roo—also major producers—filed a lawsuit because they felt the world would forever believe the habanero was from the state of Yucatán. The issue was settled more or less peacefully, and on 4 June 2010, the trade name was changed to the more diplomatic "Chile habanero de la península de Yucatán."

CULINARY USES: The habanero factors prominently in the cuisine of Yucatán: virtually no meal is consumed without at least a little. It is charred and mashed or puréed with sour orange juice to become the fiery Chile tamulado (p. 509), or it is simply carved with knife and fork, a bite of chile eaten with every bite of food. Yucatecan men (and even some women) can frequently be seen holding the stem of a whole chile and devouring it a nibble at a time with their meal. If you can't find habanero, look for the Scotch bonnet chile, a variety of the same species.

[MC]

[MC]

[MC]

CHILE DULCE

ENGLISH / bell pepper / Mayan: *ch'ujuk iik*

SCOVILLE HEAT UNITS: 0 / Diameter: 2½–3 inches (6–8 cm)

The bell pepper available in Yucatán looks rather different from that with which we are familiar: it is round, smaller than the varieties in the United States, and characterized by vertical ridges from stem to base. Chile dulce is frequently grown in *solares*, either in the *ka'anché*—raised growing beds—or in pots to keep them away from animals.

CULINARY USES: Chile dulce is frequently used as an ingredient in *sofrito* along with onion and garlic; *sofrito* is a fragrant vegetable sauté used throughout the Caribbean to flavor soups, stews, and many other dishes.

CHILE MAX, PIQUÍN

ENGLISH / bird pepper / Mayan: *max iik*

SCOVILLE HEAT UNITS: 50,000–100,000 / Diameter ¼–½ inch (0.75–1.5 cm)

Chile max is a relative of the world's earliest chiles as they evolved in the Amazon basin, which were quite small. While the chile is cultivated in other parts of Mexico, in Yucatán it continues to grow as a wild species, dispersed by birds.

CULINARY USES: The chile max is eaten fresh or dried, ground and sprinkled onto fresh fruits and vegetables or onto the maize beverages pozole and *atole*.

CHILE PAÍS / CHILE SECO, CHILE DE PAÍS / CHILE VERDE

MAYAN / *ya'ax iik*

SCOVILLE HEAT UNITS: 5,000–15,000 / Length: 1½ inches (4 cm); width: ½ inch (1.5 cm)

The local fresh chile verde is a small, heart-shaped chile; it is most commonly consumed in its dried state, known variously as chile seco, chile de país, or simply chile país. It is one of the most popular chiles in the pueblos, and for this reason is planted in quantities in the *milpas*.

CULINARY USES: Chile país is commonly used in a simple table sauce—K'uut bi ik (p. 508)—but its most popular use is in the pungent seasoning blend, Recado negro (p. 501). The chile is set afire, the ashes gathered and mixed with other ingredients to create a thick paste that is then used as a marinade or flavoring for stock, giving dishes in which it is employed a characteristic black color and smoky flavor.

CHILE SERRANO

SCOVILLE HEAT UNITS: 10,000–20,000 / Length: 1½–2 inches (4–5 cm); width: ½ inch (1.5 cm)

The slender, finger-shaped serrano is quite picante but has a light herbaceous flavor.

CULINARY USES: It is used on a daily basis throughout Mexico, giving vigor to Salsa verde (p. 509) and Arroz rojo (p. 530).

CHILE XKAT IIK / X'CATIK

ENGLISH / Anaheim chile, blond chile, Italian sweet chile, banana pepper

SCOVILLE HEAT UNITS: 1,000–10,000 / Length: 4 inches (10 cm) on average

The x'catik belongs to the family of blond chiles known in Mexico as "*güeros.*" The flavor is lightly herbaceous.

CULINARY USES: The x'catik is usually charred and added whole to many soups and stews, such as Pavo en escabeche oriental (p. 389). It is the chile of choice for stuffing, such as in Pib x'catik (p. 344), or X'catiques rellenos de cazón (p. 344). It is also used in an egg white–based mayonnaise—Crema de x'catik (p. 363)—served in Lebanese restaurants as an appetizer with pita. As suggested by its English names, all of those chiles are from the same family and may be substituted for one another.

[MC]

[MC]

CILANTRO

BOTANICAL / *Coriandrum sativum* L. / Family Apiaceae
ENGLISH / cilantro, coriander
MAYAN / none

DESCRIPTION: Opinions aside on this culinarily divisive herb, it is widely used in the cuisine of all of Mexico, lending a characteristically light, refreshing flavor. Cilantro belongs to the large botanical family that includes celery, cumin, fennel, carrots, and parsley. In some places in Mexico, it is still called "culantro"—an old Spanish word—but should not be confused with *Eryngium foetidum* (see below), a native of the region also known as *culantro*. Some colonial-era chronicles mention cilantro but use the archaic word: the *Relaciones de Sucopó* says, "There are in this land plants brought from outside, such as garlic, mint and *culantro*, parsley and mustard." The statement establishes the fact that "*culantro*" was the name applied to *Coriandum sativum*, which was brought from "outside" (Europe), since *Eryngium foetidum* is native.

CULINARY USES: Chopped cilantro factors into almost every meal in Yucatán: with chopped chives, it is the typical garnish for Mondongo (p. 221); it lends its delicate aroma to table salsas, guacamole, and many other dishes consumed throughout Mexico. Occasionally, the seeds of the plant (known in English as coriander) are used, as in Recado para puchero (p. 499) and other vintage regional recipes.

CULANTRO / PEREJIL CRIOLLO

BOTANICAL / *Eryngium foetidum* L. / Family Apiaceae
ENGLISH / sawtooth coriander, long coriander, Mexican coriander, spiritweed
MAYAN / none

DESCRIPTION: *Culantro* is one of those wonderful ingredients native to the tropical Americas that were dispersed throughout the world after European contact, forever impacting global cuisines. Today, *culantro* appears as one of the most important flavorings in the cuisines of Thailand, Malaysia, Singapore, and Vietnam. It is also a primary component in the *sofritos* of Puerto Rico. It is rarely if ever consumed in the northern lowlands of the Maya region, including Yucatán, although it is of some importance in the Petén of Guatemala and in Tabasco, zones more favorable to its growth. However, many vintage

Yucatecan cookbooks specify "*culantro*" seeds, even though history indicates what they meant was "cilantro" seeds, or coriander (see *Cilantro*, left). The two herbs are from the same family of Apiaceae, and they do have a rather similar flavor and aroma, but that of *culantro* is much stronger and longer lasting. *Culantro* features long, spiked leaves while cilantro has rounded, convoluted leaves. Even though *culantro* is not a feature of Yucatecan cooking, I include it in this section in order to clarify the many instances of the incorrect usage of the word in vintage regional cookbooks.

CULINARY USES: In the regions where *culantro* grows, it is used in soups, stews, and even salads, as well as in certain popular table salsas in Tabasco.

[MC]

[MC]

EPAZOTE / APAZOTE

BOTANICAL / *Dysphania ambrosioides* (L.)
Mosyakin & Clements / Family Amaranthaceae
ENGLISH / Mexican tea, wormseed,
goosefoot, skunkweed, epazote
MAYAN / *lukum xíiw*

DESCRIPTION: Epazote originated in the tropical belt of Central America and in central and southern Mexico. Used for centuries throughout Mesoamerica to expel parasitic worms from the body, epazote is also incorporated into bean dishes for its alleged antiflatulence properties.

CULINARY USES: A pungent, bitter herb with a taste and smell likened variously to citrus, mint, bleach, or turpentine, epazote appears in many recipes, including bean and meat dishes, stews, and quesadillas. However, perhaps nowhere in Mexico is it used more than in the cooking of Yucatán, where, most famously, a broth of the herb is mixed with pumpkinseed paste to make the classic Maya dish, Papadzules (p. 280). Epazote grows successfully in some growing zones beyond Mexico, or can be purchased dried in the ethnic sections of supermarkets or online. While there really is no substitute for fresh epazote, the dried form can be used effectively to flavor certain dishes, such as beans and soups, in which the visual appeal and stronger taste of the fresh leaf is not of primary importance.

HIERBABUENA / YERBABUENA

BOTANICAL / *Mentha spicata* Crantz /
Family Lamiaceae
ENGLISH / mint, spearmint
MAYAN / none

DESCRIPTION: Mint originated in Europe, where the Greeks used it as an aphrodisiac and the Romans as an appetite stimulant. In Yucatán it is a common ingredient in many dishes, and it is grown in raised beds in most *solares*.

CULINARY USES: While in Europe and North America mint is frequently used in sweet dishes, in Yucatán it is almost exclusively used in savory ones. Some Yucatecans use mint instead of epazote when they cook a pot of beans; Puchero (p. 350) often includes mint, and some people even chop it and add it to scrambled eggs. Several variations of the chopped-meat mixture known as Picadillo (p. 255) also feature mint.

[MR]

[MR]

HOJA SANTA / HIERBA SANTA, MOMO, ACUYO

BOTANICAL / *Piper auritum* Kunth / Family Piperaceae
ENGLISH / Mexican pepperleaf
MAYAN / *xmakulan, mak'ulan*

DESCRIPTION: Large bushes of *hoja santa*, side by side with *chaya* (see above), can frequently be seen peeping over the white-washed stone walls of Maya *solares*. The broad, heart-shaped leaves measure between 6 and 15 inches (15–40 cm) in length. The aroma of the tender leaves is of anise, and the flavor is lightly peppery. *Hoja santa* is not commercially cultivated in Yucatán, but many people transplant it from the *monte* and grow it beside the house. Its appearance in markets is limited to smaller pueblos, and even then quite sporadically, since the plucked leaves tend to wither quickly in Yucatán's fierce heat.

CULINARY USES: The distinctive flavor of *hoja santa* lends itself well as a flavoring for soups and stews, or as a wrapper for fish. The most unusual application of *hoja santa* in Yucatán is in the giant rolled Tamal de xmakulám (p. 133), known in Mayan as *makulaniwaaj* (or "bread of *hoja santa*"). The *tamal* features a filling of lima beans and toasted, ground squash seeds; it is then rolled in a large leaf of *hoja santa* and either steamed or baked underground. The delicate anise flavor of the leaf permeates the *tamal*. Recently, the Instituto Politécnico Nacional developed a powdered seasoning incorporating *Piper auritum* Kunth that reputedly reduces indigestion and stomach infections.

MIEL (HONEY AND BEES)

SCIENTIFIC / *Apis mellifera* L., *Melipona beecheii* Bennett / Family Apidae
ENGLISH / honeybee, stingless honeybee
SPANISH / *abeja dama, abeja nativa, jicote*
MAYAN / *kab, kolel kab, xunan kab*

DESCRIPTION: Many insect species produce honey in Yucatán, including sixteen species of stingless bee as well as certain wasp species. The ancient Mayas gathered honey wherever it was found, but the only bee that they routinely domesticated by cutting down the tree trunks where the bees lived, sealing them, and bringing them to the *milpa* or *solar* was the *melipona*. Read more about bees and honey on page 411.

CULINARY USES: Since ancient times, the Mayas have boiled squash seeds in honey and poured the syrup onto a surface to form something like a nut brittle, called *sikil kab*. Squash, *yuca, makal,* and *camote* (all of which see above) are stewed in honey and served in *jícara* gourds. Honey may be used as a sweetener in pozole and *atole* and is the signature ingredient in the popular local liqueur, Xtabentún (p. 289). Several recipes in this book call for "Mexican honey" because of its distinct and excellent flavor, although other honeys may be substituted. See Resources, p. 539.

[MC]

[MC]

ORÉGANO

BOTANICAL / *Lippia graveolens* L. / Family Verbenaceae
ENGLISH / Mexican oregano
MAYAN / *ak'ilche', xaak che'*

DESCRIPTION: Not to be confused with European, or so-called Italian, oregano, *Lippia graveolens* is in a completely different botanical family, Verbenaceae; European oregano is in the Lamiaceae family. The two bear a faint resemblance in terms of fragrance, but the flavor of *L. graveolens* is much stronger due to its higher concentration of essential oils. There are several varieties of *Lippia graveolens* found throughout Mexico, each slightly different according to its growing environment. The variety here is referred to as *orégano yucateco*; it grows wild, and women and children often go in search of it to dry and sell in the market. It is also cultivated in family *solares* and orchards.

CULINARY USES: Virtually every traditional savory dish in Yucatán includes greater or lesser quantities of Mexican oregano. It is always used dried, never fresh. Women lay out branches of the plant in their *solar* to dry, then gather it up, break the leaves away from the larger stalks, and keep it in a bag or box. Fistfuls of it are toasted on the comal, then ground in the *tamul* before being tossed into this or that stew. Mexican oregano was even adapted into *criollo* cooking and now appears in *escabeches* and several other traditionally Spanish dishes. Outside of Mexico, the herb is now widely available as Mexican oregano.

OREGANÓN / ORÉGANO OREJÓN, ORÉGANO CUBANO

BOTANICAL / *Plectranthus amboinicus* (Lour.) Spreng. / Family Lamiaceae
ENGLISH / Cuban oregano, Spanish thyme, Mexican thyme, Indian borage
MAYAN / none

DESCRIPTION: Related to the common garden ornamental coleus, *oreganón* is also in the same family as the fragrant herbs basil, mint, thyme, sage, rosemary, lavender, and European oregano. The broad, heart-shaped leaf of *oreganón* is serrated and fuzzy; a gentle pinch will easily bruise it, releasing an intoxicating aroma that is reminiscent of sage. *Oreganón* is a native of eastern Africa, but it now grows widely throughout the tropics. It is unclear when it arrived in Yucatán, although the adjective "*cubano*" suggests that it came during the colonial era, when Yucatán and Cuba were close trading partners. Easily grown from cuttings, it is frequently kept in large pots in family *solares*.

CULINARY USES: *Oreganón* is always consumed fresh: the high oil content of the leaves keeps them moist, supple, and almost impossible to dry. In urban settings, people may use it as a substitute for dried oregano (*Lippia graveolens* L.; see above), and it appears in some recipes from Campeche. But to the campesino, *oreganón* is rarely for eating; rather, it is an herbal cure for many ailments such as coughs and colds, a bronchodilator, an aid to digestion, or for alleviating earaches. Although frost sensitive, it can be grown in cooler climates if potted and wintered indoors. For recipes that might include *oreganón*, I have substituted Mexican oregano.

PIMIENTA GORDA / PIMIENTA DE TABASCO, PIMIENTA DULCE

BOTANICAL / *Pimenta dioica* (L.) Merr. / Family Myrtaceae
ENGLISH / allspice
MAYAN / *nukuch pool*

DESCRIPTION: Allspice is the only common pantry spice native to the New World. The natural zone of the tree that produces the berry stretches from the Yucatán Peninsula to the Antilles, where it grows to great heights in the wild. In Yucatán, many people plant it in their *solares* for the excellent shade it provides. The dried berry looks quite similar to black pepper, but is about twice as large, measuring about ¼ inch (6 mm) in diameter. The Spanish noted the use of the spice, calling it "pepper of these parts." In Jamaica, it is cultivated on a commercial scale, and its flavor and aroma are more intense than the Mexican variety.

CULINARY USES: Allspice is well documented as a flavoring used in the chocolate beverage since the pre-Columbian era. It is a versatile flavoring, appearing in sweet as well as savory dishes, and is a key component of many Yucatecan *recados*. The leaf of the tree smells and tastes like the berry and is often used in regional cooking; in vintage cookbooks, the leaf frequently appears as an ingredient in stews like *estofado*.

[PEDRO ACEVEDO-RODRÍGUEZ, COURTESY OF SMITHSONIAN INSTITUTION]

RECADOS / *XA'AK'* / SEASONING BLENDS

First-time visitors to any of the colorful markets throughout Yucatán invariably reach for their cameras when they spot one thing: the rows and rows of towering cones of the fragrant spice pastes known as *recados*.

Not unlike the *moles* of Oaxaca, *recados* are such a feature of Yucatecan cuisine that the food would be incomprehensible without them. Few are the dishes of Yucatán that are not flavored with one *recado*—and sometimes two or three. Mastering the art of the Yucatecan *recado* is like accomplishing the finesse in a French sauce, a Oaxacan *mole*, or an Indian curry. The *recado* is the sine que non of our cuisine.

A *recado* is a Yucatecan seasoning blend that may be considered an early convenience food. Rather than suffer the monotony of measuring, toasting, grinding, and blending chiles and herbs each time they were needed for a specific dish, the Maya woman made larger quantities of these blends and employed the mixture as needed.

Recados are used in two primary ways: as a thick, creamy marinade for meat, fowl, or fish when dissolved in vinegar or sour orange juice; or as a flavoring and coloring agent when diluted in water or stock, resulting in an aromatic sauce.

Some Yucatecan cooks still prepare their own *recados*, but nowadays most rely on the artisanally made blends found in every market. These are prepared in small quantities, usually by families or by lone vendors. Some *recados* are so popular that they are prepared on a commercial scale, too: most supermarkets—even beyond Mexico—offer commercial brands like Marín, La Anita, and El Yucateco, packaged in small, dense bricks.

Some *recados* that you will see in the market are simply ground dried herbs and spices, resulting in a powder, such as Recado para escabeche. Others are prepared as a paste using vinegar to bind the ground spices and herbs together, such as Recado para bistec. Recipes for *recados* begin on page 497.

VAINILLA

BOTANICAL / *Vanilla planifolia* Jack.ex. Andrews / Family Orchidaceae
ENGLISH / vanilla
MAYAN / *siis bik*

DESCRIPTION: Vanilla must surely be the most widely used flavoring in history. Both the fragrance and the flavor come from the so-called vanilla bean—actually, a seed pod that grows only after a specific orchid (*Vanilla planifolia*) is pollinated. The Spanish word "*vainilla*" comes from "*vaina*," meaning "sheath," and describes the appearance of the seedpod. The vanilla orchid is native to Mexico; the Totonacs of Veracruz were the first to cultivate it, and all vanilla produced globally today is descended from those primal flowers. The ancient Olmecs valued the aroma of the pod and burned it as incense; the Mayas valued its taste and were probably the first to include it as a flavoring in the chocolate beverage. After the arrival of the Spanish, many attempts were made to cultivate the orchid elsewhere in the world, but all efforts failed until the mid-nineteenth century, when botanists realized that the orchids were pollinated exclusively by the native *melipona* bee (see more on p. 411). A happy accident occasioned by a twelve-year-old slave in Reúnion, a French island east of Madagascar, later demonstrated that the orchids could be hand pollinated—and from that moment on, vanilla production expanded globally. Vanilla orchids grow in the wild in Yucatán, but they are not commercialized. It is believed that the best-quality vanilla grows above 6,500 feet (2,000 m), and some gastronomical experts insist that the best vanilla in the world is still that which is produced in its home in Veracruz.

CULINARY USES: The use of vanilla in Yucatán is much the same as it is in the rest of Mexico and the world. Desserts like Caballeros pobres (p. 348), ice cream, and flan, as well as sweet breads like Conchas (p. 202), feature vanilla as a delicate top note. Unfortunately, high-quality "real" vanilla is difficult to find in Yucatán, and virtually all of that offered in the markets (or in airport shops targeting tourists!) is in large bottles for a low price, a sure sign that it is artificial. Thankfully, many gourmet stores and online businesses offer excellent, pure Mexican vanilla—for a price. Buy the best you can afford and use a few drops at a time (see Resources, p. 539).

[RENE DROUYER / DREAMSTIME.COM]

2

The

MAYA

HEARTLAND

Countless times, I find myself playing tour guide through Yucatán, driving along highways as straight as taut thread, giving visitors a bug's-eye view of the peninsula's vast limestone plateau. To me, it's as powerful and inscrutable as the sea. Not all of my guests see it that way; all too often I hear myself talking louder and faster, trying to jolt passengers out of the hypnotic state induced by the drive by spotlighting the many features in the seeming featurelessness.

But perhaps—much like the allure of a lover—it isn't what you see that makes Yucatán so seductive; it is what you don't see.

Uxmal, a Late Classic Maya city in southwest Yucatán. [DK]

The flatness of Yucatán's terrain is broken occasionally by the remains of ancient Maya cities. [MR]

D ESCRIBED SCIENTIFICALLY, YUCATÁN'S PHYSIQUE doesn't paint a very poetic portrait: "A subtropical dry broadleaf forest atop a flat karst limestone plateau with 10- to 30-feet-high outcrops. Mean annual temperature of 78°F. Average annual rainfall of about 37–47 inches decreasing south to north with a six month dry season."

But for the attentive lover, the description is like a veil that begs to be lifted.

Dry forest? How did the original inhabitants of Yucatán survive in this harsh environment, with so little rain and virtually no surface water? And not merely survive, but also build great cities and an enduring civilization?

Water: first mystery solved. Even though there is a scarcity of rain and surface water, that limestone table beneath the wheels of my speeding car is as porous as a sponge. And, like a sponge, it is full of freshwater absorbed during intense downpours in the rainy season. In fact, the world's longest underground river snakes its way 95 miles (153 km) through Quintana Roo, connecting caves and subterranean tributaries. With many such underground rivers throughout the peninsula at depths averaging 75 feet (23 m), gradual erosion has caused the limestone to collapse at weak points, forming water-filled sinkholes, known as *cenotes*, from the Mayan word "*dzonot*." Maya cities were always situated near these freshwater sources. The Spanish followed suit and built their colonial cities nearby. Dive to the bottom of a *cenote* and you may find bones of sacrificial victims or Spanish coins or jadeite—all hidden from sight until you take the plunge.

So many of Yucatán's charms and mysteries remain

invisible to the untrained eye. The endless limestone plateau numbing our tour is porous due to the impact of a city-sized asteroid that struck the peninsula 65 million years ago, virtually liquefying the surrounding stone. It is that porosity that gives the limestone its water-holding capabilities. Scientists continue to argue about the possibility that the impact unleashed a shroud of dust that covered the sun and caused the extinction of many species—including the dinosaurs. Undisputed, though, is the tangible evidence of the cataclysmic impact: a massive crater 110 miles (175 km) wide, known as the Chicxulub Crater, that encircles the upper quarter of the peninsula and extends far out into the Gulf of Mexico—visible only from outer space (see map, p. 3).

Back down at ant level, the jungle guards its secrets, too. Those endless thickets of wild, dry forest beyond the windshield are often not really wild at all, but, rather, feral

gardens that the Mayas once tended. Look for large groves of similar trees, like the *ramón*: especially near the royal cities, the Mayas practiced a form of silviculture in which large numbers of economically useful plants were cultivated beneath the protection of forest canopy—grand orchards hidden throughout the jungle.

So, this seemingly inhospitable environment was for the Mayas a haven of almost limitless resources, transformed by the ingenious ways in which they lived with and responded to the land in order to survive. And it was not just water systems and managed forest orchards that nourished them, but also sustainable hunting in the *monte*, or outback; communally farmed shifting agriculture in which cropland was "borrowed" from forest deities to create the *milpa*, or crop field; and the *solar*, or kitchen garden, in which a wide variety of domesticated plants and animals was tended close at hand. Far from any notions of

Sacred cenote at Chichén Itzá. [KONSTIK / DREAMSTIME.COM]

a "collapsed civilization," these practices continue to the present as uninterrupted demonstrations of the Mayas' prodigious survival and success.

The heart of the land of the Mayas has always been the land itself.

A NATURAL CONTINUUM

According to many scholars, the lowland Maya culture was the most successful in all of Mesoamerica in terms of several key characteristics: the area occupied; population size; cultural longevity and continuity; and diversification of the language. This success was due in large part to the Mayas' relationship to nature and the ingenious use of the land they revered.

The most ancient food source, the *monte*, is still employed for hunting and gathering practices that date back millennia. The Maya tradition of beekeeping started here, too.

The *milpa* brought Maya ingenuity full circle, combining their extensive knowledge of silviculture with their well-honed skills in plant domestication. They learned from a very early time how to plant domesticated crops in small forest clearings and created an adaptive land-management practice far more sustainable than modern methods.

Another important step in plant and animal domestication took place in the *solar*. A variety of fruits, vegetables, and animals were tended on the grounds of the household compound, ensuring at least a modest supply of food year-round.

(above) The Yucatán wilderness, 1899. [THE FIELD MUSEUM LIBRARY]
(opposite page) A thin line divides the monte *from the* milpa. [MC]

THE MONTE

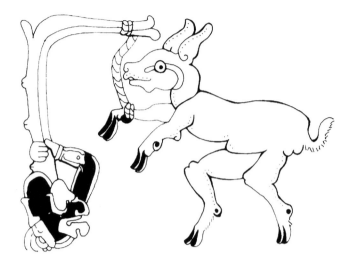

Y EARS AGO, I WENT TO COOK with Guadalupe Aké Darza of Peto, in southern Yucatán. I asked what the menu was for the day, and doña Guadalupe's answer was "pavo del monte." A hushed murmur spread among family members in the room, from aging uncles to young mothers and their children. Wild turkey, bagged just that morning, was to be cooked in *k'óol rojo*, a maize-thickened sauce stained blood red with *achiote*.

The reverence for the dish that I sensed among the family had to do with much more than just the recipe. I understood that the "del monte" qualifier guaranteed the best, the freshest, the most "real" food there was. In Yucatán, there remains an undying respect and awe for all things from the *monte*.

The *monte* long ago ceased being the sole source of sustenance among the Mayas as other food production systems proved more controllable. Still, it remains indispensable. It is in the *monte* where foods are hunted or gathered, and it is the *monte* that is partly destroyed in order to produce crop foods in the *milpa*. In this way, there is a striking ambiguity between the two entities: *milperos* (farmers) know that they must cut down and burn the *monte* in order to plant their *milpas*. On the other hand, *milperos* need the *monte* to thrive and produce more nutrients for the crops, as well as to nurture the wild animals the Mayas still hunt for food. The Maya *milpero*—both past and present—treads a very thin line between the two realms, for the *milpero* is also the hunter.

MAYA HUNTING PRACTICES

Among modern concerns for species extinction, the Maya way of hunting appears to be self-restricting and non-threatening. A 2007 study in the Petenes Biosphere Reserve of Campeche indicates that for a least a century, hunting has been sustainable at the local level. This is due to a couple of significant factors, both natural and cultural/religious. Regional environmental conditions, such as long periods of intense rains and flooding, naturally limit hunting to a few months of the year, specifically, during the dry season, from December through May, when dwindling water sources lure many species to watering holes. Perhaps more important, there is an ideology of conservation inherent in Maya culture that guides hunters not to hunt pregnant females, and not to hunt more animals than necessary to cover the basic subsistence needs of the hunter and his family.

(above) Deer hunting and trapping (from the pre-Columbian Madrid Codex).
[AUREA HERNÁNDEZ AFTER THE MADRID CODEX]

A water-filled bajo in Quintana Roo. One hunting method still used by the Mayas is simple stalking (ch'uuk). Yucatán's terrain features great shallow depressions in the limestone substrate, known in Spanish as bajos. *There, moisture accumulates, attracting thirsty animals. These depressions are easy for a hunter to spot from a distance, since nearby trees grow considerably taller than surrounding plants. Hunters often camp out overnight near the* bajos, *waiting patiently for prey to come to drink.* [LUNAMARINA / DREAMSTIME.COM]

The ocellated turkey of Yucatán. [MG]

PAVO DEL MONTE

SCIENTIFIC / *Meleagris ocellata* Cuvier / Family Phasianidae
ENGLISH / ocellated turkey
MAYAN / *cutz, kutz*

DESCRIPTION, ORIGIN, AND HISTORY: The bird that elicited so much enthusiasm from doña Guadalupe's family is the ocellated turkey. Native to Yucatán, the birds bear similarities to the peacock, with iridescent blue and green feathers. Although they can fly, they are usually seen strutting about during the day; at night they sleep in tall trees. In his sixteenth-century chronicle of Yucatán, Fray Diego de Landa mentions the birds and explains how the Mayas hunted them in the trees with arrows but also how they gathered the eggs and bred the hatchlings in the *solar*. Bone deposits suggest that the ocellated turkey was widely and frequently consumed. It was a very important ritual food: the Dresden Codex contains various glyphs that have been interpreted as distinct recipes for the bird. One glyph reads *kutz waaj*, which translates to "wild turkey *tamal*."

PAVO DEL MONTE EN K'ÓOL ROJO / CHAK K'ÓOL

TURKEY IN MAIZE-THICKENED RED SAUCE

As with so many other recipes in this book, the first step for Pavo del monte en k'óol rojo is to grill the poultry, then finish cooking it in a flavorful liquid. This is a vestige of ancient Maya practices in which hunted animals were often cooked on the spot, then refreshed back home in a finished dish. Today the custom continues, partly by tradition and partly for the added flavor the grilling achieves. "*K'óol*" translates to "thick soup" and generally refers to any kind of stock that has been thickened, traditionally with *masa de maíz* (nixtamalized corn dough). *K'óol* is prepared in the four sacred colors of the Mayas, and the Mayan prefix serves as the identifier: *chak* = red; *sak* = white; *boox* = black; and *k'an* = yellow. In addition to many other meanings, the colors symbolize the cardinal directions east, north, west, and south, respectively, and the deities that govern each are honored with their own special *k'óol*. *Kóol rojo* ("thick red soup") is a Mayan/Spanish hybrid title for the dish. Recipes for Sak k'óol and Boox k'óol can be found on pages 141 and 424.

The wild turkey of Yucatán is a somewhat scrawny creature, not fed on grain and hormones like the ones we eat at Thanksgiving. Therefore, it isn't unusual to use an entire bird for a dish that will feed only six to eight people, with no leftovers. Considering the size of the behemoths available in the United States and Canada, I suggest that you use only turkey parts instead of a whole bird.

Prepare ahead note: Brining should be done several hours in advance or overnight (see Basic Techniques on p. 516). Finished Pavo del monte en k'óol rojo keeps well under refrigeration and improves with age; reheat gently, adding a bit more stock or water to achieve the desired sauce consistency.

YIELD: 8–10 SERVINGS

PREPARE *SOFRITO*

Heat the lard in a stockpot until shimmering. Add the onions and garlic and cook until the onion is translucent. Add the remaining ingredients and cook another 5 minutes. Remove the pot from the heat and set aside.

PREPARE STOCK

Remove the turkey from the heat before it is completely cooked; there should be charring and grill marks, but it should still show pink juices. Transfer the grilled turkey to the stockpot and cover with 9 cups (2.25 L) of water. Pour the remaining cup (250 ml) of water into a blender jar; add the garlic, *recado*, chile, and bouillon and liquefy thoroughly. Transfer the liquid to the stockpot. Bring to a boil, reduce the heat, and cook at a gentle boil for 30 minutes, or until the meat is cooked to an internal temperature of 165°F (74°C). Remove the turkey from the stock and set aside.

TO PREPARE AHEAD

Enriched Lard (p. 513)
Recado para escabeche (p. 498)
Pollo asado (p. 270), using turkey pieces instead of chicken
Recado rojo (p. 500)
Masa prepared from either nixtamalized corn or *masa harina* (p. 518)

FOR THE *SOFRITO*

2 Tbs. (28 g) Enriched Lard
1 medium onion (10 oz. / 275 g), peeled, charred, and finely chopped
4 medium cloves garlic (1 oz. / 24 g), peeled, charred, and finely chopped
3 medium Roma tomatoes (10½ oz. / 300 g), charred and coarsely chopped
1 Tbs. (2 g) dried whole Mexican oregano, lightly toasted and ground
1 tsp. (3 g) Recado para escabeche
2 sprigs fresh epazote (Substitute: 1 tsp. / 1.5 g dried, crumbled)

FOR THE STOCK

3 lbs. (1.5 k) Pollo asado, using turkey pieces instead of chicken
10 cups (2.5 L) water, divided
1 medium head garlic (1¾ oz. / 50 g), charred, peeled, and separated into cloves
5 Tbs. (75 g) Recado rojo
1 chile chipotle in adobo (⅓ oz. / 10 g), drained
2 Tbs. (24 g) powdered chicken bouillon

¾ cup (170 g) *masa*

½ cup (40 g) chives, chopped

FOR SERVING

Tortillas (p. 518)

K'uut bi ik (p. 508), or the chile
   sauce of your choice

FINISH *K'ÓOL ROJO*

Strain the stock through a sieve into a saucepan. Mash and press as much liquid through as possible; discard the residue. You should have about 8 cups (2 L) of stock; discard or reserve any extra for another use. Mix 2 cups (500 ml) cooking liquid with the *masa* and mash to incorporate. Transfer the *masa* slowly to the cooking liquid, whisking constantly. Return the mixture to a boil, then reduce to a simmer. Simmer 10 minutes, until the mixture thickens slightly, whisking frequently to prevent lumps. If lumps do form, continue whisking or use an immersion blender to smooth. Stir in the chives and serve. (Note: If you will be using the K'óol rojo as a filling for any of the tamales in this book, increase the quantity of masa to 1¼ cups [280 g] in order to create a thicker sauce.)

TO SERVE

Carve or pull the turkey meat into serving portions. Place the meat in shallow soup bowls and ladle on some of the red sauce. Serve with warm tortillas and chile sauce.

VARIATIONS

K'óol de venado / Venado en k'óol rojo / Chak k'óolil kéej (Venison in Maize-Thickened Red Sauce): Brine, marinate, and grill or roast the venison as per the instructions for Pibil de venado (p. 421), removing it from the heat source while it is still very rare since it will finish cooking in the stew. Cut the meat into cubes and finish per the master recipe for Pavo del monte en k'óol rojo (p. 86). Serving instructions are the same.

Many Yucatecan tamales are filled with shredded meat from K'óol rojo as well as the sauce. Prepare K'óol rojo using Pollo asado (p. 270), Cochinita pibil (p. 420), or Pibil de venado (p. 421). See Cháamchamitos de jolo'och and other *tamal* recipes starting on page 103.

A WILD MENU

Like other Yucatecan campesinos, Artemio Moo Cauich divides his day working in his *milpa*, tending his *solar*, and occasionally going hunting in the *monte* to supplement his family's diet. Moo (pronounced "moe-oh") avers there are many unusual—and edible—animals found there.

At the top of a menu familiar to all campesinos are two birds and two rodents: the mourning dove (*sakpakal*) and the quail (*beech*); and a pouched, burrowing rodent known as *tuza* in Spanish (*baj* in Mayan), and the hare (*t'u'ul*). The *tuza* is hunted vigorously because of the damage it can do to crops.

Iguana (*juuj*) has long been consumed in Yucatán and throughout Mexico. The Spaniards first encountered it on the island of Hispaniola in the early 1500s, and chronicler to the king Peter Martyr described their reaction. After recovering from their initial disgust, "they made complete gluttons of themselves, and spoke of nothing but the deliciousness of the serpents [*sic*], and that their meat was more exquisite than our own peacocks, pheasants or partridges."

Other animals popular in the campesino diet include the agouti, a rodent known in central Mexico as *tepezcuintle* or paca (*jaleb* in Mayan). Even more enticing species like the collared peccary (*kitam*), the tapir (*tsíimin*), and the deer (*kéej*) are also hunted in the *monte*. Because these animals yield meat that is superior to the other meats and much sought after, they are protected by government restrictions, and the furtive hunting of them is prohibited to avoid extinction. All are usually marinated in sour orange juice and *achiote*, wrapped in banana leaves, and cooked in a *píib*.

Although Moo doesn't care for armadillo (*weech*), he does have an appreciation for raccoon (*k'ulu'*) and badger (*chi'ik*), both of which, he says, can be prepared in a variety of tasty Yucatecan recipes.

(above) Iguana is cooked in Yucatecan recipes much like any other animal protein. [MR]

Mourning dove. [STEVE BRIGMAN / DREAMSTIME.COM]

Peccary. [SCOTT GRIESSEL / DREAMSTIME.COM]

The tapir as well as the collared peccary—a member of the Suidae family—were replaced in the Maya diet when the Spanish brought domesticated pigs to the New World. [OM]

CODORNIZ EN PIPIÁN DE CHAYA Y HABANERO

ROASTED QUAIL WITH A PURÉE OF SQUASH SEEDS, *CHAYA*, AND HABANERO

TO PREPARE AHEAD

Pepita molida (p. 497)

Enriched Lard (p. 513)

Semiboned quail, brined (p. 536)

Longaniza de Valladolid (p. 481),
  or substitute

Seville orange juice substitute
  (p. 514), unless fresh Seville
  oranges are available

FOR THE *PIPIÁN*

½ lb. (250 g) *chaya* (Substitute:
  chard or kale)

3 cups (375 g) Pepita molida

4 medium tomatillos (14 oz. /
  400 g), husk removed, charred

½ medium white onion (5 oz. /
  137.5 g), peeled, charred, and
  coarsely chopped

2 medium cloves garlic (½ oz. /
  12 g), peeled and charred

1–2 medium chiles habaneros
  (¼ oz. / 7 g each), charred and
  seeded

1 cup (250 ml) chicken stock or
  bouillon

½ tsp. (3 g) sea salt

2 Tbs. (28 g) Enriched Lard
  (Substitute: Spanish olive oil)

This recipe for quail in a green *pipián*, or squash seed sauce, is an inventive play on several regional dishes and is quick and easy to prepare. The *pipián* gets its color from *chaya* as well as tart tomatillos. The roasted quail is served atop a bright smear of the *pipián* and a mound of puréed white *camote* (sweet potato, also known as *boniato*, available in some Mexican markets). Both the *pipián* and the sweet potato purée make excellent accompaniments for other dishes.

Olga María Frías Cámara shared this recipe with me. Olga is a dynamic cook who, after raising her children through college, decided to return to school to complete her culinary certification. Her intelligent approach to food and her thorough knowledge of both Mexican and Yucatecan traditions have earned her several scholarships as well as cooking gigs in Peru, Germany, Israel, and Taiwan.

[JC]

FOR THE SWEET POTATO PURÉE

1½ lb. (680 g) white *camote* (Substitute: standard sweet potato), peeled and boiled until tender

4 Tbs. (60 ml) Mexican *crema* (Substitute: whipping cream, sour cream, or plain yogurt)

3 Tbs. (42 g) butter

1 tsp. (0.65 g) dried whole Mexican oregano, lightly toasted and ground

1½ tsp. (9 g) sea salt

½ tsp. (2 g) freshly ground black pepper

FOR THE QUAIL

12 semiboned quail (about 3¼ oz. / 90 g each, total weight approximately 2½ lbs. / 1.1 k), brined

Spanish olive oil

Vegetable oil for frying

Sea salt

FOR THE GARNISHES

2 Longaniza de Valladolid (Substitute: chorizo, commercial longaniza, or other smoked sausage), about 7½ oz. / 215 g total, removed from casing, fried, and crumbled

¾ cup (95 g) green hulled squash seeds, gently toasted in 1 Tbs. (15 ml) vegetable oil and lightly salted

Pickled onions: ¼ medium red onion (2½ oz. / 68.75 g), thinly sliced top to bottom and separated into half-moon shapes, dressed with ¼ cup (62.5 ml) Seville orange juice or substitute

¼ cup (15 g) cilantro leaves, thinly cut in chiffonade

Prepare ahead note: Both the *pipián* and the sweet potato purée can be prepared in advance and reheated just before serving. Add a bit of stock to the *pipián* and milk or cream to the potatoes if needed to achieve the desired consistency.

YIELD: 6 SERVINGS

PREPARE *PIPIÁN*

Bring a pot of water to a rapid boil and add salt. Wash the *chaya*, remove the thick stems and discard. Blanch the *chaya* for 1 minute in the boiling water. Remove the pan from the heat and drain the *chaya* thoroughly in a fine-mesh sieve; press out as much liquid as possible and set aside.

Place the Pepita molida in the bowl of a food processor, add the *chaya* and remaining ingredients except the lard and process until thoroughly puréed. Check the seasonings. (If you are heat shy, add only ½ habanero at a time.)

Heat the lard in a large skillet until shimmering. Add the purée all at once; it should sputter and splatter, so stand back. Reduce the heat to low and cook 3–4 minutes, stirring constantly to prevent sticking, until some of the liquid has evaporated and the mixture is slightly thickened; the consistency should be like creamy oatmeal. Remove the skillet from the heat and set aside.

PREPARE SWEET POTATO PURÉE

In a food processor or the bowl of an electric mixer, whip the potatoes with the remaining ingredients until smooth; keep warm until time to serve.

ROAST QUAIL AND FINISH

Preheat the oven to 350°F (176°C). Rub the quail with a bit of olive oil and arrange them in a baking dish large enough to hold them in one layer. Roast for 15–20 minutes, or until they are just firm when you press a breast with your finger. Remove the pan from the oven.

Pour 2 inches (5 cm) of vegetable oil into a deep skillet and heat to 350°F (176°C). Add the quail a few at a time and fry until the skin is golden brown and crisped and no pink juices flow, a total of 1–2 minutes depending on the size of the birds and how done they were when they came out of the oven. Transfer the quail to paper towels to drain, sprinkle with salt, and continue with the remaining quail.

TO SERVE

Reheat the *pipián* and potatoes. Spoon some of the *pipián* onto an individual serving plate; mound potatoes to one side. Arrange 2 of the quail straddling the potatoes and the *pipián* and garnish with crumbled sausage, squash seeds, and onions and finish with the cilantro.

SALMÍ DE CONEJO
RABBIT RAGOÛT WITH *ALCAPARRADO*

TO PREPARE AHEAD
Brined rabbit (p. 536)
Recado para todo (p. 499)
Enriched Lard (p. 513)
Longaniza de Valladolid (p. 481),
   or substitute

FOR SAUTÉING AND STEWING THE RABBIT

1 large rabbit (2½–3 lbs. /
   1.2–1.5 k), brined and cut into
   serving pieces: 2 forelegs, 2 hind
   legs, and the saddle cut into
   2–4 pieces
1 cup (125 g) all-purpose flour
1 tsp. (6 g) sea salt
1 tsp. (3 g) Recado para todo
3 Tbs. (42 g) Enriched Lard
3–4 links Longaniza de Valladolid
   (Substitute: chorizo, commercial
   longaniza, or other smoked
   sausage, approximately 9 oz. /
   255 g total)
2 Tbs. (32 g) grated *piloncillo*
   (Substitute: dark brown sugar)
4 cups (1 L) beef stock or bouillon
1 medium head garlic (1¾ oz.
   / 50 g), charred, peeled, and
   separated into cloves

Hares have always been plentiful in Yucatán's dry forest, and rabbit breeding is a popular hobby—whether for fun or for food. Vintage regional cookbooks always feature at least one recipe for rabbit, although it is rare to find rabbit dishes in restaurants here. This recipe is a hybrid of two from the 1944 *Cocina yucateca* by Lucrecia Ruz *vda.* de Baqueiro. *Salmí* is a wine-based ragoût, the wine being sherry in this case. The rabbit is fried first, then slowly stewed in the wine and seasonings, and finished, as in so many regional dishes, with the *alcaparrado* mixture (p. 400) of capers, raisins, olives, and almonds. Burnt sugar deepens the flavor of the wine.

Prepare ahead note: Salmí de conejo only improves with age; prepare a day ahead and reheat just before serving.

YIELD: 6–8 SERVINGS

SAUTÉ RABBIT

Remove the rabbit from the brine, rinse, and pat dry; discard the brining solution. On a broad plate, mix the flour, salt, and *recado* and set aside. Heat the lard in a large flameproof casserole with a lid until shimmering. Dredge the rabbit pieces in the flour mixture; reserve any remaining flour. Add the rabbit pieces a few at a time to the hot fat and sauté until well browned, turning once, 2–3 minutes per side. Transfer the browned pieces to a platter. Add the sausages to the casserole and sauté until just browned; remove to the platter with the rabbit. Leave the fat in the casserole.

STEW RABBIT

If your rabbit includes a liver, place it along with 1 cup (250 ml) of the stock in a blender jar and liquefy. Combine the purée with the remaining stock and set aside.

Return the casserole with the cooking fat to medium-high heat. When the fat is shimmering, sprinkle the *piloncillo* evenly over the bottom of the casserole; as the sugar melts it will froth and bubble over the surface. Watch it closely; as the bubbles become dark to black, immediately add the beef stock mixture. Stir to dissolve the burnt sugar. Transfer the sautéed rabbit pieces to the casserole, add the charred garlic cloves, and bring to a boil. Reduce the heat to low, cover, and cook slowly while you prepare the rest of the dish.

FOR THE *SOFRITO* AND FINISHING THE RAGOÛT

2 Tbs. (28 g) Enriched Lard

1 medium onion (10 oz. / 275 g), finely chopped

4 medium cloves garlic (1 oz. / 24 g), peeled and finely chopped

1 cup (5 oz. / 140 g) green bell pepper, chopped

6 medium Roma tomatoes (1⅓ lbs. / 600 g), seeded and chopped

¼ cup (45 g) almonds, blanched and slivered

20 medium green olives, whole unpitted, pitted, or pimiento-stuffed and sliced

2 Tbs. (30 g) black raisins

1 Tbs. (15 g) small capers, drained

1 tsp. (6 g) sea salt

1 tsp. (3 g) Recado para todo

1 cup (250 ml) sweet sherry

FOR SERVING

Arroz blanco (p. 529) or Pan francés (p. 194), optional

K'uut bi ik (p. 508), optional

PREPARE *SOFRITO*

Heat the lard in a skillet until shimmering. Add the onion and garlic and cook over medium heat until the onion is translucent, 2–3 minutes. Add the remaining ingredients except the sherry and cook over medium heat until the tomatoes are tender and most of the liquid has evaporated, 5–6 minutes. Add 2 Tbs. (16 g) of the reserved flour mixture and cook 1 minute, stirring constantly.

FINISH RAGOÛT AND SERVE

Transfer the *sofrito* to the casserole containing the rabbit and stir. Add the sherry and sausages and bring to a boil. Reduce heat to a simmer, cover, and cook on low heat 30–40 minutes, or until the rabbit is very tender and the sauce has thickened. Alternatively, you may bake the dish at 350°F (176°C) for 1 hour.

TO SERVE

Remove the sausage and slice each piece in half across the width. Plate pieces of the rabbit with a slice of the sausage and spoon on some of the sauce, evenly distributing the *alcaparrado* mixture and garlic. Accompany with Arroz blanco or Pan francés and a mixed green salad if desired. Diners add chile sauce to taste.

Yucatán brocket deer. [COURTESY ECOMUSEO DEL CACAO]

VENADO / VENADO COLA BLANCA / VENADO TEMAZATE

SCIENTIFIC / *Odocoileus virginianus* Zimmerman / *Mazama americana* Erxleben / *Mazama pandora* Merriam / Family Cervidae
ENGLISH / Yucatán white-tailed deer / Yucatán brocket deer
MAYAN / *keh (ceh)*, *kéej*, *yuk*

DESCRIPTION, ORIGIN, AND HISTORY: Venison is one of the most prized foods of the Yucatecan table. Several species are plentiful: the white-tailed *virginianus* is distributed throughout the Americas, and several varieties have evolved, including the *yucatanensis*, unique to the peninsula. The *Mazama* sp. (brocket deer) is a medium-to-small animal: shoulder heights vary between 14 and 31 inches (35–80 cm). The *M. americana* and *M. pandora* are quite similar: the former is distributed from northern Mexico into South America; the latter is found exclusively in the Yucatán Peninsula, Guatemala, and Belize. Among the ancient Mayas, deer were hunted so systematically that the practice bordered on domestication. Vast tracts of forest were left intact even in highly populated zones to ensure an accessible deer population. In certain Maya communities, hunters still trap infant deer and raise them in the *solar*. Fray Diego de Landa refers to the practice during the colonial era, saying that women coddled the little ones so much that they grew to be tame and could no longer live in the *monte*. Many representations and glyphs on vessels, in texts, and on murals graphically depict the deer or suggest recipes such as venison tamales. Venison continues to be so popular on the Yucatecan menu that efforts to breed the white-tailed deer are being undertaken by several conservationist and economic-development groups to avoid overhunting.

FAISÁN

SCIENTIFIC / *Crax rubra* / Family Cracidae
ENGLISH / Great curassow
MAYAN / *k'anbul, k'ambul*

DESCRIPTION, ORIGIN, AND HISTORY: This animal presents but one more example of why we would do best to refer to the scientific names of things if we really want to know what each other is talking about. The Spanish saw in Yucatán a bird they thought they recognized and called it *faisán*, or pheasant. In truth, however, the bird they saw was the great curassow (*Crax rubra*), which does bear similar physical characteristics to the European pheasant, so perhaps the Spanish are to be excused. The great curassow is distributed from the Yucatán Peninsula into northern Central America. It is described as "vulnerable" on the International Union for Circumpolar Health Red List of Threatened Species, so for dinner we substitute farmed pheasant or Cornish game hens.

Great currasow. [IMAGEBROKERRF / INMAGINE.COM]

LAND OF THE PHEASANT AND THE DEER

A colonial legend relates the story of three animals blessed by Yuum K'áax, the lord of the *monte*: the pheasant, the deer, and the rattlesnake. The three were charged with awakening the Maya peoples when it was time to rebel against the conquerors and reclaim their land. Alas, the call has not yet come, and the Mayas continue to await the signal. Yucatán is still known as *la tierra del faisán y del venado* (land of the pheasant and the deer).

Adult and adolescent painted deer decorate a three-legged ceramic plate probably made in a workshop in Campeche. Since the Mayas often decorated their ceramic vessels with glyphs or images of the foods they held, this plate was most likely created as a serving platter for venison. [MC]

VENADO EN PIPIÁN ROJO / ÓOM SIKIL BI KÉEJ

VENISON IN RED SQUASH—SEED SAUCE

TO PREPARE AHEAD

Recado rojo (p. 500)

Pepita molida (p. 497)

Pibil de venado (p. 421)

Masa prepared from either
nixtamalized corn or *masa barina*
(p. 517)

FOR THE COOKING LIQUID

4 cups (1 L) beef stock or bouillon

1 medium white onion (10 oz. /
275 g), peeled, charred, and cut
in quarters

2 medium heads garlic (3½ oz. /
100 g), charred, peeled, and
separated into cloves

5 chiles país (Substitute: 3 dried
chiles de árbol), stemmed and
seeded

1 Tbs. (2 g) dried whole Mexican
oregano, lightly toasted

5 allspice berries

3 Tbs. (45 g) Recado rojo

2 chiles chipotles in adobo (¾ oz. /
20 g), drained

1 cup (250 ml) water

The creamy nuttiness of *pipián* is about as close as one can come to savoring a taste of ancient Mexico. Guadalupe Aké Darza of Peto, in southern Yucatán, shared her venison in *pipián rojo* recipe with me. Her husband had acquired from a neighbor a tiny saddle of native *venado*, which had already been cooked in a *píib*. The second cooking of the smoked venison, in *pipián*, is a tradition that stretches back in history.

In pre-Columbian times, after slaying an animal like a deer, hunters would salt or cook the meat on the spot to avoid spoilage during what might be a long trip home. The methodology would likely have been to roast or smoke the meat in a *píib*—a convenient strategy in the middle of the wilderness. Later, the meat would be refreshed by cooking it again in one of a variety of sauces. *Pipián—óom sikil* in Mayan—is still a popular sauce for many game animals, including iguana and pheasant, as well as certain vegetables like *camote* and *chaya*.

With our roasted venison now in the stewpot, doña Guadalupe stressed the importance of adding some sourness to the *pipián*. She told me that Yucatecan cooks customarily add *ciruela* (*Spondias purpurea*, p. 29), also known as Spanish plum or purple mombin—a fruit indigenous to a broad swath of the New World tropics. But since it is available only in the summer months, there were none to be found on the day we cooked. Her solution, used by many local cooks, was to substitute the acidic *tomate verde* (tomatillo), which is the ingredient I have suggested here, since *ciruela* may be difficult to find north of the border. Doña Guadalupe also gave me another tip: as the stew finishes cooking, puddles of delicious, bright-red fat will accumulate on the surface; skim it off and use a few drops as a garnish on each serving.

Prepare ahead note: Pibil de venado must be prepared in advance; you may do so one or two days ahead and refrigerate until ready to use. The finished *pipián* only improves with age; refrigerate up to one week and reheat prior to serving. Leftovers can also be frozen successfully for three to four months.

YIELD: 10 SERVINGS

PREPARE COOKING LIQUID

Pour the stock into a saucepan, add the onion and half of the garlic. Bring the stock to a simmer and cook 15 minutes, or until the onion is tender. Strain the liquid through a fine-mesh sieve placed over a stockpot and use a spatula or wooden spoon to mash the vegetables and extract as much liquid as possible. Discard any pulp that remains.

Place next 3 ingredients in a spice grinder or coffee mill reserved for the purpose and grind until very fine. Sift the powder through a fine-mesh sieve into a blender jar; use your fingertips to crumble and press through bits of leaf or chile; discard the residue.

Place the remaining garlic, *recado*, chipotles, and water in the blender jar with the ground spices and chiles and process 1–2 minutes, or until the ingredients are liquefied.

FOR THE *PIPIÁN*

3 cups (375 g) Pepita molida

4 cups (1 L) water, divided

1 recipe Pibil de venado (or beef), cooked until very rare, cut into 1 in. (2.5 cm) cubes

3 medium Roma tomatoes (10½ oz. / 300 g), charred, peeled, seeded, and chopped

3 medium *tomates verdes* (tomatillo, 10½ oz. / 300 g), husked and coarsely chopped

½ cup (40 g) chives, chopped

2 sprigs fresh epazote (Substitute: 1 tsp. / 1.5 g dried)

Strain the liquid through a fine-mesh sieve into the stockpot. With a spatula, press out as much liquid as possible; discard the residue.

PREPARE *PIPIÁN*

Place the Pepita molida in the bowl of a food processor, add half of the water, and process until creamy, 1–2 minutes. Pour the mixture through a fine-mesh sieve into the stockpot. With a rubber spatula, press as much of the liquid through as possible. Pour half of the remaining water into the sieve and press through again; repeat with the rest of the water. (Note: The process of straining the seeds with water through the sieve requires patience, a strong wrist, and about 10 minutes of your time.) Discard any solids that remain in the sieve. Stir the liquid in the stockpot to incorporate. Simmer over low heat, stirring constantly, as the stock thickens slightly, 2–3 minutes.

Add the remaining *pipián* ingredients to the stockpot, return it to a simmer, and cook 30 minutes, stirring frequently to avoid scorching.

Venado en pipián rojo. [DS]

FOR THICKENING

1 cup (225 g) *masa*
1 cup (250 ml) beef stock or
  bouillon
Sea salt to taste

FOR THE GARNISH

1 cup (125 g) hulled green squash
  seeds
1 Tbs. (15 ml) Spanish olive oil
2 tsp. (4 g) crushed red pepper
  flakes
¼ cup (20 g) chives, chopped
Sea salt to taste

FOR SERVING

Mexican *crema* (Substitute: crème
  fraîche, sour cream, or plain
  yogurt)
K'uut bi ik (p. 508), or the chile
  sauce of your choice

THICKEN

Mix the *masa* with the stock until thoroughly dissolved. Strain the mixture through a fine-mesh sieve into the stockpot and use a rubber spatula to press the mixture through. Simmer 15–20 minutes, stirring frequently to avoid sticking, until the sauce has thickened. As it simmers, frequently skim off any of the bright red oil that rises to the surface and reserve for a garnish (optional). Check the seasonings.

PREPARE GARNISH AND SERVE

For an updated garnish, lightly toast the squash seeds in a small skillet on high heat until they start to pop, turn fragrant, and brown lightly, 1–2 minutes. Reduce the heat to low, add the olive oil, and cook another 30 seconds, stirring constantly to coat seeds with the oil. Remove the skillet from the heat and immediately transfer the seeds to a serving bowl. Add the red pepper flakes, chives, and salt and toss to combine.

TO SERVE

Ladle the *pipián* into plates with a rim or shallow serving bowls. Garnish with some of the squash seeds and a dribble of *crema* and serve extra of both. Pipián de venado is usually accompanied by the fiery red salsa K'uut bi ik, which diners add to taste.

VARIATIONS

Pipián de frijol (Black Beans in Red Squash–Seed Sauce): In addition to appearing as a sauce for venison, quail, pheasant, and other game (including iguana!), Pipián rojo is also the background for black beans in this dish, offered by the Maya women of Tetiz in *Recetario gastronómico: Cocina indígena*. Prepare 1 recipe Frijol k'abax (p. 504), omitting the optional ingredients and enrichments; cook only until the beans are barely tender, about 30 minutes prior to finish time (they will finish cooking in the *pipián*). Drain, discard the epazote, and set the beans aside. Prepare the *pipián*, replacing the venison with the drained beans. Cook as instructed until the beans are tender and the sauce has thickened (there will be no red oil in the beans). For a vegetarian option, use vegetable stock instead of beef bouillon. Serving instructions are the same.

Faisán en pipián rojo (Pheasant in Red Squash–Seed Sauce): Prepare Pollo asado (p. 270), substituting pheasant, quail, or Cornish game hens in the desired quantity. Roast until char marks appear, but leave the birds slightly undercooked. Set aside. Prepare the *pipián* sauce as in the recipe for Venado en pipián rojo (p. 96), omitting the venison. Heat the *pipián* sauce until barely simmering around the edges, adding more beef bouillon or water if needed: the consistency should be like thick pancake batter. Add the roasted birds and continue to simmer until they are cooked and the flavors amalgamated. Finishing and serving instructions are the same as for Venado en pipián rojo.

(opposite page) Before walking to his milpa, don Hernán fills a calabazo with water. [MC]

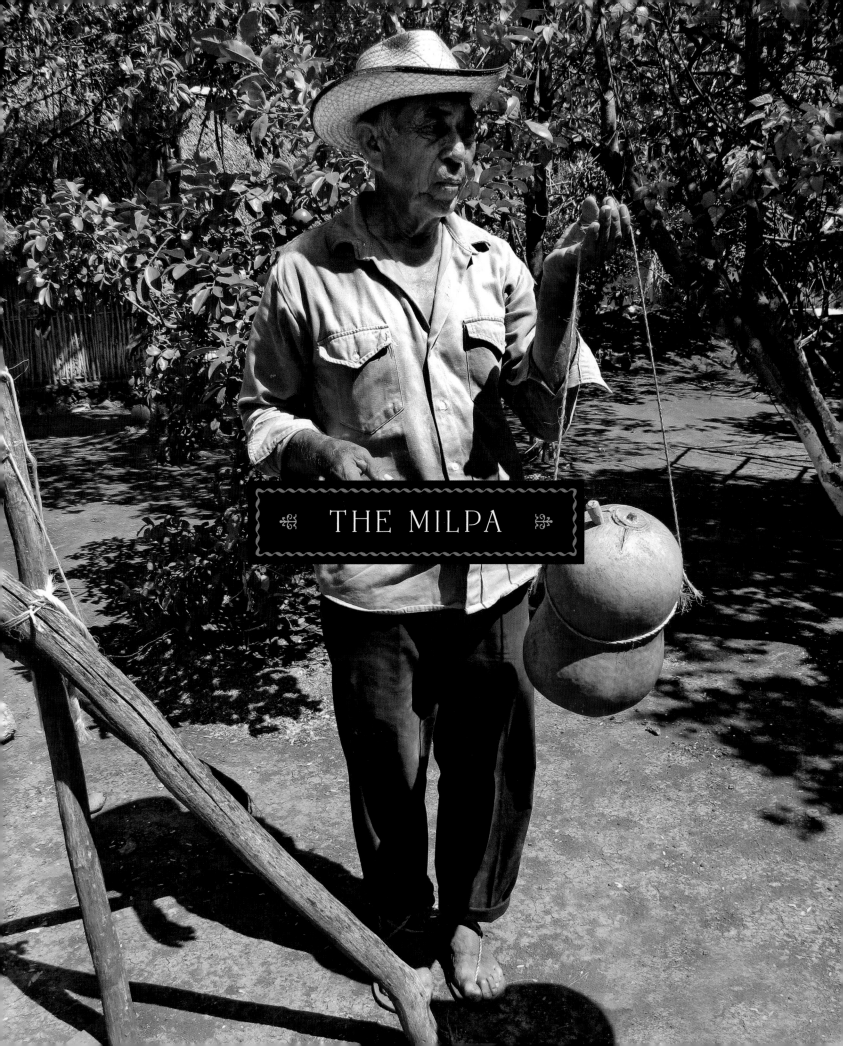

THE MILPA

F OR SEVENTY-THREE-YEAR-OLD Hernán Perrera Novelo, the day starts at 4:00 am. "The first thing I do when I wake up is light a fire. Then I grab a bit of *masa*, put it in a pot with water, and make my *atole*. That is my breakfast. I like it with a little red chile on top."

By 5:00 am, don Hernán is at work in his nearby *milpa*—the plot where he grows three primary crops of corn, beans, and squash for his family, much as his father and grandfather and a string of ancestors did before him.

His *milpa* is a terrain of about five acres (two hectares) that is part of communal *ejido* lands farmed by several Maya families in Santa Elena, in southern Yucatán. He carries to the job a *calabazo*, a large gourd for storing the day's water.

Don Hernán returns home at noon and tends to chores in the *solar* for a couple of hours. By 2:00 pm, his wife, Asaria Caamal, has the big family meal ready—enough for thirteen people. She has been up since dawn, too, her first task being to rinse the *nixtamal* (p. 517), or rehydrated corn, that she cooked the night before, then carry it to the mill to be ground into *masa*. To feed herself and her husband, as well as any of their six children, fifteen grandchildren, and five great-grandchildren who might show up to eat, she must prepare six kilos (over thirteen pounds) of *masa* every single day—more on holidays.

MAIZE: A VARIED STAPLE

Atole for breakfast; pozole (p. 227) to drink throughout the day; a lunch of tortillas, perhaps with beans or cooked *chaya*; and on special days, tamales—this is the maize-centered diet to which don Hernán has become accustomed, which he admits he loves, and which has kept him unbelievably healthy and strong for his age.

Far from being monotonous, the elaboration of maize dishes over the centuries has taken so many forms that it is impossible to list them all. From beverages and thickened porridges to tamales and tortillas, maize has formed the major part of the diet throughout Mesoamerica and is still the staple diet of indigenous peoples in Yucatán.

The coat of arms of Santa Elena depicts the town church flanked by farm tools and ears of corn. [MR]

MAYA MAIZE BREADS

Waaj—Mayan for "bread"—takes on many forms in Yucatán, from small, thin tortillas to large, thick tamales. The one constant in the formula is the corn dough known as *masa*.

The hieroglyphic record suggests an extensive repertoire of tamales in precontact times. Some recently interpreted glyphs detail the ancient recipes for several: *tamal* made of "green," or new, corn; *tamal* with honey; *tamal* that includes pieces of meat and a thickened sauce (*k'óol*, p. 86); and *tamal* that includes *sikil* squash–seed paste (p. 285). The glyphs depict the tamales' round form and vegetal wrappers, and even the technique for preparing them, such as sprinkling or scattering a sauce or seeds on top.

Pre-Columbian Maya drawings depicting tamales with filling (left) and tamales with sauce (right). [AUREA HERNÁNDEZ AFTER MAUDSLAY 1889–1902: PL. 5; AUREA HERNÁNDEZ AFTER REENTS AND BISHOP 1984: FIG. 1]

ATOLE CON PEPITA MOLIDA / SIKIL SA'

HOT MAIZE PORRIDGE WITH TOASTED GROUND SQUASH SEEDS

Atole (*sa'* in Mayan) is widely consumed throughout Yucatán, although hardly ever in public. While in other parts of Mexico, big pots of *atole* simmer and steam on street corners, here it remains a dish prepared at home before the start of the workday. This delicious version is flavored with toasted ground squash seeds, making it a very healthful choice for breakfast. Atole con pepita molida is often consumed sweetened, but try don Hernán's suggestion and add a pinch of salt and chile instead.

Prepare ahead note: The *masa* for Atole con pepita molida can be made well in advance and frozen. Once prepared, *atole* should be served immediately.

YIELD: 4 SERVINGS

TO PREPARE AHEAD

Masa prepared from either nixtamalized corn or from *masa harina* (p. 517)

Pepita molida (p. 497)

FOR THE *ATOLE*

4 cups (1 L) water, divided

1 cup (225 g) *masa*

½ cup (62.5 g) Pepita molida

FOR SWEET *ATOLE*

Honey or sugar to taste

Flavorings such as vanilla, allspice, or ground *canela* (Mexican cinnamon)

FOR SAVORY *ATOLE*

Sea salt to taste

K'uut bi ik, or the chile sauce of your choice

COOK *ATOLE* AND SERVE

Place half of the water and the *masa* in a saucepan and use your fingers or a potato masher to incorporate; the mixture will be lumpy. Add the remaining water and, with a whisk or an immersion blender, beat until smooth. Add the ground squash seeds and stir to dissolve. Bring the mixture to a boil, then reduce the heat to a simmer. Cook, stirring constantly, until the mixture thickens to the consistency of oatmeal, about 5 minutes.

TO SERVE

Ladle the *atole* into individual serving bowls or mugs. Diners add their own flavorings to taste.

CHÁAMCHAMITOS DE JOLO'OCH

TAMALES OF *ACHIOTE*-STEWED CHICKEN WRAPPED IN CORN HUSKS

TO PREPARE AHEAD

Masa para tamales yucatecos
(p. 522)

Pavo del monte en k'óol rojo
(p. 86), using chicken (Pollo
asado, p. 270) instead of turkey

FOR THE TAMALES

26 dried maize husks, soaked and
prepared per instructions on
p. 524

1 recipe Masa para tamales
yucatecos

1½ cups (450 g) chicken from
making the K'óol rojo, shredded

1½ cups (375 ml) K'óol rojo, plus
more for serving

1 bunch fresh epazote

FOR SERVING

Chile k'uut (p. 508), or the chile
sauce of your choice

K'óol rojo (left over from
assembly)

In many regions of Mexico, the corn husk is often used for wrapping tamales prior to steaming, whereas in Yucatán the great majority of tamales are wrapped in banana leaves. This particular Yucatecan *tamal* is one exception. Cháamchamitos can sometimes be seen in the market, although at least 50 percent of the time, the corn husk–wrapped ones are Mexican tamales in disguise, *estilo mexicano*, or Mexican style, which generally have a spiced ground beef filling. If you want the Yucatecan original, you have to ask for Cháamchamitos.

I have been taught this recipe on a few separate occasions: by Angelina Magaña of Muna, María Lorenza Quintal Martín and María Esther Ceballos Quintal of Mérida, and others. As is not always the case, the recipes are virtually identical, the only difference being that some cooks specify pork and others, chicken. I present the basics, and you may use either one. When the filling is pork, some cooks call the *tamal* To'biholoch.

Prepare ahead note: The chicken and red maize sauce (k'óol) for Cháamchamitos de jolo'och may be prepared several days or even weeks in advance and refrigerated or frozen.

YIELD: APPROXIMATELY 2 DOZEN

FORM TAMALES AND STEAM

See the illustrations for filling corn husks on p. 524. After soaking the husks, cut 2 of them lengthwise into 24 narrow strips to use for tying the tamales. Divide the *masa* into approximately 2 dozen balls, each weighing about 2 oz. (60 g). In the palm of your hand, pat one ball into a tortilla 5 inches (13 cm) in diameter. Spread a heaping tablespoon (25 g) of the shredded chicken along the center. Spoon 1 tablespoon (15 ml) of the *k'óol* on top of the chicken. Finish with a leaf or 2 of epazote. Fold in half to make an empanada shape and seal the edges. Fill the husks, wrap, and cook per instructions on page 526; allow to rest at least 15 minutes prior to serving.

TO SERVE

Place 2 or 3 unwrapped tamales on individual serving plates. Diners open them and spoon on more *k'óol* and chile sauce to taste.

VARIATION

To'biholoch (Tamales of *Achiote*-Stewed Pork Wrapped in Corn Husks): Follow the master recipe but use Cochinita pibil (p. 420) instead of chicken for preparing the K'óol rojo.

VAPORCITOS / TAMALITOS / CHAN OOXONTBIL WAAJ

SMALL STEAMED TAMALES

TO PREPARE AHEAD

Banana leaves, prepared to
the small (SM) size; see Basic
Techniques, p. 525

Masa para tamales yucatecos
(p. 522)

K'óol rojo (p. 87), using Pollo
asado (p. 270), Cochinita pibil
(p. 420), or Pibil de venado
(p. 421) to make the sauce

or Picadillo (p. 255) for Vaporcitos
de carne molida

or Cazón frito (p. 312) for Tamales
campechanos

FOR THE TAMALES

1 recipe Masa para tamales
yucatecos

1¼ cups (375 g) meat of your
choice (see above)

1½ cups (375 ml) K'óol rojo, plus
more for serving, except as
noted

1 bunch fresh epazote

FOR SERVING

Leftover K'óol rojo is served with
Vaporcitos de pollo, Vaporcitos
de puerco, and Tamalitos de
venado pibil

Tomate frito (p. 507) is served
with Vaporcitos de carne molida
and Tamales campechanos

Salpicón (p. 511), optional

Chile tamulado (p. 509), or the
chile sauce of your choice

The tiny tamales called Vaporcitos (also known as Tamalitos) are daily fare throughout the peninsula. In Yucatán, the traditional Vaporcito is quite small, as the diminutive *-ito* suggests. And it is usually steamed, as *"vapor"* describes. The recipe for Vaporcitos is identical to that for Cháamchamitos de jolo'och, but the tamales are wrapped in banana leaves instead of maize husks. A variety of filling options broadens the repertoire.

Prepare ahead notes: The fillings for Vaporcitos may be prepared several days or even weeks in advance, frozen, and reheated at the time of assembly.

YIELD: APPROXIMATELY 2 DOZEN

VAPORCITOS DE POLLO
(TAMALES WITH CHICKEN AND MAIZE-THICKENED RED SAUCE)
Use shredded chicken from preparing the K'óol rojo

VAPORCITOS DE PUERCO
(TAMALES WITH PORK AND MAIZE-THICKENED RED SAUCE)
Use shredded pork from preparing the K'óol rojo

TAMALITOS DE VENADO PIBIL
(TAMALES WITH VENISON AND MAIZE-THICKENED RED SAUCE)
Use shredded venison from preparing the K'óol rojo

VAPORCITOS DE CARNE MOLIDA (TAMALES WITH MINCEMEAT AND
TOMATO SAUCE; ALSO KNOWN AS TAMALITOS TICULEÑOS)
Use Picadillo (p. 255), omitting the K'óol rojo

TAMALES CAMPECHANOS (TAMALES WITH DOGFISH AND TOMATO SAUCE)
Use Cazón frito (p. 312), omitting the K'óol rojo

FORM, WRAP, AND FINISH TAMALES
Follow the instructions in Basic Techniques, on page 521, for forming tamales, choosing the small (SM) size. Pat the *masa* in a tortilla shape on a section of banana leaf. Fill with approximately 2 teaspoons (10 g) of meat and a spoonful of K'óol for each. (Omit the K'óol for the Picadillo and Cazón versions). Wrap as instructed and steam for 1 hour.

TO SERVE
Place the tamales on individual serving plates. Diners open them and spoon on sauce, optional Salpicón, and chile to taste.

Horneados (Large Baked Tamal Loaves with Chicken and Maize-Thickened Red Sauce): This super-sized *tamal* is often shared by Yucatecan couples. The *tamal* is easy to spot: it is large and rectangular and notable by its wrapping of burned banana leaves. Follow the recipe for Vaporcitos de pollo, but choose the large (L) size banana leaves as instructed in Basic Techniques on page 525. Divide the *masa* into 6 equal balls of approximately 7 ounces (200 g) each. Flatten 1 ball on a banana leaf section to a rectangle measuring about 7 inches × 10 inches (18 cm × 25 cm). Spread approximately 3 tablespoons (60 g) shredded chicken along the center and top with 3 tablespoons (60 ml) K'óol rojo. Garnish with 2–3 slices of tomato, 2–3 thinly sliced white onion rings, and a few leaves of epazote. Use the leaf to lift and fold the long sides of the *masa* to cover the filling and seal the edges. Wrap the leaves to cover, press to form the *tamal* in a tight rectangle, then tie and bake according to instructions in Basic Techniques, page 526.

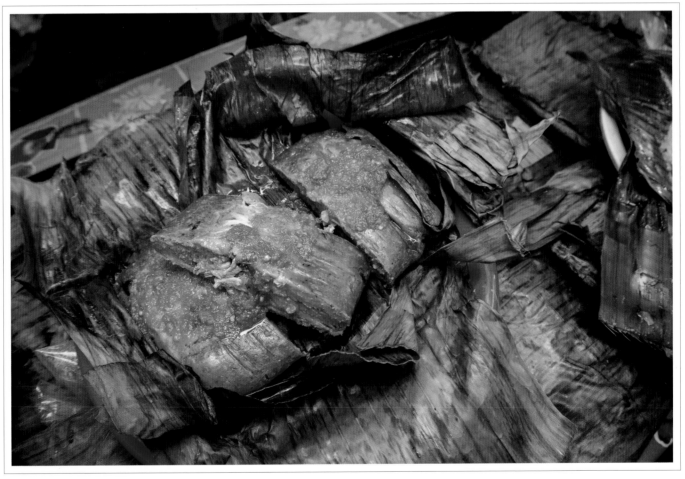

Horneados. [EC]

PIMES / PIIM

LARGE BAKED TAMAL LOAVES WITH BLACK-EYED PEAS

TO PREPARE AHEAD

Masa para tamales yucatecos
   (p. 522)

Pepita molida (p. 497)

Banana leaves prepared as per the
   instructions on page 525, choosing the extra-large (XL) size

---

FOR THE BEANS AND *MASA*

1½ cups (250 g) fresh *x'pelones*
   (Substitute: fresh black-eyed
   peas, or dried black beans
   cooked until just tender and
   drained)

1 recipe Masa para tamales
   yucatecos

On the opposite end of the spectrum from the diminutive Vaporcitos, Pimes are large, saucer-shaped tamales seen piled high in brightly colored washtubs in markets throughout the peninsula. "*Piim*" in Mayan means "thick or fat thing," and these indeed are. Some Pimes are sold still wrapped in banana leaves; others are bared of their covering to entice passing customers. The loaves are an intense earthy orange color—the *masa* is tinged with *achiote*—and dotted top to bottom with specks of black—hundreds of little *x'pelones*, or black-eyed peas. The discs are sliced into wedges like a pie and served with cooked tomato sauce and a medley of chopped cabbage, chile, and sour orange juice. María del Socorro Rodríguez Larrache and Mariela Silveira Rodríguez of Mérida shared this recipe with me.

YIELD: 2 LARGE TAMALES, EACH SERVING 5–6

PARBOIL BEANS AND PREPARE *MASA*

For fresh beans only: Clean thoroughly. Place the beans in a saucepan, cover completely with salted water, and bring to a boil. Cook on high heat for 10 minutes. Remove the pan from the heat and drain the beans thoroughly. (Note: Whether using fresh or dried beans, they should not be overcooked but, rather, be left slightly al dente, since they will finish cooking during baking.) Mix the beans into the *masa* with your hands, making sure to distribute them evenly throughout the dough.

Pimes *and other tamales for sale in the market.* [MR]

FOR FORMING THE TAMALES

FOR FORMING THE TAMALES

½ cup (62.5 g) Pepita molida, divided

6 eggs, hard-boiled, peeled, and coarsely chopped

FOR SERVING

Tomate frito (p. 507)

Pepita molida (p. 497)

Salpicón (p. 511), optional

Chile tamulado (p. 509), or the chile sauce of your choice

FORM TAMALES

Preheat the oven to 350°F (176°C). You will be forming 2 large round tamales, each with a bottom and a top. On a work surface, place enough sections of banana leaf to form 2 squares at least 20 inches × 20 inches (50 cm × 50 cm). Divide the dough in quarters. Form 4 thick disks about 9 inches (23 cm) in diameter: 2 disks will be the *tamal* bottoms; the other 2 will be the tops. Locate each bottom in the center of a square of banana leaf. Sprinkle half of the Pepita molida onto the surface of each, spreading it evenly over all with your fingertips. Next, spread half of the chopped boiled eggs evenly over the Pepita molida. Place the remaining 2 disks of *masa* on top of the *masa* bottoms and press firmly to seal. Use your palms to pat around the circumference, giving each *tamal* the shape of a cake. Fold over the banana leaves to wrap the filling completely and tie securely with the reserved ribs. Place the 2 wrapped tamales on a baking sheet.

BAKE AND SERVE

Bake for 45 minutes, then invert each *tamal* on the baking sheet. Bake an additional 45 minutes, or until the banana leaves are singed and crisp on the edges and the tamales feel firm when you press them in the center with your finger. Open a bit of the banana leaf to check the *masa*: it should be firm and rather crisp. Remove the tamales from the oven and allow them to rest at least 15 minutes before serving.

TO SERVE

For a dramatic presentation, leave the tamales in the banana leaves and place them on a large serving platter. Unwrap and slice them at the table. Alternatively, cut each *tamal* into 5 or 6 large wedges and place them on individual serving plates. Diners add garnishes and sauces to taste.

VARIATIONS

Vaporcitos de x'pelon / P'ich ich (Small Steamed Tamales with Black-Eyed Peas): You may use the same basic recipe for Pimes to prepare finger-sized tamales known as Vaporcitos de x'pelon. These are often served in *cantinas* or at parties. Prepare the black-eyed peas as in the master recipe. Rather than form 2 large tamales, form 24 individual tamales, choosing the small (SM) size (see Basic Techniques, p. 525). Divide the *masa* into 2 dozen balls. Pat 1 ball into a tortilla shape on a section of banana leaf and spread the surface evenly with 2 teaspoons (4 g) of Pepita molida. Place 2 teaspoons (7 g) of chopped boiled egg in a row down the middle. Fold and wrap as instructed and continue until you have completed all 24 tamales. Follow the steaming instructions on page 526. Accompany with garnishes and salsas as suggested for Pimes.

Bu'uliwah (Small Steamed Tamales with Enriched Black Beans): The translation from Mayan for this delicious *tamal* is simply "bean bread." It is a good way to make use of leftover Frijol k'abax, which is what the recipe calls for instead of black-eyed peas. The beans are such a rich filling there is no need to add the squash seeds or eggs. Proceed with the recipe for Vaporcitos de x'pelon, replacing the *x'pelones* with 1½ cups (250 g) drained Frijol k'abax (preferably with the optional enrichment, p. 504). Omit the Pepita molida and boiled egg. Wrap, steam, and serve as per Vaporcitos de x'pelon.

Rebirth of the maize god from a crack in the surface of the earth, represented as a turtle's back.
[AUREA HERNÁNDEZ AFTER FREIDEL ET AL. 1993]

MAÍZ IN MAYA RELIGION

As expressed in legends and cosmology, Maya culture and civilization were born hand in hand with the development of agriculture, specifically, the domestication of maize.

Maize was the Maya symbol of life, and maize rituals marked the beginning and the end: the umbilical cord of a newborn was cut over a maize cob, and a ball of maize dough was placed in the mouth of the recently deceased.

As told in the *Popul Vuh*, after the creation of the earth and its animals, the gods formed man out of mud. But because the mud dissolved, the gods next tried wood. When they saw this wooden man had no soul, the gods finally chose maize. Thus it is said that man is made of maize and lives by maize and maize flows through his veins.

The Yucatán is a land of less soil than any I know, being all live flat stones with very little earth . . . It is a marvel how much fertility exists in the soil, on or between the stones, where is to be found all there is, more among the stones than there is elsewhere.

—FRAY DIEGO DE LANDA, 1566

It wasn't only Landa who marveled at the fertility of Yucatán's harsh environment and the resourcefulness of the Mayas at extracting a living from it. Archaeologists and anthropologists since the turn of the twentieth century have proposed a variety of theories regarding how the Mayas did not merely subsist, but, rather, thrived, enough to build monumental cities that supported many thousands of people.

SEEDS OF CULTURE

The synergistic evolution of agriculture and maize resulted in new hybrid species adaptable to a range of environments. And as agriculture developed, so did culture: the colonization of the arid north of the Maya lowlands in the Yucatán Peninsula—the region covered in this book—was facilitated as a direct result of the *milpa* agricultural system dedicated to an evolved maize race complex known as Chapalote-Nal Tel (*nal t'eel* in Mayan). This maize grows well in warm climates and low elevations, is widely adaptable in terms of soil requirements, and matures quickly, making it well suited to the lowlands. Evolutionary advances such as these subsequently ameliorated Maya agriculture, liberating certain classes of society from food production, thereby clearing the path toward the building of a great civilization in the rugged dry tropical forests of the Yucatán Peninsula.

THE *MILPA* TRIAD

Some of the most timeless dishes of Yucatán are simple reflections of the harvest. A theme and variation of the three basic crops—corn, beans, and squash—combine to comfort you with a gently earthy flavor and provide balanced nutrition.

From ancient times to the present, however, flavor and variety have not been limited to the triad. As many as 32 species and 95 varieties may have shared the same soils in the *milpa*. Further, many foods we take for granted still have wild ancestors in the Yucatán Peninsula and may have been the subject of cultivation since at least 3400 BCE. Among these are *cacao*, chile, papaya, *pitahaya*, guava, lima beans, jicama, and vanilla. Other species were already domesticated when they were introduced sometime after 3400 BCE and have been cultivated here ever since: pineapple, soursop, avocado, peanut, squash, beans, corn, sweet potato, *yuca*, tomato, chayote, and *achiote*, as well as many other species not well known outside Mexico.

(left) Whole corn on the cob also finds bountiful interpretations in Yucatán: píibinal is corn that has been smoked in the underground oven known as a píib. [MC] (right) Squash nestles at the foot of maize stalks, the monte looms in the background. [DS]

JOROCHES

MINCEMEAT-FILLED MAIZE DUMPLINGS IN BLACK BEAN PURÉE

TO PREPARE AHEAD

Masa prepared from either
  nixtamalized corn or *masa harina*
  (p. 517)
Enriched Lard (p. 513)
Picadillo (p. 255)
Frijol colado (p. 505)

FOR THE DUMPLINGS

2 lbs. (1 k) *masa*
2 Tbs. (28 g) Enriched Lard
1 tsp. (6 g) sea salt
¾ cup (about 200 g) Picadillo
1 recipe Frijol colado "aguado"
  (should be approximately 10
  cups / 2.5 L. Add water or
  chicken broth if necessary to
  achieve the required amount
  and proper consistency, like that
  of buttermilk or thin pancake
  batter)

FOR SERVING

Tomate frito (p. 507)
Mexican *crema* (Substitute: crème
  fraîche, sour cream, or plain
  yogurt)
Queso cotija (Substitute: feta),
  crumbled
Chile k'uut or K'uut bi ik (p. 508),
  recommended accompaniment

Dumplings of maize *masa* appear in various regions of Mexico. Usually small balls with a deep impression in the center, allowing hot liquid to enter and cook the *masa* through, these dumplings are featured in an assortment of soups and stews and are known by several names. In Oaxaca, they are called "*chochoyotes*" and are enriched with lard and *asiento* (the crispy bits rescued from the bottom of the lard-rendering vat, known in Mayan as *xix*), then simmered in broth, beans, or *mole verde*. In Veracruz, they are called "*ombliguitos*" (little navels) for their characteristic form. In Yucatán, the dumplings are generally known as "*joroches*;" older generations call them *pocitos*, or "little wells." The traditional recipe calls for forming little balls of *masa* around your index finger, giving the dumplings a hollow, conical shape, then simmering them in creamy black beans, Frijol colado, or plopping them into Frijol con puerco. More recent innovations feature a variety of fillings for the dumplings, such as Picadillo, Cazón frito, or even Mexican cheese. María Lorenza Quintal Martín and María Esther Ceballos Quintal of Mérida shared this recipe with me using the Picadillo.

Prepare ahead notes: Dumplings can be assembled and filled, layered on waxed paper, and frozen several days in advance. Cook only those that you plan to serve for one meal and add the rest when you reheat leftover beans on another day. Leave at room temperature 30 minutes prior to cooking. Joroches are best consumed immediately after preparing.

YIELD: APPROXIMATELY 10 SERVINGS

FORM AND COOK DUMPLINGS

Mix the *masa* with the lard and salt and knead to incorporate. Form the *masa* into approximately 30 balls weighing about 1 ounce (30 g) each. Keep the finished balls covered with plastic wrap as you work. Use your index finger to make a deep impression in one of the balls. Insert about 1 heaping teaspoon (6 g) of the Picadillo into the hole, then seal the ball closed. Form the ball into an elongated egg shape; repeat until you have finished all the dumplings.

  In a stockpot, bring the bean purée to a very gentle simmer; check seasonings. Carefully drop the dumplings into the simmering bean purée. Shake the pot back and forth periodically to nudge the purée on top of the dumplings and so that neither beans nor dumplings stick to the bottom of the pot. After 20–25 minutes, the dumplings will begin to float to the surface. Simmer an additional 15 minutes, or until the dumplings are firm (35–40 minutes total).

TO SERVE

Place 3 dumplings in the bottom of a soup bowl and ladle on some of the bean purée. Diners add tomato sauce, cream, cheese, and/or chile sauce to taste.

Joroches Plain and Simple. As noted above, you may also leave the dumplings as hollow cones without sealing the top (the traditional method) and cook as directed.

Jorochitos de frijol con puerco (Maize Dumplings in Pork and Beans): Using the Joroches Plain and Simple, drop the formed dumplings gently into simmering Frijol con puerco (p. 262) 45 minutes prior to the completion of cooking time. Serve with the accompaniments suggested for Frijol con puerco.

Joroches de longaniza (Sausage Dumplings in Black Bean Purée): Substitute crumbled, browned Longaniza de Valladolid (p. 481) for the Picadillo when you form the dumplings. You may use commercial *longaniza* or chorizo if you prefer.

Joroches de cazón (Dogfish Dumplings in Black Bean Purée): Substitute Cazón asado frito (p. 312) for the Picadillo when you form the dumplings.

Joroches de queso (Cheese Dumplings in Black Bean Purée): Nontraditional but popular in some families. Substitute grated *queso oaxaqueño* or mozzarella for the Picadillo as you form the dumplings.

POL'KANES

MAIZE, LIMA BEAN, AND SQUASH-SEED FRITTERS

TO PREPARE AHEAD

Masa para tamales I or II (p. 521) or the vegetarian choice Toksel (p. 113)

FOR THE FRITTERS

1 recipe Masa para tamales
½ recipe Toksel, prepared immediately before you will be forming the fritters
Vegetable oil or lard for frying

FOR SERVING

X'nipek (p. 512)

"*Pol'kan*" is Mayan for "snake head" (*pol* = head and *kan* = serpent). This scrumptious Maya fritter takes its name from its shape: an elongated oval resembling the threatening head of the rattlesnake—an important deity in Maya culture. The simple *milpa*-derived ingredient list of corn, beans, and squash seeds suggests that Pol'kanes likely date to the preconquest era, although until the Spanish introduced the domesticated pig and lard, they would have been cooked on a *comal* instead of fried.

Prepare ahead note: The *masa* for Pol'kanes may be made in advance and frozen. The Toksel filling should be prepared at the moment you plan to use it. The fritters may be kept warm in a low oven up to 30 minutes.

YIELD: APPROXIMATELY 15 FRITTERS

FORM POL'KANES

Form the *masa* into 15 2½-ounce (75 g) balls. Pat 1 ball into a 3-inch (7.5 cm) tortilla in the palm of your hand. Top the tortilla with 1 tablespoon (about 10 g) of the Toksel in a straight row down the center. Fold the tortilla in half, creating an empanada shape and tightly seal the edges. Cupping your hands and rolling the dough in your palms, form it into a smooth and elongated egg shape. Set it aside and continue with the remaining balls of *masa*.

Add the fat to a deep skillet to a depth of 1½ inches (4 cm). Heat to 350°F (176°C). Add 3 to 4 of the Pol'kanes at a time, being careful not to crowd. Fry until deep golden brown, then flip and fry the other side. Drain on paper towels.

TO SERVE

Slit the Pol'kan along one side, break it open, and spoon in salsa to taste.

Pol'kanes. [EC]

TOKSEL

TOASTED GROUND SQUASH SEEDS WITH LIMA BEANS

TO PREPARE AHEAD
Pepita molida (p. 497)

FOR THE BEANS
2 cups (9 oz. / 250 g) fresh *ibes*
(Substitute: fresh or frozen lima beans *or* dried limas *or* white great northern beans, cooked and drained)

FOR THE TOKSEL
2 cups (9 oz. / 250 g) Pepita molida
⅔ cup (4 oz. / 113 g) spring onions, finely chopped
¼ cup (¾ oz. / 20 g) chives, finely chopped
1 medium chile habanero (¼ oz. / 7 g), seeds intact, finely chopped
¼ cup (½ oz. / 15 g) cilantro, chopped
1 tsp. (6 g) sea salt

The ladies of Tetiz still make Toksel in the traditional way. First, they heat a special hard stone (known in Mayan as *tok'tunich*) in the hearth. They then place it in a pot along with all the ingredients. They cover the pot, and when the stone has cooled, the dish is done. Like other traditional recipes from the *milpa*, Toksel is simple in its ingredient list. The *ib* (*Phaseolus lunatus*), the bean typically used in this dish, is gently heated in a bed of toasted, ground squash seeds and lightly flavored with members of the Allium genus: chives and spring onions.

Toksel is consumed in several ways in Yucatán: it is rolled up in a tortilla and eaten taco-style; it is a spectacular side dish for grilled meats or fish; and it is used as a filling in the Maya "fritter," Pol'kanes (p. 111) as well as in tamales like Ibewahes (p. 136).

Prepare ahead note: Toksel is best prepared just before serving or using in other recipes. Leftovers can be refrigerated for one or two days, but because the beans continue to exude liquid, they dry out and the ground squash seeds become soggy. Furthermore, the herbs wilt, discolor and become very unappetizing. The only real use for it at that point is disguised inside a *tamal* or Pol'kan. If you anticipate having extra, I recommend leaving out the chives and cilantro until you are ready to use the Toksel. Reheat the mixture briefly and add the herbs.

YIELD: APPROXIMATELY 4 CUPS (630 G)

COOK BEANS
Cook fresh beans in salted water until just tender, 10–15 minutes. (Note: If using dried beans, cook according to package instructions, drain, and proceed with this recipe using 2 cups of cooked beans. Beans should be tender but not falling apart.)

PREPARE TOKSEL AND FINISH
Place the Pepita molida in a dry cast-iron skillet over low heat. Add the beans, onions, chives, and chile, stirring constantly to avoid scorching. Heat 3–4 minutes, or until the mixture is very warm and the onions are slightly softened. Add the cilantro and salt, stir, and check for seasonings. Immediately transfer the Toksel to a bowl and set aside (do not leave in the skillet; the residual heat can scorch the ground squash seeds). Serve or use immediately as a filling, as noted above.

Before burning the milpa, the undergrowth must be cut down and left to dry. [MC]

FROM *MILPA* TO TABLE

I have known don Hernán and his family for several years and visit them frequently. I asked if I could accompany him through a full *milpa* cycle—from clearing the land and burning the rubble to planting and, finally, the harvest. It was important for me to witness firsthand how a little seed of hard, dried corn eventually winds up on the dinner table.

El Quemado / *Burning the* Milpa

In the dry season, from November through January, clearing the forest for a new *milpa* takes place. Clearing is a labor-intensive process, since the brush and any obstructing trees must be removed. Useful trees are almost never cut down; others may be cut to waist height around the periphery of the plot to serve as protective barrier. Remaining stumps within the *milpa* may serve as support for beans or other vining crops.

Once the cutting was complete, don Hernán left the rubble to dry, and sometime between March and May, before the start of the rainy season, he systematically burned it, a little at a time over a period of a few months. Don Hernán waited for a day of relatively strong wind, then lit the fire on the upwind side. He had cleared paths around the *milpa*—*guardarrayas* (*mis pach kol* in Mayan)—so that the fire wouldn't spread.

As the fire burned, the winds whipped and shifted and appeared to come from all different directions. "That's dangerous," said don Hernán. "We call that *suut'suut'iik'*. It can cause your fire to get out of control." "*Suut*" in Mayan means "to spin" or "to turn around." *Iik'* means "wind." I have also heard him explain this phenomenon as being the fault of the *aluxes*—Maya trickster spirits.

SHIFTING AGRICULTURE, SHIFTING VIEWS

The method of agriculture employed by don Hernán, as well as by most Yucatecan farmers today, is variously called slash-and-burn, swidden, or shifting agriculture. Individual plots are used only two to three years, then abandoned to the forest, and a new plot is cleared elsewhere—hence the term "shifting agriculture."

Many environmental scientists and archaeologists have pondered if perhaps environmental degradation caused by slash-and-burn agriculture led to the so-called collapse of Maya civilization. However, theories change, and many scholars now doubt that environmental apocalypse was the sole cause of the transformation of Maya civilization.

One reason for this shift in attitude has to do with an understanding of the Mayas' limited technology. The highly destructive "clear-cut" forest management used in slash-and-burn agriculture today would have been labor-intensive and expensive, if not impossible, in a time when there were no steel cutting implements. The fact that the Mayas would have worked with stone axes and adzes would preclude the removal of old-growth trees, suggesting that pre-Columbian *milpa* farming was likely more sustainable for longer periods of time. Further, when practiced properly and on a limited scale, shifting agriculture can actually benefit the environment, since, due to the nature of the method, it provides a rest period during which forests have the chance to recuperate after a couple of years of planting.

La Siembra / *Sowing the* Milpa

For many generations, he told me, don Hernán and his family have begun planting precisely on Día de San Pedro, and the job is finished by Día de San Pablo—that is, between

(left) The fire is carefully started in a place where paths have been cleared to prevent the spread of wildfires. [MC] *(right) The* milpa *fire burns at the edge of the* monte. [MC]

13 and 19 June. Coincidentally or otherwise, this roughly corresponds to the start of the rainy season. And so it was.

To prepare for the planting, don Hernán first emptied from his *sabukán* (a sisal shoulder bag) about 4½ pounds (2 k) of seed corn into a *ch'óoy leek*, a large gourd used throughout the region as a storage container. Using a length of sisal twine that he himself had twisted, don Hernán strapped the gourd to his waist.

Carrying a long, sharp wooden stick that he called a *sembrador* (planter), don Hernán walked about the *milpa*, perforating a hole with every stride. Into the holes he deftly tossed two or three corn seeds; later he'd return to plant beans and squash. Planting each variety takes don Hernán about four 8-hour days, longer if he works fewer hours per day. He clears, burns, plants, and harvests his *milpa* with no helpers.

In a smaller section of the *milpa*, off to one side, don Hernán planted some peanuts. This traditional compartment of Yucatecan *milpas* is known as the *paach pak'al* and is characterized by richer soils, good for certain species. Primarily, however, having the smaller patch offset in the *milpa* facilitates more intensive management of the plants there. Other *milperos* in the region will plant cantaloupe, watermelon, cucumber, and sweet potato in the *paach pak'al*.

LA *COSECHA* / THE HARVEST

Harvest extends over a considerable amount of time; cobs mature by early fall, and although some young corn may be consumed, most is left on the stalks to dry until December, at which time stalks are cut down and the dried cobs are removed and stored until they are needed. Only by early February has all the maize been harvested.

To feed all the members of his extended family, don Hernán harvests 700 kilos (1,543 lbs.) of maize from his *milpa* each year. The harvested maize lasts about seven months. He showed me two large burlap bags stuffed with dried maize cobs. "That's all we have left from last year. It will be used up by the end of this month. We'll have to buy from others for the next five months, until we harvest again in December."

(top) Don Hernán fills a gourd with maize seeds for planting. On the wooden ka'anche' at right, he will place offerings of pozole *for the rain god.* [MC]
(bottom) Don Hernán with his planting stick. [MC]

Don Hernán with the fruits of his labor. [MR]

CHULIBU'UL

MAYA "SUCCOTASH" OF NEW CORN AND BLACK-EYED PEAS

TO PREPARE AHEAD
Enriched Lard (p. 513)
Recado para escabeche (p. 498)

(continued on next page)

This timeless autumn dish makes good use of fresh harvest ingredients: new corn, tender shell beans, squash seeds, tomatoes, and chiles. It bears a striking resemblance to New England succotash. The name in Mayan is an affectionate reference to the tastiness of the dish: "*bu'ul*" means "bean," and "*chul*" refers to the act of scooping out the delicious last drops of a meal with your fingers. In *La verdadera cocina regional*, doña Manuela calls the dish Xchul de frijol y elote nuevo, a hybrid Mayan/Spanish descriptive title that means something like "finger-licking good beans and new corn." Other sources call it Chul de frijol verde. In a published project (2004) to preserve traditional Maya recipes coordinated by the National Commission for the Development of Native Peoples in Tetiz, Yucatán, it is called Chulibu'ul, which is the name I have adopted. The bean typically used for this dish is *x'pelon* (*Vigna unguiculata*, p. 58), the cowpea or black-eyed pea. Even though it may not be the most photogenic dish on the block, Chulibu'ul will hook you with its nostalgia for autumn fields and just a hint of sun peeking through in a citrusy hot salsa.

Prepare ahead note: Like so many stews, Chulibu'ul only improves with age. Prepare a day or two in advance, refrigerate, and reheat just before serving.

YIELD: APPROXIMATELY 10 SERVINGS

FOR THE BEANS

1 lb. (500 g) fresh *x'pelones*
  (Substitute: fresh or dried
  black-eyed peas)
4 cups (1 L) water
2 tsp. (12 g) sea salt
2 sprigs fresh epazote
  (Substitute: 1 tsp. / 1.5 g dried)

FOR THE *SOFRITO*

½ cup (125 g) Enriched Lard
  (Substitute: Spanish olive oil)
4 cups (500 g) fresh corn kernels
  (5–6 large ears), divided
1 cup (170 g) white onion, finely
  chopped
1 cup (140 g) red bell pepper,
  cut into medium dice
2 medium cloves garlic (½ oz. /
  12 g), peeled and finely chopped
3 medium Roma tomatoes (10 oz.
  / 300 g), seeded and finely
  chopped
½ tsp. (1.5 g) Recado para
  escabeche

FOR SERVING

6 hard-boiled eggs, peeled, sliced
1 cup (125 g) Pepita molida
Tomate frito (p. 507)
K'uut bi ik (p. 508), or the chile
  sauce of your choice

COOK BEANS

Thoroughly rinse and pick through fresh beans, place them in a stockpot, and cover with the water. Add the salt and epazote, bring to a boil, reduce to a simmer, and cook, uncovered, about 30 minutes, or until the beans are just tender but not fully cooked. Remove the pan from the heat; do not drain. Remove the epazote and discard. (Note: If using dried beans, add more water as it evaporates and adjust cooking time; cook until just tender.)

PREPARE *SOFRITO* AND FINISH

Heat the lard in a large skillet until shimmering. Add 1 cup (125 g) of the corn kernels and sauté until the kernels are just beginning to turn golden, about 4 minutes. Add the next 3 ingredients and cook until the onion is soft and translucent, about 5 minutes. Add the tomatoes and *recado* and cook until most of the liquid has evaporated, about 5 minutes. Transfer the mixture to the beans and cook over low heat, stirring occasionally as you finish the dish.

While the corn mixture is cooking, place the remaining 3 cups (375 g) of corn kernels in a blender jar, add 3–4 ladles of the cooking liquid from the beans, and purée until smooth. Transfer the corn purée to the pot containing the beans. Return the beans to a simmer, stirring frequently to prevent scorching. Continue cooking, stirring until the mixture thickens, 5–6 minutes.

TO SERVE

Ladle Chulibu'ul into individual serving bowls and top with a few slices of egg. Diners add Pepita molida, Tomate frito, and K'uut bi ik to taste. Chulibu'ul is a hearty main course dish, but it may also be served as an accompaniment for grilled meats, chicken, or fish.

VARIATION

Although not traditional, it makes for a more attractive dish to use white beans instead of black.

(opposite page) Don Hernán and doña Asaria in front of one of the outbuildings in their household compound. [MR]

THE SOLAR

Doña Asaria spends much of the day in her kitchen making tortillas for the family. [MR]

THE PICTURE-PERFECT *NAH*, or traditional Maya house, of Hernán Perrera Novelo and family is bright and welcoming, doors wide open and surrounded by fragrant herbs and flowers. It is whitewashed with *cal*—the calcium hydroxide powder that has perennially served the Mayas for everything from softening dried corn to making mortar for building. The roof, don Hernán told me, is made of leaves from the *guano* palm (*Coccothrinax argentata*, silverpalm), woven so tightly that it has never once leaked in even the heaviest downpour. The roof is more than fifty years old.

As I approached the house, I heard the friendly hushed voices of don Hernán and his wife, Asaria, speaking Spanish and calling "Pase," or "Come on in!" I extended my hand, don Hernán took it, and I noticed that I was still moved, although I have experienced this moment a hundred times throughout Yucatán: the Maya handshake is soft, passive, evanescent. No tight squeezing or hearty gripping, the hand is presented gentle as a feather, and the outsider follows the Mayas' lead so that one does not hold on too long.

The Maya *nah* is elliptical, always with two doors, one on

each of the wide sides of the house, defining front and back. Adjacent to the *nah* stands a similar structure, the kitchen. On the floor is the traditional Maya *k'óoben*, or cooking hearth. Three stones are arranged in a triangle shape; the formation traditionally symbolizes the feminine, but in practical terms it serves to contain the fire and support a comal or other cooking utensil. Doña Asaria spends many hours a day here, squatting on a tiny stool, push-pulling logs into and out of the fire to control the heat. Once every week or two, don Hernán and his son go into the *monte* to gather *ja'abin*, *boox káatsim*, *sak káatsim*, and other tropical hardwoods to supply the women's cooking needs.

The rust-red plot of dirt that encompasses the handful of outbuildings in the family compound is known as the *solar*. The *solar* is considered a vitally important agroecological activity in Yucatán, second only to the *milpa* system. *Solares* not only provide subsistence food and cash income for the families who maintain them, but they also protect a great number of plant varieties and provide a natural "laboratory" for experimenting with domestication of new species. It is likely, in fact, that it was right outside the open doors of the Maya *nah* that much important plant domestication took place in ancient times.

The *solar* fulfills many invaluable needs beyond the culinary. It is the place where children play, run, and learn to climb trees; where youths and adults rest and chat beneath the shade of trees, refreshing themselves in the late afternoon heat. And it is here where clothes are washed and dried, water drawn from the well for family needs, and tools fabricated or repaired. It is also where corn is cooked, washed, and drained in preparation for daily meals.

A WORD ABOUT WORDS

The Spanish word "*solar*" has recently been absorbed into Mayan as a loan word, spelled "*soolar.*" The original Mayan name is *táankab*, although nowadays most Mayas call it simply "*afuera*"— "outside" in Spanish. In larger pueblos or cities it may be called the patio or *traspatio*. In English, anthropologists and ethnobotanists have burdened it with an almost ridiculous list of names, including homegarden, housegarden, dooryard garden, and kitchen garden.

(top) The large open well is still in use. Don Hernán uses the tobacco plant for remedies. [MR] *(middle) Drying clothes and edible plants all have their place in the solar.* [DS] *(bottom) The Perrera family house, Santa Elena, Yucatán.* [MR]

(left) Don Hernán works in the solar *for many household necessities. Here, he uses a long wooden plank to scrape the large leaves of the henequen agave to extract the sisal fibers.* [MR] *(right, top) Green strands of henequen dry to a pale golden color in an hour or two.* [MR] *(right, bottom) Don Hernán grasps and twists multiple strands of sisal fiber to create twine and rope for family needs.* [DS]

A DAY IN THE *SOLAR*

As I followed corn through an entire day in Maya life, I observed that its rhythm coincides primarily with the life of the Maya woman. And, interestingly enough, beyond its brief months of life in the *milpa*, the real story of corn takes place in the *solar*.

Doña Asaria spends most of every day in some way involved with corn. Early in the morning, she rinses the *nixtamal*, or dried maize cooked in water mixed with slaked lime (p. 517). She boils it the night before and in the morning must wash away the pericarp. After cleaning it thoroughly, she takes it to be ground into *masa* at a public *molino*, or mill. The *masa* is used throughout the day for tortillas, tamales, and other foods. Before retiring, she boils more *nixtamal* for the next day's meals, thereby completing the cycle.

(left) Nixtamal *must be thoroughly washed and rinsed to remove the pericarp. Women spend hours stooping over a battered tin rubbing the maize between their palms, resulting in a pail full of yellow sludge.* [DS] *(right)* *At the end of every day, Maya women bring the* nixtamal *to a rapid boil for an hour or two in preparation for the next day's meals.* [DS]

The last step in the process is to grind the finished *nixtamal* into *masa*. Doña Asaria explained to me that only the poorest people still grind their own: anyone with even a few pennies won't waste the time. Really poor people in remote regions may still use a *ka'* or metate (grinding stone), but even the humblest have graduated to the cast-iron hand grinders so commonly seen clamped to table edges throughout the peninsula. Still, most head for a commercial *molino*. For those one rung up the economic ladder, you can skip making your own *nixtamal* altogether and purchase ready-to-go *masa* from these commercial *molinos*. And such is the socioeconomic hierarchy of traditional Yucatán, with doña Asaria located squarely in the middle.

SOPA DE JOROCH'

ZUCCHINI AND SQUASH-BLOSSOM STEW WITH TINY CORN PANCAKES

TO PREPARE AHEAD
Enriched Lard (p. 513)
Masa prepared from either
   nixtamalized corn or *masa harina*
   (p. 517)

FOR THE SQUASH STOCK
8 cups (2 L) water
3 tsp. (18 g) sea salt
10 squash blossoms, plus 10 more
   for garnish, washed, stalks and
   sepals removed
3 lbs. (1.5 k) small zucchini, stems
   removed, cut into large dice
   (bite-sized pieces)
½ cup (112 g) Enriched Lard
   (Substitute: Spanish olive oil)

FOR THE CORN PANCAKES
1 lb. (500 g) *masa*
½ tsp. (3 g) sea salt

FOR SERVING
1 cup (75 g) grated Edam cheese
Tomate frito (p. 507)
Mixture of chopped red onion
   and cilantro lightly dressed with
   Seville orange juice or substitute
Chile k'uut (p. 508)

Joroches in Yucatán are generally little hollow conical dumplings of maize *masa* simmered in a pot of black bean purée. But Angelina "Lina" Magaña of Muna, a skilled and intelligent cook, insists that her Sopa de joroch'—which features small, flattened *masa* pancakes instead of the dumplings and is simmered in squash stock instead of the beans—is the real thing. I am not one to argue over semantics when the results are so delicious. The squash blossoms are not essential if you can't find them, but they do make a wonderful presentation. The *Recetario gastronómico* of Tetiz calls this soup Joroch de flor de x-caitas, a title that refers to the blossoms (*flor*) as well as the squash (*x-caitas*: [x] ka' is Mayan for the squash variety *Cucurbita argyrosperma*, the species most typically used for this dish, although any variety will do). Contrary to doña Lina's pancakes, the dumplings prescribed by *las tetizeñas* are indeed conical, like those for Joroches (p. 110), using Pepita molida as the filling. I list that as an option here. The Enriched Lard is an essential flavoring for this dish, but if you just can't bring yourself to use it, the only suitable substitute for my taste would be a fruity Spanish olive oil. The salsas suggested for serving are really more like requisites: they complete the many layers of flavor of this basically simple dish.

Prepare ahead note: Sopa de joroch' keeps well 2–3 days under refrigeration, but the dumplings tend to fall apart with reheating. This does not impact flavor; rather, it serves to continue to thicken the soup.

YIELD: APPROXIMATELY 10 SERVINGS

PREPARE SQUASH STOCK
Combine the water and salt in a stockpot and bring to a boil. Coarsely chop 10 of the squash flowers. Add the chopped flowers and squash to the pot, cover, and simmer for 8 minutes. When the squash is soft, add the lard, cover, and simmer while you proceed.

FORM CORN PANCAKES AND FINISH
Mix the *masa* with the salt. Divide the *masa* into 50 balls weighing about ⅓ ounces (10 g) each. Pat 1 ball in the palm of your hand into a thin 2-inch (6 cm) round tortilla. As you work, set each pancake aside until you have 10.

Gently add the first 10 to the gently simmering stock. Use a wooden spoon to move them very delicately in order to prevent their sticking together, taking care not to break them. Simmer 3 minutes as you flatten another 10 balls, then add those to the stock. Repeat until you have added all 50 pancakes. Periodically shake the pot to move the pancakes, or baste them with hot stock and cover them with squash in order to cook them.

When all the pancakes have been added, gently simmer uncovered for 30 minutes. Remove the pan from the heat, cover, and let stand until ready to serve. (Note: Invariably, some of the pancakes will fall apart, which is unavoidable. This actually benefits the soup, since the broken pieces lightly thicken the stock.)

Use a large spoon to delicately lift 4–5 of the pancakes into an individual serving bowl. Pour hot stock and squash on top and garnish with the reserved squash blossoms, centering one atop each serving. Accompaniments are offered on the side; for the full flavor experience, diners are encouraged to use a little bit of all of them.

VARIATIONS

If you like, you may make the Joroches as the ladies of Tetiz suggest. Follow the instructions for forming the traditional conical Joroches on page 110, but use Pepita molida (p. 497) instead of meat as the filling for the dumplings. Continue as in the rest of this recipe.

[DS]

A LIVING PANTRY

Maya *solares* typically contain a rich mixture of minor crops, fruits, medicinal plants, and ornamentals as well as plants that provide useful nonedible things such as *jícaras* (drinking gourds) and cotton.

These plants grow in much the same way that the Mayas managed silviculture plantations: beneath a protective canopy of taller trees. Some *solares* may contain over thirty different tree species that not only provide shade but that also have other specific uses. Fruit trees dominate, with a range of citrus such as lime and sweet and sour oranges. Mangoes, *ciruela*, several species in the Annonaceae family, such as *saramuyo*; coconuts, mamey, and other members of the Sapotaceae family; pineapple, tamarind, papaya, and *pitahaya* as well as avocado and allspice are common. (See The Yucatecan Market, p. 11.)

Fowl are the second most frequent foodstuff found in the *solar*, with a substantial percentage of modern Maya households managing chickens and turkeys (only a few still manage ducks and doves). Rabbits are typically kept as pets, although they may also be consumed.

Beneath the sheltering canopy, the Maya garden grows: *yuca*, *chaya*, peanuts, a colorful assortment of chiles, bananas, tomato, cucumber, chayote, as well as lettuce and radishes. Condiments are grown, too, especially *achiote*. Herbs like epazote, mint, cilantro, chives, and various medicinal herbs like Cuban oregano (*Plectranthus amboinicus*) are just a few of the dozens of species I have spotted in regional *solares*. Many Maya families will also plant a small patch of corn, beans, and squash to supplement harvests from the *milpa*.

(above) Achiote, *also known in English as annatto, was used by the ancient Mayas as a pigment for dyes and paint, as well as a colorant for the chocolate beverage.* [DS]

(top, left) Mamey in the Perrera compound. [MC] *(top, right)* Most Maya household solares have a pig or two. [MR] *(bottom)* The Maya k'áanche'—a raised planter constructed of tree limbs and trunks—contains rich alluvial soils dug from the monte. It keeps fragile seedlings out of reach of scratching turkeys and rooting pigs and maintains plants at a comfortable height for the intensive tending that they require. The k'áanche' may hold tomatoes, chiles, or herbs (pictured are chives), or anything not requiring deep soil. [DS]

CHAYAS FRITAS / TSAAJBI CHAAY

SAUTÉED CHAYA WITH SMOKED BACON

FOR THE BACON AND *SOFRITO*

2 Tbs. (30 ml) Spanish olive oil

4 oz. (114 g) smoked slab bacon, cut into large dice (omit for a vegetarian option)

1 cup (170 g) red onion, finely chopped

1 cup (140 g) red bell pepper, cut into small dice

5 medium cloves garlic (1¼ oz. / 30 g), peeled and finely chopped

1 medium chile habanero (¼ oz. / 7 g), seeded and minced (Substitute: chile serrano)

FOR SAUTÉING THE *CHAYA* AND FINISHING

10½ oz. (300 g) fresh *chaya* leaves (Substitute: chard or kale), thick stems removed and cut into chiffonade or coarsely chopped

1 Tbs. (15 ml) sherry vinegar or red wine vinegar

½ tsp. (3 g) sea salt

½ tsp. (2.5g) freshly ground black pepper

(opposite page) Chaya is considered the "miracle food" of the Mayas. Indigenous to the Maya region of southeastern Mexico and northern Guatemala, the nutritional value of this green, leafy plant is two to three times greater than that of most edible leafy green vegetables such as kale or chard. [MC]

Chronicler Diego de Landa mentioned *chaya* in 1566, when he observed that the leaves were especially delicious when cooked with plenty of bacon. What isn't? Chayas fritas is an excellent side dish; it also stars in the scrambled egg dish Huevos revueltos con chaya. *Chaya* continues in popularity to the present, with exuberant chefs pushing the envelope of its many possibilities: how about a *chaya* margarita? Or *chaya* mousse? Deep fat–fried whole *chaya* leaves also appear as a decorative and edible garnish on many "fusion" dishes at contemporary restaurants. *Chaya* is slowly becoming available in southern-tier states in the United States, but if you can't find it, my favorite substitute is kale, which is hearty, robust, and nutty, much like *chaya*.

Prepare ahead note: Chayas fritas keeps well under refrigeration for a couple of days. Heat a bit of oil or lard in a covered skillet, add *chaya*, cover, and cook until heated through. Use leftovers to make Huevos revueltos con chaya (below).

YIELD: APPROXIMATELY 6 SERVINGS

FRY BACON AND *SOFRITO*

Choose a large, heavy casserole equipped with a tight-fitting lid. Heat the olive oil in the casserole, add the bacon if using, and cook, uncovered, over low heat until the bacon is thoroughly browned, 6–8 minutes. Remove the bacon and set aside; reserve the cooking fat.

Adjust the heat to medium. Add the remaining *sofrito* ingredients to the reserved cooking fat and cook, stirring frequently, until the onion is translucent and the bell pepper is softened, 2–3 minutes.

SAUTÉ *CHAYA* AND FINISH

Add the *chaya*, stir to thoroughly incorporate into the cooked vegetables, reduce the heat to low, and cover. Cook 20–25 minutes, or until the *chaya* is tender, stirring frequently to prevent scorching. Return the bacon to the casserole, add the remaining ingredients, and toss to incorporate. Check the seasonings and serve.

VARIATION

Huevos revueltos con chaya / Chay-je' (Scrambled Eggs with Sautéed *Chaya*): This is another Yucatecan favorite that makes use of leftovers from the day before. Chayas fritas from the afternoon meal are repurposed for breakfast the next day in this quick yet nourishing dish. Scramble the quantity of eggs desired, adding Chayas fritas just as the eggs are beginning to set. Season with sea salt and freshly ground black pepper and serve immediately. If you wish, you may serve these topped with Cebolla frita con frijol (p. 234) and garnished with slices of Plátano frito (p. 371). As a taco, mound the Huevos revueltos con chaya atop a fresh tortilla; as a *torta*, serve it on Pan francés (p. 194). Garnish tacos and *tortas* with Cebolla frita con frijol (p. 234). Diners add chile sauce to taste.

DZOTOBILCHAY / DZOTO-BIL-CHAY / DS'OTOBICHAY / TS'OTOBICHAY

TAMAL WRAPPED IN *CHAYA* LEAVES

The Mayan name of this uniquely Yucatecan *tamal* refers to the leafy green vegetable in its last syllable, and "*dzot*" refers to something thin. This diminutive *tamal* is wrapped in *chaya* leaves before steaming. Traditionally, only *chaya* leaves are used as the wrapper; however, cooks sometimes resort to an outer layer of banana leaves to help hold the *tamal* together. When the banana leaves are removed, the *chaya* stays in place, creating a beautiful and wholly edible little package that looks ever so much like Middle Eastern stuffed grape leaves.

YIELD: APPROXIMATELY 2 DOZEN

TO PREPARE AHEAD

Masa para tamales yucatecos
   (p. 522, or the vegetarian option)
Banana leaves, prepared for
   the small (SM) size (see Basic
   Techniques, p. 525)
Pepita molida (p. 497)

FOR THE TAMALES

½ lb. (250 g) fresh *chaya* leaves
   (Substitute: chard, a variety
   with flatter leaves), thick stems
   removed and discarded
1 recipe Masa para tamales
   yucatecos
1 cup (125 g) Pepita molida, plus
   additional for serving
6 hard-boiled eggs, peeled and
   chopped

FOR SERVING

Tomate frito (p. 507)
Pepita molida
Salpicón (p. 511)
Chile tamulado (p. 509), or the
   chile sauce of your choice

PREPARE TAMALES

Bring a large pot of salted water to a boil. Plunge the whole *chaya* leaves into the boiling water and blanch for 1 minute; drain immediately and rinse under cold water to stop cooking. Allow the *chaya* to cool, then gently pat it dry.

Divide the *masa* into 24 balls, each weighing about 1¾ ounces (50 g). Overlap 2–3 sections of banana leaf on a work surface to create a rectangle. Arrange 2–3 *chaya* leaves on top, leaving a border of banana leaves around all sides. Overlap the *chaya* slightly in order to prevent leaks when rolled (if there are small gaps, it won't harm the finished product). Gently pat 1 ball of *masa* onto the *chaya* to form a rectangle measuring approximately 3½ inches × 5½ inches (9 cm × 14 cm) and ⅛-inch (3 mm) thick, leaving a border of *chaya* on all sides of the dough.

Sprinkle 1 tablespoon (8 g) of the Pepita molida onto the *masa* and spread to cover evenly. Arrange 1 tablespoon (15 g) of the chopped boiled egg in a tight row down the middle.

Gently lift 1 side of the *chaya* leaves to fold the *masa* over onto itself to the ⅔ point; repeat with the other side, closing completely. (Note: The *chaya* can be a bit fussy, sticking to the *masa* and not cooperating when you roll. Don't worry, since you will use the banana leaves to roll and seal tightly at the end.) Roll and tuck the banana leaves. Finish and steam the *tamal* for 1 hour per the instructions in Basic Techniques, page 526. Remove the tamales from the heat and allow them to rest at least 15 minutes prior to serving.

TO SERVE

Remove the banana leaves prior to serving, but leave the *chaya* intact. Diners add their own garnishes and chile to taste.

BRAZO DE REINA

TAMAL "LOG" WITH *CHAYA*, SQUASH SEEDS, AND EGG

TO PREPARE AHEAD
Masa para tamales I or II (p. 521),
   or the vegetarian option (p. 522)
Banana leaves, cut to extra-large
   (XL) size, plus reserved ribs
   for ties (p. 525)
Pepita molida (p. 497)

FOR THE *MASA*
½ lb. (250 g) fresh *chaya* leaves
   (Substitute: chard or kale),
   tough stems removed and
   discarded
1 recipe Masa para tamales

FOR THE FILLING
½ cup (62.5g) Pepita molida, plus
   additional for serving
6 eggs, boiled, peeled, and sliced
   in half lengthwise

[MC]

Yucatán boasts several unique, large tamales that must be sliced into serving pieces: Pimes (p. 106); Tamal de xmakulam (p. 133); Mucbilpollo (p. 430); and this one, which, curiously, translates to "Queen's arm." Chopped *chaya* is kneaded into the *masa*, which is then flattened on a banana leaf. After receiving its fillings, the whole is rolled into a log shape, jelly-roll style, and steamed. The *tamal* ladies sell slices of Brazo de reina as well as Pimes for a few cents every day in the market. Grab a slice to go and you'll also receive two tiny bags: one filled with Tomate frito and the other with cabbage Salpicón for you to use as garnishes. Substituting olive oil for the lard in the *masa* makes this a vegetarian dish. In fact, Brazo de reina (probably with a bit of lard, but who will tell?) is a very popular comestible during Lent.

YIELD: 2 LARGE TAMALES OF 6 SERVINGS EACH

PREPARE *MASA*
Bring a large pot of salted water to a boil. Plunge the *chaya* into the boiling water, reduce the heat to medium and cook, uncovered, for 20 minutes. Transfer the *chaya* to a colander, allow it to cool, and press out as much liquid as possible (too much moisture will make the *masa* soggy). Coarsely chop the *chaya* and combine it with the *masa* in a large mixing bowl. Knead the *chaya* into the dough until it is thoroughly incorporated.

FILL AND FORM TAMALES
Divide the dough in half and shape into 2 large balls. On a work surface, overlap enough

large sections of banana leaf to form a rectangle about 15 inches × 20 inches (38 cm × 50 cm). Place 1 ball of *masa* in the center of the leaves and pat and extend it into a rectangle about 10 inches × 14 inches (25 cm × 35 cm) and ¼ inch (6.35 mm) thick.

Sprinkle half of the Pepita molida onto the *masa*, spreading evenly. Arrange half of the boiled eggs tip to tip lengthwise along the center of the *masa*, leaving a bit of space on either end.

Finally, roll the *tamal*. Using the section of leaf along 1 of the long sides of the *masa*, lift the *masa* up and fold it over itself to reach the two-thirds point. Press the *masa* in place and gently peel away the leaf, allowing it to rest again on the work surface. Lift the opposite side of the leaf and fold the *masa* to cover the first section. Do not peel away the leaf; rather, continue to roll the *tamal* into a log shape. Tuck the ends under and pack and compress the log into a tight loaf. (Note: Make sure to check the size of your steamer; if the *tamal* is too large, you may pack and form the loaf to be smaller without ruining it.)

Repeat with the remaining components to create 1 more large *tamal*. Use the reserved ribs from the banana leaves (or kitchen twine) to tie and secure and steam according to instructions in Basic Techniques, page 526, for approximately 1½ hours, or until the tamales are firm when pressed with your finger. Allow them to rest at least 15 minutes prior to slicing and serving.

TO SERVE

Slice each "log" into 6 equal pieces. For a dramatic party presentation, leave the tamales in the banana leaves and unwrap and slice at the table. Invite diners to spoon on their own salsas and garnishes. Alternatively, unwrap and slice beforehand, plate, and spoon on some of the Tomate frito, Pepita molida, and Salpicón. Diners add chile sauce to taste.

VARIATION

Tamalitos de chaya / Chay'wah / Chaayil waaj (Small Steamed Tamales with *Chaya*, Squash Seeds, and Eggs): The Mayan name *chay'wah* is a simple descriptor meaning "*chaya* bread." The ingredients are the same as those for Brazo de reina, but these little tamales are rolled individually rather than in the style of the "queen's arm." Follow the recipe for Brazo de reina, choosing the small (SM) size as described in Basic Techniques, page 525. Form approximately 24 balls of the *masa*. Pat each into a tortilla shape on a section of the banana leaf and spread the surface evenly with approximately 2 teaspoons (5 g) of the Pepita molida. Place 2 teaspoons (7 g) of chopped (rather than halved) boiled egg in a row down the middle and wrap as instructed on page 522. Steam for 1 hour. Allow the Tamalitos to rest at least 15 minutes prior to serving. Serving instructions are the same as for Brazo de reina.

TAMAL DE XMAKULAM / MAKULANIWAAJ

BEAN AND SQUASH-SEED *TAMAL* WRAPPED IN *HOJA SANTA* LEAVES

TO PREPARE AHEAD

Pepita molida (p. 497)

Masa para tamales I or II (p. 521), or the vegetarian option (p. 522)

3 pieces banana leaf, cut slightly larger than *hoja santa* leaf (see below); reserve ribs of banana leaves for ties

(continued on next page)

My first taste of a Tamal de xmakulam was prepared by Linda de Jesús Tun Jiménez of Chichimilá, near Valladolid, where huge bushes of *hoja santa* are abundant, nestling next to every home to protect their floppy, velvety leaves against the wind. Like several other large Yucatecan tamales, this one is in the form of a log that is sliced before serving. In the 1910 *La verdadera cocina regional*, it is titled Jotobí-xmakulam (*jotobí* may be an outmoded transcription of the Mayan word for *tamal*, currently transcribed as "to'obil." The spelling *xmakulam* with an "m" is a Yucatecan peculiarity. The author and cook, Sra. Manuela Navarrete A., explains that the *tamal* may either be baked or boiled (a technique of the era), but she notes that "they turn out much better when they are cooked in a *píib*."

Doña Linda cooked one in a *píib*, another in a steamer. Steaming left the *hoja santa* leaf intact and lent more of its subtle flavor to the *masa*. The stovetop smoking method (p. 527) also gives excellent results and yields a *tamal* with a lightly smoky flavor similar to the one cooked in a *píib*. Lacking fresh *hoja santa* leaves, you may use dried leaves instead (see Resources, p. 540). The taste will not be the same, but they make a nice visual presentation. Proceed as directed in the master recipe: place one whole, dried leaf on top of each *tamal* before you finish wrapping it with the banana leaves. It will rehydrate and soften as it cooks.

YIELD: 3 LARGE TAMALES, EACH YIELDING ABOUT 4 SERVINGS

[DS]

FOR THE BEANS AND FILLING

1 lb. (500 g) fresh *ibes* (Substitute: fresh or frozen lima beans)

4 cups (1 L) water

2 sprigs fresh epazote (Substitute: 1 tsp. / 1.5 g dried, crumbled)

1 tsp. (6 g) sea salt

2 cups (250 g) Pepita molida

½ cup (40 g) chives, finely chopped

1 Tbs. (6 g) chile país, seeded and finely ground (Substitute: chile de árbol or crushed red pepper flakes). (Note: To control heat, add ground chile a bit at a time, tasting between additions.)

FOR THE TAMALES

1 recipe Masa para tamales

3 large *hoja santa* leaves (these will naturally vary in size. The ones I find are approximately 10 in. × 18 in./ 25 cm × 46 cm), thick central stems removed to the base of the leaf

FOR SERVING

Tomate frito (p. 507)

Pepita molida

Chile tamulado (p. 509), or the chile sauce of your choice

Xmakulán / Hoja santa (p. 71) is known for its delicate flavor reminiscent of anise and black pepper. It is a broadleaf tropical plant native to the Maya region. Large bushes of hoja santa can be found growing wild across the peninsula, and it is also cultivated in solares. It is sometimes mashed or puréed for inclusion in stews or sauces, but in Yucatán its most common culinary use is as a wrapper for tamales or other foods. [MR]

COOK BEANS

Cover the *ibes* with the water. Add the epazote and salt and bring to a boil. Skim off any foam that rises to the surface. Reduce the heat to medium and cook at a gentle boil until the beans are just tender, 15–20 minutes. Pour off most of the cooking liquid leaving just enough to reach the top of the beans; discard the epazote.

PREPARE FILLING

On medium heat, add the Pepita molida to the beans and cooking liquid and cook, stirring occasionally, for about 1 minute, or until thickened. The mixture should be mostly dry with little visible liquid; if any liquid is left, continue cooking and stirring until it evaporates. Add the chives and chile to taste and stir to incorporate. Remove the pan from the heat as you continue.

FORM TAMALES AND FINISH

Divide the *masa* into 3 equal balls and set aside. Prepare the banana leaves as instructed above. (These will hold the *tamal* together during steaming, but will be discarded afterward.) Place 1 section of the banana leaf on a work surface and arrange 1 *hoja santa* leaf underside up on top of the banana leaf. Pat 1 ball of *masa* out on the *hoja santa* leaf and extend it into a large, irregular tortilla that covers most of the leaf. Spoon one-third of the bean mixture onto the *masa* and spread to completely cover.

Starting with the end where the stem was, begin to roll the leaf and *masa* into a log shape. Some of the filling will fall out of the ends, and the leaf will likely break or tear around the remaining central spine. Don't worry; just keep rolling and push as much of the dough and filling as you can back into the *tamal*. Once the *hoja santa* leaf and the *masa* are rolled, resume rolling again, this time using the banana leaf to roll and wrap, then tie. Repeat with the other 2 tamales. Steam, bake, or smoke for 1½ hours, or until firm, as instructed in Basic Techniques, p. 526. Allow the *tamal* to rest at least 15 minutes before serving.

Yucatecan beans, x'pelones (cowpeas or black-eyed peas), photographed growing along a country roadside. Yucatecan farmers plant beans wherever they have room— certainly in the milpa *and* solar, *but also in more unexpected places.* [DS]

FOR SERVING

Carefully remove the banana leaves and discard. Since the *hoja santa* leaf is edible and delicious, it should not be removed. Slice the *tamal* across the width or on the diagonal and arrange slices on serving plates. Diners add their own salsas and more of the Pepita molida to taste.

VARIATION

Chan chan de x'pelon (Bean and Squash-Seed Tamal Wrapped in Corn Husks): If the transliteration is correct, then the name of this *tamal* translates to "tiny little bean" *tamal* (*chan* is Mayan for small). It is more likely, however, that the ladies of Tetiz who shared this recipe in *Recetario gastronómico* used a common misspelling for "*cháamcham*," which means empanada. Like several others in its class, this *tamal* is formed first as a tortilla, then folded in half to create the empanada shape before being tucked into its corn husk wrapper. The recipe is similar to that for Tamal de xmakulam, featuring a cooked bean and squash-seed filling. The variations on the theme are that the bean of choice for this *tamal* is the black-eyed pea (although you may use the lima bean if you prefer), and that it is a small tamal wrapped in corn husks rather than a large loaf wrapped in *hoja santa* and banana leaves.

Prepare 26 corn husks as described on page 524. Cut 2 of the husks into enough long, narrow strips to use as ties. Prepare the bean and squash-seed mixture as directed in the master recipe for Tamal de xmakulám, using black-eyed peas instead of lima beans.

Divide the *masa* into 24 balls. Pat 1 ball into a tortilla in the palm of your hand, about 5 inches (13 cm) in diameter. Spoon approximately 2 teaspoons (10 g) of the bean-and-squash seed filling in a row down the center. (See illustrations for forming tamales in corn husks on p. 524.) Fold the *masa* in half, place inside the corn husk, seal, tie, and steam per instructions. Allow to rest at least 15 minutes prior to serving. Serving suggestions are the same as for Tamal de xmakulam.

IBEWAHES

BEAN AND SQUASH-SEED *TAMAL* WRAPPED IN BANANA LEAVES

TO PREPARE AHEAD
Banana leaves, prepared for
    medium (M) size (see Basic
    Techniques, p. 525)
Masa para tamales I or II (p. 521),
    or the vegetarian option on
    p. 522
Toksel (p. 113)

FOR THE TAMALES
Banana leaves
1 recipe Masa para tamales
2 cups (315 g) Toksel

Like many of its relatives, this satisfying little *tamal* features all the products of the *milpa*: corn, beans, and squash seeds. Referring to the *tamal* family tree, this one appears to be the offspring of Vaporcitos and Chan chan de x'pelon. It is small and wrapped in banana leaves like the former, and filled with a bean and squash-seed medley like the latter. The Mayan name of this *tamal*—which refers to the preferred bean, the *ib* (*Phaseolus lunatus*) or lima bean—translates simply to "lima bean bread."

YIELD: APPROXIMATELY 1 DOZEN TAMALES

FORM THE TAMALES
Divide the *masa* into 12 balls, each weighing about 3⅓ ounces (95 g). Place a section of banana leaf on a work surface, pat 1 ball of *masa* into a tortilla shape as directed in Basic Techniques (p. 523). Fill with approximately 1 rounded tablespoon (14 g) of Toksel, arranging the mixture in a row down the center of the tortilla. Fold, wrap, and steam for 1 hour, following the instructions in Basic Techniques.

TO SERVE
Place 1 or 2 unwrapped tamales on individual serving plates. Follow the serving suggestions for Tamal de xmakulam on page 133.

IBES EN ESCABECHE

LIMA BEANS AND CHAYOTE IN PICKLED ONIONS

TO PREPARE AHEAD
Recado para escabeche (p. 498)
Recado rojo (p. 500)
Enriched Lard (p. 513)
Seville orange juice substitute
    (p. 514), unless fresh Seville
    oranges are available
Cebollas en escabeche (p. 511)

FOR THE ENRICHMENT
½ cup (125 ml) water
½ medium red onion (5 oz. /
    137.5g), coarsely chopped
2 medium cloves garlic (1/2 oz. /
    12g), peeled and chopped

(continued on next page)

This lovely, humble side dish taught to me by doña Guadalupe Aké of Peto is quick, easy, and, with a minor adjustment, can be vegetarian. The *ib* (*Phaseolus lunatus*) is in the lima bean family and is available fresh here almost all year long, but when it is out of season, dried ones are used instead. Beyond the region, frozen beans would be preferred.

Prepare ahead note: The Cebollas en escabeche required for this recipe may be prepared a day or two in advance and refrigerated. Ibes en escabeche is best served immediately after preparing.

YIELD: APPROXIMATELY 10 SERVINGS

PREPARE ENRICHMENT
Place the ingredients in the jar of a blender and process until thoroughly puréed; set aside.

½ tsp. (1.5g) Recado para escabeche

½ tsp. (2.5g) Recado rojo

1 tsp. (6 g) sea salt

2 Tbs. (28 g) Enriched Lard, melted
(Substitute: Spanish olive oil)

FOR THE BEANS

1 medium *jícama* (1½ lb. / 680 g),
peeled, thinly sliced, and cut
into triangles

¼ cup (62.5 ml) Seville orange
juice or substitute

½ lb. (250 g) fresh *ibes* (Substitute:
fresh or frozen lima beans)

1½ cups (375 ml) water

2 medium chayotes (about 10½ oz.
/ 300 g each), seeded and sliced

½ recipe Cebollas en escabeche

2 hard-boiled eggs, peeled and
quartered

FOR SERVING

Chile con limón (p. 511)

COOK BEANS AND FINISH

Cover the jicama with the sour orange juice and allow to stand at room temperature as you proceed.

Place the beans in a saucepan and pour on the enrichment. Add the water and bring to a boil. Reduce the heat to a simmer, and cook 10 minutes. Add the sliced chayotes, cover, and cook another 10–15 minutes, or until the chayotes and *ibes* are tender. Add a bit more water if needed.

Retrieve the chiles from the Cebollas en escabeche, rub off the skin, slit along the side, remove veins and seeds, and slice lengthwise into strips. Remove the chayote slices from the beans and line them up around the edge of a large serving platter, alternating with the jicama wedges. Arrange the beans in the center of the platter, top with the Cebollas en escabeche and the chile strips, and garnish with the eggs.

TO SERVE

This dish is usually passed around the table so that diners may serve themselves; add chile to taste.

Ibes en escabeche. [MC]

[MR]

DON HERNÁN'S PEANUT PATCH

Don Hernán takes special pride in the peanut patch in front of his house and always shows it to me when I visit. I love peanuts as much as he does, so I understand his obsession. No chips and dip for don Hernán: he plucks up some peanuts, and wife, Asaria, roasts them on the comal before grinding with tomatoes and chile to make a simple spread for fresh tortillas. Peanuts also play a leading role in one of the region's most unusual sorbets: Sorbete de cacahuate (p. 246).

PAVO DEL PATIO / PAVO DOMÉSTICO / GUAJOLOTE

SCIENTIFIC / *Meleagris gallopavo* L. / Family Phasianidae
ENGLISH / turkey
MAYAN / *tso'* (male), *ulum* (female)

DESCRIPTION, ORIGIN, AND HISTORY: In 1511, King Ferdinand ordered that aboard every ship the *conquistadores* brought back from the Americas there should be a minimum of ten turkeys. The bird became so popular in Europe after Columbus brought the first ones that it quickly displaced the peacock as the banquet fowl of choice. *Meleagris gallopavo* is native to a broad region between the western and eastern ranges of the Sierra Madre. It was domesticated in the southern *altiplano* of central Mexico around 4,000 or 5,000 years ago. From there, it dispersed in all directions; by 1,800 to 3,500 years ago, it was a well-established food source, and turkey bones are frequent finds in many archaeological digs. The domesticated turkey reached the Yucatán Peninsula by the Postclassic period (900–1521 CE). Prior to that time, the Mayas consumed *Meleagris ocellata*, the ocellated wild turkey. Today, both turkey species are consumed year-round, and special dishes are prepared on feast days.

(opposite page) Domesticated turkeys kept by families in Yucatán are described as "indio"— descended from ancient stock and nothing like the hybrids of commercial breeding. [MC]

PAVO EN SAK K'ÓOL

TURKEY IN MAIZE-THICKENED WHITE SAUCE

FOR THE MARINADE

8 Tbs. (120 g) Recado blanco

8 Tbs. (120 ml) Seville orange
  juice or substitute

2 Tbs. (28 g) Enriched Lard,
  melted

2 tsp. (12 g) sea salt

3 lbs. (1.5 k) turkey pieces, brined

"*K'óol*" in Mayan translates to "thick soup" and "*sak*" means "white." The translation for this recipe, then, becomes "turkey in thick white soup." But surely "turkey and gravy" takes on a whole new meaning in this classic Yucatecan dish. Traditionally, poultry stock seasoned with herbs and chiles is lightly thickened with nixtamalized corn *masa*. Postcontact adaptations included finishing the sauce with almonds and raisins for an Andalusian touch as well as a taste and texture contrast. The dairy enrichment and wine are nontraditional but delicious; omit if you prefer. With this "gravy" as the background for charcoal-grilled poultry, the layers of flavors are worthy of the finest holiday celebration.

Prepare ahead note: The turkey and white sauce for Pavo en sak k'óol may be prepared in advance and refrigerated 1–2 days; reheat gently, thinning the sauce if necessary with a bit of milk or stock.

YIELD: 8–10 SERVINGS

MARINATE AND GRILL TURKEY

Dilute the *recado* with the orange juice, add the lard and salt, and stir to incorporate. Add a bit more juice or *recado* to get the right texture: thick, yet pourable, like barbecue sauce. Remove the turkey from the brine, rinse, and pat dry; discard the brining solution. Place the turkey in a resealable plastic bag or in a large bowl and cover completely with the marinade. (Your hands are the best tools for this job.) Allow the turkey to marinate under refrigeration at least 1 hour or up to 12 hours.

Light a gas or charcoal grill following instructions for using wood smoking chips

Pavo en sak k'óol. [MC]

FOR THE SOFRITO

3 Tbs. (45 ml) Spanish olive oil

1 cup (6 oz. / 170 g) white onion, finely chopped

2 medium cloves garlic (½ oz. / 12 g), peeled and minced

½ tsp. (1.5 g) Recado para puchero

¼ cup (15 g) fresh mint leaves, chopped

1 medium chile x'catik (about 1¼ oz. / 35 g), left whole

FOR THE STOCK

½ cup (125 ml) dry white wine

2 bay leaves

9 cups (2.25 L) water

2 Tbs. (24 g) powdered chicken bouillon

1 three-in. (7.5 cm) stick *canela* (Mexican cinnamon)

FOR THICKENING THE SAUCE

¾ cup (170 g) *masa*

½ cup (125 ml) milk (optional)

½ cup (125 ml) Mexican *crema*, optional (Substitute: crème fraîche, plain yogurt, or whipping cream)

4 Tbs. (60 g) black or golden raisins, coarsely chopped

4 Tbs. (60 g) almonds, blanched and slivered

20 medium green olives, whole unpitted, pitted, or pimiento-stuffed and sliced

Several big grinds of fresh white pepper, to taste

Sea salt, to taste

FOR SERVING

Tortillas (p. 518)

Tomate Frito (p. 507)

Mexican *crema*, or substitute as above

Fresh mint or epazote leaves

Chile k'uut (p. 508), or the chile sauce of your choice

---

in Basic Techniques, page 537. Leave the turkey at room temperature in the marinade while the grill is heating. Remove the meat from the marinade and grill it over the hottest part of the fire. It should acquire grill marks and some charring but not be cooked through; pink juices should still be flowing. Remove and set aside.

PREPARE SOFRITO

Heat the oil in a stockpot until it is shimmering. Add the garlic and onions and cook until the onions are translucent, 2–3 minutes. Add the remaining ingredients and cook an additional minute. (Note: To control the heat of this sauce, do not puncture the chile.)

PREPARE STOCK

Add the wine and bay leaves to the stockpot and simmer 2–3 minutes to concentrate the flavors and evaporate the alcohol. Add the grilled turkey, water, bouillon, and *canela*, bring to a boil, then reduce the heat and cook at a gentle boil for 30–45 minutes, or until turkey is cooked through. (It should reach an internal temperature of 165°F / 74°C.) Remove the pot from the heat, remove the turkey from the stock, and set aside. Remove the chile and *canela* from the stock and discard. Line a sieve with cheesecloth, place it over a saucepan, and strain the stock through, mashing the vegetables to extract as much liquid as possible; discard the residue. You should have approximately 7 cups (1.75 L) of stock.

THICKEN SAUCE AND FINISH

Return the stock to a gentle simmer. Place the *masa* in a mixing bowl. Add 2 cups (500 ml) of the hot stock and mash until the *masa* is completely dissolved. Stream the *masa* mixture back into the saucepan, whisking constantly over medium heat. Simmer, stirring frequently, until lightly thickened, 5–10 minutes. Use a whisk or immersion blender to break up any lumps that may form. (Note: The thickness of *k'óol* is a matter of taste in Yucatán. For a thicker gravy, add a bit more dissolved *masa*.)

Mix the milk and *crema* and add it gradually to the saucepan, whisking constantly. Simmer a few minutes, or until the sauce rethickens; do not boil. Add the remaining ingredients and check for seasonings. Remove the pan from the heat and serve.

TO SERVE

Carve the turkey and place pieces of it in shallow serving bowls. Ladle on some of the white sauce, distributing the raisins, almonds, and olives evenly. Top with a spoonful of Tomate frito, add a squiggle of *crema*, and garnish with the herbs. Serve with warm tortillas. Diners add chile sauce to taste.

VARIATION

K'óol blanco / Sak k'óol (Maize-Thickened White Sauce): Several Yucatecan dishes call for a big ladleful of this white sauce, sans turkey. Omit the turkey; prepare the *sofrito*. Replace the water and powdered bouillon with 7 cups (1.75 L) of good poultry stock or bouillon. Add the *sofrito* and heat 15 minutes to amalgamate the flavors; strain as instructed and proceed with the recipe.

3

FERTILE
SHORES

Tʜᴇ ᴍᴀɴʏ ᴅɪᴠᴇʀsᴇ ᴍɪᴄʀᴏᴇɴᴠɪ-ronments making up the 1,100 miles (1,700 km) of coastline that trace the Yucatán Peninsula harbor an almost limitless bounty of foods and tools as vital to survival as those harvested from the land. Along with *monte*, *milpa*, and *solar*, the sea is an integral part of the natural continuum that has sustained the Maya peoples for centuries.

(previous page spread) Assorted botanas in San Felipe: mixed seafood salad (left) and grilled octopus (right). [MC] (this page) Cocos. [DS]

Off the coast of Yucatán and well on the way from the island of Cozumel, the Spaniards encountered a canoe filled with fishermen. There were nine of them, and they fished with golden hooks.

—JUAN DE GRIJALVA, 1521

ALTHOUGH PRECONTACT MAYAS developed a successful agricultural system, the peculiar ecology of the entire Maya zone—partly too dry, partly too wet—presented significant challenges. However, some scholars believe that Maya civilization rose not in spite of these limitations, but, rather, because the Maya peoples recognized their unique location—a peninsular body of land surrounded by nonagricultural resources—and took advantage of it, supplementing the production of the mainland with riches from the sea. The coastal Mayas and contemporary Yucatecans continue to exploit these resources.

We'll take a tour of fishing villages along the Maya coast, starting at Celestún, close to the Campeche border, continuing on to Chunchucmil and Sisal in the state of Yucatán, around the curve past Progreso and San Felipe toward the state of Quintana Roo, through the Riviera Maya and the popular resort of Tulum, finishing our trip in Punta Allen in the breathtaking Sian Ka'an Biosphere.

(above) Coastal fishing scene on a mural in the Temple of the Warriors, Chichén Itzá. [AUREA HERNÁNDEZ AFTER A REPRODUCTION BY ANN AXTELL MORRIS, 1931]

(opposite page) The Celestún Biosphere Reserve—a protected wetland of some 147,500 acres (600 km²)—is winter home to great flocks of flamingoes, which come to feed and nest. [AMYBBB / DREAMSTIME.COM]

CELESTÚN

WHEREVER YOU ARE IN THE PENINSULA, a beach is never far away. A few times a year, the lure of Celestún captures me, and I hop in the car and head west on a two-hour drive toward tranquillity, 100 percent nature, and a cheap seafood lunch. The first stop is always the piers, from which for a few pesos you can ride a launch into the estuary to wonder at the pink horizon—a miles-long stroke of crayon color created by thousands of flamingoes perched on one leg, snakelike necks twisting and bobbing as the birds feed on the abundant shrimp larvae found in the mud of the shallow waters.

Celestún is a tranquil fishing community of only about 6,000 people, a population that doubles during octopus fishing season. A lot of the best seafood we get in Mérida—such as the *jaiba*, or blue crab, not to mention octopus—comes from Celestún.

But the main occupation in Celestún seems to be the restaurant business: dozens of seafood shanties line the beach, and a favorite pastime is to settle at a table beneath a big red (brand name omitted) umbrella, kick off your shoes, and scrunch your toes in the sand before ordering lots of beers and rounds of seafood to be shared by the table.

(above) Restaurant "Los Pámpanos" in Celestún. [MR]

CAMARONES AL MOJO DE AJO

SHRIMP IN GARLIC/CITRUS SAUCE

TO PREPARE AHEAD
Mojo de ajo (p. 514)

FOR THE MARINADE
1 lb. (500 g) shrimp (see recipe note about quantities), shelled and deveined, tails intact
½ cup (125 ml) freshly squeezed lime juice

FOR SAUTÉING
Sea salt
Freshly ground black pepper
Paprika
4 Tbs. (60 ml) Spanish olive oil
4 medium cloves garlic (1 oz. / 24 g), peeled and thinly slivered
½ tsp. (0.5 g) crushed red pepper flakes
¾ cup (187.5 ml) Mojo de ajo

FOR SERVING
Chopped cilantro, parsley, or a combination
Arroz blanco (p. 529), suggested accompaniment
Totopos para botanas (p. 515)
Saltines
Pan francés (p. 194) or French rolls

Along the Yucatecan coastline, scores of seafood stands sell this dish accompanied by tortilla chips and saltines as well as slices of Pan francés (p. 194). The chips and saltines serve as scoops for the garlic shrimp, and the Pan francés is used to sop up the fragrant oil at the end of the meal.

Prepare ahead note: The Mojo de ajo should be made at least 1 day or up to a week in advance. The sautéing should be done moments before serving.

YIELD: 6 SERVINGS

(*Note*: Make as large or small a quantity of Camarones al mojo de ajo as you like. Four large shrimp totaling about 3 ounces [90 g] is the typical portion in Yucatán for a single main course serving. Or you may serve it as an appetizer using 1–2 large shrimp, 2–3 medium shrimp, or 4–5 small shrimp.)

MARINATE SHRIMP
Place the shrimp in a shallow baking dish; pour lime juice over all to cover. Refrigerate at least 15 or up to 30 minutes as you proceed (longer marinating will result in rubbery shrimp).

SAUTÉ SHRIMP AND FINISH
Remove the shrimp from the refrigerator, drain, and discard the juice. Just before sautéing the shrimp, give them a light sprinkle of salt, pepper, and paprika on both sides.

In a large nonstick skillet, heat the olive oil until shimmering. Add the garlic and cook until pale golden. Add the shrimp and red pepper flakes and sauté, turning once, about 10–15 seconds per side, depending on size, until just pink. Add the Mojo de ajo and stir until just heated, about 30 seconds. Remove the pan from the heat immediately to avoid overcooking.

TO SERVE
Transfer the shrimp to individual serving plates and sprinkle with the chopped herbs. Accompany with Arroz blanco and a mixed green salad if you wish, and breads as noted above.

VARIATIONS
Pulpo al mojo de ajo (Octopus in Garlic/Citrus Sauce): Follow the master recipe for Camarones al mojo de ajo, replacing the shrimp with 1 small whole octopus (or the desired quantity), cleaned, pounded, and boiled for 1 hour in water with 1 tablespoon (15 ml) white vinegar. Cut the octopus into bite-sized pieces or leave the tentacles intact for a dramatic presentation.

Filete al mojo de ajo (Fish Fillet in Garlic/Citrus Sauce): Follow the master recipe for Camarones al mojo de ajo, replacing the shrimp with 6 grouper fillets (about 1¾ lbs. / 810 g; substitute: any firm, white-fleshed fish).

Mariscos en verde al mojo de ajo (Seafood in Herbed Garlic Sauce): Another version I have seen frequently on the beaches is seafood bathed in a green *mojo de ajo*, rather more like pesto or chimichurri. Create the sauce by puréeing 2 cups (120 g) tightly packed flat-leaf parsley, cilantro, or basil (or a combination totaling 2 cups) with ¾ cup (187.5 ml) Mojo de ajo in a blender. Heat the sauce briefly in a little olive oil and keep it warm as you prepare the seafood or fillets of your choice per the master recipe, omitting the Mojo de ajo after sautéing the seafood. Serve the seafood topped with the warm green sauce.

The Indians in the early times had the custom of going to gather the salt, taking the lumps from the water and carrying them off to dry. For this purpose they had places marked in the lagoon where the salt was richest and there was less water and mud. . . . Still today a great deal is gathered to carry to Mexico, and to Honduras and Havana.

—FRAY DIEGO DE LANDA, 1566

CHUNCHUCMIL AND THE SALINAS DE CELESTÚN

Just 17 miles (27 km) from the Gulf of Mexico in northwestern Yucatán, the city of Chunchucmil peaked in the Early Classic period (c. 200–600 CE) with a population of around 40,000 people. Since the region has little arable land, inhabitants survived through long-distance maritime trade, exchanging goods to supplement what could not be produced on the land. In addition, the city's port was strategically situated between what may have been the single largest producer of salt in all of pre-Columbian Mesoamerica—the Salinas de Celestún—and the major consumers in highland Mexico and Guatemala.

*Salinas de Celestún. In the shallow coastal waters of Celestún, ocean water evaporates, leaving behind many tons
of salt annually. Workers break up salt in the shallows, haul it out of the water, and leave it in piles to dry.* [DS]

Sodium chloride—salt (*ta'ab* in Mayan)—not only played an important role as a valued medium of exchange among the pre-Columbian peoples of Mesoamerica, but it also was used as a preservative, as a fixing agent for textile dyes, and as a component in soaps and other cleansers. In addition to the Celestún Salinas, other areas along the Yucatán coast were also significant producers of salt in the pre-Columbian era. In fact, the Mayas of the Yucatán coast—where the elite and ruling classes controlled much of the trade in salt and other luxury goods—savored what was essentially a monopoly of the salt trade in Mesoamerica.

Salt was produced in a variety of ways: it was leached from saline soils; it was collected by boiling seawater in large earthenware pots and gathering the evaporated residue (known as *sal cocida*, or cooked salt); and it was harvested from shallow coastal salt pans where ocean water was left to evaporate (known as *sal solar*, or solar salt). The primary method for salt production along the northern Yucatán coast was salt pans. Some scholars theorize that this Yucatecan *sal solar* was a finer grade and better tasting; thus its use was restricted to the elite classes.

Salt remains an important industry in present-day Yucatán. While it is still extracted by hand at the Salinas de Celestún and supports only a few families, the local economy of Las Coloradas (p. 3) on the northern coast relies heavily on salt production, a modern industry established there in 1946. Aided by mammoth extraction equipment, production at Las Coloradas reaches 500,000 tons a year, making it the second-largest salt producer in Mexico. Sea salt is specified in the recipes in this book, and several companies are packaging salt from Yucatán (see Resources, p. 541).

SISAL

Muscovy duck. [SALLY WALLIS / DREAMSTIME.COM]

JUST AROUND THE BEND to the north and east of the Salinas lies the old port of Sisal, another charming fishing village and beach attraction for families from Mérida for vacations during Semana Santa (Holy Week) and summer holidays. Boys and their fathers dangle their legs off the edge of the quaint pier, using string and a bit of bait to catch whatever they can. But for many years, Sisal was the most important port in the region.

In 1811, Sisal was developed as the port for Mérida, to expedite its trade with the United States and Cuba. By 1845, Sisal had evolved into its powerful position as the port from which the valuable henequen fiber was shipped abroad. Extracted from the leaves of agave plants, the fiber was processed into rope, burlap bags, and a range of utilitarian items. In fact, the fiber acquired the name "sisal" because bundles of henequen were labeled with the shipping port's name; confused recipients thought the name referred to the product itself. By 1871, maritime customs was moved to the port of Progreso, which offered greater accessibility to Mérida, as well as more favorable natural conditions for the construction of a grand pier.

MUSCOVY DUCK

Sisal continues to attract sport hunters from north of the border who come to take advantage of the wide variety of ducks found here. The Muscovy duck (*Carina moschata*)—a popular game bird in the region—is a native of Yucatán, as well as other parts of the American tropics. It was the Muscovy duck that Columbus reported seeing when he visited the West Indies. In the 1500s, both Spanish and Portuguese explorers took the duck back to Europe, where it became a popular table fowl. The Muscovy duck is distinctive in appearance, with a black body, white patches on the wings, and a featherless red face.

PATO CON GLASEADO AL XTABENTÚN

DUCK MAGRETS IN HONEY-ANISE LIQUEUR GLAZE

TO PREPARE AHEAD
Enriched Lard (p. 513)

[EC]

Duck is a rare find on menus in Yucatán—a fact that strikes me as strange, since ducks of many species have always been plentiful here, especially in the area around Sisal. According to colonial chroniclers, the Mayas of the sixteenth century consumed duck, although we aren't quite certain how they cooked it, since recipes for it rarely appear in historical sources. Sweet glazes of various flavors (cherry and orange come to mind) are common in the French repertoire, a fashionable cuisine in late-nineteenth-century Yucatán. But I was immediately smitten after my first taste of this *glace de cuisine* (glaze), prepared with a famous local liqueur known as Xtabentún (p. 289). Its honey-anise flavoring makes it the perfect counterpoint to the richness of the duck. The magrets (boned duck breast) as served at Hacienda Xcanatún are always accompanied by a couple of plantain croquettes inspired by the Cuban dish Machuquillo (p. 156), a paste of mashed plantain and pork cracklings.

This recipe and the one for the accompaniment, Machuquillo, were shared with me by Cristina Baker, the charming hostess/owner of Hacienda Xcanatún, and her executive chef, José Andrey Vázquez Manzanilla, a native-born Yucatecan who does inventive plays on Yucatecan themes incorporating local ingredients.

Prepare ahead note: The rich brown poultry stock or even the complete glaze/sauce can be made a week or two in advance and frozen. Reheat immediately before serving.

YIELD: 6 SERVINGS

2 Tbs. (28 g) Enriched Lard

1 lb. (500 g) chicken or duck neck,
  gizzard, heart, wing tips, or
  bones saved from the carcass

1 medium white onion (10 oz. /
  275 g), peeled and quartered

1 medium carrot (3½ oz. / 100 g),
  halved across the width

8 cups (2 L) beef stock or bouillon

1 tsp. (4 g) black peppercorns

2 large sprigs flat-leaf parsley
  (¼ oz. / 6g)

2 whole bay leaves

2 sprigs fresh thyme, or ½ tsp.
  (0.5 g) dried

FOR THE GLAZE

2 cups (500 ml) sweet orange juice

1 cup (200 g) sugar

½ cup (125 ml) Mexican honey

¼ cup (62.5 ml) white wine
  vinegar

¼ cup (62.5 ml) soy sauce

½ cup (125 ml) Xtabentún liqueur
  (Substitute: anisette)

FOR THE DUCK

6 duck magrets, each weighing
  about 7 oz. / 200 g

Sea salt and freshly ground black
  pepper

FOR SERVING

Machuquillo (p. 156), recommended accompaniment

PREPARE POULTRY STOCK

In a large, heavy stockpot, heat the lard until shimmering. Add the chicken or duck pieces and vegetables and cook over medium heat, stirring frequently, until the meats are well browned and the onions are beginning to caramelize, 5–6 minutes.

Add the remaining ingredients for the stock to the pot with the browned poultry pieces. Place over medium heat, and bring to a simmer; do not allow to boil. Partially cover the pot and simmer for 1 hour, skimming fat as needed during the first 15 minutes of cooking. At the end of the cooking time, pour the stock through a fine-mesh sieve into another stockpot and discard the contents of the sieve. Cool the stock to room temperature and refrigerate it overnight. You should have approximately 6 cups (1.5 L).

PREPARE GLAZE

Skim any congealed fat on the surface of the stock and discard. Bring the stock to a boil and continue over high heat until it is reduced by two-thirds, about 35 minutes (you should end with 2 cups / 500 ml of stock).

Meanwhile, in a medium saucepan, bring the orange juice to a boil and continue over high heat until it is reduced by half. Add the sugar and honey and cook over medium high heat for about 8 minutes, or until the caramel reaches the soft-ball stage (234°F / 112°C). Add the vinegar and soy sauce to the caramel, stirring until well combined, and continue cooking over medium heat for about 10 minutes, or until the caramel reaches the hard-ball stage (250°–265°F / 121°–129°C).

Add the caramel reduction to the poultry stock and simmer 15 minutes, or until it reaches the firm-ball stage (245°F / 118°C). Add the Xtabentún, bring to a boil, and cook over high heat for 2 minutes. Take the pan off the heat; the glaze should have the consistency of syrup and will thickly coat a spoon. At this point, it may be refrigerated or frozen until ready to use. (Yield: approximately 2¼ cups / 562.5 ml.)

SEAR MAGRETS AND SERVE

Bring the magrets to room temperature. Score the skin and fat side of the magrets with a sharp knife and season with salt and pepper. Place the magrets skin side down in a dry, cold, heavy skillet (preferably cast iron). Turn the heat to medium-high and cook until the skin is browned and crispy and much of the fat has rendered, 8–10 minutes (time will depend on the thickness of your magrets). Flip the magrets to the other side, baste with some of the rendered fat, and continue cooking to the preferred temperature (130°F / 55°C is recommended for medium rare). Remove the magrets from the skillet and allow them to rest 10–15 minutes. Meanwhile, reheat the glaze. Slice the duck on the diagonal just before serving.

TO SERVE

Arrange the sliced magrets on individual serving plates and spoon some of the honey-anise glaze on top. Accompany with three warm Machuquillo croquettes per person.

MACHUQUILLO

MASHED PLANTAIN CROQUETTES WITH PORK CRACKLINGS AND GOAT CHEESE

FOR THE FILLING

9 oz. (250 g) plain goat cheese, chilled

FOR THE CROQUETTES

8 cups (2 L) water

3 whole star anise

3 sticks *canela* (Mexican cinnamon)

8 allspice berries

3 medium plantains (1¾ lbs. / 795 g), peeled and sliced into six pieces. (Note: The plantains should be medium ripe, that is, green-to-yellow rather than yellow-to-black. To peel the plantains, use a sharp knife to slice the skin lengthwise at the ridges, then peel)

½ cup (125 ml) Spanish olive oil

1 cup (170 g) white onion, peeled and coarsely chopped

4 medium cloves garlic (1 oz. / 24 g), peeled and chopped

2 oz. (60 g) *chicharrón* (homemade or commercial pork cracklings; see p. 214), crumbled

1 tsp. (6 g) sea salt

½ tsp. (2.5 g) freshly ground black pepper

Vegetable oil for frying

In its West African home, this dish is known variously as Fu Fu, Foufou, or Foutou. In many parts of Cuba it is called Machuquillo; it is known as Mofongo in Puerto Rico. The African original is a thick paste made by boiling starchy root vegetables and then pounding them into a mush. Transformations occurred once the dish reached the Caribbean islands, where cooked plantain is mixed with garlic and pork cracklings, then heaped in a bowl and covered with broth. This version takes it a decadent step further by forming the plantain paste into croquettes, stuffing them with goat cheese (not a local product but delicious nonetheless), then deep-fat frying them. The croquettes are an excellent accompaniment to a variety of dishes, but they also make a delicious first course or cocktail party finger food.

Prepare ahead note: The paste for Machuquillo may be made a day ahead and refrigerated; you may also form the fritters and fill them with the goat cheese several hours or a day in advance of frying. Refrigerate; remove them from the refrigerator 15 minutes prior to finishing. Machuquillo is best served immediately after frying.

YIELD: 6 SERVINGS OF 3 CROQUETTES PER PERSON

PREPARE FILLING

Divide the goat cheese into 18 equal portions, shaped into balls approximately ½ ounce (12 g) each; refrigerate until ready to use.

PREPARE CROQUETTES

Place the first 4 ingredients in a large saucepan, bring to a boil, cover, then reduce heat to a simmer and cook for 5 minutes. Take the pan off the heat and steep for 30 minutes. Discard the spices. Add the plantains to the flavored water and return to a boil. Reduce the heat to a simmer and cook, uncovered, for 15 minutes. Drain, discard the cooking water, and allow the plantains to cool slightly as you proceed.

In a medium skillet, heat the oil until shimmering. Add the onions and garlic and cook, stirring frequently, until the onions are translucent, 2–3 minutes. Allow the mixture to cool briefly. Place the plantains and pork cracklings in the bowl of a food processor and process briefly, until just combined. Add the seasonings and the onion/garlic mixture with its cooking oil and process again until well blended but not completely puréed. Check the seasonings.

Form the plantain paste into 18 equal balls weighing about 2 ounces (50 g) each. Make a deep impression in 1 ball with your index finger. Fill the impression with a ball of the goat cheese and seal. Form the plantain ball into an elongated egg shape, pressing the paste firmly around the cheese to avoid any cracks or gaps, which can cause the croquette to fall apart during frying; set aside as you form the rest. Refrigerate at least 1 hour, then bring to room temperature 15 minutes before frying.

Pour 1½ inches (4 cm) vegetable oil into a deep skillet (the oil must be deep enough to completely cover the croquettes) and heat to 375°F (190°C). Working with a few at a time so as not to crowd, fry the croquettes until golden brown, turning once, about 30 seconds to 1 minute per side. (Note: You must maintain the temperature of the oil, or the croquettes may melt and fall apart. Pause between additions so that oil returns to the proper temperature.) Drain the croquettes on paper towels. You may keep the croquettes warm in a low oven (250°F / 120°C) up to 1 hour before serving.

Machuquillo garnished with crispy Platanitos (p. 371). [EC]

PROGRESO

FOR TEN MONTHS OF THE YEAR, the Gulf port of Progreso is the defifnition of a sleepy fishing village: shops are empty, businesses shuttered, beach homes barricaded against the hurricane season. Then suddenly, in late June, a caravan of small moving trucks loaded with furniture, kitchen utensils, suitcases, and even pets trolls 20 miles (30 km) north on the highway out of Mérida.

Families relocate en masse to the beach for two months to take advantage of *la temporada*—"the season"—when kids are out of school and working folk enjoy some vacation time. Popular restaurants and nightclubs that function most of the year in Mérida move temporarily to the beach to serve the teeming hordes. And in an annual reversal of fortune, the great metropolis to the south becomes a ghost town while Progreso experiences a population explosion.

In the mid-twentieth century, this rite of summer gave people from the city the chance to enjoy fresh seafood, an infrequent pleasure in inland locations at the time. Although seafood is now plentiful in the urban matrix, the perennial refrain of "Vamos a la playa" (Let's go to the beach) still serves as the cue to head to Progreso for ceviche or fried fish, a few tranquil hours by the sea, and more than a few beers.

THE PORT OF PROGRESO

During the initial economic boom of the nineteenth century, Yucatán's only international ports of entry were Campeche, Sisal, and Salamanca (now Bacalar). Due to its superior location, Progreso became an official port in 1866. A battery of three piers was built where the ocean was only 11 feet (3.35 m) deep, such that ships had to anchor 3 miles (5 km) out in the ocean. To accommodate deepwater docking, construction of a new pier was begun in 1937, and a further extension was built in 1985. Today, the dramatic pier is a total of a little over 4 miles (6.5 km) in length with a service area totaling 462,848 square feet (43,000 m²). Aside from its role in maritime trade, Progreso is a pit stop for day-trippers arriving on a steady stream of cruise ships.

(above) *Port of Progreso.* [ENRIQUE GÓMEZ / DREAMSTIME.COM]

SOPA DE CABEZA DE PESCADO

FISH HEAD SOUP WITH ROASTED GARLIC AND *ALCAPARRADO*

TO PREPARE AHEAD
Pan francés (p. 194), or substitute
Mojo de ajo (p. 514), or substitute
Recado para todo (p. 499)

TO PREPARE AHEAD

Pan francés (p. 194), or substitute

Mojo de ajo (p. 514), or substitute

Recado para todo (p. 499)

FOR THE FISH STOCK

3 Tbs. (45 ml) Spanish olive oil

4½ lbs. (2 k) porgy or red snapper heads

12 cups (3 L) fish stock or bottled clam juice

FOR THE CROUTONS

Mojo de ajo (Substitute: Olive oil mixed with minced garlic)

Pan francés (Substitute: baguette or French rolls), sliced into 1 in. (2.5 cm)–thick rounds

FOR THE *SOFRITO* AND FINISHING

2 Tbs. (30 ml) Spanish olive oil

1 medium onion (10 oz. / 275 g), peeled, charred, and finely chopped

2 medium heads garlic (3½ oz. / 100 g total), charred, peeled, separated into cloves, and mashed

4 medium Roma tomatoes (14 oz. / 400 g), charred and chopped

2 cups (280 g) green bell pepper, cut into medium dice

2 medium chiles x'catiques (about 1¼ oz. / 35 g each), charred, peeled, seeded, and cut lengthwise into strips

1 Tbs. (9 g) Recado para todo

¼ cup (15 g) *each* cilantro and parsley, chopped

(continued on next page)

No trip to Progreso is complete without sampling this light yet satisfying soup. There is a surprising amount of meat on fish heads. It ranges from dark to light and has a particularly wonderful nutty flavor. But if you are just too squeamish about such things, you can prepare this soup using fish fillets or mixed seafood with excellent results. Substitutions are offered below.

Prepare ahead notes: Sopa de cabeza de pescado is best served immediately after preparing. Leftovers can be refrigerated for 1 or 2 days, but reheat gently so as not to overcook the fish.

YIELD: 8–10 SERVINGS

PREPARE FISH STOCK

Heat the oil in a stockpot until shimmering. Add the fish heads and sauté until lightly browned, 2–3 minutes. Add the fish stock, bring to a boil, reduce heat to a simmer, and cook 10–15 minutes, or until the fish is firm when pressed with your finger. Remove the heads from the stock and set aside to cool. Strain the stock through a fine-mesh sieve into another stockpot and set aside. Discard the contents of the sieve.

PREPARE CROUTONS

Preheat the oven to 350°F (176°C). Brush both sides of the bread rounds with the Mojo de ajo or garlic/olive oil mixture and place on a baking sheet. Bake for about 15 minutes, or until pale golden brown, turning once. Turn off the heat and leave the bread rounds in the oven until time to serve.

PREPARE *SOFRITO* AND FINISH

Heat the oil in a large skillet until shimmering. Add the next 5 ingredients and cook, stirring frequently, until the bell pepper is softened and the liquid has reduced, 5–6 minutes. Add the *recado*, cilantro, and parsley to the vegetables and cook for 1 minute, stirring constantly. Add the next 3 ingredients and stir to mix. Transfer the *sofrito* to the stockpot. Pull the meat from the fish heads and add to the stock; simmer 5 minutes to amalgamate the flavors. Add the lime juice and vinegar; check the seasonings and add salt if necessary (this will depend on the saltiness of your fish stock or clam juice). Serve immediately.

TO SERVE

Ladle the soup into individual serving bowls. Place 1 crouton on top of each serving and sprinkle with chopped cilantro if desired.

4 Tbs. (60 g) black raisins

2 Tbs. (30 g) small capers, drained

20 medium green olives, whole
 unpitted, pitted, or pimiento-
 stuffed and sliced

½ cup (125 ml) fresh lime juice

¼ cup (62.5 ml) white wine
 vinegar

1½ tsp. (9 g) sea salt, or to taste

FOR SERVING

Cilantro, chopped

VARIATION

If you prefer not to use fish heads, substitute 1½ pounds / 750 grams cubed lean, firm-fleshed fish fillets, or the same weight of assorted seafood. Omit browning the seafood. Combine the fish stock, seafood, *sofrito*, and remaining ingredients. (Note: If you are using cubed fish fillets or mixed seafood, add the fillets first, followed by the shrimp or other shellfish a minute or 2 later.) Simmer 5 minutes, or until the fish is just firm to the touch, and serve with croutons as suggested above.

Pescado frito, a Gulf Coast favorite. [MR]

SAN CRISANTO

All things coconut at doña Teresita's stand in San Crisanto. [DS]

Another product of Yucatán's coast—one that has nothing to do with fish—is found in the seemingly endless stretch of coconut palm groves lining the beach, most planted by nature as coconuts washed ashore in the tide. Every year during the first week of August, the village of San Crisanto, about 18 miles (29 km) east of Progreso and just a few steps from the water's edge, hosts the annual Festival del Coco, or Coconut Festival.

During the festival, everyone goes loco for *coco*, and the town fills with every possible incarnation of the nut—from seedlings and small coconut trees for sale, to healing coconut oil soaps and utilitarian items carved from the shell. And of course there's the food—mostly sweet treats made of not much more than coconut and sugar. Teresita Guadalupe Sánchez Lope and her family run a little roadside stand year-round where they sell their homemade coconut candies, jellies, and pies. She shared a couple of recipes with me: Pay de coco, an addictive pie featuring coconut macaroon filling in a crust with meringue topping; and Negritos, coconut caramel cooked until the sugar burns and turns pitch black.

(opposite page) *Playa de Coco.* [DS]

PAY DE COCO

COCONUT MACAROON PIE WITH LIME-SCENTED ITALIAN MERINGUE

TO PREPARE AHEAD
Enriched Lard (p. 513)

FOR THE COCONUT
15½ oz. (440 g) fresh coconut, grated, divided (2–3 whole drained, peeled coconuts, depending on size)

FOR THE CRUST
1¼ cups (156.25 g) all-purpose flour
¼ tsp. (1.5 g) sea salt
⅓ cup (75 g) Enriched Lard, chilled
3 Tbs. (45 ml) ice water

The first time I tasted doña Teresita's Pay de coco was on a sweltering day in August. I hid from the sun beneath the rustic roof of her coconut stand—itself cooled by the shade of a grove of swaying coconut palms. The pie, recently retrieved from the refrigerator, was coolly refreshing. Pay de coco is a dream of the tropics: the crunchy sweetness of coconut softened by creamy lime-scented meringue. Follow this same recipe to make Cocadas, Yucatán's popular coconut macaroons.

Prepare ahead note: You can make Pay de coco a day in advance and refrigerate; bring to room temperature before serving.

YIELD: 8 SERVINGS

TOAST COCONUT

Preheat the oven to 350°F (176°C). Spread the grated coconut in a thin layer in a large roasting pan and toast about 30 minutes, stirring every 10 minutes, or until it is pale golden in places but still generally white; avoid overbrowning. Turn off the oven and allow the coconut to dry for 1 hour. At the end of the drying time, remove the coconut from the oven and set aside ¼ cup (40 g) for the topping. Bring the oven back to 350°F (176°C) as you continue.

PREPARE CRUST

In the bowl of a food processor, pulse the flour and salt until combined; add the lard and pulse several times until the mixture resembles fine meal.

Continue pulsing while adding the ice water through the feed tube 1 tablespoon (15 ml) at a time. Add only enough water for the dough to clump into a smooth, pliable mass (pinch to test); do not overwork. Transfer the dough to a lightly floured surface

[MC]

2 large egg whites, at room
temperature

2 Tbs. (24 g) sugar

¼ cup (31 g) all-purpose flour

½ tsp. (2 g) baking powder

¼ tsp. (1.5 g) sea salt

½ cup (125 ml) sweetened coconut
cream (sold for use in tropical
cocktails)

4 Tbs. (¼ cup / 56 g) butter,
melted

½ tsp. (2.5 ml) Mexican vanilla
extract

FOR THE MERINGUE FROSTING

2 large egg whites, at room
temperature

1 Tbs. (12 g) *plus* ¼ cup (50 g)
sugar, divided

2 Tbs. (30 ml) water

Zest of 1 large lime, finely grated

and roll out into a circle approximately 12 inches (30 cm) in diameter. Gently lift the dough by wrapping it around the rolling pin and lifting it from the surface. Transfer it to an 8-inch (20 cm) pie plate or springform pan. Trim off the excess and crimp the edges. Prick the bottom of the crust with a fork and set aside.

PREPARE PIE FILLING

Beat the egg whites until soft peaks form. Add the sugar and continue beating until firm peaks form; set aside. Place the toasted coconut except for the reserved portion in a large mixing bowl; add the dry ingredients and stir to combine. Add the last 3 filling ingredients to the dry ingredients in the mixing bowl and stir to combine. Gently fold in the beaten egg whites to incorporate.

FILL PIE AND BAKE

Pour the coconut mixture into the pie shell and bake 45–50 minutes, or until the coconut and crust are both golden brown; a toothpick inserted into the center of the pie should come out clean. Remove the pie from the oven and allow it to cool. Place the reserved coconut in a shallow baking dish and bake 10–15 minutes, or until it is toasted and golden brown. Remove and set aside.

MAKE FROSTING

In the bowl of a stand mixer, beat the egg whites until they form soft peaks. Add 1 tablespoon (12 g) of the sugar and beat until stiff peaks form. Set aside.

In a small saucepan, heat the water and the remaining ¼ cup (50 g) sugar, swirling gently until the sugar dissolves and the liquid turns clear. Increase the heat to a boil and cook without stirring until a candy thermometer registers the soft-ball stage, 234°F (112°C). Immediately remove the pan from the heat and, with your beater set to highest speed in the bowl containing the egg whites, slowly stream the hot syrup into the whites. Continue beating until all the syrup has been added. Add the lime zest and continue beating until the meringue is cooled, stiff, and glossy, 4–6 minutes.

Mound the meringue on top of the pie, spreading to the edges of the crust. Use a spatula or knife to swirl decorative shapes into the surface of the meringue. Sprinkle it evenly with the reserved toasted coconut and refrigerate. Bring the pie to room temperature at least 30 minutes prior to serving.

VARIATION

Cocadas (Coconut Macaroons): These melt-in-your-mouth treats are sold everywhere in Yucatán, from bakeries to market stalls—even door-to-door by street vendors. Use the oven temperature recommended in the master recipe. Toast the coconut as in the master recipe (no need to set aside coconut for the garnish). Omit the crust and prepare the filling; refrigerate it 30 minutes before proceeding. Line a baking sheet with parchment or a nonstick silicon baking mat. Working with 2 spoons or an ice cream scoop, form 1-ounce (30g) balls of the filling, spacing them about 2 inches (5 cm) apart on the baking sheet. Bake 50–60 minutes, or until the cookies are a deep golden brown. Transfer them to a rack to cool, then store in an airtight container. *Yield: 18 cookies.* You can beautifully revivify leftover Cocadas by heating them at 375°F (190°C) for 2–3 minutes.

NEGRITOS

BURNT-SUGAR AND COCONUT CARAMELS

FOR THE COCONUT MILK

8 oz. (225 g) freshly grated
   coconut
1½ cups (375 ml) very hot tap
   water
1 cup (250 ml) evaporated milk
¼ tsp. (1.5 g) sea salt

FOR THE BURNT-SUGAR
CARAMEL

2 cups (400 g) muscovado or
   unrefined sugar
4 Tbs. (60 ml) light corn syrup
8 Tbs. (112 g) butter, melted

Negritos aren't for sissies: burnt sugar is definitely a grown-up taste, not to mention the fact that making caramel requires considerable vigilance and precision. Be sure to arm yourself with a reliable candy thermometer before you even think of forging ahead with these darkly addictive treats.

Prepare ahead note: Stack Negritos in layers separated by waxed paper; they will keep well in an airtight container in the refrigerator for about one month.

YIELD: APPROXIMATELY 60 PIECES

PREPARE COCONUT MILK

Place the coconut and water in the jar of a blender and process about 30 seconds, or until thoroughly puréed. Transfer the mixture to a bowl and allow to cool to room temperature. Add the evaporated milk and salt, stir to combine, and set aside.

PREPARE CARAMEL

Place the sugar and corn syrup in a deep saucepan with a heavy bottom (copper is ideal for this task) and stir to combine. With the saucepan over high heat, maintain vigilance as the sugar begins to melt; swirl the pan frequently to dissolve the sugar. Continue cooking and swirling over high heat until a candy thermometer reaches the burnt-sugar stage, 350°F (177°C), and the syrup is a dark-brown color.

Remove the pan from the heat and slowly drizzle in the melted butter, stirring constantly; add it gradually to avoid splattering. Once the butter is incorporated, return the pan to medium heat and slowly stream in the coconut milk mixture. Cook, stirring frequently, until a candy thermometer reaches the hard-ball stage, 250°F (121°C), about 20–30 minutes. Immediately pour the candy into a buttered nonstick sheet cake pan, about 13 × 18½ inches (33 × 47 cm). The surface will be very textured. To create a smooth and shiny surface, when the candy is barely cool, place lightly buttered waxed paper on top of the candy and press firmly with a wooden mallet or smaller pan.

While the candy is still very warm but just cool enough to touch, place the pan over low heat for a few seconds to melt the bottom of the caramel and loosen it from the pan. Working quickly before candy hardens, turn it out onto a cutting board lined with waxed paper and immediately cut it into 1-inch (2.5 cm) squares. (Alternatively, cut the candy into large diamonds, as does doña Teresita.) Allow it to cool, then store as suggested above.

(opposite page) A rainbow of coconut possibilities (clockwise from top): ice-cold coconut water, sweet coconut "tortillas," Negritos, and coconut praline. [MC]

SAN FELIPE

A S YOU DRIVE EAST THROUGH COWBOY COUNTRY toward Tizimín, a sharp turn north onto a narrow road takes you to the fishing village of San Felipe. From one moment to the next, your focus shifts from cautiously observing cattle-crossing signs to dodging hundreds of red crabs skittering sideways across the road. Mornings around 6:00 am are hectic along the shoreline as scores of men prepare for a day of fishing. Wheelbarrows full of ice whoosh through the streets toward waiting launches. The ice is dumped into coolers, motors are fueled, and the men are off.

San Felipe is also popular with sport fishermen; birders, too, visit the impressive estuary that is home to hundreds of varieties, including nesting flamingoes. San Felipe is located within the awe-inspiring Ría Lagartos Biosphere Reserve, a protected estuary environment that spans almost 150,000 acres (60,348 hectares). Ría Lagartos and a few other tidal zones in Yucatán contain 52 percent of Mexico's biologically rich mangroves.

Because the popular Celestún Biosphere is so much closer to the main hub of Mérida, Ría Lagartos has scarcely caused a bleep on the tourist radar, preserving the charming village of San Felipe as a tranquil and relaxing getaway at water's edge.

(above) Squat, broad-planked houses define the San Felipe aesthetic, somewhere between Martha's Vineyard and Disneyland. Each house is painted one of a rainbow of garish neon colors; their corrugated tin roofs signal in Day-Glo red-orange. [MC]

*The Indians put signs on the trees to mark the way going
or coming by boat from Tabasco to Yucatán.*

—FRAY DIEGO DE LANDA, 1566

Maya canoe and oars from a drawing in the Temple of the Warriors, Chichén Itzá.
[AUREA HERNÁNDEZ AFTER MORRIS, CARLOT AND MORRIS 1931: PL. 159]

MAYA NAVIGATION   Over the course of centuries, the Mayas developed sophisticated navigation routes, signal systems, and even hydraulic works that improved and extended existing waterways. When the Spanish arrived, they noted that the Maya area was politically divided among independent rulers, each of whom participated in and competed for a vigorous long-distance trade network that was principally maritime in nature. By circumnavigating the Yucatán Peninsula, the Mayas linked key trading ports of the Gulf of Mexico with those of Honduras in the Caribbean. Knowledge of these networks and the Mayas' impressive oceangoing skills led archaeologist Eric Thompson to call them "the Phoenicians of the New World."

PARA LLEVAR

The Marrufo family has acquired a reputation in San Felipe for having the best food for takeout—*para llevar*. The head cook of the family is Sofía del Socorro Marrufo-Marrufo, but as in so many Yucatecan families, it takes a household of Marrufos to get the daily job done.

With a couple of fishermen in the family, the Marrufos' specialties tend to be made of the freshest seafood imaginable. My visit luckily coincided with lobster season, and so it was that we enjoyed Langosta en relleno negro: Stuffed Lobster Tails in Charred Chile Sauce. The unique recipe doña Sofía shared with me was one she learned from her mother, doña María Olga Marrufo Escamillo, who in turn learned it from her mother. A quick tabulation of years dates the recipe to around 1890. It is this dish that has made the Marrufos famous in San Felipe, and rightly so.

(opposite page) Doña Sofía with more of today's catch. [MC]

LANGOSTA EN RELLENO NEGRO

LOBSTER TAILS IN CHARRED CHILE SAUCE

TO PREPARE AHEAD

Enriched Lard (p. 513)

Recado negro (p. 501)

FOR THE *SOFRITO*

¼ cup (56 g) Enriched Lard

1 medium red onion (10 oz. /
   275 g), finely chopped

4 medium cloves garlic (1 oz. /
   24 g), peeled and minced

4 medium Roma tomatoes
   (14 oz. / 400 g), seeded and
   finely chopped

2 sprigs fresh epazote, leaves only,
   chopped (Substitute: 1 tsp. / 1.5 g
   dried epazote, crumbled) *plus*
   1 Tbs. / 4 g chopped parsley

1 tsp. (0.65 g) dried whole
   Mexican oregano, lightly toasted
   and ground

4 Tbs. (60 g) Recado negro

1 tsp. (6 g) sea salt (Note: If you
   are using commercial *recado*, it
   is probably already salted; check
   seasonings before adding more)

1 cup (250 ml) water

Pavo en relleno negro—turkey stuffed with meatloaf and simmered in a charred chile sauce—is a classic of Yucatecan cuisine (p. 424). Langosta en relleno negro is a creative take on the original. This signature dish of the Marrufo family is one of the most unusual and elegant I have encountered in my travels through the peninsula. A "meat-loaf" of minced lobster tails, *sofrito*, and Recado negro (p. 501) is stuffed into the lobster tail shells and sealed in with a boiled egg yolk (this may seem odd, but it is the custom in Yucatán to include whole boiled yolks in *rellenos*; see p. 423). Finally, the tails are slowly simmered in charred chile sauce. To eat it, you scoop out some of the *relleno* (stuffing) and fold it into a tortilla with a spoonful of the black sauce.

Prepare ahead note: Frozen tails work well for this dish; leave them in a container overnight in the refrigerator to defrost. To save time, make the sauce and stuff the lobsters a few hours ahead. Reheat the sauce and poach the tails immediately before serving.

YIELD: 6 SERVINGS

PREPARE *SOFRITO*

Heat the lard in a large skillet until shimmering. Add the onion and garlic and cook over medium heat until the onions are translucent. Add the tomatoes, epazote, parsley, and oregano and cook over medium heat until the tomatoes are softened, 3–4 minutes. Dissolve the *recado* and salt in the water and strain into the skillet through a sieve lined with one layer of cheesecloth. Use a wooden spoon or spatula to press through as much of the liquid as possible; discard any residue. Bring the mixture to a boil, reduce the heat to a simmer, and cook 3–4 minutes, or until the liquid has reduced and thickened slightly.

PREPARE SAUCE

Transfer half of the vegetable mixture to a medium stockpot or Dutch oven just large enough to hold the lobster tails in one layer. (Do not add the tails at this point.) Add the wine, bring to a boil, and continue over high heat for 2–3 minutes to reduce slightly. Add the fish stock, bring to a rapid boil, and continue over high heat 4–5 minutes to amalgamate flavors. Remove the pan from the heat and set aside.

PREPARE LOBSTER STUFFING

Do not cut or break the shell of the tails, since they will be stuffed with the lobster meat at the end. Insert the tip of a very sharp, long knife, such as a boning knife, into the open end of one tail and push it all the way to the end where the fin is. Work the knife around the perimeter of the tail, gently cutting away the meat, which is attached to the shell by a membrane. Once the meat is thoroughly loosened, gently tug it out and set the meat and shells aside. (Note: The tail meat usually slides out in one piece, but since the meat will be processed, it is not a problem if it is stubborn and must be cut or torn to remove.)

FOR THE SAUCE
½ cup (125 ml) dry white wine
4 cups (1 L) fish stock or bottled
  clam juice

FOR THE LOBSTER STUFFING
6 whole small lobster tails
6 eggs, hard-boiled and peeled
1 egg, lightly beaten
½ cup (60 g) breadcrumbs

FOR FILLING AND FINISHING
1 cup (125 g) all-purpose flour
¼ cup (62.5 ml) water
½ tsp. (3 g) sea salt

FOR SERVING
Chopped chives
Tortillas (p. 518)
Chile con limón (p. 511)

Sofrito *for the lobster stuffing stained black with* recado negro. [MC]

Transfer the lobster meat to a food processor fitted with the steel blade and process 1 minute, until well chopped. Stop the motor and scrape down the sides of the bowl. Process another 30 seconds, or until the meat is paste-like. Transfer the chopped meat to a mixing bowl.

Separate the whites of the boiled eggs from the yolks and set the yolks aside. Chop 3 of the whites and save the rest for another use. Transfer the chopped whites and the remaining *sofrito* in the skillet to the mixing bowl with the lobster meat and stir to combine. Add the beaten egg and breadcrumbs and mix thoroughly. Use the stuffing immediately or refrigerate it until ready to fill the tails.

FILL AND FINISH
Combine the flour, water, and salt and stir with a fork until well incorporated to make a simple dough that will seal the ends of the tails closed while they cook (the dough will be pliable yet very sticky); set aside. With a spoon, fill the reserved tails with the lobster mixture, making sure to pack the mixture tightly all the way to the fin. When each tail is filled, place 1 of the reserved cooked egg yolks at the opening of the tail, pushing to pack the filling in tightly. Form a small ball of the dough and pat

it into a miniature tortilla, about 1 inch (2.5 cm) in diameter. Place this tortilla over the egg yolk and press around the edges so that it sticks to the lobster tail and seals in the stuffing. Dip your finger in a bit of water if necessary to help the dough stick. (Note: It is important that the dough completely seal in the stuffing or it may leak out during cooking.) Set each lobster tail aside as you complete the remaining tails, then refrigerate until time to finish.

Return the sauce to a simmer. Meanwhile, make a loaf of the leftover lobster mixture by placing a large square of cheesecloth on a work surface and mounding the mixture in the center. Gather the ends of the cheesecloth and tie tightly, forming the mixture into a crude ball shape. Place the loaf in the simmering sauce, cover, and cook approximately 20 minutes, or until it is firm and a thermometer has reached 140°F (60°C). Remove the loaf and allow it to cool as you proceed.

Arrange the lobster tails in 1 layer in the simmering sauce. Return the sauce to a simmer, partially cover the pan, and cook 10 minutes, or until the tails are red and the underside feels firm. Serve immediately.

TO SERVE

Carefully unwrap the lobster loaf and slice it into 6 wedges. Using poultry shears, cut the underside of each tail along the center to expose the stuffing. Place 1 tail in a shallow soup bowl or deep serving plate, arrange a wedge of the loaf to one side, ladle on some of the black sauce, and sprinkle with chopped chives. The black liquid may be eaten with a spoon, like soup, or it may be dribbled onto a tortilla along with some of the *relleno*. Diners add chile sauce to taste.

Doña Sofía's finished dishes: Makkum (p. 315) and Langosta en relleno negro. [MC]

(opposite page) *Stuffing lobster tails with* relleno negro. [MC]

TULUM

[We sailed past] a town or village so large, that Seville could not be better or larger, and in it could be seen a very large tower.

—JUAN DE GRIJALVA, 1521

The beach at Tulum. [MR]

SOMETIME AFTER 1250 CE, Tulum became an active commercial port notable for temples and watchtowers that loomed on craggy rock outcroppings high above the Caribbean coast. It was most likely Tulum that Grijalva reported in his expedition. Today, the archaeological zone is visited by thousands of tourists each year, and the town of Tulum has become the site of trendy hotels and restaurants scattered along the strictly protected beach. It is near all the other major destinations of the Riviera Maya: the cities of Cancún and Playa del Carmen, the resort of Akumal, and the popular eco-parks Xel'ha and Xcaret, themselves ancient Maya ports dedicated to the trade in prestige goods.

HECHIZO

"Enchantment" is the translation of "*hechizo*," and you will most certainly feel bewitched when you enter this charming restaurant by the sea. Owners Stefan Schober and Ying-Hui Thai Low greet you at the door as though you were a longtime friend. Chef Stefan runs the kitchen; Hui, born in Singapore, is the pastry chef and manages front-of-house activities. There are no menus; instead, Chef Stefan kneels at your table and recites the day's specials. Local seafood and tropical fruits and vegetables are the primary focus, and the couple's youthful energy and creativity result in fresh and inspired takes on traditional Yucatecan themes.

HUACHINANGO "HECHIZADO"

PAN-FRIED YELLOWTAIL SNAPPER ON SAUTÉED *CHAYA* WITH
BRAISED CHAYOTE AND SEVILLE ORANGE/CAPER BEURRE BLANC

TO PREPARE AHEAD

Seville orange juice substitute
(p. 514), unless fresh Seville
oranges are available

FOR THE CHAYOTE

3 medium chayotes (about 8 oz. /
225 g each), peeled, cored, and
sliced lengthwise to create 8
wedges from each chayote
2 tsp. (12 g) sea salt
1 tsp. (5 g) freshly ground black
pepper
2 Tbs. (28 g) butter

[EC]

Stefan's spectacular "fusion" dish highlights local, fresh seafood while making use of
Yucatán's native *chaya* and chayote. All are dressed beautifully in a classic French sauce
sparked with Spanish colonial ingredients: capers and Seville orange juice. Yellowtail
snapper (*Ocyurus chrysurus*) is a highly prized reef fish found along Yucatán's coasts; red
snapper may be used as a substitute.

Prepare ahead note: The *chaya* and chayote accompaniments may be made up to 30 minutes in advance and kept warm until time to serve. The beurre blanc should be prepared
no more than 15 minutes in advance of sautéing the fish; maintain it at a temperature
between 100° and 130°F (37°–54°C) and whisk every few minutes to prevent separation.

YIELD: 6 SERVINGS

BRAISE CHAYOTE

Preheat the oven to 350°F (176°C). Place a large piece of aluminum foil on a baking sheet.
Arrange the chayote wedges in a single layer on the foil, sprinkle with the salt and
pepper, and toss to coat evenly. Cut the butter into small pieces and scatter it over the
chayote. Fold up the ends and sides of the foil to create a package and seal it tightly.
Place the baking sheet on the middle rack of the oven and bake 45–50 minutes, or until
the chayote is tender. If you will be serving them later, turn off the heat and leave the
chayotes in the oven to keep warm.

FOR THE *CHAYA*

3 Tbs. (45 ml) Spanish olive oil

4 medium cloves garlic (1 oz. / 24 g), peeled and finely chopped

½ lb. (250 g) small *chaya* leaves (Substitute: kale or chard torn into small pieces), washed, thoroughly dried, and stems removed

¼ cup (62.5 ml) water

1 tsp. (6 g) sea salt

1 tsp. (5 g) freshly ground black pepper

FOR THE BEURRE BLANC

3 Tbs. (30 g) shallots, peeled and minced

1½ cups (375 ml) sauvignon blanc, or other light white wine

½ cup (125 ml) Seville orange juice or substitute

2 Tbs. (30 g) small capers, drained

1½ cups (375 ml) heavy cream

4 Tbs. (56 g) butter, thoroughly chilled and cut into ½ oz. (14 g) cubes

½ tsp. (3 g) sea salt

FOR THE FISH

6 yellowtail snapper fillets (about 4½ oz. / 130 g each) (Substitute: red snapper), skin intact

Sea salt

3 Tbs. (45 ml) Spanish olive oil

2 Tbs. (28 g) butter

SAUTÉ *CHAYA*

Place the olive oil in a large skillet and heat until shimmering. Add the garlic and sauté until softened and fragrant, 1–2 minutes. Add the *chaya* and stir to coat with the oil. Cook 30 seconds and add the water. Sprinkle with the salt and pepper and cook, stirring constantly, until the water completely evaporates, 3–4 minutes. Keep warm until ready to serve.

PREPARE BEURRE BLANC

Combine the shallots and wine in a small saucepan on high heat; bring to a boil and cook, stirring occasionally, until the wine is almost completely evaporated. Add the orange juice and capers, return the pan to a boil, and cook on high heat for 1 minute. Add the cream, return the pan to a boil, and cook over high heat, stirring frequently, until the liquid is reduced by one-half.

Reduce heat to low; whisking the cream mixture, add 1 cube of butter at a time. Whisk until each cube is almost completely melted and incorporated before adding another. Continue until all the butter has been added. Remove the pan from the heat and add the salt. (Note: If the sauce starts to separate around the edges and become thin while adding the butter, remove the pan from the heat and add the butter more quickly; if the sauce starts to thicken, add the butter more slowly.) Keep warm until ready to serve. Stefan suggests leaving the finished beurre blanc on the stove above the oven where the chayote is baking to keep the sauce at a good temperature while you finish.

FRY FISH AND FINISH

Score through the skin of the fillets with a very sharp filleting knife or razor blade; create 6–10 diagonal scores on each fillet, depending on its size. (Note: Scoring completely through the skin is important to keep the fillet from curling as it fries.) Sprinkle the skin of each fillet with a bit of the salt; wait 5 minutes, then thoroughly blot the fish dry with paper towels. Heat a large nonstick skillet until a drop of water sprinkled onto the surface sizzles. Add the oil and butter and heat until the butter is melted. Place the fillets in the skillet skin-side down and sprinkle the flesh with a bit more salt; fry about 4 minutes until the skin is lightly browned and crispy; flip to the other side and continue cooking another 30 seconds or until the flesh is just cooked and reaches an internal temperature of 145°F (63°C). Serve immediately.

TO SERVE

Arrange 4 wedges of the chayote on each plate radiating in a fan shape. Place a portion of the *chaya* next to the chayote. Arrange 1 fillet skin side up on top of the vegetables and spoon on some of the beurre blanc.

PUNTA ALLEN

[MC]

A boat has been fashioned into a cabana at Cuzan Guest House in Punta Allen. [MC]

THE END OF OUR COASTAL JOURNEY takes us to what feels like the end of the earth: the remote village of Punta Allen in the vast Sian Ka'an Biosphere. Sian Ka'an, some say, means "where the sky is born" in the Mayan language. With its endless horizon dividing the waters from the heavens, it certainly seems that way.

Sonja Lillvik and Armando López Rosado are much beloved citizens of Punta Allen. They live the life many people only dream of: they met and fell in love, then fell in love all over again with the tiny fishing village where Armando was living and working as a lobster fisherman.

In this tropical paradise they decided to build themselves a little cabana. Twenty-seven years later, they own several guest cabanas on the beach, a house for themselves, and a fleet of boats that take tourists out to sea for fly-fishing and lobster catching.

LANGOSTA CON LECHE DE COCO

LOBSTER TAILS POACHED IN SWEET COCONUT MILK

The delicate combination of sweet lobster and coconut milk is a natural at Punta Allen. This recipe was inspired by one from Sonja Lillvik's cookbook, *The Painted Fish and Other Mayan Feasts*, in which she presents many of the dishes served at her Cuzan Guest House. You may prepare your own fresh coconut milk by following the first three steps for Sorbete de coco (p. 242), or you may use canned, unsweetened coconut milk. Sonja's recipe calls for a more traditional *sofrito* of onions, garlic, and tomatoes, which you may prefer to do instead.

Prepare ahead note: Frozen lobster tails work well for this dish. Leave them wrapped overnight in the refrigerator to defrost. Prepare the poaching liquid in advance and reheat it to poach the lobster tails immediately before serving.

TO PREPARE AHEAD
Recado para puchero (p. 499)

FOR THE *SOFRITO* AND POACHING LIQUID
2 Tbs. (30 ml) Spanish olive oil
¼ cup (68.75 g) shallots, minced
1 medium clove garlic (¼ oz. / 6 g), peeled and minced
2 medium chiles x'catiques (about 1¼ oz. / 35 g each), charred, peeled, seeded, deveined, and cut lengthwise into strips
½ tsp. (1.5 g) Recado para puchero
½ cup (125 ml) sauternes, or any sweet white wine such as Riesling
1 cup (250 ml) fish stock or bottled clam juice
2 cups (500 ml) coconut milk, your own or unsweetened canned
1½ tsp. (9 g) sea salt, or to taste (amount of salt will depend on your fish stock)
Freshly ground white pepper, to taste

FOR THE LOBSTER
6 small whole lobster tails

FOR SERVING
Chopped cilantro
Pan francés (p. 194), or other bread for serving

PREPARE *SOFRITO* AND POACHING LIQUID
In a deep skillet with a lid and just large enough to hold the lobster tails in 1 layer, heat the oil until shimmering. Add the next 3 ingredients and cook over medium heat until the shallots and garlic are fragrant and translucent, 2–3 minutes. Add the *recado*, stir to combine, and cook another minute. Pour the wine into the skillet, bring it to a boil, and continue cooking on high heat for 2 minutes. Add the fish stock and coconut milk and return the mixture to a boil; reduce the heat to a simmer and cook another 5–6 minutes, or until the liquid is slightly reduced and the flavors are amalgamated. Add the salt and white pepper to taste; check seasonings.

POACH LOBSTER AND FINISH
Using kitchen shears, cut open the underside of each lobster tail, starting where the tail was connected to the body, the end opposite the tail fins. Clip along the center of the tail shell, then gently open the shell to loosen it from the meat. Lift the meat partially out of the shell through the slit, leaving it attached at the fin end. Return the poaching liquid to a simmer, arrange the lobster tails in the skillet, and cover. Cook at a gentle simmer for 6–8 minutes, turning once, or until the meat is just firm. Serve immediately.

TO SERVE
Place the lobster tails in individual soup bowls and ladle in some of the cooking liquid, making sure to evenly distribute the chile strips. Finish with a sprinkle of chopped cilantro. Serve with Pan francés for soaking up the cooking liquid.

(opposite page) Part of the "lobster-only" diet in Punta Allen: lobster-tail ceviche. [MC]

LOBSTER FISHING IN SIAN KA'AN

Covering approximately 1.3 million acres (526,091 hectares), the Sian Ka'an Biosphere Reserve is the largest protected area in the Mexican Caribbean. Sian Ka'an is recognized as a UNESCO World Heritage site and in 1986 was officially designated as part of UNESCO's Man and the Biosphere Program.

Before 1960, the cultivation of coconuts as well as fishing and other types of marine exploitation were the only economic activities in the area. In 1994, the first tourism cooperative was formed, with the purpose of offering opportunities to visitors who wanted to snorkel, fly-fish, or bird-watch. Nowadays, they can also join local fishermen in season to hunt for spiny lobster (*Panulirus argus*)—a valuable economic resource in the Caribbean. Lobster harvesting is strictly controlled by federal regulations as well as tacitly by the laws of community cooperatives. Minimum sizes are required, no egg-bearing females may be caught, and scuba equipment is prohibited; all lobsters are caught by hand by skin divers.

Two of these diving lobstermen—Edwin (aka "Chiles") and Jonathan, compadres and fishing teammates—hauled us out in their boat for a day's work. At an average depth of 10 feet (3 m) below the surface of the water are the team's *casitas*: cement boxes measuring about 3½ feet × 5 feet (1 m × 1.5 m) that are sunk to the shallow ocean floor. Two sides of each *casita* are closed; the other two are open, allowing easy access for the lobsters. They don't crawl in for bait; they simply prefer a dark environment. Chiles and Jonathan boast 100 *casitas* in their fishing range, making them the most important team in town, with an average daily haul of 55 pounds (25 k). Whole lobsters are cryogenically frozen at the cooperative, where prices are determined. The Japanese are premier buyers at the co-op. Good years with big hauls can bring considerable prosperity.

Surprising us that there could ever be too much of a good thing where lobster is concerned, Chiles joked about the diet of the lobster fisherman in this remote zone: "When we're feeling poor, we just eat lobster and crab. But when we have some money, we have scrambled eggs!"

(above) Equipped with nothing more than snorkeling gear, and a protective glove, and a long pole with a small bag net, Chiles plunged into the water about 20 times that morning, each time bringing up 3–4 lobsters. [MC] *(opposite page) Spiny lobster and the fisherman known as "Chiles."* [MC]

4

The

PEOPLE'S

FOOD

F INDING THE BEST FOOD IN YUCA-
tán often requires looking beyond
the restaurant table and instead following your taste buds to some rather out-
of-the-way places. Front porches, rolling carts, butchers' storefronts, even
makeshift stands along lonely jungle
roads serve up the *real* food of Yucatán.
Prepared by families that cook together
in their homes, by older women who
sustain themselves by baking cakes, by
patriarchs preserving recipes created
by their grandfathers, or by a host of
others for whom the act of cooking
sets the rhythm of their days—the best
food in Yucatán is made by the people,
for the people.

The wood-burning oven at Panadería Liz. [MR]

LA PANADERÍA

Panadería *choices*. [MC]

URING MY FIRST VISIT TO MEXICO in the early 1970s, I embraced the local routine of taking my place in line at a corner bakery—tray and tongs in hand—to buy delectable bread and sweet treats for my breakfast. I always overbought: oh, the temptation! *Cuernos*—flaky, sugary horns oozing with fluffy white cream. Or *orejas*—"ears" of puff pastry that whorl and spiral inward toward a gooey, buttery center.

With a preponderance of puff pastry and piles of slender, baguette-shaped loaves, the much-loved Yucatecan bakery beckons with a pronounced French accent.

Daily bread in Yucatán (left to right): bolillos, *a French-style dinner roll;* teleras, *used for sandwiches with sauced fillings; and* pan francés. [MR]

PAN FRANCÉS

The popular bread known as *pan francés* can be seen in every bakeshop in Yucatán. Its French connection is undeniable. Early Spanish colonists recorded something known as *pan blanco de París* (Parisian white bread), although because this usually took a rounded shape, it is not likely the direct ancestor of what is affectionately referred to here as "*yuca-francés.*" Bearing many of the characteristics of its French antecedent, the baguette, Yucatecan *pan francés* is usually a bit shorter, wider, and flatter. The outer crust is crispy while the stark white interior is soft and spongy.

Yucatecans have always taken their *yuca-francés* very seriously. A Yucatecan traveling through France in 1817 wrote home about the bread she saw there: "We ate a bread called 'babete' [*baguette?*], similar to our '*francés.*' . . . That of Paris is longer and narrower, it becomes hard very quickly, and ours is much more flavorful."

THE FRENCH IN MESOAMERICA

In 1838, a French pastry chef with a business in the Tacubaya district of Mexico City claimed that Mexican officers had looted his shop during civil conflicts ten years earlier. He appealed to France's king Louis-Philippe. Coming to its citizen's aid, France demanded 600,000 pesos in damages, a sum that tipped the scales of Mexico's debt to France, aggravated relations between the two countries, and launched what came to be known as the Pastry War.

Yet these rivalries never got in the way of delicious bakery treats. French cooking in general and baking in particular got a countrywide boost when Francophile president Porfirio Díaz zealously promoted all things French during his rule between 1876 and 1911, an era now known as the Porfiriato. Throughout the 1800s, French-style bakeries in Yucatán proliferated, and right down to their wood-burning ovens and the mom-and-pop ownership of most of them today, they have not changed significantly in almost two centuries.

King Louis-Philippe. [COLLECTION OF MUSÉE NATIONAL DE CHATEAU DE VERSAILLES, PHOTO BY RLBBERLIN]

PAN FRANCÉS

FRENCH-STYLE SANDWICH LOAF

Remigio Cupul worked at a Mexican-owned bakery in Los Angeles for sixteen years before finally returning home to Yucatán to open his own. Panadería y Pastelería Liz launched in Mérida in 1985. Soon, son Oswaldo joined Remigio to learn the craft and carry on the family trade. With just eleven employees and some very basic equipment, the bakery is able to produce a daily output of 1,500 loaves of *pan francés*, 13 pounds (6 k) of *pan dulce*, 150 *teleras*, and 600 *bolillos* (the latter two are other kinds of rolls).

I have adapted this recipe to be mixed and kneaded in a stand mixer, although I always do give it a few turns on a floured board before forming the dough into shapes. Of course, you may do all of the same steps by hand.

Prepare ahead note: Pan francés keeps well for 2–3 days in an airtight container or resealable plastic bag. It freezes well, too.

YIELD: 3 LOAVES

TO PREPARE AHEAD

Enriched Lard (p. 513)

Strips of banana leaf cut to about 15 in. / 38 cm long by ½ in. / 1.25 cm wide (optional)

FOR THE SPONGE

2 cups (250 g) all-purpose flour (for best results, weigh the flour rather than measure it in cups)

2 packets (4½ tsp. / ½ oz. / 14 g) active dry yeast

1¼ cups (312.5 ml) warm water

FOR THE DOUGH

2¼ cups (280 g) all-purpose flour, plus additional for dusting and kneading

2 Tbs. (24 g) sugar

2 tsp. (12 g) sea salt

1 Tbs. (14 g) Enriched Lard, melted, plus additional for baking sheet

¼ tsp. (0.5 g) ascorbic acid (optional) (Note: Oxidation changes flour's protein structure and produces better flavor and baking results. Ideally, flour should oxidize by being frequently stirred during a period of 8–10 weeks after grinding. For commercial bakers, this is inconvenient, so the technique of adding flour improvers such as potassium bromate has been adapted. The home baker may use ascorbic acid [vitamin C] instead. If you cannot find the powder, use a mortar and pestle to finely crush unflavored Vitamin C tablets.)

PREPARE SPONGE

Place the sponge ingredients in the bowl of a stand mixer fitted with a dough hook. Mix thoroughly, scraping down the bowl as needed. Allow the sponge to rise in the bowl until doubled in volume, about 1 hour. Meanwhile, rub baking sheet with lard, dust with flour, and shake off the excess.

PREPARE DOUGH

Turn the mixer to low to deflate the sponge. Add the dough ingredients and beat on medium speed for 1–2 minutes, until the dough starts to pull away from the sides of the bowl. Turn the dough onto a lightly floured surface.

KNEAD AND SHAPE

Knead the dough 2–3 minutes by hand, incorporating more flour as necessary, until the dough is very elastic and no longer sticky. Divide it into 3 equal pieces (each will weigh approximately 11 oz. / 310 g). Shape each piece into a ball, then flatten each into a thick oval shape. Fold each in half lengthwise, cover with a towel, and allow to rest 5 minutes to relax the gluten.

Form the dough into long batons. Working with 1 piece at a time and leaving the others covered with the towel, press each piece of dough into a thick, elongated oval shape. Fold each oval in half lengthwise with the seam toward you and pinch the seam tightly closed. Roll the dough so that the seam is facing up.

Place the elongated ovals with the seam side down on the floured work surface. Roll each with floured hands and forearm to form a 12-inch (30 cm) baton; pinch the ends tightly to seal. Lift the batons onto the prepared baking sheet with the seam side down. Cover with a towel and allow to rise at room temperature for 60–75 minutes, or until doubled in volume.

(left, top) *Mounds of dough are cut into uniform pieces that serve for all three types of bread pictured in the photo on page 192: pan francés, bolillos, and teleras.* [MR]

(left, bottom) *Bakers use their forearms to roll pan francés.* [DS]

(right) *A strip of palm leaf is inserted into a groove on top of the pan francés (a tradition carried forward from the days before thermostats regulated oven temperature: the changing color of the leaf indicated doneness of the bread). It also adds a light, herbaceous flavor to the bread. In place of palm leaves, you may use a strip of banana leaf.* [DS]

BAKE AND FINISH

Thirty minutes into the rising time, preheat the oven to 425°F (218°C). Fill a spray bottle with water and set aside.

When the bread has risen and just before baking, use a sharp knife or razor blade to cut a shallow slit down the center of each loaf. For a Yucatecan touch, insert a thin strip of banana leaf into the slit. Lightly mist the loaves with water.

Place the baking sheets in the upper third of the oven and bake 3 minutes. Open the oven and quickly spray more water onto the loaves. Repeat 2 more times, baking and spraying at 3-minute intervals. Reduce the heat to 350°F (175°C) and bake 20–25 minutes, or until the loaves are a deep golden brown. They should sound hollow when you tap them and reach an internal temperature of about 200°F (93°C). If you do not have a convection oven, after the first 10 minutes rotate the baking sheet. (Note: If you have a baking stone in your oven, transfer the loaves onto the stone 5 minutes before finishing for a crisper bottom.)

Remove the loaves to a rack to cool.

LECHÓN AL HORNO

SMOKY SLOW-ROASTED PORK WITH CRACKLINGS

TO PREPARE AHEAD

Brined pork (Basic Techniques,
  p. 536)
Mojo de ajo (p. 514)

Lechón al horno is popular throughout the Spanish Diaspora, from the Philippines to Yucatán. Traditionally, the recipe calls for roasting a whole suckling pig—the literal translation of the word "*lechón*"—but nowadays more common cuts are pork shoulder or rump, with plenty of fat and skin. Traditional recipes specify long marination in an adobo of garlic, an acid such as citrus or vinegar, coarse salt and cracked pepper, and other flavorings. My strategy of overnight brining followed by a three-hour marinade in Mojo de ajo achieves a similar effect.

There are two key secrets to the best Yucatecan Lechón al horno: the first is its smoky flavor, accomplished by slow roasting in a wood-burning oven; the second is the crunchy skin, achieved by placing the meat close to the flames in its final minutes of roasting. By using one of the smoking methods outlined in Basic Techniques (p. 537), and by finishing the pork in a very hot oven, you can come close to don Remigio's results. If you don't live near a Latin American *carnicería* (meat market), you may need to ask your butcher in advance to set aside some skin for you.

Prepare ahead note: The full process for Lechón al horno takes about 24 hours, so be sure to start a day in advance. Leftovers keep well under refrigeration. Reheat gently in some of the accumulated juices and recrisp the skin quickly under a hot broiler.

YIELD: 6–8 SERVINGS

A DAY IN THE LIFE OF A *TORTA*

Wood-burning ovens continue to play a vital role in Yucatecan bakeries. Don Remigio estimates that there are still probably 100 such ovens in Mérida alone, fired up daily for baking everything from sweet breads to *pan francés*.

Further, because these ovens are still hot after the morning's baking, *taquería* owners and other vendors who sell meat sandwiches (*tortas*) line up at night with impressive quantities of marinated Cochinita pibil (p. 420) or Lechón al horno to take advantage of the oven's residual heat—a strategy used for centuries in many countries among the poorer classes, who could not afford firewood. So, whether bread or meat, morning to night the bakery is busy preparing the components for the best *tortas* in town.

Torta de Lechón al horno in the market. [MR]

FOR THE MARINADE

3 lbs. (1.5 k) pork shoulder or
    rump, preferably bone in,
    brined per instructions in Basic
    Techniques, page 536 (Note:
    Brine the meat, not the skin)
Pork skin, enough to cover the
    top and part of the sides of the
    meat
1 Tbs. (12 g) black peppercorns,
    coarsely crushed in a *molcajete*
    or mortar and pestle
¼ cup (62.5 ml) Mojo de ajo
Vegetable oil
½ cup (160 g) coarse sea salt
Banana leaves, cut to extra large
    (XL; see Basic Techniques, p. 525)

FOR SERVING

Pan francés (p. 194) or Tortillas
    (p. 518)
Cebollas encurtidas (p. 510)
Chile tamulado (p. 509), or the
    chile sauce of your choice

MARINATE MEAT

Remove the meat from the brine, rinse thoroughly, and pat dry; discard the brining solution. Place the skin on the pork; it should extend down to cover three-fourths of the sides of the meat. Trim off any excess and discard; remove the skin and set aside.

Rub the cracked peppercorns into the meat on all sides, then brush the meat over all with a thick coating of Mojo de ajo. Cover the meat again with the skin. Tie kitchen string several times around the width of meat and skin. With the skin facing up, use a very sharp filleting or utility knife to score the surface of the skin every ½ inch (1.25 cm), cutting through the skin but not the pork.

Spread the salt in the bottom of a baking dish. Pat the skin dry one more time, brush it with a bit of vegetable oil, then invert the meat so that the skin rests on top of the salt. Refrigerate 2–3 hours (this step will draw moisture out of the skin so that it will crisp more evenly).

ROAST MEAT

Remove the meat from the refrigerator and bring it to room temperature. Overlap the whole banana leaves on a work surface. Remove the meat from the salt and dust off any excess. Place the meat skin side up on the banana leaves. Fold the sides and ends of the leaves over to cover the meat completely. Follow the instructions in Basic Techniques for the stovetop smoking method, gas grill smoking method, or charcoal grill smoking method (p. 537). (A grilling basket works well to contain the meat for outdoor grills.) Roast until a meat thermometer reads 135°F (57°C).

CRISP SKIN AND FINISH

Preheat the oven to 425°F (220°C). Remove the roast from the grill or stovetop smoker; remove the leaves and discard. Place the meat skin side up in a roasting pan and place the pan on the highest rack of the oven. Roast until the meat registers just under 145°F (63°C). The skin will have blistered and browned; it should sound hollow when you tap it. (Note: Roasting time will depend on the cut of meat you use and your oven; it can take anywhere from 30 minutes to 1 hour.) Remove the meat from the oven and allow to rest 15–20 minutes before serving.

TO SERVE

Break or pull the skin away from the meat and set aside. Shred the meat coarsely, mixing it with some of the cooking juices.

If you wish to make a *torta*, cut a loaf of Pan francés in half widthwise, then slice each half along the length to create two *tortas*. Dip each half face down into some of the juice. Place shredded meat, a piece of crispy skin, and some of the Cebollas encurtidas on the bottom half, close the sandwich, and serve. For tacos, top tortillas with some of the shredded meat, a piece of the skin, and onions. Diners add chile sauce to taste.

VARIATION

Although not a common practice in Yucatán, for an elegant presentation, use a pork loin wrapped in the skin, then carve at the table just before serving, accompanied by your choice of rice, beans, and salsas.

Conchas. [MR]

PAN DULCE

An almost infinite variety of *pan dulce* (sweet breads) entices Yucatecans throughout the day. Many of them are made of *hojaldra*—French *pâte feuilletée*, or puff pastry—and all of them sparkle with sugar. Ears, braids, and airplanes are English translations for just a few of their whimsical names. And while in Yucatán, be sure to sample the unique Hojaldra de jamón y queso—sugar-dusted puff pastry filled with ham, cheese, and pickled jalapeño for an eye-opening burst of heat at breakfast time.

HOJALDRA DE JAMÓN Y QUESO

SWEET AND SAVORY HAM AND CHEESE PASTRY

Descended from the flaky French pastry *pâte feuilletée*, *hojaldra* treats of all kinds are so popular throughout Yucatán that *señoras* of a certain age often generate a modest income for themselves by producing them for sale in their own kitchens—not only the treats themselves, but also thick slabs of the layered butter-and-flour dough. Bakers or housewives purchase the dough, roll it out, form it into the desired delicacy, and bake until it is puffed and golden.

The first time I was offered a slice of this Yucatecan specialty for breakfast, I confess I was rather put off by the idea: flaky pastry filled with ham, cheese, and pickled jalapeño—the whole dusted with granulated sugar! Since that time I have eaten many a slice of Hojaldra de jamón y queso and have come to appreciate the Yucatecan taste for sweet/savory combinations that shows up in many regional dishes. Yucatecans use inexpensive sliced ham and cheese, but I suggest you experiment with finer ingredients: thinly sliced serrano and aged Manchego are two examples. You may certainly prepare your own puff pastry—recipes are widely available—but you can just as well purchase it refrigerated or frozen, as most people do here.

Prepare ahead note: Hojaldra de jamón y queso may be refrigerated after cooling and will keep for several days. In Yucatán it is served at room temperature, but I prefer mine warm: reheat for 5–6 minutes in a 350°F (175°C) oven or in a toaster oven.

YIELD: 15 PIECES

Some bakers form Hojaldra de jamón y queso in large rounds, others in rectangular slabs. [MR]

FOR THE BÉCHAMEL

2 Tbs. (28 g) butter

1 Tbs. (15 g) shallots, minced

2 Tbs. (16 g) all-purpose flour

2 cups (500 ml) milk, heated to
   just below boiling

1 tsp. (6 g) sea salt

⅛ tsp. (0.75 g) ground nutmeg

FOR THE PASTRY

1½ lbs. (680 g) homemade,
   refrigerated, or frozen slab
   puff pastry

1 egg, well beaten

17 oz. (480 g) excellent-quality
   smoked ham, thinly sliced

14 oz. (400 g) cheese (aged
   Manchego, Monterey jack, etc.),
   thinly sliced

15 pickled jalapeño rings or slivers

½ cup (100 g) granulated sugar

PREPARE BÉCHAMEL

Melt the butter in a saucepan over low heat. Add the shallots and cook until softened, about 2 minutes. Raise the heat to medium and add the flour all at once; stir continuously until the flour turns a pale golden color, 2–3 minutes. Add all of the hot milk at once, whisking continuously. Use a wooden spoon to scrape the bottom of the pan to release any flour that may have congealed there. Reduce the heat to a simmer and cook 15 minutes, alternately stirring and whisking, until the béchamel is thickened and reduced: the consistency should be rather like pancake batter. Remove the pan from the heat, add the salt and nutmeg, and allow to cool as you proceed with the next steps. (*Yield: About 1½ cups / 375 ml*)

ASSEMBLE PASTRY

Preheat the oven to 410°F (210°C). Butter a shallow baking sheet (approximately 10 in. × 15 in. × ½ in. / 25 cm × 38 cm × 1.25 cm), line it with baker's parchment, then butter the parchment. (Note: As some Yucatecan bakers do, you may instead form a round pastry by shaping it on a pizza baking sheet, but because your dough will be rectangular in form, my method is easier and produces less waste.) Divide the dough in half and cover and refrigerate one of the halves to prevent the dough from softening as you proceed. Working on a lightly floured surface, roll out the dough to a rectangle slightly larger than the baking sheet. Place the baking sheet onto the dough rectangle and use a sharp knife to trim away any excess, reserving trimmings for another use. Carefully lift the trimmed dough onto the baking sheet and prick it evenly with a fork. Brush the beaten egg around the edges to a width of about 1 inch (2.5 cm).

Place half the ham slices on top of the pastry dough, making certain to cover all the dough except the area covered by the egg wash. Arrange the cheese on top of the ham. Spoon on the béchamel to cover the cheese, avoiding the egg-washed edges. Space the pickled jalapeño rings evenly on top of the béchamel, 3 across, 5 down (you want to get a piece of chile centered in each square when you cut the *hojaldra* into 15 pieces after baking). Arrange the remaining ham to cover the béchamel and chiles.

Roll out the other half of the pastry dough to the same size as your sheet, trim as before, and place it on top of the last ham layer. Use your fingers to seal the edges and further seal around the perimeter using a fork or pastry crimper. With a sharp knife, pierce the surface of the dough evenly to create 15–20 small air vents. Thoroughly brush the surface of the pastry with the remaining beaten egg.

BAKE AND FINISH

Depending on your climate and oven conditions, bake 30–45 minutes, or until puffed and golden. If you do not have a convection oven, start with the baking sheet on the bottom rack for the first half of the baking, then rotate the sheet and transfer it to the top rack for the remaining time. Remove the sheet from the oven and sprinkle the pastry with sugar. Allow it to cool 20–30 minutes before cutting. Slice in thirds vertically and in fifths across the width to create 15 pieces. Serve immediately.

PASTELITOS

FRUIT-FILLED CRESCENT PASTRIES

FOR THE SUGAR SYRUP AND FILLINGS

¾ cup (150 g) sugar
¼ cup (62.5 ml) water

CAMOTE (BONIATO, OR SWEET POTATO)

9 oz. (255 g) sweet potato, peeled, boiled until very tender, and mashed
1 Tbs. (15 ml) Mexican honey
¼ tsp. (0.75 g) ground *canela* (Mexican cinnamon)
⅛ tsp. (0.375 g) ground cloves

COCO (COCONUT)

6 oz. (170 g) fresh coconut, shredded
2 Tbs. (30 ml) sweetened coconut cream (sold with drink mixes)
3 Tbs. (12 g) cornstarch
¼ tsp. (1.25 ml) Mexican vanilla extract

PIÑA (PINEAPPLE)

9 oz. (255 g) fresh very ripe pineapple, chopped, mashed, and all juices thoroughly pressed out in a fine-mesh sieve
3 Tbs. (12 g) cornstarch
¼ tsp. (1.25 ml) Mexican vanilla extract

FOR THE PASTRY DOUGH

1½ lbs. (680 g) homemade, refrigerated, or frozen slab puff pastry
Flour for dusting
Softened butter, as needed
1 egg, well beaten

FOR FINISHING THE PASTRIES

Powdered sugar for dusting

These powdered sugar–dusted pastries look like delicate white empanadas. In addition to finding them in the bakery, neighborhood women walk door to door selling an assortment of Pastelitos in Yucatecans' favorite flavors: *coco* (coconut), *piña* (pineapple), and *camote* (sweet potato), or a mixture, known whimsically as *atropellado* (see below).

Prepare ahead note: Pastelitos may be made in stages. Make fillings on one day and refrigerate or freeze until ready to use. Fill and form Pastelitos on another day and bake immediately, or freeze for a couple of days until ready to use. Finished Pastelitos keep well at room temperature for 2–3 days in an airtight container.

YIELD: APPROXIMATELY 2 DOZEN

PREPARE SUGAR SYRUP AND FILLINGS

Have all the ingredients for the fillings measured and ready before you make the sugar syrup. Combine the sugar and water in a small saucepan and bring to a boil. Cook until the syrup reaches the soft-ball stage, 234°F (112°C).

Finish the 3 fillings 1 at a time. Place the ingredients for the *camote* filling in the bowl of a food processor fitted with the steel blade and process until thoroughly puréed. With the processor running, slowly stream about one-third of the sugar syrup through the feed tube and process just until incorporated; transfer to a bowl.

Clean the processor bowl and repeat this step with the ingredients for *coco* and *piña*. (Note: As the remaining syrup cools between additions, it may begin to harden. If so, add a spoonful of water, heat, and return to the soft-ball stage. If you have more than 1 processor, you will be able to work more quickly and avoid the issue.)

Place the puréed coconut in a small saucepan and heat 3–4 minutes, stirring constantly to prevent scorching, or until the cornstarch begins to thicken; remove from heat and transfer to a small bowl. Repeat with the pineapple filling. Refrigerate the fillings for at least 30 minutes before proceeding; as they chill, they will become a more pliable paste for you to work with.

PREPARE DOUGH AND FINISH PASTRIES

Preheat the oven to 350°F (176°C). Divide the dough in thirds; work with one-third at a time and keep the rest wrapped in plastic under refrigeration. Place the dough on a lightly floured surface, dust with a bit of flour, and roll out to a thickness of ⅛ inch (3 mm). Use a 4 inch (10 cm)–diameter circular cookie cutter or other round form to cut dough into disks. Each third of dough should yield 8 disks. Use a smear of softened butter to paste together any scraps, layering them and rolling out as before.

Working with one filling at a time, form a tightly packed egg shape using about 1½ tablespoons (20 g) of filling. Place the filling just below the center of one of the dough circles. Lightly brush around the circumference of the disk with beaten egg. Fold the circle in half and press tightly around the ridge of the filling to remove air bubbles and firmly close the Pastelito; use a fork to crimp the edges and seal. Continue until all the Pastelitos have been filled.

Arrange the Pastelitos on a baking sheet lined with parchment or a silicone baking mat and bake for 30–40 minutes, or until golden brown. Cool on a cooling rack. When cool, dust the Pastelitos lightly with powdered sugar. Serve immediately or store in an airtight container.

VARIATIONS

Pastelitos de atropellado (Crescent Pastries with Camote and Pineapple or Coconut): A mixture of *camote* with *piña* or *coco* is also popular, known whimsically as *atropellado*, or "run over." These often feature a couple of tiny leaves of epazote tucked inside, which offer a somewhat bizarre yet delicious herbaceous scent to complement the sweetness. Make the mixture of your choice using the above formulas. Only fresh epazote works here.

Pastelitos de guayabate con queso filadelfia (Crescent Pastries with Guava Paste and Cream Cheese Filling): A family that frequently appears at my door with freshly baked Pastelitos creates several interesting variations like this one. These are easy to make since you don't have to prepare special fillings. Press a ⅓-ounce (10 g) slice of guava paste (see Resources, p. 539) and a ⅓-ounce (10 g) slice of cream cheese together, then place on 1 of the pastry rounds. Seal, proceed with the others, and bake as instructed in the master recipe.

CONCHAS

SWEET BREAKFAST BREADS WITH FLAVORED SHELL-SHAPED TOPPINGS

The Conchas I enjoyed on my first trip to Mexico many years ago still stand out as the benchmarks: gently sweet, yeasty dough—almost creamy—topped with crumbly, sugary caps in different flavors. None that I have tried since come close to that original ecstasy—except for homemade ones. "*Conchas*" means "shells" and refers to the characteristic pattern traced in the flavored toppings.

Prepare ahead note: Like many breads, Conchas are unbelievably addictive eaten right out of the oven, but they will keep well for 2–3 days in an airtight container. Reheat before serving by wrapping in paper towels and heating in the microwave oven for 20 seconds, or heat without a wrapper for 2–3 minutes in a toaster oven.

YIELD: 1 DOZEN

PREPARE DOUGH

Place the water and yeast in the bowl of a stand mixer fitted with a dough hook and beat to incorporate. Allow the mixture to rest a few minutes as you continue.

FOR THE DOUGH

½ cup (125 ml) warm water

2 packets (4½ tsp. / ½ oz. / 14 g) active dry yeast

½ cup (125 ml) canned evaporated milk

⅓ cup (75 g) butter, melted

1 egg, beaten

4 cups (500 g) all-purpose flour

¼ cup + 2 Tbs. (74 g) granulated sugar

1 tsp. (6 g) sea salt

½ tsp. (1.5 g) ground *canela* (Mexican cinnamon)

FOR THE FLAVORED TOPPINGS

⅔ cup (135 g) granulated sugar

½ cup (112 g) butter

1 cup (125 g) *plus* 1 Tbs. (8 g) all-purpose flour, divided

1 tsp. (5 ml) Mexican vanilla extract

1 tsp. (3g) ground *canela*

1 Tbs. (8 g) unsweetened cocoa powder

Mix the milk, butter, and egg together in one bowl and the remaining dry dough ingredients in another. With the mixer on low speed, add the liquid ingredients to the yeast mixture and beat 15 seconds, until incorporated. Add half the dry ingredients and beat slowly until blended, about 1 minute. Add the remaining dry ingredients and beat again until blended. With the mixer on medium-high, beat 3–4 minutes, or until the dough starts pulling away from the sides of the bowl. Stop and pull some of the dough between your fingers: it should be very elastic and only slightly sticky.

FIRST RISING

Transfer the dough to a lightly floured surface and knead until smooth, 3–4 minutes. Place it in a large buttered bowl and turn to coat with the butter. Cover with a towel and allow to rise in a warm place 1 hour, or until doubled in volume.

PREPARE FLAVORED TOPPINGS

Cream the sugar and butter in the bowl of the mixer until lightened and fluffy. Beat 1 cup (125 g) of the flour into the mixture until a stiff paste forms. Divide this paste into thirds and place each third in a small mixing bowl.

Mix the vanilla and the remaining 1 tablespoon (8 g) of flour into one-third of the paste; mix the *canela* into another; and mix the cocoa into the final third. Divide each of these flavored toppings into 4 equal balls of about 1 ounce (32 g) each. Pat them into thin, flat tortilla shapes and set aside. You will have 12 of the flavored toppings.

FORM *CONCHAS* AND SECOND RISING

Butter a baking sheet and set aside. When the yeast dough has doubled, punch it down and transfer to a lightly floured surface. Pat the dough into a large pie shape and, with a long knife, cut it into 12 equal wedges as you would a pie. Shape the wedges into balls, turning the floured, dry side in and the damper side out.

Place the dough balls on the baking sheet about 3 inches (8 cm) apart. Pat them into round and slightly flatter shapes. Place the circles of flavored toppings on top of the dough balls and pat down lightly to seal; the toppings will cover the entire top of the dough ball and extend down the sides about halfway. Cover with a towel and allow to rise in a warm place until doubled in volume, about 45 minutes.

Preheat the oven to 375°F (190°C). When the Conchas have risen and just before baking, use a sharp knife or a razor blade to cut radiating grooves like a scallop shell into the topping. Bake until pale golden brown, 30–45 minutes, depending on your climate and oven conditions. Serve warm.

BREAD AND CHOCOLATE The oldest café in Mérida, La Flor de Santiago was established in 1926 and continues in operation to the present. It still boasts a functioning wood-burning oven, which stocks the café's own baked-goods vitrine as well as supplies local orders. In addition, the oven is still used for Lechón al horno as well as the restaurant's signature *chamorro pibil*, *achiote*-basted ham hock. A rare find in the peninsula nowadays, *laban*, or Lebanese yogurt, is a popular breakfast offering. The charming décor of La Flor de Santiago provides a perfect setting for enjoying *pan dulce* or *churros* and a hot cup of cinnamon-spiced Chocolate (recipe on p. 464).

La Flor de Santiago. [MR]

BAKE SALE

Alot of baking and selling go on every day in Yucatán. Aside from the *panaderías*, an incalculable number of Yucatecan women operate small cottage industries in their homes to boost family income. Laundry, ironing, and tailoring are some of the chores these women execute for others, but by far the most popular of these vocations has to do with food and cooking. Some operate *cocinas económicas* (p. 252), others make meringues and candies, while still others have a reputation for their fine cakes.

One of the most in-demand cakes among these women nowadays is Pastel de queso de bola. Brainchild of Alfonso Lara Ruiz—son-in-law of Ana María de Fernández, a well-known Mérida baker, born in 1919, who opened a successful bakery that continues in operation to the present—the cake has become the family's signature product. You most likely will never see this dessert in a restaurant, since it is considered a "special" cake, ordered for *quinceaños*, weddings, or baptisms. An instant hit, Pastel de queso de bola has been co-opted by many bakeries and *pastelerías*, but the most coveted are those baked to order by individual women.

A YOUNG LADY'S EDUCATION

Rather than purchase from a bakery, many Yucatecan women still prefer to make their own cakes. It is a tradition that goes back at least to the early nineteenth century, when the education of upper-class girls focused on preparing them for a life as wife and mother. During Mexico's Gilded Age, great strides were made in the education of girls and young women. A new school for females was founded in Mérida so that parents no longer had to send their daughters abroad for an education. In addition to science and mathematics, girls were taught drawing, embroidery, sewing, and also many kitchen skills, such as how to manage kitchen staff or organize a banquet. At the end of the school term, students were required to present their handiwork, evident in this photo of confectionery students with a table full of pastries.

(above) Pastry class in Mérida, ca. 1900. [FPG]

PASTEL DE QUESO DE BOLA

VANILLA LAYER CAKE WITH EDAM CHEESE FILLING

FOR THE CAKE BATTER

1¾ cups (218 g) all-purpose flour, plus additional for dusting the baking pans

2 tsp. (8 g) baking powder

¼ tsp. (1.5 g) sea salt

2 eggs, separated

½ cup (112 g) butter, at room temperature

1 cup (200 g) sugar, divided

1 tsp. (5 ml) Mexican vanilla extract

½ cup (125 ml) milk

Queso de bola (literally, "ball cheese"), or Edam cheese, is frequently used in Yucatán as the counterweight for something sweet. It is a favorite garnish for the honeyed Dulce de payapa (p. 414), and in recent history it was confected into this sugary cake.

Prepare ahead note: The sponge cakes for Pastel de queso de bola may be made several days in advance and frozen. Assemble the cake at least 2 hours before serving. Pastel de queso de bola is best kept refrigerated; it will keep well 2–3 days.

YIELD: 8–10 SERVINGS

PREPARE CAKE BATTER

Preheat the oven to 350°F (176°C). Butter three 6-inch (15 cm) round by 2-inch (5 cm) deep cake pans. Line the bottom of each pan with waxed paper and butter the paper. Dust the pans with flour, turn to coat evenly, and shake out the excess.

Sift the first 3 batter ingredients together into a large bowl and set aside. Lightly beat the egg yolks and set aside, reserving the whites. In a stand mixer, beat the butter on medium speed until light and creamy. Add ¾ cup (150 g) of the sugar and beat on high speed until the mixture is fluffy, 2–3 minutes. Scrape down the sides of the bowl. Add the vanilla and continue beating to incorporate. With the mixer still running, slowly drizzle in the beaten yolks. Scrape the sides of the mixing bowl as necessary and beat another 3 minutes. Continue beating on low as you add the flour mixture and milk a little at a time, alternating additions until all is incorporated.

Place the 2 reserved egg whites in another bowl and beat until soft peaks form. Continue beating as you gradually add the remaining ¼ cup (50 g) sugar. Beat until stiff peaks form. Using a rubber spatula, transfer one-third of the beaten whites into the batter and stir briefly to incorporate. Gently add the remaining whites, folding just until incorporated in order to avoid deflating the batter; a few spots of unmixed egg white will not affect the cake.

[MC]

6 oz. (170 g) cream cheese,
    at room temperature

3 Tbs. (42 g) butter, at room
    temperature

½ tsp. (2.5 ml) Mexican vanilla
    extract

¾ cup (90 g) confectioner's
    sugar, sifted

6 oz. (170 g) Edam cheese,
    grated, divided

¼ cup (62.5 ml) dark or aged rum

2 Tbs. (32 g) brown sugar

FOR THE MERINGUE FROSTING

4 egg whites, at room
    temperature

2 Tbs. (24 g) *plus* 1 cup (200 g)
    sugar, divided

⅓ cup (85 ml) water

Zest of 2 limes, finely grated

Divide the batter evenly among the 3 cake pans. Use a spatula to gently spread and smooth, taking care not to deflate the batter. Bake 20–25 minutes, or until pale golden. If your oven is not a convection oven, rotate the pans once midway through the baking. Test for doneness by inserting a toothpick into the center of the cake: if it pulls out clean, the cake is done. (Note: The cakes will not rise as much as some other cakes; this is normal.)

Remove the cakes from the oven and cool for 15 minutes in the pans. Run a knife around the sides of the pans to loosen, then turn the cakes out onto cooling racks. Carefully peel off the waxed paper and invert the cakes so that they are right side up. Allow them to cool as you make the filling and the frosting. (Note: You may also freeze the cakes before filling them and finish just prior to serving. In fact, freezing helps keep the cake intact during the filling and frosting process.)

PREPARE FILLING

Place the cream cheese and butter in the bowl of a food processor fitted with the steel blade and process until smooth. Scrape down the bowl, add the vanilla, and process again. Add the confectioner's sugar a bit at a time, processing between each addition. Add half of the grated Edam and pulse 1 or 2 times to incorporate. Set the remaining Edam and filling aside.

ASSEMBLE LAYERS

Heat the rum with the brown sugar until the sugar melts; allow the mixture to cool. Place 1 cake on a platter or cake stand. Liberally sprinkle it with about one-third of the rum mixture. Spoon on half of the cream cheese filling and spread to cover the top of cake completely. Sprinkle the filling with half of the remaining grated Edam.

Place the second cake on top of the first and douse with another third of the rum mixture. Repeat with the remaining filling and grated cheese.

Top with the final cake, the "dome" facing upward. Douse the top cake with the rest of the rum mixture. Refrigerate the cake at least 1 hour to set filling before frosting.

PREPARE MERINGUE FROSTING AND FINISH

In the bowl of a stand mixer, beat the whites until they form soft peaks. Add 2 tablespoons (24 g) sugar and beat until the whites form stiff peaks; set aside.

In a small saucepan, heat the water and remaining 1 cup (200 g) sugar, swirling gently until the sugar dissolves and the liquid turns clear. Bring to a boil and cook without stirring until a candy thermometer registers the soft-ball stage, 234°F (112°C). Immediately remove the pan from the heat. With your mixer set to the highest speed, beat the egg whites as you slowly stream in the hot syrup. Continue beating until all the syrup has been incorporated. Reserve a spoonful of the lime zest as a garnish for the finished cake if desired and add the remaining zest to the whites and resume beating until the meringue is stiff, glossy, and cool, 4–6 minutes.

Spread the frosting over the cake, starting with the sides. With a spatula, use a swirling/lifting motion to create an attractive pattern. Sprinkle the cake with the reserved lime zest, if using. Refrigerate 2 hours. Bring to room temperature 30 minutes prior to serving.

Dondé façade. [PRODUCTOS DE HARINA, S.A. DE C.V.]

MODERNIZATION AND INDUSTRIALIZATION

In 1905, Luis A. Dondé founded Productos de Harina, S.A. de C.V.—the region's first commercial baked-goods factory. The founder took it as his challenge to distribute bakery products into the most remote reaches of the peninsula, from the floodplains of Tabasco and the rainforests of Campeche east to the jungles of Quintana Roo. Soon, a flood of cookies, crackers, and snack items appeared in places reachable at that time only by donkey or barge. By the mid-twentieth century, thanks in large part to television advertising, the name Dondé had become synonymous with family fun, and fat, smiling cracker and cookie characters in baker's uniforms began appearing as cartoons and life-sized puppets. Today, Dondé distributes more than 130 products throughout Latin America and in Hispanic communities in the United States for those who yearn for treats that remind them of home.

(opposite page) Chicharronería *"La Lupita."* [MR]

LA CHICHARRONERÍA

THE CHICHARRONERÍA OFFERS a taste of one of Yucatán's most visceral gastronomical delights: *tacos de chicharra*. While it might not be everyone's fancy to wolf down bits of fried pig offal, all those to whom I have introduced this delicacy go away with a newfound appreciation for pork's potential.

Chicharronerías are a vibrant part of urban life in Yucatán. These family-run shops play an important supporting role in the slaughter and consumption of pigs, for the *chicharronería* is where the leftover scraps of the carcass are salvaged and cooked, and where precious lard is rendered.

Chicharronería "La Lupita" in Xcalachén is the pantheon of pork: a corner altar enshrines a statue of the Virgin of Guadalupe; at her feet a plastic pig clock ticks in adoration; and overhead, a mobile of piglets flits and floats, looking ever so much like plump, pink angels.

Up to 440 pounds (200 k) of pork fat, organs, skin, and extremities are processed each day at La Lupita. Organ meats are ground for Buche relleno; blood and brains are confected into *morcilla*; skin is parboiled and twice fried to make crispy *chicharrrón* (cracklings). The remaining organs, along with feet, ears, and faces are parboiled, then tossed into enormous vats along with thick slabs of pork fat. Raging fires superheat the contents until the lard is rendered and the meats are browned and crispy.

In the front of the shop, assorted meats (*chicharra*) are ordered and chopped, the *chicharrón* crumbled, and tables spread with baskets of fresh tortillas so that diners can assemble their own *tacos de chicharra*. These are typically eaten for breakfast or as a mid-morning snack; nothing of this carnage will be left by noon.

CASTACÁN / K'ASTAK'ÁN / CHICHARRA ESPECIAL

PORK BELLY CONFIT

FOR THE CHICHARRA ESPECIAL

3 lbs. (1.5 k) unhydrogenated pork lard

1 lb. (500 g) pork belly, skin intact

8 oz. (225 g) smoked slab bacon, cut into 4 equal portions (optional; if omitting the bacon, add 8 oz. / 225 g of the pork belly)

1 tsp. (6 g) sea salt

FOR SERVING

Salpicón (p. 511)

Chile sauce of your choice

Lime wedges

Sliced avocado

Chicharra especial is quite simply pork belly simmered in copious quantities of its own fat. It is also known as *castacán* (from the Yucatek Mayan vernacular *k'astak'án*, or "half-cooked"), which in Yucatán is often curiously pronounced with a final "m" instead of "n." (Listen, too, for "Yucatám.") For this recipe and the Chicharra surtida, the optional smoked slab bacon helps capture the flavor created by the hours of rolling boil at which the lard of *chicharronerías* is maintained. Tacos of Castacán are extremely popular street food prepared at an abundance of local stalls (p. 212). (Note: The lard used for Chicharra especial and surtida can be strained, refrigerated, and used for recipes that call for Enriched Lard [p. 513]).

Prepare ahead note: Chicharra especial is best eaten immediately after preparing. However, the meats can be fried in the lard a day in advance and refrigerated. Just before serving, coarsely chop and reheat quickly in a bit more lard.

YIELD: 6 SERVINGS

FRY MEATS

Place the lard in a deep, heavy stockpot and turn the heat to low. Add the pork belly and continue to heat until the lard is completely melted. It should cover the meat; if not, add more lard. Cook on medium high, maintaining the temperature at 375°F

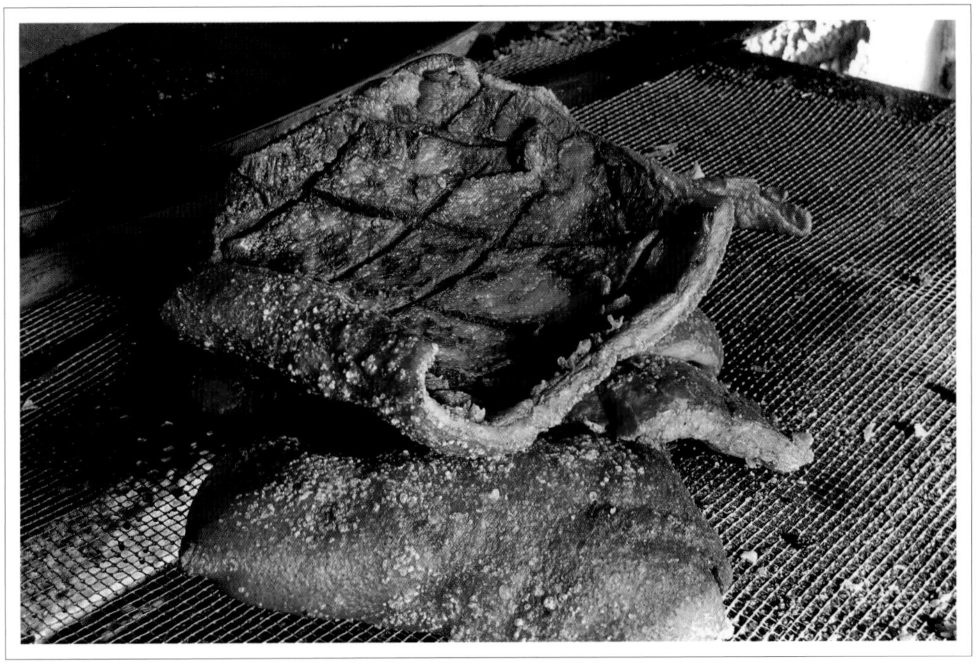

Crispy pork belly, castacán. [MR]

(190°C), turning the meat from time to time, for about 30 minutes, or until the meat is beginning to brown. Add the bacon and cook another 15 minutes, or until both meats are evenly browned and the skin of the pork belly is crisp. Remove the meats, drain, and cool. Coarsely chop the meats and sprinkle with salt. Use immediately in one of the following options.

VARIATIONS

Chicharra en salpicón (Chopped Vegetable and Pork Confit "Cobb Salad"): The classic way of eating Chicharra is to chop it and mix with the shredded-cabbage mixture known as Salpicón. Use 1 recipe of Chicharra (either especial or surtida, below), coarsely chopped. Add 3 ounces (75 g) Chicharrón (p. 214, or commercial), coarsely crumbled, and 1 teaspoon (6 g) sea salt, or to taste. Mix the meats and toss with 1 recipe Salpicón immediately before serving. Serve with tortillas and chile sauce and invite diners to assemble their own tacos.

Taquitos de castacán (Pork Belly Confit Tacos): This little taco is a favorite at the popular Taquería Wayan'e (p. 232). Place coarsely chopped Castacán atop warm tortillas and garnish with Cebolla frita con frijol (p. 234). Diners add their own K'uut bi ik (p. 508) or other chile sauce to taste. Garnish the plate with sliced avocado if you wish.

Chicharra surtida (Pork Offal Confit): Not just fine pork belly is fried for Chicharra; in Yucatán, just about every part of the pig is put to use in Chicharra surtida. Create an assortment that conforms to your particular threshold of squeamishness: start with 1 pound (500 g) mixed pork pieces such as liver, kidneys, some ribs, perhaps a foot or tail. You will also always want to include a piece of fatty leg or rump so that you have some more "conventional" meat in the dish. Parboil the meat in salted water 20–30 minutes, or up to 1 hour, depending on the quantity and size of pieces you have, skimming frequently. Drain, dry thoroughly, and fry the meat in lard with the bacon as described in the master recipe. If you have access to Spanish *morcilla*, fry it separately, slice it, and add it with the other chopped meats. Finish per Chicharra en salpicón, above.

Chicharra en salpicón. [MR]

Chicharra surtida. [MR]

The proper way to eat chicharra. [MR]

CHICHARRÓN

CRISPY FRIED PORK SKIN

FOR THE CRACKLINGS

12 oz. (340 g) fresh pork skin,
    preferably scraped by the
    butcher and ready to use

3 lbs. (1.5 k) unhydrogenated
    pork lard

1 tsp. (6 g) sea salt

Commercially packaged pork cracklings can be rather flavorless; worse, they can easily become rancid. The solution: make your own! If you live near a Latin American *carnicería* (meat market), you can probably find fresh pigskin already cleaned and prepared for making Chicharrón. If you would rather purchase the Chicharrón already fried and ready to use, try to get it from a *carnicería* rather than the potato chip aisle of your supermarket, since the quality will be far superior.

Prepare ahead note: You will need about 2–3 days for making Chicharrón. On the first day, parboil and dry the skin. On the last day, finish the frying. Chicharrón keeps well in a resealable plastic bag for about 2 weeks. You may also process the Chicharrón through the drying step and store the dried skin in a resealable plastic bag in the refrigerator. When ready to use, bring it to room temperature, then fry.

YIELD: APPROXIMATELY 9 OZ. / 250 G CRACKLINGS

PARBOIL SKIN

If you are cleaning the skin yourself, turn the skin flesh side up on a work surface. Using a very sharp filleting knife, scrape away any remaining fat or meat and discard. The trick to this is to end up with a very thin, almost translucent, piece of skin with no membrane, fat, or meat whatsoever. You should be able to see the pores on the underside of the skin. Commercial *chicharronerías* may leave some of this fat intact, but

Owner Elda Rodríguez with three stages of chicharrón *(right to left): parboiled and dried; first frying; final product.* [MR]

(left) Parboiled pigskin is hung out to dry for several days, until it turns into tough leather. After drying, the skin is fried at a low chicharronería temperature to produce a brittle shell. [MR]

(right) In chicharronerías, chicharrón goes through two fryings: after the first frying at low heat, the skin is fried again at extremely high temperatures, causing it to inflate to the size of a sheet—the crisply addictive chicharrón. [DS]

you should not: the heat of the lard on your stovetop can never compete with that of the commercial vats, meaning that your *chicharrón* will likely never crisp properly.

Check the reverse side of the butcher's or your cleaned skin for any bristle and scrape away as much stubble as you can. Any really stubborn hairs will be burned off during the frying. Place the cleaned skin in a large stockpot and completely cover with water. Bring to a boil, and cook at a rapid boil for 1 hour. Remove the pan from the heat, drain, and allow to cool.

DRY SKIN

Place the skin flat on an oiled baking rack located on a baking sheet and refrigerate for 3–4 hours, or overnight. (The rack will allow air to circulate around the skin so that it dries more evenly.)

Preheat the oven to 250°F (121°C). Bake the skin on the rack and baking sheet for 2 hours; turn it over and bake an additional hour. Turn off the oven and leave the skin in the oven for another 2–3 hours or overnight. (Alternatively, you may place it in a dehydrator for about 12 hours.) The finished "leather" should be shiny and look and feel rather like plastic.

FRY CHICHARRÓN

Place lard in a large stockpot and heat it on high until a thermometer reaches a temperature of 390–400°F (198–204°C). Meanwhile, break or cut the dried pigskin into small pieces, roughly 1½ inches (4 cm) square. Have a slotted spoon or wok strainer ready and, working a few at a time, drop the dried skin pieces into the hot fat. Allow the skins to inflate until you hear no more crackling and they are lightly browned (this happens quickly, after about only 30–45 seconds). Remove with the strainer and drain on paper towels. Sprinkle with salt and store in an airtight container or resealable plastic bags.

THE REWARD OF PORK Yucatecan masons and other labor guilds play key parts in annual parish celebrations. On 3 May, the masons receive their own special day of honor. It coincides with the Día de la Santa Cruz, or Day of the Holy Cross, significant in Yucatán due to a miracle that occurred during the horrific Caste War. Nowadays it is traditional for masons to erect a Holy Cross—always homemade and festooned with scraps scavenged from job sites—atop work in progress whenever a roof is completed. Once the cross has been erected, the masons are rewarded with an on-the-job party featuring plenty of cold beer and *tacos de chicharra*. Each worker is assigned a culinary task: chopping the meats, tomatoes, and chiles or squeezing the sour orange juice.

Masons assembling an impromptu lunch of Chicharra en salpicón. [DS]

CHICHARRÓN EN SALSA ROJA

PORK CRACKLINGS IN TOMATO SAUCE

TO PREPARE AHEAD
Tomate frito (p. 507)
Chicharrón (p. 214), or substitute

FOR THE SAUCE AND CHICHARRÓN

1 recipe Tomate frito
  (about 4 cups / 1 L)
2 medium cloves garlic (½ oz. /
  12 g), peeled, charred, and
  mashed
2–3 chiles chipotles in adobo
  (about 30 g), drained, quantity
  according to your preferred heat
  level
2 cups (500 ml) chicken stock
  or bouillon
¼ cup (62.5 ml) white vinegar
2½ oz. (75 g) Chicharrón (or
  commercial cracklings), broken
  into bite-sized pieces, plus a few
  extra pieces for garnish
½ tsp. (3 g) sea salt, or to taste

FOR SERVING

Mexican *crema* (Substitute: crème
  fraîche, sour cream, or plain
  yogurt)
8 oz. (225 g) *queso panela* or *cotija*
  (Substitute: fresh mozzarella or
  feta), cubed or crumbled
1 Tbs. (5 g) cilantro, finely
  chopped
Salpicón (p. 511), optional

Doña Elda shared this easy recipe with me—a delicious way to make use of leftover cracklings. This, she said, is her family's version of comfort food; a big plate of it demonstrates a mother's love.

Prepare ahead note: The sauce may be prepared in advance and refrigerated or frozen. Reheat and add the Chicharrón 5 minutes before serving.

YIELD: 6 SERVINGS

PREPARE SAUCE AND CHICHARRÓN

Fill the jar of a blender with half of the Tomate frito. Add the garlic and chipotles and process until completely liquefied. Transfer the purée to a large a saucepan and add the remaining Tomate frito, chicken stock, and vinegar. Bring to a boil then reduce to a simmer.

Add crumbled Chicharrón to the sauce and stir to incorporate. Continue simmering about 5 minutes, or until the Chicharrón is softened but not mushy. Check the seasonings, adding salt as necessary.

TO SERVE

Ladle the sauce and some of the Chicharrón pieces into individual serving bowls or plates and drizzle on some of the *crema*. Garnish with a piece of the reserved crispy Chicharrón and sprinkle with cheese and chopped cilantro. For textural contrast, you may also top each serving with a spoonful of Salpicón if you wish.

VARIATION

Chicharrón en salsa verde (Pork Cracklings in Tomatillo Sauce): Like other dishes featuring Salsa verde, such as flautas or enchiladas verdes, this dish is considered by proud Yucatecans to be just a bit "too Mexican." Still, in households where the parents or grandparents are from other regions of Mexico, Chicharrón en salsa verde is frequently prepared. Heat 1 tablespoon (14 g) Enriched Lard (p. 513) in a large saucepan until shimmering. Add 1 recipe Salsa verde (about 4 cups / 1 L; p. 509), bring to a boil, reduce to a simmer, and cook, uncovered, for 5–6 minutes, stirring frequently, until the sauce thickens and darkens slightly. Add 2 cups (500 ml) chicken stock or bouillon and return to a simmer. Finish as for Chicharrón en salsa roja. Serving suggestions are the same.

SOPA DE CHICHARRÓN

CREAMY PORK CRACKLING SOUP

TO PREPARE AHEAD

Chicharrón en salsa verde or
Chicharrón en salsa roja (p. 217)

FOR THE SOUP

1 recipe Chicharrón en salsa roja
or Chicharrón en salsa verde

2 cups (500 ml) chicken stock or
bouillon

½ cup (125 ml) Mexican *crema*
(Substitute: crème fraîche,
whipping cream, or sour cream),
plus additional to garnish

FOR SERVING

Chicharrón (p. 214, or commercial
cracklings), broken into large
pieces

8 oz. (225 g) *queso panela* or *cotija*
(Substitute: fresh mozzarella or
feta), cubed or crumbled

1 Tbs. (5 g) cilantro, finely chopped

Cristina Baker and Executive Chef José Andrey Vázquez Manzanilla of Hacienda Xcanatún shared this recipe with me for a spectacular, creamy soup based on Chicharrón en salsa verde. You may also follow this same formula using Chicharrón en salsa roja.

Prepare ahead note: Sopa de chicharrón reheats very well. If you like, prepare the soup a day in advance and refrigerate. Reheat immediately before serving, adding a bit more stock if needed.

YIELD: 8 SERVINGS

PREPARE SOUP

Bring the Chicharrón en salsa verde (or roja) to a simmer in a stockpot. Add the chicken stock. Using a food processor or handheld immersion blender, process until the Chicharrón is thoroughly puréed. Add the cream and process again until well blended. Check the seasonings and serve.

TO SERVE

Serve in soup bowls. Place one piece of Chicharrón in the center of the soup, drizzle on some of the cream, and garnish with cheese and cilantro.

BUCHE RELLENO / GIANT FRIED PORK SAUSAGE

Cousins of this "offal" delicacy are prepared worldwide, including ponce in New Orleans and haggis in Scotland. In Yucatán's *chicharronerías*, a pig stomach is filled with chopped pork offal, parboiled, and then fried in lard. Doña Elda stuffs, boils, and fries 20 *buches rellenos* three times a week, and they are either sold in slices or chopped and mixed with Chicharra surtida to order. Her recipe for filling all those stomachs includes 22 pounds (10 k) pork meat, 33 pounds (15 k) pork heart, 11 pounds (5 k) pork fat, 5 dozen raw eggs, 5 dozen hard-boiled eggs, and two large rolls of mint and chives (about 2 lbs. / 1 k) each.

(left) Chopped organ meats, raw eggs, and herbs make up the filling for buche relleno. [MR] *(middle) Pork stomachs, or buches, are stuffed and sewn before parboiling and frying.* [MR] *(right) Parboiled buches rellenos ready to fry.* [MR]

(opposite page) Breakfast in the Santiago market, Mérida. [MR]

COMIDA CALLEJERA

J UST AS IN ALL BIG CITIES around the world, street food is a prominent aspect of the daily rhythm of life in Yucatán. Yucatán's tropical climate means that people enjoy al fresco snacks, sweets, even entire meals all day long, 365 days a year.

Churros *are popular morning street fare.* [MR]

THE MARKETS

The early morning air wafting from the prepared-food stalls of Yucatán's public markets is saturated with many heady aromas, but most particularly that of *mondongo*—a rich tripe stew that fortifies and is considered a remedy for hangovers.

Two kinds of *mondongo* are offered: a la andaluza or k'aab-ik. The former is a Spanish import and includes not only tripe but also sausage, bacon, ham, and chickpeas. The latter version is stripped of all but the basics in humble Yucatecan fashion: tripe, beef hooves, *achiote*, tomatoes, and local chile. Both stews are served with a sprinkling of chopped chives.

MONDONGO A LA ANDALUZA
YUCATECAN TRIPE STEW WITH SAUSAGES, HAM, AND GARBANZOS

TO PREPARE AHEAD
Recado rojo (p. 500)
Recado para bistec (p. 501)
Recado blanco (p. 502)
Seville orange juice substitute
   (p. 514), unless fresh Seville
   oranges are available
Enriched Lard (p. 513)
Longaniza de Valladolid (p. 481),
   or substitute

FOR PARBOILING THE TRIPE
2 lbs. (1 k) beef tripe
20 cups (5 L) water
1 Tbs. (18 g) sea salt

FOR THE MARINADE
8 Tbs. (120 g) Recado rojo
4 Tbs. (80 g) Recado para bistec
2 Tbs. (30 g) Recado blanco
1 cup (250 ml) Seville orange juice,
   or substitute
8 medium cloves garlic (2 oz. /
   48 g), peeled and charred
2 Tbs. (28 g) Enriched Lard,
   melted
1 Tbs. (18 g) sea salt

FOR THE STEW
20 cups (5 L) water
2 sprigs fresh epazote (Substitute:
   1 tsp. / 1.5 g dried, crumbled)
2 Tbs. (24 g) powdered beef
   bouillon, or 2 cubes

(continued on next page)

Put your squeamishness aside and discover the soft, creamy succulence of well-prepared beef tummy; with proper cooking it will be soft as marshmallows rather than rubbery. The name of this recipe is deceptive since here it is generally considered to be 100 percent certified Yucatecan. Perhaps the reference to Andalucía is due to the inclusion of those very Middle Eastern garbanzos. Depending on the country, the inner lining of beef stomach is known in Spanish as either *mondongo* or *menudo*—and again, depending on where you are eating it, the dish that includes it may be called by either name. As if this stew weren't rich enough with the fatty beef stomach, Yucatecans add two kinds of sausages as well as ham to take it up a notch or two.

A simpler version prepared by campesinos—Mondongo k'aab-ik—features a much shorter ingredient list. The Mayan name means "chile broth" (*k'aab* = broth; *ik* = chile) and reveals its primal simplicity. Noemi Gómez García of Tizimín in Yucatán's cattle country (p. 489) shared both recipes with me. She used a combination of *toalla* (smooth) and *colmena* (honeycombed)—both meticulously cleaned—to succulent result.

Prepare ahead note: Both of the *mondongo* recipes are best prepared over a 2-day period. Parboil the tripe a day in advance, then marinate it at least 4 hours or overnight; finish cooking the next day. Alternatively, prepare everything on one day and refrigerate; reheat just before serving.

YIELD: 8–10 SERVINGS

CLEAN AND PARBOIL TRIPE
Thorough cleaning of tripe is essential to an excellent finished product; if your butcher doesn't do it, you will have to. Rinse and scrub the tripe vigorously under cold running water. (Yucatecan women also squeeze sour orange juice onto the tripe to refresh it.) Pull away all the yellowish, fatty membrane and discard. (Note: The most delicious, grease-free Mondongo will require at least 30 minutes to clean thoroughly.) Slice into long ribbons about 2½ inches (6.3 cm) wide, then cut across the width to create rough squares about 2½ inches (6.3 cm) across. Place the squares in a large stockpot, cover completely with the water, and add the salt. Bring to a boil, skimming frequently. Cook at a rolling boil for 30 minutes, adding more water as necessary. Drain and rinse.

MARINATE MEATS
While the tripe is boiling, place the marinade ingredients in the jar of a blender and process until thoroughly liquefied. Place the cooked, drained tripe in a large baking dish or in a resealable plastic bag and coat it completely with the marinade. Refrigerate at least 4 hours or overnight.

PREPARE STEW
Transfer the tripe and all of the marinade to a large stockpot, cover with the water, and add the epazote and bouillon. Bring to a boil, skimming frequently. Cover, reduce

FOR THE *SOFRITO*

2 Tbs. (28 g) Enriched Lard

9 oz. (255 g) smoked slab bacon, cubed

3 fresh chorizos (about 9 oz. / 255 g total), whole

3 Longanizas de Valladolid (about 5¼ oz. / 150 g total; substitute: commercial longaniza or any smoked sausage)

9 oz. (255 g) smoked ham, cubed

1 medium red onion (10 oz. / 275 g), peeled, charred, and finely chopped

1 cup (140 g) red bell pepper, cut into small dice

4 medium Roma tomatoes (14 oz. / 400 g), charred, seeded, and chopped

4 medium chiles x'catiques (about 5 oz. / 140 g total), charred and left whole without puncturing

FOR FINISHING THE STEW

4 cups (15 oz. / 425 g) cooked garbanzos (chickpeas), drained

1 lb. (500 g) baking potatoes, boiled, peeled, and cubed

¼–½ tsp. (0.75–1.5 g) cayenne powder, or to taste

¼ cup (62.5 ml) red wine vinegar

¼ cup (30 g) all-purpose flour

TO SERVE

Mixture of chopped chives and cilantro

Chile k'uut (p. 508)

Pan francés (p. 194), French rolls, or other bread for serving

to a simmer, and cook 3½–4 hours, replenishing the water as needed, until the tripe is very tender.

PREPARE *SOFRITO*

While the stew is cooking, heat the lard in a large skillet until shimmering. Add the bacon and cook, stirring frequently, until it is browned and crisp; transfer to paper towels, reserving the fat. In the same fat, quickly brown the chorizo, *longaniza*, and ham, working in batches as needed. As they are browned, remove the meats from the skillet. Slice the sausages on the diagonal into disks and set aside.

Drain all but 1 tablespoon (15 ml) fat from the skillet. Add the onion and bell pepper and cook, stirring frequently, until softened, 2–3 minutes. Add the tomatoes and cook until most of the liquid has evaporated, another 3–4 minutes. Add the whole chiles and stir just until heated.

When the tripe is done, add the *sofrito* and meats to the stockpot. Simmer 15 minutes to incorporate the flavors. Remove the epazote and discard; retrieve the chiles, rub off the skin under running water, remove the stems and seeds, and slice the chiles into thin strips as a garnish; set aside.

FINISH STEW

Add the remaining ingredients except the flour to the stockpot. Transfer 1–2 ladles of the hot stock to a heatproof bowl, add the flour, and whisk to blend. Transfer the flour mixture to the stockpot and stir. Simmer 15 minutes, stirring frequently, until the mixture thickens slightly. Check the seasonings.

TO SERVE

Serve the Mondongo in individual soup bowls or deep plates and top with some of the reserved chile strips. Diners add their own chive/cilantro garnish and chile sauce to taste. Use tortillas or bread for dunking.

Mondongo k'aab-ik. [MR]

VARIATION

Mondongo k'aab-ik (Rustic Yucatecan Tripe Stew in Tomato and Chile Broth): Follow the instructions for cleaning, cutting, and parboiling the tripe in the master recipe for Mondongo a la andaluza. During marination, include 1 pair beef hooves (about 4½ lbs. / 2 k) cut across the width into 6 pieces each (optional), cleaned thoroughly, burning away any bristle and removing fatty pockets between skin and bones.

Add the tripe and hooves to the stockpot and proceed with the recipe, omitting the bacon, sausages, ham, chickpeas, and potatoes. Skip the thickening step.

To serve, remove the tripe and serve it with pieces of the hooves on individual serving plates. Ladle the stock into soup bowls. Garnishes and sauces are the same as for Mondongo a la andaluza.

[MC]

THE *TAMAL* LADIES　　Markets across the peninsula are flooded early every morning with teenagers rushing to school, as well as masons and housekeepers on their way to work. And waiting for them are the *tamal* ladies—Maya women who prepare a variety of tamales favored by Yucatecans for breakfast and display them in colorful plastic tubs. Recipes for tamales appear on pages 103–107, 130–136, 376–377, and 442–444.

AGUAS FRESCAS: TROPICAL FRUIT REFRESHERS

Steamy tropical mornings are a good time for refreshing beverages and healthful juices, and markets abound with delicious *aguas frescas*—fresh fruits juiced or puréed with water and a bit of sugar, then strained. Plastic bags stretched over the top of the cups keep the bugs away. The range of fruits used to make *aguas frescas* is almost infinite, limited only by seasonal availability. Served over a bit of ice and enjoyed beneath the shade of a tree in the park—that's Yucatecan air conditioning.

AGUA FRESCA DE GUANÁBANA

GUANÁBANA REFRESHER

Prepare ahead note: Aguas frescas keep well under refrigeration 1–2 weeks.

YIELD: 10 SERVINGS

FOR THE SYRUP
AND FINISHING

1½ cups (300 g) sugar
6½ cups (1.75 L) water, divided
1-in.-wide (2.5 cm) strips lime rind
1 cup (250 ml) Puré de guanábana
  (see Sorbete de guanábana,
  p. 245; substitute: canned
  or frozen guanábana pulp
  [see Resources, p. 540])

PREPARE THE SYRUP

Place the sugar, 1½ cups (375 ml) water, and the lime rind in a small saucepan and bring to a boil. Continue over high heat for about 1 minute, or until the sugar has completely dissolved and the liquid is clear. Remove the pan from the heat, cover, and allow to steep with the rind for 30 minutes.

FINISH, CHILL, AND SERVE

Mix 1 cup (250 ml) water and your homemade purée or packaged pulp thoroughly and pour it through a fine-mesh sieve into a mixing bowl. Use a rubber spatula to press through as much liquid as possible; discard any residue. Remove the rind from cooled sugar syrup and discard. Transfer the strained liquid to a large pitcher, add the syrup, and stir until well incorporated.

Add the remaining 4 cups (1 L) water to the pitcher and stir to blend. Cover and refrigerate.

AGUA FRESCA DE TAMARINDO

TAMARIND REFRESHER

Prepare ahead note: Aguas frescas keep well under refrigeration 1–2 weeks.

YIELD: 10 SERVINGS

FOR THE INFUSION
AND FINISHING

9 oz. (250 g) tamarind pods
¾ cup (150 g) sugar
12 cups (3 L) water, divided

PREPARE THE INFUSION

Bring 4 cups (1 L) water to a boil in a nonreactive saucepan; add the tamarind pods and sugar and stir continuously while the mixture boils for 1 minute. Remove the pan from the heat, cover, and allow to steep for 2 hours.

Using a potato masher, break up the softened tamarind pods to release the seeds and dissolve the pulp. Strain the mixture through a fine-mesh sieve; use a wooden spoon to mash through as much liquid as possible; discard the residue.

FINISH, CHILL, AND SERVE

Transfer the infusion to a large pitcher, add the remaining water, and stir to incorporate. Cover and refrigerate. Stir before serving.

REFRESCO DE POZOLE CON COCO

CORN, COCONUT, AND CINNAMON REFRESHER

TO PREPARE AHEAD

Masa prepared from either nixtamalized corn or *masa harina* (p. 517)

FOR THE POZOLE

4 cups (1 L) water

1 cup (225 g) *masa*, or more for a thicker beverage

1 cup (120 g) fresh coconut, shredded

1 Tbs. (12 g) sugar or honey, or to taste

¼ tsp. (1.25 ml) Mexican vanilla

¼ tsp. (0.75 g) ground *canela* (Mexican cinnamon)

Chalky white spheres stacked like piles of cannonballs are common features of Yucatán's markets. These are used to make Refresco de pozole con coco, a refreshing corn beverage flavored with coconut and *canela* and nowadays served over ice. Customers dissolve the ball in water, adding honey or sugar to taste. (Yucatecan *pozole* has nothing to do with the Western Mexican hominy stew.)

Prepare ahead note: The *masa* for Refresco de pozole con coco may be made well in advance and frozen. The prepared drink will keep well under refrigeration for about 2 days.

YIELD: 4 SERVINGS

PREPARE POZOLE AND SERVE
Place the ingredients in the jar of a blender and process until completely liquefied.

TO SERVE
Pour the pozole over ice and garnish with a stick of *canela* if desired.

Aguas frescas. [MR]

XEK / XE'EK / XEK'

JICAMA AND MANDARIN ORANGE SNACK WITH CHILE AND LIME

In Mérida's central market you will frequently see piles of Asian mandarin oranges stacked neatly next to pyramids of Yucatecan jicama, a crispy root vegetable. These two unlikely bedfellows are displayed together because they are the ingredients for Xek (pronounced "shek"), Mayan for something like "hodgepodge." Xek is especially popular during Hanal Pixán (p. 429), when the market is overtaken by piles of the ingredients for use as offerings on family altars.

The recipe is simple. Peel the jicama and cut it into julienne strips (rub cut jicama with a bit of lime to prevent browning). Mix with peeled, seeded mandarin sections. Add the juice of a couple of limes (or Seville oranges), some chopped cilantro, a sprinkle of sea salt, and cayenne powder or red pepper flakes to taste.

Although not traditional, the basic combination can be enhanced by the addition of other ingredients to transform Xek into a refreshing salad course. Add seedless white grapes, arugula or watercress, diced cucumber, melon balls, and so on. You may also dress it with a light lime-based vinaigrette if you wish.

Bags of xek—jicama and mandarin orange wedges—and other fruit medleys in the market. [MR]

Taco stand in the market. [EC]

TAQUERÍAS

Some *taquerías* are so popular with high school students and businesspeople that lines form for *desayuno* at 8:00 am and continue growing through *almuerzo*, the mid-morning snack. By noon or 1:00 pm, almost everything prepared for the day will be sold out.

TAQUITOS DE PULPO EN SU TINTA

LITTLE TACOS OF OCTOPUS IN ITS OWN INK

FOR THE OCTOPUS

1 medium or 2 small octopus
   (3 lbs. / 1.5 k total), beaks, eyes,
   and entrails removed, reserving
   ink sac
1 Tbs. white vinegar

FOR THE *SOFRITO*

½ cup (125 ml) Spanish olive oil
½ medium white onion (5 oz. /
   137.5 g), finely chopped
3 medium cloves garlic (¾ oz. /
   18 g), peeled and minced
1 cup (140 g) green bell pepper,
   finely chopped
2 medium Roma tomatoes
   (7 oz. / 200 g), seeded and
   finely chopped
½ cup (30 g) flat-leaf parsley,
   finely chopped

TO FINISH

1 cup (250 ml) dry red wine
2 bay leaves
1 tsp. (0.65 g) dried whole
   Mexican oregano, lightly toasted
1 tsp. (6 g) sea salt
½ tsp. (2.5 g) black peppercorns
¼ cup (62.5 ml) red wine vinegar

FOR SERVING

Tortillas (p. 518)
X'nipek (p. 512)
Avocado slices
Lime wedges

The Mexican states that line the Gulf of Mexico all have versions of Pulpo en su tinta. The popular *taquería* El Tetizeño in Mérida's Parque Santiago is famous for its seafood tacos—most especially for the little tacos of *pulpo en su tinta*, updated for this recipe. Most mornings you can see a giant galvanized metal tub full of octopus being parboiled for this and several other dishes.

Prepare ahead note: Pulpo en su tinta is best made a day in advance, then gently reheated just prior to serving. It can also be prepared over several consecutive days. Clean and cook the octopus one day, assemble the stew the next, and reheat/serve on the final day.

YIELD: 6 SERVINGS

PREPARE OCTOPUS

Pound the cleaned octopus between sheets of waxed paper to soften. Cook in rapidly boiling water with 1 tablespoon (15 ml) white vinegar for 1 hour. Cut the bodies and tentacles into bite-sized pieces and set aside. (Note: This step may be done 1 day in advance. Place the octopus in a resealable bag filled with water and refrigerate. Drain well and proceed with the recipe.)

PREPARE *SOFRITO*

Heat the oil in a large, deep skillet until shimmering. Add the onion, garlic, and bell pepper. Cook, stirring frequently, until the onions are translucent and bell peppers tender, 3–4 minutes. Add the tomatoes and parsley and continue cooking until the tomatoes are softened, 2–3 minutes.

FINISH AND SERVE

Transfer the octopus to the skillet and stir to combine with the *sofrito*. Add the wine and bay leaves and bring to a simmer. Grind the oregano, salt, and peppercorns in a spice mill or coffee grinder reserved for this purpose; add to the skillet and continue to simmer.

   Place the reserved ink sacs in the jar of a blender with the red wine vinegar and liquefy. Pour the liquid through a fine-mesh sieve into a bowl; return any solids that remain in the sieve to the blender, add a bit of water, and liquefy again. Once more, pass the liquid through the sieve. Pour the collected black liquid through a clean fine-mesh sieve into the skillet with the octopus. Cook 15–20 minutes, or until the liquid has evaporated, leaving only the octopus and a puddle of olive oil at the bottom of the skillet.

(foreground) Taquitos de pulpo en su tinta. *(background)* Camarones empanizados *(p. 269), both served as* panuchos. [MR]

TO SERVE

Heap the octopus on a large serving platter or in a heated chafing dish. Serve with tortillas and salsas so that guests may assemble their own tacos with garnishes of their choice.

Alternatively, prepare individual servings. Place a mound of the octopus on a tortilla. Top with some X'nipek and a slice of avocado, with lime wedges on the side. You may also serve the octopus plated with Arroz negro (p. 532) and a mixed green salad.

TAQUERÍA WAYAN'E

A Mérida institution since 1991, Wayan'e got its start on a street corner with just three daily *guisos*. In the ensuing years, owners Mauricio Loría Herrera and Nidia Cervera have taken the business to a total of 36 *guisos* and hundreds of diners daily. Most tacos are garnished with Mauricio's signature fried-onion-and-bean medley—Cebolla frita con frijol—the ultimate indulgence, as if these tacos needed any. When you experience the first bite of your first taco by Mauricio, you'll find yourself shouting the company name, "Wayan'e," which in Mayan means, "Here it is!"

Wayan'e offerings. [MR]

CARNE ASADA CON SALSA ROJA ("ROJO")

CHARCOAL-GRILLED PORK WITH *ACHIOTE* SAUCE

TO PREPARE AHEAD

Recado rojo (p. 500)

Brined pork loin (see Basic Techniques, p. 536)

Enriched Lard (p. 513)

FOR THE MARINADE

6 Tbs. (90 g) Recado rojo

¾ cup (187.5 ml) white vinegar

4 medium cloves garlic (1 oz. / 24 g), peeled, charred, and mashed

½ tsp. (3 g) sea salt

¼ tsp. (1 g) cayenne powder

1 ½ lbs. (680 g) pork loin, brined

FOR THE "ROJO"

1 medium Roma tomato (3 ½ oz. / 100 g), charred

2 Tbs. (28 g) Enriched Lard

At Wayan'e, listen for the cry of ¡Dame un Rojo!—or "Give me a red one!"—"Rojo" being the nickname of this dish. Thin cutlets of pork are marinated in *achiote*, then twice cooked, once on a charcoal grill, and again on a searing hot griddle, where they are doused with more *achiote*. This two-for-one recipe is flexible enough for any entertainment option: either grill the cutlets and serve them immediately—in which case the dish is known simply as Carne asada—or for convenience, grill in advance and reheat later to make Carne asada con salsa roja.

Prepare ahead note: Allow enough time for brining the pork overnight, and 30 minutes additional marinating time in the refrigerator just before grilling.

YIELD: 6 SERVINGS

MARINATE CUTLETS

Place the first 5 marinade ingredients in the jar of a blender and process until the garlic is thoroughly puréed; set aside. Remove the pork from the brine, rinse, and pat dry; discard the brining solution. Slice the loin into 6 equal portions, each weighing about 4 oz. (115 g). Working one slice at a time, place pork between 2 layers of waxed paper and pound with a wooden mallet to flatten to a uniform thickness, about ¼ inch (0.5 cm).

Place the cutlets in a large, nonreactive baking dish. Pour the marinade over the meat, turning and basting to cover the meat completely. Refrigerate 30 minutes as you preheat the grill following the instructions for using wood smoking chips in Basic Techniques, p. 537.

Remove the cutlets from the marinade, shaking off any excess. If you want to make "Rojo," reserve the marinade; if you will be making Carne asada, discard it. As soon as the coals are glowing, drain the wood smoking chips and spread half over the hot coals. Sear the cutlets quickly, 3–4 minutes per side, adding more wood chips as necessary and closing the grill's lid after each addition. The thin meat cooks very quickly, so be vigilant and don't overcook; cutlets should be a bit springy when pressed with your fingertip, with no traces of pink juice.

Remove the cutlets from the grill and serve immediately as Carne asada, or proceed with the recipe for "Rojo."

FINISH THE "ROJO"

Coarsely chop the meat and set aside, reserving any juices. Transfer the reserved marinade to the jar of a blender, adding a bit more vinegar if it is thick. Add the tomato and process until thoroughly liquefied; set aside.

FOR SERVING
Tortillas (p. 518) to make tacos, or Pan francés (p. 194) to make tortas

X'nipek (p. 512)

Cebolla frita con frijol (p. 234)

TO PREPARE AHEAD
Frijol k'abax (p. 504)

Enriched Lard (p. 513)

FOR THE BEAN/ONION MEDLEY
2 cups (15 oz. / 425 g) Frijol k'abax, drained (Substitute: plain cooked black beans)

2 Tbs. (28 g) Enriched Lard (Substitute: Spanish olive oil)

6 cups white onion (about 3 medium onions, 2 lbs. / 900 g total), peeled, thinly sliced, and separated into rings

1 tsp. (0.65 g) dried whole Mexican oregano *plus* ½ tsp. (1 g) cuminseed, both lightly toasted and ground together, then passed through a fine-mesh sieve; discard residue

½ tsp. (2.5 g) freshly ground black pepper

½ tsp. (3 g) sea salt

Heat the lard in a large, heavy skillet until shimmering. Add the meat, stirring briefly. On highest heat, add the purée from the blender all at once; it should sputter and splatter, so stand back. Cook on high heat, stirring constantly, until all of the liquid has cooked off and the meat is coated with the red sauce, 4–5 minutes. Remove the skillet from the heat.

TO SERVE
As noted above, serve the meat as Carne asada immediately after grilling. Serve whole cutlets plated with rice and beans, or chop to serve as *tortas* or tacos. Alternatively, you may grill the meat earlier in the day or a day in advance, chop, and reheat later to serve as Carne asada con salsa roja (Rojo). If you serve tacos, whether Carne asada or Rojo, top with some of the fried onions if you wish. Offer X'nipek as a garnish for all serving options.

CEBOLLA FRITA CON FRIJOL
FRIED ONION AND BLACK BEAN MEDLEY

This simple but delicious garnish is mounded on every taco served at Wayan'e. Also try it as a garnish for any of the grilled or *pibil*-style meats in this book.

Prepare ahead note: The beans for Cebolla frita con frijol should be made a day or two in advance. Slice the onions and finish the garnish immediately before serving.

YIELD: ABOUT 6–8 SERVINGS AS A GARNISH

PREPARE BEANS AND FRY ONIONS
Place the cooked, drained beans in a colander and flush with cold water; set aside to drain thoroughly as you continue.

Heat the lard in a large skillet until shimmering. Add the onions, reduce the heat, and cook 8–10 minutes, until the onions are caramelized.

Add the ground spices to the skillet with the onions. Add the pepper and salt and cook another minute. Add the drained beans to the onion mixture and stir to incorporate. Cook until just heated through. Serve.

ABOUT *TORTAS* Almost as popular in Yucatán as tacos, *tortas* are a species of sandwich made with Pan francés (p. 194)—a French-style baguette. The baguette is cut in half across the width, then each half is sliced lengthwise and filled to form one sandwich. As for fillings, the sky is the limit: fried shrimp, breaded cutlets, Carne asada—just about anything offered on the menu boards of *taquerías* can also be ordered as a *torta*. If the filling is a juicy meat, the bread is first dipped in the cooking juices. All fillings are dressed with the garnish that would normally accompany the dish: for example, pickled onions go with Cochinita pibil; shredded cabbage Salpicón goes with breaded cutlets.

Tortas. [EC]

CARNE AL PASTOR

GRILLED PORK IN YUCATECAN SPICES WITH PINEAPPLE

Descended from Lebanese *shawarma* and Turkish *döner kebab*, Carne al pastor has now been thoroughly acculturated in its Mexican home. Dried Mexican chiles serve as the potent flavoring, and in Yucatán, the meat is stained bright red with *achiote* (or nowadays, unfortunately, with other colorants).

A pineapple typically spins atop the *trompo* (or toy top), and the juices eventually drip onto the whirling cone of pork, where they caramelize and create a brilliantly flavorful crust. In addition, pineapple contains protein-digesting enzymes that tenderize the meat. For both reasons I include pineapple juice in the marinade.

Not only is it the marinade that gives Carne al pastor its characteristic flavor, but also it is the cooking method: as it rotates in front of the flame, the meat is constantly basted with its own fat and juices; and, as the grill man shaves thin slices off the outer edge of the *trompo*, each diner is promised meat that has just been seared in the flame.

Assuming few home cooks will have a rotisserie, I have tried to create a version of Carne al pastor approximating the flavor of that achieved in the outdoor stalls. First, I char thick-cut pork steaks on a gas or charcoal grill using wood smoking chips. By thinly slicing the steaks on a diagonal after grilling, the aesthetic of the meat is similar to that achieved by the most adept *taquería* grill man with his razor-sharp carving knife. Finally, for faster service, at many *taquerías* in Yucatán the meat is shaved off in quantity, then heaped in a big, juicy pile on a searing griddle washed with lard. This keeps the meat warm but also gives it another hit of flavorful fat. I have added that step at the end of this recipe.

David Ek Canul—a cook, caterer, and native of Hunucmá, Yucatán—has become famous in his new home of Coahuila in northern Mexico for his Carne al pastor. As a cultural crossover between Mexico and Yucatán, his insights were invaluable to me, not least of which was to serve the dish with real Lebanese Crema de ajo.

Prepare ahead note: Allow 12–15 hours for the brining and marinating. Carne al pastor is a great party dish, since you can brine, marinate, and grill the meat in advance. When it's time to eat, carve the meat and sear it in a hot skillet to reheat just before serving.

YIELD: 10 SERVINGS

TO PREPARE AHEAD

Recado para pastor (p. 498)

Enriched Lard (p. 513)

Brined pork (see Basic Techniques, p. 536)

Recado rojo (p. 500)

FOR THE MARINADE

1 medium Roma tomato (3½ oz. / 100 g), charred

½ medium white onion (5 oz. / 137.5 g), peeled, charred, and coarsely chopped

1 medium head garlic (about 1¾ oz. / 50 g), charred, peeled, and separated into cloves

½ cup (125 ml) pineapple juice

1 Tbs. (16 g) *piloncillo*, grated (Substitute: dark brown sugar), dissolved in ½ cup (125 ml) cider vinegar

1 Tbs. (18 g) coarse sea salt

6 Tbs. (54 g) Recado para pastor

2 Tbs. (28 g) Enriched Lard

2 lbs. (1 k) whole pork loin, brined (Note: For maximum flavor, select a pork cut with a bit of marbling)

PREPARE MARINADE

Combine the marinade ingredients except the lard and pork in the jar of a blender and process until thoroughly liquefied. Heat the lard in a deep, heavy skillet until shimmering. Pour all of the marinade into the skillet at once, which should create a sizzle. (Note: This will create a lot of splattering, so a deep skillet is recommended.) Reduce the heat to medium and simmer, stirring frequently, 4–5 minutes, or until the mixture has darkened, reduced, and thickened. Remove the pan from the heat and allow to cool thoroughly.

Remove the pork from the brine, rinse, and pat dry; discard the brining solution. Cut the loin across the width into 1-inch (2.5 cm) thick steaks. Place the steaks in a

FOR GRILLING AND FINISHING

½ large pineapple (about 1⅓ lbs. / 600 g), peeled and thickly sliced, core intact

4 Tbs. (56 g) Enriched Lard, melted

2 Tbs. (30 g) Recado rojo

FOR SERVING

Tortillas (p. 518)

Crema de ajo (p. 362) *or* Crema de x'catik (p. 363) *or* Salsa de aguacate (p. 510) *or* an assortment

Chile tamulado (p. 509) *or* K'uut bi ik (p. 508)

Mixture of chopped onion and cilantro

Lime wedges

See other serving options below

large baking dish or in a resealable plastic bag and cover with the cooled marinade, making sure to coat each steak thoroughly. Refrigerate 2–3 hours.

GRILL PORK AND FINISH

Bring the pork to room temperature in its marinade for about 30 minutes as you prepare a charcoal or gas grill (see Basic Techniques, following the instructions for using wood smoking chips, p. 538). The grill should be intensely hot, with remnants of flame. Leaving a bit of the marinade still coating the steaks, grill the pork quickly with the grill lid closed until the meat displays some charring and reaches an internal temperature of 140°F (60°C), 5–6 minutes per side. It should still be pink inside; it will finish cooking later. As the meat is grilling, nestle the pineapple slices among the steaks and grill until char marks appear. Transfer the pineapple and pork to a cutting board.

Using a carving knife held at a 45° angle, thinly carve, or shave, the pork steaks on the diagonal. Roll and toss the slices in any juices that collect to coat the exposed meat thoroughly; set aside. Thinly slice the pineapple across the width, discarding the core; set the pineapple slices aside.

Combine the melted lard and *recado* and mash with a fork to incorporate thoroughly. Heat the lard/*recado* mixture in a large nonstick skillet over medium heat. As it fries, the *recado* will tend to clump—use a spatula to break it up, scraping the bottom of the skillet frequently to keep the *recado* spread over the surface. Increase the heat to high. Working in batches so as not to crowd, quickly sauté the pork slices, moving them constantly to coat them with the *recado*, 1–2 minutes until seared; transfer the meat to a platter and keep warm. Add more lard and *recado* if needed to continue with the rest of the pork. Serve immediately.

STREET STALLS   A vestige of the wave of Lebanese immigration to Mexico at the end of the nineteenth century and into the early years of the twentieth (p. 355), Carne al pastor is now popular daily fare in Yucatán. At the Mercado de San Benito in Mérida, a broad aisle is covered with awnings and populated by more than a dozen stalls run by vendors of this Middle Eastern specialty, now fully "Mexicanized."

The inverted rotisserie cone resembles a children's top, in Spanish, trompo—the nickname for these sizzling towers of meat known as carne al pastor. [MR]

Plated: Arrange individual servings of the pork on plates and top with some of the pineapple. Serve with rice and beans of your choice (pp. 527 and 504). Serve condiments and salsas on the table.

VARIATIONS

Tacos al pastor (Grilled Pork and Pineapple on Corn Tortillas): Place the pork and pineapple on top of warm corn tortillas; plate 3 per diner. Diners add their own toppings and salsas.

Gringas (Grilled Pork and Pineapple with Cheese on Flour Tortillas): Place the pork and pineapple on warm flour tortillas and top with grated mild Cheddar or Monterey Jack cheese. Place under a broiler until the cheese is bubbling. Serve with the recommended accompaniments.

Mestizas (Grilled Pork and Pineapple with Cheese on Corn Tortillas): Place the pork and pineapple on top of warm corn tortillas and top with grated mild Cheddar or Monterey Jack cheese. Place under a broiler until the cheese is bubbling. Serve with the recommended accompaniments.

Tacos árabes (Grilled Pork and Pineapple on Pita): Place the pork and pineapple on top of warm pita bread. Drizzle on a bit of Mexican *crema* or plain yogurt, sprinkle on some crumbled *cotija* or feta cheese, and serve with the recommended accompaniments. A new garnish on the scene features finely chopped pineapple mixed with minced habanero and lime juice.

Tortas al pastor (Grilled Pork and Pineapple Sandwich on French Bread): Place the pork and pineapple on halves of Pan francés (p. 194) split down the middle. Serve with the recommended accompaniments.

MOVEABLE FEASTS

In cities and towns throughout Yucatán, you don't have to walk very far to find great food. In fact, in many cases, the food comes to you. Roving vendors in little carts—bicycles adapted with awnings, containers, and attention-getting bells or other sound effects—pedal languidly through the streets, hawking everything from fried snacks like Lebanese *kibis* and Maya *pol'kanes* to sweet breads and corn on the cob.

Elotes *man.* [MR]

ESQUITES

SAUTÉED CORN KERNELS WITH LIME JUICE, CREAM, AND CHILE

TO PREPARE AHEAD

Recado para escabeche (p. 498)

FOR THE CORN

¾ cup (187.5 ml) Spanish olive oil, divided

4 cups (700 g) fresh corn kernels (from 5–6 large ears)

1½ tsp. (9 g) sea salt

1 tsp. (3 g) Recado para escabeche

1 cup (140 g) red bell pepper, cut into medium dice

1½ cups (240 g) chiles poblanos, charred, peeled, seeded, and cut into medium dice (3 large chiles totaling about 15 oz. / 435 g)

½ cup (85 g) scallions, thinly sliced diagonally, including some green

½ cup (125 ml) lime juice or Seville orange juice

FOR SERVING

¾ cup (187.5 ml) Mexican *crema* (Substitute: crème fraîche, plain yogurt, or sour cream), in a squeeze bottle, thinned with a bit of milk

3 ½ oz. (100 g) *queso cotija* (Substitute: feta cheese), crumbled

Cayenne powder, to taste

Totopos para botanas (p. 515)

Lime or Seville orange wedges

Esquites is a fresh corn snack enjoyed throughout the country. On some days and most weekends in Yucatán, rolling carts fitted with steam bins brimming with kernels can be found without having to walk more than a couple of blocks. The vendor scoops some of the warm corn into a cup and tops it with Mexican *crema*, *cotija* cheese, powdered red chile, and a squeeze of lime juice—according to the customer's taste. I've bumped up the flavors by adding a couple of other peppers—the poblano and a bell pepper—as well as some scallions; omit them if you want a simpler dish closer to the original. Either way, Esquites is special enough to serve as a side dish for grilled meats or seafood, or in the more casual manner as a dip with Totopos. (For a Yucatecan twist, use Seville orange juice instead of lime.)

Prepare ahead note: Esquites can be prepared in advance excluding the citrus juice. Refrigerate up to 3 days. Bring to room temperature and add juice immediately before serving. Esquites is best served at room temperature.

YIELD: 10 SERVINGS

SAUTÉ CORN

Heat ½ cup (125 ml) of the oil in a large nonstick skillet over moderate heat. Add the corn, salt, and *recado* and sauté 6–7 minutes, stirring constantly and scraping the bottom of the skillet to prevent sticking. The kernels should be a slightly deeper golden color and barely softened but still al dente. Transfer the corn to a heatproof mixing bowl and allow to cool completely.

Add the remaining ¼ cup (62.5 ml) olive oil and the other ingredients except the citrus juice to the bowl of corn and toss to combine. Allow the mixture to rest at room temperature for 30 minutes to amalgamate the flavors. If you won't be serving the dish immediately, cover and refrigerate.

If the corn has been refrigerated, bring it to room temperature. Add the juice just before serving and toss to combine; check the seasonings.

TO SERVE

Esquites is typically served in individual serving bowls or cups and eaten with a spoon; it can also be eaten as a dip with chips. Top each serving with a squeeze of cream, some crumbled cheese, and a light dusting of cayenne powder. Offer Totopos para botanas for dipping if you wish. Serve additional *crema*, cheese, chile powder, chips, and lime wedges on the table. Esquites is also an excellent accompaniment for any of the seafood dishes in Mojo de ajo (p. 514), as well as grilled meats, such as Poc chuc (p. 448) or Pollo asado (p. 270).

Sharing helados. [MR]

ICE CREAM PARLORS

After a filling *comida* and perhaps a little nap, people venture out to the streets again. Steamy Yucatecan afternoons find young couples, students, and families taking shelter from the sun and refreshing themselves with a cooling *sorbete* or *helado*. "*Helado*" in Yucatecan Spanish is a generic term referring to all frozen treats. However, *helados* typically contain dairy products such as cream and eggs, whereas *sorbetes* are prepared only with juices or puréed fruit pulp and sugar.

(opposite page) Sorbete social, Itzimná, late 1800s. Embroidery on the aprons of the attendants reads "Kermesse," a Dutch term used in many Latin American countries to refer to entertainments held as fund-raisers for churches or schools. "Sorbetes y leche (sorbets and milk) may have been sold separately, but more likely they were combined for the popular Yucatecan beverage Champola (p. 245), something like an ice cream float using milk instead of soda. [FPG]

SORBETE DE COCO

COCONUT SORBET

The base for Sorbete de coco is fresh coconut milk—not to be confused with the water found inside coconuts (although that should be reserved to use in the recipe). You may substitute the fresh whole coconuts in the recipe with canned, unsweetened coconut milk and grated coconut—but you can't beat the flavor of doing it from scratch.

YIELD: APPROXIMATELY 1.5 QUARTS (1.5 L)

FOR THE SORBET, USING FRESH COCONUT

2 whole coconuts, outer shell and brown husk removed (each weighing about 9½ oz. / 270 g cleaned and drained; reserve liquid)

Reserved water from the coconuts (each coconut has about 1¼ cups / 312.5 ml liquid)

1½ cups (375 ml) water, approximately

1 cup (95 g) of the reserved shredded coconut after coconut is puréed (you may toast or freeze the remaining coconut for another use)

2 cups (400 g) sugar

⅛ tsp. (0.125 ml) Mexican vanilla extract

or

FOR THE SORBET, USING CANNED COCONUT MILK

1 cup (250 ml) water

1½ cups (142.5 g) grated unsweetened coconut

3 cups (750 ml) canned coconut milk (check label to make sure it has no artificial ingredients or sugar and that it is not sweetened "coconut cream," which is used for making tropical cocktails)

2 cups (400 g) sugar

⅛ tsp. (0.125 ml) Mexican vanilla extract

IF YOU ARE USING FRESH, WHOLE COCONUT:

PREPARE COCONUT MILK

Grate the coconut. If you are using a hand grater, cut the coconut into quarters and grate; if you are using the grating attachment of a food processor, chop the coconut into pieces small enough to fit through the feed tube. This should result in approximately 4 cups (475 g) grated coconut.

Add enough plain water to the reserved coconut liquid to reach a total of 4 cups (1 L). (Note: If you have coconuts that have already been drained, use 4 cups [1 L] water instead.) Transfer the liquid to a saucepan and heat gently to just under a simmer; remove the pan from the heat. Place half the grated coconut and half the hot liquid in the jar of a blender and liquefy for 30 seconds. Transfer the mixture to a heatproof bowl; repeat with the remaining coconut and liquid. Let the mixture cool to room temperature.

Ice cream carts have been a feature of Yucatecan life for at least a century. [EC]

Place a large sieve lined with cheesecloth over a bowl. When the coconut purée is cool, pour it into the sieve. Lift the cheesecloth, pull the edges together, and squeeze out as much of the liquid as you can into the bowl, reserving the liquid. Gather the shredded coconut from the cheesecloth and reserve. (Note: This should yield about 4 cups of coconut milk.)

PREPARE COCONUT SYRUP

Place 1 cup (about 115 g) of the reserved coconut along with 1 cup (250 ml) of the coconut milk in a blender and liquefy for 1 minute; set aside. In a heavy saucepan, combine the remaining coconut milk and sugar and stir over low heat until the sugar is thoroughly dissolved. Increase the heat and bring to a boil; boil for 30 seconds. Remove the pan from the heat. Add the vanilla and coconut purée from the blender and stir to combine. Transfer to a heatproof bowl and allow to cool. Refrigerate at least 4 hours or, preferably, overnight.

FREEZE AND FINISH

Remove the chilled sorbet base from the refrigerator and stir. (Note: The natural fats of coconut tend to separate from the water; stir to recombine.) Process in an ice cream freezer according to manufacturer's directions. Place the finished sorbet in a covered freezer container and freeze for 2–3 hours before serving.

**IF YOU ARE USING CANNED COCONUT MILK
AND PACKAGED GRATED COCONUT:**

PREPARE COCONUT MILK

Place the water and coconut in the jar of a blender and liquefy for 1 minute; set aside. Combine the coconut milk and sugar in a medium saucepan and stir over low heat until the sugar is thoroughly dissolved. Increase the heat and bring the mixture to a boil; boil for 30 seconds. Remove the pan from the heat. Add the vanilla and coconut purée from the blender and stir to combine. Transfer the mixture to a heatproof bowl and allow it to cool. Refrigerate at least 4 hours or, preferably, overnight. Proceed with freezing as described above.

SORBETE DE GUANÁBANA

GUANÁBANA SORBET

FOR THE SIMPLE SYRUP

1½ cups (300 g) sugar

1½ cups (375 ml) water

2 one-in.-wide (2.5 cm) strips
   lime rind

FOR THE GUANÁBANA PURÉE

2½ lbs. (1.2 k) *guanábana*

1½ cups (375 ml) water

Surely the ugly duckling of the large *Annonaceae* family (p. 33), *guanábana*—"soursop" in English—is off-putting in ways beyond its appearance and English name: the sticky pulp clings to both the leathery, prickly skin and to the scores of seeds inside, making extracting the flesh of soursop a labor of love. But for the truehearted, the effort pays off. *Guanábana* pulp is creamy, sweet, aromatic, and vaguely reminiscent of pineapple—in short, ambrosial. This dessert as well as Agua fresca de guanábana (p. 226) and Crema de guanábana (p. 384) all begin with a purée of the fruit. Once the pulp has been extracted, the purée is easy enough to make. But good, unadulterated purées are also available frozen or canned under several brand names. (Note: Both pulp and purées are available. For this recipe use the purée; see Resources, p. 540.)

Prepare ahead note: If you are using a large *guanábana* (I recommend here 2½ lbs. / 1.2 k), you will have enough pulp for several recipes in this book. The purée freezes very well for several months. For convenience, place 1-cup (250 ml) measures of purée in sandwich bags and freeze.

PREPARE SIMPLE SYRUP

Place the sugar, water, and rind in a small saucepan and bring to a boil. As the mixture heats, swirl the pan to dissolve the sugar. Cook about 1 minute, or until the sugar has completely dissolved and the liquid is clear. Remove the pan from the heat, cover, and allow the syrup to steep for 30 minutes.

PREPARE *GUANÁBANA* PURÉE

(Note: If you are using frozen purée, skip to the finish and freeze step.) Slice the fruit in quarters lengthwise. Remove the fibrous core that runs down the center of each quarter. Peel away the leathery skin; if it is stubborn and sticks to the pulp, separate it with a sharp knife or scrape the pulp away with a large spoon. Pull the pulp apart in sections. Using your fingertips, squeeze the seeds out of each section and discard. Continue until you have removed and seeded all the pulp. You should have approximately 3 cups (650 g) of the skinned, seeded pulp.

   Place the pulp and water in the jar of a blender and process until the mixture is well puréed. You should have approximately 4 cups (1 L) purée. Reserve 2 cups (500 ml) for this recipe and freeze the rest for another use per the instructions above.

FINISH AND FREEZE

Remove the rind from the sugar syrup and discard. Pour the syrup into a medium mixing bowl. Add 2 cups (500 ml) of the *guanábana* purée (your own, as above, or commercial purée) and use a whisk to blend thoroughly. Cover and refrigerate at least 4 hours or overnight. Freeze in an ice cream maker according to manufacturer's directions. Place the finished sorbet in a covered container and freeze for 2–3 hours before serving.

Sorbete de mamey, Sorbete de mango, Sorbete de nance, Sorbete de piña, Sorbete de pitahaya: With the current availability of so many tropical fruits in frozen form, you can make virtually any of the exotic sorbet flavors found in Yucatán by following the above recipe. Start with about 2 cups (450 g) of any fleshy tropical fruit, cleaned and chopped (or frozen). Purée with water as in the master recipe, yielding 2 cups (500 ml) for the sorbet (freeze any extra for another batch). (Note: Since many tropical fruits contain more water than does *guanábana*, reduce the amount of water in the purée to about ½ cup [125 ml], adding more as necessary just to keep the blender moving. The result should be thick yet pourable.) Replace the *guanábana* purée with 2 cups (500 ml) of the purée of your fruit of choice. Proceed with the rest of the recipe.

Champola (Ice Cream Float): Throughout the Caribbean—from Cuba to Puerto Rico—the Champola is something like a fruit-and-milk smoothie made with milk, sugar, and *guanábana*. In Yucatán, the recipe was streamlined at least 60 years ago and, as defined in a regional vernacular vocabulary book, the contemporary Yucatecan Champola is nothing more than a tall glass of milk with a scoop of your favorite ice cream or sorbet floating on top—the traditional flavor still being *guanábana*. However, a rainbow of possibilities has opened in recent years, and nowadays it is just as common to use the delicious almond beverage Horchata (p. 437) instead of milk, and anything from strawberry or chocolate ice cream to mamey or limón sorbet as the "float." My favorite is this *guanábana* sorbet served in a glass of ice cold Horchata.

Flavors of the day: mamey (left) and nance. [MR]

SORBETE DE CACAHUATE

PEANUT SORBET

FOR THE SIMPLE SYRUP

2 cups (400 g) sugar

3 cups (750 ml) water

2 one-in.-wide (2.5 cm) strips
Seville orange or lime zest

FOR THE PEANUTS

1¼ cup (335 g) chunky peanut
butter with salt (Note: Choose a
brand marked "natural chunky"
with no ingredients except
peanuts and salt. Alternatively,
you can make your own in a
food processor. Place 2½ cups
[350 g] roasted, salted peanuts in
the bowl of a food processor fitted with the steel blade. Process
about 5 minutes, or until the
desired consistency is reached.
If you are not a "chunky"
fan, process the peanuts until
completely smooth)

⅛ tsp. (0.375 g) cayenne powder
(optional)

[MC]

Peanuts are abundant in Yucatán. While goobers may seem an odd ingredient in a sorbet, Sorbete de cacahuate is one of the most popular offerings in Yucatecan *sorbeterías*.

YIELD: APPROXIMATELY 1.5 QUARTS (1.5 L)

PREPARE SIMPLE SYRUP

In a heavy saucepan, combine the sugar and water. Stir over low heat until the sugar
is completely dissolved. Increase the heat and bring the mixture to a boil. Add the zest
and boil for 1 minute. Remove the pan from the heat, cover, and allow to cool.

PREPARE PEANUTS

When the simple syrup has cooled, remove the zest and discard. Transfer 2 cups
(500 ml) of the syrup to the jar of a blender. Add the peanut butter and cayenne powder, if using, and liquefy. Transfer the mixture to a mixing bowl and add the remaining
syrup; whisk well to combine. Cover and refrigerate at least 4 hours or, preferably,
overnight.

FREEZE AND FINISH

Process the mixture in an ice cream freezer according to manufacturer's directions.
Place the finished sorbet in a covered container and freeze 2–3 hours before serving.

ESQUIMOS

COCONUT SORBET ICE POPS DIPPED IN CHOCOLATE AND COCONUT

TO PREPARE AHEAD

Sorbete de coco (p. 242)

FOR THE COATING

12 oz. (340 g) unsweetened dark
    chocolate, chopped
2 cups (200 g) freshly grated
    coconut (Substitute: sweetened
    shredded coconut)

A summertime favorite in Yucatán, Esquimos (pronounced "ess-SKI-mos") are a "catch-them-if-you-can" treat—few people make them nowadays, and when they do, the treats sell out before all other flavors. Look for them in the rolling carts labeled "PALETAS" (literally, "paddles"; the word refers to frozen treats on a wooden stick.)

Prepare ahead note: Prepare the base for the coconut sorbet a day in advance and refrigerate overnight. Once you have formed the ice pops, freeze them at least 4 hours or overnight to set.

YIELD: 8–10 ICE POPS, DEPENDING ON THE SIZE OF YOUR MOLD

PREPARE SORBET

Prepare and process the Sorbete de coco in an ice cream freezer. (Note: The finished sorbet should be slightly slushy, not completely frozen.) Immediately after finishing in the ice cream freezer, pour or spoon the sorbet into prepared ice pop molds (alternatively, you may use small disposable paper or plastic cups covered with plastic wrap secured with a rubber band to hold the sticks erect). Insert the sticks or stems into each mold and freeze at least 4 hours or until very hard.

PREPARE CHOCOLATE AND COCONUT COATING

Place the chocolate in a double boiler or in a small saucepan set over a larger pan of boiling water. Reduce the heat to a simmer and stir the chocolate frequently until it is completely melted.

Remove the chocolate from the heat and allow it to cool until it is cool to the touch. Spread half the coconut on a large baking sheet or plate. Line a separate tray or large plate with waxed paper. Working one at a time, remove the ice pops from the freezer and take them out of the mold. Holding onto the stick, quickly dip each pop into the chocolate. (Note: If the chocolate cools too much, it may start clumping on the frozen ice pop; simply reheat and continue.) Immediately roll the chocolate-dipped ice pop in the coconut to cover completely. Place each ice pop on the waxed paper and store in the freezer as you complete the others. Spread more coconut as needed. When all have been completed, layer the ice pops between sheets of waxed paper and store in the freezer.

SORBETE DE ELOTE

FRESH CORN SORBET

FOR THE SORBET

3 cups fresh corn kernels (525 g,
 from about 5 medium ears),
 divided
2 cups (500 ml) water
1½ cups (300 g) sugar
⅛ tsp. (0.625 ml) Mexican
 vanilla extract

Although some visitors are not so sure about the idea of corn sorbet, they are usually won over by its earthy, natural sweetness. Part of the joy of this sorbet is finding whole kernels in every bite.

PREPARE SORBET

Place 2 cups (320 g) of the kernels in the jar of a blender and reserve the rest; add the water and process 1 minute to thoroughly liquefy. (Note: If you prefer a smooth texture rather than encountering whole kernels in the finished product, process all 3 cups of the kernels in batches as per these instructions.)

In a heavy saucepan, combine the sugar and the corn purée and stir over low heat until the sugar is thoroughly dissolved. Increase the heat and bring the mixture to a boil. Add the reserved corn kernels, reduce the heat to a simmer, and cook, stirring frequently, for about 3 minutes, or until the kernels are cooked but still al dente. Stir in the vanilla, transfer the mixture to a heatproof bowl, and allow it to cool. Refrigerate at least 4 hours or, preferably, overnight.

FINISH AND FREEZE

Process the mixture in an ice cream freezer according to manufacturer's directions. Place the finished sorbet in a covered container and freeze for 2–3 hours before serving.

[MC]

HELADO DE CREMA MORISCA

GUAVA, MARASCHINO CHERRY, AND SHERRY FROZEN CUSTARD

FOR THE FRUIT BASE

1½ cups (300 g) sugar
1 cup (250 ml) water
2 pounds (1 k) ripe guavas
  (Substitute: 3 cups / 750
  ml frozen guava pulp with
  no additives or sugar),
  preferably pink

FOR THE CUSTARD

1 can (14 oz. / 397 g) sweetened
  condensed milk
½ cup (125 ml) amoroso or
  sweet sherry
½ cup (125 ml) maraschino
  cherry juice or liqueur
1 Tbs. (15 ml) Mexican vanilla
  extract
¼ tsp. (1.5 g) sea salt
¼ tsp. (0.75 g) ground *canela*
  (Mexican cinnamon)
¾ cup (150 g) maraschino cherries,
  drained, pitted, stems removed,
  and chopped, divided
2 cups (500 ml) whipping cream
5 large egg yolks

FOR FREEZING AND FINISHING

½ cup (100 g) candied fruit,
  diced. (Note: Use a colorful
  assortment of the candied
  fruits of your choice—lime peel,
  pineapple, etc.)
½ cup (100 g) *guayabate* (guava
  paste), diced (see Resources,
  p. 539)

Helado de crema morisca is a rare regional ice cream flavor fondly remembered by previous generations, yet verging on extinction in today's *sorbeterías*. The first time I ever sampled the fantastical flavor was at Sorbetería Colón in Mérida, which purports that its 1876 recipe is the "original." The ingredient list for its version calls for *guayabate* (guava paste), vanilla, *canela*, and rum. However, when I asked Vicente Heredia Muñoz, whose family has been making ice creams and sorbets in Yucatán for over 100 years, he claimed that Crema morisca was his family's formula, which they made until the 1990s. According to don Vicente, their Crema morisca was a custard-type ice cream flavored with candied fruits like figs and dates in equal ratio to real maraschino cherries—and of course a splash of the maraschino liqueur. (Don Vicente said that his father created the title, tweaking the original name of the "marasca" cherry to "*morisca*," or "Moorish," in honor of Yucatán's Middle Eastern heritage.) The dictionary of Yucatecan vernacular published by the Archivo Histórico de Mérida defines Helado de crema morisca simply as "tutti-frutti"—close to don Vicente's description. A combination of the two versions became the basis for my reconstructed recipe: a guava ice cream base flavored with sweet sherry, Mexican vanilla, and *canela* and finished with colorful nuggets of candied fruits and maraschino cherries (splurge on real ones—marasca cherries preserved in maraschino liqueur). You will forget the giddy childishness of the candied fruits when you savor the sensuality of the exotic bottom note of guava.

PREPARE FRUIT BASE

Combine the sugar and water in a saucepan and bring to a boil. Reduce the heat and simmer, swirling the pan occasionally, until the sugar is completely dissolved, about 1 minute. Cover and set aside as you proceed.

(Note: If using frozen pulp, skip this step.) Wash the guavas thoroughly under cold running water. Cut off the tips, slice the fruit into quarters, and use a spoon to scrape the seeds into a fine-mesh sieve placed over a bowl. Use the spoon to press the seeds to extract as much of the pulp and juice as possible; discard anything that doesn't pass through. Reserve the contents of the bowl.

Coarsely chop the guavas and add them along with the collected juice and pulp in the bowl to the saucepan containing the syrup. (Note: If using frozen pulp, add to the syrup now.) Bring the mixture to a boil. Reduce the heat to a simmer, stirring frequently, and use a potato masher to break up the fruit. Cook 6–8 minutes, or until the fruit is cooked and very soft (adjust the cooking time for the frozen pulp, which will cook more quickly). Remove the pan from the heat and transfer the pulp to a heatproof measuring cup; you should have about 3 cups (750 ml) of syrup and fruit.

PREPARE CUSTARD

Mix all the ingredients except the cherries, cream, and egg yolks in a large saucepan and whisk to combine. Pour half of this mixture into the jar of a blender. Add ¼ cup (50 g) of the cherries and process about 1 minute, or until the fruit is completely liquefied. Working in batches, add the cooked guava/syrup mixture to the blender and liquefy. As you finish each batch, pour the purée through a fine-mesh sieve back into the saucepan, using a rubber spatula to press as much liquid through as possible; discard any residue. Continue until all the guava mixture has been puréed and strained into the saucepan.

Place the saucepan over medium heat and whisk in the whipping cream; bring to a simmer. Place the egg yolks in a large heatproof mixing bowl. Using a whisk or hand-held electric mixer, beat the yolks until light and fluffy. Still beating, slowly stream a ladle (about 1 cup / 250 ml) of the warm milk mixture into the beaten eggs. Beat thoroughly; repeat 2–3 times, until the eggs are heated through. Very slowly stream the hot egg mixture back into the saucepan, whisking or beating constantly. With heat on medium-low, constantly stir the mixture with a wooden spoon for 2–3 minutes, or until it is thick enough to coat the back of the spoon. A candy thermometer should read 180°F (82°C). *Do not allow to boil* or the eggs may scramble. The mixture will be thick.

Immediately remove the pan from the heat to stop cooking and transfer the custard back into the heatproof bowl. Allow to cool to room temperature, cover, and refrigerate several hours until thoroughly chilled, preferably overnight.

FREEZE ICE CREAM AND FINISH

Process the chilled custard in an electric ice cream maker according to manufacturer's directions. Just before removing the ice cream from the machine, add the chopped fruits, guava paste, and remaining ½ cup (100 g) of maraschino cherries and process for 1 minute. Place the finished ice cream in a covered container and freeze for 2–3 hours before serving.

(opposite page) Menu at Sorbetería Colón, a Mérida institution in the same location on the main square since 1908. [MR]

CREMA MORISCA
ZAPOTE
COCO
NARANJA
GUANABANA
MELON
MAMEY
LIMON

LA COCINA ECONÓMICA

Family members pitch in at Cocina Económica "Doña Lupita," Hunucmá. [MR]

T HE MOST GENUINELY YUCATECAN DISHES will be those made by *mamás* and *abuelas* for the daily *comida*, or big afternoon meal, a family affair largely off-limits to outsiders. But for those who want a taste of the real thing, the *cocina económica*—an inexpensive family-run restaurant often operated in the front room of a private home—offers much the same family-style menu of true regional cuisine.

I feel that this section is, if not the most important, at least the most useful one in this book for the modern cook. The recipes are by nature economical, quick, and very easy to prepare. Most are one-pot meals, cooked on the stovetop and accompanied only by plain white rice. Ingredients in these recipes are simple, as well, and all but one or two of them can be found in any urban supermarket. The handful of unusual items required are easy to locate as long as you have access to an "ethnic" market or can do a bit of shopping online. (See Resources, p. 539).

In present-day Yucatán, the term "*cocina económica*" is used to refer both to the type of food and to the establishment in which it is prepared and served. (In other parts of Mexico, the establishment that sells *cocina económica* is more often called a *fonda*.) Meals are complete—soup or rice, beans, a meat of some kind, and often a beverage or dessert—and very inexpensive—around 40 pesos, which at today's exchange rate is $3.50 U.S. The food is characterized as *casera*, or "home cooking," just like *mamá* would make.

Dishes are extremely simple—just a few basic ingredients—and can be prepared quickly, since everything is made fresh in the morning and is sold out by early afternoon.

TO SERVE

In *cocinas económicas*, several or all of these *guarniciones* (side dishes) and salsas are served with the main dish. Suddenly a series of accompaniments turns something simple into a fully satisfying meal.

- Arroz blanco (p. 529), or the rice of your choice
- Frijol colado or Frijol k'abax served in bowls, *or* Frijol refrito (p. 506) served on the plate and garnished with Totopos para botanas (p. 515)
- Plátano frito (p. 371)
- Chile tamulado (p. 509), or the chile sauce of your choice
- Salpicón (p. 511), or a simply dressed mixed green salad
- Tortillas (p. 518)
- Lime or Seville orange wedges

Originally a term used to describe an efficient stove that both heated the house and cooked food, between 1880 and 1910, "*cocina económica*" in Spain came to refer to what in English might be called a "soup kitchen." In these modest but comfortable dining halls, people of few resources could enjoy a free breakfast, as well as two other meals a day for just a few cents. These *cocinas económicas*—established as charitable works by both Catholic and secular donors—soon sprouted up in towns and cities across Spain.

In colonial Mexico, a different notion of *cocina económica* took form in the Catholic convents, where many culinary concepts evolved. The convents were known for their *cocina de pobre*, or "poor man's food." This cuisine "was based on local products, on easy-to-prepare dishes and stews that formed the basis of a simple and *economical cuisine* [my emphasis] (*cocina económica*)."

By the 1940s, the humble cooking of *cocina económica* was popularized for the masses in cookbooks like *Cocina popular: 30 menús económicos* (Popular cooking: 30 economical menus) and *Cómo cocinar en tiempos de carestía* (How to cook in hard times), both by Josefina Velázquez de León.

The phenomenon of the *cocina económica* took root in Yucatán in the mid-twentieth century, as women took on a more independent role in the family. To supplement income, the women of a single family, with occasional help from the men, prepared food in the household kitchen; seating for customers was offered in the front parlor, on the porch, or in other space accessible from the street and retrofitted as a dining room.

PICADILLO

PORK AND BEEF MINCEMEAT

Ground meat mixtures (*picadillo*) flavored with spices and *alcaparrado* were bequeathed to Yucatán by early Andalusian colonists, who had inherited the recipes from the Moors. Because of their economical nature, many versions of Picadillo are to be found in Yucatán's *cocinas económicas*, appearing as a plated meal, or as the foundation for everything from Albóndigas (p. 257) to Queso relleno (p. 345). Local ingredients make other versions distinctly Yucatecan, as in Picadillo en chilmole and Pavo en relleno negro (p. 424).

PICADILLO EN CHILMOLE

MINCEMEAT IN CHARRED CHILE SAUCE

Older recipes for Chilmole feature cubed pork simmered in the pitch-black charred chile condiment known as Recado negro. While attending an artisans' fair sponsored by indigenous Maya women, I discovered this version using ground meat instead. At the fair, I met doña Guadalupe Aké, of Peto, who with her daughter had a booth where they were selling several food items, but the dish that immediately won me over was their deeply flavored tacos of Picadillo en chilmole. If you use a commercial *recado*, take a pinch to taste first; this will tell you if you want to add more or less heat, salt, and so on. For extra heat, toss a drained chile chipotle in adobo into a blender with the water and *recado* while preparing the *sofrito*. And since commercial *recados* are already salted, additional salt may not be necessary.

Longaniza de Valladolid (p. 481),
   or substitute
Enriched Lard (p. 513)
Recado negro (p. 501)

FOR THE MEAT MIXTURE

12 oz. (340 g) *each* ground pork
   and beef
3½ oz. (100 g) Longaniza de
   Valladolid (Substitute: chorizo,
   commercial longaniza, or other
   smoked sausage)
9 oz. (250 g) smoked ham

FOR THE *SOFRITO* AND FINISHING

2 Tbs. (28 g) Enriched Lard
1 cup (170 g) white onion, finely
   chopped
½ cup (70 g) green bell pepper,
   cut into small dice
4 medium cloves garlic (1 oz. /
   24 g), minced
2 medium Roma tomatoes (7 oz. /
   200 g), seeded and chopped
1 Tbs. (2 g) dried whole Mexican
   oregano *and* 1 tsp. (2 g) cuminseed, both lightly toasted and
   ground together, then passed
   through a fine-mesh sieve;
   discard residue
5 Tbs. (75 g) Recado negro
1½ cups (375 ml) water
1 chile chipotle in adobo (⅓ oz. /
   10 g), optional
2 tsp. (12 g) sea salt, or to taste.
   (Note: If using commercial
   recado, salt may not be necessary.
   Check seasoning before adding)

Prepare ahead note: Picadillo en chilmole only improves with age. It may be prepared in advance and refrigerated or frozen. Reheat prior to serving.

YIELD: 6 SERVINGS

PREPARE MEATS

Place the ground beef and pork in a large mixing bowl. Remove the skin from the sausage and discard. Pass the sausage meat and ham through the fine blade of a meat grinder into the bowl containing the beef and pork. (If you don't have a meat grinder, you can finely chop the meats in a food processor.) Mix to combine and set aside.

PREPARE *SOFRITO* AND FINISH

Heat the lard in a large, heavy skillet until shimmering. Sauté the next 3 ingredients over medium heat until the onions are translucent, 3–4 minutes. Add the tomatoes and ground spices and cook another 2–3 minutes, or until the tomatoes are tender and the liquid has mostly evaporated.

   Add the meat mixture to the *sofrito*. Using a spatula or wooden spoon to crumble, cook over medium-high heat 4–5 minutes, or until lightly browned; skim off any accumulated fat. Reduce the heat to simmer.

   Meanwhile, mix the *recado* in the water and stir until dissolved. (Note: If you like more heat, place a drained chile chipotle in adobo in the jar of a blender with the water and *recado* and process until thoroughly liquefied.) Strain the mixture through a sieve lined with cheesecloth into the skillet; gather the cheesecloth to squeeze out as much liquid as possible and discard residue. Bring the mixture in the skillet to a boil, then reduce the heat to a simmer. Simmer until the liquid has mostly evaporated and the Picadillo has thickened and is mostly dry, 40–45 minutes. Check the seasonings and add salt if necessary.

TO SERVE

For a plated meal, see the serving suggestions on page 253. Or you may serve the Picadillo en chilmole as tacos by spooning it onto fresh tortillas. Top with Salpicón (p. 511) and offer the chile sauce of your choice. It is also delicious as a simple appetizer served with Totopos para botanas (p. 515) for dipping.

VARIATIONS

Picadillo (Simple Mincemeat): Probably the grandfather of all subsequent *picadillo* incarnations, this simple mincemeat mixture is daily fare at the *cocinas económicas*, served atop a bed of white rice. Follow the master recipe for Picadillo en chilmole, but eliminate the Recado negro; instead, mix the water with the salt and finish as instructed.

   Picadillo rojo / Picadillo "San Carlos" (Mincemeat in *Achiote* with Potatoes): Cut 1–2 large baking potatoes (1 lb. /500 g) in half across the width and cook in boiling water until just tender. Cool, peel, and cut into ¾-inch (2 cm) cubes; set aside. Proceed with the master recipe for Picadillo en chilmole, substituting Recado rojo (p. 500) for the Recado negro. Add the cubed potatoes 15 minutes before the end of cooking.

PICADILLO DE ESPECIAS

SPICED MINCEMEAT FOR FILLINGS

TO PREPARE AHEAD

Enriched Lard (p. 513)
Recado para todo (p. 499)
Longaniza de Valladolid (p. 481),
 or substitute

FOR THE *SOFRITO*

4 Tbs. (56 g) Enriched Lard
1 cup (170 g) white onion, finely
 chopped
½ cup (70 g) green bell pepper,
 cut into small dice
4 medium cloves garlic (1 oz. /
 24 g), minced
1 medium chile habanero (¼ oz. /
 7 g), seeded and minced
 (optional; for more heat,
 keep seeds)
2 medium Roma tomatoes (7 oz. /
 200 g), seeded and chopped
2 Tbs. (8 g) fresh mint leaves,
 chopped
1 Tbs. (9 g) Recado para todo
2 tsp. (12 g) sea salt, or to taste

FOR THE MEAT MIXTURE

12 oz. (340 g) *each* ground pork
 and beef
3½ oz. (100 g) Longaniza de
 Valladolid (Substitute: chorizo,
 commercial longaniza, or other
 smoked sausage)
9 oz. (250 g) smoked ham
15 small pimiento-stuffed green
 olives, coarsely chopped
4 Tbs. (44 g) almonds, blanched
 and coarsely chopped
2 Tbs. (30 g) small capers,
 drained and coarsely chopped
2 Tbs. (30 g) black raisins,
 coarsely chopped
2 eggs, beaten
½ cup (67.5 g) *masa harina*

This exotically spiced (not hot!) Picadillo de especias is the multipurpose raw meat mixture that serves for several of the spiced mincemeat fillings found in this book, such as Queso relleno (p. 345) and Pavo en relleno negro (p. 424). It is also the meat mixture used in Albóndigas (p. 257) and Sopa de rabioles (p. 392).

Prepare ahead note: Picadillo de especias may be prepared in advance and frozen or refrigerated. Bring to room temperature before using. Many dishes in this book call for half of this recipe. It is easily halved, but you may also prepare the entire quantity and freeze half for future use. Use leftovers for Albóndigas (p. 257) or Sopa de rabioles (p. 392).

YIELD: APPROXIMATELY 3½ LBS. (1.6 K)

PREPARE *SOFRITO*

Heat the lard in a large, heavy skillet until shimmering. Add next 3 ingredients and the habanero, if using, and sauté over medium heat until the onions are translucent, 3–4 minutes. Add the tomatoes and mint and cook another 2–3 minutes, or until the tomatoes are tender. Add the *recado* and salt, stir to incorporate, and cook another minute. Remove the pan from the heat and allow the *sofrito* to cool a few minutes.

PREPARE MEATS

Place the ground pork and beef in a large mixing bowl. Remove the skin from the sausage and discard. Pass the sausage and ham through the fine blade of a meat grinder and add to the bowl containing the beef and pork. Add the *sofrito* along with its cooking fat. Stir or mix with your hands to combine thoroughly.

FINISH *PICADILLO*

Add the remaining ingredients to the ground meats and mix thoroughly. Check the seasonings by frying a small amount and tasting. Refrigerate or freeze the *picadillo* until you are ready to proceed with the recipe in which it will be used.

VARIATION

Buut' blanco (Spiced Mincemeat): Also sometimes known as Picadillo de especias, this is virtually the same formula as the raw version above used for stuffing and meatballs, the significant difference being that this one is cooked. It may be served plated with rice like other *picadillos*, but it is also often used as a cooked filling for tamales, empanadas, and other foods. Follow the master recipe for Picadillo de especias to prepare the *sofrito*. Add the ground meats from that recipe to the skillet and cook until browned and crumbled. Add the remaining ingredients except the beaten eggs and *masa harina*. Dissolve 1 Tbs. (15 g) Recado blanco (p. 502) in ¼ cup (62.5 ml) white vinegar, add to the skillet, and cook, stirring frequently, until most of the cooking liquid has evaporated, 6–8 minutes. Serve immediately or allow to cool before using in a recipe. Buut' blanco may also be frozen until ready to use. (Note: If serving as a plated dish, hard-boil 6 eggs. Separate the whites from the yolks, chop the whites, and add them to the skillet as you finish the *picadillo*. It is also traditional to place one of the boiled egg yolks atop each serving. This step is not necessary if the meat mixture will be used as a filling.)

ALBÓNDIGAS

SPANISH MEATBALLS

There may be no other "theme-and-variation" dish more beloved—and ubiquitous in Yucatán—than Albóndigas. They appear in one form or another—black or white, spicy or mild—on every menu board of every *cocina económica* throughout the peninsula.

Both the dish and the word "*albóndigas*" trace to Islamic/Andalusian genealogy in our cuisine. The spiced, chopped meat is a Middle Eastern formula, and the dictionary of the Real Academia Española tells us that the Spanish word derives from the Arabic "*al-búnduqa*," or "hazelnut," by inference describing anything of that shape and size. Albóndigas are a great party buffet food: keep them warm in a chafing dish, with steaming white rice on the side. And, since it is a theme-and-variation dish, you can easily prepare several versions so that guests can sample an assortment.

Prepare ahead note: Meatballs are easy to make and form in advance and freeze. On the day of the meal, defrost the meatballs at room temperature for 30 minutes prior to cooking while you prepare the sauce. Finished Albóndigas only improve with age: refrigerate 3–4 days and reheat just before serving.

YIELD: 8 SERVINGS OF APPROXIMATELY 5 MEATBALLS PER PERSON

TO SERVE
Albóndigas are typically served atop a *colchón*, or "mattress," of Arroz blanco (p. 529).

ALBÓNDIGAS CON YERBABUENA (HIERBABUENA)

MINTED MEATBALLS IN BROTH

Both the meatballs and the cooking liquid of this version feature a generous bouquet of mint, giving the finished dish a light and refreshing taste to counterbalance the richness of the meat.

TO PREPARE AHEAD
Picadillo de especias (p. 256)
Recado para puchero (p. 499)

FOR THE MEATBALLS
¾ cup mint leaves (1½ oz. / 45 g), finely chopped, divided
½ recipe Picadillo de especias (approximately 1¾ lbs. / 800 g)
1 Tbs. (15 ml) Spanish olive oil

FOR THE SOFRITO
2 Tbs. (30 ml) Spanish olive oil
1 cup (140 g) mixed red and green bell pepper, cut into small dice
1 cup (170 g) white onion, finely chopped
4 medium cloves garlic (1 oz. / 24 g), peeled, charred, and finely chopped
4 medium Roma tomatoes (14 oz. / 400 g), seeded and chopped
1½ tsp. (4.5 g) Recado para puchero

FOR THE STOCK
6 cups (1.5 L) beef stock or bouillon
1 medium head garlic (about 1¾ oz. / 50 g), charred, peeled, and separated into cloves
1 five-in. (12 cm) stick canela (Mexican cinnamon)
¼ cup (62.5 ml) sherry vinegar
20 medium green olives, whole unpitted, pitted, or pimiento-stuffed and sliced
1 Tbs. (15 g) small capers, drained
½ cup (60 g) breadcrumbs

FORM AND SAUTÉ MEATBALLS

Add ½ cup (30 g) mint to the *picadillo* and mix well. Form balls of *picadillo* weighing ¾ oz. (20 g) each. Pack them tightly in your palms to keep them from falling apart as they cook. Place the meatballs on a platter as you finish each one; you should have 35–40 *albóndigas*. (Note: If you are working with *picadillo* that you made in advance and froze, you may wish to add another egg and more *masa harina* to hold the mixture together as you form the balls.) Heat the olive oil in a large, non-stick skillet until shimmering. Working in batches as needed, sauté the meatballs until lightly browned overall. Swirl the skillet to rotate the meatballs; using a spatula may result in breaking them. Transfer the meatballs to a platter as you finish.

PREPARE SOFRITO

Heat the oil in a medium stockpot or a large, deep skillet until shimmering. Add the next 3 ingredients and cook, stirring frequently, until the onions begin to sweat, 3–4 minutes. Add tomatoes, *recado*, and remaining ¼ cup (15 g) mint and cook over low heat until vegetables are tender, 3–4 minutes.

PREPARE STOCK AND COOK MEATBALLS

Add the stock to the *sofrito*, along with the whole garlic cloves and *canela*. Bring to a boil, reduce to a simmer, and cook 3–4 minutes to incorporate the flavors. Carefully drop the meatballs into the simmering liquid and shake the pot or skillet to cover them with the hot stock. At this stage they are still fragile, so avoid stirring. Simmer 10–15 minutes, shaking the pot from time to time, or until the meatballs are firm and cooked through.

Add the vinegar, olives, and capers and simmer 3 minutes to incorporate the flavors. Remove the *canela*, add the breadcrumbs to the stock, and stir gently to incorporate. Simmer 10–15 minutes more, or until the stock thickens. Follow the serving suggestions on page 257.

HOY

- FRIJOL CON PUERCO
- POLLO EN BISTEC
- FILETE PESCADO
- UGA POLLO

COCINA ECONÓMICA "DOÑA LUPITA"
Hunucmá, Yucatán

Rita Guadalupe Canul Méndez—like so many women of her generation—opened her *cocina económica* to support her growing family. Twenty-five years later, she has seven sons, two daughters, and twenty-one grandchildren—and a thriving business. While she is unquestionably the driving force behind the operation, everyone pitches in: even the men can be found chopping and cooking with doña Rita, or at least keeping the kids out of the way.

Cocina económica *menu.* [MR]

ALBÓNDIGAS EN ESCABECHE BLANCO

MEATBALLS WITH *ALCAPARRADO* IN WHITE WINE SAUCE

TO PREPARE AHEAD
Picadillo de especias (p. 256)

FOR THE MEATBALLS
½ recipe Picadillo de especias
   (approximately 1¾ lbs. / 800 g)

FOR THE *SOFRITO*
2 Tbs. (28 g) butter
1 Tbs. (15 ml) Spanish olive oil
¼ cup (42.5 g) white onion, finely
   chopped
2 medium cloves garlic (½ oz. /
   12 g), peeled and finely chopped
1 medium chile x'catik (about
   1¼ oz. / 35 g), whole

FOR THE STOCK
2 cups (500 ml) sauternes or other
   sweet white wine
2 cups (500 ml) chicken stock or
   bouillon
2 bay leaves
1 sprig fresh epazote (Substitute:
   ½ tsp. / .75 g dried, crumbled)

[MC]

A version of this recipe appeared in the 1910 cookbook from Valladolid, *La verdadera cocina regional*, by Manuela Navarrete A. The butter and cream are my touches; use only olive oil if you prefer, and, for a lighter sauce, omit the cream.

FORM AND SAUTÉ MEATBALLS
Form and sauté the meatballs as in Albóndigas con yerbabuena, omitting the mint. Set aside.

PREPARE *SOFRITO*
Heat the butter and olive oil in a large, deep skillet. Add the remaining ingredients and cook until the onion is translucent, 2–3 minutes. (Note: To control the heat of this sauce, avoid puncturing the chile.)

PREPARE STOCK
Add the stock ingredients to the onions in the skillet, bring to a boil, reduce heat to a simmer, and cook 10 minutes, or until the liquid is slightly reduced and the flavors are incorporated.
   Remove the chile, bay leaves, and the sprig of epazote and discard. Using a blender, food processor, or immersion blender, process the mixture until the onions are puréed and the liquid is smooth.

TO THICKEN AND FINISH

¼ cup (33.75 g) *masa harina*

½ cup (125ml) Mexican *crema*
(Substitute: crème fraîche, plain
yogurt, or whipping cream)

3 Tbs. (45 g) almonds, blanched
and slivered

2 Tbs. (30 g) golden raisins,
coarsely chopped

2 Tbs. (30 g) small capers, drained

⅛ tsp. (0.25 g) ground nutmeg

Sea salt and freshly ground white
pepper, to taste

Mint leaves or golden raisins,
chopped, or blanched almonds,
slivered, to garnish

THICKEN SAUCE, COOK MEATBALLS, AND FINISH

Place the *masa harina* in a heatproof mixing bowl. Slowly add 1 ladle of the hot cooking liquid, whisking constantly. Repeat. Slowly pour the *masa* mixture back into skillet, whisking constantly over medium heat. Use a whisk or immersion blender to break up any lumps. Add the next six ingredients and stir to combine. Carefully add the meatballs 1 at a time and gently shake the pan so that they are completely submerged in the simmering stock. Simmer about 15 minutes, or until the *albóndigas* are firm.

Simmer a few minutes, or until the sauce rethickens. Check for seasonings. Remove the skillet from the heat and serve as suggested on page 257, garnished with chopped mint leaves, raisins, and/or almonds if you wish.

VARIATION

Albóndigas en chilmole (Meatballs in Charred Chile Sauce): When making Pavo en relleno negro (p. 424), some cooks prefer to form a multitude of meatballs rather than the more typical baseball-sized ones and serve them as a stand-alone dish, or with a few shreds of turkey. Follow the master recipe for Pavo en relleno negro. Form the *buut'* into balls (without the egg yolks) weighing ¾ ounce (20 g) each. (Note: If you choose to omit the turkey, prepare the *buut'* and the *sofrito*. To prepare the stock, replace the 9 cups water with 4 cups [1 L] and proceed. To finish, omit the additional *recado* and use just ⅓ cup [45 g] *masa harina*.) Serve the meatballs (with a few strips of turkey, if you used it) and cooking liquid atop rice or in soup bowls. Accompaniments are the same as for Pavo en relleno negro.

Doña Rita with granddaughter Valentina and grandson Víctor. [MR]

FRIJOL CON PUERCO

BLACK BEANS WITH PORK

TO PREPARE AHEAD
Enriched Lard (p. 513)

FOR THE BEANS
1 lb. (500 g) dried black beans

16 cups (4 L) water, divided

2 lbs. (1 k) pork loin or leg, with some fat, cut into 1 in. (2.5 cm) cubes

6 medium cloves garlic (1½ oz. / 36 g), peeled and charred

2 oz. (60 g) smoked slab bacon (optional)

2 sprigs fresh epazote (Substitute: 1 tsp. / 1.5 g dried)

If it's Monday, it must be Frijol con puerco. Like clockwork, every Monday throughout Yucatán, menu boards at *cocinas económicas* announce this revered dish, and an *abuela* is remiss in her duty if she doesn't prepare it for the family on that day. When serving, *abuela* will ask: "¿Cómo lo quieres? ¿Vas a hacer tu puuch'?" (How would you like it? Are you going to make your *puuch'*?) This is to distinguish who would like to mash the beans and meat together (*puuch'*—see Puchero, p. 350) to eat as a taco, in which case she will lovingly drain the pot and serve the cooking liquid in a bowl like soup, and plate the pork and drained beans separately. For everyone else, she will ladle meat, beans, and liquid all together into individual serving bowls or plates. To keep it traditional, swap out some of the pork leg with an equal weight of back ribs. Pig tails and ears are also traditional ingredients of Frijol con puerco, but beyond private family kitchens those are increasingly considered optional.

Prepare ahead note: Like so many bean dishes, Frijol con puerco only improves in flavor over the course of a few days. Keep refrigerated or freeze and reheat just before serving, adding a bit more water if necessary.

YIELD: 10 SERVINGS

PARBOIL BEANS AND PORK
Rinse, clean, and pick through the beans. Place them in a heavy pot and cover with half of the water. Bring to a boil, remove the pan from the heat, cover, and let the beans stand for 2–3 hours. (Alternatively, cover the beans with water and allow them

This variation, Frijol blanco con puerco (next page), also includes Butifarras (p. 377) in homage to the Catalán classic, Botifarra amb mongetes. [MC]

4 Tbs. (56 g) Enriched Lard

1¼ cup (212.5 g) white onion,
peeled, charred, and chopped

1 tsp. (0.65 g) dried whole
Mexican oregano *and* ½ tsp.
(1 g) cuminseed, lightly toasted
and ground together and passed
through a fine-mesh sieve;
discard residue

½ tsp. (2.5 g) freshly ground black
pepper

1 medium chile x'catik (about
1¼ oz. / 35 g) or chile habanero,
whole

2 tsp. (12 g) sea salt, or to taste

FOR SERVING

Arroz negro (p. 532)

Garnish of chopped radish,
white onion, and cilantro lightly
dressed with a squeeze of Seville
orange juice, or substitute

Chile tamulado (p. 509) or
Chile con limón (p. 511)

Chiltomate (p. 451)

Lime wedges

Avocado slices, optional garnish

to soak overnight, at least 12 hours.) Remove any beans that float to the surface. Drain. (Note: Save that black liquid from the precooking step. It can be repurposed in Arroz negro [p. 532], either refrigerated or frozen until ready for use.) Meanwhile, parboil the cubed pork in salted water for 10–15 minutes, scooping off foam as it accumulates; as soon as foam has stopped forming, remove the pork from the heat, drain, rinse well to remove any coagulated juices, and set aside.

COOK BEANS

Add the remaining fresh water to the drained beans; add the parboiled pork and the next three ingredients. Bring to a boil, reduce to a simmer, and cook uncovered for 1½–2 hours. (Note: About 1 hour through the cooking time, check the level of the liquid. You may need to add up to 8 cups [2 L] more water to keep the beans completely covered.)

PREPARE ENRICHMENT

Heat the lard in a large skillet until shimmering. Add the onions, reduce the heat, and cook slowly, until the onions are beginning to caramelize, 8–10 minutes. Add the ground spices and black pepper, stir, and cook another minute. Transfer the fat/onion mixture to the beans and stir to incorporate. Add the whole chile and cook 30 minutes to 1 hour, or until the beans are tender but still intact.

FINISH AND SERVE

Remove the chile and epazote and discard. Check the seasonings, adding salt as necessary, and stir to incorporate.

TO SERVE

As noted above, you may serve the cooking liquid in bowls and the beans and pork separately. Alternatively, ladle everything together into individual shallow bowls or plates. Serve the garnishes and salsas at the table; diners add their own to taste. Frijol con puerco is often served atop a bed of black rice (Arroz negro, p. 532), which you can prepare with the liquid from the first cooking of the beans, but you may also serve plain white rice.

VARIATIONS

Frijol blanco con puerco (White Beans with Pork): For a bit of variety, some *mamás* use white beans instead of black for Frijol con puerco. The flavor and texture are only slightly different but the change keeps family members from getting bored. In Yucatán, we use the local *ib* (*Phaseolus lunatus*), a member of the lima bean family. You may use any dried white bean such as lima, navy, or great northern, using a quantity equal to that specified in the master recipe. Serve with Arroz blanco (p. 529), K'uut bi ik (p. 508), the chopped radish and onion garnish noted above, Seville orange wedges, and slices of avocado.

In homage to the Catalán classic Botifarra amb mongetes, prepare Frijol blanco con puerco, replacing the cubed pork with an equal weight of sautéed Butifarras (p. 377), adding them to the beans during the last 30 minutes of cooking. Serve with aïoli or Crema de ajo (p. 362).

POLLO EN BISTEC

CHICKEN AND POTATOES STEWED IN OREGANO AND BLACK PEPPER SAUCE

TO PREPARE AHEAD

Brined chicken (see Basic Techniques, p. 536)

Recado para bistec (p. 501)

Seville orange juice substitute (p. 514), unless fresh Seville oranges are available

Enriched Lard (p. 513)

FOR THE MARINADE

3–4 lbs. (1.5–2 k) chicken (about 1 whole fryer), brined and cut into 6–8 serving pieces (Note: You may use cut up chickens, or any combination of pieces you wish, preferably with bone and skin intact)

5 Tbs. (75 g) Recado para bistec

⅔ cup (165 ml) Seville orange juice, or substitute

¼ cup (62.5 ml) white vinegar

4 medium cloves garlic (1 oz. / 24 g), peeled

1 Tbs. (18 g) sea salt (use less salt or omit if using commercial *recado*)

Like all clever businesswomen, doña Rita listens to her customers and adapts dishes to their special requests. For several years, she prepared Bistec a la cazuela—an imported Cuban classic—which features cubed stewing beef marinated in Seville orange juice and Recado para bistec (p. 501), potatoes, onions, tomatoes, and chiles all stacked in neat layers in a giant skillet. Several of her customers requested the same preparation, but "light"—with chicken instead of beef—and her specialty, Pollo en bistec, was born. (The word "*bistec*" in the title refers to the heady oregano/garlic Recado para bistec, but the *recado* is used for many more things than beef.) Just as she substituted chicken for beef, she reminded me that one can also use pork chops or fish fillets with equal success.

Prepare ahead note: Pollo en bistec keeps well under refrigeration for several days and improves with age.

YIELD: 6–8 SERVINGS

MARINATE CHICKEN

Remove the chicken from the brine, rinse, and pat dry; discard the brining solution. Transfer the chicken to a shallow baking dish or resealable plastic bag. Place the remaining marinade ingredients in the jar of a blender and process until thoroughly liquefied. Pour the marinade over the chicken and allow to rest 30 minutes at room temperature.

Everyone has a task. [MR]

3 Tbs. (42 g) Enriched Lard

2 cups (500 ml) water

1 lb. (500 g) baking potatoes,
unpeeled, sliced into rounds
about ¼ in. (6.5 mm) thick (place
sliced potatoes in water to avoid
oxidation)

1 medium white onion (10 oz. /
275 g), cut into quarters top
to bottom, then each quarter
thinly sliced top to bottom and
separated into half-moon shapes

1 medium green bell pepper
(6½ oz. / 185 g), sliced into thin
rounds and seeded

3 medium Roma tomatoes (10½
oz. / 300 g), seeded and sliced
lengthwise into thin wedges

1 medium chile x'catik (about
1¼ oz. / 35 g), left whole

8 whole chiles de árbol

8 whole medium chiles serranos

SAUTÉ CHICKEN

In a very large, deep skillet that has a lid, heat the fat until shimmering. Remove the chicken from the marinade, reserving any extra marinade. Brown the chicken over high heat a few pieces at a time to avoid crowding, turning once, 2–3 minutes per side. Transfer the browned pieces to a platter.

Return the chicken to the skillet. Add the water and bring to a boil, then reduce the heat to a simmer. Drain the potatoes, cover them with the leftover marinade, and toss to coat thoroughly. Arrange the potatoes in a single layer on top of the chicken and pour on any remaining marinade. Layer on the onion, bell pepper, and tomatoes, in that order, distributing them evenly over the potatoes. Distribute the chiles evenly over all. Cover and cook 15–20 minutes, or until the chicken is tender and the vegetables are softened. The chicken should reach an internal temperature of 165°F (74°C); do not overcook. If the chicken is done but the potatoes aren't yet tender, remove the chicken to a plate and allow the vegetables to cook a bit longer, then return the chicken to the skillet. Remove the pan from heat, cover, and allow to rest 15–20 minutes prior to serving to enhance flavors.

VARIATIONS

Bistec a la cazuela (Beef and Potatoes Stewed in Oregano and Black Pepper Sauce): To prepare the original version of the beef dish on which doña Rita based her "light" chicken dish, follow the master recipe for Pollo en bistec, replacing the chicken with 4 ounces (110 g) cubed stewing beef per person. (Omit the brining step.)

Adobado de pollo (Chicken and Potatoes Stewed in *Achiote* and Tomato Sauce): This simple recipe was shared with me by doña Elsy de Socorro Piña Argáez of Mérida. It is virtually identical to Pollo en bistec, but uses Recado rojo instead of the Recado para bistec. The flavor is very different. The earthy taste of oregano is replaced by the pungent *achiote*. Like Pollo en bistec, the recipe can be adapted using beef, pork, or fish. Follow the master recipe for Pollo en bistec, substituting Recado rojo (p. 500) for the Recado para bistec. Finally, instead of adding the tomatoes to the sautéed chicken, char them whole and add them to the blender jar with the Recado rojo and the other marinade ingredients at the beginning. Proceed with the rest of the recipe.

HIGIENICAMENTE
PREPARADA
TORTAS
SABRITAS
REFRESCOS
GALLETAS

cuida tu sa
come

COCINA ECONÓMICA "LA COCINA DE MAMÁ"
Mérida, Yucatán

The sparkling eyes and vivacity of Elsy de Socorro Piña Argáez have built her a loyal customer following. Winking at me, she described herself as *mañosa*, meaning that she has her own special way of doing things—a polite way of saying "finicky." With two of her daughters, doña Elsy serves breakfast to twenty-five to thirty-five people starting at 6:30 am, and lunch to around forty people, between 11:00 am and 5:00 pm. Not all of doña Elsy's customers sit in the tidy dining area; many bring plastic containers—known here as "*tupers*"—which they fill with food and tote home for the family. Her Cocina Económica "La Cocina de Mamá" does a brisk business with employees of a nearby hardware store as well as neighborhood high school students. Customers come for the simply delicious food, but doña Elsy is the real attraction.

Doña Elsy. [MR]

CHILMOLE DE FRIJOL CON PUERCO

BLACK BEANS WITH PORK IN CHARRED CHILE SAUCE

TO PREPARE AHEAD

Recado negro (p. 501)

FOR THE BEANS

Ingredients for Frijol con puerco
   (p. 262)

3 medium Roma tomatoes
   (10½ oz. / 300 g), seeded and
   finely chopped

4 Tbs. (60 g) Recado negro

2 chiles chipotles in adobo
   (¾ oz. / 20 g), drained

2 tsp. (12 g) sea salt, or to taste
   (Note: Be sure to taste first;
   if using commercial *recado*,
   additional salt may not be
   necessary)

1 cup (250 ml) water

This simple variation of Frijol con puerco takes on new life with the addition of Recado negro, Yucatán's famous charred chile seasoning paste. I love this easy adaptation so much that I often make it instead of the basic Frijol con puerco. Seasonally, cooks add whole immature fruits of *ciruela* (*Spondias purpurea* L., p. 29), lending a tart burst to every few bites of meat and beans. Lacking *ciruela*, if you are a fan of sourness, substitute tomatillos for the quantity of Roma tomatoes specified in the recipe.

Prepare ahead note: As with so many bean dishes, the flavors of Chilmole de frijol con puerco only improve over the course of a few days. Keep it refrigerated or freeze and reheat just before serving, adding a bit more water if necessary.

YIELD: 10 SERVINGS

COOK BEANS

Proceed through the enrichment step of the instructions for Frijol con puerco. When the onions are almost caramelized and after adding the spices, add the tomatoes and cook until softened, 3–4 minutes. Transfer the tomato/onion mixture to the beans and stir to combine. Place the *recado*, chipotles, salt, if using, and water in the jar of a blender and process until thoroughly liquefied. Strain the liquid through a fine-mesh sieve into the beans, pressing out as much liquid as possible; discard the residue. Add more water if necessary (this dish should have a bit more liquid than Frijol con puerco.) Cook 30 minutes, or until the beans are tender but still intact and the flavors have amalgamated. Remove the chile and epazote and discard.

TO SERVE

Follow the serving suggestions for Frijol con puerco, but serve white rice instead of black.

VARIATION

Chilmole de frijol con costillas ahumadas (Black Beans with Smoked Ribs in Charred Chile Sauce): A special dish from the smokehouses of Temozón, this simply substitutes an equal quantity of your own smoked Costillas ahumadas (p. 479) for the pork. Or use your favorite mixture of smoked ribs, Longaniza de Valladolid (p. 481), and/or Carne ahumada (p. 478). Proceed with the recipe for Chilmole de frijol con puerco.

EMPANIZADO

BREADED DEEP-FRIED CUTLETS

TO PREPARE AHEAD

Seville orange juice substitute
(p. 514), unless fresh Seville
oranges are available
Recado para escabeche (p. 498)
Pan molido para empanizado
(p. 515)

FOR THE MARINADE

½ cup / 125 ml citrus juice: Seville
orange juice (or substitute) for
the pork and lime juice for the
chicken or beef are the typical
marinades in Yucatán
1 tsp. (6 g) sea salt
½ tsp. (1.5 g) Recado para
escabeche
Thinly sliced *milanesa* pork,
chicken breast, or beef cutlets,
in the quantity desired (see
Basic Techniques, p. 533; finished
cutlet should be no more than
¼ in. / 6.25 mm thick)

[MC]

A popular workhorse of all *cocinas económicas* is Empanizado. It is a kind of comfort
food, served with white rice, mashed potatoes, or, nowadays, even French fries. Thin
cutlets—known here as *milanesas*—are breaded in a seasoned coating, then fried in
sizzling oil. Beneath the crispy breading is a refreshing breath of citrus, because in
Yucatán, the cutlets are briefly marinated in either lime or Seville orange juice before
frying. Even though the menu board may just read Empanizado, you will always be
offered a choice: *pechuga* (chicken breast cutlets), *puerco* (pork cutlets), or sometimes
filete (beef cutlets). This basic recipe serves for all of them.

Prepare ahead note: If you wish, you may proceed through the breading step and freeze
the breaded cutlets in a single layer on waxed paper. Do not defrost before frying.
Empanizado is best served immediately after frying.

Yield: You may make as large or small a quantity of Empanizado as you like. The typical
portion in Yucatán for a single serving cutlet is about 4½ oz. (125 g).

MARINATE CUTLETS

Mix the juice, salt, and *recado*. Place the cutlets in a large baking dish or casserole, add
the juice mixture, and turn to coat all the cutlets. Refrigerate no less than 30 and no
more than 45 minutes.

Vegetable oil for frying

1 cup (125 g) all-purpose flour

2 cups (250 g) Pan molido para
empanizado

3 eggs, well beaten

Sea salt

FOR SERVING

Salpicón (p. 511)

Crema de ajo (p. 362) *or* Crema
de x'catik (p. 363)

Chile tamulado (p. 509), or the
chile sauce of your choice

BREAD AND FRY CUTLETS, ASSEMBLE, AND SERVE

Pour 1½ inches (4 cm) of oil into a broad, deep skillet and heat to 375° F (190°C). While the oil is heating, bread the cutlets. Because the flour and the Pan molido para empanizado will eventually get mixed with the egg, work with small batches. Spread half the flour evenly on a large plate. Spread 1 cup (125 g) Pan molido on a separate large plate. Remove the cutlets from the marinade and dredge each cutlet in the flour, dip in the beaten eggs, then roll in the Pan molido.

Immediately transfer the breaded cutlets one at a time to the hot oil and fry them, turning once, 1½–2 minutes per side, or until a deep golden color. Transfer to paper towels to drain. Allow the oil to return to temperature before adding another cutlet. Repeat with the remaining cutlets, refreshing flour and breadcrumbs as needed. Just before serving, sprinkle each cutlet with salt to taste. Serve immediately, or keep warm on a baking sheet in a low oven (250°F / 120°C).

TO SERVE

Serve as suggested on page 268. You may also top the cutlets with Salpicón and serve *crema* and salsas on the side. In some private homes in Yucatán, *mamás* also serve Chiltomate (p. 451) or Tomate frito (p. 507) as a sauce for the cutlet. You may also serve Empanizado as tacos or *tortas* instead of as a plated dish.

VARIATIONS

Filete de pescado empanizado (Breaded Deep-Fried Fish Fillet): Follow the master recipe for Empanizado, but instead of pork, chicken, or beef, substitute 6 fish fillets (about 4½ oz. / 125 g each). Marinate them in lime juice 30 minutes before proceeding with the rest of the recipe.

Camarón empanizado (Breaded Deep-Fried Shrimp): This is considered breakfast food to many Yucatecans: a *torta* of a French roll stuffed with fried shrimp. A popular condiment in Yucatán for breaded fried fish or shrimp is, of all things, mayonnaise. Yucatecans have taken to it with gusto and spoon it onto everything from fish and meats to corn on the cob. I confess that its tangy creaminess goes well with many seafood dishes, especially fried fish. Try homemade mayonnaise, or use Crema de ajo (p. 362) or Crema de x'catik (p. 363). Follow the master recipe for Empanizado, but instead of pork, chicken, or beef, substitute 1½ pounds (750 g) medium shrimp (43–50 count), deveined, shells and tails removed, butterflied. Marinate in lime juice 30 minutes before proceeding with the rest of the recipe.

Mariscos empanizados (Breaded Deep-Fried Mixed Seafood): Follow the recipe for Camarón empanizado but use an equal weight of mixed seafood, such as cleaned and cooked octopus or squid, raw cubed whitefish fillet, or scallops, instead of the shrimp.

Tortas de empanizado (Sandwiches on French Bread): Tortas filled with any of these fried foods are also extremely popular in Yucatán (p. 235). Cut a Pan francés (p. 194) or baguette in half widthwise to create 2 *tortas*, then open by slicing along the length. Smear the inside of both pieces of one of the sandwiches with Frijol refrito (p. 506). Add the breaded cutlet of your choice (for seafood, omit the beans and use one of the *cremas* instead) and garnish with leaves of romaine or other lettuce and a few tomato slices. Diners add their own sauces to taste.

POLLO ASADO

CHARCOAL-GRILLED CHICKEN IN *ACHIOTE* MARINADE

TO PREPARE AHEAD

Recado rojo (p. 500)

Seville orange juice substitute
   (p. 514), unless fresh Seville
   oranges are available

Enriched Lard (p. 513)

Brined chicken (see Basic
   Techniques, p. 536)

FOR THE MARINADE

8 Tbs. (120 g) Recado rojo

8 Tbs. (120 ml) Seville orange
   juice, or substitute

2 Tbs. (28 g) Enriched Lard,
   melted

2 tsp. (12 g) sea salt

3 lbs. (1.5 k) chicken, about
   1 medium, halved and brined

Wood- or charcoal-grilled Pollo asado features a *recado* made of *achiote* (p. 500) diluted with Seville orange juice to create a pungent marinade. Carved into pieces, the chicken can be plated and served like other *cocina económica* dishes, but it may also be finely shredded for a variety of uses such as in Tsi'ik (p. 421), or on top of *panuchos* (p. 434).

Prepare ahead note: The chicken for Pollo asado should be brined 4–8 hours in advance. Once removed from the brine, it can be covered with the marinade and refrigerated for another 8–12 hours, although this is not necessary.

YIELD: 8 INDIVIDUAL PIECES, OR 10 SERVINGS OF CARVED OR SHREDDED MEAT

MARINATE CHICKEN

Dissolve the *recado* in the orange juice. Add the lard and salt and stir to incorporate. Add a bit more juice or *recado* to get the right texture: thick, yet pourable, like barbecue sauce. (Note: If you are using commercial *recado*, you will have better results if you prepare the enrichment as described in Pantry Staples, p. 500.)

Remove the chicken from the brine, rinse, and pat dry; discard the brining solution. Place the chicken in a resealable plastic bag or large baking dish and cover completely with the marinade. (Your hands are the best tools for this job.) Refrigerate 30 minutes or up to 12 hours.

GRILL CHICKEN AND FINISH

Light a gas or charcoal grill following the instructions for using wood smoking chips in Basic Techniques (p. 538). Grill the chicken 20–30 minutes on each side, or until a meat thermometer registers just over 160°F (71°C). Remove the chicken from the grill and allow it to rest 15 minutes prior to carving or shredding; the temperature should reach 165°F (74°C).

VARIATION

Codorniz asado (Charcoal-Grilled Quail in *Achiote* Marinade): Roasted quail is very popular in Yucatán and can be found skewered on long sticks at street stalls in many pueblos. Originally a creature hunted in the *monte* (p. 88), today it is most often bred and sold live in the markets. This dish is extremely quick and easy to prepare, yet makes an impressive dish for dinner guests. Quail requires less brining time than chicken, so monitor to avoid mushy meat. Scale this recipe to accommodate the number of guests: allow 2 quail per person. You may also use Cornish game hens, each of which can serve 2–4 people, depending on the hens' size. Follow the master recipe for Pollo asado, adjusting cooking time according to the type of fowl you are using. Serve with Arroz verde (p. 531) or the rice of your choice, or any of the side dishes in this book, such as Esquites (p. 239), Calabacitas fritas (p. 276), or Chayas fritas (p. 129).

(opposite page) Cantina *"El Gallito."* [EC]

EL GALLITO

LA CANTINA
AND EL RESTAURANTE FAMILIAR

*Prohibida la venta de
bebidas alcoholicas a menores
de edad asi como su consumo
en la via pública.*

*Di no a las drogas.
Usa Conductor Modelo.*

*Para Clientes:
contamos con:
Estacionamiento
enfrente.*

Atte: El Gallito

Michelada. [MR]

SALOON DOORS—THOSE LOUVERED, SWINGING PANELS that are fixtures on the set of every cheap Hollywood Western—are still very much present at the entrances to *cantinas* throughout Yucatán. I was surprised to learn that they are required by ordinances governing the sale of liquor in public places: if the large, full doors are left open for ventilation, these half-doors must be left closed in order to shield passersby from the sight of what might be going on inside.

I spent a few years in Yucatán before venturing inside a *cantina*. After all, aren't these rugged, all-male enclaves dangerous dens of smoke, prostitutes, and raucous drunks? No matter how much fun that might sound to some, I confess I always felt somewhat intimidated, especially as I am, to my great annoyance, rather quickly identified as a gringo.

Eventually, though, my curiosity to see what was behind those seductive doors got the better of me and led me to try several *cantinas*—in the company of a local male friend well versed in the social code of these places.

El Gallito (translated as "The Little Rooster" but also vernacular for cocky) was the first *cantina* we entered. Its pert façade with a painted relief of a whimsical rooster above the door and its public parking lot just across the street were more comforting than intimidating. Once past those swinging doors, I was surprised to feel my trepidation turning to disappointment. Where were all the drunks? The smoke? The cheap women? All those delightfully tawdry images I had collected through the years were instantly shattered. The tidy interior of El Gallito was decorated with ceramic figurines of roosters and blue and white tiles reminiscent of old bars in Spain. Customers were equally divided among clusters of men and groups of well-dressed female friends taking their afternoon break from work. And El Gallito—like so many public places in today's world—is by law a smoke-free environment.

I rested my foot on the bar rail—just like in the Pedro Infante movies—and ordered our first round.

MICHELADA

BEER "ON THE ROCKS" WITH CHILE, LIME, AND WORCESTERSHIRE SAUCE

FOR THE FLAVORED LIQUID

1⅓ cup (335 ml) fresh lime juice
1 bottle Worcestershire sauce
  (about ⅔ cup / 148 ml)
4½ tsp. (14 g) chile powder,
  divided

FOR SERVING

1 Tbs. (18 g) sea salt
1 lime, halved
Lime slices or wedges for garnish
10 chilled beers (lagers are more
  common for this drink in
  Yucatán, but you may also use a
  darker beer such as León Negra)
Straws

There is something wonderfully appropriate in the tropics about tossing back a fizzy, ice-cold beer with the citrusy tartness of lime, the zing of chile, and the vinegary sweetness of Worcestershire sauce. Bartenders here never mix the beer with the dark, tangy liquid; rather, the glass arrives with the liquid at the bottom, and you top it off with your own beer as you go. You have to pace it so that you still have some of the liquid left as you add the last drops of beer.

There are at least a dozen legends about how this drink came to have its name, but ask Yucatecans and most will stick to the same story. It starts with the root *"chelada"*— the name of another popular beverage consisting of beer poured over ice with a squeeze of lime juice. The *"mi,"* or *"my,"* distinguishes the two drinks. *"Ch'eel"* in Mayan means "blond" or "light-colored." It is the name that has for several generations been used to refer to all the lager-style beers so popular here. And coincidentally, the pale Bavarian lagers that were introduced into Yucatán in the late 1800s were known in German as *"helle"*—"bright" or "light." Last clue: *"helada"*—a Spanish word—means "ice cold." Now, put it all together: *mi + chel* (or *helle*) + *helada* = *michelada*. Translation: "my ice-cold lager." At least that's the local story.

Prepare ahead note: The lime/Worcestershire sauce mix can be made several days in advance and refrigerated. Divide the recipe for fewer drinkers, but the flavored mixture keeps well under refrigeration for about a week.

YIELD: 10 SERVINGS

PREPARE FLAVORED LIQUID
Mix the lime juice, Worcestershire sauce, and 2½ teaspoons (8 g) chile powder; stir well and refrigerate at least 10–15 minutes as you proceed.

PREPARE GLASSES AND SERVE
Mix the salt and remaining 2 teaspoons (6 g) chile powder and pour onto a shallow plate. Prepare 10 Tom Collins or pilsner glasses by rubbing the rim of each glass with the lime half. Dip the rims of the glasses into the salt/chile mixture, fill the glasses with ice, garnish each glass with a lime slice and a straw.

TO SERVE
Pour 1½ ounces (45 ml) of the chilled lime/Worcestershire sauce mix into each glass. Serve the decorated glass alongside a bottle of beer.

MARGARITA YUCATECA

YUCATECAN SEVILLE ORANGE AND MEZCAL COCKTAIL

TO PREPARE AHEAD
Seville orange substitute (p. 514), unless fresh Seville oranges are available

FOR THE MARGARITA MIX
1½ oz. (44 ml) Yucatecan mezcal reposado (Substitute: any reposado tequila or mezcal)
1 oz. (30 ml) Seville orange juice, or substitute
½ oz. (15 ml) Cointreau or Triple Sec

FOR SERVING
1 Tbs. (18 g) sea salt
1 lime, halved
Lime slices or wedges for garnish

Since it is illegal to produce an agave beverage and call it "tequila" anywhere in Mexico outside the sanctioned growing region, a couple of Yucatecan distilleries have side-stepped the issue and are exploiting Yucatán's plentiful indigenous *Agave fourcroydes*, or henequen—the plant from which sisal fiber is extracted—to create a flavorful mezcal. Brand names are Mayapán and Izamal, among a few others. The recipe for this cocktail—relatively new to the scene—puts a Yucatecan spin on the Mexican margarita, employing local mezcal as well as the beloved Seville orange.

Prepare ahead note: Multiply this recipe by the number of guests. The entire mixture may be made several hours or days in advance and refrigerated until time to serve.

YIELD: 1 SERVING

PREPARE MARGARITA MIX
Mix the ingredients, stir, and chill thoroughly.

PREPARE GLASSES AND SERVE
Chill a margarita or cocktail glass in the freezer at least 15 minutes, or until frosty. Rub the rim of the glass with the halved lime. Dip the rim into the salt and garnish the glass with a slice of lime. Pour the chilled mix into the glass and serve either up or on the rocks.

Plantations of Agave fourcroydes *once served Yucatán's lucrative sisal industry.* [MC]

First round of botanas. [MR]

As we nursed our Micheladas in El Gallito, several small plates of food began to appear. These are the *botanas*—or snacks—that are required by Yucatecan health codes to be given free to anyone who orders booze. All those little plates constituted a big meal: chicken livers in tomato sauce, pickled vegetables, rich little cakes of maize *masa* and crispy pork cracklings, Lebanese *kibis* (p. 358), an assortment of tamales. The flow of food ends only when you finish the last drop of your last beer and ask for the check.

CALABACITA FRITA / TZAAJBIL TS'OL

WARM SAUTÉED ZUCCHINI DIP

Calabacita, or "little squash," is the name used in Yucatán to refer to the zucchini (*Cucurbita pepo* L., p. 24). Calabacita frita is a great party dip for the health-conscious; it is also a wonderful side dish for fish or grilled meats. In *cantinas,* Calabacita frita is deliciously picante—good for tempting patrons to order more beer. But if you are heat shy or plan on using this as a side dish, you may wish to use just one seeded serrano (or even a half for the truly timid).

Prepare ahead note: Calabacita frita can be made a day in advance and refrigerated. Either gently reheat or bring to room temperature just before serving.

YIELD: 8–10 SERVINGS

TO PREPARE AHEAD
Recado para escabeche (p. 498)

FOR THE ZUCCHINI
4 cups (1⅓ lbs. / 650 g) zucchini, unpeeled, cut into large dice

FOR THE *SOFRITO*
¼ cup (62.5 ml) Spanish olive oil

1 cup (175 g) fresh corn kernels, from approximately 2 medium ears

1 medium white onion (10 oz. / 275 g), finely chopped

6 medium cloves garlic (1½ oz. / 36 g), peeled and finely chopped

½ cup (70 g) green bell pepper, finely chopped

1½ tsp. (9 g) salt

1½ tsp. (4.5 g) Recado para escabeche

1 or 2 medium chiles serranos, charred, peeled, seeded, and finely chopped

3 medium Roma tomatoes (10½ oz. / 300 g), seeded and chopped

½ cup (30 g) cilantro, chopped

FOR SERVING
Cotija or feta cheese, crumbled

Totopos para botanas (p. 515)

PARBOIL ZUCCHINI

Bring a medium saucepan of water to a boil, add the zucchini, and return to a boil. Cook on high heat for 10 minutes, or until very tender. Drain and set aside to cool.

PREPARE *SOFRITO* AND FINISH

Heat the olive oil in a large nonstick skillet until shimmering. Add the corn and sauté 3–4 minutes, stirring constantly to prevent sticking, until the kernels are lightly browned and tender. Add the next 5 ingredients in order, stirring to combine after each addition. Sauté until the onions are beginning to caramelize, 5-6 minutes.

Add the chiles and tomatoes to the skillet and cook, stirring frequently, 3–4 minutes. While the chile/tomato mixture is cooking, place the drained zucchini in a bowl and mash with a potato masher until well broken up. Transfer the mashed zucchini to the skillet with the chile/tomato mixture and continue cooking over medium heat another 4–5 minutes, stirring frequently, until most of the liquid from the squash and tomatoes has evaporated. Add the cilantro, stir, and serve immediately.

TO SERVE

Mound the zucchini in a serving bowl, sprinkle with the crumbled cheese, and serve with Totopos para botanas for dipping. Alternatively, you may serve the squash as a side dish, as noted above.

THE NUT GUY Ever since *cantinas* first opened their swinging doors in Yucatán, roving vendors have capitalized on the captive audience inside, many of whom at some point lose their sales resistance and can be talked into a spontaneous purchase. Some vendors sell gum and cigarettes, others sell snacks not offered in the *cantinas.* One of these vendors in Mérida is affectionately referred to as "the nut guy." Shuttling from one *cantina* to the next, he carries a wooden tray filled with bags of colorful and delicious nuts, with the requisite lime and chile sauce at the ready.

[MR]

CODZITOS

FRIED TORTILLA ROLLS WITH TOMATO SAUCE AND DUTCH CHEESE

TO PREPARE AHEAD
Tortillas (p. 518)
Tomate frito (p. 507)

FOR THE CODZITOS
20 corn tortillas, fresh or day-old
Vegetable oil, for frying

FOR SERVING
½ tsp. (3 g) sea salt
1½ cups (375 ml) Tomate frito
4 oz. (115 g) finely grated Edam
  cheese
Fresh cilantro leaves for garnish,
  coarsely chopped

Codzitos are a simple pleasure. Stale tortillas are given new life as they are tightly rolled, fried, drowned in tomato sauce, then sprinkled with cheese. Because they are made of the cheapest ingredients—usually leftovers—Codzitos are served liberally as *botanas* at *cantinas*.

"*Codz*" is a transliteration of the Mayan word "*koots*'" or "*kots*'," meaning "to roll." In Yucatán, you often hear phrases like "La tía Lisa está hecha kots' en su hamaca" (Aunt Lisa is all rolled up in her hammock). The Spanish diminutive suffix *-ito* creates a Spanish/Mayan hybrid word that describes these delicious "little rolls."

Traditionally, the tightly rolled tortillas were secured with *sosquil*, or threads of dried, unprocessed henequen fiber; nowadays, cooks usually resort to toothpicks.

Prepare ahead note: The Tomate frito should be made in advance: refrigerate or freeze, then heat immediately prior to serving. If you have time, use fresh tortillas: roll and secure them a day in advance and allow to air-dry overnight. If using leftover tortillas, you will need to lightly heat them in a skillet with a bit of oil to soften before rolling, then immediately fry and finish. Once fried and dressed, Codzitos must be served immediately.

YIELD: 10 SERVINGS

PREPARE CODZITOS

If using fresh tortillas: Roll tortillas very tightly and secure as described above. Arrange on a tray in one layer and allow to air-dry overnight.

If using leftover tortillas: Heat 1 tablespoon (15 ml) vegetable oil in a small skillet until very hot but not smoking. Lightly heat each tortilla one by one on both sides until just softened, about 5 seconds per side, replenishing oil as needed. Working quickly, roll and secure each tortilla while it is still warm; set aside.

Fill a small, heavy skillet with about 1 inch (2.5 cm) of oil; heat to 350°F (175°C). Fry the Codzitos a few at a time so as not to crowd. Cook until golden brown on all sides. Drain on paper towels.

TO SERVE

When the Codzitos are cool enough to handle, remove the string or toothpicks and arrange Codzitos on a serving platter. Sprinkle on the salt, then ladle on the Tomate frito, leaving the ends of the rolls unsauced. (Note: In *cantinas*, Codzitos are generally considered finger food, which is why you should leave the ends sauceless.) Sprinkle with the cheese first, followed by the cilantro, and serve immediately.

VARIATIONS

You may also fill the Codzitos before rolling them up. Use approximately 1 tablespoon (15 g) of your favorite filling in each tortilla before rolling: shredded Pollo asado (p. 270), Cochinita pibil (p. 420), Picadillo en chilmole (p. 254), or grated Edam cheese. Secure, fry, and finish as instructed above.

HIGADILLO ENTOMATADO

SAUTÉED CHICKEN LIVERS AND ONIONS IN SMOKY TOMATO SAUCE

TO PREPARE AHEAD
Enriched Lard (p. 513)
Tomate frito (p. 507)
Recado rojo (p. 500)

FOR THE CHICKEN LIVERS
5¼ oz. (150 g) smoked slab bacon, coarsely diced (about ⅜ in. / 1 cm cubes)
1 Tbs. (14 g) Enriched Lard
½ medium white onion (5 oz. / 137.5 g), cut into quarters top to bottom, then each quarter thinly sliced top to bottom and separated into half-moon shapes
½ tsp. (3 g) sea salt
¼ tsp. (1.25 g) freshly ground black pepper
1 lb. (500 g) chicken livers, fatty membranes removed, cut into bite-sized pieces
1 Tbs. (15 g) Recado rojo, dissolved in an equal amount of water
2 cups (500 ml) Tomate frito

FOR SERVING
Fresh cilantro leaves for garnish, coarsely chopped
Totopos para botanas (p. 515)
Chile tamulado (p. 509), or the chile sauce of your choice

Viscera are, not surprisingly, the least-expensive animal proteins available in Yucatecan markets. A pound (500 g) of chicken livers (*hígado*) costs about 3 pesos—less than 25 cents U.S.—making it a popular dish at the frugal *cantinas*, where food is given away. Poultry vendors display giant trays full of innards, with the gutted chickens and turkeys bobbing about from the necks on hooks just overhead. Don José Fernández, manager of El Gallito in Mérida, recited this easy recipe to me.

Prepare ahead note: You can prepare Tomate frito well in advance and refrigerate or freeze; reheat before using in this recipe. Higadillo entomatado is best served immediately after preparing.

YIELD: 10 SERVINGS

SAUTÉ CHICKEN LIVERS

In a large skillet, cook the bacon in the lard slowly over low heat until browned. Add the onions, salt, and pepper and continue cooking on high, stirring frequently, until the onions begin to caramelize, 2–3 minutes.

Add the livers and sauté until no longer pink, 3–4 minutes.

Add the *recado* mixture to the Tomate frito and whisk to combine; add to the skillet with the livers and stir. Continue cooking until the sauce reduces and thickens slightly, 5–6 minutes. Serve immediately.

TO SERVE

You may transfer Higadillo entomatado to a heated chafing dish for guests to serve themselves or place a small amount on individual buffet plates. Sprinkle with chopped cilantro and serve with Totopos para botanas and chile to taste for eating *botana*-style.

(opposite page) Piles of botanas *with every drink: Papadzules (background); round* kibis *(middle); and Empanadas de cazón (right).* [MR]

PAPADZULES

EGG-STUFFED TORTILLAS BATHED IN
SQUASH-SEED AND TOMATO SAUCES

TO PREPARE AHEAD

Recado para papadzul (p. 503)
Tortillas (p. 518)
Tomate frito (p. 507)

FOR THE SQUASH-SEED SAUCE

3 cups (750 ml) water
4 large sprigs fresh epazote
   (¼ oz. / 8 g; substitute:
   2 tsp. / 3 g dried, crumbled
   epazote leaves)
2 Tbs. (24 g) white onion,
   coarsely chopped
2 tsp. (10 g) sea salt (Substitute:
   powdered chicken or vegetable
   bouillon)
1 recipe Recado para papadzul

[EC]

To traditionalists or proud Yucatecans, it may seem heretical to place the recipe for luxurious Papadzules in this section on the lowly *cantina*. But the dish is such a fixture in the daily fare of *cantinas* and *restaurantes familiares*—perhaps more than at any other dining establishment—that this just seemed like the most logical section in which to include it.

Papadzules are unquestionably a hallmark—even the pinnacle—of Maya cuisine, and indeed are quite possibly one of the most ancient traditional dishes of Yucatán. In her panoramic review, *America's First Cuisines*, Sophie D. Coe mentions a native Maya dish that involved dipping tortillas in a sauce made of ground squash seeds and an herb-infused liquid—possibly the predecessor of the modern incarnation. While the boiled egg filling is common today, earlier versions employed Chayas fritas (p. 129), blue crab, or chicken cooked in the squash-seed sauce.

The meaning of the word "*papadzul*" in Mayan is contested: some say that it means "dipped and soaked"; others claim that it means "food of the lords."

Papadzules may be eaten as an appetizer, as a brunch or breakfast item, or as a light supper. If you have the Recado para papadzul and the Tomate frito already prepared, Papadzules are quick and easy to assemble.

Prepare ahead note: You should prepare the Recado para papadzul and the Tomate frito at least a day ahead. You may also finish the squash-seed sauce in advance. Gently reheat just before serving, adding a bit of chicken stock or water to dilute to the proper consistency. Papadzules must be assembled quickly and served immediately.

YIELD: 10 SERVINGS

FOR ASSEMBLING
THE PAPADZULES

20 fresh, warm Tortillas
  (Note: If you are using packaged
  tortillas instead of your own,
  look for the smallest ones you
  can find. With tortillas larger
  than 5 inches [12 cm], you will
  need to adjust the quantities of
  this recipe using more egg and
  possibly reducing the number
  of servings)
10 hard-boiled eggs, peeled
  and coarsely chopped

FOR SERVING

Fresh epazote leaves for garnish
  (or a mix of whole flat-leaf
  parsley and cilantro leaves)
2 Tbs. (30 ml) squash- or
  pumpkinseed oil preferably
  green rather than amber
  (optional: see notes below)

PREPARE SQUASH-SEED SAUCE

Place the first 4 ingredients in a saucepan and bring to a boil. Reduce to a simmer, cover, and cook 5 minutes. Remove the pan from the heat and allow the broth to steep at least 15 minutes.

Strain the epazote broth. You should have about 2½ cups (625 ml). If not, add water to complete the measure. Place the *recado* in a broad, deep skillet. In a saucepan, return the broth to a boil. Add the hot broth to the squash-seed paste and blend. For best results, use an immersion blender to break up the paste and thoroughly emulsify it with the liquid. Alternatively, you may use a spatula or wooden spoon to break up the paste, then a whisk to blend until smooth. The final consistency should be like pancake batter. Add a bit more water or stock as needed to keep the batter-like consistency.

ASSEMBLE PAPADZULES AND SERVE

Warm a large serving platter. If the green sauce has cooled, warm it gently over very low heat. (Note: Do not allow the sauce to boil or it may curdle and separate. Also, as it heats it will continue to thicken; stir and scrape the bottom of the skillet frequently.) Working very quickly so that the ingredients stay warm, use a pair of tongs or your fingers to dip one side of a tortilla into the sauce, coating completely. Flip and repeat on the other side. Place the sauced tortilla to one side of the platter and spoon about 2 tablespoons (30 g) of the chopped egg down the center of the tortilla. Roll into a flute shape; repeat until you have 20 Papadzules lined up in neat rows. (Note: This process will make a mess all over your platter; wipe off excess sauce with a clean, damp towel when you have finished all the rolling.)

TO SERVE

Pour the remaining squash-seed sauce over the Papadzules. Spoon on the Tomate frito in one or two strips perpendicular to the Papadzules, then decorate with the epazote leaves. Immediately before carrying to the table, use a small spoon to sprinkle droplets of the optional pumpkinseed oil over all, making sure that each Papadzul gets its fair share. Serve immediately.

THE SQUASH-SEED OIL CONTROVERSY

Whether the scant droplets of emerald green squash-seed oil that appear scattered like tiny jewels on the surface of Papadzules—the hallmark, some say, of "real" Papadzules—was an ancient practice or not is unclear: scholars are not in agreement on how the Mayas might have been able to produce vegetable oils without extraction tools. Most, however, acknowledge that they boiled chocolate paste and collected the fat that rose to the surface; the Mayas also produced small quantities of oils during the process of grinding seeds or nuts; and finally, over time, ground seed pastes will naturally separate—like peanut butter.

Regional cookbooks seem to be divided on the subject, too: some tell how to extract squash seed oil, but most make no mention of it whatsoever. Those that do include it—even as far back as 1896—instruct the cook to sprinkle hot water on the squash seed paste and then to knead it (*amasar*) until a few precious drops trickle out.

I have experimented with all of the above methods, to greater and lesser degrees of success; you may want to do the same. If not, you can achieve a similar aesthetic by using one of the excellent pumpkin seed oils now on the market; only a few drops are required (see Resources, p. 541). It is pretty, but the flavor it adds is barely distinguishable.

[MR]

My drinking buddy and I proceeded to get a bit woozy from the beer, the *botanas*, and the heat in El Gallito and listened with increasing rapture as owner don José entertained us with tales about the sea change that the Yucatecan *cantina* has undergone in the past few decades.

"El Gallito was established on this very spot right after World War II ended. It was well known and very popular for many years. I took over the business 20 years ago, but even by that time it had been bought by Grupo Modelo (p. 272). I just rent it from them, and they take care of the rest. I would estimate that today around 80 percent of all *cantinas* in Yucatán are owned by Modelo. Very few are still run by individuals—and those, well, most likely they are not *familiar*, if you know what I mean."

Don José was telling us a lot with few words. As was evident from the tidy physical appearance of El Gallito, as well as from its clientele, the place was what is increasingly referred to as a *cantina familiar*—or family saloon. The other establishments to which don José referred are those that still populate my *cantina* image-bank, where the occasional fistfight erupts, and where the *meseras* (waitresses) are known for offering considerably more than efficient table service.

VERDURAS EN ESCABECHE
PICKLED MIXED VEGETABLES WITH JALAPEÑOS

The heap of chiles among these mixed vegetables gives the dish an impressive zing, making it a wonderful accompaniment to beer or mixed drinks. Control the heat by using more or fewer chiles, or by seeding them or not. Perhaps surprisingly, the chile of choice in the *cantinas* is the jalapeño, although you may use a more "Yucatecan" chile, such as the x'catik (any blond chile will do), or for the truly daring, the habanero. While a frequent vegetable mix in *cantinas* is often beets and onions, you can use whatever vegetables you prefer. I like this medley of cauliflower, carrots, potatoes, and jalapeños. I also suggest some paper-thin cucumber slices.

Prepare ahead note: Verduras en escabeche is best made several hours or a day in advance to allow flavors to combine. The pickled vegetables store well under refrigeration up to 1 week. Bring to room temperature before serving.

YIELD: 10 SERVINGS

TO PREPARE AHEAD
Recado para escabeche (p. 498)

FOR THE VEGETABLES
1 lb. (500 g) baking potatoes
1–4 medium jalapeños (about 1¼ oz. / 35 g each), sliced into rings across the width, seeds left in or removed (see note at right)
½ medium red bell pepper (3¼ oz. / 92.5 g), seeded and cut into thin julienne strips about 2 in. (5 cm) long
1 cup (115 g) carrots, peeled and thinly sliced across the width on a diagonal
1 cup (115 g) cauliflower, separated into bite-sized florets

FOR DRESSING AND FINISHING
1 medium head garlic (1¾ oz. / 50 g), charred, peeled, and separated into cloves
½ medium white onion (5 oz. / 137.5 g), cut into quarters top to bottom, then each quarter thinly sliced top to bottom and separated into half-moon shapes
½ small cucumber (the half should weigh about 7 oz. / 200 g), peeled and very thinly sliced across the width
1 cup (250 ml) white wine vinegar
1 tsp. (6 g) sea salt
½ tsp. (2 g) sugar
½ tsp. (1.5 g) Recado para escabeche, plus 1–2 bay leaves from the *recado*

FOR SERVING
3 Tbs. (12 g) fresh cilantro leaves, coarsely chopped
Totopos para botanas (p. 515)

PARBOIL VEGETABLES
Cut the potatoes in half across the width, place them in a large pan, and cover with water. Bring to a boil, reduce heat to a simmer, and cook, uncovered, about 15 minutes, or until just tender when pierced with a fork. Drain and allow to cool.

Fill a large saucepan with water and bring to a boil. Add the jalapeños and bell peppers and blanch for 1 minute. Immediately remove the peppers with a wok strainer or slotted spoon and transfer to a large heatproof and nonreactive bowl. Add the carrots and cauliflower to the boiling water, reduce the heat to a simmer, and cook 3–4 minutes, or until the vegetables are just tender when pierced with a fork. Drain well and transfer to the bowl with the peppers.

DRESS VEGETABLES AND FINISH
Add the garlic, onions, and cucumber to the vegetables in the bowl. Peel the potatoes, cut them into ¾-inch (2 cm) cubes, and add to the vegetables. Mix the vinegar with the salt, sugar, and *recado* and stir to dissolve. Pour over the vegetables, toss to combine, and allow to macerate at room temperature at least 2 hours, tossing from time to time to keep the vegetables covered with the vinegar. Refrigerate until ready to serve. Bring to room temperature, add the cilantro, and toss just before serving

TO SERVE
Cantina patrons eat the vegetables with tortilla chips, but you may use a fork.

VARIATIONS
For a light summer salad, place chilled Verduras en escabeche atop a leaf of romaine or baby lettuce and arrange some sliced avocado on the side.

Papas en vinagreta (Pickled Potatoes with Jalapeños): Another *cantina* favorite. Increase the quantity of potatoes to 1½ pounds (680 g) and omit the carrots, bell pepper, and cauliflower. Cucumber is optional; proceed as in the master recipe.

PIMITOS DE CHICHARRA / PIMIWAH

THICK MAIZE PANCAKES WITH PORK CRACKLINGS

TO PREPARE AHEAD

Chicharra "especial" (p. 211)
Enriched Lard (p. 513)
Chicharrón (p. 214)
Masa para tamales yucatecos
  (p. 522)

FOR THE PIMITOS

½ recipe Chicharra "especial"
  (Note: You may use any
  combination of meats, including
  smoked slab bacon or Castacán
  and/or Chicharrón, to a finished
  total of ½ lb. [225 g], or 2 cups of
  Chicharrón by itself)
1 Tbs. (15 g) Enriched Lard
1 recipe Masa para tamales
  yucatecos
Sea salt

FOR SERVING

Salsa x'nipek (p. 512), or Tomate
  frito (p. 507)
Chile con limón (p. 511), or the
  chile sauce of your choice

When the Pimitos de chicharra arrived, our drinking scene became a feeding frenzy, with friend vying against friend to grab the last crumbs. *Cantinas* make these little maize breads a bit saltier than usual—for obvious reasons—but something about their fatty crunchiness makes them a natural with cold beer.

The regional name for this snack is Pimiwah: "*pim*" or "*piim*" is Mayan for "thick" or "fat"; "*wah*" means "maize bread" or "tortilla." The Spanish diminutive -*ito* means "little," making this a "thick little tortilla." In Mexico, the same snack is called *gordita*— Spanish for "little fatty" or "little fat girl." Pimitos can be filled with anything—from peas and potatoes to sausage or *picadillo*—but *chicharra* is the crowd pleaser here. Vegetarians, take heart: these same little maize breads can be made with the green leafy *chaya* (p. 27), in which case they are called Tortitas de chaya—and they are equally delicious (see below).

Prepare ahead note: The *masa* for Pimitos can be made in advance and frozen. The meats can be made a day ahead and refrigerated. Pimitos are best served immediately after cooking, but you can keep them warm in a 150°F (65°C) oven for about an hour. Left-overs can be refrigerated or frozen. Allow them to come to room temperature, then quickly reheat in a skillet or on a griddle, or bake in a 350°F (176°C) oven for 10–15 minutes.

YIELD: 1–1½ DOZEN PIMITOS

FORM PIMITOS AND FINISH

Finely chop the Chicharra and/or bacon. If you are using Chicharrón, coarsely crumble the cracklings, then finely chop. Heat the lard in a heavy skillet until shimmering. Add the meats and Chicharrón and reheat for 2–3 minutes, or until it is heated through and mixed with the lard. Remove the skillet from the heat and proceed.

Add the meat mixture with all the fat to the *masa* and knead with your hands to incorporate thoroughly.

Shape the *masa* into 3½-ounce (100 g) balls. In the palm of your hand, pat one ball into a fat tortilla, about 4 inches (10 cm) in diameter and ⅜-inch (5 mm) thick. Place 3–4 Pimitos at a time in a non-stick skillet over medium heat and fry 3–4 minutes. Turn to check for doneness: they should be a deep golden brown in patches over the entire surface. Repeat on the reverse side. (Note: Cooking for a longer time over medium rather than high heat will ensure that the *masa* is cooked through.) Repeat with all the Pimitos. As they are cooked, transfer them to paper towels and sprinkle lightly with salt.

TO SERVE

Serve warm. Pimitos are usually accompanied by tomato sauce, either Tomate frito or X'nipek; diners add chile sauce to taste.

Tortitas de chaya (Thick Maize Pancakes with Chaya): While *cantina* patrons would start a brawl if they were served porkless Pimitos, you can easily transform the original recipe into a vegetarian version that appears in some vintage regional cookbooks. Use the vegetarian option of Masa para tamales yucatecos on page 522. Prepare one recipe Chayas fritas (p. 129), omitting the bacon. Allow the mixture to cool, then combine the greens with the *masa*, using your hands to incorporate completely. Proceed as in the master recipe for Pimitos.

SIKIL P'AAK

VEGETABLE DIP OF TOASTED SQUASH SEEDS, ROASTED TOMATOES, AND CHILE

Few dishes so sensually conjure the full flavors of the *milpa* at harvest time as does Sikil p'aak: squash seeds, tomatoes, and chiles consumed atop a corn chip, tortilla, or Pimito come together as a comforting reminder of all things of the earth. In the pueblos, Sikil p'aak is still consumed by using a corn tortilla to scoop up a fistful, but in urban settings such as at parties and in *cantinas*, it is served as a dip and eaten with crispy fried tortilla chips. The name—also variously transcribed as Sikilpak, P'aak i tsikil, and, occasionally, Ha' sikil p'aak—reads like a shopping list for the dish's simple formula: "*sikil*" is Mayan for "squash seed"; "*p'aak*" means "tomato"; and "*ha'*" is "water." If you plan to serve this at a party, you should double the recipe; it goes fast.

[MC]

Seville orange juice substitute
(p. 514), unless fresh Seville
oranges are available

Pepita molida (p. 497; you
may use either the Verde or
the Menuda, but I prefer the
former)

FOR THE TOMATO PURÉE

2 medium Roma tomatoes (7 oz. /
200 g), charred

2 medium cloves garlic (½ oz. /
12 g), peeled and charred

1 medium chile habanero
(7–14 g), charred, seeded,
and finely chopped

½ cup (125 ml) water

¼ cup (62.5 ml) Seville orange
juice, or substitute

2 tsp. (12 g) sea salt or powdered
chicken or vegetable bouillon,
or to taste

FOR FINISHING THE DIP

2 cups (250 g) Pepita molida

¼ cup (20 g) chives, chopped

½ medium white onion (5 oz. /
137.5 g), charred and finely
chopped

3 Tbs. (11 g) fresh cilantro leaves,
finely chopped

FOR SERVING

Totopos para botanas (p. 515)

Prepare ahead note: Sikil p'aak should be made at least 30 minutes in advance so that the pulverized seeds have a chance to soften and absorb the tomato purée. It is best served on the day it is prepared, but it can be refrigerated for 2–3 days. Bring it to room temperature and stir. You may wish to thin it with a bit of water or stock and refresh it with a bit more fresh chopped chives and cilantro.

YIELD: 6–8 SERVINGS

PREPARE TOMATO PURÉE

Place the ingredients in the jar of a blender and process until thoroughly liquefied; set aside. You should have 2 cups of the purée; if not, add water to complete the amount.

FINISH DIP AND SERVE

Place the Pepita molida in a large mixing bowl. Different conditions will cause the ground seeds to absorb the liquid at different rates, so add the tomato purée to the seeds gradually. Start by adding only about ¾ of the contents of the blender and stir to blend thoroughly. Let the mixture rest for 5–10 minutes; the seeds will absorb the liquid and the dip will thicken. Add more of the liquid if you wish. In *cantinas*, Sikil p'aak is served in a thinner state, something like yogurt, but I prefer mine to be a thicker paste. You will add between 1½ and 2 cups of the purée. Stir in the chives, chopped onion, and cilantro and check for seasoning; add salt if necessary. (Note: Pepita menuda is much more absorbent than Pepita verde. If using the Menuda, you may need to add more water or juice to achieve the desired consistency.)

TO SERVE

Serve Sikil p'aak as a dip with crispy Totopos para botanas. It is also delicious spread on Yucatecan fritters such as Pol'kanes (p. 111) and Pimitos (p. 284).

VARIATIONS

In homage to Middle Eastern flavors, add a scant ⅛ teaspoon (less than 0.625 g) ground *canela* (Mexican cinnamon) in the finishing step.

Sikil abal (Vegetable Dip of Toasted Squash Seeds, Spanish Plums, and Chile): This regional variation of Sikil p'aak found in eastern Yucatán is made with the local fruit *ciruela* (*Spondias purpurea*—"*abal*" in Mayan, p. 29) instead of tomatoes. Since *ciruela* is available only at certain times of year, cooks may elect to substitute the *tomate verde* (tomatillo) in the off-season to simulate *ciruela*'s tart taste. Both recipes are provided here.

With *ciruela* (available frozen in some regions): The ingredients for Sikil p'aak, substituting tomatoes for 7 oz. / 200 g *ciruela* (finished weight after pitting), parboiled until tender. Proceed as in the master recipe.

With tomatillo: The ingredients for Sikil p'aak, substituting 2 cups (500 ml) Salsa verde (p. 509) for the tomato purée 1. Proceed as in the master recipe.

Yucatecan cantina, early 1900s. Rum bottles crowd the shelves, and plates of food are displayed atop a vitrine, right. A painting on the wall advertises Habanero Berreteaga, always ordered by name. "Habanero" was a popular blend of sweet Spanish wine and sugarcane spirits; this particular brand was produced in Tabasco. [FPG]

TAMING MACHISMO

From All-Male Watering Hole to Coed Cabaret

The phenomenon of the modern *restaurante familiar* evolved out of the old *cantina*: around 1950–1960, many *cantinas* began to open what was known as the "*salon familiar*," or family room—a side room of the main *cantina* into which women and, later, children were allowed. Relaxing social mores during the next few decades dissolved the barriers between the *cantina* proper and the *salon familiar*, and whole families soon spilled out of the room set aside for them and into the bar itself. This new format soon became known as the "*cantina familiar*"—the genre to which El Gallito belongs—and quickly surged in popularity. And close on the heels of that success, the concept of the *restaurante familiar* emerged, following the tried-and-true *cantina* format of "beer and *botanas*" but also offering full menus and entertainment.

LA HORA CRISTAL

The custom of coed mingling in Yucatecan *cantinas* began in the middle of the twentieth century, thanks in large part to a popular radio program of the time. The program was called *La Hora Cristal* and began broadcasting in 1953 on XEMH Radio Mérida Monday through Friday. Its joint sponsors were Cervecería Yucateca (p. 289) and Embotelladora Peninsular, which had been founded in 1947 as the region's official bottler of Coca-Cola and the manufacturer of the popular Cristal soft drink brand. *La Hora Cristal* featured popular music by request and was hosted by Víctor Manuel Barrios Mata, a local personality known for his success with the women as well as his straight-shooting commentaries on Yucatecan politics. It aired from noon until 2:00 pm, and people left work or home to meet friends or family at the local *cantina* to listen to the program together, enjoy a beer or other refreshment, and to eat a little something. It was this phenomenon that underwrote the growth of certain *restaurantes familiares* that are still in existence, such as Eladio's, which opened as Eladio's Bar in Mérida in 1952 and now is a chain with several venues across the peninsula. To the present, Yucatecans still refer to "*la hora cristal*" as the time of day to stop the regular routine, relax, and enjoy a beer and a bite.

The Indians are very dissolute in drinking and becoming intoxicated.

—FRAY DIEGO DE LANDA, 1566

It is difficult to know what the fiercely Catholic eyes of de Landa and others really saw regarding the Mayas' interaction with alcohol. Of course, as did peoples in most ancient cultures, the Mayas concocted fermented beverages that they used to contact the spirit world, to offer sacrifice, and occasionally just to get plain silly.

Whatever transpired in history, times have changed. Yucatecans are, statistically, moderate drinkers. And, when they do drink, the alcoholic beverage of choice in Yucatán is unquestionably beer, followed by rum, vodka, whisky, tequila, and brandy, in that order. Tequila ranks low for a number of reasons, not least of which is the perception that it is "Mexican" rather than Yucatecan. Wine is consumed so infrequently that it does not even make the list. In fact, three times more beer per liter is consumed in Yucatán than any other alcoholic beverage. Drinkers revealed that beer was their favorite primarily because of the relatively cheap price, but also because of the relief it provided in the intense Yucatecan heat.

YUCATECAN BEER AND BOOZE

Beer

Notwithstanding its current popularity, the early presence of beer in Yucatán met with significant production and storage problems in an environment of year-round hot

(above) Cervecería Yucateca, c. 1900. [FPG]

weather. With the importation of cooling technology in the late nineteenth century, Yucatán was finally ready to establish its first brewery. On 7 April 1899, in Mérida, José María Ponce & Co. founded the Gran Cervecería Yucateca, which produced the Cruz Roja, Estrella, Conejo, and Mestiza brands. In 1900, the company simplified its name to Cervecería Yucateca and built a major plant that soon became an icon in the heart of the city, on Calle 70 at Calle 63, near Parque Santiago.

The premier offering of the Cervecería Yucateca was a Vienna amber–style beer called León Negra, which continues in popularity. Later, the brewers released the lager-style Carta Clara, and finally in the 1960s, the pilsner-style Montejo, named after Yucatán's first governor, Francisco de Montejo.

In 1979, the Mexican giant Cervecería Modelo acquired Cervecería Yucateca, retaining the León Negra and Montejo brands, and in 2002, it moved production to central Mexico, where it continues to the present. Other Mexican beer brands, such as Superior, Sol, and Dos X (all produced by Cuauhtémoc Moctezuma in Monterrey), are consumed, too, but most locals still exhibit Yucatecan pride by ordering the beers that originated on their own soil.

Rum

The consumption of rum dates back at least two centuries and is due in large measure to Yucatán's regional trade relationships with the United States and most particularly the Caribbean. While most rums are imported, the D'Aristi distillery at Hacienda Vista Alegre produces the award-winning Caribe rum.

Balché *and* Xtabentún

Some say that no Yucatecan meal is complete without a glass of ice-cold Xtabentún to finish it off. How that came to be is rooted in ancient Maya ceremonial practices.

Xtabentún—a vining morning glory (*Turbina corymbosa*) native to the region—is rich in psychotropic ergoline alkaloids. Honey from the plant's blossoms, produced by the local stingless *melipona* bee (p. 411), is thought to have the same psychotropic characteristics. The ancient Mayas used *xtabentún* honey medicinally, but it was also frequently fermented to produce a mead, or "honey wine," to which the bark of the leguminous *balché* tree (*Lonchocarpus violaceus*, lilac tree) was added during the fermentation process.

Cuba Libre: *Two shots light rum, juice of ½ lime, cola to fill the glass.* [MR]

L. violaceus, like several other members of the Fabaceae family, is itself psychoactive due to its rotenone content—nowadays classified as a botanical insecticide. When combined with *xtabentún* honey's ergoline alkaloids, the effect must have been transcendental indeed! This inebriant, known as *balché*, was used to induce trances in the shaman and offer him a glimpse into the other world.

Balché is still used by the Mayas in Yucatán as an offering in planting ceremonies and to ward off pesky *aluxes* (trickster spirits), that might try to damage crops. Any promises of hallucination, however, must now be fulfilled by its more straightlaced descendant, the liqueur known as Xtabentún.

In 1935, suffering from losses in revenue due to a sagging

The xtabentún *plant from an 1843 book on botany.* [EDWARDS'S BOTANICAL REGISTER, LONDON, 1843]

Xtabentún Cocktails

Serve chilled or over ice as a digestif or add to coffee or serve in a shot glass alongside coffee.

D'Aristi also offers some poetic cocktails featuring Xtabentún:

- *Xaman eek'* (North Star): Mix equal parts Xtabentún and quality tequila; serve over ice with a squeeze of lime juice
- *K'iin* (Sun): Mix 1 part Xtabentún with 4 parts fresh orange juice; serve over ice
- *Sak nikte'* (White Flower): Mix 1½ parts Xtabentún with 4 parts chilled white wine
- *Yuum k'áax* (Spirit of the *Monte*; see p. 95): Place 1 part honey, 2 parts rum, 3 parts Xtabentún, and the juice of 1 lime in a blender with ice; process until smooth and serve.

YUCATECAN HANGOVER REMEDIES

It would be irresponsible if not downright cruel to close this chapter without offering some remedies for "*la cruda*"— the hangover. An informal survey yielded these tips. You'll find recipes for several of these purported cures throughout this book.

- Orange juice as soon as you wake up
- Sopa de cabeza de pescado (p. 160) "con un chingo de chile" (with a helluva lot of chile—their exact words, not mine)
- Mondongo (p. 221), with a lot of chiles habaneros and a cola beverage
- A *caguama* (Mexican slang for a liter of beer) at the point of freezing
- Chilpachole de jaiba, a spicy crab stew
- Chilaquiles with red or green sauce, "pero que piquen un chingo" (as long as it's as hot as hell)
- Michelada (p. 273) with a lot of ice, lime, and chile, drunk all in one gulp
- Ojo rojo, a beer beverage featuring Clamato
- Vampiro—I provide the simple recipe here: liquefy some eggplant; pour equal measures of the eggplant purée and orange juice into a glass filled with ice
- Huevos motuleños (p. 454), but the tomato sauce has to be very spicy

national economy, the owners of Hacienda Vista Alegre decided to devote their infrastructure to the production of a new, distilled version of the ancient mead, which they christened Xtabentún in honor of its history. The liqueur is still made from fermented honey—now a blossom blend, since the *xtabentún* vine is increasingly rare. White rum is added to increase alcohol content, and anise gives a pronounced flavor and bows to the historical taste of the early Spanish colonists for anise liqueurs. Today, Xtabentún is produced by several distilleries in the region and is thought of as the quintessential Yucatecan liqueur.

(opposite page) Xtabentún. [MC]

5

The

URBAN

MATRIX

THE URBAN CENTERS OF YUCATÁN are hubs of commerce and culture, the matrix where Mayas and Europeans met and still meet to exchange ideas, trade goods, and, most important, swap recipes.

In the urban matrix, the gastronomical possibilities are dizzying. Modern-day Campeche, Mérida, and Valladolid—the three largest cities in the peninsula—share many foods that lend a sense of cultural connection among their residents. Yet, each city boasts its own special dishes, too, that foster a sense of local pride.

(previous page spread) Pescado en tikin xiik' (p. 316) [EC]
(this page) Twilight at Mérida en domingo. [KO]

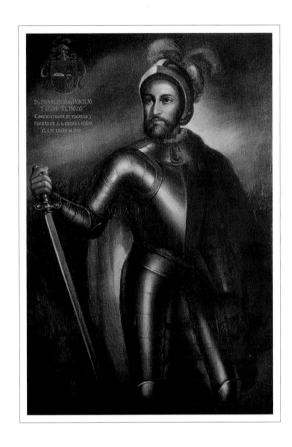

EMPIRE BUILDING

Campeche, Mérida, and Valladolid grew up together rather like triplets. All three cities were founded and governed by one family. The Montejos—father, son, and nephew—from Salamanca solicited and were granted a royal contract to conquer Yucatán in 1526. Just one year later, the three landed with 500 men in Cozumel and began a steady march across the peninsula. Maya resistance was fierce, however, and apparently the family decided it was wiser to divide and conquer.

Montejo "El Adelantado" (the elder) retreated to Tabasco in 1534, which he governed for many years. Montejo "El Mozo" (the son) took over for his father in Yucatán and by 1540 had subdued the Mayas enough that he was able to found Campeche. From there he returned east to finish what the trio had started almost fifteen years earlier: the conquest of T'Ho, later called Mérida, which he founded in 1542. And Montejo "Sobrino" (the nephew) claimed his share of the booty by establishing Valladolid in 1543. For at least two decades, the three Montejo men enjoyed the power that came with dominating the vast terrain of Yucatán, as well as the wealth that was soon generated there.

(above) Conqueror and founder: Francisco de Montejo, "el Mozo." [ERMILIO TORRE GAMBOA, 16TH CENTURY]

(opposite page) Casa de Montejo, the conqueror's mansion in Mérida, built in the mid-sixteenth century. [RAZIEL ROSAS NOVELO / SECRETARÍA DE FOMENTO TURÍSTICO, MÉRIDA]

CAMPECHE

FOR CENTURIES, THE SEA has defined the commerce, culture, and history of Campeche—and also its cuisine. If Mérida is a culinary melting pot and Valladolid a quaint time capsule of Spanish colonial recipes, then Campeche is a copious treasure chest of the bounties of the sea. The recipes in this section, logically, focus on seafood.

Campeche's undulating coasts, sheltered lagoons, and vast tracts of estuaries, seagrass meadows, and mangroves supplied the Mayas and later explorers with a rich variety of seafood. Many species, such as *Octopus maya*, are unique to the region and coveted in national as well as global markets. Fishing for export grew steadily during the twentieth century, establishing Campeche as the largest fishery on the Gulf Coast of the Yucatán Peninsula and a primary seafood exporter, particularly to U.S. markets.

In Campeche, the presence of the sea is felt at every turn. Stroll through the quaint cobblestoned streets of the city—a UNESCO World Heritage site—and from time to time through arched gates piercing the mammoth protective wall that encircles the city, you will glimpse gently rippling turquoise waters. And along the *malecón*, a seafront walkway that traces the shoreline for many kilometers, hundreds of small fishing launches dock at various points and offer up the day's catch to satisfy a steady flow of customers throughout the day.

(above) Walled fortress. [MC]

PIRATES OF YUCATÁN

Campeche's rapid rise to power occurred in part because of the valuable raw materials native to the area, but mostly as a result of its prime location. Not only was it a necessary point of departure for a wealth of local products, but it was also the port of entry for galleons from Cádiz, bringing casks of wine, oil, figs, raisins, olives, and iron from the Old World. And as the ships returned to Spain, their holds were restocked with peninsular products: logwood, chicle (see Zapote, p. 53) and the valuable fiber sisal (p. 453).

Pirates of many nationalities established bases in Hispaniola and Jamaica in order to stage attacks on Caribbean ports. But when they discovered the riches that were to be had in the Gulf of Mexico, they seized Isla de Términos (now Isla del Carmen in Campeche), from which they could more conveniently plan attacks on the Yucatán Peninsula.

The first assaults by pirates on Campeche began in 1559. Fortification became an ongoing military goal for the next several decades, especially as pirates plotted to raid inland cities such as Mérida and Valladolid. In 1683, plans were finished for the grand defensive wall that would ultimately surround Campeche. The massive wall—over 8,200 feet (2,500 m) long, some 25 feet (8 m) tall, 8 feet (2.5 m) thick, and pierced with four fortified gates controlling entrance to the city—took eighteen years to build. Ironically, by the time of its completion in 1704, a string of political and economic changes had resulted in the decline of piracy, such that the wall never had to perform its intended function. Much of it is still visible today.

(above, left) Sugarcane fields in Campeche. [JFMT] *(above, middle) Felipe IV, Madrid, 1628, by court painter Diego Velázquez. The popularity of black clothing in seventeenth-century Spain as captured in many of the artist's paintings was made possible by a valuable dye extracted from Campeche's native logwood tree* (Haematoxylum campechianum), *known colloquially as "campeachy." Logwood was a key target for pirates.* [ALBUM / ART RESOURCE, NY]
(above, right) Cathedral of Campeche. [DS]

In spite of the atrocities enacted by these opportunists, pirates were not without their gastronomical impact (read about Edam cheese on p. 347).

CONQUEST AND SHAME: SLAVERY IN THE NEW WORLD

An unhappy by-product of the great wealth generated in Europe's tropical colonies was the trade in slaves. Some of the new colonial industries—such as sugar production in the vast cane fields of Yucatán and the Caribbean islands—were highly labor intensive, and slavery was legitimized as an inexpensive solution to the problem.

Recently discovered evidence documents the earliest unmistakable physical link between Africa and the New World to date and places the arrival of African slaves to the Americas just a few years after the arrival of Columbus. The study draws on isotope ratios in the teeth of four individuals found in a burial ground originally located in what is now Campeche's main plaza near the cathedral. Distinctive dental mutilations commonly practiced among West African tribes at the time leave little doubt as to the origin of the remains.

This tragic episode left behind a gastronomical legacy: many African foods were brought to Yucatán in the early years after contact, including cowpeas and watermelon. And the exchange worked both ways: American sweet potatoes, *yuca*, and peanuts were soon thoroughly incorporated into African cooking.

THE *MERENDEROS*

Starting at dawn, a synergistic dance between fishermen and seafood vendors enlivens the oceanfront and satiates passersby with the freshest seafood imaginable. As soon as a fishing launch touches shore, bicycle- or *moto*-powered

Portable merendero. [MR]

carts equipped with serving dishes, spoons, and chile sauces whoosh up alongside piles of fresh fish. The vendor descends, sets up his equipment, and buys seafood to transform into quick, simple dishes. Soon he sings: "¡Hay coctel! ¡Campechanos! ¡Hay ceviche!"

These are the *merenderos*, or "picnic stands," which are a feature of the undulating Gulf Coast highway that stretches 130 miles (212 km) southwest from San Francisco de Campeche all the way to Ciudad del Carmen. Enjoying a fresh shrimp or oyster cocktail here is one of the great pleasures of *campechano* life.

Some of Campeche's signature dishes are named after the city and playfully describe an attitude about the place. "*Campechano*" is the demonym that describes one who or that which hails from Campeche. But to those who live in Mexico, it also means so much more. The dictionary of the Real Academia Española lists ten meanings, ranging from "affable" and "fun-loving" to "a kind of puff pastry" and "a mixture of different alcohols or food ingredients."

During your visit to Campeche, you cannot overlook *campechanas* or *campechanos*—a sweet flaky pastry and a seafood cocktail, respectively—both like heartbeats in the daily rhythm of eating. They say that the seafood cocktail was invented in Campeche, but true or not, a contrived verb has emerged from this Neptunian medley: "*campechanear*" in the vernacular Spanish of the region has come to mean the act of mixing a bunch of stuff together.

Campechano. [MR]

CAMPECHANO

OYSTERS AND SHRIMP IN TANGY TOMATO SAUCE

Whether or not the shrimp cocktail was invented in Campeche, seafood "*cocteles*" in a tomato-based sauce are so associated with this genteel city by the sea that people across Mexico refer to them as Campechanos. While the mixture of seafood remains open to interpretation, the essential ingredient for a Campechano in its native habitat is raw oysters. Cooks jealously guard their secret formulas for the sauce, although most recipes seem to have one thing in common: catsup. One cook told me her special touch was orange soda, which I must admit adds a citrusy tang and also a bit of effervescence—refreshing on steamy tropical afternoons.

Prepare ahead note: The sauce and cooked shrimp for Campechano should be prepared in advance and refrigerated. Assemble the *coctel* immediately before serving.

YIELD: 6 SERVINGS

FOR THE SAUCE

3 medium Roma tomatoes
  (10½ oz. / 300 g), seeded and
  chopped
1 cup (250 ml) tomato juice
½ cup (125 ml) fresh lime juice
½ cup (125 ml) Spanish olive oil
3 Tbs. (45 ml) white wine vinegar
2 Tbs. (30 ml) catsup
½ tsp. (2.5 g) freshly ground black
  pepper

FOR THE COCKTAIL

2 lbs. (1 k) large raw oysters,
  freshly shucked or canned with
  liquor, weighed with liquor
1 lb. (500 g) medium shrimp
  (43–50 count), heads and tails
  removed, shelled and deveined,
  and parboiled for 1 minute until
  just pink, then refrigerated
6 Tbs. (90 ml) Worcestershire
  sauce, divided
1½ cups (375 ml) canned orange
  soda, chilled (Substitute: mix
  ½ cup / 125 ml Seville orange
  juice or substitute with 1 tsp.
  / 4 g sugar and 1 cup / 250 ml
  sparkling water)

FOR SERVING

Mixture of chopped white onion
  and cilantro
Avocado slices (optional)
Totopos para botanas (p. 515)
Chile con limón (p. 511), or the
  chile sauce of your choice
Lime wedges

PREPARE SAUCE

Combine the sauce ingredients in the jar of a blender and process until liquefied. Refrigerate at least 1 hour before assembling the cocktail. (Note: In Campeche, *merenderos* use only tomato juice instead of fresh tomatoes, which is easier and results in a redder sauce; the addition of fresh tomatoes results in a brighter taste and a bit of texture, although the color is somewhat pink. If you opt to take the shortcut and omit the fresh tomatoes, increase the juice to 2 cups [500ml]).

ASSEMBLE COCKTAIL

Immediately before serving, create the cocktail in layers in 6 tall parfait or Tom Collins glasses. Place about 3½ ounces (100 g) oysters and their liquor at the bottom of one of the glasses. Add 5–6 shrimp (about 2½ oz. / 85 g). Pour on 1 tablespoon (15 ml) Worcestershire sauce and ¼ cup (62.5 ml) orange soda or Seville orange mixture. Finish with about ½ cup (125 ml) of the chilled tomato sauce.

TO SERVE

Top the cocktail with a spoonful of the onion/cilantro mixture and garnish with avocado slices if you wish. Serve with a long spoon accompanied by Totopos and/or saltines. Diners add squeezes of lime juice and chile sauce to taste.

VARIATION

Coctel de camarón (Shrimp Cocktail): Follow the master recipe, omitting the oysters and increasing the shrimp to 3 pounds (1.5 k). Distribute the shrimp evenly among the 6 glasses.

Fishmonger with pámpano in the Pedro Sainz de Barrada market. [MR]

FISH MARKETS OF CAMPECHE

There are three principal fish markets in Campeche. San Román de Justo Sierra and 7 de Agosto are small markets located at the water's edge on the *malecón*. The largest fish market—which occupies two square blocks of the interior of the central Pedro Sainz de Barranda market—features a brilliant display of all the major species of the region.

Although thousands of species are found in Campeche's waters, the following are the most representative varieties and the recipes for them are those you are likely to sample in restaurants.

CALAMARES RELLENOS

BREADED FRIED SQUID STUFFED WITH SHRIMP AND LONGANIZA

The seafood restaurants that line the beachfront of San Francisco de Campeche seem to have a competition going for who can serve the biggest, fattest, most overstuffed Calamares rellenos. A poetic blend of surf and turf, the filling for Calamares rellenos consists of chopped shrimp and the local smoked sausage, Longaniza de Valladolid. Once stuffed, the creature is breaded and deep-fat fried. This recipe is adapted from one shared with me by Campeche-born Palmira Rodríguez Tejeda de Angele.

Prepare ahead note: Calamares rellenos should be served immediately after the frying step. You can clean and fill the squid ahead of time and freeze them; defrost for a few minutes prior to finishing.

YIELD: 6 SERVINGS AS A FIRST COURSE

TO PREPARE AHEAD

Longaniza de Valladolid (p. 481), or substitute
Pan molido para empanizado (p. 515)

FOR FILLING

2½ oz. (75 g) Longaniza de Valladolid (Substitute: chorizo, commercial *longaniza*, or other smoked sausage)
2 Tbs. (30 ml) Spanish olive oil
¼ cup (35 g) *each* red, yellow, and green bell pepper, cut into small dice
½ medium white onion (5 oz. / 137.5 g), finely chopped
4 medium cloves garlic (1 oz. / 24 g), peeled and minced
1 medium chile habanero (¼ oz. / 7 g) *or* 2 medium chiles serranos (¾ oz. / 20 g total), charred, peeled, seeded, and finely chopped
9 oz. (250 g) shrimp, tails, heads, and shells removed, deveined, and finely chopped
1 tsp. (6 g) sea salt, or to taste
18 small squid, approximately 6 inches (15 cm) in length, each weighing about 4 oz. (113 g), cleaned, tentacles reserved

FOR BREADING AND FRYING

½ cup (62.5 g) all-purpose flour
½ tsp. (3 g) sea salt
4 egg whites
Vegetable oil for frying
1½ cups (180 g) Pan molido para empanizado
Sea salt

PREPARE FILLING

Remove the casings from the sausage and discard. In a heavy skillet, heat the oil until shimmering. Add the sausage and cook, stirring constantly, 2–3 minutes, using a wooden spoon to crumble the meat. Raise the heat to medium, add the bell pepper, onion, garlic, and chile and cook until the peppers are very tender, 4–5 minutes. Add the shrimp and cook, stirring constantly, 1–2 minutes, or until just pink. Check the seasonings and add salt if needed. Remove the pan from the heat and allow to cool.

Pat the squid dry. Fill each squid body with approximately 2 teaspoons (1 oz. / 25 g) of the stuffing. Use a toothpick to seal the open end and hold in the filling. If you wish, freeze the squid at this stage and finish later.

BREAD, FRY, AND FINISH

Mix the flour and salt in a bowl. Roll each filled squid in the seasoned flour and set aside. Beat the egg whites until soft peaks form.

Pour the oil into a skillet to a depth of 1½ inches (4 cm) and heat to 350°F (176°C). Working one at a time, pass the floured squid through the egg whites, roll in the Pan molido, and immediately add to the hot oil. Fry until golden brown, turning once, 1–2 minutes per side. Transfer the squid to paper towels to drain and remove the tooth-picks. Carefully add the reserved tentacles, 1 or 2 at a time, to the hot oil (if they are damp they will splatter, so stand back) and fry 10–15 seconds. Transfer the tentacles to the paper towels with the squid, sprinkle all with salt, and serve immediately.

FOR SERVING

Tomate frito (p. 507)

Chopped cilantro

Arroz con camarón (p. 528),
   optional

Chile tamulado (p. 509), or the
   chile sauce of your choice

TO SERVE

Arrange 3 squid per person on individual serving plates. Mask the opening where the stuffing was inserted by placing one set of tentacles where they were once attached. Spoon on some of the Tomate frito and sprinkle with chopped cilantro. Turn this into a complete meal by serving with Arroz con camarón and a mixed green salad if you wish. Diners add chile sauce to taste.

[MR]

CALAMAR / SQUID

Loligo pealei / Loligo plei / Dosidicus gigas

In Campeche's fish markets you'll notice that the squid for sale is much smaller than the behemoths of movie fame. While there is a commercial industry for the jumbo squid (*Dosidicus gigas*), which can reach a mantle length of almost six feet (1.75 m), virtually all of these giants are prepared for export.

The other two varieties are smaller and typically a by-catch that may be discarded, used for bait, or sold in the markets. *Loligo plei* and *L. pealei* reach mantle lengths of only 10 and 11.4 inches (250 and 285 mm), respectively. These are the most typical market squid in Campeche.

CAMARONES EN CHILMOLE

SHRIMP IN CHARRED CHILE SAUCE

TO PREPARE AHEAD
Recado negro (p. 501)

**FOR CHILE SAUCE
AND SHRIMP**

6 Tbs. (90 g) Recado negro,
  dissolved in 1 cup (250 ml) water
1 medium head garlic (1¾ oz. /
  50 g), charred, peeled, and
  separated into cloves
4 cups (1 L) fish stock or bottled
  clam juice
3 medium Roma tomatoes
  (10½ oz. / 300 g), seeded
  and chopped
2 sprigs fresh epazote
  (Substitute: 1 tsp. / 1.5 g dried)
⅓ cup (45 g) *masa harina*
1 lb. (500 g) large shrimp
  (31/35 count), tails, heads, and
  shells removed, deveined

FOR SERVING

Arroz negro (p. 532), recommended accompaniment
Salpicón (p. 511), recommended
  accompaniment
Tortillas (p. 518)
Chile tamulado (p. 509), or the
  chile sauce of your choice

Dressed head to toe in black, this stylish dish is never out of date. Recado negro gives Camarones en chilmole its characteristic graphite color, and it is typical in Yucatán to serve many *chilmole* dishes atop Arroz negro—rice steeped in the cooking liquid of black beans. This recipe was adapted from the 1944 cookbook *Cocina yucateca*, by Lucrecia Ruz *vda*. de Baqueiro.

Prepare ahead note: The chile sauce can be prepared several hours or a day in advance and refrigerated. Reheat, add the shrimp, and finish immediately before serving. If you anticipate having leftovers, add only the shrimp you plan to eat at one sitting; cook the rest when you reheat the sauce for another meal.

YIELD: 6 SERVINGS

PREPARE CHILE SAUCE AND SHRIMP

Strain the *recado* liquid into a blender jar through a piece of cheesecloth placed in a sieve. With a rubber spatula, press through as much liquid as possible. Gather the ends of the cheesecloth and squeeze to extract more liquid; discard the residue. Add the garlic to the blender and process at high speed until puréed; set aside.

Pour the fish stock into a stockpot. Add the *recado* mixture, tomatoes, and epazote and bring to a boil. Cook at a rapid boil for 10 minutes to reduce the stock and intensify the flavors.

Ladle some of the stock into a heatproof bowl. Add the *masa harina* and whisk to blend. Return the flour mixture to the stockpot, whisking vigorously to remove any lumps. Simmer gently for 5 minutes to thicken, stirring frequently. Check the seasonings. (Note: If you used homemade *recado*, it contains no salt, so you may wish to add ½–1 teaspoon [3–6 g] sea salt at this stage. Check the seasonings: the amount of salt you need will depend on the saltiness of your fish stock.)

Add the shrimp to the simmering sauce and cook 3–4 minutes, or until the shrimp just turns pink and is still firm. Remove the pan from the heat and serve the shrimp immediately.

TO SERVE

Heap Arroz negro in the middle of a shallow soup bowl. (Alternatively, you may mold the rice by packing it into a custard cup or ramekin, then inverting it in the center of the bowl.) Spoon some of the shrimp and sauce onto the rice and garnish with Salpicón. To eat, place some of the rice, shrimp, and Salpicón onto warm tortillas, adding chile sauce to taste.

Camarones asados en chilmole (Grilled Shrimp in Charred Chile Marinade): Combine the strained Recado negro–water mixture with the garlic in a blender as described in the master recipe. (Omit the remaining ingredients and steps.) Pour this marinade over the shrimp and refrigerate for 1 hour. Remove the shrimp from the marinade and shake off the excess; discard the marinade. Grill the shrimp quickly over charcoal, about 2 minutes per side. Sprinkle with sea salt and serve with a mixed green salad and white or black rice.

[MR]

CAMARÓN / SHRIMP

Penaeus duorarum (pink shrimp) / *Penaeus setiferus* (white shrimp) / *Penaeus aztecus* (brown shrimp)

In the mid-twentieth century, the Campeche Bank—a shallow underwater plain that extends into the Gulf 150 miles (240 km) from the shoreline—was considered the best shrimp habitat in North America. Three shrimp species—pink, white, and brown—make up more than 99 percent of all shrimp caught in the Gulf of Mexico.

While hauls have diminished, the Campeche Bank still represents a major source for all three varieties. The pink shrimp is most extensively fished in the Bay of Campeche, where it makes its habitat in the plentiful seagrass beds found there.

CAZÓN ASADO
CHARCOAL-GRILLED DOGFISH

FOR MARINATING AND GRILLING THE DOGFISH

¼ cup (72 g) *plus* 1 tsp. (6 g) sea salt, divided

1 gallon (4 L) water

3½ lbs. (1.6 k) dogfish, head, tail, and fins removed, skinned, cut across the body into steaks; finished weight after cleaning should be about 2¾ lbs. (1.25 k)

¼ cup (62.5 ml) Spanish olive oil, plus additional for the grill

5 medium cloves garlic (1¼ oz. / 30 g), peeled and finely chopped

The enormous fish market in Campeche's central market displays a rainbow of Gulf seafood, most of it fresh, but some salted or roasted, such as Cazón asado. Rarely consumed as is, this charcoal grilled dogfish is usually cooked two more times before being included in a dish. First it is boiled in lightly salted water and shredded, then it is sautéed with a *sofrito* mixture. Roasting the dogfish gives the finished dish a noticeably smoky flavor. You may grill it whole, but it is more manageable if you cut it into thick steaks sliced across the girth of the fish or use fillets.

Whole *cazón* must be well cleaned and removed of head, tail, and fins. It should also be skinned: *campechano* cooks usually do this after cooking, but since the skin can deteriorate into a sandy residue in cooking liquid, I find it more manageable to skin beforehand. That said, I don't recommend doing these things yourself, since a perfectly sharp filleting knife is essential, not to mention knowledge, skill, and experience in the task. Your fishmonger should be able to oblige.

All shark meat contains urea, which thoroughly decomposes during cooking. However, untreated meat can have an ammonia-like smell and taste that is unpleasant to some. A half-hour marinade in milk or brine will neutralize the urea.

Prepare ahead note: Cazón asado may be prepared in advance and refrigerated or frozen until ready for use.

YIELD: APPROXIMATELY 1¾ LBS. (850 G)

MARINATE DOGFISH

Dissolve ¼ cup (72 g) sea salt in the water. Add the fish and allow it to rest at room temperature for 30 minutes.

Remove the dogfish from the brine, rinse, and pat dry; discard the brining solution. Spread the dogfish steaks in a baking dish large enough to hold them in 1 layer, sprinkle both sides with the remaining 1 tsp. (6 g) sea salt, add the olive oil and garlic, and turn the steaks to coat thoroughly. Allow the steaks to rest at room temperature for 1 hour.

[MR]

While the steaks are resting, prepare the grill. Brush the grates with a bit of oil to prevent sticking. Follow the instructions for gas or charcoal grills using wood smoking chips in Basic Techniques, page 538.

Remove the fish steaks from the marinade and shake off any excess marinade. Grill the steaks 6–8 minutes per side, depending on thickness, or until the fish feels firm to the touch. Remove the fish from the grill and allow to cool before proceeding.

[MR]

CAZÓN / DOGFISH SHARK

Squalus sp.

Local fishermen rank the seventy species in the Squalidae, or "dogfish shark," family by size, regardless of species: large ones are known as *tiburón*; small ones are labeled *cazón*. It is the latter that can be seen in piles that overwhelm tables in all local fish markets. *Cazón* is incredibly popular and culturally important in the region: *campechano* cookbooks from the last century to the present feature more recipes for *cazón* than for any other seafood. Today, Campeche shares with Veracruz the largest shark catches in the country.

Sharks have been caught in the waters off Campeche since pre-Columbian times. Fish were important symbols in the complex Maya counting system. The word "*xok*" (pronounced "shok") was a term for "count," and in Yukatek Mayan was also used to describe a large fish, specifically a "shark, the teeth of which the Indians remove to shoot arrows with." According to Mayanist David Stuart, the English word "shark" derives from the Mayan "*xok*."

The meat of *cazón* has a mild, sweet flavor and firm texture. Although it is low in fat, it has a higher oil content than mako or other sharks. More recipes for *cazón* can be found on pages 310, 344, and 437.

Substitutes: Swordfish, mahimahi, marlin, or steaks of larger shark species

CAZÓN ASADO FRITO

GRILLED DOGFISH FRIED IN TOMATO SAUCE

TO PREPARE AHEAD
Cazón asado (p. 310)
Enriched Lard (p. 513)

FOR STEWING THE DOGFISH
1 recipe Cazón asado
8 cups (2 L) water
1 Tbs. (18 g) sea salt
2 sprigs fresh epazote
  (Substitute: 1 tsp. / 1.5 g dried,
  crumbled)

FOR THE *SOFRITO*
8 Tbs. (112 g) Enriched Lard
1 cup (170 g) white onion, finely
  chopped
4 medium cloves garlic (1 oz. /
  24 g), peeled and minced
¾ cup (105 g) green bell pepper,
  cut into medium dice
1 sprig fresh epazote (Substitute:
  ½ tsp. / .75 g dried)
2 medium chiles serranos (¾ oz.
  / 20 g), charred, peeled, seeded,
  and finely chopped
4 medium Roma tomatoes
  (14 oz. / 400 g), seeded and
  finely chopped
½ tsp. (3 g) sea salt, or to taste

Cazón frito—twice- or thrice-cooked dogfish—is the way *cazón* is usually consumed in Campeche. After being grilled or parboiled, it is shredded and then fried for use in a range of dishes. It can be consumed simply as a taco with the meat heaped atop a fresh tortilla, but it is more typically used as the filling for Panuchos campechanos, Joroches, Empanadas de cazón, and the hallmark *campechano* dish, Pan de cazón. This recipe is for Cazón asado frito and employs the grilled dogfish; the variation below is for Cazón fresco frito and uses parboiled dogfish instead. They may be used interchangeably unless your recipe specifies otherwise.

Prepare ahead note: Cazón frito can be prepared in advance and refrigerated or frozen until ready for use. Freeze leftovers to use in one of the many other recipes in this book that call for Cazón frito.

YIELD: APPROXIMATELY 2½ LBS. (1.2 K)

STEW DOGFISH

Place the stewing ingredients in a stockpot and bring to a boil. Reduce the heat and simmer for 10 minutes. Remove the pot from the heat and drain. When the fish is cool enough to handle, remove any residual skin and cartilage and discard. Finely shred the fish and set aside.

PREPARE *SOFRITO*

Heat the lard in a large skillet until shimmering. Reduce the heat, add the next 4 ingredients, and cook, stirring occasionally, until the onions are translucent. Add the next 2 ingredients and continue cooking until the tomatoes are softened and most of the liquid has evaporated, about 10 minutes. (If you used fresh epazote, remove it now.) Add the shredded dogfish and cook until the mixture is dry, stirring constantly, 8–10 minutes. Add the salt, check seasoning, and use immediately in one of the recipes in this book or refrigerate or freeze for later.

VARIATION

Cazón fresco frito (Boiled Dogfish Fried in Tomato Sauce): Some cooks prefer the lighter flavor of simple boiled-then-fried shark to the grilled (or perhaps they're just saving a step). In this case, it is called Cazón fresco frito. Marinate the shark as in Cazón asado, using ¼ cup (72 g) sea salt. After the marinating time, remove the shark from the marinade and drain. Do not grill the fish. Complete as in the master recipe for Cazón asado frito.

PAN DE CAZÓN

LAYERED "PIE" OF DOGFISH, TORTILLAS, BLACK BEAN PURÉE, AND TOMATO SAUCE

TO PREPARE AHEAD

Cazón frito, either Asado or
   Fresco (p. 312)
Frijol colado "espeso" (p. 505)
Enriched Lard (p. 513)
Tortillas (p. 518)
Tomate frito (p. 507)

**FOR ASSEMBLING
THE PAN DE CAZÓN**

½ recipe Cazón frito (about 21 oz.
   / 600 g of the mixture)
2 cups (500 ml) Frijol colado
   "espeso"
½ cup (112 g) Enriched Lard
Tortillas (You will need 24 tortillas
   if you make all 6 servings)
1 recipe Tomate frito

(continued on next page)

Unquestionably the signature dish of Campeche, Pan de cazón has become so popular that it has been embraced throughout the peninsula. "Shark pie" may sound unappetizing to some, but this simple dish of layers of tortillas, Cazón frito, and Frijol colado bathed in a lightly picante tomato sauce is a Yucatecan's idea of comfort food. Which Cazón frito to use—Fresco or Asado—remains a polarizing issue among local cooks, but to my taste buds, the only answer is the Asado.

Prepare ahead note: The Cazón frito, Frijol colado, and Tomate frito should be made in advance and refrigerated or frozen. Reheat just before assembling.

YIELD: 6 SERVINGS

ASSEMBLE PAN DE CAZÓN

In separate pans, reheat the Cazón frito and the Frijol colado and keep warm as you fry the tortillas.

Heat the lard in a large skillet until shimmering. Working quickly, use tongs to pass tortillas through the hot fat, turning once, about 10 seconds per side. Transfer to paper towels to drain as you proceed.

Quickly dip one fried tortilla in the Tomate frito to coat completely. Place it on an individual serving plate and spread the top completely with about 1 tablespoon (15 ml) of the beans. Top that with 2 tablespoons (30 g) of the dogfish mixture and carefully spread to cover the beans. (Note: Tortillas in Yucatán are quite small—only

[MC]

Sliced avocado

6 whole chiles habaneros
  for garnish (optional)

Chile tamulado (p. 509), or
  the chile sauce of your choice

about 4 inches [10 cm] in diameter. If you are using larger tortillas, you may need to adjust the quantities of the other ingredients.) Dip a second tortilla in the Tomate frito, place it on top of the first, and again spread on some of the beans followed by the fish. Repeat with a third tortilla, beans, and fish. Smear beans onto a fourth, *undipped*, tortilla, invert it, and place it on top of the stack. Ladle hot Tomate frito over the "pie" to cover completely. (Note: Mothers in Yucatán will ask how hungry you are. You may ask for just 2 layers or as many as 5 or 6.)

TO SERVE

Arrange avocado slices on the side of the plate and center a chile on top of the pie as a garnish. People in Yucatán eat Pan de cazón much like a stack of pancakes, slicing the layers into wedges with a knife and fork, adding chile sauce to taste.

[MC]

HUACHINANGO / RED SNAPPER

Lutjanus campechanus

Red snapper ranges throughout the Gulf of Mexico. Its characteristic red skin and red eyes make it easy to spot in the market, although several other species may be sold under the name *huachinango*. In the United States, the only species that can legally be sold as "red snapper" is *Lutjanus campechanus*.

Huachinango has lean, moist meat with a firm texture and a slightly sweet, nutty flavor adaptable to a variety of seasonings—from delicate to strong—making it a great choice for Yucatán's pungent *achiote*.

Substitutes: Red porgy, grouper, halibut, catfish

MAKKUM

BAKED RED SNAPPER IN *ACHIOTE*

TO PREPARE AHEAD

Recado rojo (p. 500)

Seville orange juice substitute (p. 514), unless fresh Seville oranges are available

Enriched Lard (p. 513)

Banana leaves, prepared for extra-large (XL) size (see Basic Techniques, p. 525)

FOR THE MARINADE

8 Tbs. (120 g) Recado rojo

2 medium heads garlic (1¾ oz. / 50 g each), charred, peeled, and separated into cloves

1 cup (250 ml) water

½ cup (125 ml) Seville orange juice, or substitute

2 Tbs. (30 ml) Spanish olive oil

1 Tbs. (18 g) sea salt

6–8 4-oz. (115 g) red snapper fillets (Note: As doña Sofía did, you may use about 3 lbs. [1.5 k] whole fish, cut widthwise into steaks. Doña Sofía even included the head and tail, which you may elect to do or not.)

FOR THE *SOFRITO*

¼ cup (56 g) Enriched Lard

½ medium white onion (5 oz. / 137.5 g), thinly sliced and separated into rings

3 medium cloves garlic (¾ oz. / 18 g), peeled and finely chopped

1 medium green bell pepper (6½ oz. / 185 g), seeded and thinly sliced into rings

2 medium Roma tomatoes (7 oz. / 200 g), thinly sliced across the width

(continued on next page)

"*Maak*" in Mayan means "lid," "*kuum*" means "pot," which describes the traditional cooking method for this dish. It is especially lovely baked and served in a lidded clay *cazuela*. Makkum (sometimes transcribed as Makum or Mac-cum) shares much with another Yucatecan classic, Pescado en tikin xiik' (recipe follows), the only significant difference being the cooking method. This recipe is based on one shared with me by Sofía del Socorro Marrufo-Marrufo. As tradition dictates, she used whole *pargo* (porgy), but since some diners may not appreciate such a bony fish, many cooks use red snapper. You may also use fillets instead of the whole fish.

Prepare ahead note: Makkum may be assembled to the baking step and refrigerated 4–5 hours. Bring the dish to room temperature, bake, then serve immediately.

YIELD: 6–8 SERVINGS

MARINATE FISH

Place the first 6 ingredients in the jar of a blender and process until thoroughly liquefied. Place the fish in a shallow baking dish large enough to hold it in a single layer and cover with the marinade. Refrigerate 30 minutes.

PREPARE *SOFRITO*

While the fish is marinating, heat the lard in a large skillet until shimmering. Add the next 3 ingredients and cook over medium heat, stirring occasionally, until the onions are translucent and the peppers are softened, 3–4 minutes. Add the tomatoes and continue cooking until they are tender, 2–3 minutes.

Remove the fish from the marinade, shaking off any excess marinade, and set aside. Pour the remaining marinade into the skillet and stir to combine. Simmer on low heat as you continue.

BAKE FISH AND FINISH

Preheat the oven to 350°F (176°C). Line the inside of a large, covered, ovenproof casserole with the banana leaves, letting the leaves extend well beyond the pot. Arrange half of the fish pieces in one layer on the banana leaves. Spoon on half of the *sofrito*, making certain to distribute the vegetables evenly. Place half of the chile strips on the *sofrito*, followed by half of the olives, capers, and herbs. Sprinkle the casserole with half of the wine, if using. Repeat, making 1 more layer. Fold the banana leaf extensions up and over to cover the fish. Place the lid on the casserole and bake 20–30 minutes, or until the fish feels firm when you press it with your finger. (Note: If you refrigerated the Makkum, bring it to room temperature before baking. If you have a small casserole, you may need to make more than two layers of the fish. Baking time will vary depending on how many layers you have. Avoid overcooking.)

FOR BAKING THE FISH

4 medium chiles x'catiques
   (about 1¼ oz. / 35 g each),
   charred, peeled, seeds removed,
   and cut lengthwise into strips
20 medium green olives, whole
   unpitted, pitted, or pimiento-
   stuffed and sliced
1 Tbs. (15 g) small capers, drained
4 bay leaves
2 sprigs fresh epazote or cilantro
2 sprigs flat-leaf parsley
¼ cup (62.5 ml) dry white wine
   (optional)

FOR SERVING

Cebollas encurtidas (p. 510)
Arroz blanco (p. 529), or the
   rice of your choice, suggested
   accompaniment
Chile tamulado (p. 509), or the
   chile sauce of your choice
Seville orange or lime wedges
   to garnish

TO SERVE

Place the casserole on the table and fold back the leaves for a dramatic presentation. Alternatively, transfer the fillets to individual serving plates, making sure to spoon some of the cooking juices, vegetables, and chile strips onto each portion. Garnish with Cebollas encurtidas and accompany with Arroz blanco. Place citrus wedges on the side and allow diners to squeeze on the juice and add their own chile sauce to taste.

VARIATIONS

Makkum negro (Baked Red Snapper in Charred Chile Sauce): Follow the master recipe, using Recado negro (p. 501) instead of Recado rojo. Dissolve the *recado* in the water and strain through a sieve lined with cheesecloth into the blender jar. Press and squeeze to extract as much of the black liquid as possible; discard any residue. Continue with the master recipe.

Pescado en tikin xiik' (Grilled Red Snapper in *Achiote*): Substitute 3 pounds (1.5 k) whole red snapper (or, more traditionally, grouper, or any of the substitutes listed on p. 316), cleaned and butterflied (or fillets). Marinate the fish as directed in the master recipe for Makkum. Omit the lard and the frying step, leave the vegetables raw, and discard the marinade. Light a grill following the instructions for wood smoking chips in Basic Techniques, page 538. Line 2 grilling racks with the banana leaves. Brush the leaves with vegetable oil to prevent sticking. Place the fish in one layer on the leaves, top with slices of raw vegetables and other garnishes in the order instructed, fold and tuck the leaves to cover. Move the coals to one side of the grill so as not to burn the banana leaves. Place the wrapped fish away from the heat source, lower the cover, and bake, 10–15 minutes, or until the fish is firm when pressed with your finger. Avoid overcooking. Serve as suggested for Makkum. See the photo of Pescado en tikin xiik' on p. 292.

(opposite page) For her Makkum, doña Sofia cooked everything in a large skillet and omitted the banana leaves. You may do the same although it's less traditional. [MC]

JUREL EN ESCABECHE
GRILLED YELLOWTAIL AMBERJACK STEAKS IN PICKLED ONIONS

TO PREPARE AHEAD

Seville orange juice substitute
   (p. 514), unless fresh Seville
   oranges are available
Recado para escabeche (p. 498)
Cebollas en escabeche (p. 511)

FOR THE MARINADE

½ cup (125 ml) Seville orange
   juice, or substitute
½ cup (125 ml) Spanish olive oil
5 medium cloves garlic (1¼ oz. /
   30 g), peeled and charred
1 Tbs. (9 g) Recado para escabeche
1 tsp. (6 g) sea salt
6 4-oz. (115 g) yellowtail steaks,
   approximately 1 in. (2.5 cm)
   thick
2 bay leaves

FOR GRILLING AND FINISHING

1 recipe Cebollas en escabeche
Vegetable oil

TO SERVE

Rice of your choice (p. 527)
Chile con limón (p. 511), or the
   chile sauce of your choice

The earliest reference to this dish appears in *Libro de guisados*, the 1529 translation by Ruperto de Nola of a Catalán cookbook. The dish is called Escabeig a peix fregit, or "Pickled Fried Fish". Most subsequent recipes feature the fish served at room temperature or, in later years, chilled. I find this *campechano* recipe for *pescado en escabeche* particularly interesting in that the dish veers from the original by grilling the fish rather than frying it and includes the local chile x'catik. The smoky flavor from the grill marries wonderfully with the tang of the vinegar and the heat of the chiles.

Prepare ahead note: The fish should be grilled approximately 1 hour before serving. Some old Spanish recipes for fish *en escabeche* specify serving it cold, in which case you may prepare Jurel en escabeche one day in advance and refrigerate.

YIELD: 6 SERVINGS

MARINATE FISH

Place the first 5 ingredients in the jar of a blender and process until liquefied. Place the steaks in a large nonreactive bowl or baking dish large enough to hold the fish in a single layer and cover with the marinade. Add the bay leaves and allow to rest at room temperature up to 30 minutes.

GRILL FISH AND FINISH

While the grill is heating, extract the chiles from the Cebollas en escabeche and set aside. Pour the rest of the pickled onion mixture into a medium saucepan and bring to a simmer.

Remove the fish from the marinade. Add the leftover marinade to the onion mixture in the saucepan and simmer for 3 minutes. Remove the pan from the heat.

Brush the grilling racks with vegetable oil to prevent sticking. Grill the fish 4–5 minutes per side, turning once. It should acquire grill marks and some charring but should still be slightly moist inside, since it will finish cooking in the hot onion mixture. Transfer the fish to a heatproof serving platter large enough to hold it in a single layer.

Gently rub the blackened skin off of the reserved chiles under running water. Slit them open along the side and remove the seeds and veins. Slice the chiles lengthwise into 4–6 strips and set aside as a garnish. Return the onions in the saucepan to a boil. Pour the hot onion mixture over the fish and garnish with the chile strips. Cool to room temperature before serving, or refrigerate as noted above.

TO SERVE

Accompany Pescado en escabeche with the rice and chile sauce of your choice and a mixed green salad if you wish.

Camarones en escabeche (Pickled Shrimp): A popular *botana* with beer served in the *cantinas* (p. 271), these pickled shrimp are addictive. Follow the master recipe, replacing fish steaks with 1½ pounds (680 g) large (31/35 count) cleaned, shelled, and deveined shrimp. Use a grilling basket to grill over charcoal, or simply sauté the shrimp in olive oil with a bit of minced garlic until just pink. Add 1 finely chopped habanero for more heat if you wish. Mound the shrimp on a large serving platter, cover with the pickled onions, and serve at room temperature or chilled.

[JFMT]

JUREL / YELLOWTAIL AMBERJACK

Seriola dorsalis lalandi

One of the many members of the large amberjack family, *jurel* is characterized by its long, aerodynamic body, pointed snout, a blue upper back, silver-white sides and belly, yellow fins and tail, and a distinguishing thin bronze stripe along the middle of the body that turns yellow toward the tail.

Jurel meat is rich, fatty, and full-flavored and is a favorite in Asian countries for sushi and sashimi.

Substitutes: Tuna, mackerel

CAVIAR CAMPECHANO

STRIPED MULLET ROE APPETIZER

FOR PARBOILING THE ROE

1 fresh mullet roe sac (approximately 9 oz. / 250 g; substitute: shad or cod roe) (Note: If the roe has been frozen, allow it to defrost overnight in a pot of salted water in the refrigerator)

6 medium cloves garlic (1½ oz. / 36 g), peeled and mashed

1 tsp. (6 g) sea salt

1 tsp. (0.65 g) dried whole Mexican oregano

FOR THE TOMATO SAUCE AND FINISHING

1 medium head garlic (1¾ oz. / 50g), charred, peeled, and separated into cloves

2 medium Roma tomatoes (14 oz. / 200 g), charred

½ medium white onion (5 oz. / 137.5 g), charred and coarsely chopped

1 medium chile habanero (¼ oz. / 7 g), charred, peeled, and seeded (Substitute: For less heat, use half of the chile or a medium chile serrano instead)

¼ cup (62.5 ml) Spanish olive oil

2 oz. (56 g) smoked slab bacon, minced

1 Tbs. (2 g) dried whole Mexican oregano, lightly toasted and ground

½ tsp. (3 g) sea salt

½ tsp. (2.5 g) freshly ground black pepper

FOR SERVING

Spanish olive oil

Cilantro, chopped

1 Tbs. (15 g) small capers, drained

Pan francés (p. 194), baguette, or cocktail crackers

Lime wedges

Another spectacular dish served at upscale restaurants in Campeche is Caviar campechano. The surprisingly rich, garlicky, and lightly picante appetizer features roe of *lisa* (striped mullet) or *esmedregal* (cobia) cooked with bacon, garlic, onions, tomatoes, and spices, then molded artfully and served rather like pâté. To find fresh roe, befriend a fishmonger, who will be able to procure different varieties for you depending on your location and the season. You can also use frozen roe with no sacrifice in flavor. This recipe was adapted from one by Ligia Beatriz Bates Pérez of Campeche.

Prepare ahead note: Caviar campechano can be prepared a day in advance and refrigerated. Unmold and bring to room temperature 30 minutes prior to serving.

YIELD: 6 SERVINGS

PARBOIL ROE

Place the roe sac in a medium saucepan and cover completely with water. Add the remaining ingredients and bring to a boil. Reduce the heat to a simmer and cook, uncovered, 5–7 minutes, or until the roe is firm. Remove the pan from the heat, drain, and discard the garlic. When the roe sac is cool to the touch, peel away the outer membrane and discard. Crumble the roe into small pieces.

PREPARE TOMATO SAUCE

Place the first 4 ingredients in the jar of a blender and process until thoroughly liquefied; set aside. In a large, deep skillet, heat the olive oil and bacon. Cook the bacon slowly until it is crisp and the fat is rendered. Add the tomato mixture from the blender all at once; it should sizzle and sputter, so stand back. Add the crumbled roe and the oregano, salt, and pepper and stir to blend. Simmer, stirring constantly and using the spoon to break up any whole pieces of roe, for 20 minutes; the mixture should be very dry and stiff, resembling thick oatmeal. Remove the pan from the heat and allow to cool slightly.

MOLD CAVIAR AND SERVE

While the roe is cooling, prepare the molds. If you are serving Caviar campechano as an appetizer shared by several people, work with a small soufflé mold; if you wish to prepare individual servings, work with 6 half-cup (125 ml) custard cups or ramekins. Wipe the insides of the molds with a bit of vegetable or olive oil and line with plastic wrap, leaving some of the wrap extending beyond the mold. Wipe the plastic wrap with more oil, pressing so that the plastic adheres to the walls of the mold. Pack the Caviar campechano tightly into the molds. (Note: If you are using individual molds, fill them only about halfway.) Turn the edges of the plastic over to cover and press to compact. Refrigerate at least 2 hours to set or, preferably, overnight.

Invert the mold over a serving plate; remove the mold, then carefully remove the plastic wrap. Allow the caviar to rest at room temperature for 30 minutes. Drizzle a bit of olive oil over the caviar and sprinkle with cilantro and capers. Diners eat the caviar in the style of pâté: a squeeze of lime juice first, if desired, then spread some of the caviar onto the bread of your choice.

[MC]

LISA / STRIPED MULLET

Mugil cephalus / Mugil liza

While *Mugil cephalus* can be found in many oceans, the species *Mugil liza* has so far been discovered ranging only from the north coast of Yucatán to northwestern Cuba. Mullets are dark blue-green with some brown along the spine and silvery on the sides. Conspicuous stripes along both sides are formed of dark spots located at the base of the scales. Mullets range in size from 10 to 14 inches (25–35 cm) and can reach 3 pounds (1.4 k).

Mullet is a firm-textured, lean fish with both light and dark meat that has a somewhat nutty flavor, making it a popular fish in many markets. Particularly prized is the roe, which is salted and dried and used as a specialty food in Taiwan, Korea, Japan, and Italy. The fish meat is consumed year-round in Campeche, but during the primary spawning months of November–December, the roe is the favored delicacy and appears on menus as Caviar campechano.

Substitutes for the fish: mahimahi, Spanish mackerel, pompano, amberjack

Substitutes for the roe: shad, cobia, or cod roe

PÁMPANO EMPAPELADO

POMPANO EN PAPILLOTE

French culinary influences replace the local banana leaf with parchment paper for this dish. The recipe is featured in regional cookbooks dating to 1832, and again in the Porfiriato of the early twentieth century. The parchment presentation must have been—and still is—considered very elegant, indeed. Pámpano empapelado continues to be a topline item on the contemporary menu at upscale *campechano* restaurants (although, unfortunately, many restaurants are now using aluminum foil instead of parchment, to disastrous aesthetic effect). Modern variations may be prepared either with a white (garlic) or green (parsley and herb) sauce. All the vintage recipes I have found specify a *recado* formula virtually identical to Recado blanco, which is what I include here. These recipes, too, recommend baking the fish on a *parrilla*, or wood-fired grill.

Prepare ahead note: Pámpano empapelado can be prepared and wrapped up to 1 hour in advance and refrigerated. Bring to room temperature for 30 minutes before baking.

YIELD: 6 SERVINGS

TO PREPARE AHEAD
Recado blanco (p. 502)

FOR THE MARINADE
6 4-oz. (125 g) pompano fillets
1 cup (250 ml) water
¼ cup (62.5 ml) fresh lime juice
1 tsp. (6 g) sea salt

FOR THE SAUCE
4 Tbs. (60 ml) Spanish olive oil
½ medium white onion (5 oz. / 137.5 g), finely chopped
2 cups (240 g) green bell pepper, cut into small dice
2 medium cloves garlic (½ oz. / 12 g), peeled and minced
2 Tbs. (8 g) flat-leaf parsley, finely chopped
1 Tbs. (15 g) Recado blanco
½ cup (125 ml) white vinegar
10 small pimiento-stuffed green olives, sliced
1 Tbs. (15 g) small capers, drained
1 tsp. (6 g) sea salt

FOR BAKING
Parchment paper squares cut to triple the size of one fillet
Spanish olive oil
6 slices Seville orange (Substitute: large Persian lime), seeded
6 small sprigs fresh epazote (Substitute: cilantro or flat-leaf parsley)
Banana leaf ribs or kitchen twine

FOR SERVING
Salpicón (p. 511)
Rice of your choice (p. 527), suggested accompaniment
Chile tamulado (p. 509), or chile sauce of your choice

MARINATE FISH
Place the fish in a nonreactive container large enough to hold it in a single layer. Combine the water, lime juice, and salt, pour over the fish, and refrigerate 30 minutes.

PREPARE SAUCE
Heat the olive oil in a large skillet until shimmering. Add the next 4 ingredients and cook slowly until the vegetables are very soft, 4–5 minutes. Dissolve the *recado* in the vinegar and pour into the skillet. Add the remaining ingredients and simmer, stirring occasionally, about 5 minutes, or until the liquid has evaporated and the mixture is almost dry. The resulting sauce will be chunky.

BAKE FISH
Preheat the grill following the instructions for wood smoking chips in Basic Techniques, page 538. Move the coals to one side of the grill so as not to set the paper alight.

While the grill is heating, place the 6 squares of parchment on a work surface and brush the top side of each with the oil. Place a slice of citrus in the center of each square and top the citrus slices with about 2 heaping tablespoons (55 g) of the sauce, distributing it evenly.

Drain the fish and pat it dry; discard the marinade. Place the fillets on top of the sauce and garnish with the herbs. Lift the corners of the parchment, gather, crimp, and tie closed using the banana-leaf ribs or kitchen twine. Place the packages on a removable grilling rack. Add wood chips to the grill and place the rack with the packages away from the heat source. Lower the lid and bake 10–15 minutes, or until the fish is firm when pressed with your finger.

Alternatively, you may bake the fish in the oven. Preheat the oven to 325°F (162°C). Bake for 20–25 minutes, or until fish is firm.

TO SERVE
Place the packages on individual serving plates and allow guests to open them themselves. Serve with Salpicón and the rice of your choice. Diners add their own chile sauce to taste.

[MC]

PÁMPANO / FLORIDA POMPANO
Trachinotus carolinus

Pámpano is another member of the large Carandigae, or Jack, family and is related to the *jurel*. Lone fishermen of Campeche catch *pámpano* from piers, small launches, and jetties, since its habitat in the Gulf is along sandy beaches with calm waters. This also makes it an attractive target for brown pelicans, which can be seen dive-bombing to catch the fish from heights of two or three stories into the waters along the coast of Champotón. *Pámpano*'s distinctive oval shape, compressed body, and greenish-silver color—to say nothing of its delicious lean meat—make it one of the most attractive fish in the market, where it commands a higher price per kilo than most other fish. *Pámpano* is a firm-textured, lean, and mild fish.

Substitutes: mullet, mahimahi, or snapper

RÓBALO EN VERDE / PÁMPANO EN VERDE

SNOOK OR POMPANO IN TOMATILLO AND PARSLEY SAUCE

In Campeche, the most common fish used in this recipe is pompano, although sometimes the recipe is based on "fish of the day," in which case it will be listed on the menu as the more generic Pescado en verde. Actually, this delicious fusion dish comes to us from País Vasco—Spain's Basque region—as Róbalo en salsa verde and bears a strong resemblance to a medieval dish from Moorish dominated Spain. You may use either fish or any of the listed substitutes. The *campechano* adaptation includes tomatillo and cilantro as well as the more typical parsley to impart the green color of the title.

Prepare ahead note: The fillets should be fried and finished just before serving.

YIELD: 6 SERVINGS

TO PREPARE AHEAD
Mojo de ajo (p. 514)
Recado para escabeche (p. 498)
Salsa verde (p. 509)

FOR THE MARINADE
6 snook or pompano fillets
  (about 1½ lbs. / 680 g)
½ cup (125 ml) Mojo de ajo
½ cup (125 ml) freshly squeezed
  lime juice

FOR FRYING
1½ cups (187.5 g) all-purpose flour
2 tsp. (6 g) Recado para escabeche
½ cup (125 ml) Spanish olive oil
4 medium cloves garlic (1 oz. /
  24 g), peeled and slivered

FOR THE SOFRITO
Spanish olive oil, if needed
¼ cup (42.5 g) shallots or
  scallions, minced
½ cup (70 g) red bell pepper,
  finely chopped
¼ cup (15 g) flat-leaf parsley,
  finely chopped
¼ cup (15 g) cilantro,
  finely chopped

FOR THE SAUCE
3 cups (750 ml) fish stock or
  bottled clam juice
½ cup (125 ml) dry white wine
1 Tbs. (15 ml) white wine vinegar
½ tsp. (3 g) sea salt, or to taste

MARINATE FISH
Place the fillets in a shallow baking dish large to hold them in a single layer. Brush both sides with Mojo de ajo. Cover with lime juice and refrigerate up to 30 minutes.

FRY FISH
Combine the flour and *recado* and set aside. Heat the olive oil in a large, deep skillet over medium heat until shimmering. Add the garlic and cook until it starts to turn pale golden and rises to the surface. Remove the garlic with a slotted spoon and reserve.

Working in batches, remove the fillets from the marinade, leaving any of the Mojo that may still be clinging to them. Dredge the fillets well in the flour mixture and add to the skillet. Sauté 1–2 minutes per side, or until lightly golden but not fully cooked. Remove the fillets to a platter and repeat until all have been sautéed.

PREPARE SOFRITO
Add a bit more olive oil to the skillet if it is dry. Add the reserved garlic and *sofrito* ingredients and cook until the shallots are translucent, the bell pepper is soft, and the herbs are wilted, 2–3 minutes.

FINISH SAUCE AND SERVE
Add the fish stock to the skillet and bring to a boil, scraping the bottom of the skillet with a wooden spoon or spatula to remove residual flour stuck there, which will help thicken the sauce. When the stock reaches a boil, return the fillets to the skillet, reduce the heat to a gentle simmer, cover, and continue cooking 5–6 minutes, or until the fish is firm when pressed with your finger. Transfer the fillets to a warm platter.

Add the wine to the skillet and bring to a boil. Cook 4–5 minutes, or until the sauce has thickened and reduced by about one-third. Add the vinegar and salt and check the seasonings.

FOR SERVING

1 cup (250 ml) Salsa verde
Chopped flat-leaf parsley
or cilantro

Place the Salsa verde in a small saucepan and cook over medium heat, stirring occasionally, until it has reduced and is slightly thickened, 5–6 minutes.

TO SERVE

Place the fillets in shallow individual serving bowls and ladle some of the cooking liquid around the fish. Spoon some of the cooked Salsa verde onto each fillet and sprinkle with parsley or cilantro.

[MC]

[MR]

RÓBALO / SNOOK

Centropomus undecimalis

PULPO / OCTOPUS

Octopus vulgaris / Octopus maya

Róbalo is found along the coastline of Campeche, where spawn and juveniles seek protection in the plentiful seagrass beds there. It is fished year-round, but principal catches happen May to October.

Róbalo has a long, slender body, silvery-yellow skin, and a yellow tail with an unmistakable black lateral line. An adult *róbalo* in the Gulf of Mexico can grow to be over 40 inches (103 cm) long and live on average 13.5 years.

In addition to its value in sport fishing, it is caught for its delicious meat, which is soft and mild-flavored with a low-to-medium oil content.

Substitutes: striped bass, snapper, grouper

Octopus is a particularly important catch in the waters off Campeche and Yucatán. The government-managed co-op fishery employs some 20,000 fishermen in both states and catches some 90 percent of all the octopus in Mexico. Primary species are the common octopus (*Octopus vulgaris*) and the Maya octopus (*Octopus maya*), a species identified in 1966 and unique to the Bay of Campeche. The Maya octopus is particularly prized in Japan and the European Union and competes strongly with local species in spite of its higher price. Octopus season in the region is 1 August–15 December.

Recipes for octopus can be found on pages 149 and 230.

SIERRA / SPANISH MACKEREL

Scomberomorus maculatus

Many fish species of Campeche are aesthetically beautiful—but the *sierra* must be one of the loveliest. Its sleek, aerodynamic body and sharp, splayed tail, as well as its smooth, silvery skin flecked with neat rows of yellowish polka dots make it a very stylish fish, indeed, and easily recognized in the market.

Sierras are migratory fish that travel in large schools along coastlines and appear seasonally in the Gulf of Mexico, "wintering" in the zone from September through March before heading north for cooler waters. Females grow larger than males, achieving sizes of up to 2¾ feet (83 cm) and weights of around 11 pounds (5 k). *Sierra* meat is fatty and flaky-textured.

Sierra frita (Fried Spanish Mackerel in Wine and Caper Sauce): When in Campeche, look for the popular Sierra frita—a quick and easy dish to prepare. Marinate steaks in sweet white wine, dredge in flour, and fry until golden. Finish cooking in a light sauce of the leftover marinade, fish stock, a splash of white vinegar, and capers and serve with a chopped red onion and radish *salpicón*.

Substitutes: mackerel, shad, herring, tuna

[MC]

ABOUT *MARAÑÓN*

Marañón—or "cashew apple"—is the fruit that gives us the cashew nut (see more on p. 42). The popularity of the nut in so many cultures unfairly eclipses the absolutely ambrosial flavor of the fruit. *Marañón* is cultivated extensively in Campeche and is anticipated seasonally throughout the peninsula to be consumed as a hand fruit. Unlike so many other tropical fruits, it only rarely appears here as an ingredient in a recipe. A cookbook from 1947, *Tropical Cooking in Panama: A Handbook of Tropical Foods and How to Use Them*, lists a sauce, jam, preserves, and a beverage called Cashew Frost. A more recent book on the cooking of Campeche offers two dishes: preserves and a sorbet. But you aren't likely to find treats such as these outside of private homes. So I decided to take a few liberties by creating the two recipes included here: the preserves are adapted from both books mentioned; the ice cream is my own invention. Not readily available fresh outside the tropics, *marañón* is being sold frozen by a few companies north of the border (see Resources, p. 540).

CONSERVA DE MARAÑÓN

CASHEW APPLE PRESERVES

FOR THE CONSERVE

3 lbs. (1.5 k) *marañones* (approximately 15–20 medium fruit, weighed with seeds removed; substitute: 1½ lbs. / 680 g frozen *marañones*)

2 cups (400 g) sugar

2 cups (500 ml) water

2 whole cloves

This exquisite conserve can be enjoyed in many ways: it is delicious as an accompaniment to grilled meats or poultry, or, for a conceptual treat that reunites the nut with the fruit, try it atop some cashew butter spread on a warm piece of toast. The complete recipe for the *conserva* is also used in Helado de marañón, following.

Prepare ahead note: Conserva de marañón keeps well in an airtight container under refrigeration for 2–3 weeks. If you plan to use it for Helado de marañón, prepare it a day or two in advance and refrigerate until needed. Conserva de marañón is best served at room temperature; stir before serving.

YIELD: ABOUT 2 CUPS (500 ML)

PREPARE FRUIT

If using frozen fruit, skip to the last step. For fresh fruit, twist off the seed at the top of the fruit and discard. (Note: The seeds of *marañón* contain a potent toxin; do not be tempted to try to open them [read more on p. 42]). *Marañón* fruits are quite tannic, and most of the tannins reside in the peel, making it necessary to peel them. Place a cutting board inside a large roasting pan in order to collect the juices that will be pressed out as you peel. Working with one *marañón* at a time, slice the fruit in quarters. Lay each piece on the cutting board and use a very sharp paring or boning knife to slice or scrape the flesh away from the skin. Leave the skins on the side of the board as you continue (later you can squeeze more juice from them.) Finely chop the *marañones*, reserving the accumulated juices. Place a sieve over a large measuring cup and pour through any juices that accumulated in the pan. Add the peels to the sieve and mash with a wooden spoon to extract as much juice as possible; discard the peels. Add the chopped fruit to the juice: you should have about 4 cups (about 1.3 k) total of fruit and juice.

FINISH CONSERVE

Place the chopped fruit and juices (or finely chopped frozen fruit) in a saucepan. Add the sugar, water, and cloves and bring to a boil. Reduce the heat to a simmer. Cook, uncovered, over medium heat, stirring frequently, for 30–40 minutes, or until the liquid has reduced and is syrupy. Make certain the sugar does not caramelize; add extra water a bit at a time if the juices evaporate and the syrup starts to darken. Remove the pan from the heat and allow the conserve to cool. Transfer the conserve to an airtight container for storage, or use in the ice cream recipe that follows.

HELADO DE MARAÑÓN

CASHEW APPLE ICE CREAM

This fruit-and-cream dessert reminds me of the peach ice cream I enjoyed as a boy—but from a tropical paradise rather than the windswept prairies of Oklahoma. Top with salted cashews or homemade cashew brittle for a conceptual touch and a sweet/savory/textural contrast.

Prepare ahead note: The fruit base, Conserva de marañón, must be made in advance. Bring Helado de marañón to room temperature 5–10 minutes before serving to soften.

YIELD: APPROXIMATELY 1½ QUARTS (1.5 L)

TO PREPARE AHEAD

Conserva de marañón (p. 328)

FOR THE FRUIT PURÉE

2 cups (500 ml) milk
¼ cup (62.5 ml) aged rum
¼ tsp. (1.25 ml) Mexican vanilla extract
¼ tsp. (1.5 g) sea salt
1 recipe Conserva de marañón, cloves removed and discarded

FOR THE CUSTARD BASE

1 cup (250 ml) whipping cream
1 can (14 oz. / 397 g) sweetened condensed milk
6 egg yolks

PURÉE FRUIT

Place the first 4 ingredients in the jar of a blender. Add half the Conserva and set the rest aside. Process 1–2 minutes, or until the fruit is completely liquefied. Transfer half the milk/fruit purée to a saucepan. Add the remaining Conserva to the blender and pulse 4–5 times, just until the fruit is coarsely broken up, so that the finished ice cream will have a few small pieces of fruit in each bite. Transfer the blender contents to the saucepan.

PREPARE CUSTARD BASE

Add the cream and condensed milk to the saucepan and stir to blend. Cook over medium heat until the mixture reaches a simmer. While the mixture is heating, in a heatproof mixing bowl, use a handheld electric mixer to beat the egg yolks until light and creamy.

Slowly stream one ladle of the hot cream into the egg yolks, beating constantly. Repeat until you have added 3–4 ladles full. Slowly pour the heated egg yolk mixture back into the saucepan, stirring constantly with a wooden spoon. Cook over medium heat until a thermometer reaches 180°F (82°C). Immediately remove the custard from the heat and allow to cool.

CHILL, FREEZE, AND FINISH

Cover the cooled custard and refrigerate at least 4 hours or overnight. Process in an ice cream maker according to manufacturer's instructions. Transfer the finished ice cream to an airtight container and freeze 2–3 hours prior to serving.

MÉRIDA

S ECOND-BORN OF THE TRIPLET CITIES and midway between her two sisters, Mérida has traditionally served as the ambassador of the region—a cosmopolitan *grande dame* standing at the crossroads, graciously welcoming home her global family.

An early morning stroll to Mérida's colorful central market will introduce you to a veritable United Nations of culinary offerings: Lebanese *kibis* garnished with Mexican *pico de gallo*; a pile of bright red, bowling ball–sized Dutch Edam cheeses; a wooden tray full of buttery French *palmiers*, known here as *orejas* (ears); stacks of rust-colored, smoky Portuguese sausages—the *longaniza*.

Mérida is a melting pot that for centuries has attracted people from around the world. Prior to European contact, the Yukatek Mayas had extensive trade networks that exposed them to "foreign" influences from other regions of Mexico as well as the Caribbean, enriching their cultural and culinary options. And from the sixteenth century forward, the European empires of Spain, Portugal, Germany, the Netherlands, and points as far-flung as Africa, Lebanon, and Cuba, have all contributed their own unique piquancies to the pot.

It is as though all roads lead to Mérida—and it has ever been thus.

T'HÓ: THE CENTER OF THE COSMOS

Long before Europeans were aware that there were powerful civilizations to the west, the Maya city known as Ich Caan Ziho, or "The City in Heaven Born" (occasionally transcribed as Tiho, eventually shortened to just T'Hó and, during colonial times, changed to Mérida) was one of four principal capitals of the northern Maya lowlands. Along with Izamal, Chichén Itzá, and Uxmal, T'Hó stands out among the 2,000 archaeological sites registered in the state of Yucatán.

The Maya cosmic vision was based on the four cardinal directions, with a middle axis pinpointing the center of the universe. Street grids of ancient cities were aligned in this manner, as were groupings of five cities: four cities marked north, south, east, and west, and a fifth city always

A recently excavated sak beh *once connected the palace complex of Xoclán with the ancient city center of T'ho.* [MM]

dominated the midpoint. Mérida has long been viewed as one such cosmic center. An illustration in the *Chilam Balam de Chumayel* (p. 331)—a colonial manuscript recounting historical events that transpired before European contact—depicts Mérida (Tihoo) at the center of a cosmic wheel, with radiating spokes pointing to Campeche (Campech'), Maní, Valladolid (Zaci), and Izamal (Yz mal). (Typical of Maya maps, west is at the top of the wheel.)

Mérida "La Blanca"

From a bird's-eye view, a flat green jungle so dense it looks like moss saturates the bulging outline of the Yucatán Peninsula. Long, thin, straight white lines slash through the green and scrape the surface of the white limestone substrate. Many of these lines are new roads, bike paths, train tracks. But some of them were there in ancient times, too—an expansive highway system built by the Mayas to facilitate communication and trade between and among their ritual cities. Known in Mayan as "*sacbeob*" (or white roads; *sak beh* or *sacbé* is singular), the thoroughfares were paved with the region's plentiful white limestone. These white roads are one of several explanations for the origin

of Mérida's nickname—"The White City"—chanted proudly at every public function, ¡Mérida "La Blanca"!

By the time Europeans arrived in Yucatán, the great Maya cities lay in ruins—white stone ghost towns that reminded the strangers of the Roman ruins in their Spanish home—and the great white highways were being slowly digested by the jungle. On 6 January 1542, the Spaniard Francisco de Montejo "El Mozo" founded the colonial capital of the province of Yucatán and named it Mérida. On the heels of the conquest, opportunists from other European powers flocked to the region, threatening to eradicate the indigenous culture. However, as powerful as the Europeans were, they could not erase the steadfast Maya people. Their language and customs were strong glue that held their culture intact, an adhesive that continues unweakened to the present.

Through the centuries and amidst the influxes of so many other cultures into the region, the Mayas continue to hold their own. Walk along any street in The White City and this reality quickly dawns. A remarkable percentage of the people you pass are of Maya descent, with names like Canché and Uc and Canul. And many of these will be wearing the traditional clothes of Yucatán: women in the white cotton shift with fanciful floral embroidery at the neck and hem, known as the *huipil*; men in white *guayabera* and pants, with a white straw hat and white sandals.

And yes, their white clothing is one more theory of how Mérida got its nickname.

But this is not the theory I subscribe to. The most credible theory to me is certainly not the prettiest. Some scholars have suggested that the name originated during the horrific Guerra de las Castas (Caste War, 1847–1901), which marred the peninsula for decades. In this rebellion, incited and exacerbated by ancient feuds between the *hacendados* and their Maya workers, the Maya insurgents at one point quite literally cornered the Spanish gentry in Mérida, which became their stronghold and sanctuary for several years during the war. Mérida had become a prison for the Europeans, and the Mayas were the guards. Say it with a snarl, and the timbre skews dramatically: ¡Mérida "La Blanca"!

The cultural divisions that caused so much suffering are still there to some extent, but it seems to me that of far greater importance to the Mayas is their sense of connection—much like the ancient white roads that connected Mérida to all other places in their world. And the connections they describe are to nature, to their history and heritage, to their religion and city and state, to their ancestors and their families.

The enduring foundation of Mérida "La Blanca" always has been and always will be the beautiful brown of the Maya people.

MÉRIDA EN DOMINGO

Mérida en domingo (see pages 333–339) is the joyous weekly fair where visitors can indulge in a culinary smorgasbord. Starting Saturday night, streets surrounding Mérida's Plaza Principal are closed to all but pedestrian traffic; by early Sunday morning, colorful umbrellas and canopies have sprouted at the feet of centuries-old buildings. Insulated from the usual workweek rumble of traffic, the square fills to overflowing with strolling families, friends, and lovers, all drawn by the temptations offered by the scores of vendors who have set up for the day under the shade. Politely, they'll wink or wave to lure you to purchase their fare: Lebanese Carne al pastor or a flight of typical Maya tamales; Cuban fried plantains or good old American *perros calientes* (hot dogs)—foods that guide you on a whirlwind tour of Mérida's rich history.

[DK]

EMPANADAS

SAUSAGE-FILLED FLAKY PASTRY TURNOVERS

TO PREPARE AHEAD

Enriched Lard (p. 513)
Longaniza de Valladolid (p. 481),
  or chorizo, or the filling of
  your choice

FOR THE PASTRY DOUGH

3 cups (375 g) all-purpose flour
1 tsp. (6 g) sea salt
1 tsp. (6 g) baking powder
1 tsp. (4 g) sugar
3 Tbs. (42 g) butter, chilled
6 Tbs. (84 g) Enriched Lard,
  chilled
¼ cup (62.5 ml) ice water
1 egg
1 egg yolk

On Sundays in Mérida, the main square is flooded with the tempting aroma of *frituras*, "fried foods". One of these is the empanada. What originated in Spain were convenient packages of meat and bread for carrying on pilgrimages; similarly, modern Mexican empanadas are the ultimate "to go" snack. They also are a great way to make use of leftovers—a frugal trick common in Yucatán. The variety of fillings to choose from is limited only by your imagination. The recipe I provide here is for *longaniza* or chorizo. Or freeze leftovers of other recipes in this book and use as fillings: shredded Pollo pibil, Cochinita pibil, or Cazón frito, or for vegetarians, Calabacita frita, Chayas fritas, or simply a strip of jalapeño and a bit of goat cheese.

Prepare ahead note: The entire process of making Empanadas can be done in stages. Make the dough on one day and refrigerate or freeze until ready to use. Fill the Empanadas with your choice of fillings on another day, form and refrigerate or freeze until ready to use. Fry Empanadas immediately before serving.

YIELD: APPROXIMATELY 2 DOZEN

PREPARE PASTRY DOUGH

Place the first 4 ingredients in the bowl of a food processor fitted with the plastic dough blade and pulse until combined. Add the butter and lard and pulse just until the mixture is crumbly and resembles coarse meal.

Combine the water, egg, and egg yolk in a bowl and whisk with a fork until thoroughly incorporated. With the motor of the processor running, slowly dribble half of the egg mixture through the feed tube. Check the consistency: the dough should be smooth but slightly tacky; if it still seems dry, add a tablespoon of the water/egg mixture at a time until the dough feels smooth. Add only enough liquid to create a

[DK]

FOR THE FILLING

2 Tbs. (28g) Enriched Lard

12½ oz. (350 g) Longaniza de
Valladolid (Substitute: chorizo,
commercial *longaniza*, smoked
sausage, or the filling of
your choice)

½ medium white onion (5 oz. /
137.5 g), finely chopped

1 medium clove garlic (½ oz. /
6 g), peeled and minced

2 medium chiles serranos (¾ oz. /
20 g), charred, peeled, seeded,
and minced

2 Tbs. (16 g) all-purpose flour

¼ cup (62.5 ml) milk

FOR FINISHING AND FRYING THE EMPANADAS

All-purpose flour for dusting

1 egg, well beaten

Vegetable oil for frying

FOR SERVING

Salsas: X'nipek, Conserva de
marañón, Salpicón, and/or
hot sauces

---

smooth dough and process just enough to blend. Wrap the dough in plastic wrap and refrigerate for at least 1 hour or overnight.

PREPARE FILLING

Heat the lard in a medium skillet. Remove the sausage from the casings and add to the skillet. Use a wooden spoon or spatula to break the sausage up until it is well crumbled; continue heating until browned. Drain the sausage in a sieve placed over a bowl; return 2 tablespoons (30 ml) of the fat to the skillet and discard the rest.

Add the next 3 ingredients to the skillet and sauté over medium heat until the onions are translucent, about 2–3 minutes. Return the sausage to the skillet. Sprinkle the flour over everything and stir to combine. Cook, stirring frequently, 2–3 minutes. Add the milk, stir, and cook 1–2 minutes, or until the mixture has thickened and the ingredients are coated with the white sauce. (The sauce will hold the mixture together as you form the Empanadas.)

FORM AND FILL EMPANADAS

Divide the dough into 4 equal parts. Wrap and refrigerate the dough that you are not working with.

Turn the dough onto a lightly floured work surface; do not knead. Dust the dough with a bit of flour and roll it out to a thickness of ⅛ inch (3 mm). Use a 4 inch (10 cm)–diameter circular cookie cutter, a bowl, or other round form to cut the dough into rounds. Place approximately 1 tablespoon (15 g) of the filling of your choice just below the center of one of the dough circles and lightly brush around the circumference of the dough with the beaten egg. Fold the circle in half and press tightly around the ridge of the filling to remove air bubbles and firmly close the empanada; use a fork to crimp the edges and seal. Do not overfill, since the filling can expand and leak out during frying.

FRY EMPANADAS

Just before serving, pour 1½ inches (4 cm) of oil into a deep skillet. Heat to a temperature of 350°F (176°C). Working with a few at a time, fry the Empanadas until golden brown, turning once, 2–3 minutes per side. Remove them to paper towels to drain. Serve immediately or keep warm in a slow oven for 1–2 hours.

TO SERVE

For finger food, serve with any one or a combination of your favorite salsas: X'nipek, Conserva de marañón, Salpicón, and/or hot sauces (pp. 507). To serve as an appetizer or main course, accompany with Esquites (p. 239), Verduras en escabeche (p. 283), or guacamole and a tossed green salad.

VARIATION

Empanadas de cazón (Dogfish-Filled Flaky Pastry Turnovers): For this Campeche favorite, follow the master recipe, substituting an equal weight of Cazón frito (p. 312) for the sausage. Omit all the filling ingredients except the lard, flour, and milk. Reheat the *cazón* in the lard and proceed with the instructions for the filling.

Enjoying Tamal colado. [MR]

SUNDAY TAMALES

The variety of Yucatecan tamales offered during Mérida en domingo hits all the main themes of the genre. Learn to recognize them: Colados (p. 442) are small square tamales usually eaten with a spoon. Horneados (p. 105) means "baked" in Spanish; you will recognize them by their large rectangular shape and their singed and scorched banana-leaf wrappers. And Vaporcitos de x'pelon (p. 107) appear as little golden fingers studded with black beans. Tamales are so popular that recipes for them appear in several sections throughout this book.

MARQUESITAS

SWEET FLUTE-SHAPED WAFERS FILLED WITH EDAM CHEESE

FOR THE BATTER

3 eggs
¾ cup (150 g) sugar
¼ tsp. (1.5 g) sea salt
3 Tbs. (42 g) butter, melted
  and cooled
½ cup (125 ml) milk
½ tsp. (2.5 ml) almond extract
½ cup (62.5 g) all-purpose flour

FOR BAKING AND FINISHING

Vegetable oil
1½ cups (150 g) Edam cheese,
  grated

No one who visits Yucatán can leave without trying Marquesitas, another of the sweet/savory foods Yucatecans seem to love. The fanciful flute-shaped snack is composed of a sweet, crispy wafer filled with gooey, salty Edam cheese. Marquesitas were invented in 1938 by Vicente Mena, son of the founder of a famous Mérida institution, Sorbetería "El Polito." The original was simply an ice cream cone that don Vicente filled with cheese and sold to the children of wealthy *hacendados* during school recesses. Two of those children were granddaughters of a marquis ("*marqués*" in Spanish). When the girls made a special request for him to make the wafer elongated rather than the standard cone shape, he dubbed the new product Marquesitas. For a crispier product, you will achieve best results using an electric griddle especially made for waffle cones. Lacking that, you can cook these in a small nonstick skillet as you would crêpes, although they will remain somewhat soft as they cool.

Prepare ahead note: The batter for Marquesitas can be made a day in advance and refrigerated until ready to use. Bring it to room temperature and whisk before cooking. Marquesitas are best served immediately after rolling. Set up a station at your next party and prepare Marquesitas to order.

YIELD: APPROXIMATELY 10 MARQUESITAS

Preparing Marquesitas in the main square: form the wafer; sprinkle on cheese; roll. [MR]

PREPARE BATTER

Break the eggs into a medium mixing bowl and whisk or use an electric mixer to beat for 10–15 seconds. Add the sugar and salt and beat vigorously until frothy, 1–2 minutes. Add the butter, milk, and almond extract and beat until blended. Beat in the flour until well incorporated; the consistency of the batter should be quite thin, slightly thinner than pancake batter.

COOK WAFERS AND FINISH

Following manufacturer's instructions, preheat a waffle cone griddle to moderate-to-high. (Note: Alternatively, cook the batter as you would a crêpe in a 6-inch [15 cm] nonstick skillet, flipping once.) Lightly brush the griddle surfaces with oil. Pour a scant quarter cup (60 ml) of the batter onto the griddle (the amount depends on the size of your griddle; check manufacturer's specifications.) Cook for the required time. You may need to test this 1 or 2 times; the finished wafer should be golden brown all over. Use a fork or blunt knife to gently remove the wafer and transfer it immediately to a work surface.

As the wafers cool, they will become too brittle to roll, so work quickly. Place about 1 tablespoon (15 g) grated cheese on the wafer in a straight row along the side closest to you. Lift up the closest edge and roll the wafer away from you to form a flute shape. Set the finished Marquesita on a cooling rack as you proceed with the others. Repeat with the remaining batter, brushing a bit of oil on the griddle each time to avoid sticking. Serve immediately.

The Canul family enjoys Sunday afternoon comida at San Ildefonso Teya, a restored seventeenth-century hacienda. [MR]

"LLEGA LA FAMILIA"

Sundays in Mérida are a time for families to get together for a large afternoon meal and a weekly visit. While this tradition is, sadly, almost completely a thing of the past in many "developed" countries, in Yucatán it is still a strong—even tenacious—custom. In fact, it is almost impossible to get together with friends on Sunday afternoons because the standard response to an invitation will usually be, "No puedo. Llega la familia" (I can't. The family is coming). "Real" Yucatecans understand that activities with friends can happen any day *except* Sunday.

In earlier times, people ate at home, and they still do. But today it is just as common for the entire family to converge at a *restaurante familiar* (p. 271), or even a more upscale establishment for food and drink. The camaraderie starts by 2:00 pm and frequently stretches on until the restaurant closes at around 6:00 pm. The dishes served on Sunday afternoon are considered somewhat "fancy"—foods usually not consumed during the week.

(opposite page) Family meal in Yucatán, 1899. The urban solar is food-centered with rows of lettuces, fruit trees, and pots of herbs and medicinal plants. [THE FIELD MUSEUM LIBRARY]

CREMA DE CILANTRO
PURÉED SOUP OF LEEK, POTATO, SQUASH, AND CILANTRO

FOR THE SOUP BASE

10 cups (2.5 L) chicken stock or bouillon

2–3 small zucchini (10 oz. / 275 g), cubed

20 oz. (600 g) baking potatoes, peeled and cubed

FOR THE *SOFRITO*

1 stick (113 g) butter

3 cups (415 g) leek, cleaned and sliced (about 1 medium leek, 22 oz. / 630 g)

3 cups (290 g) scallions, coarsely chopped (3–4 medium bunches, 13 oz. / 390 g)

4 medium cloves garlic (1 oz. / 24 g), coarsely chopped

2 medium chiles serranos (¾ oz. / 20 g), charred, peeled, seeded, and chopped

TO FINISH

2 cups (120 g) cilantro, rinsed, coarsely chopped, and tightly packed into a measuring cup, divided

½ cup (125 ml) Mexican *crema* (optional) (Substitute: crème fraîche, sour cream, plain yogurt, or whipping cream)

FOR SERVING

Totopos para sopa (p. 515)

Squash blossoms (optional)

Mexican *crema* (Substitute: crème fraîche, sour cream, or plain yogurt) (optional)

Chopped cilantro (optional)

Cotija or *queso para sopa*, crumbled (Substitute: feta) (optional)

A favorite at Hacienda Teya, Crema de cilantro is based on vichyssoise—a relatively recent arrival on the Yucatecan table. The puréed leek and potato soup dates only to 1917 and is credited to Louis Diat, chef at the Ritz-Carlton in New York City. This recipe "Mexicanizes" vichyssoise with the addition of squash for texture and taste, chiles serranos for a bit of bite, and two full cups of cilantro to give a light aromatic flavor to this otherwise rather hearty soup. It is served hot in Yucatán, but it is equally delicious chilled, in the true tradition of vichyssoise.

Prepare ahead note: Crema de cilantro keeps well under refrigeration for 4–5 days. Reheat before serving or serve chilled.

YIELD: 10 SERVINGS

PREPARE SOUP BASE

Pour the stock into a large pot, add the squash and potatoes, and simmer approximately 20 minutes, or until the potatoes are tender.

PREPARE *SOFRITO*

While the vegetables are cooking, in a large skillet, melt the butter and cook the remaining ingredients until the leeks are translucent; do not allow them to brown. Transfer the vegetables to the pot containing the potato/squash mixture, cover, and simmer 6–8 minutes.

FINISH AND SERVE

To give the soup its characteristic bright green color, ladle 1 cup (250 ml) of the stock into a blender jar, add ½ cup (30 g) of the cilantro, and liquefy. Return the mixture to the stockpot. Using a handheld immersion blender, a blender, or a food processor, purée the ingredients in the stockpot until smooth. Add the remaining cilantro and cream, if using, and purée again to incorporate all the ingredients.

TO SERVE

Ladle the soup into individual bowls. Top with Totopos para sopa and garnish each serving with the squash blossom, if using. Drizzle on some *crema*, if using, and sprinkle with chopped cilantro and cheese if you wish.

SOPA DE LIMA

CHICKEN SOUP WITH SWEET LIME ESSENCE

TO PREPARE AHEAD

Salpimentado (p. 352), or
  substitute

Recado para escabeche (p. 498)
  (Note: As described in Pantry
  Staples, Recado para escabeche is
  also known as Recado para salpimentado and is the requisite
  seasoning for this dish.)

FOR THE SOUP BASE

10 cups (2.5 L) stock from making
  Salpimentado (p. 352; substitute:
  chicken stock or bouillon)

½ medium chicken
  (about 1½ lbs. / 680 g)

1 sprig fresh thyme (Substitute:
  ¼ tsp. / .25 g dried)

Sopa de lima is *the* classic soup of Yucatán. The *lima* (*Citrus limetta*)—also known as limetta or sweet lime—is more aromatic and less acidic than the Persian or Mexican lime and gives this soup its characteristic floral taste. The traditional preparation method for Sopa de lima is gradually being lost. Nowadays, most cooks simply squeeze some *lima* juice (tightwads use lime juice) into a pot of chicken soup and call it a day. However, the original recipe evolved out of a Yucatecan stew known as Salpimentado, a potpourri of pork, chicken, and vegetables seasoned with a special *recado*. Like so many other recipes in the *olla podrida* family, the meats of Salpimentado are removed and served separately, while the cooking liquid is served in bowls on the side. It is this cooking liquid that was eventually transformed into Sopa de lima as cooks pondered what to do with leftovers. A quick *sofrito* with the special Recado para salpimentado and some slices of *lima* turn it into a wholly unique dish. Since *lima* is not available beyond the growing zone, substitutions are suggested.

Prepare ahead note: Sopa de lima can be prepared in advance, refrigerated, and reheated just before serving. As noted below, it is also delicious served chilled.

YIELD: 10 SERVINGS

PREPARE SOUP BASE

Place the stock, chicken, and thyme in a stockpot and bring to a simmer, skimming frequently. Continue to cook gently until the chicken is cooked through, 25–30 minutes.

[MR]

Zest of 1 *lima* or lime, finely
grated
2 Tbs. (30 ml) Spanish olive oil
1 medium white onion (10 oz. /
275 g), finely chopped
4 cloves garlic (1 oz. / 24 g), peeled,
charred, and finely chopped
1 cup (140 g) green bell pepper,
cut into small dice
½ tsp. (1.5 g) Recado para escabeche (Note: omit if using the
stock from Salpimentado)
3 medium Roma tomatoes
(10½ oz. / 300 g), seeded and
finely chopped
⅓ cup (85 ml) fresh *lima* juice
(Substitute: Mexican or Persian
lime juice)

FOR SERVING
Chopped cilantro
Totopos para sopa (p. 515)
Slices of *lima* or lime
Chile con limón (p. 511)

Remove the chicken and set aside to cool. Pull the meat from the bones into large pieces or slice into julienne strips; set aside.

Strain the stock through a fine sieve into another pot. If time allows, refrigerate the stock several hours or overnight and skim off any fat before finishing.

FOR THE *SOFRITO* AND FINISHING

Place the stock in a stockpot and return to a simmer. Add the citrus zest, cover the pot, and remove it from the heat to allow the stock to steep as you continue.

While the stock is steeping, heat the oil in a large skillet until shimmering. Add the next 3 ingredients and cook, stirring frequently, until the onions are translucent, 2–3 minutes. Add the *recado* and tomatoes and continue to cook until the tomatoes are softened, about 3 minutes. Add the *sofrito* to the stock. Stir in the chicken and simmer 2–3 minutes to heat through. Add the citrus juice and serve immediately.

TO SERVE

Ladle the soup into individual bowls, distributing the chicken evenly. Sprinkle on some of the cilantro and top with Totopos para sopa and slices of *lima* or lime. Place additional Totopos and cilantro on the table along with the chile sauce so that diners can adjust their soup to taste.

VARIATIONS

Wanting *lima*, you may mimic its floral note by substituting a 5-inch (13 cm) stalk of lemongrass cut in half lengthwise for the zest. Add it to the stock and simmer for 10 minutes only. Remove the pan from the heat, cover, and allow the stock to steep for 15 minutes as you prepare the *sofrito*. Remove the lemongrass and proceed with the rest of the recipe.

While not traditional, for a refreshing summer soup, serve Sopa de lima chilled. Omit adding the chicken in the soup base. Instead, prepare Tsi'ik de pollo asado (p. 422) using shredded Pollo asado (p. 270). To serve, pack Tsi'ik into individual ramekins and unmold in the center of a soup bowl. Pour in the chilled soup and garnish with Totopos para sopa and slices of *lima* or lime.

(opposite page) A groaning board of Yucatecan specialties at Hacienda Teya: Longaniza de Valladolid and Panuchos; in the background, Papadzules and Empanadas de cazón. [MR]

PIB X'CATIK

BLOND CHILES STUFFED WITH PIT-SMOKED PORK IN ACHIOTE MARINADE

TO PREPARE AHEAD
Cochinita pibil (p. 420)

FOR THE STUFFED CHILES
12 large chiles x'catiques
2 cups (about 600 g) Cochinita pibil, finely shredded

FOR SERVING
Tomate frito (p. 507)
Cebollas encurtidas (p. 510)

Chiles rellenos—or stuffed chiles—are popular throughout Mexico. The chile most commonly used for stuffing is the poblano, due in large part to its mildness and generous size. In Yucatán, however, the favorite for *rellenos* is the blond chile x'catik. In Mérida, the common filling is Cochinita pibil, while in Campeche the most in-demand filling is *cazón* (see below). Pib x'catik is meant to make use of leftover Cochinita pibil, so plan ahead to get two dishes in one.

Prepare ahead note: The chiles may be prepared and stuffed in advance. Cover with plastic wrap and reheat in a microwave oven for 1–1½ minutes. Serve immediately.

YIELD: 6 SERVINGS

STUFF CHILES
Char the chiles without puncturing them over an open flame or in a heavy skillet until generally blackened. Immediately place the chiles in a plastic bag, seal, and allow to steam for 10 minutes. Remove the chiles one by one from the bag and under running water, rub off as much of the charred skin as possible. Carefully slit each chile down the length of one side, open, and remove the seeds and veins, taking care to leave the stem intact.

Heat the Tomate frito while you continue with the rest of the recipe. Warm the Cochinita pibil in a skillet or saucepan with its juices; keep warm.

Generously stuff the chiles with the shredded pork (quantity depends on the size of the chile); tuck the filling in tightly and lift the sides of the chile over the top to cover. Reshape the chiles to their original form. Serve immediately or reheat as noted above.

TO SERVE
Arrange 2 stuffed chiles on each of 6 individual serving plates or all together on a large serving platter. Spoon on the hot Tomate frito and top with Cebollas encurtidas.

VARIATION
X'catiques rellenos de cazón (Blond Chiles Stuffed with Dogfish): In Campeche, stuffed chiles feature Cazón frito (p. 312) instead of Cochinita pibil. Quantities and serving suggestions are the same.

QUESO RELLENO

DUTCH EDAM CHEESE STUFFED WITH SAVORY MINCEMEAT

TO PREPARE AHEAD

Picadillo de especias (p. 256)

Banana leaves prepared to
  extra-large (XL) size (see Basic
  Techniques, p. 525)

K'óol blanco (p. 140)

Tomate frito (p. 507)

(continued on next page)

The traditional way of eating Edam has been to cut an opening in the top of the cheese and scoop out the quantity desired. In this way the cheese is slowly consumed until nothing but the firm rind remains. Although the true history of the invention of Queso relleno is clouded in mystery, surely some frugal cook sought a creative way to make use of the rind, filled the hollow with ground meat, and a Yucatecan classic was born.

Since most people beyond Yucatán will not keep a ball of Edam on their table at all times until the soft cheese inside has been consumed, many recipes instruct the cook to scoop out the cheese and save it for another use. This is somewhat labor intensive, so in addition to the traditional method, I present an alternate, if less dramatic, assembly technique, using grated cheese instead of the entire ball.

Prepare ahead note: The Picadillo de especias, K'óol blanco, and Tomate frito can be made in advance and refrigerated or frozen. Leftovers of Queso relleno can be refrigerated for 2–3 days; reheat in a moderate oven or in the microwave oven before serving.

YIELD: 8–10 SERVINGS

TRADITIONAL METHOD

Remove the wax coating from the ball of cheese and discard. Slice off the top of the cheese to form a "cap" approximately ½-inch (1.25 cm) thick; reserve. Scoop out the insides of the cheese using a melon baller or spoon, leaving walls about ½-inch (1.25 cm)

[MC]

FOR THE CHEESE AND FILLING

1 whole Edam cheese, approximately 5 pounds (2.25 k) (Note: You will only need 1 lb. [500 g] of cheese for the alternate method, below)
½ recipe Picadillo de especias (about 1¾ lbs. / 800 g)
Vegetable oil
Cheesecloth
Kitchen twine

FOR SERVING

10 whole chiles habaneros, optional garnish
Avocado slices, optional garnish
Tortillas (p. 518)
Chile tamulado (p. 509) or the chile sauce of your choice

thick. Grate the leftover cheese and refrigerate or freeze it for other Yucatecan dishes like Codzitos (p. 277), Marquesitas (p. 337), or Pastel de queso de bola (p. 206).

Lay 2 squares of cheesecloth large enough to wrap around the cheese on a work surface. Crisscross several sections of banana leaf on top of the cheesecloth, making sure you have enough to cover the ball completely.

Place the hollow ball in the center of the banana leaves and pack tightly with the raw Picadillo de especias. Replace the cap. Brush the exterior of the cheese and the exposed side of the banana leaves with vegetable oil. Fold the banana leaves over the top of the cheese to cover completely. Wrap both layers of cheesecloth around the ball, gather the cheesecloth at the top, and tie it securely with kitchen twine. Place the cheese in a heatproof steep-sided bowl in which it fits snugly (this will help the cheese maintain its spherical form during steaming).

Place the wrapped cheese in its bowl on a rack in a large *tamal* steamer. (Alternatively, place the wrapped cheese in its bowl in a deep baking pan filled with boiling water. Cover the pan securely with foil and bake at 350°F / 176°C.) Steam for 1 hour (a meat thermometer inserted into the center should register 160°F / 71°C). Remove the cheese ball from the steamer and allow to rest in the bowl 30 minutes before slicing.

Remove the cheesecloth and gently peel away the banana leaves. To serve, place the entire cheese on a platter and slice into wedges at the table or serve it already sliced and plated according to serving suggestions below.

ALTERNATE METHOD

Cut the banana leaves into 3-inch × 9-inch (7.6 cm × 23 cm) strips. Rub the leaves with a bit of vegetable oil, then line 10 6-ounce (170 g) soufflé molds or ramekins with 2 pieces of leaf, crossed in the center.

Grate 1 pound (500 g) Edam cheese and set aside. Shape the raw Picadillo de especias into 10 balls weighing about 3 ounces (80 g) each, then form into patties to a diameter that will fit snugly in your mold. Cover the bottom of each ramekin with about 1 ounce (25 g) of the grated cheese and pack tightly, edge to edge. Place a patty of meat on top of the cheese and finish with another ounce (25 g) of cheese. Fold the banana leaves over the top and press firmly to seal and pack. Repeat with the rest of the ramekins.

Preheat the oven to 350°F (176°C). Place the ramekins in a deep baking pan and add boiling water three-quarters of the way up the sides of the ramekins. Cover the pan securely with foil and bake for approximately 1 hour, or until a meat thermometer inserted into the center of the meat registers 160°F (71°C). Allow the ramekins to cool 10 minutes to set, then unmold and serve. You may remove the banana leaves prior to serving, or guests may do so themselves. Serve sauces on the side.

TO SERVE

Ladle a puddle of K'óol blanco onto each serving plate and place a slice or individual serving of Queso relleno on top. Spoon on some Tomate frito and garnish with a chile on top and a slice of avocado to the side. In Yucatán, people often put bite-sized bits of the Queso relleno onto a tortilla along with a few sprinkles of chile sauce and eat it taco-style.

VARIATIONS

Queso relleno de cazón (Dutch Edam Cheese Stuffed with Savory Dogfish Filling): Hacienda Teya offers a novel version of Queso relleno, filling it with dogfish instead of meat. Substitute the Picadillo de especias with about 3 cups (800 g) Cazón asado frito (p. 312). Allow the fried dogfish to cool, then place it in a large mixing bowl and add 1 tablespoon (4 g) fresh mint leaves (about 4 large sprigs), chopped; 10 small pimiento-stuffed green olives, sliced; 3 tablespoons (45 g) blanched and slivered almonds; 2 table-spoons (30 g) small whole capers, drained; 2 tablespoons (30 g) black raisins; 2 eggs, beaten; and ½ cup (60 g) bread crumbs. Mix thoroughly to combine and stuff and steam the cheese in either the traditional or the alternate method of the master recipe for Queso relleno.

Queso relleno de mariscos (Dutch Edam Cheese Stuffed with Savory Seafood Filling): You may also use mixed seafood in this recipe shared with me by Ramón Lara Cárdenas, aka "Moncho," the son of the owner of the popular regional restaurant El Faisán y el Venado in Playa del Carmen. For the mixed-seafood version, follow the master recipe for Cazón asado frito (p. 312), replacing the grilled dogfish with 1¾ pounds (800 g) mixed seafood (cooked octopus or squid, raw peeled shrimp, raw lobster tail meat, raw whitefish fillets, raw scallops), finely chopped. Finish as per Cazón asado frito. After the mixture has cooled, continue with the recipe as described for Queso relleno de cazón (above), adding the mint and other ingredients followed by stuffing and steaming the cheese.

[MC]

EDAM: THE PIRATES' LEGACY

In 1621, the Dutch West India Company was chartered to establish trade with Spanish and Portuguese colonies in the Americas and Africa and to attempt the settlement of Dutch colonies in the New World. Dutch contact with the Yucatán Peninsula occurred mostly in the form of piracy: Dutch pirates took it upon themselves to fight out the Catholic/Protestant rivalry that defined relations between the Netherlands and Spain—and to pillage and sack along the way.

Whether the Dutch ever actually used their hard, spherical Edam cheeses as cannonballs shall remain the subject of folklore; still, Edam is a notable vestige of the Dutch presence in Yucatán. It was the most popular cheese in Europe from the fourteenth through the eighteenth centuries, especially at sea and in the far-flung European colonies due to its ability to travel well. Once the cheese is aged, a thick rind protects the soft, rich interior. In more recent times, the Edam has continued to flow into the peninsula via the free port of Chetumal.

CABALLEROS POBRES

BREAD PUDDING "SOUFFLÉ" WITH CINNAMON SYRUP AND NUTS

TO PREPARE AHEAD
Pan francés (p. 194), or substitute

FOR THE SYRUP

1 cup (250 ml) water

1 cup (200 g) sugar

1 cone *piloncillo*, chopped
(Substitute: 1 cup / 250 g
dark brown sugar)

2 whole cloves

2 three-in. (8 cm) sticks *canela*
(Mexican cinnamon)

½ cup (50 g) almonds or pecans,
whole or chopped

¼ cup (62.5 ml) brandy, coffee
liqueur, or aged rum

FOR THE BREAD

2 cups (500 ml) milk

3 Tbs. (36 g) sugar

2 tsp. (10 ml) Mexican vanilla
extract

4 small or 2 large loaves stale Pan
francés (Substitute: French rolls
or baguettes), sliced into ¾ in.
(2 cm) thick rounds

6 egg whites

3 egg yolks

Vegetable oil for frying

Every culture has its recipe for using up stale, leftover bread, and bread pudding is probably as old as bread itself. In Tudor England, the dish was dubbed "poor knights" pudding signifying its humble birth. Caballeros pobres—as it is translated literally in Spanish—has by now become a quintessentially Yucatecan dessert. It descends from the tradition of French *pain perdu* and Spanish *torrijas* and is a kissing cousin of Cuban *torrejas*. Somewhere between bread pudding and French toast, the recipe for Caballeros pobres specifies dipping stale Pan francés (p. 194) in sweetened milk, bathing it in beaten egg whites, after which it is fried then drowned in sugar syrup. In Yucatán, Caballeros pobres is typically served chilled or at room temperature, but serving it warm out of the oven and à la mode with a scoop of your favorite ice cream makes it more like "*caballeros ricos*" (rich knights)!

Prepare ahead note: Caballeros pobres can be assembled a day in advance and refrigerated, then baked just before serving, or simply refrigerated after finishing. Either reheat 15–20 minutes in a moderate oven, or serve chilled or at room temperature, as is the style in Yucatán.

YIELD: 10 SERVINGS

PREPARE SYRUP

Place the first 5 ingredients in a saucepan. Simmer, stirring frequently, until the sugars are completely dissolved. Continue cooking until the syrup coats the back of a spoon. Strain into another small pan and discard the *canela* and cloves. Add the nuts and liquor and continue cooking another 5 minutes, or until the syrup rethickens. Remove the pan from the heat and set aside.

PREPARE BREAD

Combine the first 3 ingredients and stir to dissolve the sugar. Pass each slice of bread through the milk mixture to moisten lightly and transfer to a colander placed over a bowl to drain. (Note: Do not allow the bread to become soggy or it will fall apart during frying.)

Beat the egg whites until stiff but not dry. Beat the 3 egg yolks well. Fold the beaten yolks gently into the beaten egg whites, being careful not to deflate the whites.

Fill a large skillet with oil to a depth of 1½ inches (4 cm). Heat the oil until a thermometer reaches 350°F (176°C). Working in batches, roll each bread slice in the egg white mixture to coat, then fry. When deep golden brown, flip the bread to cook the other side. Drain on paper towels.

BAKE AND SERVE

Preheat the oven to 350°F (176°C). Meanwhile, place 1 layer of the fried bread in a deep baking dish, soufflé mold, or individual soufflé ramekins. Pour on a large spoonful of the syrup/nut mixture. Repeat until all the bread and syrup have been used. Bake for

25–30 minutes, or until the syrup begins to bubble and you see caramelization occurring at the edges. Remove the dish from the oven and allow the pudding to rest at room temperature for 15 minutes before serving.

TO SERVE
As noted above, Caballeros pobres may be served warm, at room temperature, or chilled.

VARIATIONS
Caballeros pobres often features raisins instead of nuts. Add them alone or with the nuts.

Serve warm and à la mode with your favorite ice cream. Rum raisin, coffee, or vanilla are excellent choices, or try Helado de chocolate maya, page 468.

[MC]

PUCHERO DE TRES CARNES

BEEF, PORK, AND CHICKEN STEW WITH VEGETABLES AND PLANTAIN

TO PREPARE AHEAD
Enriched Lard (p. 513)
Recado para puchero (p. 499)

FOR THE MEATS
3 Tbs. (42 g) Enriched Lard

1 medium chicken (about 3 lbs. / 1.5 k), cut into serving pieces

1 lb. (500 g) stewing beef, cut into 2 in. (5 cm) cubes

1 lb. (500 g) pork leg, with some fat, cut into 2 in. (5 cm) cubes

20 cups (5 L) water

2 medium heads garlic (approximately 1¾ oz. / 50 g each), charred, peeled, and separated into cloves

1 medium white onion (10 oz. / 275 g), peeled, charred, and quartered

1 five-in. (12 cm) stick *canela* (Mexican cinnamon)

2 Tbs. (24 g) powdered chicken bouillon, or 2 cubes

1 Tbs. (18 g) sea salt

1 Tbs. (8 g) Recado para puchero

Big pinch saffron

FOR THE VEGETABLES
9 oz. (250 g) *each* kohlrabi, sweet potato, potato, and carrot, peeled and halved

9 oz. (250 g) *each* zucchini and chayote, halved lengthwise, seeds removed from chayote

½ medium white cabbage (about 1 lb. / 500 g total), quartered

1 medium semiripe plantain (9 oz. / 250 g), ends sliced off but left whole and unpeeled

Puchero is another one-pot, feed-the-whole-family meal that belongs to the Spanish *olla podrida* family. But it has been so assimilated into Yucatecan gastronomy that it has created many spinoff dishes and even vocabulary. It is customary to serve Puchero by ladling the cooking liquid into a bowl, with the meats and vegetables served separately. Then begins what can only be described as a Yucatecan dinnertime ritual: diners use a fork to mash together their preferred meat and vegetables, then heap the result on a tortilla, taco-style. In the last century, this mash was used as the filling for *salbutes* (p. 435), a regional taco variant. In fact, in honor of the stew, the mash has been dubbed "*puuch*'," a Mayan word meaning "to squash, press, or mash," now absorbed into Yucatecan vocabulary and appearing in regional dictionaries with additional meanings beyond the culinary. A local campaign for breast cancer awareness sported the slogan, "Haz puuch' en tu chuchú"—a vernacular Mayan/Spanish way of saying, "Press your breast."

There is a certain rhythm employed by Yucatecan cooks when making Puchero, and it is a wise tip to follow: start by cooking the meats (if you are using a stewing hen, it goes in first); then add the vegetables in the order listed, starting with the ones that take longest to cook. While "one-pot stew" may sound simple, there's a real trick to timing the addition of ingredients so that the chicken doesn't fall apart but the vegetables are perfectly tender at the end. Puchero is also the start of several other stew variations, a couple of which follow.

Prepare ahead note: Leftovers of Puchero de tres carnes can be reheated another day, but do so gently so as not to overcook the vegetables. Or make the *puuch*' from leftovers and use in the original version of the local tacos, *salbutes* (p. 435).

YIELD: 10–12 SERVINGS

PREPARE MEATS
In a large stockpot, heat the lard until shimmering. Working in batches, brown the chicken, beef, and pork; transfer the browned meats to a platter as you finish. When all the meats are browned, return them to the stockpot along with any accumulated juices, cover with the water, and add the next 3 ingredients. Bring to a boil, skimming frequently. After 5 minutes, when the foam subsides, add the last 4 ingredients and reduce the heat to medium.

COOK VEGETABLES
Add the kohlrabi to the stockpot and cook over medium heat for 10 minutes. Add the sweet potato, potato, and carrot in this order, with 5 minutes between additions. After these vegetables have been added, cook 5 minutes, then add the remaining vegetables all at once.

4 cups (15 oz. / 425 g) cooked
  garbanzos (chickpeas), drained
½ cup (30 g) fresh cilantro leaves,
  chopped
½ cup (30 g) fresh mint leaves,
  chopped
¼ cup (62.5 ml) fresh *lima* juice
  (Substitute: lime juice)

FOR SERVING

Arroz amarillo (p. 529)
Tortillas (p. 518)
Mixture of chopped radish and
  cilantro with one minced chile
  habanero, dressed with Seville
  orange juice, or substitute,
  and sea salt
Lima or lime wedges

FINISH STEW

Add the garbanzos, cilantro, and mint and bring the stew to a boil. Reduce the heat to a simmer and cook 10–15 minutes, or until the vegetables are just tender and the meats are cooked. Add the *lima* juice and serve immediately.

TO SERVE

Remove the vegetables and meats from the stockpot, arranging the vegetables attractively on one platter and the meats on another. Peel the plantain, slice it into rounds, and place it on the platter of vegetables. Use a slotted spoon or wok strainer to retrieve all of the *canela* pieces in the stockpot and discard. Mound the rice in a separate serving bowl. Pour the cooking liquid into a tureen or ladle it into individual bowls.

To consume Puchero traditionally, place some meat and vegetables on your plate and mash thoroughly with a fork. Scoop this *puuch'* onto tortillas and garnish with the radish/cilantro mixture and a squeeze of lime juice. The stock and garbanzos are eaten with a soup spoon.

VARIATIONS

Instead of serving rice on the side, some cooks add rice and/or elbow macaroni or broken spaghetti to the cooking liquid at the same time as the vegetables.

Puchero vaquero (Cowboy-Style Beef Stew): Salting and drying meats was a Maya strategy for preservation; coincidentally, the Spanish brought their own version—*cecina*, or salted, dried beef—which became a staple in the pantries of Yucatán's ranches. Follow the master recipe for Puchero, replacing the meats with 1½ pounds (690 g) *each cecina* and cubed stewing beef. Soak the *cecina* overnight to remove the salt. Pass it through two more rinses of fresh water prior to using.

Cooking puchero for the Sunday afternoon meal with the Rodríguez family. [MR]

Trim off any fat or sinew from both meats, cut the meat into bite-sized pieces, and set aside. Brown the stewing beef and proceed with the master recipe, adding the *cecina* at the same time you add the water. Replace the chicken bouillon with beef bouillon. Add 2 tablespoons (40 g) Recado para bistec (p. 501) dissolved in ¼ cup (62.5 ml) white vinegar. Add vegetables and cook until they are tender. Remove the vegetables and meat and arrange on platters as explained in the master recipe.

Add ½ cup (100 g) long-grain white rice, 5¼ ounces (150 g) uncooked spaghetti broken in half, and ½ pound (250 g) fresh *chaya* leaves, chard, or kale, thick stems removed and cut into chiffonade. Cook until the pasta and rice are soft, about 15 minutes. Serving suggestions are the same.

Potaje de lentejas con huevo (Vegetarian Lentil Stew with Poached Eggs): In the same bottomless-pot family as Puchero, lentil stews assume a multitude of forms in the peninsula. This one is (mostly) vegetarian, depending on your orthodoxy; it traditionally includes a poached-egg garnish. Follow the master recipe for Puchero but omit the first 4 ingredients. Place the water in a stockpot and add 1 pound (500g) green lentils along with the garlic, onions, and salt and substitute vegetable bouillon for the chicken. Bring to a gentle simmer.

While the lentils are cooking, make a *sofrito*. Heat 1 tablespoon (15 ml) Spanish olive oil in a medium skillet. Sauté 1 cup (170 g) chopped white onion, 4 medium cloves garlic (1 oz. / 24 g), chopped, and 1 cup (140 g) chopped green bell pepper until pepper is tender, about 5 minutes. Add 2 chopped Roma tomatoes (7 oz. / 200 g) and continue cooking over low heat until tomatoes are softened, about 5 minutes. Dissolve 3 tablespoons (45 g) Recado rojo (p. 500) and 3 tablespoons (60 g) Recado para bistec (p. 501) in ½ cup (125 ml) white vinegar, add to the *sofrito*, and cook 30 seconds.

Transfer the *sofrito* to the stockpot and raise the heat to high. When the liquid reaches a boil, reduce to a simmer and cook until the lentils are barely tender, about 10 minutes.

Peel the vegetables and cut into 1-inch (2.5 cm) cubes. Halve the cabbage then quarter each half. Peel the plantain and cut into thick rounds. Add all the vegetables and the plantain at once. Cook 25–30 minutes; the vegetables should be very tender and the liquid should have reduced and thickened somewhat. Discard the *canela* and check the seasonings. Add 2 teaspoons (12 g) sea salt or to taste.

Poach one egg per diner in some of the cooking liquid, as is the custom in Yucatán, or in water. Ladle the *potaje* into individual soup bowls and top each serving with one poached egg. Accompany with Arroz blanco (p. 529) and Pan francés (p. 194).

Salpimentado ("Spiced-Up" Stew): I must give at least cursory attention to Salpimentado, since it plays a prominent role in another Yucatecan classic, Sopa de lima (p. 341). A complete recipe will not be useful since one of the key components of Salpimentado is the *pepino kat* (p. 48), or "tree cucumber," which is unavailable outside the region. Salpimentado bears a striking resemblance to Puchero de tres carnes, but uses Recado para escabeche (p. 498) instead of the Recado para puchero. Its use transforms this "everything-but-the-kitchen-sink" stew into something quite "spiced-up." Beyond that change, it also omits the beef and uses only chicken and pork pieces and ribs; a couple of chiles x'catiques are thrown in for good measure; and it is finished with an even more generous dousing of *lima* (p. 37) juice, preparing it for its later reincarnation as Sopa de lima.

CHANCLETAS

BAKED CHAYOTE WITH SPICED MINCEMEAT FILLING

TO PREPARE AHEAD

Picadillo en chilmole or Picadillo
   (p. 254)
Pan molido para empanizado
   (p. 515)

FOR THE STUFFED CHAYOTES

5 medium chayotes (about 10½ oz.
   / 300 g each)
2 tsp. (12 g) sea salt
½ recipe Picadillo en chilmole
   or Picadillo
¾ cup (90 g) Pan molido para
   empanizado
¼ cup (62.5 ml) Spanish olive oil

FOR SERVING

Tomate frito (p. 507)
Cotija or feta cheese, crumbled
Cebollas encurtidas (p. 510),
   recommended accompaniment

Mexican native chayote (p. 28) is a member of the squash family. "*Chancletas*" is a Spanish word meaning "flip-flops" or sandals and is applied to this dish as a whimsical reference to the shape of the chayote when cut in half. Although it is traditional to use standard Picadillo for the filling, the best Chancletas I ever tasted used Picadillo en chilmole, which is my suggestion here, although you may use either. (Note: Be sure to select only fresh, young chayotes for this dish. Check the skin of the chayote: if it looks dry and wrinkled, it is not fresh. It should appear smooth and without blemish and lose a bit of water if you press a fingernail into the flesh.)

Prepare ahead note: The Picadillo filling can be made well in advance and refrigerated 1–2 days until needed, or frozen for several months. Chancletas are best served hot out of the oven.

YIELD: 10 SERVINGS

PARBOIL CHAYOTES

Slice the chayotes in half lengthwise following the line of the natural indentation at the base. Place them in a large pot of boiling water with the salt and return to a boil. Reduce the heat to a simmer, cover the pan, and cook 20–25 minutes, or until the chayotes are barely tender when pierced with a fork. Drain and set aside to cool.

STUFF CHAYOTES, BAKE, AND SERVE

Preheat the oven to 400°F (205°C). While the oven is preheating, with a spoon or melon baller, remove the soft center seed from the middle of each chayote and discard. Scoop out and reserve some of the chayote flesh, being sure to leave the sides and bottom of the squash thick enough to support the filling. Mash the reserved flesh and mix it with the Picadillo. Stuff each chayote with some of the Picadillo mixture and place on an oiled baking sheet or in an oiled baking dish. Top with a sprinkle of Pan molido, then drizzle on a bit of Spanish olive oil. Bake until the tops are lightly golden, about 30 minutes.

TO SERVE

Heat the Tomate frito while the Chancletas are baking. You may arrange all of the Chancletas together on a large serving platter, or a half on each of 10 individual plates. Ladle on some of the hot Tomate frito, sprinkle with the cheese, and top with Cebollas encurtidas if desired.

Chancletas for Sunday dinner as prepared by Palmira Rodríguez Tejeda and Rosa Tejeda. [MR]

The general aspect of Mérida is Moorish, as it was built at a time
when the Moorish style prevailed in Spanish architecture.

—JOHN LLOYD STEPHENS, 1843

THE LEBANESE EMIGRATION

It is virtually impossible to avoid bumping into vendors on every street corner selling Lebanese *kibis*—egg-shaped fritters of bulgur wheat, a surprising ingredient to find here amidst indigenous maize, beans, and squash. And not just bulgur, but also limes and garbanzos and lentils and cloves and a litany of other flavorful vestiges of centuries of Arabic/Islamic global trade can now be found in markets throughout Yucatán. This Middle Eastern heritage arrived in the New World onboard the first ships from Spain; a second wave occurred in the last half of the nineteenth century.

Early Arrivals

Many of the first Spaniards to arrive in Yucatán in the early sixteenth century were from southern Spain, in particular regions now known as Andalucía and Extremadura. In 711, Iberia was invaded by the Moors—Islamic warriors from North Africa— who claimed the vast region for themselves and named it al-Andalus. The Moors ruled virtually the entire lower two-thirds of the Iberian peninsula for 781 years, marking it with the stamp of their own culture, known for its ornate palaces, manicured gardens, fountains, and, of course, culinary riches.

On 2 January 1492, Los Reyes Católicos, Fernando and Isabel, captured the Alhambra and reclaimed it for what was soon to become a unified Spain. In a sweeping drama that only true history can write, on 3 August 1492, just months after this major coup, Columbus set sail from an Andalusian port along a route thought to be a western passage to Asia.

Naturally, the ships' crews wanted to enjoy all the familiar comforts and foods of home, and so they brought with them the things that in turn had been introduced by the Moors. Ship inventories of the time read like the shopping list from a souk. In just a few years, the New World was stocked with a cornucopia of unfamiliar foods largely credited to Arabic cultivation and trade: cherries, apricots, melons, parsley, cilantro, eggplant, garbanzos, fava beans, lentils, cardamom, cinnamon, ginger, almonds, sesame seeds, pistachios, capers, raisins, and olives. Still other ingredients of Arabic pedigree—for example, mango, citrus, coffee, and sugarcane—soon became adapted to New World soils.

Later Infusions

Between 1878 and World War I, turmoil in the Mideast launched the first great wave of what became known as "the Lebanese emigration" in the Ottoman provinces of Greater Syria and Mount Lebanon. Many of those emigrants arrived in Mexico through Veracruz; others entered through Tampico, Tamaulipas, and still others via the port of Progreso in Yucatán.

During the 1920s and 1930s, Middle Eastern migration to Mexico quadrupled. In an atmosphere tolerant of their customs, immigrants from the Levant succeeded in conserving a large part of their traditions, including their culinary heritage.

By the mid-twentieth century, Lebanese culture had

(opposite page) Alberto's Continental: Moorish arches trace the courtyard of a seventeenth-
century mansion that has served as a Lebanese restaurant since the 1960s. [EC]

Garbanzos in Mérida's central market. [MC]

strongly rooted in Mexico, with social clubs and civic organizations linking immigrants to each other as well as to their new communities. The cuisine, too, was by now well established throughout the country, and a woman from Mérida attained prominence as its champion. María Manzur de Borge published *Manual práctico de cocina libanesa* (Practical manual of Lebanese cooking) in 1952, and the cookbook became so popular throughout Mexico that it is still in print, now in its eighth edition. Several recipes in this section have been adapted from her book.

The Moorish Pantry

Thanks to the ingredients brought to the New World by Andalusian explorers, nineteenth-century immigrants from the Levant found it relatively easy to make their favorite foods: garbanzo beans were turned into hummus, lentils into *potaje*, and bulgur into *kibis* or tabbouleh. The pantry had been conveniently stocked for these new citizens some 400 years earlier. Fascinating fusions were made out of necessity or, sometimes, simple curiosity: Seville oranges replaced lemons; pork or beef replaced lamb; and several chiles sneaked their way into Old World recipes as if to awaken staid ways to this brave new world.

BULGUR

Bulgur is a common Middle Eastern cereal food made of durum or other wheat varieties that have been parboiled, dried, debranned, and coarsely crushed. The technique dates to almost 6000 years BCE, revealed in archaeological sites in Bulgaria. Its capacity to store for long periods without going rancid made it a logical staple for seagoing travelers. Today it is common, if rather anachronistic, to see traditionally dressed Maya women selling bags of bulgur in Yucatecan markets, crying, "¡Hay trigo para kibis!" ("Wheat for *kibis* here!")

All recipes using bulgur in this section provide measurement in weight, but because bulgur can vary dramatically due to humidity levels or the grade of bulgur you purchase, you will have better results if you use the U.S. standard cup volume measure.

(opposite page) Kibi *man.* [MC]

KIBI FRITO

BEEF AND BULGUR FRITTERS

TO PREPARE AHEAD

Recado para todo (p. 499)

Stacked in neat pyramids inside glass boxes resembling aquariums, fried *kibis* are hawked day and night by street vendors. They are often displayed side by side with the Maya fritter known as *Pol'kanes* (p. 111), which is almost identical in appearance, so you may have to ask which is which. The best *kibis* are to be found in local Lebanese restaurants, where they include beef (street *kibis* are often pure bulgur) and where they will arrive fresh, hot, and crispy to your table. Yucatecan fried *kibis* veer from the traditional: habanero adds a light heat to the fritters, which are served with the Yucatecan version of *pico de gallo*, and more chile. A meatless version—Kibi de pescado—appears annually during Lent.

Prepare ahead note: Kibis can be made in advance and frozen in their raw state. Place them on a tray in a single layer to avoid flattening. Bring them to room temperature before frying. Fried *kibis* can be kept warm for about 1 hour in a 200°F (93°C) oven.

YIELD: 10 SERVINGS

[EC]

FOR THE *KIBI* MIXTURE

1 cup (140 g) fine bulgur

1½ lbs. (680 g) lean sirloin,
  finely ground

½ cup (85 g) white onion,
  finely chopped

¼ cup (15 g) mint leaves,
  finely chopped

½ tsp. (3 g) sea salt

¼ tsp. (1.25 g) freshly ground
  black pepper

FOR THE FILLING

¼ cup (62.5 ml) vegetable oil,
  plus additional for frying

9 oz. (250 g) lean sirloin,
  finely ground

1 cup (170 g) white onion,
  finely chopped

2 medium cloves garlic (½ oz. /
  12 g), peeled and minced

1 medium chile habanero (¼ oz. /
  7 g), seeded and minced

¼ cup (15 g) mint leaves,
  finely chopped

¾ cup (100 g) pine nuts

½ tsp. (1.5 g) Recado para todo

FOR SERVING

Salsa x'nipek (p. 512) or Salpicón
  (p. 511)

Chile sauce of your choice

PREPARE *KIBI* MIXTURE

Place the bulgur in a bowl and add cold water to cover; drain and add more water to rinse thoroughly. Pour the bulgur into a sieve and press out as much liquid as possible.

Place the drained bulgur and sirloin in the bowl of a food processor fitted with the steel blade. Add the remaining ingredients and process about 1 minute, or until smooth. Fry a small amount to check the seasonings. Refrigerate.

PREPARE FILLING

Heat ¼ cup oil in a skillet until shimmering. Add the sirloin and cook over medium heat until lightly browned, using a wooden spoon or spatula to crumble the meat. Add the remaining ingredients and simmer until the cooking liquids have evaporated, 5–6 minutes. Remove the skillet from the heat and allow to cool.

FORM *KIBIS* AND FINISH

Remove the *kibi* mixture from the refrigerator. Working with wet hands to keep the mixture from sticking, form 20 balls, about 1¾ ounces (50 g) each. One at a time, flatten the balls in the palm of your hand, shaping each into an oval that measures approximately 2¾ inches (7 cm) long and 2 inches (5 cm) wide. Place approximately 1 tablespoon (10–12 g) of the cooked meat filling in the center of the oval. Carefully close the *kibi* mixture around the filling, sealing to avoid leakage during cooking. Cup your hands to shape the *kibi* into an elongated egg shape. Pinch each end to form a gentle point and place the finished *kibis* on a tray. Continue until you have used all of the *kibi* mixture and the filling. Refrigerate 30 minutes.

Fill a deep skillet with 2 inches (5 cm) vegetable oil and heat over medium-high heat until a thermometer reads 375°F (190°C). Working in batches to avoid crowding, fry the *kibis* until golden brown, turning once, about 5 minutes. Drain on paper towels and serve immediately.

TO SERVE

Serve 2 *kibis* per person with a choice of Salpicón or X'nipek. Diners crack open the *kibis* and spoon on salsas to taste.

VARIATION

Kibi de pescado (Dogfish and Bulgur Fritters): Substitute 1 recipe Cazón frito (p. 312) for the sirloin, weighed and divided as described, using one portion for the outer coating (*kibi* mixture) and the other for the filling. Reheat the *cazón* gently in the oil, omitting the other ingredients except the mint, pine nuts, and *recado*. Check the seasonings and proceed as directed in the master recipe.

KIBI DE PAPA

POTATO AND BULGUR FRITTERS

TO PREPARE AHEAD

Recado para escabeche (p. 498)

FOR THE POTATO *KIBIS*

2 cups (280 g) fine bulgur

¾ lb. (340 g) baking potatoes,
  peeled, quartered, and boiled
  until tender

½ medium white onion (5 oz. /
  137.5 g), finely chopped

2 medium cloves garlic (½ oz. /
  12 g), peeled and minced

1 medium chile habanero (¼ oz. /
  7 g), seeded and minced

1 cup (60 g) mint, finely chopped

1 two-in.-long (5 cm) strip orange
  rind, minced

1 cup (125 g) all-purpose flour

1½ tsp. (9 g) sea salt

1 tsp. (3 g) Recado para escabeche

1 tsp. (4 g) baking powder

Vegetable oil for frying

If you are having a party and want to serve *kibis* on your buffet spread, you can easily whip up these potato *kibis* for your vegetarian guests at the same time you prepare the standard beef *kibis*.

Prepare ahead note: The dough for Kibi de papa should be prepared at least an hour or up to several hours in advance and refrigerated. Form into fritters and fry immediately before serving.

YIELD: 10 SERVINGS

PREPARE *KIBIS*

Place the bulgur in a bowl and add cold water to cover; drain and add more water to rinse thoroughly. Pour the bulgur into a sieve and press out as much liquid as possible; allow it to drain and dry as you continue.

Place the potatoes in a large mixing bowl and mash coarsely. (Note: Food processors and similar devices will make the dough pasty; for best results, use the manual method described here.) Add the remaining ingredients except the vegetable oil and mash until incorporated and smooth. Add the drained bulgur and mash again until just blended. Refrigerate the mixture at least 1 hour before finishing.

Pour 2 inches (5 cm) oil into a deep skillet; heat to 375°F (190°C). Divide the dough into 20 equal balls, each weighing about 1¾ ounces (50 g). Form fritters a few at a time just before frying. Pat balls into thick rounds about 2½ inches (6.35 cm) in diameter. Fry a few at a time to avoid crowding, turning once, until they are golden brown, about 5 minutes. Transfer to paper towels to drain. When all have been fried, serve immediately, following the serving suggestions for Kibi frito.

VARIATION

Kibi de chaya (*Chaya* and Bulgur Fritters): Another vegetarian *kibi* features the local leafy green vegetable, *chaya* (p. 27); you may substitute kale or chard. Remove and discard thick stems from ½ pound (250 g) fresh *chaya* leaves and parboil the leaves until just tender, 10–15 minutes. Drain well, pressing out excess moisture, and coarsely chop.

Omit the potatoes. Place the *chaya* along with the remaining ingredients except the bulgur and vegetable oil in the bowl of a food processor fitted with the steel blade and process until the mixture becomes a creamy paste. Transfer to a mixing bowl and combine with the drained bulgur. Check the seasonings and add an extra 1½ teaspoons (9 g) sea salt or to taste; proceed as directed in the master recipe.

KIBI LABNILLE

BULGUR AND BEEF DUMPLINGS IN MINTED YOGURT

TO PREPARE AHEAD
Kibi frito (p. 358), without frying
Enriched Lard (p. 513)

FOR THE *KIBIS*
Ingredients for Kibi frito, formed
  but not fried

FOR THE *SOFRITO*
2 tsp. (10 g) Enriched Lard
½ cup (85 g) white onion, finely
  chopped
3 medium cloves garlic (¾ oz. /
  18 g), peeled and minced
½ cup (30 g) fresh mint leaves,
  finely chopped
¼ cup (15 g) fresh cilantro leaves,
  finely chopped
1 tsp. (6 g) sea salt
½ tsp. (2.5 g) freshly ground
  black pepper

FOR THE YOGURT SAUCE
4 cups (1 L) Lebanese *laban* yogurt
  (Substitute: plain unsweetened
  yogurt)
2 cups (500 ml) water
1 egg white, lightly beaten
1 Tbs. (6 g) cornstarch
1 tsp. (6 g) sea salt

FOR SERVING
Chopped mint leaves
Tabbouleh, optional
  accompaniment
Pita, warmed

Alberto Salum of Alberto's Continental—iconic Lebanese restaurant and Mérida institution since the 1960s—shared this recipe with me, taken from the 1975 cookbook *Mis platillos favoritos*, by his sister-in-law, Vivianne Francis de Salum. A version also appears in doña María's book, transcribed as Kibi con lavin. The dish features beef *kibis* simmered in mint-flavored *laban* (here called *lavin*)—Lebanese yogurt—but you may use plain unsweetened yogurt. Alberto told me that this dish is considered one of the most prestigious of all Middle Eastern dishes, the sort of thing one would serve only on special occasions. He lamented that because it has so many steps, few have the patience to prepare it nowadays. Its exquisite subtlety motivated me to streamline the processes for the modern cook: if you prepare the *kibis* ahead and freeze them, it takes only about an hour to finish just before serving.

Prepare ahead note: Kibi labnille is best served immediately after preparing. You may prepare the *kibis* in advance and freeze them; defrost just before cooking. You may also prepare the yogurt base in advance; refrigerate, then reheat before final assembly.

YIELD: 6 SERVINGS

PREPARE *KIBIS*
Prepare the *kibis* through the form and finish step of Kibi frito: do not fry. Refrigerate 30 minutes to 1 hour as you proceed.

MAKE *SOFRITO*
Heat the lard in a medium skillet until shimmering. Add the onions and garlic and cook over medium heat until the onions are translucent, 2–3 minutes. Add the remaining ingredients and cook an additional minute. Remove the skillet from the heat and set aside.

PREPARE YOGURT SAUCE
Bring the yogurt and *kibis* to room temperature. (If the *kibis* were frozen, defrost before proceeding.) In a medium stockpot, combine the ingredients for the yogurt sauce and whisk until the cornstarch is dissolved. Bring to a simmer over moderate heat, stirring constantly until bubbles appear around the edges. Add the *sofrito*, lower the heat, and cook, stirring constantly, another 3–4 minutes, or until the mixture begins to thicken.

COOK *KIBIS* AND FINISH
Carefully add the *kibis* to the yogurt sauce, one at a time, taking care not to break them as they enter the liquid; gently shake the pot to submerge them. Maintain the heat at a gentle simmer, shaking the pot occasionally, for 30–45 minutes. (Note: Do not allow the liquid to boil, which may cause curdling, although if that happens, it won't affect

the flavor. Some of the *kibis* may open and spill a few of the pine nuts into the liquid; this is normal and only helps the finished aesthetic.) Serve immediately.

TO SERVE
Serve 2 *kibis* per person in individual bowls. Ladle in enough of the cooking liquid to just cover the *kibis* and garnish with mint. Serve with pita and tabbouleh on the side.

CREMA DE AJO
GARLIC AND EGG-WHITE MAYONNAISE

FOR THE GARLIC PURÉE

6–10 medium cloves garlic (about 1½–2½ oz. / 36–60 g), peeled. (Note: As explained at right, you may adjust the quantity of garlic to your taste with no effect on the finished product. The full 10 cloves is explosive but delicious!)

2 tsp. (10 ml) *plus* 3 Tbs. (45 ml) fresh lime or Seville orange juice, divided

⅛ tsp. (0.85 g) sea salt

5–6 big grinds of fresh white pepper

2 egg whites, at room temperature

1⅓ cups (330 ml) neutral vegetable oil (safflower or canola)

2 Tbs. (30 ml) cold water

FOR SERVING

Totopos para botanas (p. 515) or toasted pita chips

Thum—the name of this dish in Arabic—translates to "garlic," and to be sure, this creamy egg-white mayonnaise is for serious garlic lovers only. Sauces of oil and garlic are ancient: in the first century CE, Pliny recorded a sauce he saw in Tarragona called "*alioli*," composed of olive oil pounded with garlic until the mixture emulsified. The French aïoli is similar but adds egg yolk to facilitate the emulsion. *Thum* is the Middle Eastern counterpart of aïoli although most Lebanese restaurants in Yucatán use egg whites instead of yolks. There are two more changes to the standard formula that have been made in Yucatán. First, it is common to use lime or Seville orange instead of lemon juice, since the latter is rarely available here. And most people use plain vegetable oil rather than olive oil, which tends to be expensive and found only in supermarkets. I actually like these adaptations: the other citrus varieties give the cream a fresh, tropical taste rather than a Mediterranean one, although you may use whichever you prefer; and I like the lighter vegetable oil because it doesn't compete with the intensity of the garlic. Depending on your taste for garlic, you can adjust the number of cloves you use with no compromise to the formula.

Prepare ahead note: Crema de ajo keeps well under refrigeration for up to 2 weeks.

YIELD: 8–10 SERVINGS

[MC]

Place the garlic, 2 teaspoons (10 ml) lime juice, salt and pepper in the jar of a blender. Process 2–3 seconds to break up the garlic. Stop the motor, push the garlic down toward the blade with a spatula, and repeat. The garlic does not have to be finely chopped to continue.

Add the egg whites to the garlic in the blender jar. Process for 1 minute, scraping down the sides of the jar as needed. Process an additional 1½ minutes, until the emulsion turns white and creamy and bits of garlic are no longer visible. With the motor running, through the hole in the blender lid slowly drizzle about one-quarter of the oil in a thin stream, aiming for the center where the blade is. Scrape down the jar and repeat 2 more times. Continue to drizzle in the oil until about three-quarters has been used. When you get to the last quarter of the oil, drizzle in the remaining lime juice and the rest of the oil simultaneously. If you go slowly, your emulsion should hold together. If it separates, transfer half of it to a small bowl, add one more egg white to the mixture in the blender, and process until it becomes creamy, then add the emulsion you removed. Process until smooth and frothed.

FINISH PURÉE AND SERVE

With the motor off, pour the water into the blender jar and stir. (Because the emulsion is thick and oily, the water will sit on top unless stirred to mix.) Once the water is incorporated, purée on high until the mixture becomes light and fluffy, about 30 seconds. Transfer to an airtight container and refrigerate until ready to serve.

TO SERVE

Let the mixture sit at room temperature for 30 minutes before serving. Serve with corn chips or pita for dipping as an appetizer, as a dip for Kibis fritos (p. 358) or crudités, or as a salsa/topping for Tacos al pastor (p. 238), Camarón empanizado (p. 269), Pollo asado (p. 270), or any other grilled meat or fish.

VARIATION

Crema de x'catik (Blond Chile and Egg-White Mayonnaise): The Lebanese of Yucatán made ingredient substitutions out of necessity. But they also incorporated New World ingredients into Old World recipes out of sheer curiosity and creativity. Wonders were born, including Crema de x'catik, based on the standard recipe for *thum* (Crema de ajo) but employing Yucatán's ubiquitous chile x'catik instead of garlic. This uniquely Yucatecan formula is now widely available at many local restaurants and supermarkets. The x'catik has a light, herbaceous flavor with just the right amount of zing. Careful, though: depending on the specimen, the heat level can vary wildly—from 500 to 10,000 Scoville Heat Units. If you don't want a zippy sauce, sample a small seeded cross section of the chile before using the whole thing. Follow the master recipe except replace the garlic with 2 medium chiles x'catiques (about 1¼ oz. / 35 g each), charred, peeled, and seeded. When you finish the *crema* and check for seasoning, if you want a bigger chile flavor or more heat, add 1–2 more charred, peeled, and seeded chiles to the mayonnaise and purée until thoroughly incorporated and smooth.

THE CUBA CONNECTION

A popular café in Mérida frequently leads me into temptation with the top item on their menu: Torta cubana (p. 365). This famously proletarian and high-calorie sandwich from Cuba—legendarily popularized among cigar factory workers—may seem anachronistic next to Maya tamales, yet there is an almost palpable cultural and gastronomical connection between Yucatán and Cuba.

The connection shouldn't be too surprising, at least inso-far as geography is concerned: just 124 miles (200 km) of ocean stretch between Cabo Catoche on the northern coast of the Yucatán Peninsula and Cabo San Antonio in the extreme western part of Cuba. But this physical proximity is only one explanation for the strong and continuing bonds that exist between Yucatán and Cuba.

Ancient Ties

According to the geological record, the island of Cuba has sunk and reemerged from the ocean several times. During one or more of its emergences, the island and the landmass of Yucatán were connected. The same limestone comprises both, and the organic and animal life found in both are related.

Lithic remains unearthed in the late 1990s have led some archaeologists to conclude that the first colonizers of the islands of the Greater Antilles—particularly Cuba—were most probably early Mayas who arrived from the Yucatán Peninsula as early as 4000 BCE. The theory is further sup-ported by the knowledge that these peoples were skilled mariners, traveling in canoes along the coast as far south as Honduras, and possibly even Panama.

In the fifteenth century, Cuba was the first colony in the Caribbean to be established by Spain. Havana became an important port of entry, and Spanish immigrants and trad-ers passed through before locating in the Yucatán Peninsula or elsewhere in Mexico. This movement worked in reverse, too: each time Cuba was threatened by pirates or flotillas of other European conquerors, Mexican military might arrived along with laborers for building defensive construc-tions and other projects. The majority of this workforce was from Yucatán.

(above) Dutch map of the West Indies showing Yucatán and Cuba, by Joan Vingboons, 1639. [LIBRARY OF CONGRESS GEOGRAPHY AND MAP DIVISION]

Yucatán and Cuba enjoy many similar foods as a result of these ancient ties. Ingredients like chile habanero, *achiote*, Seville orange, and many others insinuated themselves so seamlessly into both gastronomical traditions that it would appear they had always been present. Recipes and cooking methods, such as *alcaparrado* and *sofrito*, are shared, too.

In a final note, as a result of the triangular trade routes between Europe, Africa, and the Americas, both Yucatecan and Cuban tables share many ingredients with Africa. Cassava (*yuca*), yams (*ñame*), black-eyed peas (*x'pelon*), and plantain (*plátano macho*) are just a few foods that shaped a distinctive *criollo* cuisine linking all three.

TORTA CUBANA

PRESSED SANDWICH OF ROAST PORK, SMOKED HAM, AND CHEESE

Some say (perhaps not too delicately) that this sandwich is called "Cubana" because it is bigger, juicier, and more filled out than any other sandwich, just like a Cuban woman. To be sure, it's loaded, and the possible combination of ingredients is exponential. Whatever form it finally takes, it will invariably feature two kinds of pork (roasted and ham), cheese, and dressings. The emphasis here is on using up leftovers. This version of Torta cubana makes use of several recipes found in this book. If you don't have a sandwich press, use a pancake griddle with a heavy preheated cast-iron skillet for the top press.

Prepare ahead note: All of the components for Torta cubana must be prepared in advance.

YIELD: 1 SANDWICH

TO PREPARE AHEAD

Mojo de ajo (p. 514)
Lechón al horno (p. 196)
Longaniza de Valladolid (p. 481), or substitute
Frijol refrito (p. 506)
Crema de ajo (p. 362)
Your own guacamole

FOR THE SANDWICH

Cuban sandwich bread or a large sourdough bun
The above ingredients, prepared in advance (you may substitute commercial *longaniza*, chorizo, or other smoked sausage for your own homemade *longaniza*)
Vegetable oil
Sliced smoked ham
Sliced cheese (Swiss, Cheddar, Manchego, Chihuahua)
Pickled jalapeño slices

FOR SERVING

Tostones (p. 370)

ASSEMBLE SANDWICH

Preheat the griddle or sandwich press. Slice the bread in half across the girth to create two pieces resembling hamburger buns. Pinch out a bit of the bread from the insides of both pieces to create room for the fillings. Brush both pieces inside and out with Mojo de ajo. Place the bread on the hot griddle to lightly toast both sides, turning once.

While the bread is toasting, thinly slice the Lechón al horno. Thinly slice the Longaniza on the diagonal into thin disks. Pour a bit of oil into a large skillet and quickly heat the Lechón, sliced ham, and Longaniza. Remove the skillet from the heat and leave the meats in the skillet to keep warm.

Spread the inside of one of the toasted buns with a couple of spoonfuls of warm Frijol refrito (this will be the bottom), the other half with Crema de ajo. Stack the following ingredients on the bottom half in this order: slices of Lechón, ham, Longaniza, a dollop of guacamole, jalapeño slices, and slices of cheese. Place the other half of the bun on top. Press and grill the sandwich until the bread is crispy and the cheese begins to melt. Serve immediately.

TO SERVE

Cut the sandwich in half diagonally and serve with Tostones.

HOT STUFF Margarita danced and sang most of the day as we cooked together—chopping rhythmically, tossing things into the pot percussively. Her songs, many of them racy, all had to do with food. I'll translate one that warns of distractions in the kitchen. Remember that Cuba has an extensive population of African origin:

No me toques la puerta
que el negro está cocinando.
Está adobando la carne
y la yuca se está ablandando.

Don't knock on my door
because the black guy is cooking.
He's marinating the meat
and the yuca is getting soft.

[EC]

"CUBATECAN" CUISINE

Like so many immigrants around the world who have found happy lives in new countries, Margarita Rodríguez stays in touch with her roots by cooking the foods of her homeland, Cuba. A native of Havana, she settled in Mérida in the late 1990s. Cooking is her life's passion, and she has acquired a reputation for having a great *sazón*—cook's touch.

(opposite page) *Margarita Rodríguez.* [EC]

AJIACO

GARLICKY PORK, POTATO, AND SQUASH STEW WITH PLANTAINS

TO PREPARE AHEAD

Enriched Lard (p. 513)

Recado rojo (p. 500)

FOR THE GARLIC AND
VEGETABLES

6 medium heads garlic (approximately 1¾ oz. / 50 g each),
whole, unpeeled

Spanish olive oil

16 cups (4 L) water

1½ cups (approximately 245 g) *each*
of potato, chayote, and sweet
potato, peeled and cut into 1 in.
(2.5 cm) dice

1½ cups (approximately 245 g)
zucchini, cut into 1/2 in.
(1.5 cm) dice

1½ cups (approximately 245 g)
carrot, peeled and cut into ½ in.
(1.5 cm) rounds

1 medium baking potato (7 oz. /
190 g), peeled and cut into
1/2 in. (1.5cm) dice (the extra
potato cut into smaller pieces
will help thicken the sauce)

1 medium semiripe plantain
(9 oz. / 250 g), peeled and cut
into ½ in. (1.5 cm) rounds

2 Tbs. (24 g) powdered chicken
bouillon, or 2 cubes

2 tsp. (12 g) sea salt

Ajiaco is one of those great bottomless stews with as many interpretations as there are cooks. It descends from the classic Spanish *olla podrida* family related to Puchero (p. 350). When I said to Margarita that in fact the recipe reminded me very much of Puchero, she uttered a breathless, "¡¡No no no no no!!" With pork, plantains, potatoes, squash, sweet potatoes, and carrots, it looked an awful lot like Puchero to me. In a friendly debate, I coaxed her to define the differences for me. We finally settled on a few important distinctions: Ajiaco contains tomatoes, while Puchero does not; Ajiaco cooks such a long time that the potatoes and plantain break down and thicken the sauce, but the cooking liquid of Puchero is more like broth; Ajiaco features almost vulgar quantities of garlic and cuminseed, double or triple the amount in Puchero, and no other spices. In fact, we used three whole heads of garlic and later wished we had added more (I increased the quantity for this recipe), and a full tablespoon and then some of cuminseed was toasted, ground, and tossed into the pot. When I mentioned to Margarita that I had once enjoyed a version of Ajiaco in Campeche that featured shrimp instead of pork, she glanced heavenward, as if to pray for this poor, lost heathen. In any case, the shrimp version was delicious, and I offer it as an option below.

Prepare ahead note: Like so many stews, Ajiaco only improves with age. Prepare a day or two in advance and reheat just before serving.

YIELD: 10—12 SERVINGS

[MC]

FOR THE *SOFRITO*

3 Tbs. (42 g) Enriched Lard

4 medium cloves garlic (1 oz. / 24 g), peeled and thinly sliced

1 medium red onion (10 oz. / 275 g), chopped

1 cup (140 g) *each* red bell pepper and green bell pepper, cut into small dice

1 Tbs. cuminseed (6 g), lightly toasted and ground

FOR STEWING THE MEAT

4 medium Roma tomatoes (14 oz. / 400 g), charred

1 Tbs. (15 g) Recado rojo

1 chile chipotle in adobo (⅓ oz. / 10 g), drained

2 lbs. (1 k) pork leg or shoulder, with some fat, cut into 2 in. (5 cm) cubes

FOR SERVING

1 recipe Tostones (p. 370), recommended accompaniment

ROAST GARLIC AND COOK VEGETABLES

Preheat the oven to 350°F (176°C). Slice about ⅛ inch (3 mm) off the top of the whole garlic heads. Place the heads in a shallow baking dish and drizzle them with a little olive oil. Bake approximately 45 minutes, or until just tender. Remove the garlic from the oven and allow it to cool as you continue.

Pour the water into a large stockpot and add the remaining ingredients. Bring to a boil and continue at a rapid boil while you prepare the *sofrito*.

PREPARE *SOFRITO*

Squeeze the cloves from the roasted garlic heads and coarsely mash in a bowl. Heat the lard in a large skillet until shimmering. Add both the sliced and the mashed garlic, the onion, and the bell pepper and cook, stirring occasionally, until the onions are translucent, 3–4 minutes. Add the ground cuminseed, stir, and set the skillet aside.

STEW MEAT AND FINISH

Place the first 3 ingredients in a blender and process until liquefied; pour into the stockpot. Add the meat and *sofrito* to the stockpot and continue cooking at a full boil, stirring occasionally, for 1 hour 45 minutes–2 hours, or until the stock has thickened and reduced by about half.

TO SERVE

Unlike Puchero, Ajiaco is not separated into parts for serving. Instead, arrange both the meat and the vegetables in individual bowls and ladle on some of the cooking liquid. Place one of the Tostones on top of each serving as a garnish. Alternatively, transfer to a large tureen or cazuela, top with the Tostones, and serve at the table.

VARIATION

Ajiaco con camarón (Garlicky Shrimp, Potato, and Squash Stew with Plantains): Proceed with the master recipe for Ajiaco, but substitute fish stock or bottled clam juice for the water and omit the salt. Continue through the end of the recipe, omitting the pork. After the full cooking time, and just before serving, reduce the heat to a simmer, add 2 pounds (1 k) large shrimp (31–35 count), heads and tails removed, peeled and deveined. Cook another 1–2 minutes, or until the shrimp just turn pink. Serve immediately following the serving suggestions for Ajiaco.

TOSTONES

TWICE-FRIED PLANTAIN CHIPS

FOR THE TOSTONES

2 large green plantains
Vegetable oil for frying
Sea salt

Tostones are the ever-present "twice-fried" plantain chips that accompany so many Cuban meals. They are fried slowly once to cook through, then mashed flat and deep-fried a second time in very hot oil to crisp them. Margarita stressed the importance of using green, unripe plantains for this garnish. Since then, I have tried to make Tostones with semiripe plantains and, while the flavor is good, the issue is texture: they are so soft that they become a bit mushy during the second frying, making them difficult to handle. Nonetheless, if you only have ripe plantains available, don't let that stop you from trying Tostones.

Prepare ahead note: Tostones are best served immediately after the second frying. However, I have successfully left them at room temperature for a couple of hours, then brushed them with Mojo de ajo (p. 514) and quickly fried them a third time in a non-stick skillet to heat through before serving. The results are delicious. Since I always have Mojo in the refrigerator, it is a quick and easy way to refresh Tostones and add a surprising layer of flavor.

YIELD: 10 TOSTONES

FIRST FRY

Slice off the tips of the plantains, then use a thin knife to cut lengthwise slits along the ridges of the skin; remove the peel. Pour 1¼ inches (3 cm) oil into a heavy skillet and place over medium heat. While the oil is heating, slice each plantain across the width into 5 equal sections, yielding 10 pieces total. When the oil is shimmering, lay the plantain sections flat in the skillet; the oil should come to about three-quarters of the way up the side of each piece. Cook slowly over medium heat, turning from time to time, until the pieces are pale golden all over, 6–8 minutes. Remove to drain on paper towels.

SECOND FRY

Turn the heat to high. While the oil is heating, place one section of plantain upright on a work surface and use a wooden mallet or the bottom of a heavy jar to mash the plantain section flat, to a thickness of about ¼ inch (6 mm). (Note: If you are using ripe or semiripe plantains, you will need to place the sections between waxed paper to prevent sticking.) When the oil reaches 375°F (190°C), add the plantain sections a few at a time so as not to crowd. Fry, turning once, about 2 minutes per side, or until deep golden brown (ripe plantains will take longer to brown). Transfer the Tostones to paper towels to drain. Just before serving, sprinkle with sea salt to taste.

TO SERVE

Tostones may be used as a plate garnish for any Cuban or Yucatecan meal.

PLÁTANO FRITO

FRIED PLANTAIN

FOR THE FRIED PLANTAINS

3 Tbs. (42 g) butter

1 Tbs. (15 ml) vegetable oil

2 large ripe plantains, peeled, cut
   in half across the width, then
   sliced lengthwise into 3–4 pieces

This simple garnish is placed alongside the rice and beans that accompany many Yucatecan dishes and is a requisite accompaniment to Huevos motuleños (p. 454). It's also a good substitute if you don't have time to make Tostones, or if you have only ripe plantains available.

FRY THE PLANTAINS

Heat the butter and oil in a nonstick skillet until the foam subsides. Immediately add the plantain slices a few at a time. Fry, turning once, until browned on both sides, about 2 minutes per side. Transfer to a platter; repeat with the remaining plantains, adding more butter and oil if needed. Serve with any of the dishes in Part Four, La Cocina Económica, or as specified.

Platanitos (Crispy Plantain Chips) are popular street snacks. For these you must use green plantains. Peel and shave into very thin, long strips. Plunge into hot oil, drain, and sprinkle with salt. Serve with any of your favorite salsas for dipping. [MR]

VALLADOLID

VINEGAR AND PEPPER. Capers, raisins, and olives. Few are the dishes of Valladolid that do not contain these ingredients. Bittersweet, savory, piquant—summoning images of faraway lands—their flavors coalesce to produce the exotic *sazón* that characterizes the cuisine of this timeless colonial town in eastern Yucatán.

"La Sultana del Oriente" (Sultaness of the East) is the nickname frequently applied to Valladolid, a city of about 40,000 inhabitants just 100 miles (162 km) east of Mérida.

In its Arabic references and feminine overtones, the nickname sounds like something spun out of nineteenth-century Spanish romantic poetry. The romantic label fits perfectly: while Mérida has long been the cultural capital of the peninsula, and Campeche its defensive fortress, Valladolid is its heart and soul, its veiled sensuality.

It is also the legendary birthplace and namesake of a number of popular regional dishes, such as Pavo en escabeche oriental. It is fitting that several dishes of Valladolid employ vinegar and old Spanish pickling techniques, metaphorically serving up the city's sometimes bitter history.

"SULTANNESS OF THE EAST"

Valladolid captures the essence of the fiercely independent Yucatecan spirit and is the stage upon which much of the peninsula's legend and history was enacted. Almost immediately after its founding in 1543, Valladolid began to play a pivotal role in both Yucatecan and Mexican history, serving as the locus of great social movements—from indigenous uprisings to national cries for independence.

In 1546, a group of rebel Mayas—bent on revenge for a series of complaints, including their conscripted servitude

(above) Woodcut by José Guadalupe Posada Aguilar depicts the Porfirio Díaz antireelection struggle that was ignited in Valladolid. [COLLECTION OF MUSEO NACIONAL DE ARTE, MEXICO, D.F., PHOTO BY ALEJANDRO LINARES GARCÍA]

Colonial home in Valladolid boasts a family coat of arms above the doorway. [EC]

and the tribute extracted from them by the Spanish crown—rose up against hacienda owners, torturing and killing 18 Spaniards and slaughtering some 600 of their own on suspicion of being Spanish sympathizers. Although the revolt was quickly squelched, the conflict fanned the flames for further Maya uprisings and would ultimately serve as the banner for indigenous rights.

Perhaps the bloodiest chapter of Yucatecan history was drafted in Valladolid, where the infamous Guerra de las Castas (Caste War) erupted in 1847. When a Maya rebel was executed for his alleged involvement in Yucatán's separatist movement, there arose such an outcry among the indigenous population that by the end of that year, the entire eastern half of the peninsula lay in the hands of Maya rebels and separatists.

This strongly independent Yucatecan spirit shed its light beyond Valladolid on the rest of the country, for in June of 1910, just a few years after the last flames of the Caste War had flickered and died, the first sparks of the Mexican Revolution were ignited. It was here that the Yucatecan-bred antireelection campaign against Porfirio Díaz—who served as Mexico's "elected" president" for thirty-four years—resulted in the imprisonment or execution of more than 100 revolutionaries at the hands of progovernment troops. Ten years later, Mexico had won its second independence.

Rebellious. Spirited. Independent. None of these words

seem to have much resonance here and now in this tranquil town. Today, Valladolid is a pit stop for day-trippers to Chichén Itzá. Sons of freedom fighters and landed gentry alike all now seem to live here amicably side by side and nod and smile as tourists descend from charter buses to stroll the quaint cobbled streets for a few minutes before heading back toward Cancún.

SPANISH RECIPES ON A MAYA HEARTH

More than elsewhere in Yucatán, many foods of Valladolid are precious time capsules of vintage Spanish recipes. For years after its founding, and well into the nineteenth century, the people of Valladolid considered themselves the elite among the Spanish gentry of the peninsula and were proud of their Iberian heritage. Principal streets were lined with mansions emblazoned with Castilian coats of arms above their doorways, and both pure-blooded Mayas and mestizos were restricted from the city center.

The cuisine of the colonial era naturally projected the cultural image to which the gentry aspired. Elegant recipes from the various regions of Spain, particularly Andalucía and Extremadura, located in the former Moorish empire known as al-Andalus, characterized the Yucatecan table of the eighteenth and nineteenth centuries. Yet, while early-nineteenth-century cookbooks made only cursory acknowledgments of an indigenous past, by the turn of the twentieth century, Maya recipes had taken their rightful place in the company of classic Spanish dishes—if at the back of the book. And soon, as local ingredients were adopted to fill gaps in the pantry, culinary fusions began to occur that would eventually blur boundaries and give birth to a wholly independent cuisine.

Cathedral of San Gervasio, Valladolid. [MR]

TAMAL REDONDO

ROLLED *TAMAL* WITH BANANA, ANISE, AND SPICED MINCEMEAT

The late colonial period throughout the Yucatán Peninsula witnessed social changes that would eventually result in the independence struggle launched in Valladolid, changes that coincided neatly with a surge in *criollo* dishes on the menu. One example is the Tamal redondo, a heavenly food dating to an 1832 regional cookbook that perfectly exemplifies the marriage of Maya and Spanish traditions. The *tamal* is unique from the ground up: the *masa* is flavored with anise water and plantain or banana, and the Andalusian-style ground meat filling is flecked with capers, raisins, olives, and almonds, making this unquestionably one of the most unusual and flavorful tamales I have ever eaten.

YIELD: APPROXIMATELY 1 DOZEN TAMALES

TO PREPARE AHEAD
B'uut blanco (p. 256)

Enriched Lard (p. 513)

Masa, prepared from either nixtamalized corn or from *masa harina* (p. 517)

Recado para todo (p. 499)

Banana leaves cut to medium (M) size as instructed in Basic Techniques, p. 525, and ribs reserved

FOR THE FILLING
½ recipe B'uut blanco

FOR THE *MASA*
8 Tbs. (112 g) Enriched Lard, chilled

1 Tbs. (12 g) baking powder

1 recipe (about 2 lbs. / 1 k) *masa*

2 tsp. (6 g) Recado para todo

2 tsp. (12 g) sea salt

1 tsp. (6 g) ground anise

2 Tbs. (30 ml) hot water

1 medium banana (about 5¼ oz. / 150 g), peeled and coarsely mashed. (Note: For a less sweet *masa*, use an equal weight of ripe plantain instead)

½ cup (62.5 g) all-purpose flour

3 Tbs. (45 ml) Mexican honey

1 medium clove garlic (½ oz. / 6 g), peeled, charred, and minced

FOR SERVING
Tomate frito (p. 507)

Chile tamulado (p. 509), or the chile sauce of your choice

PREPARE FILLING
If it has been refrigerated, gently warm the cooked B'uut blanco. Remove the pan from the heat and set aside.

PREPARE *MASA*
Place the chilled lard and baking powder in the bowl of a stand mixer. Beat on high speed until the lard turns light, fluffy, and creamy, about 3 minutes.

With the mixer on medium-high, continue beating the lard as you add the *masa* little by little; allow it to become thoroughly incorporated with the lard before you add more. Mix the *recado*, salt, and anise with the hot water and stir to dissolve. Add the *recado* mixture and the remaining ingredients to the bowl with the *masa*. Beat on high speed until the dough is lightened, about 5 minutes. Cover the bowl with a damp towel until ready to use, up to 30 minutes, or wrap the dough in plastic and refrigerate.

FILL TAMALES AND STEAM
Form the *masa* into balls weighing about 3½ ounces (100 g) each. Center 1 ball on a section of banana leaf. Pat the *masa* into a rough rectangle measuring 6 × 8 inches (15 cm × 20 cm), leaving plenty of space around the edges (use 2 overlapping leaves if necessary). Turn the rectangle to horizontal in front of you. Place 2 heaping tablespoons (40 g) of the B'uut blanco on top of the *masa* along the long side closest to you, leaving a 1-inch (2.5 cm) space at side, top, and bottom of the *masa*. Using the banana leaf to form the *tamal*, turn the edge of the leaf closest to you up, over, and away from you to begin rolling the *masa* into a cylinder. Continue to roll, using the leaf to lift, until you have formed a cylinder. Press the ends of the *masa* closed, then roll and wrap to completely cover the *masa* cylinder with the leaf. Tuck under the loose ends of the leaf, then use the reserved ribs (or kitchen twine) to tie around the *tamal* about 1 inch (2.5 cm) from each end to secure.

Follow the instructions for steaming in Basic Techniques on page 526. Steam for 1 hour and allow to rest 15 minutes prior to serving.

TO SERVE

Place the tamales on individual serving plates and allow diners to unwrap and add salsas to taste.

BUTIFARRAS
SPICED CATALONIAN SAUSAGE

Butifarra (*botifarra* in Catalán) is the mascot sausage of Barcelona and indeed all Cataluña. Even though originally from northern Spain, Butifarras bear a hint of Andalusian/ Moorish influence with their inclusion of Spice Island flavorings like black pepper, cloves, nutmeg, *canela*, and anise. The 1910 *La verdadera cocina regional* from Valladolid also adds a New World touch of allspice (*Pimienta dioica*, p. 73). Valladolid's women made hams, sausages, and other preserved meats that took many days to execute. Smoking and other meat-preservation techniques have been utilized in the peninsula for centuries, and Europeans brought new methods, so no doubt author doña Manuela was familiar with the processes.

Prepare ahead note: Allow 3–4 days for the complete production of Butifarras. The meat mixture should rest in the refrigerator for at least 8 hours or overnight. Once stuffed into the casings, the sausages should dry in the refrigerator 48–72 hours. Once dried, the sausages can be poached and consumed immediately, or vacuum-packed and frozen for 2–3 months.

YIELD: APPROXIMATELY 1 DOZEN SAUSAGES

FOR THE SPICE MIXTURE

4 tsp. (24 g) sea salt
1 tsp. (5 g) black peppercorns
12 allspice berries
8 whole cloves
2 star anise
¼ tsp. (0.75 g) cayenne powder
½ tsp. (1.5 g) ground *canela*
  (Mexican cinnamon)
1 cup (250 ml) dry white wine

FOR MEAT MIXTURE AND STUFFING

3 lbs. (1.5 k) lean boneless pork leg
  or rump, trimmed of connective
  tissue
1 lb. (500 g) smoked slab bacon
About 8 ft. (1.8 m) medium hog
  casings

PREPARE SPICE MIXTURE

Place the salt and spices in a spice mill or coffee grinder reserved for the purpose. Grind until very fine and pass through a fine-mesh sieve into a bowl. Return any particles that remain in the sieve to the grinder, grind again, pass through the sieve, and discard the residue. Mix the spices with the wine and set aside.

PREPARE MEAT MIXTURE

Working with the coarse plate of a meat grinder, grind the meat and bacon into a large mixing bowl. Change to the fine plate and pass the meats through again. Add the spice/ wine mixture and mix well to combine. To test for seasoning, fry a small batch; correct the seasonings if necessary. Cover and refrigerate overnight.

  If your casings were packed in salt, rinse them well, place in a bowl of cold water, and leave them at room temperature for 1 hour. (Note: If using fresh casings, soak them overnight in water with ½ cup / 125 ml white vinegar. Drain and rinse. Turn the casings inside out and remove the fatty membrane. Turn the casings right side out, rinse, and continue.) Pour off the water, rinse the casings, and drain.

When you are ready to stuff the sausages, cut one length of casing at a time, approximately 36 inches (90 cm) in length. Place one end of the casing on the nozzle of your kitchen faucet and slowly run cold water through to open it and prepare it for stuffing.

STUFF AND DRY SAUSAGES

For best results, use a stand mixer with a sausage-stuffing attachment. Follow manufacturer's instructions for the equipment, filling complete, thick lengths about 1½ inches (4 cm) in diameter. Twist off Butifarras into 5-inch- (12.7 cm) long sausages. Tie the ends to seal in the stuffing. Repeat until all the meat has been used. Place the finished sausages in one layer on a baking rack placed on a baking sheet lined with paper towels (the sausages need to have air circulating around them to dry properly, and the paper towels will absorb any juices that seep out). Refrigerate at least 48 hours or up to 72 hours prior to cooking.

POACH SAUSAGES

Bring a large pot of water to a boil and add the sausages. Reduce the heat to a simmer and check the water temperature: it should be maintained at 160°F (71°C) throughout the cooking process. Higher temperatures can cause the sausages to rupture. Poach the sausages for 30–40 minutes, or until they are firm and the juices run clear when you pierce one sausage with a needle. A meat thermometer should read 160°F (71°C). Allow the sausages to cool, then serve them, use them in a recipe, or store as noted above.

TO SERVE

If the sausages have been refrigerated or frozen, reheat in simmering water and serve. Alternatively, fry or grill the sausages prior to serving. The poached sausages may be served as they are accompanied by a mixed green salad, Chayas fritas (p. 129), Esquites (p. 239), or Verduras en escabeche (p. 283). To grill the sausages, follow technique and serving instructions for Longaniza asada (p. 482). Whole grilled or fried sausages can be added to Frijol blanco con puerco (p. 263) during the last half hour of cooking, in homage to *botifarra amb mongetes*, the Catalonian dish in which Butifarras and white beans are cooked together.

ESTOFADO DE CARNE DE CERDO CON LONGANIZA

PORK, HAM, AND SMOKED SAUSAGE STEW

TO PREPARE AHEAD

Enriched Lard (p. 513)

Longaniza de Valladolid (p. 481), or substitute

Butifarras (p. 377), or substitute

Recado para todo (p. 499)

FOR THE MEATS

1 Tbs. (14 g) Enriched Lard

6 oz. (170 g) smoked slab bacon, cut into medium dice

8 oz. (225 g) Longaniza de Valladolid (Substitute: chorizo, commercial *longaniza*, or other thin smoked sausage)

8 oz. (225 g) Butifarras (Substitute: Weisswurst or other mild sausage)

2 lbs. (1 k) pork loin, cut into roughly 2 in. (5 cm) cubes

8 oz. (225 g) smoked ham, cut into large dice

2 Tbs. (16 g) all-purpose flour

3 cups (750 ml) red wine

3 cups (750 ml) beef stock or bouillon

(continued on next page)

Carnivores will surely mobilize to help rescue this recipe from the verge of extinction. A highlight of the 1910 cookbook from Valladolid, *La verdadera cocina regional*, but now disappearing, this rich, smoky stew features a panoply of regional pork products: Longaniza de Valladolid, Butifarras, as well as pork loin and ham. The stew slowly simmers in red wine, and doña Mañuela cautions us to be sure to add more wine at the end if the cooking liquid has reduced too much.

Prepare ahead note: The Longaniza and Butifarras must be made several days in advance, although substitutions are offered. The finished dish improves with age: prepare a day ahead and reheat just before serving.

YIELD: 8–10 SERVINGS

SAUTÉ MEATS

In a large, heavy casserole or Dutch oven, heat the lard until shimmering. Add the bacon and reduce heat to low. Cook the bacon until crisp; remove it with a slotted spoon and reserve, leaving the fat in the casserole. Over medium heat, quickly brown the Longaniza and the Butifarras; remove them from the casserole and set aside. With the fat just below the smoking point, brown the pork cubes a few at a time so as not to

Longaniza in the Valladolid market. [EC]

FOR THE ENRICHMENT AND FINISHING

1 medium white onion (10 oz. /
  275 g), charred and coarsely
  chopped
5 medium cloves garlic
  (1¼ oz. / 30 g), peeled, charred,
  and chopped
2 medium Roma tomatoes
  (7 oz. / 200 g), charred and
  coarsely chopped
1 tsp. (3 g) Recado para todo
1 Tbs. (14 g) Enriched Lard
5 chiles país (Substitute: 3 chiles
  de árbol), lightly toasted in a
  skillet but left whole
1 bay leaf
1 tsp. (6 g) sea salt, or to taste

FOR SERVING

Pan francés (p. 194), or
  French rolls
Arroz blanco (p. 529), optional
  accompaniment
Chile k'uut or K'uut bi ik (p. 508),
  or the chile sauce of your choice

---

crowd. As they brown, remove them to a platter. Return the pork and any accumulated juices along with the diced ham to the casserole (you will add the bacon and sausages later). Add the flour and stir to coat the pieces evenly. Cook over medium heat, stirring constantly, until the flour turns a pale golden brown, about 1 minute. Add the wine and bouillon and bring to a boil, scraping the bottom of the casserole with a wooden spoon. Reduce the heat and simmer while you continue.

PREPARE ENRICHMENT

Place the first 4 ingredients in the jar of a blender and process until thoroughly liquefied. Heat the lard in a large skillet until shimmering. Pour the liquid from the blender into the skillet all at once; it should splatter and sizzle, so stand back. Add the chiles and bay leaf to the skillet and stir to combine. Cook over medium heat until the mixture thickens and darkens somewhat, 3–4 minutes. Transfer the mixture to the casserole.

FINISH STEW

Simmer the stew, uncovered, over medium-low heat for about 30 minutes; the liquid should begin to thicken slightly and reduce. Return the reserved sausages to the casserole and cook an additional 20 minutes, or until the cooking liquid coats the back of a spoon. Transfer the sausages to a cutting board and slice on the diagonal into thick rounds. Return the sausages and bacon to the casserole, check the seasonings, and add salt if needed.

TO SERVE

Place pieces of pork and sausage in soup bowls or shallow serving plates and ladle on some of the sauce. Serve with white rice or Pan francés for dipping. Diners add their own chile sauce to taste.

BUÑUELOS DE YUCA

HONEY-DRENCHED YUCA FRITTERS

FOR THE *YUCA*

1 lb. (500 g) *yuca*

FOR THE DOUGH

1 egg *plus* 1 yolk, lightly beaten
1 Tbs. (12 g) sugar
1 Tbs. (8 g) all-purpose flour
1 tsp. (4 g) baking powder
½ tsp. (3 g) sea salt
½ tsp. (1.5 g) ground *canela*
  (Mexican cinnamon)
Vegetable oil for frying

FOR SERVING

Yucatecan or Mexican honey

In the early colonial era, wheat flour was often in short supply, leading *criollo* cooks to look for ready substitutes. One was the starchy tuber known as *yuca* (p. 52), which worked well in various guises, including the sweet Spanish fritter, the *buñuelo*. Buñuelos de yuca are common in Yucatecan pueblos, but rare in the cities. I was delighted to find them sold in little plastic bags—six to the order—one morning as I strolled through the market in Valladolid. Ask the vendor to open the bag and squeeze some of our incomparable Yucatecan honey onto the warm fritters for you. Eumelia Villanueva *vda.* de Castillo shared this easy recipe with me.

Prepare ahead note: The dough for Buñuelos de yuca can be made up to 24 hours in advance. Form it into balls and refrigerate or freeze until ready to fry and serve. Bring the balls to room temperature before frying. *Buñuelos* are best eaten while still warm, but if, like me, you hate to see leftovers go to waste, you can quickly reheat them by frying in a bit of butter with a spoonful of honey until the honey begins to caramelize.

YIELD: APPROXIMATELY 2½ DOZEN

PREPARE *YUCA*

Cut the *yuca* into rough chunks, cover with water, and let stand 10–15 minutes. (This step will help loosen dirt and soften the skin, making it easier to peel.) Leave each piece in the water as you peel the rest. Working with a vegetable peeler or paring knife, peel the *yuca* and immediately place it in a saucepan of clean water to prevent oxidation. When all the *yuca* is peeled, slice each piece in half lengthwise. Look at the center: some *yuca* has a woody, fibrous core that should be removed. Pull at it with your fingers or extract it with a paring knife and discard. Return the *yuca* pieces to a saucepan of fresh water. Bring to a boil, then simmer, uncovered, 1–1¼ hours, or until the *yuca* is very tender when pierced with a fork. Drain and set aside until cool.

  Yuca is extremely starchy, and the dough for Buñuelos will be gluey. For best results, use a stand mixer with a grinding attachment and the finest blade, or a cast-iron hand grinder with plates at the tightest setting. (Note: A food processor is not recommended, since the stiff paste may cause the motor to jam.) Grind the *yuca* into a mixing bowl.

PREPARE DOUGH

Add all the ingredients except the oil to the mixing bowl containing the *yuca* and beat with the flat beater attachment of your stand mixer until the dough is stiff and sticky, about 2 minutes. If you do not have a stand mixer, use a potato masher. (Note: Small chunks of unblended yuca are difficult to avoid but will not affect the finished product.)

FORM FRITTERS

Line a tray with waxed paper and set aside. Turn the dough onto a well-floured work surface and knead 1–2 minutes, or until the surface of the dough is less sticky. With floured hands, form the dough into balls of about 1 heaping tablespoon (20 g), rolling the balls in flour as needed to keep them from sticking to your hands. Place the balls on the tray as you continue.

FRY FRITTERS AND SERVE

Pour 3 inches (7 cm) of vegetable oil into a deep skillet and heat until a thermometer reads 300°F (149°C). (Note: This lower-than-typical temperature for deep-fat frying is recommended in order to cook the Buñuelos inside and slowly brown them outside.) If the Buñuelos have flattened as you've worked, quickly reshape them into balls before plunging them into the hot oil. Fry Buñuelos a few at a time until a deep golden brown. Transfer to paper towels to drain.

TO SERVE

Arrange warm Buñuelos on a serving platter and pour a generous amount of honey over them. In Valladolid, people eat Buñuelos de yuca with their fingers, but you may prefer a fork or spoon.

(opposite page) Buñuelos de yuca. [EC]

CREMA DE GUANÁBANA

GUANÁBANA CRÈME BRÛLÉE

TO PREPARE AHEAD

Guanábana purée (see Sorbete de guanábana, p. 244), or you may use frozen pulp

FOR THE *CREMA*

12 egg yolks

¾ cup (150 g) granulated sugar, divided

4 cups (1 L) whipping cream, divided

1 cup (250 g) *guanábana* purée (your own or frozen)

½ tsp. (2.5 ml) Mexican vanilla extract

FOR SERVING

Muscovado or brown sugar, for the glaze

This unique Old World/New World "fusion" recipe from the 1910 cookbook *La verdadera cocina regional* was obviously based on Spanish *crema catalana*, itself derived from the French crème brûlée, although chefs from both countries will joust over which came first. Ironically, most food historians agree that crème brûlée was in fact an English invention known as "burnt cream," appearing first in a seventeenth-century cookbook from Dorsetshire. A special iron tool was heated, then pressed onto a thin layer of sugar sprinkled onto the finished cream to burn and caramelize the sugar. Even author Manuela Navarrete A. refers to the *plancha* (iron) at the end of her recipe. The twist in doña Manuela's recipe is the addition of the American tropical fruit *guanábana* for the flavoring instead of the more typical sweet orange zest in the Spanish version and vanilla in the French dessert. Creamy like French crème brûlée, but scented with ambrosial tropical fruit, Crema de guanábana is the dessert of dreams.

Prepare ahead note: Crema de guanábana needs to be prepared several hours to one day in advance in order to chill. It can remain under refrigeration for 3–4 days; finish the burnt-sugar glaze 10 minutes before serving.

YIELD: 10 SERVINGS

PREPARE *CREMA*

Preheat the oven to 300°F (150°C). In a large, heatproof mixing bowl, combine the yolks and ¼ cup (50 g) of the sugar and beat until the mixture is pale, thickened, and creamy. Set aside.

Place 2 cups of the whipping cream and the fruit purée in the jar of a blender and process until thoroughly liquefied. Pass the mixture through a sieve placed over a medium saucepan and use a rubber spatula to press through as much liquid as possible. Scrape any accumulated cream from the bottom of the sieve into the saucepan and discard any *guanábana* pulp in the sieve. Add the remaining cream, the remaining ½ cup (100 g) sugar, and the vanilla to the saucepan. Cook over medium heat, stirring constantly, until the sugar has dissolved and small bubbles appear around the edges. Continue cooking over low heat while you prepare the rest of the recipe.

While beating constantly, slowly drizzle in one ladle of the hot cream into the bowl containing the egg mixture and beat until it is incorporated. Repeat 3 more times, beating constantly, until the egg mixture is heated through.

Slowly pour the hot egg/cream mixture back into the saucepan and stir constantly over low heat until the mixture is quite thick and coats the back of a spoon, 2–3 minutes. Remove the pan from the heat.

BAKE *CREMAS*

Bring a kettle of water to a boil. Place 10 ¾-cup (6 oz. / 175 ml) ramekins or shallow *crema catalana* molds in a deep roasting pan. Divide the cream evenly among the ramekins (approximately ½ cup / 125 ml per ramekin). Fill the roasting pan with enough boiling water to reach halfway up the side of the ramekins. Bake 30–45 minutes, or until the custards are set but still quite wobbly in the middle. Remove the pan from the oven and immediately remove the ramekins from the water bath to halt cooking. Allow them to cool to room temperature, cover with plastic wrap, then refrigerate at least 8 hours or overnight.

TO SERVE

Sprinkle the top of each *crema* with 1 teaspoon (4 g) brown sugar. For best results, use a chef's torch to caramelize the sugar until it is browned and crisp but not burned (alternatively, place the ramekins briefly under a broiler). Allow the *cremas* to rest at room temperature for 10 minutes before serving.

MAZAPÁN DE PEPITA

SQUASH-SEED MARZIPAN

FOR THE SQUASH SEEDS

21 oz. (600 g) *pepita verde* (see Resources, p. 539)

(continued on page 387)

Straight from the Middle East by way of Andalucía, the little candies known as Mazapán de pepita now stock the displays of every *dulcería* (sweet shop) in Yucatán. Although it resembles traditional marzipan, Yucatecan *mazapán* has some notable differences. First, local cooks long ago substituted the more plentiful (and affordable) *pepitas* (squash seeds) for rare and costly almonds. And while Andalusian marzipan may be formed in the shape of peaches, plums, or other European fruits, Yucatecan *mazapán* mirrors New World iconography: ears of corn, pineapple, mamey, and even skulls during our Day of the Dead festivities. Vintage recipes call for *agua de azahar*, or essence of orange blossom oil, another Arabic inheritance.

Several families of Valladolid are dedicated to making Mazapán de pepita, and it is a common sight to see large wooden trays full of seeds drying in the sun on people's front porches. If you make this easy treat with your children, they will enjoy forming and coloring animal shapes, or whatever fantasies their hearts desire. Or you may form the candies as simple cone shapes and dust them with *canela*—a common practice in Yucatán—in which case they are known as Zapotitos.

Prepare ahead note: Cleaning and drying the *pepitas* should begin 2–3 days prior to finishing the candies. Mazapán de pepita keeps well in an airtight container at room temperature for 1 week, and for 3 weeks under refrigeration.

YIELD: APPROXIMATELY 3 DOZEN CANDIES

PREPARE SQUASH SEEDS

Place the squash seeds in a stockpot and cover with water at least 2 inches (5 cm) above the seeds. Bring to a rapid boil, cover the pot, remove it from the heat, and allow it to come to room temperature.

Mazapán de pepita. [MR]

When the water has cooled, plunge your hands into the pot and rub the seeds between your palms or squish them through your fingers to remove the green outer paper and reveal pale cream-colored seeds. Drain, cover the seeds with cold water, and repeat. Continue until the seeds appear white. (Note: This process can take up to 30 minutes. As the paper comes off the seeds, it will turn into a green slime that looks like algae. Various techniques of removing the slime have worked for me: place the stockpot in the sink and keep cold water running into one side of the pot; on the other side, look for the residue floating to the surface and remove it with a small sieve. When the water appears clean, use your hands or a spoon to agitate the seeds again and bring more residue to the surface. Repeat until the water is mostly clean. Alternatively, place the seeds in a colander with large holes and flush with water repeatedly until it runs clean.) Turn the cleaned seeds into a colander and drain thoroughly.

For the initial drying, spread the seeds in a thin layer on a surface and allow to dry for several hours or until barely damp. (Note: In Valladolid, cooks spread the seeds on wooden tables or trays, and in fact, the best surface by far is wood [you may use a pastry board or pizza peel]. The wood continues to absorb moisture from the seeds, and the seeds don't stick. Other surfaces I have tried with success are silicon baking mats or nonstick baking sheets. Do not use any form of paper: it will become soggy and tear, and the seeds will stick to it almost permanently. Sun drying is the method used in Valladolid, but if you are working indoors, place a fan near the seeds to speed up the drying process.) If you are drying the seeds in the sun, turn them and leave them another day or two or until completely dry. Otherwise, after the initial drying, spread them in a thin layer on baking sheets, place them in a very slow oven (250°F / 120°C), and bake for 3–4 hours, stirring every 30 minutes. Turn off the oven and leave them overnight. Alternatively, you may use a dehydrator. The seeds should not be brown but

1 cup (250 ml) water

2½ cups (500 g) sugar

½–1 tsp. (2.5–5 ml) pure orange oil, or to taste

Optional: Liquid food coloring or ground *canela* (Mexican cinnamon)

must be thoroughly dry before you proceed. You should have about 1 pound (500 g) seeds, accounting for loss.

Place the dried seeds in the bowl of a food processor and process until pulverized. With the motor running, continue processing until the powder turns into a stiff paste resembling modeling clay. Process again until the paste turns into something like thick mud (see instructions for Recado para papadzules, p. 503); set aside.

PREPARE SUGAR SYRUP

Place the water and sugar in a saucepan and bring to a boil. Continue cooking without stirring until the syrup reaches the soft-ball stage (234°F / 112°C). With the motor of the food processor running, slowly drizzle the hot syrup through the feed tube. Add the orange oil and process another 15 seconds, until incorporated.

FORM CANDIES AND FINISH

Carefully turn the hot paste onto a large sheet of waxed paper and allow to cool about 10 minutes, or until just cool enough to handle. Divide the paste into approximately 36 balls, each weighing about 1 ounce (30 g). Form the balls into the desired shapes. (Note: The balls will remain pliable enough to work with for about 1 hour, but as they dry, the surfaces will begin to crack. Not to worry. When this happens, dip your fingers in a bit of water, or if the balls become quite dry, dip them quickly in water one at a time before shaping.) Decorate finished marzipan with food coloring if desired. Simple finger or spherical shapes may be rolled in *canela* instead. Allow the candies to dry at room temperature for 2 hours. Store in layers separated by waxed paper in an airtight container.

Sun-drying pepitas. [DS]

VINEGARED FOODS

Vinegar, wine, and olive oil traveled in kegs in the ships' holds of Columbus' first American expedition. All these precious liquids had their uses, but vinegar was especially important for preservation. Various forms of pickles (*escabeches*) were soon made in the New World, using Spanish vinegar to flavor and preserve indigenous Mexican ingredients ranging from chiles to turkey. The apotheosis of this fusion is Pavo en escabeche oriental—one of the most beloved dishes of Yucatán and one that must be tasted when in Valladolid. Turkey is marinated for several hours in a special Spice Island blend, then, after a good roasting over a wood fire, it is finished in a stew of vinegar, pickled onions, and the local blond chile x'catik.

Vinegar and Preservation

The use of vinegar as a preservative is credited to the Arabs, and their word *sikbâg* (pronounced "iske-bech") defined a meat dish prepared with vinegar and other ingredients. *Sikbâg* is cited in the Persian *The One Thousand and One Nights* and was introduced into Spain sometime in the eleventh century during the anti-Moorish campaigns of El Cid. The word "*escabeche*" first appeared in print in *Libro de guisados* by Ruperto de Nola—his 1529 translation of a Catalán cookbook to Castilian Spanish—in which was presented a recipe for "Escabetx o escabeig a peix fregit" (pickled fried fish; recipe on p. 318).

PAVO EN ESCABECHE ORIENTAL

SOUSED TURKEY STEWED IN ONIONS AND CHILES

TO PREPARE AHEAD

Brined turkey (see Basic
  Techniques, p. 536)
Recado blanco (p. 502)
Enriched Lard (p. 513)
Cebollas en escabeche (p. 511)

FOR THE MARINADE

5½ lbs. (2.5 k) turkey, halved or
  pieces, brined (Substitute: an
  equal weight of chicken)
5 Tbs. (75 g) Recado blanco
5 Tbs. (75 ml) white vinegar
1 Tbs. (18 g) sea salt
2 Tbs. (28 g) Enriched Lard

FOR GRILLING

3 medium chiles x'catiques
  (about 1¼ oz. / 35 g each)
2 medium heads garlic
  (about 1¾ oz. / 50 g each),
  whole, unpeeled

FOR THE STEW

16 cups (4 L) water
2 Tbs. (36 g) sea salt
4 bay leaves
2 Tbs. (30 g) Recado blanco
2 Tbs. (30ml) white vinegar
1 recipe Cebollas en escabeche

Another pinnacle of the Yucatecan table, this dish is known variously as Pollo en escabeche oriental or Pavo en escabeche oriental (depending on whether the cook uses chicken or turkey) or simply Escabeche oriental or even Escabeche de Valladolid. The proper version calls for *pavo* (turkey), but many people use chicken instead, which indeed is more manageable. You may use either, but I find the robust taste of turkey more capable of standing up to the intense pepperiness in this dish.

Prepare ahead note: Pavo en escabeche oriental benefits from an overnight rest. Refrigerate and reheat just before serving.

YIELD: 10—12 SERVINGS

MARINATE POULTRY

Remove the poultry from the brine, rinse, and pat dry; discard the brining solution. Mix the remaining ingredients and stir to create a thick cream. Liberally coat the poultry on all sides with the mixture and allow it to marinate under refrigeration at least 1 hour or overnight.

GRILL POULTRY

Bring the poultry to room temperature. Preheat a gas or charcoal grill following instructions for using wood smoking chips in Basic Techniques, p. 538. Grill the poultry over a very hot fire, with the grilling rack close to the flame and the lid closed. It should acquire charring and grill marks overall, but it will not cook through and should still present some pink juices. Char the garlic and chiles at the same time, making sure not to puncture the chiles. Remove the poultry and vegetables from the grill and place

[MR]

the poultry in a large stockpot. Peel the garlic and separate it into cloves. Add the charred chiles and garlic to the pot with the poultry.

STEW POULTRY AND FINISH

Cover the poultry with the water and add the salt and bay leaves. Bring to a boil, then reduce to a simmer, skimming off any foam that surfaces. Cook until the poultry is cooked through but not falling apart, about 30 minutes.

Dilute the *recado* in the vinegar and add it to the stockpot along with the Cebollas en escabeche (include all the marinade, garlic, and chile). Simmer another 5 minutes to combine the flavors. Check the seasoning and add more salt if necessary. Remove all the chiles and gently rub off their skin under running water. Slice them open along one side and remove the stem, seeds, and veins. Cut the chiles lengthwise into thin strips and set aside for the garnish.

TO SERVE

Pull large pieces of meat off the bones. Place some of the meat in individual serving bowls and ladle on some of the stock, making sure to include pickled onions and garlic cloves with each serving. Garnish with a few strips of chile. (Note: In Yucatán, each diner is usually given a whole charred chile, which you may do for heat-loving friends.)

The Mesón del Marqués restaurant, in the center of Valladolid, is famous for its Pavo en escabeche oriental. [EC]

SOPA DE RABIOLES

VINEGARED SOUP WITH MINCEMEAT AND CAPER–STUFFED RAVIOLI

TO PREPARE AHEAD

Picadillo de especias (p. 256)

Recado para puchero (p. 499)

FOR THE RAVIOLI

3 cups (375 g) all-purpose flour

4 large eggs

½ recipe Picadillo de especias

This exquisite 100+-year-old recipe from *La verdadera cocina regional* may be the region's ultimate fusion dish: Italian ravioli are stuffed with a meat filling flavored by the exotic spice formula that characterized the Moorish cooking of Andalucía; the peppers and tomatoes are clearly from Mexican soils; and a faint hint of Spanish vinegar from Jerez unites all in blissful harmony.

Prepare ahead note: Except for the ravioli, which can take close to 2 hours to prepare, the soup can be assembled in under 30 minutes. Form the ravioli in advance and refrigerate or freeze until ready to use. The soup stock, too, can be prepared in advance and refrigerated. Just reheat, cook the ravioli as instructed, and serve.

YIELD: 8 SERVINGS

PREPARE RAVIOLI DOUGH

Place the flour in a mound on a pastry board, make an indentation in the center, and add the eggs. Using a fork, beat the eggs in the center as if you were making scrambled eggs. Gradually incorporate a little of the flour into the egg mixture as you continue beating. When the eggs are well beaten, use your fingers to fold more flour into the egg mixture. Little by little, collect the dough in your hands, kneading and blending in more flour as needed. You will want to use only enough flour to make a soft dough that is smooth and no longer sticky. You may test the dough by inserting your finger deep into the center of the ball: if it comes out clean, stop adding flour.

With just enough flour on the pastry board to keep the dough from sticking, vigorously knead the dough until it is smooth and elastic, 6–8 minutes. Roll it into a log shape about 12 inches (30 cm) long, then cut it into 12 equal portions. Form each portion into a ball and wrap each ball tightly with plastic wrap. Refrigerate all the balls except the one you are working with. (Note: Pasta dough dries out very quickly at room temperature. For this reason it is very important that you work with only one portion of the dough at a time and leave the rest wrapped in plastic.)

FILL RAVIOLI

Shape 48 half-ounce (15 g) balls of the Picadillo de especias (about 1 rounded teaspoon each) and place on a large platter; cover with plastic and refrigerate while you work. Unwrap one of the balls of dough and knead it briefly on a lightly floured work surface, about 1 minute, to restore its elasticity. Set the rollers of a pasta machine at the widest opening, flatten the ball, and pass it through the opening starting with the narrow end. Fold the dough in half, then in half again. Pass it through the rollers again, starting with the narrow end. Repeat 3 more times.

Close the rollers one notch and feed the dough through again. Repeat, closing the rollers by one notch each time, until the pasta sheet is approximately 4½ inches (11.5 cm) wide, 12 inches (30 cm) long, and ¹⁄₁₆th-inch (2 mm) thick. Carefully transfer

FOR THE *SOFRITO*

2 Tbs. (30 ml) Spanish olive oil

1 medium green and 1 medium
red bell pepper (about 6½ oz. /
185 g each), cut in half lengthwise, seeded, and sliced into
thin julienne

1 medium white onion (10 oz. /
275 g), peeled, thinly sliced
across the width, and separated
into rings

4 medium cloves garlic (1 oz. /
24 g), charred and finely chopped

4 medium Roma tomatoes (14 oz.
/ 400 g), seeded and chopped

1 Tbs. (8 g) Recado para puchero

3 Tbs. (15 g) flat-leaf parsley,
chopped

FOR THE SOUP

8 cups (2 L) chicken stock or
bouillon

1 medium head garlic (1¾ oz. /
50 g), charred, peeled, and
separated into cloves

1 four-in. (10 cm) stick *canela*
(Mexican cinnamon)

¼ cup (62.5 ml) sherry vinegar

FOR SERVING

Queso para sopa (Substitute:
crumbled *queso cotija* or feta)

the pasta sheet to a lightly floured work surface. (Note: If you are rolling the dough by hand, roll/fold in the same steps listed above to create a strip with the same measurements.)

Place the pasta strip horizontally in front of you; lightly dust the exposed surface with flour, fold the top edge down to meet the bottom edge, and quickly open it again to leave a faint horizontal crease along the center; this will help you with the place-ment of the meatballs. Align 4–5 of the meatballs just below the crease on the side closest to you, making sure that they are about 2 inches (5 cm) from each end and from each other. Lightly brush some water onto the pasta around each meatball. Fold the dough to cover the meatballs, bringing the long side at the top over to meet the side closest to you. Use your fingertips to press a U-shaped seal around each meatball on the 3 sides without the fold. Using a 3-inch (7.5 cm) circular cookie or biscuit cutter (pref-erably fluted), locate it above one of the meatballs, with the folded edge of the dough at the halfway point of the cutter, in other words, running through the diameter. Cut out the ravioli into half-moon shapes and set each one aside as you continue with the rest. Place the finished ravioli on large trays covered with waxed paper and refrigerate or freeze until ready to use.

PREPARE *SOFRITO*

Heat the olive oil in a stockpot until shimmering. Add bell peppers, onion, and garlic and cook, stirring frequently, until the onions begin to sweat. Add the remaining ingredients and cook over low heat until the tomatoes are tender.

PREPARE SOUP

Add the first 3 ingredients to the stockpot containing the *sofrito* and bring to a boil. Reduce the heat to a simmer and cook 5–6 minutes to incorporate the flavors. Add the vinegar and simmer an additional 3 minutes. Remove the pan from the heat, cover, and allow the ingredients to steep as you continue.

Bring a pot of salted water to a boil. A few at a time, drop in the amount of ravioli you intend to serve (if frozen, do not defrost). Cook the ravioli in the salted water, uncovered, 6–8 minutes, or until they float to the surface. Return the soup to a sim-mer; retrieve the *canela* and discard.

TO SERVE

Immediately transfer the ravioli with a wok strainer or slotted spoon to individual serving bowls, 6 ravioli per person. Use tongs to extract the vegetables from the stockpot and arrange them on top of the ravioli. Ladle stock around the ravioli and vegetables. Top with crumbled cheese if you wish and serve extra cheese at the table.

LOMITOS DE VALLADOLID

CUBED PORK LOIN IN TOMATO/CHILE SAUCE
WITH CREAMY STRAINED LIMA BEANS

TO PREPARE AHEAD
Enriched Lard (p. 513)

FOR BROWNING THE PORK

2 Tbs. (28 g) Enriched Lard

1 medium white onion (10 oz. / 275 g), thinly sliced and separated into rings

8 medium garlic cloves (1½ oz. / 48 g), peeled

2 lbs. (1 k) pork loin or leg, with some fat, cut into ¾ in. (2 cm) cubes

FOR STEWING THE PORK

2 lbs. (1 k) medium Roma tomatoes, coarsely chopped

1 Tbs. (18 g) sea salt

6 whole chiles país, or 3 chiles de árbol (about 3 g total), toasted in a skillet until darkened

2 sprigs fresh epazote (Substitute: 1 tsp. / 1.5 g dried, crumbled)

½ cup (125 ml) white vinegar

1 tsp. (3 g) cayenne powder (optional)

FOR SERVING

Ibes colados (p. 506), recommended accompaniment

8 hard-boiled eggs, peeled and halved

Tortillas (p. 518)

K'uut bi ik (p. 508), or the chile sauce of your choice

This lightly picante pork stew was included in the 1910 *La verdadera cocina regional* and today is served at virtually every regional Yucatecan restaurant. It is typically nested atop a creamy bed of pureed *ibes* (lima beans), although some vendors in Valladolid's market serve it as a *torta* on a special pit-baked *masa*-and-lima-bean bread known as *pibilhua*. Author Manuela Navarrete A. stresses twice that the cook should ensure that the Lomitos turn out *picantito* (lightly spicy, but definitely spicy). When I prepared the dish with Sra. Angelina "Linda" de Jesús Tun Jiménez, she used ground red chile instead of whole chiles. The Mesón del Marqués restaurant in the center of Valladolid employs whole charred dried red chile país, which makes a nice presentation. Following doña Manuela's advice, I have opted to use both for this recipe. Although this dish is not very spicy, sensitive tongues should taste the sauce before adding the cayenne at the very end.

Prepare ahead note: Lomitos de Valladolid refrigerates well for a couple of days and is excellent reheated.

YIELD: 6–8 SERVINGS

BROWN PORK

In a deep casserole or Dutch oven, heat the lard until shimmering. Add the onions and garlic cloves and cook until the onions are translucent. Add the pork and sauté over high heat until it is browned and the onions are caramelized, about 6–8 minutes.

STEW PORK AND FINISH

Add the first 4 ingredients to the pork. Simmer, uncovered, over medium heat about 30 minutes. Use a wooden spoon to mash down the tomatoes periodically so that they break apart and are completely rendered and reduced. Add the vinegar and cook another 15 minutes, stirring constantly, until most of the liquid has evaporated. The resulting sauce should thickly coat the pork pieces, and the bottom of the pot should be almost dry. Check the seasoning and add optional cayenne if desired.

TO SERVE

Mound the Ibes colados in the center of individual serving plates, top with the Lomitos and two egg halves to garnish. Serve with corn tortillas and chile sauce.

(opposite page) Lomitos served on pibilhua—maize bread baked on a píib. [EC]

[MC]

PEPPERY FOODS

In addition to the liberal use of vinegar in the cooking of Valladolid, the pungent Recado blanco (p. 502) is used here more than elsewhere in Yucatán, adding a distinctive and potent pepperiness to many *vallisoletano* dishes. Contrary to its name, Recado blanco isn't white at all, but, rather, a rich slate black due to its scale-tipping quantity of black pepper. Considering that pepper was an expensive import item in the colonial era, such prolific use of it would have demonstrated prestige. Recado blanco adds an unmistakable zing to everything from Mechado and Escabeche oriental to the local Longaniza de Valladolid.

MECHADO

PEPPERED CHICKEN AND PORK STEW WITH CHICKPEAS, CAPERS, AND OLIVES

TO PREPARE AHEAD

Pork and chicken, brined
  separately (see Basic Techniques,
  p. 536)
Recado blanco (p. 502)
Enriched Lard (p. 513)

FOR THE MARINADE

2½ oz. (70 g) smoked slab bacon,
  cut into 40 half-inch (1.5 cm)
  cubes
2 lbs. (1 k) pork leg or shoulder,
  preferably with bone, brined
1 large whole chicken (about 3 lbs.
  / 1.5 k), halved and brined
8 Tbs. (120 g) Recado blanco
½ cup (125 ml) white vinegar
2 Tbs. (28 g) Enriched Lard
1 tsp. (6 g) sea salt

FOR THE STEW

12 cups (3 L) water, or enough to
  cover the meats
1 cup (225 g) dried garbanzos
  (chickpeas), parboiled for 1 hour
  then drained (Substitute: you
  may use 2½ cups / 450 g drained
  canned garbanzos; add them
  30 minutes prior to finishing
  the dish)
¾ cup (180 g) raisins
½ cup (120 g) small capers, drained
¾ cup (100 g) unpitted green
  olives
2 medium white onions (about
  10 oz. / 275 g each), charred and
  quartered
3 medium chiles x'catiques (about
  1¼ oz. / 35 g each), charred
  without piercing

(continued on page 399)

This popular *vallisoletano* dish will surprise you: is it *really* Yucatecan? The complex Asian flavor profile of hot/sour/sweet is not what you might expect of foods from Mexico. Nonetheless, this is the *true* and historical food of Spanish-influenced Valladolid. *Mechado* in Spanish means "stuffed" or "larded," and in fact, the typical preparation method specifies liberally piercing whatever meat is being cooked and filling the slits with garlic, ham, bits of fat, or spices. In this case, the spices are those in Recado blanco, the lightly picante Yucatecan spice blend based on black pepper. Sra. Angelina "Linda" de Jesús Tun Jiménez, who shared this recipe with me, told me that it is best prepared a day in advance and eaten on the second day, in which case it is known as Mechado. But if the aroma is too tempting and you eat it right away, it is called Mechadillo (little Mechado).

Prepare ahead note: The chicken and pork should be brined for several hours. As noted above, the entire dish is best prepared a day in advance; reheat just prior to serving.

YIELD: 8–10 SERVINGS

MARINATE AND GRILL PORK AND CHICKEN

Bring a small saucepan of water to a boil, add the bacon, return to a boil, and cook 1 minute; drain and set aside to cool. Remove the pork and chicken from the brine, rinse, and pat dry; discard the brining solutions. Dissolve the *recado* in the vinegar, mashing with a fork to break up any large pieces. Add the lard and salt and mix thoroughly to form a thick cream. Using a sharp knife, pierce the pork and chicken 20 times each, spacing the slits evenly on all sides, about 1 inch (3 cm) apart, to a depth of about ½ inch (2.25 cm). Twist the knife as you make each hole to widen it to accommodate the stuffing. Fill each hole with one piece of the bacon. Rub the meats all over with the *recado* mixture, pushing it deep into the gashes to seal in the bacon. Allow the meats to marinate, refrigerated, for at least 30 minutes or up to 2 hours.

While the meats are marinating, preheat a charcoal or gas grill following instructions for using wood smoking chips in Basic Techniques, page 538. Remove the meats from the refrigerator and bring them to room temperature while the grill preheats. Shake the excess marinade off the meats; reserve the marinade. Grill the meats over a very hot fire with the lid closed until they are seared and charred with some grill marks but not cooked through.

STEW MEATS

Put the grilled meats in a large stockpot and cover with the water. Add the reserved marinade and the remaining ingredients. Bring to a boil, then reduce to a simmer. Continue cooking until the meats are tender and the garbanzos are cooked through, about 1½ hours.

1 medium red bell pepper (about 6½ oz. / 185 g), charred and left whole

2 medium heads garlic (about 1¾ oz. / 50 g each), charred, peeled, and separated into cloves

2 medium Roma tomatoes (about 7 oz. / 200 g total), charred and coarsely chopped

1 cup (250 ml) white vinegar

2 Tbs. (24 g) powdered beef bouillon, or 2 cubes

1 Tbs. (15 g) Recado blanco, dissolved in ½ cup (125 ml) water

FINISH AND SERVE

Remove the chicken and pork from the stockpot and allow to cool until cool enough to handle. Strip the chicken from the bones and pull the pork. Retrieve the bell pepper and the chiles x'catiques from the stockpot and gently rub off the skin under running water. Make a slit along the length of the chiles, remove the seeds and veins, and slice into thin julienne strips; set aside as the garnish.

TO SERVE

Place the pieces of the meats in individual serving bowls and ladle on some of the cooking liquid, making sure to distribute the garlic, garbanzos, raisins, capers, and olives in each serving. Garnish with the chile strips.

OLD WORLD SPICES IN THE NEW WORLD

On his second American voyage in 1493, Christopher Columbus brought small quantities of Asian spices like black pepper and cinnamon to show to native residents in hopes that they could point him to local sources of the same things. It was not until the 1520s, however, that Old World spices began appearing more widely in Mexico. At that time, saffron, cinnamon, cloves, and black pepper were sold separately, or could be purchased as a proportioned mixture, similar to today's *recados*. In de Nola's 1529 Spanish cookbook, a common sauce is described as containing "three parts cinnamon, two parts cloves, one part ginger, one part pepper."

Although the Mayas had probably been concocting simpler versions of *recados* since pre-Columbian times, these new, more elaborate spice blends eventually took root in creole kitchens. From 1565 to 1815, the legendary Spanish galleon *La Nao de China* brought many trade goods, including spices, from Asia to the Mexican port of Acapulco and then overland in exchange for New World silver. Increased trade brought costs down, such that the use of these spice blends soon spread beyond the tables of the Yucatecan gentry and into the pueblos, proliferating in variety, too, as individual cooks tinkered with the formulas.

(above) Spanish galleons on the East Indian spice route. Braun and Hogenberg, "Calicut 1572." Civitates Orbis Terrarum, 1572. [BASED ON COPY AT HISTORISCHES MUSEUM, FRANKFURT]

Jars of capers, raisins, and olives appear in every market in Yucatán. [EC]

ALCAPARRADO

Many foods of Valladolid bear the imprint of their Andalusian/Moorish origins, but perhaps none so much as the ingredient mixture known as *alcaparrado*.

The literal translation from the Spanish term "*alcaparrado*" is "capered," and it describes any number of dishes that include capers (*alcaparras*). In Yucatán as well as in parts of Cuba and Puerto Rico, the term also refers to a mixture of capers, green olives, and, often, raisins, lending foods cooked with *alcaparrado* an alluring sweet/savory complexity and Moorish timbre. Almonds are also sometimes thrown into the medley, and all four ingredients are stocked side by side in big jars in most Yucatecan markets, much as they were in the ships' holds of early explorers.

PESCADOS BLANCOS FRITOS CON ALCAPARRAS

FRIED FISH WITH CAPER PESTO, OLIVES, AND CHILES IN VINAIGRETTE

This unusual dish makes use of a caper pesto—sophisticated for early-twentieth-century Valladolid, when this recipe first appeared. Fish fillets are marinated in the pesto for half an hour, then fried and doused with vinaigrette, sliced olives, and pickled jalapeños.

Prepare ahead note: You may prepare the marinade and the vinaigrette several days in advance and refrigerate. Marinate the fish 30 minutes prior to cooking. Once marinated, the fish should be fried and served immediately.

YIELD: 6 SERVINGS

TO PREPARE AHEAD
Recado para todo (p. 499)

FOR THE MARINADE
1 cup (150 g) small capers, drained
¼ cup (62.5 ml) freshly squeezed
  lime juice
2 Tbs. (15 ml) Spanish olive oil
1 tsp. (3 g) Recado para todo
6 firm-fleshed fish fillets
  (striped bass, snapper, grouper,
  pompano, robalo; about 1½ lbs. /
  680 g)

FOR THE VINAIGRETTE
¼ cup (62.5 ml) Spanish olive oil
½ cup (125 ml) white wine vinegar
1 medium clove garlic (¼ oz. /
  6 g), peeled and mashed
½ tsp. (2.5 ml) tarragon mustard
½ tsp. (3 g) sea salt
½ tsp. (2.5 g) coarsely ground
  black pepper
10 medium pimiento-stuffed
  green olives, sliced

FOR FRYING THE FISH
1 cup (125 g) all-purpose flour
1 tsp. (6 g) sea salt
½ tsp. (2.5 g) freshly ground
  black pepper
¼ cup (62.5 ml) vegetable oil

FOR SERVING
Chopped flat-leaf parsley or
  cilantro
Pickled jalapeños, drained, in
  strips or "nacho" rings, or
  Verduras en escabeche (p. 283)
Lime wedges
Arroz blanco or Arroz
  verde (p. 529), suggested
  accompaniment

MARINATE FISH
Place the first 4 ingredients in the bowl of a small food processor and process about 30 seconds, or until the capers are broken up but still have some texture. Place the fillets in a shallow baking dish large enough to hold them in a single layer and cover with the marinade, making sure all sides of the fish are well coated. Use your fingers to press the capers into the flesh of the fish. Refrigerate 30 minutes while you prepare the vinaigrette.

PREPARE VINAIGRETTE
Place all the ingredients but the olives in the jar of a blender and process about 1 minute, or until the ingredients are emulsified. Transfer the vinaigrette to a nonreactive bowl, add the sliced olives, and allow to rest at room temperature while you finish.

FRY FISH AND SERVE
Remove the fish from the refrigerator and allow to sit at room temperature for 15 minutes. Mix the flour, salt, and pepper on a large, shallow plate. Heat the oil in a large skillet until shimmering. Working in batches, remove the fish from the marinade, leaving as much of the caper pesto clinging to it as possible. Dredge the fillets in the flour. Fry the fish until lightly browned, turning once, 3–4 minutes per side (time will depend on the thickness of your fillet). Check for doneness by pressing the center of the fillet with your finger; it should be springy, not soft or mushy. Remove the fish to a warmed platter.

TO SERVE
Place the fillets on individual serving plates and divide the vinaigrette among the plates, distributing the olives evenly. Sprinkle with the herbs and top each fillet with jalapeño or a few pieces of Verduras en escabeche. Garnish with lime wedges and accompany with a scoop of Arroz Blanco or Arroz verde and a mixed green salad if you wish.

PAVO EN NARANJA CHINA

TURKEY WITH CAPERS, RAISINS, AND OLIVES IN SWEET ORANGE SAUCE

TO PREPARE AHEAD
Brined turkey (see Basic
  Techniques, p. 536)
Recado para todo (p. 499)
Enriched Lard (p. 513)

FOR THE MARINADE
3–4 lbs. (1.3–2 k) turkey pieces,
  brined
1 Tbs. (9 g) Recado para todo
1 medium head garlic (about
  1¾ oz. / 50 g), charred, peeled,
  and separated into cloves
1 cup (250 ml) freshly squeezed
  sweet orange juice
1 tsp. (6 g) sea salt

[EC]

The term "*china*" is used in Yucatán to refer to the sweet orange, differentiating it from the popular *naranja agria*, or sour orange. This recipe as recorded in *La verdadera cocina regional* is impressive; I translate and paraphrase here: "One whole turkey, cut into pieces and fried; juice of 40 sweet oranges; one bushel of tomatoes (peeled); four bell peppers and six onions with a bunch of parsley. Chop the vegetables and fry to create a *sofrito*. Then proceed to make the *recado*: six heads garlic and six onions and six chiles x'catiques (all roasted underground); grind together with pepper, cloves, and nutmeg. Mash and dissolve the resulting paste with wine and add to stewpot. Toss in 24 each of olives, raisins, and capers. Cook for 2 hours." Hopefully, my version of doña Manuela's recipe is more user-friendly but just as delicious.

Prepare ahead note: Brine the poultry several hours in advance. Pavo en naranja china improves with age; make it a day in advance and reheat just before serving.

YIELD: 6–8 SERVINGS

MARINATE POULTRY
Remove the poultry from the brine, rinse, and pat dry; discard the brining solution. Transfer the poultry to a shallow baking dish or resealable plastic bag. Place the remaining marinade ingredients in the jar of a blender and purée 1–2 minutes, or until

FOR THE *SOFRITO*

2 Tbs. (28 g) Enriched Lard

1 medium white onion (10 oz. / 275 g), cut into quarters top to bottom, then each quarter thinly sliced top to bottom and separated into half-moon shapes

4 medium cloves garlic (1 oz. / 24 g), peeled and minced

1 medium green bell pepper and 1 red bell pepper (about 6½ oz. / 185 g each), cut in half lengthwise, seeded, and sliced into thin julienne strips

2 medium Roma tomatoes (7 oz. / 200 g), seeded and chopped

¼ cup (15 g) flat-leaf parsley, chopped

1 Tbs. (3 g) sweet orange rind, finely grated

1 large pinch saffron

FOR SAUTÉING AND FINISHING

3 Tbs. (42 g) Enriched Lard

¾ cup (187.5 ml) freshly squeezed sweet orange juice

¼ cup (62.5 ml) sweet sherry

20 (about 1 oz. / 30 g) almonds, blanched and slivered

2 Tbs. (30 g) raisins

1 Tbs. (15 g) small capers, drained

20 medium green olives, whole unpitted, pitted, or pimiento-stuffed and sliced

1 two-in. (5 cm) square piece of sweet orange rind, thinly slivered

2 whole medium chiles x'catiques (about 1¼ oz. / 35 g each), charred without puncturing

FOR SERVING

Arroz blanco (p. 529), optional accompaniment

Slices of sweet orange

thoroughly liquefied. Pour the purée over the poultry and allow to rest 30 minutes at room temperature as you prepare the *sofrito*.

PREPARE *SOFRITO*

Heat the lard in a medium skillet until shimmering. Add the onion, garlic, and bell peppers and cook over medium heat until the onions are translucent and the peppers are softened, 3–4 minutes. Add the remaining ingredients and cook until the tomatoes are softened. Remove the skillet from the heat and set aside.

SAUTÉ POULTRY AND FINISH

In a large, deep skillet with a lid, heat the lard until shimmering. Remove the poultry from the marinade, reserving any leftover marinade. Brown the poultry over high heat a few pieces at a time so as not to crowd, turning once, 2–3 minutes per side. Remove the browned poultry to a platter.

When all of the poultry has been browned, pour the fat out of the skillet, return the turkey and any accumulated juices to the skillet, and add the reserved marinade along with the vegetable *sofrito*, orange juice, and sherry. Bring to a boil, cover, and cook over medium heat 20–25 minutes. Add the remaining ingredients, cover, and simmer another 5 minutes to meld the flavors, or until the poultry reaches a temperature of 165°F (74°C).

Remove the chiles and rub off the skin under running water. Slit the chiles open along the side and remove the seeds and veins, then slice them lengthwise into thin strips; set aside for the garnish.

Transfer the poultry to a platter. Bring the cooking liquid to a boil and boil uncovered over high heat for 6–8 minutes to reduce by about one-quarter.

TO SERVE

Carve the poultry and place pieces on individual serving plates. Spoon on some of the sauce, including the *alcaparrado* mixture, and garnish with chile strips and slices of sweet orange. Accompany with Arroz blanco if desired.

POLLO EN MACALÚ

CHICKEN STEWED IN SPICED WINE

TO PREPARE AHEAD
Enriched Lard (p. 513)
Brined chicken (p. 536)

FOR BROWNING AND SAUTÉING THE CHICKEN
1 Tbs. (14 g) Enriched Lard

6 oz. (170 g) smoked slab bacon, cut into large dice

5 lbs. (2.25 k) chicken parts (whole chickens cut into pieces, all drumsticks, breasts, or your favorite parts), skin and bone intact, brined

FOR STEWING THE CHICKEN
6 cups (1.5 L) red wine

2 cups (500 ml) beef stock or bouillon, or as needed to cover the chicken

6 medium cloves garlic (1½ oz. / 36 g), peeled, charred, and mashed

1 oz. (24 g) fresh ginger root, peeled and sliced

1 four-in. (10 cm) stick *canela* (Mexican cinnamon)

6 allspice berries

4 whole cloves

3 Tbs. (36 g) sugar

1 tsp. (2 g) ground ginger

1 tsp. (3 g) ground *canela*

1 tsp. (6 g) sea salt

½ tsp. (2 g) black peppercorns

¼ tsp. (.25 g) dried thyme

With an ingredient list that walks the line between coq au vin and mulled wine, this elegant and exotically flavored dish preserves a glimpse of *vallisolitano* cuisine in the Gilded Age. The basic recipe of chicken stewed in wine could perhaps be found anywhere in the Mediterranean, but the Spice Islands flavorings and the *alcaparrado*/almond mixture summon memories of al-Andalus. And don't forget the pickled peppers at the end—a distinctive creole touch. The dish was named after a famous nineteenth-century personage: Macalú was a Cuban-born *picador* (bullfighter) of African blood who became one of the most popular players in Yucatán's bullrings.

Prepare ahead note: Pollo en Macalú benefits from a day's rest in the refrigerator to amalgamate flavors. Prepare it a day in advance and reheat just before serving.

YIELD: 8–10 SERVINGS

BROWN BACON AND SAUTÉ CHICKEN
Heat the lard in a large, heavy stockpot or casserole. Add the bacon and cook slowly until it is crisp. Remove it with a slotted spoon and reserve; leave the fat in the casserole.

Working a few pieces at a time so as not to crowd, brown the chicken over medium-high heat, turning once, about 2–3 minutes per side. Transfer the pieces to a platter.

STEW CHICKEN
Drain off all but 2 tablespoons (30 ml) of fat from the casserole. Return the chicken and any accumulated juices to the casserole and cover with the wine and bouillon, adding enough bouillon to just cover the chicken. Add the remaining ingredients, bring to a boil, reduce to a simmer, and cook, uncovered, 20–25 minutes, or until the chicken is tender and reaches an internal temperature of 165°F (74°C). Transfer the chicken to a platter while you finish the sauce.

TO THICKEN THE SAUCE AND FINISH

3 Tbs. (42 g) Enriched Lard

3 Tbs. (24 g) all-purpose flour

½ cup (65 g) almonds, blanched and slivered

2 Tbs. (30 g) small capers

20 medium green olives, whole unpitted, pitted, or pimiento-stuffed and sliced

5 whole pickled jalapeños, cut in half lengthwise, seeded, and cut into julienne strips

¼ cup (62.5 ml) red wine vinegar or sherry vinegar

FOR SERVING

Arroz blanco (p. 529), optional accompaniment

THICKEN SAUCE AND FINISH

Pour the cooking liquid through a sieve held over a large heatproof bowl; discard the spices. Wipe out the casserole and return the cooking liquid to it. Bring the liquid to a boil and cook over high heat until the liquid has reduced by about half (you should have 4 cups / 1 L).

Use a fork to mash the lard and flour together in a heatproof bowl. Add a ladle or two of the hot cooking liquid to the flour/fat mixture and whisk to combine. Reduce the heat to a simmer, add the flour mixture to the cooking liquid, and whisk vigorously to prevent lumps (if lumps do occur, an immersion blender works well to remove them). Continue whisking until the sauce thickens slightly, 1–2 minutes.

Return the chicken to the casserole. Add the reserved bacon and the remaining ingredients. Stir to blend, ladling liquid over the chicken. Cover and cook at a gentle simmer an additional 5 minutes to heat the chicken and amalgamate the flavors.

TO SERVE

Serve directly from the casserole at the table. Alternatively, plate individual portions, making certain each plate receives some of the olives, capers, almonds, and jalapeño. Accompany with Arroz blanco and a mixed green salad if you wish.

DOÑA MANUELA'S HOUSEHOLD HINTS

In addition to recipes for food, many cookbooks of yesteryear presented their female authors with an opportunity to share with other women their beauty, health, and cleaning secrets in an era well before Heloise, much less Martha Stewart! The 1910 *La verdadera cocina regional*, published in Valladolid by Manuela Navarrete A., is no exception, and the entire second and third sections are devoted to such tips, with over 200 separate formulas. Many of them call for peninsular plants, barks, and flowers, most with Mayan names. I do not include any of the recipes here, but cannot resist the urge to tantalize you with some of the titles:

- Saint Michael's Toothpaste Elixir
- Soap to Dye Your Hair Black
- Water to Preserve Beauty
  [which consists of strained boiled rice and river water with just a smidgen of watercress juice, in case you were curious]
- To Frighten Away Ants
- To Make Your Piano Keys Shine
- To Banish Freckles Completely
- To Cure a Cough No Matter How Bad
- For Tarantula Bite
- To Avoid Chapped Breasts
- To Remove Facial Wrinkles
- For Memory
- For Nervous Hiccups
- To Destroy Warts
  [Caution: this recipe calls for using a toasted scorpion]
- To Prevent Children from Eating Dirt

6

The

PUEBLOS

ONE OF MY FAVORITE PASTIMES is to do what is colloquially referred to in Mexico as "*pueblear*," to leisurely travel from village to village. Escape the superhighways, take any of the small state roads that link one little town to the next, and trace a giant game of connect the dots.

Beyond the bustling metropolises, pueblo life quite literally slows you down. The first sign you are approaching a pueblo is the teeth-jarring speed bumps known as *topes*. Ignore them, and you can rip out your vehicle's undercarriage. They do an excellent job of controlling speeders.

Each pueblo has its own history, stretching from ancient Maya dominance through the Spanish colonial period to the present. And, happily, many pueblos are known for their unique culinary specialties.

Pueblo turkeys. [DK]

FELIPE CARRILLO PUERTO

NECTAR OF THE GODS

Beekeeping is an ancient practice in Yucatán, and honey remains a big business. The region is the top honey producer in all of Mexico, and the country ranks among the top ten in global honey production.

Through the centuries, honey production has been a family affair in Yucatán; many homes in the pueblos have at least a couple of hives, generating important supplemental income for the household. The so-called *mundo maya* in eastern Quintana Roo is home to a number of traditional beekeepers.

HONEY IN MAYA HISTORY AND CULTURE
The Yucatán Peninsula is home to a unique species of stingless bee, *Melipona beecheii*, known for creating hives in hollow trees. This allowed precontact Mayas to easily cut away the section containing the colony and take it to their *solar* for easier honey harvesting. When Francisco Hernández de Córdoba arrived in Yucatán from Cuba in 1517, he noted vast zones with thousands of such hives, producing sufficient honey for the Mayas' expansive trade routes.

So central was the role of beekeeping and honey in Maya

(above) Ranging in hue from palest amber to darkest black, Yucatecan honey from small producers is often packaged in recycled beverage bottles. [MR]

(opposite page) Unlike the combs constructed by the common bee (Apis mellifera), melipona bee honey is stored in pitch-black wax spheres. [MC]

life, culture, and religion that "bee gods" populated the Maya cosmos. This is evident in one of the three surviving Mayan texts, the Madrid Codex, in which several sections are devoted to apiculture, with illustrations of bees and hives as well as gods sporting what appear to be antennae.

The culture of honey changed significantly after the arrival of Europeans. Immediately thereafter, the Mayas were required to pay tribute to the Spanish in both honey and wax. The first tribute register, from 1549, states that a total of approximately 32 tons (29,300 k) of wax and 3½ tons (3,300 k) of honey were collected.

Unfortunately, loss of habitat is threatening the native bee and, along with it, the centuries-old tradition of stingless beekeeping. Also, while a *melipona* colony may produce a few pounds of honey per year, Africanized bees can produce 220 pounds (100 k) in the same-size hive, clearly a more economically attractive option for beekeepers, one that is further sealing the doom of traditional ways. At present, there are only about 500 producers of *melipona* bee honey in Yucatán.

Enter Pablo Dzib, a burly Maya who seems to have been weaned on honey. In Felipe Carrillo Puerto, Quintana Roo,

a small city of 26,000, he lives on a rustic *terreno* where he has fashioned a spectacular condominium complex for bees.

With help from an economic development organization, in just a few years don Pablo has developed a colony of twenty trunks/hives, known as *jobones*, each hosting between 3,000 and 10,000 of the disappearing *melipona* bees. The government program is implementing experiments like this all over the peninsula in hopes of saving the bee while at the same time providing a viable income source for indigenous families and reestablishing ties to traditional practices.

Melipona bee honey is so rare that it commands a royal price for a small flask. This makes selling his *melipona* honey difficult for don Pablo; the marketing strategy that works best, he says, is to play up its purported medicinal value.

(above, left) Traditional beekeeping strategy: Cut down the section of tree where bees have made their hives and store it in the *solar*. [MR]
(above, middle) Maya bee god, also known as the "Descending God." [AUREA HERNÁNDEZ AFTER A POSTCLASSIC CERAMIC CENSER, MAYAPÁN] [COLECCIÓN DEL MUSEO REGIONAL DE ANTROPOLOGÍA E HISTORIA, MÉRIDA] *(above, right)* Beekeeper Pablo Dzib. [MC]

(opposite page) A female sentinel stands guard at the entrance to the hive to ward off invaders like ants. The carved cross demonstrates right side up because if logs are laid upside down, the bees will drown. [MC]

DULCE DE PAPAYA

PAPAYA IN BURNT-SUGAR AND HONEY GLAZE

FOR SOAKING THE PAPAYA

6½ lbs. (3 kg) green or underripe
   papaya, peeled and seeded

3½ oz. (100 g) calcium hydroxide
   ("slaked lime" or "pickling
   lime;" see Resources, p. 540)

FOR THE SYRUP

2 cups (400 g) sugar

1 lb. (500 g) *piloncillo*, chopped
   (Substitute: 2½ cups / 500 g dark
   brown sugar)

1 cup (250 ml) Mexican honey

2 cups (500 ml) water

2 tsp. (10 ml) Mexican vanilla
   extract

2 five-in. (13 cm) sticks *canela*
   (Mexican cinnamon)

10 allspice berries

5 whole cloves

Many local fruits and vegetables are preserved in honey or sugar syrup in Yucatán, but Dulce de papaya must be the most popular. When served with cubes of Edam cheese, as it usually is, it is reminiscent of the fruit and cheese course of a French meal. The complex blend of New World honey, fruit, and allspice with Old World spices and cheese is a defining feature of Yucatecan cuisine.

In Yucatán, papaya (*Carica papaya*, p. 47) is frequently consumed fresh, but preserving it in honey has long been a way of enjoying it beyond the fruit's shelf life. The burnt sugar is a postcontact addition. Yucatecan cooks soak the papaya in a solution of water and calcium hydroxide (slaked lime) prior to cooking in the syrup; the process transforms the texture of the fruit, keeping it soft on the inside yet firm on the outside so that it remains intact during cooking.

Prepare ahead note: Dulce de papaya should be prepared a day in advance and chilled overnight. It keeps well under refrigeration for 2–3 weeks.

Yield: 30 servings. Papayas in Yucatán are enormous, some the size of watermelons. The recipe that follows makes use of only one of our papayas. Further, since the sugar acts as a preservative, Dulce de papaya is typically prepared in quantities sufficient to last a family for a couple of weeks or more. Halve the recipe if you wish.

PREPARE AND SOAK PAPAYA

Cut the peeled papaya into small triangles by slicing it lengthwise into strips about ¾-inch (2 cm) wide. Lay one strip flat; at one end, make a diagonal cut, resulting in a small triangular piece. Reverse the diagonal and cut again to result in another triangle. Place the triangles in a stainless steel bowl and add water to cover. Mix the slaked lime with 1 cup (250 ml) water to dissolve, add to the papaya, and stir. (Note: Use only stainless steel or enameled utensils for all contact with the slaked lime. It will permanently alter the surface of glass, plastic, wood, and many other materials.) Allow the papaya to stand at room temperature for 1 hour. (Note: Longer soaking time can toughen the fruit.) Drain and rinse thoroughly several times to remove all traces of the slaked lime.

PREPARE SYRUP, COOK, AND FINISH

Place the sugar and *piloncillo* in a large, deep stockpot on high heat; cook, stirring constantly, until the sugars completely melt and darken, 6–8 minutes. Continue another 1–2 minutes or until the syrup begins to foam and smoke. Reduce the heat to low and very carefully stream in the honey, then the water; stand back since this can cause intense steam and splattering. Add the remaining syrup ingredients, stir to dissolve the honey and burnt sugar, and bring to a boil. Reduce the heat to a simmer and add the papaya. Partly cover the pot and cook at a gentle simmer for 1 hour. Remove the lid and push the papaya down to cover with the syrup. Cook, uncovered, 45 minutes. Check the papaya for tenderness. The syrup should coat the back of a spoon. If it does not, remove the papaya with a slotted spoon and boil the syrup until it coats a spoon.

Remove the pot from the heat and allow the syrup to cool. Transfer the papaya and syrup to a covered container and refrigerate.

TO SERVE

Bring the papaya to room temperature. Place the fruit on individual serving plates or bowls and top with some of the Edam.

VARIATIONS

You may also create other popular Yucatecan preserved-fruit desserts by following the master recipe. Many regional fruits like nance, *ciruela*, and *ciricote* can now be found frozen in some areas (see Resources, p. 540). Sweet potato and *yuca* are also popular. Omit soaking in calcium hydroxide; adjust sugar/water quantities for the amount of fruit you wish to preserve. Information on each fruit is available starting on page 19.

Dulce de calabaza (Pumpkin in Burnt-Sugar and Honey Glaze) is one of the traditional offerings to ancestors during Hanal Pixán (p. 429). It is usually cooked over a wood fire, giving it a lightly smoky flavor, but during the autumn rituals it is cooked *enterrada* ("buried," p. 418). Use unpeeled pumpkin or winter squash in the weight desired. Remove the seeds and cut the squash or pumpkin into large wedges (the traditional way here) or into bite-sized cubes or triangles instead and proceed as per the master recipe. For a true taste of Yucatán, lightly smoke the squash or pumpkin before cooking in the syrup. Soak the squash or pumpkin as directed in the master recipe, rinse, and drain thoroughly, then wrap very loosely in foil. Smoke with wood smoking chips following the instructions for gas or charcoal grills (Basic Techniques, p. 538). After smoking for 30 minutes, continue as directed in the master recipe.

Dulce de papaya and other sweetened fruits in the market. [MR]

Tajonal *blossom.* [JFMT]

YUCATECAN HONEY FLAVORS

Although many tropical trees and plants produce nectar collected by bees, the most common honey-producing florations come from two prominent plants.

Dzidzilché (Gymnopodium floribundum) is a plant unique to Yucatán and has no English name. It is a woody bush that from March through May produces a tiny pale green flower with a lightly sweet floral fragrance. *Dzidzilché* honey is pale amber in color, has an unmistakable tropical flavor and low moisture content, and is recognized among connoisseurs as one of the world's finest honeys.

Tajonal (Viguiera dentata), or "toothleaf goldeneye," is a member of the aster family. The genus occurs primarily in Mexico and South America and reaches its northern limit of distribution in the southwestern United States. *Tajonal* produces a bright yellow flower that covers the countryside from December through February. Traditional Mayas use its dried stalks and stems to make brooms and other household items. At 78.5 percent sugar content, it is Yucatán's sweetest honey. *Tajonal* honey is dark gold in color.

(opposite page) Altar at Hanal Pixán. [DS]

HUNUCMÁ

BURIED FOODS

Comida enterrada—or "buried food"—is the signature cooking method of Yucatán. Holes are dug, fires are lit, and whole sides of pork or other foods are laid to rest atop a bier of glowing embers. The resurrection happens when it's time to eat.

Hunucmá, a pueblo in northwest Yucatán, has acquired a reputation of being *the* place for the best Cochinita pibil, or pit-roasted pork, in all of Yucatán, and many families there are devoted to the art of *comida enterrada*.

THE MAYA *PÍIB*

The underground ovens where Yucatecan pit cooking happens are known in Mayan as *píib* (sometimes spelled *pib*);

dishes prepared in them acquire the descriptor "*pibil*." Anything and everything may be cooked *pibil*-style, from meats and fowl to tamales and pots of beans. The method is simple: a hole is dug, a pile of firewood is stacked in the pit, and stones are placed on top. The fire is lit and burns

(above) Don Felipe spreads fragrant branches on top of buried food before covering the whole thing with soil. [MC]

(left) A side of pork marinated in achiote and covered with ja'abin *leaves is ready for the* píib. [MC] *(right) Unearthing the* píib. [DS]

for about an hour; at the end of this "preheating" time, the firewood and the stones have collapsed to the bottom of the pit. Any coals still burning are removed; foods are cooked not by flames but by the white-hot stones. Wrapped meats or pots of foods are lowered into the pit, and a covering of branches is put in place and sealed completely closed with a few shovels full of soil.

Since the 1990s, Felipe Humberto Méndez Quintal has supported his family with his *comida enterrada* business in Hunucmá. He learned the art from his father, and together they have built a "vertically integrated" operation that includes a battery of pens housing pigs, turkeys, and chickens. Income spikes during the busy Hanal Pixán season (October 31–November 2), when the demand for a pit-baked *tamal*, Mucbilpollo, keeps the family working twenty-four hours a day.

The ample terrain that stretches behind the family house has a roofed area sheltering ten *píibs* so that the family can deliver *comida enterrada* to their customers rain or shine.

As sacred as going to mass, eating a *torta* of Cochinita pibil or Lechón al horno is a Sunday morning ritual in Yucatán. So Saturdays are hectic for Felipe's family: pigs are slaughtered early in the morning; meats are marinated for several hours; giant tins full of the meat are buried by 2:00 pm; and at 4:00 am Sunday morning they are unearthed and taken to market.

"BURIED FOODS" IN THE HOME KITCHEN

As I began to translate a true taste of Yucatán for the home kitchen beyond Mexico, it quickly became clear to me that I faced a unique challenge: how to prepare *pibil* dishes, Yucatán's most characteristic food, when I could scarcely expect people to dig holes in their backyards. I analyzed what to me were the essential elements of the *píib* environment that gave these foods their unique flavors. There were three immediate answers: (1) smoke, (2) steam, and (3) leaves. Branches of any number of regional trees (particularly the *ja'abin*) are placed in the pit along with the food; gradually, they begin to smolder from the intense heat of the stones, producing smoke. The juices of the meat or the liquids of the stocks evaporate, producing steam. And the banana leaves in which most *pibil* foods are wrapped add a light herbaceous taste. Putting all this together, it occurred to me that the stovetop smoking method could meet all the criteria: a sealed environment full of intense heat, steam, and smoke. The method achieves flavors very similar to those of the *píib*, although you may also use a charcoal or gas grill effectively. All methods are described in Basic Techniques on page 537.

COCHINITA PIBIL

PIT-SMOKED PORK IN *ACHIOTE* MARINADE

FOR THE MARINADE

8 Tbs. (120 g) Recado rojo

4–8 Tbs. (60–120 ml) Seville
orange juice, or substitute

2 Tbs. (28 g) Enriched Lard

2 tsp. (12 g) sea salt

2 lb. (1 k) pork rump or leg,
with fat, brined

FOR GARNISHING AND WRAPPING

3 oz. (85 g) smoked bacon, thickly
sliced (optional)

½ medium white onion (5 oz.
/ 137.5 g), thinly sliced and
separated into rings

1 medium green bell pepper
(6½ oz. / 185 g), seeded and
thinly sliced into rings

1 medium Roma tomato (3½ oz. /
100 g), thinly sliced across the
width

1 bunch fresh epazote, separated
into leaves (Substitute: about
1 tsp. / 1.5 g dried epazote)

Avocado leaves or bay leaves
(optional)

The most "real" Cochinita pibil in the peninsula employs the whole pig: leg, loin, and rump, yes, but also liver, head, ears, and tail. Most vendors today, though, use just *pierna*, or "leg." I have modernized the traditional recipe by brining the pork for a few hours. And to lend an even smokier flavor and more juicy fat, I suggest placing a few thick slices of smoked slab bacon on top of the meat; as it cooks, it will render smoky fat onto the pork for a lovely result. Since this is not traditional in Yucatán, I list it as an option.

Prepare ahead note: Cochinita pibil is best served immediately. Leftovers can be reheated in the cooking juices, so be sure to save them.

YIELD: 10 SERVINGS

PREPARE MARINADE

Dilute the *recado* with the orange juice; if you made your own *recado*, add only enough juice to create a thick yet pourable liquid, rather like barbecue sauce. Add the lard and salt and stir to incorporate. (Note: If you are using commercial *recado*, you will achieve better results if you enrich it as described in Pantry Staples, p. 500.)

Remove the meat from the brine, rinse, and pat dry; discard the brining solution. Place the meat in a resealable plastic bag or large baking dish and cover completely with the marinade. (Your hands are the best tools for this job.) Marinate under refrigeration at least 30 minutes or up to 12 hours.

GARNISH AND WRAP PORK

Arrange large pieces of banana leaf on a work surface, overlapping to avoid leaks. Place the marinated meat in the center of the leaves and garnish the top with slices of bacon (if using), onion, bell pepper, tomato, epazote, and avocado leaves or bay leaves (in that order). Fold the sides of the banana leaves up and over, then tuck in the ends, wrapping the meat as you would a package. Tie with the reserved ribs from the leaves or kitchen twine. Allow the meat to come to room temperature before proceeding with one of the following cooking methods:

- Stovetop smoking method (p. 537)
- Charcoal grill smoking method (p. 538)
- Gas grill smoking method (p. 538)

SMOKE MEAT AND FINISH

Cook the meat until it reaches an internal temperature of 145°F (63°C). (Note: Cooking time will vary according to the size and cut of meat you choose, but you should allow at least 1 hour.) Remove the meat and allow it to rest 10–15 minutes prior to carving or using in another recipe.

FOR SERVING

Cebollas encurtidas (p. 510)

Tortillas (p. 518) or Pan francés
  (p. 194)

Chile tamulado or Chile con
  limón (p. 509), or the chile sauce
  of your choice

TO SERVE

In Yucatán, Cochinita pibil is typically "pulled," that is, shredded or torn into small pieces, then briefly baptized in the cooking juices. Create tacos by placing bits of meat onto warm tortillas and topping with pickled onions. But perhaps the most popular way to eat Cochinita in the peninsula is as a *torta*: cut Pan francés (p. 194) in half across the width, then slice each half lengthwise. Dip the cut sides of the bread in the cooking juices. Fill the *torta* with pork and garnish with pickled onions.

VARIATIONS

You may follow the lead of some contemporary restaurants by serving hefty hunks of Cochinita pibil as a fully plated main course, with accompanying rice and beans.

For an elegant if nontraditional presentation at the table, use a crown rib of pork. Wrap and garnish as directed in the master recipe, or use thick-cut pork chops with as much fat and bone still intact as possible. Reduce brining time accordingly, and take care during cooking, since thinner cuts dry out more quickly.

Pollo pibil (Pit-Smoked Chicken in *Achiote* Marinade): This makes for an entertaining presentation at a dinner party. Serve the chicken breasts still wrapped in banana leaves. Guests unwrap their own, then pass a bowl around the table to collect discarded leaves. Follow the master recipe for Cochinita pibil substituting 6–8 chicken breast halves, with bone and skin, brined, or enough drumsticks or mixed thighs and legs to serve the number of diners. (See Basic Techniques, p. 536, for brining instructions.) Proceed with the rest of the recipe, omitting the bacon and wrapping each breast in large (L) banana leaves, prepared per instructions on page 525. Cook approximately 45 minutes to 1 hour to an internal temperature of 165°F / 74°C. Remove the chicken from the heat and allow to rest 10–15 minutes prior to serving. Serve plated with rice and beans and accompanied by Cebollas encurtidas and chile sauce.

Pibil de venado / Venado en píib / Píibil kéej (Pit-Smoked Venison in *Achiote* Marinade): Hunting restrictions in Yucatán limit access to wild deer, leading chefs to get creative with ingredients. Although certain deer species are now being farmed, beef is a frequent substitute. Follow the master recipe for Cochinita pibil, replacing the pork with 2 pounds (1 k) venison top round or tenderloin, brined. (See Basic Techniques, p. 536, for brining instructions; substitute: beef loin, without brining.) (Note: If using unbrined beef, increase the salt in the marinade to 1 tablespoon.) Proceed as directed in the master recipe and cook to an internal temperature of 134°F (57°C) for medium-rare, the recommended finish for venison to prevent its becoming too dry. If you will be using the meat for Venado en pipián rojo (p. 96) or K'óol de venado (p. 87), cook until very rare at an internal temperature of 120°F (48°C) since it will finish cooking in the stew. If you will be using the meat for the shredded salad known as Tsi'ik de venado, cook the meat to medium-well at an internal temperature of 150–55°F (66–68°C).

Tsi'ik de venado (Chopped Vegetable and Venison "Cobb Salad"): Salads of chopped vegetables and shredded meat rather like Cobb salad are very common in Yucatán. Chicharra en salpicón (p. 212) is a classic example. The grandfather of all these mixtures must surely be Tsi'ik de venado. "*Tsi'ik*" in Mayan means simply "to shred, unravel, or tear apart." After roasting in the *píib*, venison is shredded then mixed with chopped vegetables. Other meats may be used instead (see below). Tsi'ik is usually served at room temperature with warm tortillas. Use a tortilla to grab a fistful, or more delicately spoon some onto the tortilla before folding and eating. It also makes a beautiful salad served chilled atop bibb or romaine lettuce leaves and accompanied by sliced avocado and lime wedges. Tsi'ik is a good way of using leftover meat. Prepare the meat component, whether venison, beef, turkey, or chicken, a day in advance and use part for a main meal. Shred the rest and refrigerate. (Note: Meat shreds more easily before refrigeration.) When ready to serve Tsi'ik, chop the vegetables and assemble the salad, reserving the juice, salt, and cilantro until moments before serving to reduce wilting. Mix 1 recipe Salpicón (p. 511) with approximately 2 cups (about 250 g) shredded meat.

Tsi'ik de pollo asado (Chopped Vegetable and Grilled Chicken "Cobb Salad"): You can also use shredded Pollo asado (p. 270) or any cooked meat for Tsi'ik with excellent results.

Tsi'ik de langosta (Chopped Vegetable and Lobster "Cobb Salad"): Sonja Lillvik of Punta Allen in Quintana Roo does a delicious version of Tsi'ik using lobster. Yours can be boiled, steamed, or grilled.

Tsi'ik de carne ahumada (Chopped Vegetable and Smoked Pork "Cobb Salad"): Maruja Barbachano of La Taberna de los Frailes in Valladolid makes a unique regional version using locally smoked Carne ahumada (p. 478).

Tsi'ik de venado. [EC]

(left) Cleaning turkeys for Pavo en relleno negro. [JFMT] *(right) A group of men preparing quantities of Pavo en relleno negro in a píib for a village festival.* [MIPA]

As Felipe busied himself with marinating an entire pig half for Cochinita pibil, the other for Lechón al horno, his mother, doña María Candelaria Quintal Cetina, walked me through the steps of another of their popular "buried" dishes, Pavo en relleno negro. Once a ceremonial food, this smoky turkey cooked with meatloaf in a pitch-black, charred chile sauce is now commonplace throughout the peninsula. Nonetheless, seeing it prepared in a *píib* evokes its primal origins and profound symbolism.

BURIED BLACK TURKEY: THE SUN AT NIGHT

Pavo en relleno negro is not merely a popular Yucatecan dish, it is also chock full of rich symbolism for the Maya people, expressing the archetypes of life and death. The traditional way of preparing the stuffing for the turkey is to boil eggs and separate the whites from the yolks; a ground meat mixture stained pitch black with the Recado negro (p. 501) is then formed into balls around the yolk, and the balls are subsequently stuffed inside the cavity of the turkey. The turkey is submerged in water flavored and colored with the black *recado*, then buried in the *píib* to cook. Diners receive slices of the turkey and the meatloaf with its contrasting colors of the blackness of night and the yellow of the sun all bathed in graphite-colored gravy.

To the Mayas, this gravy is *sangre negra*, "black blood." In Maya cosmology, black is the feminine, the color of death, and a signal of illness. For this reason, the Mayas always include a bit of Recado rojo (p. 500), the earthy color of *achiote*, to balance the *sangre negra* with the living color of red blood. The eggs inside the turkey are considered masculine, the symbol of life. The turkey itself is the Mother: she is buried in black death then resurrected, returning life to the people. In this way, Pavo en relleno negro is thought of as a "dish of the night sun."

PAVO EN RELLENO NEGRO / BOOX BUUT'IL TSO'

CHARCOAL-GRILLED TURKEY AND MINCEMEAT STUFFING IN CHARRED CHILE SAUCE

TO PREPARE AHEAD

Recado negro (p. 501)

Seville orange juice substitute (p. 514), unless fresh Seville oranges are available

Enriched Lard (p. 513)

Brined turkey (see Basic Techniques, p. 536)

Picadillo de especias (p. 256)

Recado rojo (p. 500)

Masa prepared from either nixtamalized corn or *masa harina* (p. 517)

FOR THE MARINADE

8 Tbs. (120 g) Recado negro

½ cup (125 ml) Seville orange juice, or substitute

2 Tbs. (28 g) Enriched lard, melted

1 Tbs. (2 g) dried whole Mexican oregano *and* 1 tsp. (3 g) cuminseed, both lightly toasted in a small skillet

1 tsp. (4 g) whole black peppercorns

4 medium cloves garlic (1 oz. / 24 g), peeled and charred

1 Tbs. (18 g) sea salt

3 lbs. (1.5 k) turkey pieces, brined

FOR THE *BUUT'*

½ recipe Picadillo de especias (1¾ lbs. / 800 g)

2 Tbs. (30 g) Recado negro

2 Tbs. (30 ml) water

4 hard-boiled eggs, peeled, yolks and whites separated

The preparation of Pavo en relleno negro, originally a feast food, was traditionally a labor shared by the community. Amazingly, however, nowadays it is prepared and served every day of the week, in market stalls and at *cocinas económicas*. The ingredients list and steps for this recipe may seem overwhelming, and in fact it does require the strategizing of a Thanksgiving feast. Streamline the workflow by spending a couple of hours a day in advance to prepare the components; finish on the day you plan to serve. Today, it is rare for cooks to fill the turkey with the egg yolk–stuffed meatballs, known as *buut'* in Mayan ("stuffing"). Instead, the meatballs (curiously, rather like Scotch eggs) are gently lowered into the stock in which the turkey is cooking, then retrieved and sliced for serving. The pitch-black, maize-thickened sauce that creates the backdrop for the turkey and *buut'* is known as *Boox k'óol* and is one of four such colored sauces typical of Maya cuisine (see p. 86). This recipe specifies only 3 pounds (1.5 k) of turkey pieces; you can easily scale up to use a half or whole bird for a larger group.

Prepare ahead note: The *buut'* can be prepared in advance and refrigerated or frozen. The finished dish reheats well and can be made a day ahead.

YIELD: 8 SERVINGS

MARINATE AND GRILL TURKEY

Dilute the *recado* with the orange juice. Add the lard to the mixture and stir to incorporate. Using a mortar and pestle or a spice grinder adapted to the purpose, grind the oregano, cuminseed, peppercorns, garlic, and salt to a paste. Transfer the spices to the *recado* mixture and stir to combine. Add a bit more juice or *recado* to get the right texture: thick yet pourable, like barbecue sauce.

Remove the turkey from the brine, rinse, and pat dry; discard the brining solution. Place the turkey in a resealable plastic bag or in a large baking dish and coat thoroughly with the marinade. (Your hands are the best tools for this job.) Allow the turkey to marinate under refrigeration at least 30 minutes or overnight.

Preheat a gas or charcoal grill; follow the instructions in Basic Techniques (p. 538) for the use of wood smoking chips. Remove the turkey from the marinade, reserving any extra marinade. Grill the turkey with the lid closed until it acquires some charring and grill marks; it should not be fully cooked, and there should still be some pink juices flowing. Remove the turkey and set aside.

PREPARE *BUUT'*

While the turkey is cooking, place the Picadillo de especias in a large mixing bowl. Dissolve the *recado* in the water and strain the mixture directly into the mixing bowl through a sieve lined with cheesecloth. Squeeze out as much liquid as possible and

FOR THE *SOFRITO*

FOR THE *SOFRITO*

2 Tbs. (28 g) Enriched Lard

1 medium onion (10 oz. / 275 g), charred and finely chopped

4 medium cloves garlic (1 oz. / 24 g), charred and finely chopped

3 medium Roma tomatoes (10½ oz. / 300 g), charred and coarsely chopped

1 Tbs. (2 g) dried whole Mexican oregano, lightly toasted and ground

1 sprig fresh epazote (Substitute: ½ tsp. / .75 g dried, crumbled)

FOR THE STOCK

9 cups (2.25 L) *plus* 1 cup (250 ml) water

1 medium head garlic (1¾ oz. / 50 g), charred, peeled, separated into cloves

5 Tbs. (75 g) Recado negro

1 Tbs. (15 g) Recado rojo

2 Tbs. (24 g) powdered chicken bouillon, or 2 bouillon cubes

1 chile chipotle in adobo (⅓ oz. / 10 g), drained

(continued on next page)

discard anything that doesn't pass through the cheesecloth. Finely chop the whites of the boiled eggs and add to the meat mixture; combine thoroughly.

Separate the *buut'* into 4 equal-sized balls, each weighing about 7 ounces (200 g). Working with 1 ball at a time, insert a finger into the side to create a cavity. Place one of the cooked yolks inside, toward the center, then cover it with meat and reshape it into a meatball. Repeat with the remaining meat and yolks. Refrigerate until ready to use.

PREPARE *SOFRITO*

Heat the lard in a large stockpot until shimmering. Add the onions and garlic and cook until the onion is translucent. Add the tomatoes and herbs and cook 5 minutes, or until most of the liquid from the tomatoes has evaporated.

PREPARE STOCK

Place the grilled turkey in the stockpot containing the *sofrito*. (Note: Depending on the pieces you use, you may need to cut the turkey into smaller sections so that it can be completely submerged in the stock.) Add 9 cups (2.25 L) water and any reserved marinade and bring to a boil, then reduce to a simmer. Place the remaining 1 cup (250 ml) of water and the rest of the ingredients in the jar of a blender and process until thoroughly liquefied. Pour the contents of the blender into the stockpot through a sieve lined with cheesecloth. Mash through and squeeze the cheesecloth to extract as much of the liquid as possible; discard the residue.

Gently lower the meatballs into the simmering stock, return to a boil, reduce to a simmer, and cook 30 minutes, or until the turkey and meatballs are cooked through.

Two buried foods appear in the market as toppings for salbutes: *Pavo en relleno negro (left) and Cochinita pibil (right).* [MR]

FOR FINISHING THE SAUCE
2 Tbs. (30 g) Recado negro
¾ cup (170 g) *masa*

FOR SERVING
Cebollas encurtidas (p. 510)
Chile tamulado (p. 509)
Tortillas (p. 518)

(The turkey should reach an internal temperature of 165°F / 74°C, and the meatballs will float to the surface.)

FINISH THE SAUCE

Carefully remove the meats and set them aside. Strain the cooking liquid through a sieve lined with cheesecloth into a smaller stockpot; mash and squeeze through as much cooking liquid as you can and discard the residue. You should have about 8 cups (2 L) of stock; discard or reserve any extra for another use.

Dissolve the *recado* in 1 cup (250 ml) of the cooking liquid. Pour the mixture through a sieve lined with cheesecloth back into the stockpot; discard the residue. Bring the cooking liquid to a rapid boil and cook 8–10 minutes to reduce slightly.

Mix 1 cup (250 ml) cooking liquid with the *masa* and beat until well incorporated. Transfer the *masa* mixture to the cooking liquid, return it to a boil, reduce heat to a simmer, and whisk constantly until the *masa* is thoroughly incorporated. Simmer 10 minutes, or until the cooking liquid is slightly thickened, whisking occasionally to prevent lumps. (Note: If lumps do form, use an immersion blender to smooth.)

TO SERVE

Carve or pull the turkey meat off the bones into serving portions and place in shallow soup bowls or deep plates. Cut the meatballs in half and place a half in each bowl. Ladle 1 cup (250 ml) of the black sauce into each bowl and garnish with pickled onions. Diners use tortillas to make tacos, heaping on the turkey, meatloaf, gravy, onions, and chile sauce to taste before folding and eating.

VARIATION

Pavo en relleno blanco / Sak buut'il tso' (Charcoal-Grilled Turkey and Mincemeat Stuffing in Maize-Thickened White Sauce): This traditional feast dish is the twin of Pavo en relleno negro, but features a subtle white sauce (*sak k'óol*) instead of the pungent black sauce. You may find Pavo en relleno blanco served at weddings or on special occasions such as Christmas. For the turkey, stock, and sauce, follow the recipe for Pavo en sak k'óol on page 140; form meatballs as described in the recipe for Pavo en relleno negro, omitting the Recado negro; cook as described in this recipe using the stock prepared for Pavo en sak k'óol. When meats are done, strain and thicken stock and serve as instructed in the recipe for Pavo en sak k'óol, placing a halved meatball with each serving.

(opposite page) Pavo en relleno negro cooked in a píib, freshly disinterred, and ready to eat. [MC]

FEAST OF THE SPIRITS

The Maya harvest festival known as Hanal Pixán, or "Feast of the Spirits", poetically combines food and death in an ancient ritual in which ancestors are revered, foods are buried then resurrected, and everyone living and dead alike gets plenty to eat.

Coinciding with north-of-the-border Halloween and Mexico's Día de los Muertos, Hanal Pixán is a particularly Yucatecan autumnal rite. The Spanish observed that Hanal Pixán occupied a week when it was believed that departed ancestors came back to earth. If the souls were propitiated with properly prepared and delicious foods, they returned to the other world for another year, leaving the living alone.

Hanal Pixán Meals

October 31 marks the first celebration with a day of feasting for the "child souls," or *chichan pixán*. Breakfast consists of *atole nuevo* (a porridge made with fresh maize) and freshly boiled corn on the cob. Cookies, sweet rolls, and hot Chocolate (p. 464) complete the meal. For the midday meal, the preferred dish is chicken and vegetable stew, with sweetened *yuca* or papaya as dessert. The evening meal is more frugal: Vaporcitos (tiny tamales, p. 104), bread, and chocolate milk. On the dining table are placed various children's trinkets and treats, such as clay whistles, tops, and honey candies.

November 1 is celebrated with the feast of the "adult souls," or *noboch pixán*. Breakfast and dinner are similar to those for children, but the midday meal is more robust, with dishes like Pavo en escabeche oriental (Soused Turkey Stewed in Onions and Chiles, p. 389) or Pavo en relleno negro (p. 424). A bowl of water is left near the dining table so that the spirits can wash their hands. Rum or the honey-anise liqueur Xtabentún (p. 289) is always nearby for those spirits who wish to imbibe.

November 2 is nowadays celebrated as All Souls Day, borrowed from Catholic rites. All of the feasts are characterized by flowers, gourds full of chocolate, and the ubiquitous Mucbilpollo (p. 430) a kind of giant *tamal*. On the eighth day, a variety of tamales is served, and the spirits begin to depart, carrying with them their take-away meals.

For these feasts, certain rules must be followed. All foods must be cooked in a *píib* (p. 418). And only hens may be cooked, because roosters may crow and scare away the otherworldly visitors.

(opposite page) Family altars are beautifully decorated and foods are served to ancestors during Hanal Pixán. [MR]

MUCBILPOLLO / MUUKBI'KAAX / PIBIPOLLO

LARGE BAKED FESTIVAL TAMAL WITH CHICKEN FILLING

TO PREPARE AHEAD

Pollo asado (p. 270) *or* Cochinita pibil (p. 420) or ½ recipe of each

K'óol rojo (p. 86)

Banana leaves, prepared for the extra-large (XL) size per instructions in Basic Techniques, p. 525, ribs reserved

Masa para tamales yucatecos (p. 522), using *masa* prepared from either nixtamalized corn or *masa harina*

FOR THE FILLING

K'óol rojo and your choice of meat (see above)

FOR THE TAMALES

1 recipe Masa para tamales yucatecos

1½ cups (250 g) x'pelones (Substitute: black-eyed peas), parboiled until just tender, drained

The defining dish of *comida enterrada* must surely be Mucbilpollo, which translates literally to "buried chicken" (*muuk* in Mayan and *pollo* in Spanish; *kaax* is Mayan for hen). It is another of Yucatán's super-sized tamales. Although it can be as small as a dinner plate, it more typically boasts an impressive square yard and larger. Whole chicken pieces and sometimes chunks of pork are stewed in *achiote* gravy, pushed deep into mounds of *masa*, then shrouded in banana leaves before being buried in the *píib*. The black *x'pelon* beans are plentiful in late fall and appear in the diminutive *tamal*, Vaporcitos de x'pelon (p. 107), a junior-sized companion to Mucbilpollo, but increasingly they are incorporated into the *masa* for this large *tamal*, too. In pueblo festivities, once cooked, the Mucbilpollo is ritualistically disinterred or resurrected by a *x'men*, Maya priest. It is still a traditional courtesy to share slices of Mucbilpollo with neighbors and even strangers.

Much as at Thanksgiving north of the border, a feeding frenzy erupts in Yucatán around the end of October, as families and businesses place their orders for "*pibipollos*" or "*pibes*," nicknames for Mucbilpollos. During the three-day period, trucks can be seen completing deliveries, pulling up to private homes and restaurants, their beds laden with trays full of the fragrant tamales still wrapped in their burnt leaf vestments. The prize of a well-baked Mucbilpollo is the crispy, jaw-breaking crust around the edges, still clinging to a bit of warm *masa* sodden with heady, bright red *achiote* gravy and a snippet of chicken or pork nestled in there somewhere. I have heard many a Yucatecan complain if the *masa* wasn't crispy enough, so that becomes an important goal of this recipe. Mucbilpollo is traditionally accompanied by T'anchukwa' (p. 466), a warm maize porridge flavored with chocolate and spices.

Prepare ahead note: All of the components for Mucbilpollo can be prepared several days ahead and frozen, or one day ahead and refrigerated. Similarly, you can prepare and wrap both of the large tamales a day in advance, refrigerate, then bake on the day you plan to serve.

YIELD: 2 LARGE TAMALES, EACH SERVING 5–6

PREPARE FILLING

Follow the directions for making K'óol rojo, using your choice of grilled meat (Pollo asado, Cochinita pibil, or a combination). When the meat has thoroughly cooked in the stock, remove it, allow it to cool, then shred it; you should have approximately 4 cups (510 g) shredded meat. Finish by thickening the K'óol as instructed. Set the sauce and meat aside as you continue.

FORM TAMALES

Preheat the oven to 350°F (176°C). Working with 8 sections of the prepared banana leaves, create 2 squares measuring about 20 inches × 20 inches (50 cm × 50 cm). Place

2 medium Roma tomatoes
   (7 oz. / 200 g), thinly sliced
½ medium white onion
   (5 oz. / 137.5 g), thinly sliced
   and separated into rings
1 sprig fresh epazote (Substitute:
   flat-leaf parsley)

2 of the leaves on a flat work surface, overlapping 1 inch (2.5 cm) along the length. Lay the other 2 banana leaves on top, running perpendicular to the first two. (This double strength will help hold the *tamal* together during baking.) Repeat with the remaining leaves to create a second square.

Place the *masa* in a large mixing bowl. Add the beans and use your hands to knead them into the dough. Divide the *masa* in half and pat it into 2 balls with which you will be forming 2 "pies." Separate one-third of the *masa* from each ball and pat both pieces into smaller balls; these will ultimately serve as the tops of the pies. Center the larger ball on 1 of the squares of banana leaves and pat into a tortilla measuring about 11 inches (28 cm) in diameter and ½ inch (1 cm) thick. Pinch up the edges to form thick, vertical walls around the circumference, creating something resembling a pie without a pie pan. When you finish, the resulting circle will have reduced to 8 inches (20 cm) in diameter. On waxed paper or a spare banana leaf, pat the smaller ball into a flat circle the same diameter as the walled circle; this will be the top of the pie. Repeat these steps with the remaining *masa* to create a second pie.

GARNISH AND BAKE

Use half of the shredded chicken and/or pork to fill one of the pies and pat down to compact. Pour on about 1 cup (250 ml) of the K'óol rojo, cover with the *masa* "lid," and seal the edges. Cup your hands and gently pat around the circumference of the *tamal* to compact the ingredients and give it a round shape. Garnish the top with tomato and onion slices, arranging them in a decorative pattern, and finish with a few leaves of epazote. Fold the edges of the banana leaves over the top of the *tamal*, tuck edges

An assortment of tamales baked in a píib. [DS]

K'óol rojo left over from assembly

Chile k'uut (p. 508)

T'anchukwa' (p. 466), suggested
   accompaniment

in, and tie securely with reserved banana leaf ribs or kitchen twine. Use enough ties to hold the package completely closed. Repeat.

Place the tamales on baking sheets, bake for 45 minutes, then invert each *tamal*. Bake another 45 minutes, or until a knife inserted in the center comes out clean. To make sure that the crust is crisp, gently open the banana leaves on the side of one *tamal* to check. Tap the *masa*; top, bottom, and sides should be very firm to the touch.

TO SERVE

Turn the Mucbilpollos right side up and place them on large serving platters. Open the banana leaves and slice at the table. Alternatively, slice the Mucbilpollos into wedges and place on individual serving plates. Serve with the remaining K'óol rojo and chile to taste. Accompany with T'anchukwa' if desired.

VARIATIONS

For an authentic smoky flavor, bake the Mucbilpollos in a charcoal or gas grill following the instructions for using wood smoking chips on page 538. Baking time may vary; check the tamales as described above to test for doneness.

Chachacuahes (Miniature Chicken and Pork Tamal Pies): These are individual-sized versions of Mucbilpollo. Because of their convenient size, they are an excellent dinner option, especially when served with another Hanal Pixán favorite: Xek' (p. 228), a refreshing salad of crispy jicama and mandarin oranges. The spelling for the name as given here is a common if rather sloppy transliteration of "*chanchakwaah*," Mayan for "little red bread." Follow the master recipe for Mucbilpollo, but make the pies smaller. Divide the prepared *masa* into 10 balls, each weighing about 5½ oz. (160 g). Work with banana leaves cut to the medium (M) size. Form the base of each pie into an approximately 5-inch (13 cm) circle. Pinch up the edges, fill each with approximately 2 ounces (52 g) of the shredded meat and some sauce, and seal with the top as instructed. Garnish, wrap, and bake (or cook in a gas or charcoal grill) per the master recipe. Serve unopened Chachacuahes on individual plates with the suggested accompaniments.

(opposite page) Panucheria La Susana del Oriente in Kanasín. [MR]

KANASÍN

In an effort to stay competitive, some vendors have taken to making panuchos *in awesome proportions.* [MR]

NEXUS OF YUCATECAN TACOS

The little village of Kanasín has acquired a patina of fame, at least among Yucatecans, for having the most delicious *panuchos* in the region, and people come from miles around, especially on Saturday evenings, to hang out in the park and visit any one of dozens of *panucherías* for a snack before going to a party or to the movies. It's a tradition that goes back at least to the mid-twentieth century, when it was common to see young lovers, always accompanied by the girl's older female chaperone, sitting outdoors and sharing two or three rounds of *panuchos* among the three of them.

PANUCHO DEFINED

The *panuchos* of yesteryear evolved in the hands of house-wives and cooks who wanted to make use of leftovers, most notably, Frijol colado and Cebollas encurtidas. The hollow of a tortilla was filled with the puréed beans, a sliver of boiled egg was slipped inside, then the whole was fried before being topped with a modest clump of pickled onions. The Mayan name says it all: Waaj ixi'im yéetel bu'ul (maize bread with beans). Since its origins, the *panucho* has undergone many fashion changes, including a period in which it was topped with Pavo en escabeche. Today, just about any shredded meat will appear as a topping, but the bean filling and pickled onion garnish remain unchanged.

Although the *panucho* probably originated in the late nineteenth century, it did not emerge into the public realm until the early twentieth century, when the first *panucherías*, or *panucho* shops, began to appear. The most venerated was for many years La Flor de Mayo, located in an old mansion on the Camino Real to Campeche in Mérida's San Sebastián, the parish said to be the birthplace of the *panucho*.

SALBUTES DEFINED

Another gastronomical innovation devised to repurpose leftovers, the original *salbut* made use of yesterday's Puchero (p. 350), a stew of chicken, beef, or pork and several varieties of vegetable. On subsequent days, leftover meats and vegetables were mashed together to form a mixture known in Mayan as "*puuch*'," then the mash was heaped on a fresh uncooked tortilla, another one was placed on top, and the edges were pressed together before being toasted on a comal.

Today, the *salbut* bears but a faint resemblance to its ancestor. The current incarnation features a previously uncooked tortilla that is plopped into hot oil, where it instantly inflates and turns golden brown. The top of the resulting crispy pillow is punched down, and the hollow is adorned with a variety of toppings.

Salbutes. [MR]

FOR *PANUCHOS*

2 cups (500 g) *masa*

1 cup (250 ml) Frijol colado
  "espeso"

FOR *SALBUTES*

2 cups (500 g) *masa*

¼ cup (31.25 g) all-purpose flour

½ tsp. (3 g) sea salt

1 Tbs. (15 ml) water

TO FINISH AND GARNISH
PANUCHOS OR *SALBUTES*

Vegetable oil for frying

Leaves of romaine or Bibb lettuce
  (optional)

Your choice of meat, as above,
  shredded

Cebollas encurtidas, or the onions
  from Pavo en escabeche oriental

Slices of Roma tomatoes
  (optional)

Slices of avocado (optional)

Slices of pickled jalapeño
  (optional)

PANUCHOS AND SALBUTES
YUCATECAN-STYLE TACOS

Panuchos and *salbutes* may appear similar when you see them at *taquerías*, but to Yucatecans, they are worlds apart, and party lines are drawn according to one's favorite. So how do you know which is which? You'll recognize the *panucho* by the dark coloring of the beans visible through the surface; and the golden puffiness and collapsed top of the *salbut* is always easy to spot. The recipes for both tacos are similar, the significant difference being the specifics for the tortilla base of each. Recipes yield about 15 servings, and if you prefer, you can split the recipe between *panuchos* and *salbutes* for variety.

Prepare ahead note: Every component of these tacos can and should be made well in advance and refrigerated or frozen. You can even fill the *panuchos* with the beans, freeze them in a stack, and then fry without defrosting. Once fried and assembled, however, *panuchos* and *salbutes* do not keep well and should be eaten immediately.

YIELD: APPROXIMATELY 15 PANUCHOS OR SALBUTES

FORM *PANUCHOS*

Follow the instructions in Basic Techniques on page 520 for making Tortillas para panuchos. (Note: If your tortillas are stubborn and don't inflate, you can fry them and smear the beans on top just before finishing with the garnishes.) Open a slit in the side as instructed, and set aside as you finish the other tortillas.

Fill each tortilla with about 1 tablespoon (15 g) Frijol colado. Spoon beans all the way to the end opposite the slit, then use your fingertips to press and mash outward and from side to side to spread the beans evenly within. Set aside until you finish filling all of the tortillas.

FORM *SALBUTES*

Mix the ingredients to create a stiff dough. Using a tortilla press, form tortillas per the instructions in Basic Techniques on page 520. Fry each tortilla as directed below immediately after forming it.

FRY, GARNISH, AND SERVE

Pour 1½ inches (4 cm) oil into a large skillet and heat to 350°F (176°C).

For Panuchos: Working 2–3 at a time, fry the bean-filled tortillas in the hot oil until golden brown. Baste the tops to crisp them rather than turning them (the moisture from the beans makes them fragile). Remove and drain in a colander or on paper towels.

For Salbutes: Carefully slide each pressed, raw tortilla into the hot oil. When the tortilla inflates, flip it to cook the other side. When golden brown, remove and drain in a colander or on paper towels.

FOR SERVING
Chile tamulado, or the chile sauce
of your choice

Top *panuchos* or *salbutes* with a leaf of lettuce, if using, some shredded meat, a slice of tomato, and a mound of Cebollas encurtidas (Cebollas en escabeche if using Pavo en escabeche oriental), in that order. Garnish with avocado, if using, and/or jalapeño.

TO SERVE

Arrange the *panuchos* or *salbutes* on a large platter or on individual serving plates and serve immediately. Diners add their own chile sauce to taste.

VARIATION

Panuchos campechanos (Campeche-Style Dogfish Tacos): To prepare this unique taco variant, it is not necessary to open the hollow of the tortilla; instead, spread one side of each of two cooked tortillas with a spoonful of Frijol colado. Place a heaping tablespoon of Cazón frito (p. 312) in the center of the beans on one of the tortillas. Place the two tortillas together with the beans facing inward and press to seal. Fry as instructed above, holding the taco under the oil with a spatula until crisp. Top with Cebollas encurtidas.

HORCHATA

INFUSION OF GROUND RICE, ALMONDS, AND CINNAMON

FOR THE INFUSION

1¼ cups (265 g) long-grain white rice
1¼ cups (215 g) raw unsalted almonds, blanched
1 five-in. (12 cm) stick *canela* (Mexican cinnamon)
6 allspice berries
½ oz. (14 g) lime peel, in strips
4 cups (1 L) water, hot but not boiling

(continued on next page)

In Yucatán, the traditional beverage with which to wash down your *panuchos* and *salbutes* has long been Horchata, a refreshing white-as-milk but nondairy beverage of rice and almonds. Although Horchata arrived in Mexico from Spain, it has been embraced so strongly in Yucatán that many people believe it originated here. The genesis of Old World Horchata is debated, but today's version developed when almonds were introduced into the New World and Horchata evolved to include them in addition to rice. Lacking almonds, almond extract was used. Or, wanting the extract, a seed of Yucatán's native mamey (*Pouteria sapota* [Jacq.], p. 40) was added to a pitcher of the beverage. Its strong flavor, similar to almond, permeated the liquid. Sadly, disappearing in Yucatán may be real Horchata; most versions you drink when you order it will be made from commercial concentrate. Your own homemade will be noticeably superior and well worth the effort.

Prepare ahead note: Horchata can be made up to a week in advance and refrigerated. Some separation will occur; stir before serving.

YIELD: 8–10 SERVINGS

PREPARE THE INFUSION

Grind the rice in a blender or clean coffee grinder until fine. Place the ground rice along with the next 4 ingredients in a medium bowl and add the hot (not boiling) water. Cover and allow to rest a minimum of 8 hours, or overnight.

6 cups (1.5 L) water

¼ tsp. (1.25 ml) almond extract

¾ cup (150 g) sugar, or to taste

Remove the flavorings and discard. Working in batches, transfer the rice/almond mixture and its liquid to the jar of a blender and process 4–5 minutes, until very smooth. Check for any grittiness and blend more if necessary.

FINISH THE HORCHATA

Line a sieve with 2 layers of cheesecloth and place it over a large bowl or pitcher. Pour in the rice/almond mixture, pressing with a spatula to pass through as much liquid as possible. Add some of the water as needed to help pass the liquid through. Once most of the liquid has been strained, gather the ends of the cheesecloth and twist and squeeze to extract as much liquid as possible; discard the residue. Add the remaining water.

Add the extract and sugar to taste, stir to dissolve, and refrigerate until ready to serve.

TO SERVE

Serve in Tom Collins glasses over ice. Garnish with a sprinkle of Mexican cinnamon if desired.

(above) Horchata *(foreground) with two other popular Yucatecan beverages:* limonada *and* agua fresca de chaya. [MR] *(opposite page) Doña Yolanda adds a tub of herbs to the bubbling* masa *for Tamal colado.* [JFMT]

LERMA

A FEAST FOR KINGS

Feasts of reciprocity are common throughout Yucatán. Every parish in every pueblo and city in the peninsula enshrines its patron saint. Guild members and families take turns for the right to honor the saint on its special day, often paying for the privilege to do so, having saved money for years. Día de los Santos Reyes (Three Kings' Day), on 6 January is one of the most popular of these festivals, when Baltasar, Gaspar, and Melchor, the legendary kings who followed the star of Bethlehem to visit the newborn Christ, are revered with processions, fireworks, and lots of feasting.

(left) The whopping menu for the Feast of Santos Reyes put all of the Xaman family's sacrificed pigs to good use. Men were charged with the job of gutting and cleaning. [JFMT] (middle) The women had their tasks, too. Mothers and daughters, some elbow deep in buckets of black-red blood, fashioned the Spanish sausage morcilla. [JFMT] (right) Neighbors oversaw a cauldron of lard in which ribs were frying. These and other fried bits were offered as snacks while the main feast was being prepared. [JFMT]

(left) Tamal colado is made with finely strained masa. *But preparing 600 tamales for the annual celebration required heavier artillery than tiny kitchen sieves. Instead, doña Yolanda and friends used large, colorful woven plastic* sabukanes, *a modern version of the traditional Maya sisal shoulder bag, to make short work of all that straining.* [JFMT] *(middle) After 3 strainings, the* masa *was poured into a huge vat balanced over a raging wood fire.* [JFMT] *(right) At 5:00 pm, the tamales were assembled:* masa *was spooned onto the leaves; chunks of pork were placed in the center and topped with a dollop of bright red* k'óol; *and each* tamal *was tidily wrapped in banana-leaf squares before being stacked by the hundreds in steel tubs for cooking.* [JFMT]

Five families in Lerma, a little village in Campeche that clings to the slopes of a ridge of hills rising abruptly from the Gulf of Mexico, annually host the events for villagers. José Ángel Candelaria Xaman Canul is the patriarch of one of the families and began participating in the tradition in the mid-twentieth century.

Behind don José's home, the rocky hill slopes steeply upward. On the day I visited, stair-stepped from the foot of the hill to its summit were some 75 people, all engaged in various phases of preparing the feast sponsored by the Xaman family. I was greeted by Yolanda del Carmen Xaman, the ebullient granddaughter of the event's founder and the director of the massive preparation. Her work and that of other members of the family started on 4 January

and wouldn't finish until the seventh, the day after Día de los Santos Reyes.

"When my grandfather held the first Santos Reyes feast," explained Yolanda, "he told me 'If I give my pig and my maize to the Kings, it is not a sacrifice because I will get even more in return. I will have an even better harvest next year.'" Apparently, his offering was appreciated: by the second year, he was able to slaughter two pigs; the following year it was three; and by now, the number has grown to ten pigs, which are slaughtered and consumed during the course of the four days of festivities. Except for the pigs, all the rest of the food and the beverages are donated by the sponsoring families; guests pay for nothing except for their *cervezas*.

TAMAL COLADO

TWICE-COOKED *TAMAL* WITH PORK AND HERBS

TO PREPARE AHEAD

Cochinita pibil (p. 420)

K'óol rojo (p. 86) prepared using
the Cochinita pibil

Enriched Lard (p. 513)

Basic *masa* prepared from either
nixtamalized corn or *masa harina*
(p. 517)

12 pieces banana leaves, prepared
to the large (L) size per Basic
Techniques, p. 525, and reserved
ribs for ties

FOR THE FILLING

About 1 cup (300 g) Cochinita
pibil from preparing the K'óol
rojo, shredded

About 1 cup (250 ml) K'óol rojo

FOR THE *MASA*

½ cup (112 g) Enriched Lard

1 Tbs. (12g) whole *achiote* seeds

2 medium cloves garlic (½ oz. /
12 g), peeled

4 cups (1 L) chicken stock or
bouillon

4 cups (1 k) *masa*

1 cup (250 ml) water

1 tsp. (6 g) sea salt, or to taste
(optional)

¼ cup (15 g) *each* cilantro, mint,
chives, and epazote, finely
chopped (Note: If you don't have
fresh epazote available, increase
the other herbs so that you have
a total of 1 cup)

Surely Yucatán's, if not all of Mexico's, most unusual and delicate *tamal* is the Tamal colado. Creamy and pudding-like, the *masa* for this *tamal* is strained ("*colado*") then cooked to become a thick pudding before finally being wrapped in banana leaves and cooked again in a steamer. Tamal colado is nicknamed "*tamal de cuchara*" ("spoon *tamal*") not because it is eaten with a spoon, but because the cooked *masa* is spooned onto the banana leaves rather than patted out tortilla-style, as are most other tamales in Yucatán. It is also known as "*tamal de boda*" ("wedding *tamal*") because it is hugely popular at wedding parties, although now it has attained equal popularity at First Holy Communions and other special occasions.

I had never had a Tamal colado that included herbs, nor is it typical, but I quickly became a convert to doña Yolanda's special formula and use them here; they add a lightness and freshness that perfectly balance the meat filling. Yolanda told me quite emphatically that in homage to the ceremonial nature of the day, the Tamal colado should be made of *saka'* porridge from dried corn that has been boiled without *cal* rather than the more quotidian *masa* from *nixtamal* (p. 517). Since *saka'* is not well known outside the region, I recommend standard *masa*.

Alas, a custom gradually fading in the cities but still alive in the pueblos, especially at harvest festivals, is to serve hot, sweet *atole nuevo* (*áak sa'* in Mayan), a porridge made with fresh maize instead of nixtamalized corn as the beverage accompaniment to Tamal colado. A more heavenly meal I cannot imagine.

Prepare ahead note: Since you will only need about 1 cup (300 g) of shredded pork for the tamales, plan to get a couple of meals from this dish: serve Cochinita pibil on one day; refrigerate or freeze the leftovers and then use them to make the *k'óol* before finishing the tamales. Tamal colado can also be made well ahead of time and frozen; to reheat, steam 1 hour.

YIELD: APPROXIMATELY 1 DOZEN TAMALES

PREPARE FILLING

Cook the meat and prepare the K'óol rojo as instructed on page 86. Remove the meat from the cooking liquid, cool, and shred. Thicken and finish *k'óol* as instructed; set aside.

PREPARE *MASA*

Melt the lard in a heavy skillet. Over medium heat add the *achiote* seeds, stir briefly, and cook 2–3 minutes, or until the lard is stained a deep reddish-orange. Strain the fat through a sieve into a heatproof bowl and set aside; discard the seeds.

In a medium saucepan, simmer the garlic in the stock until soft, about 15 minutes. Remove the pan from the heat. Using a handheld immersion blender or in a standard blender, blend the mixture until the garlic is thoroughly puréed. Combine the stock

2 medium Roma tomatoes
  (7 oz. / 200 g), thinly sliced
½ medium white onion
  (5 oz. / 137.5 g), thinly sliced
  and separated into rings
2 sprigs fresh epazote (Substitute:
  fresh cilantro and/or flat-leaf
  parsley leaves)

with the *masa* in the saucepan. Working with a potato masher or the immersion blender again, mix thoroughly to remove any lumps.

Pass the *masa* mixture through a fine sieve placed over a clean saucepan. Using a rubber spatula, mash the contents of the sieve, pressing through as much liquid as you can. After you have pressed through about half of the liquid, add the cup (250 ml) of water to the sieve and continue to press; discard the residue. Check the seasoning and add salt if necessary.

Bring the liquid to a boil, stirring constantly. As it reaches the boil, it will begin to thicken dramatically. (Use an immersion blender again if lumps form.) Using a wooden spoon, beat vigorously as you gradually drizzle in the stained lard. Reduce the heat to low and add the herbs. Continue cooking and beating another 4–5 minutes, or until the mixture is stiff, thick, and satiny, resembling polenta. The *masa* will start pulling away from the pan and will hold its shape when dropped from a spoon.

FILL, GARNISH, AND WRAP

While the *masa* mixture is cooking, arrange the prepared banana leaves on a work surface. When the *masa* has thickened, immediately pack some of it into a half-cup (120 g) dry measure and turn onto one of the banana-leaf sections; repeat with the remaining *masa* and leaves. Center about 1 heaping tablespoon (25 g) of shredded meat on top of each *tamal*, then spoon on 1 tablespoon (15 ml) of the K'óol rojo. (Reserve the leftover K'óol to serve at the table.) Garnish with one slice of tomato, a ring of onion, and a few leaves of epazote.

[MC]

Reserved K'óol not used in the
filling, warmed
Chile tamulado (p. 509), or the
chile sauce of your choice

Fold the left side of the banana leaf over the top of the *tamal*; repeat with the right side. Do the same movements top and bottom. Use your hands to compress and shape the *tamal* to form the package into a rough square. Using the reserved banana-leaf ribs or kitchen twine, tie the *tamal* securely, as you would a package. Set aside until you have completed all of the tamales. Steam for 1½ hours according to instructions on page 526. Remove the tamales from the steamer and allow to cool at least 15 minutes before serving.

TO SERVE

The tradition in Yucatán is to open the leaves, leaving the *tamal* in place, and eat it with a spoon. Diners add warm K'óol and chile sauce to taste.

VARIATION

Tamalitos de especie (Creamy Strained Tamal with Mincemeat and Spices): This unique variant of Tamal colado appears in several regional cookbooks. To prepare in advance, replace the Cochinita pibil and K'óol rojo with 1 cup (300 g) Buut' blanco (p. 256) and 1 cup (250 ml) Tomate frito (p. 507). Hard-boil 3 eggs, peel, and slice. Follow the basic instructions for Tamal colado with the following changes: omit the herbs (the herbs are delicious and I sometimes include them, although it is not typical of this *tamal*); substitute 1 heaping tablespoon (25 g) of the cooked Buut' blanco for the pork; spoon on 1 tablespoon (15 ml) Tomate frito instead of the K'óol rojo and add a slice of boiled egg to replace the garnishes. Wrap and tie as in the master recipe, but *do not steam*. Allow the *tamal* to cool for a few minutes and serve immediately with additional Tomate frito and the chile sauce of your choice.

[MC]

MANÍ

INQUISITION TO TRANSFORMATION

Maní, "the place where everything happened," is located about 62 miles (100 km) south of Mérida, just east of the hills of Ruta Puuc. It factors prominently in one of the most compelling and tragic stories of the conquest of Yucatán.

It was here, in July of 1562, in the courtyard of the monastery of San Miguel Arcángel, that Fray Diego de Landa, bishop of Yucatán, executed a dramatic and lamentable auto-da-fé in which some twenty-seven scrolls containing the historical register of Maya civilization were burned, along with many other precious artifacts, all proclaimed by Landa to be "works of the devil." Only three texts survived. For this and other infractions, Landa was chastised by the Council of the Indies and wrote *Relación de las cosas de Yucatán* as

an apologia. In his compensatory act, Landa recorded in as much detail as he could remember all he had learned of the Mayas during his time in Yucatán. The work survives to the present as one of the most thorough records of early Maya life that we have. It is chilling to stand in the vast courtyard in front of the church, imagining the roaring flames that

---

(above) Church and former convent of San Miguel Arcángel, Maní, Yucatán. [MR]

consumed the majority of the recorded history of one of the greatest civilizations the world has ever known.

EL PRÍNCIPE TUTUL XIÚ

I won't dwell on the irony of the fact that nowadays Maní is known for Poc chuc, meat quickly grilled over an open wood fire. The popular local restaurant El Príncipe Tutul Xiú, just blocks from the monastery, displays plaques that recount the history of the event and draws hundreds of patrons from across the peninsula who converge beneath the restaurant's ample *palapa* roof to savor juicy seared pork and to inhale the smoke of history.

Grilling Poc chuc at El Príncipe Tutul Xiú. [MR]

POC CHUC / POKCHUK

WOOD FIRE—GRILLED PORK CUTLETS
WITH CHARRED TOMATO AND ONION SALSAS

TO PREPARE AHEAD

Brined pork (Basic Techniques, p. 536)

Mojo de ajo (p. 514)

Seville orange juice substitute (p. 514), unless fresh Seville oranges are available

Recado para escabeche (p. 498)

The layering of flavors in this quick, rustic dish is awe-inspiring: the light saltiness of the brined pork is freshened by crisp citrus, all wed harmoniously in earthy smokiness. A bite of the pork with a dollop of each of the typical accompaniments, Chiltomate (p. 451) and Cebollas asadas (p. 450), becomes a "must taste" flavor experience of Yucatán.

The most accurate transliteration for this dish is Póok chúuk, which in Mayan means "roasted or grilled [*póok*] in the embers of wood coals [*chúuk*]." It traces its ancestry to the ancient Maya practice of salting meat, which in the past would have been peccary or tapir (p. 88), then rinsing and cooking it on top of hot stones. Today, the preservation practice continues among campesinos who have no refrigeration, although now they are more likely to cook the meat over a wood or charcoal fire.

Follow the instructions for the accompaniments, streamlining the process by using the same fire for the vegetables that you will use for the pork. Roast the vegetables and finish the salsas first, then quickly grill the pork so that it can be served hot off the fire.

Prepare ahead note: Brining the pork must be done several hours or one day in advance. The Mojo de ajo marinade should be prepared in advance; marinating time is 30 minutes. The Frijol colado accompaniment can also be made in advance and refrigerated or frozen; reheat before serving.

YIELD: 6 SERVINGS

[MC]

FOR THE MARINADE

1¾ lbs. (750 g) pork loin, brined
½ cup (125 ml) Mojo de ajo
½ cup (125 ml) Seville orange
   juice, or substitute
½ tsp. (3 g) sea salt
½ tsp. (1.5g) Recado para escabeche

FOR THE SALSAS

Ingredients for Cebollas asadas
   (recipe follows)
Ingredients for Chiltomate
   (recipe follows)

FOR SERVING

Frijol colado "aguado" (p. 505)
Tortillas (p. 518)
Chile tamulado (p. 509), or the
   chile sauce of your choice
Chopped cilantro (optional)
Seville orange or lime wedges

MARINATE CUTLETS

Remove the pork from the brine, rinse, and pat dry; discard the brining solution. Slice the loin into 6 equal portions, each weighing about 4½ ounces (125 g). Working 1 or 2 pieces at a time, place the pork between 2 layers of waxed paper and pound with a wooden mallet or rolling pin to flatten to a uniform thickness, about ¼-inch (0.5 cm). Brush both sides of each flattened cutlet with Mojo de ajo and transfer the pork to a large, nonreactive baking dish. Mix the salt and *recado* with the juice and pour it over the meat to cover completely; refrigerate up to 30 minutes.

PREPARE SALSAS

Preheat a gas or charcoal grill using wood smoking chips as described in Basic Techniques, p. 538. Allow the pork to come to room temperature as you prepare Cebollas asadas and Chiltomate.

Place the onions, tomatoes, and chiles in a grilling basket and locate directly on the hot coals (or as close to the flame as possible if using gas.) Grill until char marks appear, remove, and follow recipe instructions to finish each salsa.

GRILL PORK

As soon as the 2 salsas are finished, sear half of the cutlets quickly, 1–2 minutes per side, using half of the wood smoking chips and lowering the lid of the grill each time. The thin meat cooks very quickly, so be vigilant and don't overcook; cutlets should be a bit springy when pressed with your fingertip. Transfer the cutlets to a large serving platter. Repeat with the other cutlets and the rest of the wood smoking chips. Serve immediately.

TO SERVE

Arrange the pork on a large serving platter with accompaniments in separate bowls so that diners may serve themselves. Alternatively, plate individual servings of pork with some of the onions and tomatoes and a bowl of the beans on the side; garnish with a wedge of sour orange and sprinkle a bit of cilantro over all. Diners arrange slices of the meat on tortillas, add a spoonful of each accompaniment, douse with some citrus juice and hot sauce, fold, and eat.

VARIATION

Poc chuc de pollo (Wood-Fire-Grilled Chicken Cutlets with Charred Tomato and Onion Salsas): The Mayan name *poc chuc* refers to the cooking method, not the ingredients of the dish: substitute boned chicken breasts, flattened in the manner described above. For seafood lovers, use firm-fleshed whitefish fillets or lobster tails instead of the pork. Do not brine or flatten the fish or lobster. Serve with the accompaniments listed above. Poc chuc is also delicious when accompanied by Esquites (p. 239), your own guacamole, or all of the above.

CEBOLLAS ASADAS

PICKLED ROASTED ONIONS

TO PREPARE AHEAD

Seville orange juice substitute
  (p. 514), unless fresh Seville
  oranges are available
Recado para escabeche (p. 498)

FOR THE PICKLED ONIONS

2 lbs. (1 k) red onions, whole
¼ cup (62.5 ml) Seville orange
  juice, or substitute
1 tsp. (6 g) sea salt, or to taste
¼ tsp. (0.75 g) Recado para
  escabeche (p. 498)
3 Tbs. (15 g) fresh cilantro leaves,
  coarsely chopped

A close relative of Cebollas encurtidas, Cebollas asadas are wonderfully aromatic onions that have been charred over a wood or charcoal fire, then pickled in Seville orange juice and spices. Cebollas asadas are a requisite accompaniment of Poc chuc and Longaniza asada (p. 482) and are delicious with any grilled meat or fish. The traditional preparation method is to char the vegetables directly on the same hot coals you will be using for the meat. And since Cebollas asadas and the companion accompaniment Chiltomate are usually served together, you can char the ingredients for both at the same time.

Prepare ahead note: Cebollas asadas can be refrigerated 2–3 days; bring to room temperature before serving.

YIELD: 8–10 SERVINGS

CHAR AND FINISH ONIONS

Char the onions in a grilling basket over a gas or charcoal fire. Roast, turning occasionally, 15–20 minutes. They should be very black on the surface and a bit soft when squeezed. Set aside to cool.

Slice off the tips of the onions and slip off the outer layers; leave any charred bits intact for more flavor. Cut the onions lengthwise into eighths, separate into sections, and place in a nonreactive bowl. Add the juice, salt, and *recado* and toss.

TO SERVE

Transfer the onions to a serving bowl. Immediately before serving, add cilantro leaves and toss.

[MC]

CHILTOMATE / K'UUT BI P'AAK

RUSTIC SALSA OF CHARRED TOMATOES AND CHILES

TO PREPARE AHEAD

Seville orange juice substitute
(p. 514), unless fresh Seville
oranges are available

FOR THE TOMATO SAUCE

2 lbs. (1 k) Roma tomatoes

1 medium chile habanero
(¼ oz. / 7 g), whole

6 cloves garlic (1½ oz. / 36 g),
peeled

¼ medium white onion
(2½ oz. / 68.75 g)

1 tsp. (6 g) coarse sea salt

2 Tbs. (30 ml) Seville orange juice,
or substitute

3 Tbs. (15 g) fresh cilantro leaves,
coarsely chopped

[MC]

Tomatoes were domesticated in Mesoamerica, and Chiltomate is possibly a vestige of one of the world's earliest cooked tomato sauces. Rustic both in preparation and final form, this elemental sauce is composed of only the simplest ingredients and cooking methods. Tomatoes and chiles are charred in a bed of hot coals, then crushed, making it quick and easy to prepare. Chiltomate is traditionally chunky, so you should avoid the temptation to use a blender or food processor.

Prepare ahead note: Chiltomate is best consumed immediately after preparation but will keep under refrigeration for 2–3 days; bring to room temperature before serving. Stir to blend, adding a bit more chopped cilantro to refresh, if desired.

YIELD: 8–10 SERVINGS

CHAR TOMATOES AND FINISH SAUCE

Char the first 4 ingredients over a charcoal or wood fire, or in a gas grill, then allow them to cool to the touch. Cut the cap off the chile and discard, leaving the seeds intact. Mash the chile with the salt and garlic in a stone *tamul* (*molcajete*) or mortar and pestle. If you don't have a *tamul*, use a large mixing bowl with a potato masher. Cut off the stem end of the tomatoes and discard. Cut the tomatoes in half, leaving the charred skin intact. Squeeze out the seeds and as much of the juice as possible and discard. Coarsely chop the tomatoes then crush together with the chile and garlic in the mortar and pestle. Mash coarsely: there should be no large pieces, but it should not be a purée. Transfer to a mixing bowl. Finely chop the onion, charred exterior intact, then add to the bowl with the tomatoes; toss to combine.

TO SERVE

Just before serving, add the juice and cilantro and stir to blend. Transfer to a serving bowl.

MOTUL

GARNISHING HISTORY

Just 28 miles (44 kilometers) northeast of Mérida, Motul was founded in the eleventh century by a Maya priest named Zac Mutul, who gave the city its name. In the mid-sixteenth century, Francisco de Montejo, captain general of Yucatán, converted the Maya ceremonial city of Mutul into the Spanish colonial city of Motul. In time it became one of the most important cities of the region due in large part to its production of sisal, a strong natural fiber extracted from the leaves of a native agave species and used for making rope and other important products.

Motul's most famous citizen was Felipe Carrillo Puerto, a reformer and state governor as well as the man for whom Huevos motuleños were created.

FELIPE CARRILLO PUERTO

Of mixed Spanish and indigenous Maya background, Carrillo Puerto was born in Motul in 1874. He was one of fourteen children, the majority of whom worked diligently to better the lives of the Maya people. A progressive favoring land reform, women's suffrage, and rights for the indigenous Mayas, Carrillo Puerto served as governor of the state of Yucatán from 1922 to 1924.

The early decades of the twentieth century were tumultuous throughout Mexico, rife with revolution and political upheaval. Although a member of the despised government, Carrillo Puerto was viewed as a savior by the indigenous Mayas. Realizing that the Mayas would never join their cause as long as Carrillo Puerto were alive, the revolutionaries began plotting to eliminate him, which they did by firing squad on January 3, 1924, along with three of his brothers and eight of his most active supporters.

HUEVOS MOTULEÑOS

The admittedly crass juxtaposition of a legendary hero with the recipe for a breakfast dish will hopefully be forgiven. But in truth the two are intricately interwoven, and I personally cannot eat Huevos motuleños without thinking of Felipe Carrillo Puerto.

During his tenure as governor, Carrillo Puerto was known to host "power lunches" in his hometown of Motul, during which he could review his agenda with staff and aides. A favorite Motul restaurant was La Sin Rival, owned by the Lebanese Siqueff family.

According to descendants of the family, the governor's preferred meal service was to receive many small plates containing a plentiful assortment of garnishes and accompaniments to the main dish. For one of these meals, in 1922, which the Siqueffs had arranged to host in the famed Motul *cenote*, so many people showed up that the cooks realized they would not have enough service pieces. In a stroke of creativity, the head chef created a new egg dish that would have all of the accompaniments and garnishes served on a single plate, and Huevos motuleños was born. In ensuing years, this same style, which is characterized by a fried tortilla topped with refried beans, fried eggs, tomato sauce, and garnishes of peas, ham, grated Edam, and fried plantain, has been applied to a handful of other foods, such as chicken, Pollo motuleño.

HUEVOS MOTULEÑOS

GARNISHED EGGS FROM MOTUL

FOR THE TOMATO SAUCE

1 Tbs. (14 g) Enriched Lard

½ medium white onion (9 oz. /
137.5 g), cut into medium dice

2 medium cloves garlic (½ oz. /
12 g), peeled and finely chopped

3 medium Roma tomatoes
(10½ oz. / 300 g), seeded,
cut into medium dice

½ recipe (2 cups / 500 ml)
Tomate frito

½ tsp. (3 g) sea salt

**FOR THE ASSEMBLY
AND GARNISHES**

12 Tostadas

3 cups (750 g) Frijol refrito,
warmed

8 oz. (225 g) smoked ham, cut
into ½ in. (1.5 cm) cubes,
lightly browned in 1 Tbs. (14 g)
Enriched Lard and kept warm

¾ cup fresh peas (about ½ lb. /
250 g peapods; substitute:
frozen peas), shelled, blanched
until just tender, tossed with
a bit of butter and sea salt,
and kept warm

8 oz. (225 g) Edam cheese, grated

½ cup (40 g) chives, chopped

1 recipe Plátano frito

Like so many Yucatecan dishes, Huevos motuleños is a cinch to assemble, providing you have all the components on hand. The original dish was invented in a time when canned goods were the order of the day, including the ham and peas. I suggest an upgrade: use the best-quality smoked ham you can find and, of course, blanch your own fresh (or frozen) peas.

Prepare ahead note: The Frijol refrito and Tomate frito should be prepared in advance; both freeze brilliantly. Except for these steps, Huevos motuleños should be assembled and served immediately.

YIELD: 6 SERVINGS

PREPARE TOMATO SAUCE

Heat the lard in a skillet until shimmering. Add the onion and garlic and sauté until the onions are translucent, 2–3 minutes. Add the tomatoes and cook until just softened, 3–4 minutes. Add the Tomate frito and salt and heat briefly; keep warm until time to serve.

PREPARE ASSEMBLY ITEMS AND GARNISHES

Have all assembly items and garnishes at hand.

Huevos motuleños as served in the Motul market. [MC]

12 eggs
6 Tbs. (84 g) Enriched Lard

FOR SERVING
Chile tamulado (p. 509)

FRY EGGS
In a small (6 in. / 15 cm) nonstick omelet pan fitted with a lid, heat 1 Tbs. (14 g) of the lard until melted. Crack 2 of the eggs into the pan, cover, and fry over low heat until they reach the desired doneness. (In Yucatán, the eggs are served with the whites firm and the yolks runny.)

ASSEMBLE, GARNISH, AND SERVE
Place one Tostada on an individual serving plate and spread approximately ½ cup (125 g) Frijol refrito over the surface. Spoon on a scant tablespoon (14 ml) of the tomato sauce, then slide the eggs from the omelet pan onto the beans and sauce. Crown with another Tostada. Spoon on about ⅓ cup (80 ml) of the tomato sauce, then garnish with 3 heaping tablespoons (45 g) of the ham. Finish with a spoonful of peas and a sprinkle of cheese followed by chopped chives. Garnish the plate with two slices of fried plantain. Repeat these steps for each serving, frying the eggs immediately before plating.

TO SERVE
Serve with Chile tamulado or the chile sauce of your choice.

VARIATION
Pollo motuleño (Garnished Fried Chicken from Motul): All sorts of spin-offs of Huevos motuleños continue to appear, each with the requisite garnishes. This version makes use of fried chicken. Prepare *milanesa*-style chicken cutlets according to the master recipe for Empanizado (p. 268). Proceed with this recipe, replacing the eggs with the fried chicken when you assemble the dish.

OXCUTZCAB

The "Puuc" style at Labná. [GRETALORENZ / DREAMSTIME.COM]

LAND OF ORANGES AND CHOCOLATE

Pronounced "ohsh-coots-COB," the Mayan translation of the name is "land of three wild turkeys" (*óox* = "three"; *kuuts* = "wild turkey"; *kaab* = "land"). Stamping it with their own style, the Spanish colonialists changed the nickname of Oxcutzcab to "Place of Oak, Tobacco, and Honey." Perhaps the slogan of Oxcutzcab should now be "Land of Oranges and Chocolate," since in recent years the region has become a wellspring of those two most delectable ingredients. Oxcutzcab stands as the municipal center of this rich region, known as La Ruta Puuc, poised between oranges on one side and chocolate on the other.

LA RUTA PUUC

South and gently west of Mérida, the tabletop of jungle-clad limestone suddenly heaves heavenward to form a serpentine range of low hills known in Mayan as *pu'uk* or *puuc*, which stretches from south-central Yucatán into eastern Campeche. Tourist literature labels the area La Ruta Puuc ("hilly route") and promotes an impressive cluster of Maya archaeological zones all within minutes of one another by car: Sayil, Labná, Kabah, Xlapak, and the unparalleled Uxmal.

The Puuc region is interesting to archaeologists for many reasons, not least of which is the quantity of ancient Maya cities. Civilization here obviously thrived, engendering what is widely considered to be one of the most sophisticated architectural styles in the pre-Columbian New World, the "Puuc style." One theory for the Mayas' success here is that the Puuc region has long been viewed as a "breadbasket," with good soils that made it possible for Puuc cities to become major food exporters to Yucatán's less agriculturally blessed zones.

THE ORANGE FAIR

The municipality of Oxcutzcab is considered Yucatán's citrus capital. With acres and acres devoted to lime, sweet and sour orange, grapefruit, and other citrus varieties, the region surrounding the village is fragrant and full of honeybees in the months that begin the principal citrus season. Every year during the last two weeks of November and the first two weeks of December, citrus in all its forms is celebrated at the annual Feria de la Naranja ("orange fair"). People come from around the peninsula to buy freshly

Traditional Maya home fabricated of several citrus varieties at the Oxcutzcab Feria de la Naranja. [COURTESY OF CASA DE LA CULTURA OXCUTZCAB]

They have sacred groves where they cultivate certain trees, like cacao.

—FRAY DIEGO DE LANDA, 1566

Young cacao *plants are sheltered beneath taller trees at Plantación Tikul.* [MR]

plucked oranges, as well as to marvel at the whimsical and colorful sculptures formed with thousands of citrus fruits.

SACRED *CACAO* GROVES

In recent years, another important species has been planted on a commercial scale to take advantage of the region's fertile growing conditions: *cacao.*

Mingling with the fragrance of citrus in Oxcutzcab, the bouquet of exotic plants at the nearby Plantación Tikul—vanilla, allspice, Mexican cinnamon, and perhaps the most

prized food of all time, *cacao*—creates an intoxicating promise of earthly delights. In recent years, entrepreneurs have planted some 11,000 specimens of the *criollo cacao* subspecies in the rich soils of the Puuc region, reinstating the ancient practice of growing *cacao* in Yucatán.

Growing *cacao* is not easy: it stubbornly refuses to grow beyond 20° latitude north or south of the equator, and much of Yucatán misses the mark by enough minutes to matter. In addition, the *cacao* tree prefers well-drained, fertile soils in regions that receive at least 2,000 mm of rainfall annually, none of which characterizes the physical environment of the Yucatán Peninsula.

By the time of European contact, *cacao* cultivation centered in the lowland Maya area, but farther south and west than Yucatán, specifically, Tabasco, the Atlantic coast of Guatemala, and the Caribbean coast of both Guatemala and Honduras. Still, apart from these major production centers, *cacao* was also cultivated farther north, in smaller groves, the so-called sacred groves of the Mayas to which Landa refers, possibly as a prestige item for consumption by families or small groups.

The Landa report and a series of other clues led research scientists to conclude that these groves had been planted in *cenotes* (see p. 80), the perfect environment for *cacao*, with plenty of shade and cooler temperatures, rich alluvial soils, and a constant freshwater source supplied by Yucatán's vast system of underground rivers. A team of botanists headed by Arturo Gómez-Pompa went on a quest for these fabled orchards and in 1990 published a paper detailing their discovery of three sacred groves in *cenotes* just south of Valladolid.

Familiar with the paper, and convinced that *cacao* could grow in the region, local master chocolatier Mathieu Brees, owner of a successful chocolate business in Yucatán since 2003, partnered with a European chocolate consortium to create Plantación Tikul, a 245-acre (100-hectare) zone in the Puuc region dedicated to *cacao* cultivation. By borrowing ancient Maya silviculture strategies and enhancing them with modern technology, each plant is shaded by old-forest canopy or fast-growing new banana trees and is watered by a tiny irrigation nozzle at its foot. Beans are destined for fine Belgian chocolates confected in Brees' shops, or for bulk shipment to European partner Belcolade, the second-largest producer of professional *couverture* chocolate in the world.

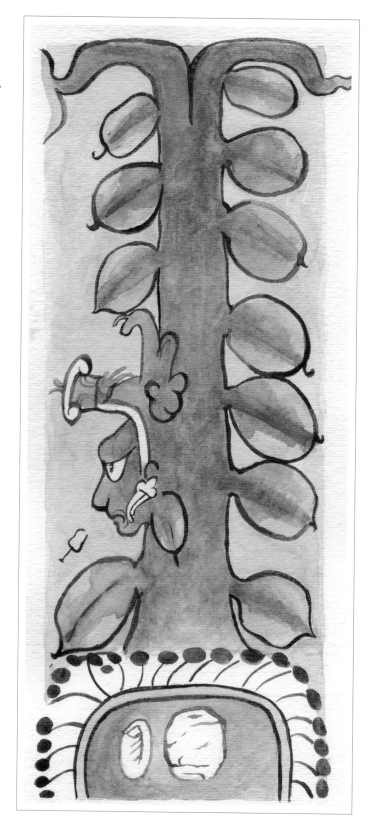

Cacao *tree with the head of Maya deity Hun Hunahpu as a* cacao *pod, from a Maya chocolate vessel.* [DRAWING BY AUREA HERNÁNDEZ]

(opposite page) Blossoms and young pods of Criollo cacao, *considered to produce the world's finest chocolate, at Plantación Tikul.* [COURTESY ECOMUSEO DEL CACAO]

PASTA DE CHOCOLATE

PURE CHOCOLATE PASTE

**FOR ROASTING
WHOLE RAW BEANS**

1 lb. (500 g) dried raw *cacao* beans

**FOR GRINDING ROASTED
BEANS OR NIBS**

3 cups (13 oz. / 375 g) roasted,
peeled *cacao* beans *or cacao* nibs
(Note: For both options, skip
to the grinding step)

Pasta de chocolate is a phase all *cacao* beans must pass through before officially being recognized as "chocolate." Raw *cacao* beans are fermented, roasted, peeled, and ground; the grinding releases natural vegetable fats in the beans, eventually resulting in a creamy, black paste known in Spanish as *pasta de chocolate*. A special smooth metate, or grinding stone, served the ancient Mayas and still serves contemporary women in the pueblos for grinding. A heat source placed beneath the stone helps break down the natural fats in the beans.

Making your own pure chocolate paste from *cacao* beans is remarkably easy, especially now that we have food processors instead of metates, although it is a bit time consuming. The heat the machine produces will aid in melting the fats, much as does the traditional method described above. Incorporate your own homemade chocolate paste in the recipes offered here. One proviso: without a commercial chocolate grinding mill, you will never be able to get the chocolate paste totally fine and smooth; instead, it will have a slightly grainy texture from bits of the nibs, which many people, myself included, enjoy.

Cacao beans and "cocoa" nibs are becoming more available. The *Criollo* variety will offer the best flavor if you can find it. Both whole beans and nibs are always sold fermented; beans often require roasting and peeling, while nibs are already roasted, peeled, crushed, and ready to be ground. Below, I give the steps for roasting and peeling whole beans and for grinding both beans and nibs.

Prepare ahead note: Refrigerate Pasta de chocolate until ready to use. It also freezes quite well. Defrost, gently warm, and stir before incorporating into a recipe.

YIELD: APPROXIMATELY 1½ CUPS (13 FL. OZ. / 375 ML)

ROAST WHOLE RAW BEANS

Heat a dry large, heavy, cast-iron skillet on highest heat for 5 minutes; add the beans. Very quickly they will begin to crack and pop; immediately flip and toss them in the skillet, or use a spatula to keep them in constant motion. Continue until they are fragrant and considerably blackened on all sides, about 5 minutes. Immediately transfer the beans to a heatproof bowl and allow to cool.

Once the beans are cool, grasp one between thumb and forefinger and squeeze: the papery shell will crumble away. Continue until all the beans are shelled. Some will likely break or crumble; just rescue the good parts as best you can and discard the rest. Accounting for loss, you should end up with about 3 cups (375 g) of peeled beans.

GRIND BEANS OR NIBS

Fill the bowl of a small, heavy-duty food processor with the roasted, shelled beans (or crushed nibs). Turn on the motor and be patient: the beans will immediately be broken into tiny bits. Continue processing for 5 minutes or so, until the beans or nibs are ground into a fine powder. Eventually, the powder will clump into a clayey mass, but continue to process until you have a creamy, shiny black paste. The time required to finish depends on your processor; mine usually takes 15–20 minutes.

For a finer product, continue running the processor for several minutes after the paste develops, or until it turns from a paste to a liquid, like hot fudge sauce. You will need to tend the machine only occasionally to scrape down the sides of the bowl with a rubber spatula. Give your poor machine a rest every 5 minutes or so to cool down. Transfer the paste to an airtight container and refrigerate or freeze until ready to use.

Fine Belgian chocolate at Ki'Xocolatl. [MR]

First-time visitors to Yucatán who get wind of the Maya/chocolate connection go on a ravenous quest for chocolate desserts in the peninsula only to be doomed to disappointment. Thanks to chocolatiers like Mathieu Brees of Ki'Xocolatl in Mérida, as well as Isabel Carreon of Ah Cacao in Playa del Carmen, we do have access to great handmade chocolate truffles and bonbons produced from top-quality Mexican *cacao* beans. But why, if we are in a major center of Maya *cacao* history, are there no delicious chocolate dessert recipes to be found in regional Yucatecan cuisine? The answer is simple: to all peoples of Mesoamerica, chocolate has traditionally been consumed primarily as a beverage, and the same is true today.

CHOCOLATE / CHUKWA'

CLASSIC MAYA BEVERAGE

TO PREPARE AHEAD
Pasta de chocolate (p. 462)

FOR THE MILK BASE
3 cups (750 ml) milk

1 cup (250 ml) whipping cream
(Note: For the diet conscious, any combination of skim/whole milk/cream will do as long as the final measure is 4 cups)

¼ cup (62.5 g) sugar (optional if using commercial bittersweet chocolate)

1 Tbs. (5 g) cornstarch

FOR FINISHING THE CHOCOLATE
8 oz. (225 g) Pasta de chocolate (Substitute: bittersweet chocolate), chopped

2 Tbs. (30 ml) Mexican honey

½ tsp. (2.5 ml) Mexican vanilla extract

¼ tsp. (0.75 g) ground allspice

⅛ tsp. (0.375 g) cayenne powder, or to taste

In cooler months, Chocolate (pronounced "cho-ko-LAH-tay") remains the beverage of choice in Yucatán for breakfast and *merienda* (afternoon teatime). It is served with a multitude of accompaniments: churros and other sweet breads for dunking, or Pan francés (p. 194) spread with imported Australian or Dutch butter, sprinkled with sugar and grilled, or topped with thick slices of Edam. The traditional Maya chocolate beverage used water as a base, was served hot or cold, sweet or savory, and included such ingredients as allspice, vanilla, honey, chile, salt, and/or *achiote*. The resulting chocolate beverage was poured back and forth between two gourds or pots to aerate it and produce a froth. The following recipe includes postcontact milk, as well as several of the traditional ingredients, and is served sweet and hot. Since many Maya chocolate beverages were thickened with *masa*, I have suggested using a member of the maize family of products, cornstarch, for a similar effect. For heavenly results, use your own Pasta de chocolate (p. 462).

Prepare ahead note: Chocolate can be made a day in advance and refrigerated. Whisk in any skin that forms and reheat prior to serving, adding a bit more milk as necessary to achieve the desired consistency.

YIELD: 6 SERVINGS

PREPARE MILK BASE
In a large saucepan, heat the first 3 ingredients. Stir until the sugar is dissolved and the milk is bubbling around the edges. Transfer one ladle of the hot milk to a small bowl, add the cornstarch, and whisk until incorporated. Whisk the cornstarch mixture back into the saucepan. Continue whisking over medium heat until the mixture thickens slightly, 3–4 minutes, stirring frequently to avoid scorching.

FINISH CHOCOLATE AND SERVE
Add the remaining ingredients to the saucepan and continue whisking over medium heat until the chocolate is completely melted and frothy. Check the flavorings and serve immediately.

TO SERVE
Serve the Chocolate in individual mugs or cups with Mexican sweet breads such as Conchas (p. 202) or churros for dunking. To froth the beverage in a traditional way, use a wooden *molinillo* (see Resources on p. 541). Alternatively, use a battery-powered bar whisk to produce froth in the cup immediately before serving. Or, for a modern touch, top the finished chocolate with steamed, frothed milk made in an espresso machine and a dash of ground *canela*, if you wish.

At Ecomuseo del Cacao, the charming chocolate museum at Plantación Tikul, visitors are invited to add their own flavorings to the pure, unadulterated chocolate beverage. Hand-ground allspice, red chile, and *achiote* are presented in little wooden boxes; honey is dipped with a tiny wooden ladle; and an assistant will scrape some seeds from a fresh vanilla pod into your drink if you wish. This presentation concept is fun for children and even adults! Just omit the flavorings in the finishing step and serve them on the table with the chocolate.

Maya deity of commerce, Ek Chuak, associated with cacao *as currency.* Cacao *pods can be seen sprouting from the trunk of the tree.*

[COURTESY ECOMUSEO DEL CACAO]

T'ANCHUKWA' / TANCHUCUÁ / XTÁAN CHUKWA'

MAIZE AND CHOCOLATE PORRIDGE

TO PREPARE AHEAD

Pasta de chocolate (p. 462)

Masa prepared from either nixtamalized corn or *masa harina* (p. 517)

Atole (*sa'* in Mayan) is a cooked corn porridge rather reminiscent of my favorite childhood breakfast: cream of wheat. Somewhere between a food and a beverage, *atole* has been consumed in Mesoamerica for thousands of years. It is well documented that many ingredients were added to *atole* to vary the flavor, not least of which was *cacao*. T'anchukwa' is *atole* mixed with chocolate. Native allspice was a common addition precontact; *canela* and anise entered later. Maize and *cacao* were intertwined in Maya religion and cosmology: the maize god was frequently depicted on vessels dedicated to the chocolate beverage, such that *cacao* was symbolically compared to the life-giving powers of maize. To savor this beverage is to drink from the vessel of time. T'anchukwa' is a contraction of two Mayan words: "*táam*" (sometimes transcribed as "*x'táan*") refers to the diluted *masa* used as a thickener; "*chukwa'*" is the Mayan word for "chocolate." And that is the recipe for the beverage. T'anchukwa' is the traditional accompaniment to the giant festival *tamal*, Mucbilpollo (p. 430), during Hanal Pixán, the Maya Day of the Dead commemoration. Bowls of it can be seen on altars next to photos of departed loved ones.

Prepare ahead note: The Pasta de chocolate and *masa* should both be made in advance. T'anchukwa' is best consumed immediately after preparing.

YIELD: 10 SERVINGS

Offering of T'anchukwa' in tree gourd bowls on a family altar during Hanal Pixán. [MR]

FOR THE FLAVORED INFUSION

5 cups (1.25 L) water, divided
½ cup (100 g) sugar
1 Tbs. (15 ml) Mexican honey
½ tsp. (3 g) sea salt
3 allspice berries
1 whole star anise

FOR THE *ATOLE*

8 oz. (225 g) Pasta de chocolate
   (Substitute: bittersweet
   chocolate), chopped
1½ cups (337.5 g) *masa*

PREPARE FLAVORED INFUSION

Place 2 cups (500 ml) of the water and the remaining ingredients in a saucepan and bring to a boil; simmer until the sugar is completely dissolved. Remove the pan from the heat, cover, and allow to steep for 10 minutes.

COOK *ATOLE* AND SERVE

In a separate saucepan, bring the remaining 3 cups (750 ml) of water to a boil. Remove the pan from the heat and add the chocolate and *masa*. Using a whisk or hand-held immersion blender, blend until the ingredients are thoroughly incorporated and there is no sign of lumps.

Remove the anise and allspice from the infusion and discard. Bring the liquid to a boil, then reduce the heat to a simmer. Whisking constantly, add the *masa*/chocolate mixture to the simmering infusion. Continue whisking or blending with the immersion blender to avoid lumps. Cook gently, stirring constantly, for 3–4 minutes, or until thickened.

TO SERVE

Just as with my childhood cream of wheat, it is up to the diner or cook to determine the degree of thickness and sweetness of T'anchukwa': add more water to thin or cook longer to thicken; add more or less sugar to taste. T'anchukwa' is delicious with any of our Yucatecan tamales, although Mucbilpollo (p. 430) is the classic partner. It is traditionally served in *jícaras* (tree gourd bowls) or, more recently, in mugs. You may do the same, or serve it in bowls à la oatmeal. Sprinkle a bit of *canela* on top. For the kids, add a few typical oatmeal garnishes such as a pat of butter, raisins, or sliced banana.

HELADO DE CHOCOLATE MAYA

CHOCOLATE FROZEN CUSTARD WITH ACHIOTE, VANILLA, ALLSPICE, AND CHILE

TO PREPARE AHEAD

Pasta de chocolate (p. 462), or
  substitute

FOR THE CUSTARD BASE

2 cups (500 ml) milk

3 Tbs. (48 g) commercial recado
  rojo (Sometimes labeled "achiote
  paste." See Resources, p. 540.
  Note: For this recipe, the
  commercial recado is preferred
  since it is ground more finely
  than your homemade will be.
  Do not add salt to this recipe,
  since the commercial recados
  already include salt.)

2 cups (500 ml) Mexican crema,
  crème fraîche, or whipping
  cream

1 cup (250 g) sugar

¼ cup (62.5 ml) Mexican honey

⅜ tsp. (1.125 g) ground allspice

⅛ tsp. (0.375 g) cayenne powder,
  or to taste

5 large egg yolks

8 ounces (225 g) Pasta de chocolate
  (p. 462; substitute: bittersweet
  chocolate, chopped)

1 Tbs. (15 ml) Mexican vanilla

When I eat this memorable and rich ice cream, I am always reminded of what the Mayas must have experienced when they were spiritually transported by chocolate. Since there are no recipes for chocolate desserts in regional cookbooks, I based my formula for this ice cream on what we know of the Maya and, later, Aztec recipes for the chocolate beverage, which at times included various combinations of chile, vanilla, allspice, and achiote. I add all four for a surprising punch, an herbaceous bottom note, and an earthy rust red color. Try using your own chocolate paste (Pasta de chocolate, p. 462), since it will create a rustic, authentic texture and an absolutely unsurpassed flavor in the finished product.

Prepare ahead note: The custard base for Helado de chocolate maya should be prepared a day in advance in order to chill thoroughly before freezing. After processing, the ice cream keeps well frozen for 1 week.

YIELD: APPROXIMATELY 1½ QUARTS (1.5 L)

PREPARE CUSTARD BASE

Place the milk and *recado* in the jar of a blender; process for 1 minute; strain the mixture through a fine-mesh sieve into a heavy saucepan, discarding any residue that does not pass through; stir in the next 5 ingredients and bring to a simmer. Cook over moderate heat, stirring constantly, 3–4 minutes, until the sugar dissolves and the mixture is hot and bubbling around the edges. *Do not allow to boil.*

Using a hand-held electric mixer or a whisk, beat the egg yolks in a heatproof bowl until light and fluffy. Still beating, very gradually add about 1 cup (250 ml) of the warm milk mixture to the eggs and beat thoroughly; repeat 2–3 times to gently heat the eggs. With the beater running in the saucepan, very slowly stream the egg mixture back into the hot milk. Reduce the heat to medium-low. Stir constantly with a wooden spoon 3–4 minutes, or until the mixture thickens enough to coat the back of the spoon; a candy thermometer should read 180°F (82°C). *Do not allow to boil* or the eggs may scramble.

FINISH ICE CREAM AND FREEZE

Remove the saucepan from the heat source and immediately add the chocolate. Stir briefly to melt then beat with the electric mixer until the chocolate is thoroughly incorporated into the custard mixture, about 1 minute. Allow the mixture to cool, stir in the vanilla, then cover and refrigerate for at least 6 hours or, preferably, overnight. The resulting base will be thick and mousse-like after refrigeration. Process the custard in an ice cream maker according to manufacturer's directions. Place the finished ice cream in a covered container and freeze to set 2–3 hours before serving.

Helado de chocolate maya as an accompaniment to Caballeros pobres. [EC]

POMUCH

Breads cool on the floor for a few minutes before being rushed to the storefront. [MR]

VILLA OF BAKERIES

Pomuch is a sleepy little village on the colonial Camino Real to Campeche. But around 4:00 pm each day, the pueblo comes to life as shop doors spring open and people bustle to bakeries to purchase treats for their afternoon *merienda*, or Yucatecan "teatime." Pomuch, nicknamed "the Villa of Bakeries," enjoys a reputation for having the peninsula's most delicious and unusual breads.

The oldest and best-known bakery in Pomuch is Panadería La Huachita, just off the main square. It has been privately run by the same family since the end of the nineteenth century. The menu board at La Huachita is a record of classic Yucatecan breads and the family's unique creations.

TUTIS

SWEET ROLLS WITH CHEESE FILLING

FOR THE DOUGH

½ cup (112 g) butter, room temperature

¾ cup (150 g) sugar

1 tsp. (6 g) sea salt

Zest of one sweet orange, finely grated

6 cups (750 g) all-purpose flour, divided

4 eggs, well beaten, room temperature

1¼ cups (312.5 ml) warm water

2 packets (5 tsp. / ½ oz. / 14 g) active dry yeast

FOR THE FILLING AND GLAZE

10½ oz. (300 g) *queso chihuahua* or mild Cheddar cheese, finely grated

½ cup (10 g) sugar, plus extra for dusting

¼ cup (62.5 ml) sweet orange juice

I had heard of Tutis for many years, but until my visit to La Huachita I had never actually seen one in captivity. This is the sort of bread old folks dream of wistfully, recounting stories of their childhood when *mamá* would buy Tutis as a special reward for good behavior. At La Huachita, Tutis are sweet, orange-scented pillows of yeasty dough inside of which nestles a golden nugget of Queso Daisy, the local brand name for *queso chihuahua*, an aged, mild Cheddar-type cheese. Big wheels of the cheese rest on shelves at the bakery. Tuti variations are legion: some versions use *hojaldra* rather than yeast bread, and instead of the cheddar, Edam or, more recently, *queso filadelfia* (cream cheese) supplies the creamy center.

Prepare ahead note: Tutis are best eaten warm out of the oven. They will last a day or two in an airtight container and benefit from a brief reheating.

YIELD: 15

PREPARE DOUGH AND FIRST RISING

Place the first 4 ingredients in the bowl of a stand mixer fitted with a dough hook (alternatively, use a food processor fitted with the plastic dough blade) and cream together until pale yellow. Add ½ cup (62.5 g) of the flour and beat until thoroughly combined. Blend the beaten eggs with the warm water. With the mixer running, slowly drizzle the egg/water mixture into the bowl and beat until well incorporated. Add another ½ cup (62.5 g) flour and beat again to combine. Add the yeast and another ½ cup (62.5 g) flour and beat. Add another ½ cup (62.5 g) flour and beat until thoroughly

A recycled butter tin is perforated and reborn as a citrus grater for Tutis. [MR]

incorporated. Add the remaining 4 cups (500 g) flour a cup at a time, beating briefly after each addition. When a stiff dough has formed, turn it onto a floured work surface. Knead for 6–8 minutes, incorporating more flour as needed to form a smooth and elastic mass that is no longer sticky. Transfer the dough to a large buttered mixing bowl, cover with a clean towel, and allow to rise in a warm place for 1½ hours.

FILL THE BREADS AND SECOND RISING

Line a large baking sheet with parchment paper. Pack ¾ ounce (20 g) of grated cheese into a tablespoon measure and release onto a plate to form a ball. Repeat until you have formed 15 cheese balls, and set aside.

Punch down the dough and turn it out onto a lightly floured work surface. Knead for 1–2 minutes to restore elasticity. Divide the dough into 15 balls, each weighing approximately 3½ ounces (100 g), reserving the remainder for decorations. Hold one of the balls as you insert your index finger into the bottom. Twist and pull to open a large hole; place a cheese ball inside the hole and pinch the dough to seal tightly; reshape into a smooth ball. Place the ball seam side down on the baking sheet. Continue until you have formed all the Tutis.

TO DECORATE

Divide the remaining dough into 15 equal pieces, each weighing about ⅓ ounce (10 g). Divide each piece again into 4 smaller pieces. Roll each of the smaller pieces into a small cylinder, then pinch one end to bring it to a point; form the opposite end to be rounded (the finished shape should look like an exclamation point.) Using a bit of water on a pastry brush to adhere the decorations, arrange four of the shapes spaced equally on top of each bread with the pointed ends at the center. The resulting decoration should look like the four cardinal points of a compass. Cover Tutis with a clean towel and let rise for 1 hour.

BAKE AND GLAZE

Preheat the oven to 350°F (176°C) while the bread is rising. Uncover the baking sheet and bake the Tutis for 15–20 minutes, or until pale golden brown. Remove the baking sheet from the oven and allow the Tutis to cool for 10 minutes. While they are cooling, combine the sugar and orange juice in a small saucepan and bring to a boil. Reduce the heat to a simmer and cook until the sugar dissolves; continue to cook for 2 minutes.

Working quickly and one at a time so that the sugar adheres, brush the tops of the Tutis with some of the orange juice mixture and sprinkle liberally with sugar. Allow the breads to finish cooling, then serve immediately or store in an airtight container.

PAN DE PICHÓN

FRENCH LOAF FILLED WITH HAM, CHEESE, AND JALAPEÑO

This long French-style loaf is stuffed with ham, cheddar-style cheese, and pickled jalapeños before it is baked. Another proprietary treat of La Huachita, the *sandwichón* ("really big sandwich"), according to legend, acquired its name when the manager, Tío Jorge, was a bit inebriated and told the on-duty baker to fashion him a large baked sandwich. As the baker worked, a baby pigeon (*pichón*) fell out of the rafters and onto the baker's table. Not missing a beat, Tío Jorge proclaimed, "*Pichón* will be the name of this new bread!" The recipe produces a sizable quantity, making it perfect for tailgate parties or any large gathering. Alternatively, whole loaves can be frozen 1–2 months and reheated prior to serving.

YIELD: 2 LARGE LOAVES OF 6–8 SLICES EACH

TO PREPARE

Follow the instructions for Pan francés (p. 194), but divide the dough into 2 equal balls instead of 3 (about 1 lb. / 465 g each). Shape the dough into long batons, then flatten each slightly into a thick, irregular rectangle. Arrange narrow strips of sliced ham and cheddar cheese (approximately 1½ oz. / 45g of each filling) and 5–6 strips of pickled jalapeños in a row down the center (make sure the filling reaches both ends so that no diner is cheated!). Fold in half lengthwise to cover the fillings, tightly pinch to seal closed, and reshape into 12-inch (30 cm) loaves. Place seam side down on the prepared baking sheets. Finish final rising and bake as instructed in the master recipe.

(above) Wheels of local Queso Daisy for filling Tutis and Pan de pichón. [MR] *(opposite page) Carne enchilada.* [MR]

TEMOZÓN

Inside the smokehouse. [MR]

THE ETHEREAL ESSENCE OF SMOKE

Whenever I am asked which flavor or ingredient most characterizes the foods of Yucatán, my first response is invariably, "Smoke." This ethereal yet all-pervasive substance stretches across the peninsula beginning in March in the months just prior to the start of the rainy season, as farmers set their *milpas* ablaze to burn off last season's dead stubble. Soon, it drifts over fields and highways like a low-flying phantasm, leaving in its wake a snowy coat of white ash on jungle flora and urban gardens alike. Or it wafts temptingly from the hearths of Maya women cooking tortillas; it drifts heavenward from mounds of smoldering copal in clay burners on altars for the ancestors. And it adds an unmistakably Yucatecan flavor to our foods.

Smoking foods is a long-standing tradition in Yucatán. In pre-Columbian times, the Mayas used smoke to preserve many foods such as chiles, meat, and fish. The *barbacoa*—a raised stick framework that held items to be cooked and smoked above a fire, a technique and word borrowed from Caribbean island tribes—was used for smoking a range of foods, including tamales.

Smoke takes on an almost palpable reality in the tiny eastern town of Temozón (a Spanish transliteration of a Mayan phrase meaning "place of the whirlwind"), capital of Yucatecan smoked meats. This area of the peninsula is known for its hardwood forests of *boox káatsim*—the Mayan name for the *Acacia gaumeri* S. F. Blake, a member of the Fabaceae family. This and several other dense, tropical hardwoods are excellent building materials and are also prized for the unique flavor they impart to foods when used as firewood. It is this scent that permeates the air as you enter the pueblo.

INSIDE THE SMOKEHOUSE

Carnicería Concepción, at the entrance to town, is buzzing with activity every day of the week: skilled smokers carry on a tradition that started centuries ago, when campesinos hung scraps of meat above the cook fire, and that emerged as an industry in the 1960s. Shop owner José Concepción Díaz Mena learned the art of smoking from his grandfather Filo Gutiérrez, considered the pioneer of meat smoking in Temozón. Now, with his wife, son, and daughter, José produces and sells fine smoked meats to local customers as well as to a variety of prestigious restaurants across the peninsula.

Smoking happens daily, but the most important day of the week at Carnicería Concepción is Thursday, when José makes the four-hour round trip to Mérida to pick up his order of pork. And a lot of it: for a single week's sales, he must purchase 2,200 pounds (1 metric ton) of pork leg.

Incredibly, the battery of giant brick ovens is left burning all day, every day throughout the year. Workers check to see if the fire is getting low; if so, more wood is added. The local woods *ja'abin* (*Piscidia communis* S. F. Blake) and *ya'ax ché* (*Ceiba pentandra* [L.] Gaertn.), José says, impart the best flavor. By 6:00 pm, José and staff begin to load the ovens with precious meats. Here the meats rest overnight, being gently smoked until 6:00 am, by which time they are deeply flavorful. Piece by succulent piece, the meats are pulled from the ovens and whisked immediately to waiting customers in the shop or wrapped in butchers' paper and packed for delivery.

Cool Smoking Method

For best results in all the following recipes for smoked meats, you will need a bullet-, offset firebox-, or cabinet-style cool smoker. Follow the recipe for preparing meat for smoking, then follow the manufacturer's instructions for your particular model of smoker. Mesquite is widely available and is the preferred wood for these recipes.

Smoking meats is not difficult, but you have to be vigilant about adding more coals, wood smoking chips, and so on, during the several-hour process. As anyone who has ever smoked meats is aware, you should prepare several meats in substantial quantities to make best use of your efforts.

Prepare ahead note: Smoked meats keep well for many months. Group in small quantities, vacuum pack, and freeze. When you anticipate using some of the meat, transfer one package from the freezer to the refrigerator to defrost overnight.

Along with smoking, woodworking is a big business in Temozón. The main road through town passes rows of stores selling the fruits of both: warehouses filled with wooden furniture sit side by side with tiny shops where meat is smoked in the back and sold in the front. [MR]

CARNE AHUMADA

SMOKED PORK

The succulent, smoky Carne ahumada and Carne enchilada (recipes follow) start with well-marbled pork leg or rump. The meat is typically marinated in a mixture of salt, Seville orange juice, garlic, and other flavorings. The technique presented here for brining and then marinating in Mojo de ajo achieves the same end. All smoked meats in Temozón are sold in roughly rectangular pieces measuring about 6 inches × 8 inches (15 cm × 20 cm) and approximately ¾-inch (1¼ cm) thick. Start out with a whole cut, then trim to shape after brining.

TO PREPARE AHEAD
Mojo de ajo (p. 514)

FOR BRINING
2½ lbs. (1.2 k) pork shoulder or rump, boned, skin removed, and trimmed of excess fat
2 Tbs. (40 g) commercial meat cure powder (see Resources, p. 540)

FOR THE MARINADE
1 Tbs. (12 g) black peppercorns, coarsely crushed in a *molcajete* or mortar and pestle
½ cup (125 ml) Mojo de ajo

FOR SMOKING
Mesquite wood smoking chips

BRINE MEAT

Follow the instructions for brining in Basic Techniques, p. 536, adding the meat cure powder to the brine solution. At the end of brining, remove the meat from the brine, rinse, and pat dry; discard the brining solution.

Place 1 piece of meat on a work surface with the grain running horizontally in front of you, left to right. Locate a very sharp knife on the right side of the pork (if you are right-handed) at the one-third point above the bottom and slice through the meat with the grain, right to left, stopping about ¼ inch (6.35 mm) from the opposite side. Rotate the meat 180° so that the slice is on the left. Now, locate your knife again on the right side, about one-third from the top of the pork and cut as before. This will result in three sections; open the sections and spread them flat to create one larger sheet of meat approximately ¾ in. / 2 cm thick (the overall size of the sheet doesn't matter). Repeat with the other piece of pork. (You may also use boned pork chops with some fat, or loin sliced to the same thickness.) If your finished sheet is thicker than ¾ inch

[MR]

(2 cm), place between two pieces of waxed paper and pound with a wooden mallet or rolling pin until you achieve the correct thickness.

MARINATE MEAT

Place the meat in a single layer in a large baking dish. Rub and press the cracked peppercorns into the flesh and cover completely with the Mojo de ajo. Refrigerate for 2 hours.

SMOKE MEAT

Remove the meat from the refrigerator and bring to room temperature, 30–45 minutes. While the meat is coming to room temperature, prepare the smoker. When it is heated, remove the meat from the marinade, shake off the excess, and arrange it in the smoker. Depending on your equipment, smoking should take 2–3 hours; pork should reach a temperature of 145°F (63°C). Alternatively, you may smoke the meat more rapidly by following the instructions for the stovetop smoking method or the gas or charcoal grill smoking methods (p. 538). (Note: Meats smoked by any of the other methods will acquire a smoky flavor but will not be preserved.) Remove the meat from the smoker and allow it to rest 15–20 minutes before serving. Vacuum pack any of the meat you will not immediately consume, then freeze.

TO SERVE

Both Carne ahumada and Carne enchilada (recipe follows) may be eaten in a variety of ways: thin slices may be used as a filling for tacos or *tortas*; larger pieces may be plated with rice and beans; or, shredded, the meat may be mixed with Salpicón to make Tsi'ik (p. 422).

VARIATION

Costillas ahumadas (Smoked Ribs): Start with 2½ pounds (1.2 k) pork back ribs. Place the rack of ribs flat on a work surface with the meat side down. Remove the membrane, a plastic-looking covering that protects the bones; this step allows the smoke to penetrate the meat more efficiently. Brine, marinate, and smoke the ribs as in the master recipe for Carne ahumada. Depending on your smoker, smoking should take approximately 4 hours; meat should reach a temperature of 145°F (63°C). Costillas ahumadas are eaten here like any ribs, but they also enjoy a guest-star appearance in Chilmole de frijol con costillas ahumadas (p. 267).

CARNE ENCHILADA

SMOKED PORK WITH CHILE RUB

TO PREPARE AHEAD
Recado rojo (p. 500)

FOR BRINING THE MEAT
2½ lbs. (1.2 k) pork shoulder or rump, boned, skin removed, and trimmed of excess fat
2 Tbs. (40 g) commercial meat cure powder (see Resources, p. 540)

FOR THE CHILE RUB
2 dried chiles chipotles, stems removed and seeded
5 Tbs. (75 g) Recado rojo
¼ cup (62.5 ml) white vinegar
1 tsp. (6 g) sea salt
1 tsp. (3 g) cayenne powder

FOR SMOKING
Mesquite wood smoking chips

This picante alternative to Carne ahumada enjoys the same serving flexibility. Serve it plated with rice and beans, use it on sandwiches or tacos, or chop it and use it as the basis for a quick (nontraditional) stovetop chili. The chile rub is also good to use on ribs, chicken, fish, or anything you plan to grill.

BRINE MEAT

Follow the instructions for brining in Basic Techniques, p. 536, adding the meat cure powder to the brine solution. At the end of brining, remove the meat from the brine, rinse, and pat dry; discard the brining solution.

Follow the instructions for dividing the pork into sheets per the recipe for Carne ahumada (p. 478).

PREPARE CHILE RUB

Place the chipotles in a spice mill or coffee grinder reserved for the purpose and grind until very fine. Pass the chipotle powder through a sieve, returning anything that remains in the sieve to the grinder. Repeat 1 or 2 more times, until the chipotles are very fine; discard any residue. Mix the Recado rojo with the vinegar to dissolve and add the salt, cayenne, and powdered chipotles; stir to mix well. Place the prepared meat in a single layer in a large baking dish and cover completely with the chile mixture, turning the meat to coat completely on all sides. Refrigerate 30 minutes to 1 hour as you prepare the smoker.

SMOKE MEAT

Remove the meat from the refrigerator and allow it to rest at room temperature for 30 minutes. Shake off any excess marinade and follow the cool smoking instructions provided by the manufacturer of your smoker.

VARIATION

Costillas enchiladas (Smoked Ribs with Chile Rub): Follow the master recipe for Costillas ahumadas (p. 479), replacing the Mojo de ajo marinade with the spice rub in Carne enchilada. Proceed with the rest of the recipe as instructed.

LONGANIZA DE VALLADOLID

SMOKED SAUSAGE OF VALLADOLID

TO PREPARE AHEAD

Recado rojo (p. 500)

Recado blanco (p. 502)

(continued on next page)

The layers of flavor in this recipe led a friend of mine to liken the sausages to coffee or red wine: many complementary tastes combine and are finished with smoke, lending a heady complexity to the finished sausage. Longaniza de Valladolid has such a prominent place on the Yucatecan table that it appears in a variety of guises: as an appetizer or main course when grilled (see Longaniza asada, below), or in meaty stews like Estofado de carne de cerdo con longaniza (p. 379).

Related to the Spanish chorizo, Portuguese *linguiça* is known as "*longaniza*" in Yucatán as it is elsewhere throughout the Spanish Diaspora, from the Philippines to Argentina. This mildly spicy, long and skinny sausage varies considerably from one region to the next. Here it is stained red-orange with *achiote* and is finished by smoking. The product has forged a booming cottage industry in Valladolid, Temozón, and the surrounding area. A peculiarly regional variation is to swap the pork for fresh venison when available, in which case the sausage is called, appropriately, Longaniza de venado.

I strongly recommend that you use a commercial meat-curing product for this recipe (see Resources on p. 540). Since the sausages will be suspended above a heat source of only about 120°F (49°C) for a couple of hours, the meat potentially runs the risk of developing nasty bacteria. That said, in Yucatán we rarely if ever eat smoked *longaniza* without frying or grilling it just before serving, ensuring the certain death of any bugs that may have sneaked past our attention.

Prepare ahead note: Allow 3–4 days for the complete production of Longaniza de Valladolid. The meat mixture should rest in the refrigerator for at least 8 hours or overnight. Once stuffed into the casings, the sausages should dry in the refrigerator 48–72 hours. And the smoking can take 2–3 hours, depending on your equipment.

YIELD: APPROXIMATELY 18 SAUSAGES (2½ LBS. / 1.2 K TOTAL)

Rows of smoky Longaniza de Valladolid in a smoker in Temozón. [DIANA KENNEDY]

FOR THE SEASONING

3 Tbs. (45 g) Recado rojo

4 Tbs. (60 g) Recado blanco

1 Tbs. (2 g) dried whole Mexican oregano, lightly toasted and ground

1 medium white onion (10 oz. / 275 g), peeled, charred, and coarsely chopped

10 medium cloves garlic (2½ oz. / 60 g), peeled, charred, and coarsely chopped

½ cup (125 ml) white vinegar

2 tsp. (12 g) commercial meat cure powder (see Resources, p. 540)

FOR THE MEAT MIXTURE AND CASINGS

2 lbs. (1 k) boneless pork leg or rump, trimmed of connective tissue

½ lb. (225 g) pork fat

Approximately 8 ft. (2.5 m) small sheep casings (19–21 mm) (Note: Typical Longaniza de Valladolid links are narrow in diameter; sheep rather than hog casings are preferred)

FOR THE SMOKING

Mesquite wood smoking chips

PREPARE SEASONING

Place the ingredients in the jar of a blender and liquefy, making sure the onion and garlic are completely puréed; set aside.

PREPARE MEAT MIXTURE

Pass the meat and fat through the coarse blade of a meat grinder into a large mixing bowl. Change to the fine blade and pass the meat through again. Add the seasoning ingredients and mix well. To check the seasonings, fry a small batch. (Note: The raw mixture will be slushy, and the fried batch will be crumbly. This is typical of Longaniza in Yucatán.) Cover and refrigerate overnight.

PREPARE CASINGS

Your casings will most likely be packed in salt. Rinse them under cold water, then place them in a bowl of cold water and leave at room temperature for 1 hour. Pour off the water and rinse. When you are ready to stuff the sausages, cut one length of the casing at a time, approximately 36 inches (90 cm) in length (experienced sausage makers may use full lengths). Place one end of the casing on the nozzle of your kitchen faucet and slowly run cold water through it to open and prepare it for stuffing.

STUFF AND DRY SAUSAGES

For best results, use a stand mixer with a sausage-stuffing attachment. Follow the manufacturer's instructions for the equipment, filling complete, narrow lengths of the sausage about ¾ inch (2 cm) in diameter. Twist the lengths into links about 8 inches (20 cm) long. Tie the ends to seal in the stuffing and set aside. Repeat until all the meat has been used.

   Place the finished sausages in one layer on a baking rack on a cookie sheet lined with paper towels (the sausages need to have air circulating around them to dry properly, and the paper towels will absorb any juices that seep out). Refrigerate at least 48 hours or up to 72 hours prior to smoking.

SMOKE SAUSAGES

Follow the manufacturer's directions for your smoker. Start with a smoker temperature of about 120°F (49°C), increasing over the course of a couple of hours to 160°F (71°C). Immediately remove sausages when they are just short of an internal temperature of 160°F (71°C). Drape them over a broom handle or on clothes hangers wrapped in aluminum foil for an hour or two, or until they are completely dry. Refrigerate or vacuum-pack and freeze until ready for use.

TO SERVE

Several recipes in this book specify Longaniza de Valladolid as a main component. But the most typical way to eat it is grilled, as in Longaniza asada.

VARIATION

Longaniza asada (Grilled Smoked Sausage with Charred Tomato and Onion Salsas): Follow the master recipes for Chiltomate (p. 451) and Cebollas asadas (p. 450). As for Poc chuc (p. 448), char the vegetables for the salsas over the same fire you will use for grilling the sausages; finish the salsas immediately before grilling the sausages. Serving suggestions are the same.

(opposite page) Longaniza asada with Chiltomate (p. 451) and Cebollas asadas (p. 450). [MC]

TETIZ

THE SWEETEST OF PUEBLOS

Tetiz is a tiny pueblo of only 4,000 people on the western road to Celestún. The name in Mayan, oddly, translates as "to choose sweet potato" (*téet* = "to choose"; *íis* = "sweet potato"). Coincidentally or not, several villagers of the town earn a living preparing sweet treats, including a few made with sweet potato, to sell in regional markets.

A particular meringue that I once sampled in the market so enchanted me with its crispy exterior and creamy and light-as-air interior faintly scented with lime that I went on a quest for the maker, who, I was told, was simply known as doña Sara. I found her in Tetiz.

Doña Sara María Caamal Poot, her daughter Ruby and son Rudi, along with patriarch don Luis Armando Canché Balam, form part of an extended family that, like so many families of Yucatán, earns a modest living by means of a variety of cottage industries. Doña Sara is dedicated to making sweet treats, principally meringues, as were her mother and grandmother before her, and now the whole family is involved in the sweets business.

Making Merengues is an all-day family affair, six days a week, seven during holiday seasons. Doña Sara's recipe (below) is for just one batch. On the day I visited, the family was going to mix eight of the large tubs of egg whites, totaling 480 eggs and yielding 1,000 meringues, all for the next day's order. First thing the next morning, a courier from the local post office would pick up the sweets and drive them to their markets. Before the first meringue would be sold and eaten, doña Sara and family would be back at work producing another thousand swirls of creamy sweetness.

DOÑA SARA'S RECIPE FOR MERINGUES

Ruby recited to me her mother's simple yet voluminous formula:

- 60 egg whites
- 4 k sugar
- ½ L water
- Rind of 2 limes

(1) *Sugar syrup was boiled in a battered tin pail above a raging wood fire, giving the syrup a slightly smoky flavor. As the syrup boiled, Ruby cracked open 60 eggs, separating yolks from whites.* [DS] (2) *Don Luis seemed to come alive the moment Ruby poured the viscous whites into a plastic tub set before him. He immediately took his cue and proceeded to whip with a fury I had not expected from a man his age.* [DS] (3) *With the speed that could only come from having done this chore a thousand times, Ruby deftly squeezed uniform mounds of the meringue, each with a perfectly formed tuft on top, onto paper-lined wooden tables.* [DS] (4) *Doña Sara's meringues are baked in a traditional way that is slowly disappearing. A round steel drum with a gently sloping conical top is placed above the meringues and hot coals are piled on top. After just 20 minutes, the meringues are beautifully golden and show the telltale cracking that signals they are done.* [DS]

(opposte page) Crispy, creamy Merengues. [DS]

MERENGUES

CRISPY/CREAMY EGG WHITE MOUNDS SCENTED WITH LIME ZEST

FOR BEST RESULTS
YOU WILL NEED
Stand mixer
Candy thermometer
Precise oven thermometer
Parchment paper
Timer

FOR THE EGG WHITES
4–5 large egg whites, room
temperature (Note: The volume
of whites is more important
than the number of eggs; you
should use enough eggs to reach
⅔ cup [160 ml] of whites)
¼ tsp. cream of tartar

FOR THE SUGAR SYRUP
AND FINISHING
½ cup (125 ml) water
1⅓ cups (265 g) *plus* 5 Tbs. (60 g)
granulated sugar, divided
Zest of ½ large lime, grated or
coarsely chopped

I have never had meringues (*merengues*) as heavenly as those I have eaten in Yucatán. Often, meringues are dry and crunchy through and through. In stark contrast, meringues in Yucatán are lightly crispy on the outside, but soft and creamy inside. The difference has much to do with the baking: most recipes for meringues that I followed in the United States called for baking them at a very low temperature for an hour and a half or more—the point being to thoroughly dry them out. But in Yucatán, the most typical ones are baked with an intense heat source on top, and the baking is finished in a much shorter period. Result: crispy top, creamy interior. This recipe has been adapted to produce similar results in a standard oven.

If you are challenged by meringues, take heart: even a *maestra* like doña Sara says that they can be very fussy. Some days they just won't cooperate. When she taught her daughters how to make them, she carefully instructed them that they should not make meringues when they were pregnant, and they should never leave the front door open because passersby could be distracting.

Prepare ahead note: Merengues keep well in an airtight container at room temperature in a cool, dry place for 2–3 days.

YIELD: APPROXIMATELY 18 "DOUBLE" MERENGUES

BEAT WHITES

Preheat the oven to 250°F (121°C). Line 2 baking sheets with parchment. For convenience, place a stand mixer next to the stove. Beat the whites on slow until they foam; add the cream of tartar, increase the speed to medium-high, and beat until soft peaks form. Turn the machine to very slow while you make the sugar syrup.

PREPARE SUGAR SYRUP AND FINISH

In a small saucepan equipped with a lid, combine the water and 1⅓ cups (265 g) of the sugar and place the pan over high heat, swirling gently to dissolve the sugar. Cover the pan and continue cooking over high heat. Lift the lid after a minute or two: the sugar should be completely dissolved and the liquid clear. Remove the lid and insert a candy thermometer into the syrup. Continue to cook on high heat until the syrup reaches the soft-ball stage, 234°F (112°C), 2-3 minutes.

Immediately turn the mixer to medium-high and continue beating as you slowly stream in the syrup. When all the syrup has been added, increase the speed to high and beat for 12 minutes.

With the mixer still on high speed, sprinkle in 1 tablespoon (12 g) of the sugar and beat 2 minutes. Repeat, adding 2 more tablespoons of the sugar one at a time, beating 2 minutes after each addition. Add the lime zest and 1 more tablespoon of sugar and beat another 2 minutes. Add the fifth and final tablespoon of sugar and beat for just 15 seconds. You will have beaten the meringue 20 minutes and 15 seconds; it will be cool and slightly grainy.

Transfer the meringue to a pastry bag fitted with a No. 8 (½ in. / 1.25 cm) plain tip (alternatively, you may use a plastic storage bag, snipping off ½ in. / 1.25 cm of 1 corner). Working on the parchment paper–lined baking sheets, pipe approximately ¾ ounce (20 g) of the meringue in a circle measuring 3 inches (7.5cm) in diameter. Continue piping in a spiral motion to fill in the circle. Continue spiraling to form a smaller circle on top of the first, fill in, then spiral upward to create a curlicue. (See full instructions below.) Proceed with the remaining meringues; you should have approximately 36.

Place the baking sheets in the preheated oven, locating one close to the top and one close to the bottom, and bake for 20 minutes; rotate the sheets. Bake another 20 minutes, then turn off the heat. Leave the baking sheets in the oven another 20 minutes, then remove them and allow to cool to the touch.

While the meringues are still slightly warm, carefully lift 2 and place them bottom to bottom to create the typical Yucatecan double meringue. (They are fragile, so handle with care.) If the bottoms are too dry to stick together, brush them very gently and lightly with a bit of water, then stick them together. As soon as they are cool and set, store them in an airtight container.

SECRETS OF YUCATECAN *MERENGUES*

Humidity is a notorious enemy of meringues, and it can seem Sisyphean to try making them in Yucatán. However, one secret to Yucatecan meringues is that they are always the Italian style: egg whites beaten with hot sugar syrup. Italian meringue is known to be very forgiving and humidity resistant.

Another reason why Yucatecan meringues last so well in a tropical environment is their domed "caps." This outer layer is almost 1/16-inch (1.5875 mm) thick, crunchy, with a light sensation of grittiness from the sugar. You can achieve something similar by adding granulated sugar up to the last minute of beating and by stopping the beating seconds after the final addition—counter to most other meringue recipes.

Because of the way meringues are baked in Yucatán—with the heat source located above—this upper cap bakes first, which creates the crust and seals in the creamy center. Locate one baking sheet as close to the top oven wall as possible, the other on the bottom rack, then rotate halfway through baking.

Guaranteeing the creamy center is another Yucatecan secret: meringues here are much larger than conventional ones, measuring 3 inches (7.5 cm) in diameter and about 1½ inches (4 cm) tall. The outside cooks evenly, but the inside never completely dries out. Be sure to mound meringues high: keep moving in a continuous spiral as you pipe a circle, fill in the circle, continue spiraling to form a smaller circle, fill it in, then finish the spiral with a curlicue at the top. You should pipe about ¾ ounce (20 g) of meringue for each piece. Practice getting size and volume correct: (1) trace a 3-inch (7.5 cm) circle on paper; (2) place the paper on a scale; (3) pipe out one meringue to a weight of ¾ ounce (20 g).

Finally, Yucatecan meringues are baked on inexpensive butcher paper, which is "dry," somewhat porous, and absorbent. Use only paper bags, butcher paper, or parchment for best results. Waxed paper and even silicon mats will stick.

TIZIMÍN

Jarana. [MR]

COWBOY COUNTRY

Near the dramatic Maya archaeological zone of Ek' Balam, due north of Valladolid, Tizimín is the capital of Yucatán's cattle country. *"Tsíimin"* means "tapir" in Mayan, and in an interesting historical footnote, it was also the word the Mayas applied to horses when the Spanish introduced them to the New World. Driving through the region offers views that remind me of West Texas: dense scrub forests give way to flat grazing land, with parcels discreetly defined by tidy, low walls of whitewashed mortarless stone.

Cattle ranching in the region started shortly after the arrival of Europeans. As Spain divided the spoils of the New World, the regal ruin of Chichén Itzá, once the mightiest city of the Mayas, was partitioned as part of a land grant, and by the 1580s, it had become a cattle ranch. By the eighteenth century, sprawling ranches flourished throughout the peninsula. The men who handled the cantankerous breed brought from Spain had little choice but to allow the cattle to graze in scrubland. The distances between the grazing grounds and the marketplace were so great that herd managers had to learn to ride horses and use ropes for snaring wanderers. This style of cattle management created what we know today as the vaquero, or cowboy, still a prominent character in Yucatán.

LA VAQUERÍA

A confluence of Spanish and indigenous traditions gave rise to the most famous festival in Yucatán: *la vaquería.* Born in the mid-eighteenth century, the festival was originally held to celebrate the branding and counting of cattle on Yucatán's many ranches. After the branding, ranchers' wives entertained their husbands and guests by performing traditional Maya dances against a backdrop of Spanish music. The dance, as well as the music, is known as "*la jarana.*"

The *jarana* is known for certain special stunts. In one instance, the more adept dancers balance a tray precariously loaded with beer bottles on their heads while their feet clack away in rhythm to the music. Each dance lasts between 20 and 30 minutes, punctuated occasionally by the cry of "¡Bomba!" at which point the music and dancing stop, and the narrator recites a ribald poem rather like a limerick, often with food references eliciting howls of laughter from the audience:

> ¡Bomba!
> *Me gusta el pan de Progreso*
> *y también el de Pomuch,*
> *pero prefiero ese queso*
> *que guardas bajo tu tuuch.*

> *I like the bread from Progreso*
> *and also the bread from Pomuch,*
> *but I prefer that cheese*
> *you keep hidden below your belly button.*

Music and dance were not the only entertainments at the *vaquería.* Ranch owners erected makeshift bullrings cobbled together from branches and sticks that they pillaged from the forest; townsfolk took their places in the rickety bleachers under the still-fierce late afternoon sun to watch an amateur bullfight. At the end of the fight, the bull was hauled off and dismembered, the meat, blood, head, ears, tail, and organs distributed among the hungry crowd. The stew made from all the carnage was called "*chocolomo,*" a Mayan/Spanish hybrid word meaning "hot loin." It is a direct descendant of "*carne de lidia,*" "meat of the bullfight," a gastronomical custom brought to the New World from Spain.

The *vaquería* and the *jarana* are still very much alive in Yucatán. Nowadays, the reverence of patron saints has replaced the branding of cattle as the raison d'être of the festival, and the *jarana* is danced at just about any time of year, including most Sunday and Monday nights in the main plaza of Mérida. To witness the whole raucous spectacle of the *vaquería,* however, you'll have to take a trip into the pueblos.

Bullfight, as part of the vaquería *festival.* [RW]

Brahman cattle, or zebus (Bos indicus), are well suited to Yucatán's harsh environment. [MC]

CHOCOLOMO

BEEF ORGAN MEAT STEW IN PEPPERY BROTH

TO PREPARE AHEAD
Enriched Lard (p. 513)
Recado para bistec (p. 501)
Recado blanco (p. 502)

FOR THE MEATS

3 Tbs. (42 g) Enriched Lard

3 lbs. (1.5 k) assorted stewing beef, beef heart, liver and/or kidneys, and brains, or all stewing beef, cleaned and cubed

1 lb. (500 g) beef stewing bones

FOR THE STEW

8 cups (2 L) beef stock or bouillon

2 cups (500 ml) red wine, optional (Note: if eliminating the wine, replace it with 2 cups [500 ml] beef stock or bouillon)

2 Tbs. (40 g) Recado para bistec

1 Tbs. (15 g) Recado blanco

¼ cup (62.5 ml) sherry vinegar

FOR THE *SOFRITO* AND FINISHING

1 Tbs. (14 g) Enriched Lard

1 medium white onion (10 oz. / 275 g), peeled, charred, and chopped

1 medium head garlic (1¾ oz. / 50 g), charred, peeled, and separated into cloves

1 Tbs. (2 g) dried whole Mexican oregano *and* 1 tsp. (2 g) cuminseed, lightly toasted and ground together, then passed through a fine sieve, residue discarded

4 medium Roma tomatoes (14 oz. / 400 g), seeded and chopped

½ cup (40 g) chives, chopped

½ cup (30 g) fresh mint leaves, chopped

Don't let "organ meat stew" put you off trying this exquisite *criollo* dish: the richness of the meats is mitigated by mint and a peppery wine-based stock. I happen to enjoy organ meats, but for a less visceral experience you can use cubed stewing beef exclusively. This recipe is a composite of several found in vintage regional cookbooks. The wine is not traditional for this essentially campesino dish, but, curiously, side by side with the recipe for Chocolomo frequently appear recipes for similar beef dishes stewed in wine, so I chose to include it. You may omit it if you wish.

The earliest record of bullfights held by the Mayas dates to around the first half of the sixteenth century. While in Spain the bullfight took on special significance as a battle with Death, for the Mayas it took on added meaning in a world dominated by conquerors. Many of the traditions from that period continue in some places: in Santa Elena, for example, on the Friday before a slaughter, the bull is tied to a ceiba tree and left to be observed by those who will consume the meat; Saturday at dawn the butchering and meat distribution take place; cooking happens in the afternoon. For this reason, in many pueblos, Chocolomo remains a dish consumed only in the evening.

Prepare ahead note: Chocolomo can be prepared a day or two in advance and reheated prior to serving.

YIELD: 6 SERVINGS

The butchering and distribution of the meat takes place immediately after a bullfight. [RW]

BROWN MEATS

Heat the lard in a stockpot until shimmering. Working in batches so as not to crowd, brown the meats and bones on all sides, about 2–3 minutes per side. Transfer the browned pieces to a platter as they are done.

STEW MEATS

Return the meats and bones to the stockpot and cover with the stock and wine. Dissolve the *recados* in the vinegar and add to the stockpot. Bring to a boil, reduce the heat to a simmer, and skim off any foam that surfaces. Continue simmering as you proceed.

PREPARE *SOFRITO* AND FINISH

Heat the lard in a skillet until shimmering. Add the onions and garlic and cook until softened, 2–3 minutes. Add the ground spices and stir to incorporate. Add the tomatoes and cook until most of the liquid has evaporated, 3–4 minutes. Transfer the *sofrito* to the stockpot and return to a simmer. Cook slowly 1 hour, or until the meat is tender and the cooking liquid has reduced by about one-quarter.

Remove the meats and discard the bones. Add the herbs to the stock and stir to combine. Simmer an additional 5–10 minutes to incorporate the flavors. Remove the pot from the heat.

TO SERVE

Distribute the meats and cooking liquid among soup bowls; alternatively, distribute the meats among individual plates and serve the cooking liquid in soup bowls on the side. Top with Totopos para sopa; diners garnish with Chiltomate, the radish/cilantro mixture, and chile sauce to taste.

PANTRY
STAPLES

Pantry Staples features recipes for the essential components that will serve you for a broad range of Yucatecan fare. Make large quantities and store them; most of these components have a long shelf life in proper conditions.

RECADOS / XA'AK' / SEASONING BLENDS

Recados are Yucatán's indispensable seasoning blends (p. 74). To the uninitiated, the number of *recados*, the minute variations in their formulas, even their names, which can change without warning or be used interchangeably, can be daunting.

During ten years of research, I, too, have occasionally been lost in the *recado* labyrinth. As much for my own culinary clarity as for that of my students, I have struggled to define the primary uses and basic formulas of the most important ones. To do so, I have delved into historical sources and vintage regional cookbooks—some dating to the early 1800s—and worked with local cooks. In the historical sources, only rarely are entire recipes given for *recados*; instead, the author lists various ingredients—with neither measurements nor methods—then instructs the cook to "prepare the *recado*." One assumes the women of the age knew just what to do.

With as much scientific method as I could muster, I extracted a range of *recado* formulas and organized them in a matrix, analyzing which ingredients were always included, which were usually included, and which were only occasionally included. I then took an average to calculate proportions. In this way, I believe that I have been able to reconstruct what might be described as "composites" of the most common Yucatecan *recados* since at least the late eighteenth century.

POWDERED *RECADOS*

Pepita molida

PRIMARY INGREDIENT: Pepita menuda (squash seeds: *Cucurbita moschata*)

USES: Brazo de reina (p. 131), Pipián rojo (p. 96), Pol'kanes (p. 111), Sikil p'aak (p. 285), Toksel (p. 113)

OTHER NAMES: Pepita para brazo de reina, Pepita para sikil p'aak

Recado para escabeche

PRIMARY INGREDIENT: Black pepper (*Piper nigrum*)

USES: Camarones en escabeche (p. 319), Cebollas en escabeche (p. 511), Pavo en escabeche oriental (p. 389)

OTHER NAMES: Recado para escabeche oriental, Recaudo oriental, Recado para salpimentado

Recado para pastor

PRIMARY INGREDIENT: Chile pasilla (*Capsicum annuum* L.)

USES: Carne al pastor (p. 236)

Recado para puchero

PRIMARY INGREDIENT: Coriander seed (*Coriandrum sativum* L.)

USES: Puchero (p. 350), Puchero vaquero (p. 351), Sopa de rabioles (p. 392)

Recado para todo

PRIMARY INGREDIENT: Orégano yucateco (*Lippia graveolens*)

USES: Picadillo de especias (p. 256)

OTHER NAMES: Recado de toda clase, Recado de especie, Recado de especias

Recado para bistec

PRIMARY INGREDIENT: Orégano yucateco ("Mexican oregano," *Lippia graveolens*)

USES: Bistec a la cazuela (p. 265), Pollo en bistec (p. 264)

OTHER NAMES: Recado blanco (in Valladolid)

Recado blanco

PRIMARY INGREDIENT: Black pepper (*Piper nigrum*)

USES: Longaniza de Valladolid (p. 481), Mechado (p. 397)

OTHER NAMES: Recado para mechado, Recado para bistec (in Valladolid)

Recado negro

PRIMARY INGREDIENT: Chile país (*Capsicum annuum*). Also known as chile de país, chile seco de país, chile seco yucateco

USES: Frijoles en chilmole (p. 267), Pavo en relleno negro (p. 424), Picadillo en chilmole (p. 254)

OTHER NAMES: Recado para chilmole, Recado para chirmole, Recado para relleno negro

Recado para papadzules

PRIMARY INGREDIENT: Pepita verde (squash seeds: *Cucurbita argyrosperma*)

USES: Papadzules (p. 280)

Recado rojo

PRIMARY INGREDIENT: *Achiote* (*Bixa orellana*)

USES: Pollo pibil (p. 421), Cochinita pibil (p. 420), Pescado en tikin'xik (p. 316), K'óol rojo (p. 86)

OTHER NAMES: Recado de achiote, Recado colorado

Note on all recado *recipes:* Formulas for *recados*—whether commercial or homemade—generally include salt in the ingredient list. However, since all recipes in this book that require a *recado* also call for salt, I do not include salt in any of the *recados*. This will allow you to adjust the salt level according to the quantity of the meal you are preparing, as well as to your own taste.

Prepare ahead note for all recados: Powdered *recados* will keep for several months. Place them in an airtight container or resealable plastic bag. Paste *recados* with organics such as garlic must be refrigerated or frozen. Place them in an airtight container or resealable bag, refrigerate for 1–2 weeks, or freeze indefinitely.

PEPITA MOLIDA

TOASTED GROUND SQUASH SEEDS

When toasted and finely ground, squash seeds (*pepitas*) turn into an earthy brown powder known as *pepita molida*. These ground seeds are used in everything from sauces and dips to fillings for tamales and fritters.

Two varieties of squash seeds regularly used in Yucatecan cooking predominate in the markets. *Pepita menuda* comes from the *Cucurbita moschata* (p. 22), a family that includes winter squashes like Hubbard and butternut as well as some pumpkin varieties. It is a brownish, small oval seed—never hulled. Another common squash seed found in the market is a larger white seed that comes from *Cucurbita argyrosperma* (p. 24), a species that includes the Cushaw. When still in its hull it is known in Spanish as *pepita gruesa*; when the hull is removed to expose the inner green seed, it is called *pepita verde* and is the seed that most closely corresponds to the commercially available pumpkinseeds (also known as "*pepitas*") that you will be able to find outside Mexico.

Since *pepita menuda* is unhulled, labor costs are low, meaning that the seeds are less than half the price of the hulled *pepita verde*. It may be for this reason that the *menuda* is the seed of choice among frugal Yucatecans for making Pepita molida to use in workaday dips and fillings, whereas the expensive *verde* is reserved for "fancy" dishes like Papadzules (p. 280).

While earthy and flavorful, Pepita molida made from the unhulled seeds of *C. moschata* gives dishes in which it is employed a rather fibrous and not altogether pleasant texture. If this is not to your liking, you may sacrifice a bit of authenticity by switching to hulled seeds for all Yucatecan recipes that call for *pepita molida*.

To make Pepita molida outside of Mexico, look for fresh *unroasted* pumpkinseeds, hulled or not, depending on your taste. (Some vendors are now selling roasted seeds; these work fine, but get unsalted ones for the recipes in this book and skip the roasting step.) You can also extract seeds from your own squash, but clean them well and allow them to dry thoroughly.

Prepare ahead note: Like all fats, the fats in squash seeds—once released after grinding—tend to oxidize and go rancid over time. Storing the powder in the refrigerator will keep it fresh for about two weeks; freezing preserves it for several months. Since so many Yucatecan dishes call for Pepita molida and since it stores so well, I always double this recipe and freeze it.

PEPITA MOLIDA (*VERDE*)

TOASTED GROUND SQUASH SEEDS, HULLED

YIELD: APPROXIMATELY 4 CUPS (500 G)

---

4 cups (500 g) green squash- or pumpkinseeds, hulled

Heat a large dry cast-iron skillet over highest heat for 5 minutes. Place the seeds in the hot skillet. As soon as they begin to pop, toss or stir them vigorously and constantly to avoid burning the seeds at the bottom. Continue toasting until the seeds are fragrant and golden brown, about 5 minutes. Immediately transfer the seeds to a metal colander or large sieve (do not leave them in the skillet: residual heat can burn the seeds at the bottom). Outdoors, or in a place where you don't mind making a bit of a mess, briskly toss the seeds in the colander to shake off the papery skins.

Once the seeds have cooled, place them in the bowl of a large food processor fitted with the metal blade. Process 3–4 minutes, until the powder begins clumping on the sides of the bowl. Stop the motor and use a spatula to scrape the powder back into the bowl. Process another 2–3 minutes. Scrape the bowl down again and process until you see very little movement of the powder (the clumping action is a result of the oils being released from the seeds). Taste a bit of the powder: it should have a pleasant texture but not be grainy. If it's grainy, process a minute or 2 more.

Transfer the powder to an airtight container and store as instructed above, or use immediately in one of the recipes in this book.

VARIATION

Pepita molida (*menuda*) (Toasted Ground Squash Seeds, unhulled): If you want to aim for authenticity and don't mind some chewy fiber, the *menuda* seeds are the ones commonly used in dishes like Sikil p'aak (p. 285). Proceed according to the recipe for Pepita molida (*verde*), but use unhulled seeds. For a finer powder, after you grind the seeds in a food processor, grind again in batches in a clean spice mill or coffee grinder. Test by pinching a small amount and tasting it; process more if it's still too fibrous.

RECADO PARA ESCABECHE
PEPPERY SPICE BLEND FOR PICKLED DISHES

"*Escabechar*" in Spanish means "to pickle." The best known use of this *recado* is for Pavo en escabeche oriental (p. 389), a classic dish of Valladolid. It also is used for pickled vegetables or fish as well as for many other dishes in which the flavors of pepper and oregano are appropriate.

YIELD: APPROXIMATELY 1½ OZ. (45 G) / 6 TBS.

FOR THE *RECADO*
3 Tbs. (36 g) black peppercorns
3 Tbs. (6 g) dried whole Mexican oregano, lightly toasted
20 cloves
20 allspice berries
13 bay leaves

Place the first 4 ingredients and 5 of the bay leaves in a spice mill or coffee grinder reserved for the purpose and grind until very fine. Strain the powder through a fine-mesh sieve over a bowl, crumbling any remaining bits of debris through the sieve with your fingers. Return anything left in the sieve to the grinder and process again. Pass through the sieve and discard any residue.

Transfer the ground spices to an airtight container, add the remaining whole bay leaves, and toss to mix.

RECADO PARA PASTOR
SEASONING BLEND FOR "SHEPHERD-STYLE" PORK

Recado para pastor has only recently begun appearing in the markets next to the more traditional powdered *recados*. Commercial recipes for this seasoning blend result in a paste, but the powdered form has a longer shelf life. Once the exclusive domain of street vendors and *taquerías*, Carne al pastor has become so popular that even home cooks have created a demand for this *recado*.

YIELD: APPROXIMATELY 4½ OZ. (126 G) / 14 TBS.

FOR THE *RECADO*
10 chiles pasillas (about 3¼ oz. / 90 g)
10 chiles guajillos (about 2¼ oz. / 65 g)
2 Tbs. (4 g) dried whole Mexican oregano, lightly toasted
1 Tbs. (6 g) cuminseed, lightly toasted
12 allspice berries
8 cloves

Preheat the oven to 350°F (176°C). While the oven is heating, use scissors to remove the stems from the tops of the chiles. Slit them along one side, open, and remove the seeds and veins. (See Basic Techniques, p. 534.) Press the chiles flat and transfer them to a large baking tray. Bake for approximately 25 minutes, or until the chiles are crisp, fragrant, and slightly darkened. Remove the baking tray from the oven and allow the chiles to cool.

Place the remaining ingredients in a spice grinder or coffee mill reserved for the purpose and grind until very fine. Strain the powder through a fine-mesh sieve into a bowl, crumbling any remaining bits of debris through the sieve with your fingers. Return anything left in the sieve to the grinder and process again. Pass the powder through the sieve and discard any residue.

Crumble the chiles into the bowl of a food processor. Process for several minutes, or until they are completely broken up and beginning to turn into a powder. Depending on the capacity of your food processor, you may be able to render the chiles into a fine powder. If not, transfer them in batches as necessary to the spice mill and grind to a very fine powder. Pass the powder through the sieve into the bowl with the other spices; repeat until all the chiles have been ground. Mix the ground spices and the chile powder thoroughly and store in an airtight container.

RECADO PARA PUCHERO
AROMATIC SEASONING BLEND FOR STEWS

Puchero is a classic Yucatecan stew descended from its Spanish ancestor. Recipes for the requisite *recado* vary dramatically, so in a quest for "realness" I sought the earliest version that I could find. Luckily, I happened upon *Prontuario de cocina para un diario regular* (Handbook for everyday cooking), a Mérida cookbook dating to 1832 that contains a recipe for the *recado* as well as for the *puchero* stew itself. The recipe for the *recado* specifies no measurements and only three ingredients—coriander seed, black pepper, and *achiote*, in that order—although when the cookbook was updated in 1896, the revised *recado* also featured anise. Further, the author's recipe for the stew in which the *recado* is used specifies a few more herbs and spices: oregano, cumin, cloves, and a pinch of saffron. (She also suggests adding some Mexican cinnamon if you are cooking a hen.) I took the liberty of combining everything in the recipe for this *recado*, since, after all, *recados* are supposed to be labor saving.

YIELD: APPROXIMATELY 1½ OZ. (48 G) / 6 TBS.

FOR THE *RECADO*
3 Tbs. (15 g) coriander seed
1 Tbs. (6 g) cuminseed
1 Tbs. (2 g) dried whole Mexican oregano, lightly toasted
1 tsp. (4 g) *achiote* seeds
1 tsp. (4 g) black peppercorns
1 tsp. (3 g) ground *canela* (Mexican cinnamon)
1 star anise
¾ tsp. whole cloves (about 30 cloves)
Big pinch saffron

Working in batches as necessary, place all of the ingredients in a spice mill or coffee grinder reserved for the purpose

and grind until very fine. Strain the powder through a fine-mesh sieve over a bowl, crumbling any remaining bits of debris through the sieve with your fingers. Return anything left in the sieve to the grinder and process again. Pass the powder through the sieve and discard any residue. Toss to mix and store in an airtight container.

RECADO PARA TODO
SPICY ALL-PURPOSE SEASONING BLEND

Most of the traditional Spice Islands flavorings can be found in this great all-purpose seasoning—black pepper, cloves, and cinnamon—as well as Yucatán's indigenous allspice (*Pimenta dioica*). One of the main ingredients is local *orégano yucateco* (*Lippia graveolens*, known outside Mexico as "Mexican oregano"), which gives the mixture an earthy bottom note. Recado para todo is featured prominently in a number of ground meat mixtures, such as the stuffing for Queso relleno (p. 345), and lends finished dishes a distinctive Middle Eastern flavor.

YIELD: APPROXIMATELY 1½ OZ. (45 G) / 6 TBS.

FOR THE *RECADO*
4 Tbs. (8 g) dried whole Mexican oregano, lightly toasted
3 Tbs. (36 g) black peppercorns
1 tsp. (3 g) ground *canela* (Mexican cinnamon)
1 tsp. (2 g) cuminseed
1 tsp. (2 g) whole cloves
1 tsp. (2 g) allspice berries
½ tsp. (2 g) *achiote* seeds

Working in batches as necessary, place all ingredients in a spice mill or coffee grinder reserved for the purpose. Grind until very fine and strain through a fine-mesh sieve over a bowl, crumbling any remaining bits of debris through the sieve with your fingers. Return anything left in the sieve to the grinder and process again. Pass the powder through the sieve and discard any residue. Toss to mix and store in an airtight container.

The three most popular paste *recados* are widely available in markets beyond Yucatán: Recado rojo (also called Recado de achiote or Recado colorado); Recado negro (also called Recado para chilmole or simply Chilmole); and Recado para bistec. The *recados* are boxed in small blocks under a variety of brand names (see Resources, p. 540). Your own homemade *recado* will be more intensely flavorful, but the commercial ones perform acceptably in a pinch.

RECADO ROJO
ACHIOTE SEASONING PASTE

Achiote (p. 63, annatto in English) is the principal ingredient in Recado rojo. Diluted with Seville orange juice, Recado rojo becomes a marinade for Yucatán's pit-cooked foods, including Pollo pibil (p. 421) and Cochinita pibil (p. 420), and is a flavoring in many other dishes.

Note about working with *achiote*: Annatto is a powerful colorant and will stain everything it touches. Cover work surfaces with paper; wear an apron if you wish to preserve your clothing; wear gloves if you wish to preserve your manicure.

TO PREPARE AHEAD
Seville orange juice substitute (p. 514), unless
    fresh Seville oranges are available

YIELD: APPROXIMATELY 2 CUPS (500 G) PASTE (33 TBS.)
(Note: Yield is large because Recado rojo is Yucatán's most-used *recado*; freeze until ready to use.)

FOR THE *RECADO*
1 cup (192 g) *achiote* seeds (also known as annatto;
   see Resources, p. 514)
¾ cup (187.5 ml) white vinegar
4 Tbs. (8 g) dried whole Mexican oregano *and* 1 tsp. (2 g)
   cuminseed, lightly toasted together
1 Tbs. (12 g) black peppercorns
12 allspice berries
1 medium head garlic (about 1¾ oz. / 50 g), charred, peeled,
   separated into cloves
¾ cup (187.5 ml) Seville orange juice, or substitute

In a spice mill or coffee grinder reserved for the purpose, grind the *achiote* seeds in batches until fine. Transfer to a fine-mesh sieve held over a plate or bowl. Tap and shake the sieve until all that remains is a coarse residue that looks like sand. Return the residue to the grinder and repeat the process one more time. Continue until all of the *achiote* has been ground; discard any residue that will not pass through the sieve.

Transfer the ground *achiote* seeds to a blender or small food processor, cover with the vinegar, and process to blend. Leave the *achiote* mixture in the processor at room temperature to soften as you continue.

Place the oregano, cuminseed, peppercorns, and allspice berries in the spice grinder and process to a fine powder. Sift the powder through a fine-mesh sieve held over a plate, as you did for the *achiote* seeds. Return any stubborn particles to the grinder. Sieve again and discard any residue.

Add the ground spices, the garlic, and the juice to the *achiote* in the processor and process 3–4 minutes, or until the mixture turns into a thick paste. (Homemade Recado rojo will be grainier than commercial versions, but this will not affect the finished product.) Store in an airtight container.

COMMERCIAL RECADO ROJO

Due to the way in which they are used in recipes, neither the commercial Recado negro nor the Recado para bistec need any doctoring; however, commercial Recado rojo benefits from the addition of natural organics like garlic and Seville orange juice to achieve the proper flavor. Following are instructions for preparing an enriched marinade using commercial Recado rojo. The recipe in which the *recado* is used will tell you if this step is necessary.

Seville orange juice substitute (p. 514), unless fresh
   Seville oranges are available

Enriched Lard (p. 513)

FOR THE ENRICHMENT

8 Tbs. (120 g) commercial Recado rojo

8 Tbs. (120 ml) Seville orange juice, or substitute

2 Tbs. (28 g) Enriched Lard, melted

1 Tbs. (2 g) dried whole Mexican oregano *and* 1 tsp. (3 g)
   cuminseed, lightly toasted together

1 tsp. (12 g) black peppercorns

4 medium cloves garlic (1 oz. / 24 g), peeled and charred

1 Tbs. (18 g) sea salt

PREPARE THE ENRICHMENT

Dilute the *recado* with the juice, add the lard, and stir to incorporate. Add more juice or *recado* to get the right consistency: thick, yet pourable, like barbecue sauce. Place the remaining ingredients in a *tamul* or mortar and pestle (or in a small food processor or blender) and grind until the garlic is thoroughly mashed and the whole turns into paste. Add the paste to the *recado* mixture and stir to blend. It is now ready to use in your recipe.

RECADO PARA BISTEC
HERBAL SEASONING PASTE

This *recado* acquires its intense flavor and forest green coloring from hefty quantities of Mexican oregano and cumin. As the name suggests, this *recado* serves as a marinade for beef (*bistec*), but it is used just as frequently for turkey, pork, and even some fish dishes.

YIELD: APPROXIMATELY 6 OZ. (170 G) / 8 TBS.

FOR THE *RECADO*

5 Tbs. (10 g) dried whole Mexican oregano *and* 2 Tbs. (12 g)
   cuminseed, lightly toasted together

1 Tbs. (12 g) black peppercorns

2 medium heads garlic (about 1¾ oz. / 50 g each), charred,
   peeled, and separated into cloves

2 Tbs. (30 ml) white vinegar

Working in batches if necessary, place the spices in a spice mill or coffee grinder reserved for the purpose and grind until very fine. Strain the powder through a fine-mesh sieve over a bowl, crumbling any remaining bits of debris through the sieve with your fingers. Return anything left in the sieve to the grinder and process again. Pass through the sieve and discard any residue.

Place the ground spices, garlic, and vinegar in the jar of a blender or a small food processor. Purée for several minutes, scraping down the sides of the jar as needed, until the mixture turns into a smooth paste. Store in an airtight container.

RECADO NEGRO
CHARRED CHILE SEASONING PASTE

Recado negro is surely Yucatán's most unusual and distinctive seasoning blend. Dishes flavored with it are always a characteristic charcoal color; it can be alarming to see people in the market eating tacos dripping with pitch-black gravy! Dried chiles are set aflame, and the ashes are ground with herbs and spices to form a pungent black paste. The little bright red chile país (sometimes known as chile seco) is the chile of choice for Recado negro, but since these may be difficult to find outside of Mexico, I offer substitutions.

In Yucatán's markets, you have your choice of two black *recados*: normal or picante. Even though chiles are the basis of the *recado*, it tends not to be very hot, so some producers toss dried habanero or other fiery chiles into the mixture. If you buy your *recado* in Yucatán, you'll want to confirm which one you are getting; if you make your own, you'll be in control of the heat. The process of burning chile país produces an acrid smoke so fierce that it causes choking, sneezing, and watery eyes, such that preparing Recado negro within the city limits in Yucatán is prohibited.

Of course, you can avoid the issue altogether by purchasing commercial Recado negro, widely available in Mexican groceries or in the "ethnic" foods sections of many supermarkets (see Resources, p. 540). But for best results, make your own. I have developed a method for oven roasting the chiles that produces quite similar results without the stress on your system. It is traditional in Yucatán to include a pinch of Recado rojo in the recipe; read why on page 423.

Prepare ahead note: Make Recado negro at least one day ahead of your needing it, since the charred chiles require an overnight soaking.

TO PREPARE AHEAD
Recado rojo (p. 500)

YIELD: APPROXIMATELY 6 OZ. (170 G) / 11 TBS.

FOR THE CHILES
6 oz. (170 g) chile país (Substitute: 2 oz. / 56 g each dried chile de árbol, chile guajillo, and chile ancho), stems removed, seeded and deveined (See Basic Techniques, p. 535)

FOR THE RECADO
3–4 corn tortillas (7 oz. / 200 g total), toasted in a cast-iron skillet over highest heat until blackened overall

1 Tbs. (12 g) black peppercorns

1 Tbs. (2 g) dried whole Mexican oregano *and* ½ tsp. (1 g) cuminseed, lightly toasted together

5 large cloves

5 large allspice berries

1 chile chipotle in adobo (⅓ oz. / 10 g), drained

1 tsp. (5 g) Recado rojo

1 medium head garlic (1¾ oz. / 50 g), charred, peeled, and separated into cloves

½ medium white onion (5 oz. / 137.5 g), peeled, charred and coarsely chopped

2 Tbs. (30 ml) white vinegar

CHAR AND PREPARE CHILES
Preheat the oven to 425°F (218°C). Place the chiles in a large roasting pan and bake for 45 minutes to 1 hour, or until they are lightly smoking, blackened, and brittle. Transfer to a stockpot full of water and use a potato masher to break the chiles into small pieces. Drain the chiles through a sieve lined with cheesecloth. Use a spatula to mash and extract as much liquid as possible; discard the soaking water but retain the residue in the cheesecloth. Fill the stockpot with fresh water and return the chile ash from the cheesecloth to the stockpot. Allow to soak overnight.

Drain the chile ash through a cheesecloth-lined sieve placed over a bowl; reserve ½ cup (125 ml) of the soaking liquid and discard the rest. Use a spatula to mash the chile ash and extract as much liquid as possible. Gather the chile ash in the cheesecloth; twist and press to squeeze as much liquid from the chile ash as possible; set aside.

GRIND *RECADO* AND FINISH
Place the charred tortillas and the reserved chile-soaking liquid in a small food processor or blender jar and process until the tortillas are dissolved. Place the peppercorns, oregano, cuminseed, cloves, and allspice berries in a spice grinder or coffee mill reserved for the purpose and grind to a powder. Pass the powder through a fine-mesh sieve; return any particles that won't pass through the sieve to the grinder and process again. Strain through the sieve one last time and discard any remaining hard particles. Add the powder to the food processor or blender jar.

Place the chile ash and remaining ingredients except the vinegar in the blender jar and process until thoroughly puréed and smooth. Collect the mixture in a piece of cheesecloth held over a sieve and twist and press to squeeze out as much of the liquid as possible. Transfer the paste to a bowl, add the vinegar, and mash with a fork until thoroughly incorporated. Form the paste into a ball and wrap it in plastic wrap. Refrigerate or freeze until ready to use.

RECADO BLANCO
PEPPERY SEASONING PASTE

This *recado* is used prolifically in the dishes of Valladolid and is also employed as a flavoring in the smoked meats of the region, like Longaniza de Valladolid (p. 481). Recado blanco is the distinctive and essential seasoning in Mechado (p. 397), a popular *vallisoletano* dish. Its strong, peppery flavor with a light clove finish is an excellent accent for large cuts of meat or fowl. Contrary to its name, Recado blanco is not white at all but, rather, a deep slate gray due to voluminous quantities of black pepper. I've asked many local cooks to explain the name, and the standard answer is invariably, "To distinguish it from Recado negro."

YIELD: APPROXIMATELY 6.5 OZ. (180 G) / 12 TBS.

5 Tbs. (60 g) black peppercorns

1 Tbs. (6 g) cuminseed *and* 1 Tbs. (2 g) dried whole Mexican
   oregano, lightly toasted together

2 tsp. (6 g) whole cloves

10 allspice berries

½ tsp. (1.5 g) ground *canela* (Mexican cinnamon)

2 medium heads garlic (approximately 3½ oz. / 100 g total),
   charred, peeled, and separated into cloves

2 Tbs. (30 ml) white vinegar

Working in batches as necessary, place the spices in a spice mill or coffee grinder reserved for the purpose and grind until very fine. Strain the powder through a fine-mesh sieve over a bowl, crumbling any remaining bits of debris through the sieve with your fingers. Return anything left in the sieve to the grinder and process again. Pass the powder through the sieve and discard any residue.

Place the ground spices, garlic, and vinegar in the jar of a blender or a small food processor. Purée for several minutes, scraping down the sides of the jar as needed, until the mixture turns into a smooth paste. Store in an airtight container.

RECADO PARA PAPADZUL
GREEN SQUASH-SEED PASTE FOR PAPADZULES

The fragrant green paste for Papadzules is sold at every Yucatecan market alongside the other *recados*, but outside the region you will have to make your own. It is very easy to do, although time consuming without commercial grinding equipment. You will need a heavy-duty food processor, and I recommend giving it a rest every once in a while so as not to overheat it.

There are a few important tips to keep in mind: (1) buy the freshest green hulled seeds possible; they should appear moist rather than dried out and papery (if you have any doubts, eat one; it should taste fresh, oily, and not rancid); (2) be as patient as you possibly can during the grinding process; Recado para papadzul is not finished until some shiny oil starts appearing on the surface of the paste, which can take as much as 30–40 minutes.

During the grinding, the seeds will pass through three main stages. Skip any of these stages at your peril!

1. A coarse powder
2. Clumps of crumbly dough resembling children's modeling clay
3. A stiff, shiny, pourable paste that looks like green frosting with an oily surface

Prepare ahead note: Recado para papadzul is labor-intensive enough that you certainly want to do it a day (or several days) ahead of making the Papadzules. Place the finished *recado* in an airtight container and refrigerate; bring to room temperature before proceeding with the recipe. It also keeps well frozen for several months.

YIELD: APPROXIMATELY 2 CUPS (16 OZ. / 500 G)

FOR THE *RECADO*

4 cups (500 g) *pepita verde* (raw, unsalted, hulled green
   squash or pumpkinseeds)

Place the seeds in a large, dry cast-iron skillet. Turn the heat to high and wait a few minutes until you hear the seeds begin to pop. Immediately start vigorously and constantly stirring them with a wooden spoon or tossing them in the skillet. The seeds should inflate and change to a slightly richer green color in 2–3 minutes; do not allow them to brown. Immediately transfer the seeds to a colander or large sieve and shake vigorously to remove as much of the papery skin as possible. Allow the seeds to cool 4–5 minutes.

Transfer the seeds to the bowl of a food processor and begin to process. After about 30 seconds, the seeds will have turned into a fine powder. Continue processing 2–3 minutes, or until the powder starts to clump on the sides of the bowl. This is a sign that the natural oils have started to be released. Scrape the powder back into the bowl and resume processing. Repeat these steps for 20–25 minutes, scraping the bowl every few minutes as needed. (Although my food processor's manufacturer might disapprove, I occasionally rock the machine back and forth so that the powder settles back into the center of the bowl without having to stop the motor each time.) After 10–12 minutes, the powder will begin to clump into a crumbly dough; after 15 minutes the clumping should be more evident and even audible; after 20 minutes or so, the crumbly dough will miraculously coalesce into a mass of green clay. Scrape down the bowl again and continue processing until the dough becomes creamy and pourable. Turn off the processor and wait a few minutes. If shiny oil begins accumulating on the surface, the *recado* is ready; otherwise, process a few minutes more. Store in an airtight container until ready to use.

 FRIJOLES / BU'UL / BEANS

In an effort to avoid waste and streamline kitchen chores, Yucatecans are in the habit of "repurposing" dishes after the first meal. This is especially true for beans: a big pot of Frijol k'abax is cooked at the beginning of the week; on Tuesday it is puréed and strained to become Frijol colado; by week's end the purée is poured into a skillet with some sizzling lard to create Frijol refrito. Thus is the life cycle of Yucatecan beans.

FRIJOL K'ABAX / K'ABAX-BU'UL

SIMPLE POT BEANS

Frijol k'abax (K'abax-bu'ul) is traditionally the first bean dish of the week in Yucatán. The Mayan name means "beans cooked simply, with no seasonings," suggesting its basic method of preparation and lack of fussiness. It corresponds to the Mexican *frijoles de la olla*. From this simple bean dish are derived several other dishes (see notes above), making it an essential pantry staple. Frijol k'abax is humble folks' food, flavored only with salt, chile, and epazote. However, all recipes for subsequent dishes in which the leftover beans are reused call for the addition of enrichments—onions, lard, and oregano among them. For this reason, I break with tradition and include those flavorings in my recipe for Frijol k'abax, thereby saving steps later and enriching this dish to a truly sublime stand-alone meal. I list my "extras" as options if you prefer to keep it "*k'abax*."

Prepare ahead note: Frijol k'abax only improves over the course of a few days. Refrigerate or freeze until ready to use. Reheat just before serving, adding a bit more water if necessary.

TO PREPARE AHEAD
Enriched Lard (p. 513)

FOR PARBOILING AND COOKING THE BEANS
1 lb. (500 g) black beans
16 cups (4 L) water, divided
2 sprigs fresh epazote (Substitute: 1 tsp. / 1.5 g dried)
6 medium cloves garlic (1½ oz. / 36 g), peeled and charred (optional)
2 oz. (56 g) smoked slab bacon (optional)

FOR THE ENRICHMENT (OPTIONAL)
1 tsp. (0.65 g) dried whole Mexican oregano *and* ½ tsp. (1 g) cuminseed, lightly toasted and ground together
4 Tbs. (56 g) Enriched Lard
1 medium white onion (10 oz. / 275 g), peeled, charred, and chopped
½ tsp. (2.5 g) freshly ground black pepper
1 medium chile x'catik (about 1¼ oz. / 35 g) or chile habanero, whole
2 tsp. (12 g) sea salt, or to taste

FOR SERVING
Arroz blanco (p. 529), optional accompaniment
Mixture of chopped red onion, radishes, and cilantro
Chile con limón (p. 511), or the chile sauce of your choice
Lime wedges

PARBOIL AND COOK BEANS

Rinse and pick through the beans. Place in a large pot and cover with half the water. Bring to a boil, remove the pot from the heat, cover, and let stand 2–3 hours. Remove any beans that float to the surface; drain. (Note: Save that black soaking liquid! It can be repurposed in Arroz negro [p. 532]; refrigerate or freeze until ready to use.)

Add the remaining water to cover the beans. Add the epazote, garlic, and bacon, if using. Bring the beans to a boil, reduce the heat to a simmer, and cook partially covered for about 1½ hours. (Note: Halfway through the cooking time, check the level of the liquid. You may need to add up to 8 cups [2 L] more water to keep beans completely submerged. Cooking time may vary according to your atmospheric conditions and the beans you are using.)

PREPARE ENRICHMENT (OPTIONAL)

Pass the ground oregano and cuminseed through a fine-mesh sieve into a bowl; set aside. Heat the lard in a large skillet until shimmering. Add the onion, ground spices, and black pepper, reduce the heat, and cook slowly until the onions are caramelized, 8–10 minutes. Transfer the lard/onion mixture to the beans and stir to blend. Add the whole chile and cook another 30 minutes, or until the beans are tender but still intact.

Remove the bacon, if used, and discard. Add the sea salt and stir to incorporate. Check the seasonings.

TO SERVE

Frijol k'abax is usually accompanied by Arroz blanco and topped with the mixture of chopped onion, radish, and cilantro. Diners add a squeeze of lime juice and chile to taste.

FRIJOL COLADO / TSAAJ BI BU'UL

CREAMY STRAINED BLACK BEANS

Bowls of creamy black liquid accompany many meals here. This is Yucatán's ubiquitous Frijol colado, or strained black beans, which might be thought of as Phase Two in the lifespan of Yucatecan beans. Leftover Frijol k'abax is enriched with lard and spices, then puréed and strained ("colado" means "strained" in Spanish). Doña María del Socorro Rodríguez Larrache of Mérida, who taught me this recipe, told me that there are three traditional textures of Frijol colado: *aguado*, *espeso*, and *seco* (watery, thick, and dry). The texture is chosen according to use (see below). The difference is simply the amount of cooking liquid left in the beans when they are puréed. In the middle of the twentieth century, Frijol colado was a common treat for *merienda*, or afternoon tea, served in a soup bowl and topped with crumbled saltines.

Prepare ahead note: Frijol colado keeps under refrigeration for up to one week or freezes well for several months.

TO PREPARE AHEAD

Frijol k'abax (p. 504), using the enrichments

YIELD: APPROXIMATELY 10 SERVINGS (if working with leftovers, the yield will naturally vary depending on the quantity of beans you start out with)

FOR THE STRAINED BEANS

1 recipe Frijol k'abax, using the enrichments

PURÉE THE BEANS AND STRAIN

Remove the bacon, chile, and epazote and discard. Reheat the beans in their cooking liquid to cover by about ½ inch (1.25 cm); add water if needed. Use a food processor, blender, or immersion blender to purée the beans until smooth. Pass the beans through a sieve, using a rubber spatula to press through as much of the liquid as possible. Discard any solids that remain.

FINISH AND SERVE

Put the strained beans in a large skillet or saucepan and cook over medium heat, stirring constantly to prevent scorching, until the beans thicken slightly. Check the seasonings. You will either add more liquid (chicken broth or water) to thin it or continue cooking to reduce it, until you achieve the desired consistency:

- *Aguado*: this should be quite liquid, rather like pea soup
- *Espeso*: the consistency should be like sour cream, spoonable yet creamy and not dry
- *Seco*: the consistency should be like oatmeal, very thick and almost dry

TO SERVE

Serve *aguado* in a small side dish with a spoon as an accompaniment to a fully plated meal; diners may eat it like soup or spoon it onto meats, rice, or tacos. Use *espeso* to fill *panuchos* (p. 434) or as a *botana*, dusted with crumbled *cotija* or feta and served with crispy Totopos (p. 515). Use *seco* for Frijol refrito (recipe follows), serving as an accompaniment to a main meal or with Totopos and cheese.

VARIATIONS

Ibes colados / Ibes fritos (Creamy Strained Lima Beans): Opposite on the color wheel of the black Frijol colado, yet similar in preparation, this creamy bean dish employs the local white bean, *ib* (pl. *ibes*, *Phaseolus lunatus* L., p. 59). The indigenous *ib* is related to the common lima bean, found outside of Mexico, which you may use as a substitute. Follow the master recipe for Frijol k'abax (p. 504), substituting fresh *ibes* or fresh or frozen lima beans for the black beans and reducing cooking time accordingly. You may also use dried white beans such as great northern, navy, or cannellini and maintain the longer cooking time. Include the enrichment and finish as directed in the master recipe for Frijol colado (p. 505), using the "*espeso*" version.

Ibes colados are the requisite accompaniment for Lomitos de Valladolid (p. 481). Some cooks in Yucatán also make the thick Naach, or Frijol refrito, using lima beans, sprinkling with a bit of Pepita molida (p. 497), and serving with Totopos para botanas (p. 515).

FRIJOL REFRITO / NAACH'

REFRIED BEANS

The Mayan name of this dish translates roughly to "reheated leftovers." Frijol refrito is the third and final incarnation of the beans prepared on the first day of the week and makes use of a subsequent stage, Frijol colado. Frijol refrito should be cooked until very thick, such that you can mold it into a log shape by scraping it with a spatula while it is still in the skillet. In the 1950s, this "bean log" would be wrapped in banana leaves to take on outings or to the beach. It was then sliced and served atop Pan francés (p. 194), usually for breakfast.

Prepare ahead note: Refrigerate or freeze leftover Frijol colado seco until ready to use in Frijol refrito. The finished Frijol refrito also keeps under refrigeration for up to one week and freezes well for several months.

TO PREPARE AHEAD

Enriched Lard (p. 513)
Frijol colado seco (p. 505)

YIELD: APPROXIMATELY 10 SERVINGS (if working with leftovers, the yield will naturally vary depending on how much you start out with)

FOR THE BEANS

1 recipe Frijol colado seco
4 Tbs. (45 g) Enriched Lard (if using leftovers, adjust the quantity according to how much of the Frijol colado you are using)

FRY BEANS AND SERVE

Reheat the beans in a saucepan, adding a bit more water as needed; they should be thick yet pourable. Heat the lard in a large, deep skillet until shimmering. Pour in the beans all at once. Cook, stirring constantly to avoid sticking, until the beans are thick, cracks start appearing on the surface, and you can mold them with a spatula as described above. Depending on the thickness of the purée you start out with, the frying should take 8–10 minutes. (Note: Frijol refrito tends to splatter terribly during the frying. A large, deep skillet is recommended. You can also just fry the quantity you plan to serve and reserve the rest for later.)

TO SERVE

Nowadays, Frijol refrito is typically served in a dollop on the plate with many meat, fowl, and fish dishes. It may also be served as a *botana*, sprinkled with crumbled *cotija* and accompanied by Totopos para botanas (p. 515).

While salsas are important throughout Mexico, they are particularly relevant in Yucatán. Here we say that the food of central Mexico is "muy condimentado" (highly seasoned); by contrast, the food of Yucatán is generally quite tame. The secret is that we finish the dish by spooning on quantities of one, two, three, or more salsas to get just the flavor and piquancy we want. Salsas in Yucatán are quick and easy to prepare, and many store well, such that there really is no excuse for purchasing the bottled kind.

Prepare ahead note: The red and green sauces in this section will keep well under refrigeration 4–5 days and can be frozen quite well for several months. The pickled onions keep well under refrigeration for up to 2 weeks; the other chopped salsas can be refrigerated for 2–3 days. All are best served at room temperature.

SALSAS ROJAS / RED SAUCES

TOMATE FRITO
ENRICHED COOKED TOMATO SAUCE

Tomate frito is an indispensable cooked tomato sauce for dousing tamales, garnishing soups, or finishing plated meals. Make it in quantity and freeze so that you always have it on hand. This recipe, shared with me by doña Angelina Magaña of Muna, Yucatán, is ridiculously simple and fast—a miracle, since it yields perhaps the richest, brightest tomato taste of any cooked salsa I have ever eaten. The only change to doña Lina's recipe that I have made is to add some tomato paste to help keep the sauce from separating, but that is optional. The heat factor of this sauce is a matter of family taste in Yucatán: some, like me, like it hot. Since blond chiles can vary wildly in heat—from just 500 Scoville Heat Units to upwards of 10,000—you should sample a cross section of yours before you toss the whole thing into the sauce. Control heat by leaving seeds in or taking them out or add the chile a few pieces at a time until you reach the desired piquancy.

TO PREPARE AHEAD
Enriched Lard (p. 513)

YIELD: APPROXIMATELY 4 CUPS (1 L)

FOR THE PURÉE
2 lbs. (1 k) Roma tomatoes, charred and quartered

½ medium red onion (5 oz. / 137.5 g), peeled, charred, and quartered

1 cup (250 ml) water

1 Tbs. (15 g) tomato paste (optional)

1 medium chile x'catik (1¼ / 35 g), charred, skin left intact, and stem removed. (Note: Read notes above about controlling heat)

FOR FRYING AND FINISHING
½ cup (112 g) Enriched Lard (p. 513; substitute: Spanish olive oil)

1 tsp. (6 g) sea salt

PURÉE SAUCE

Working in batches as needed, place the tomatoes and onion in a blender with the water and tomato paste, if using, and purée thoroughly. Slowly add slices of the chile through the feed tube until you reach the desired heat level.

FRY SAUCE AND FINISH

In a large, heavy skillet (preferably cast iron with steep sides) heat the lard or oil until shimmering. Pour all of the tomato mixture in at once; it should spatter and sizzle, so stand back. Stir to incorporate and continue cooking over moderately high heat, stirring occasionally, about 10 minutes, until the sauce begins to thicken. Reduce the heat to a simmer and continue cooking another 10 minutes, or until the sauce has turned a deep red color and has reduced by about one quarter. Add the salt and stir to incorporate. Check the seasonings and serve.

K'UUT BI IIK

SMOKY AND HOT CHILE TABLE SAUCE

It is impossible to enter a humble Maya home without seeing a pool of this flavorful deep red sauce at the bottom of a mortar and pestle. "*K'uut*" in Yukatek Mayan refers to a wooden mortar and pestle commonly used here; it also refers to anything crushed or pounded in the *k'uut*. "*Iik*" is the Mayan word for "chile." And that is the original recipe: pound and crush chiles with liquid in the *k'uut*. (Of course, a blender will produce faster results.) Local cooks often use water instead of Seville orange juice, making it surely one of the simplest salsas in Mexico. But in spite of its simplicity, it is fragrant and smoky and packs a punch.

TO PREPARE AHEAD

Seville orange juice substitute (p. 514), unless fresh
  Seville oranges are available

YIELD: 10–12 SERVINGS

FOR THE SALSA

30 chiles país plus 5 to finish (Substitute: 20 chiles de árbol,
  plus 5 to finish), stemmed and seeded
½ cup (125 ml) Seville orange juice, or substitute, or water
Pinch sea salt

Place all but 5 of the chiles in the jar of a blender with the liquid and salt. (Note: While blending, make sure you have good ventilation, since this process produces a cough-inducing vapor.) Liquefy on high for 2–3 minutes, or until the chiles are pulverized.

Add the reserved chiles to the blender jar and pulse briefly so that small pieces are still visible in the sauce. Allow the salsa to rest at room temperature for at least 15 minutes prior to serving to amalgamate flavors.

CHILE K'UUT

FIERY GREEN CHILE TABLE SAUCE

A green version of K'uut bi iik that uses fresh instead of dried chiles, this bright, herbaceous salsa can be taken up or down a notch or two, heatwise, depending on the kind of chile you use. *Cantinas* often use the serrano, which is quite hot (5,000–15,000 Scoville Units) and has a lovely "green" flavor. For more punch but still nowhere near as much as the habanero, try fresh (not dried) chile de árbol (15,000–30,000 Scoville Units), which is what many Yucatecan home cooks use.

TO PREPARE AHEAD

Seville orange juice substitute (p. 514), unless fresh
  Seville oranges are available

YIELD: 10–12 SERVINGS

FOR THE SALSA

3½ oz. (100 g) fresh green chiles de árbol (Substitute: chile
  serrano), charred, stems removed
¼ medium onion (2.5 oz. / 68.75 g), peeled, charred, and
  coarsely chopped
¼ cup (15 g) cilantro, coarsely chopped
½ cup (125 ml) Seville orange juice, or substitute
Pinch sea salt

PURÉE SALSA AND FINISH

Put all the ingredients in a blender, cover, and process until liquefied, about 30 seconds. Caution: when you remove the lid, step away from the blender and keep your face turned. A very potent aroma that can cause you to cough will emanate from the blender.

Allow the salsa to rest at room temperature at least 15 minutes prior to serving to amalgamate flavors.

CHILE TAMULADO
FIERY HABANERO TABLE SAUCE

The basis of this fiery sauce is the habanero—considered among the world's hottest chiles. Habanero salsa is Yucatán's salt and pepper: no dish is complete without at least a few drops. This simple sauce is composed only of chile, Seville orange juice, and sea salt. I have specified green chiles for no reason other than the fact that most restaurants in Yucatán serve the salsa made that way. You may use any single color available (a mix of colors results in an unappetizing greige).

TO PREPARE AHEAD
Seville orange juice substitute (p. 514), unless fresh
    Seville oranges are available

YIELD: 10–12 SERVINGS

FOR THE SALSA
12–15 medium green chiles habaneros (approximately 3½ oz. / 100 g), charred, stems removed
¼ cup (62.5 ml) Seville orange juice, or substitute
Pinch sea salt

PURÉE SALSA AND FINISH
Put all the ingredients in a blender, cover, and process until liquefied, about 30 seconds. Caution: when you remove the lid, step away from the blender and keep face turned. A very potent aroma that can cause you to cough will emanate from the blender.

Allow the salsa to rest at room temperature for at least 15 minutes prior to serving to amalgamate flavors.

VARIATION
Preserved Chile tamulado: Noemi Gómez García of Tizimín in Yucatán's cattle country makes big jars of Chile tamulado whenever she gets quantities of the chile. Her secret to keeping it well preserved is acetic acid. The white vinegar so common in Yucatán has only about 5 percent acetic acid; to preserve well for long periods of time, a percentage closer to 10 percent is advised. Pickling vinegars do the trick, with upwards of 8–10 percent acetic acid content. Several brands are available in larger supermarkets. The proportion doña Noemi gave me was 6:2:1 (chile:garlic:pickling vinegar), with salt to taste. Char the chiles and garlic, peel the garlic, and separate it into cloves, then grind all together with the vinegar and salt. Store in tightly covered jars. Doña Noemi leaves big jars of the salsa in her kitchen at room temperature for months on end, but you may prefer to refrigerate it.

SALSA VERDE
FRESH TOMATILLO AND CHILE SAUCE

Although considered to be just a bit too "Mexican," Salsa verde is showing up in Yucatán with increasing frequency. The only challenge for local cooks is that fresh husk tomatoes (*tomate verde*, aka tomatillos, p. 51) are still difficult to find here in the public markets, although supermarkets usually stock them. This sauce is most often served *cruda*, or uncooked, and eaten with chips as a dip or spooned onto tacos. When cooked it can serve as a dressing for non-Yucatecan *flautas* and *enchiladas verdes*, or for Chicharrón en salsa verde (p. 217), popular throughout the entire republic, including here in Yucatán.

YIELD: APPROXIMATELY 4 CUPS / 1 L

FOR THE SALSA
6 medium tomatillos (1⅓ lb. / 600 g), husk removed and discarded, washed
½ medium white onion (5 oz. / 137.5 g), coarsely chopped
2 medium chiles serranos (¾ oz. / 20 g) charred, peeled, seeded, and roughly chopped
4 medium cloves garlic (1 oz. / 24 g), peeled and coarsely chopped
¼ cup (15 g) cilantro, coarsely chopped
½ tsp. (3 g) sea salt

PARBOIL TOMATILLOS
Place the tomatillos in a medium saucepan, cover with water, bring to a boil, and cook, uncovered, 8–10 minutes, until barely tender. Remove the tomatillos and reserve the cooking liquid.

PURÉE SAUCE AND FINISH

Place ⅓ cup (83 ml) of the reserved cooking liquid in a blender; discard the remaining liquid. Add the next 4 ingredients and process until very smooth. Add the tomatillos and puree until smooth. Add the salt and check the seasonings. Store in an airtight container and refrigerate or freeze; bring to room temperature prior to serving.

Because of the mucilaginous properties of the tomatillo, the salsa should be stirred after it rests a while and just before serving.

VARIATION

Salsa de aguacate (Avocado Sauce): This simple sauce is a favorite with Carne al pastor (p. 236). You can get two salsas for the price of one by preparing the Salsa verde, halving it, serving half as is (or freezing it for later), and using the other half for Salsa de aguacate.

Place half a recipe of Salsa verde in the jar of a blender along with 1 large ripe avocado (10½ oz. / 300 g), peeled, seeded, and cut into cubes, and ¼ teaspoon (1.5 g) sea salt. Purée until well blended, cover, and refrigerate.

SALSAS PICADAS / CHOPPED SAUCES

Pickled Onions

Spanish has two words for "to pickle": "*encurtir*" and "*escabechar*." Perhaps the bountiful vocabulary illustrates how important pickling has traditionally been in the cuisine of Spain. All sorts of foods are pickled in Yucatán, too: cabbage, onions, radishes, beets, potatoes—even turkey. The pickling medium is naturally something acidic, sometimes vinegar, but just as often the juice from our favorite citrus, the Seville orange (*Citrus aurantium, naranja agria*, p. 46).

Most protein dishes (meat, fowl, fish) are topped with one or the other of the region's famous pickled onions: Cebollas encurtidas—a simple pickle employing diced or slivered red onions, chile habanero, and Seville orange juice—or Cebollas en escabeche—a vinegar-and-spice pickle of thinly sliced white onion rings.

CEBOLLAS ENCURTIDAS / CEBOLLA CURTIDA

RED ONIONS PICKLED IN SEVILLE ORANGE JUICE

TO PREPARE AHEAD

Seville orange substitute (p. 514), unless fresh Seville oranges are available

Recado para escabeche (p. 498)

YIELD: 8–10 SERVINGS

FOR THE PICKLED ONIONS

1 lb. (500 g) red onions, peeled and cut into quarters top to bottom, then each quarter thinly sliced top to bottom and separated into half-moon shapes

1 cup (250 ml) Seville orange juice, or substitute

1 tsp. (6 g) sea salt

½ tsp. (1.5 g) Recado para escabeche

1 medium chile habanero (¼ oz. / 7 g), cap removed, seeds intact, and finely chopped or slivered

MACERATE ONIONS

Place the onions in a large nonreactive bowl. Cover with

boiling water and let stand 1 minute; drain thoroughly and return to the bowl. Add the remaining ingredients and toss to combine. Allow the onions to macerate at room temperature for at least 1 hour, tossing occasionally to keep them covered with the juice.

VARIATION

For those who prefer less heat, omit the habanero and instead use 1 large chile x'catik, charred and tossed whole into the bowl with the onions.

CEBOLLAS EN ESCABECHE
WHITE ONIONS PICKLED IN VINEGAR AND SPICES

TO PREPARE AHEAD
Recado para escabeche (p. 498)

YIELD: 8–10 SERVINGS

FOR THE PICKLED ONIONS
1 lb. (500 g) white onions, peeled, thinly sliced across the width, and separated into rings
1 cup (250 ml) white vinegar
2 tsp. (12 g) sea salt
1 Tbs. (9 g) Recado para escabeche (p. 498), plus 2 bay leaves from the *recado* mixture
2 medium chiles x'catiques (2½ oz. / 70 g), charred
1 medium head garlic (1¾ oz. / 50 g), charred, peeled, and separated into cloves

MACERATE ONIONS
Place the onions in a large nonreactive bowl. Cover with boiling water and let stand 1 minute; drain thoroughly and return to the bowl. Add the remaining ingredients and toss to combine. Allow the onions to macerate at room temperature for at least 1 hour, tossing occasionally to keep them covered with the vinegar. (Note: It is more common in Yucatán to leave the chiles whole in Escabeche. But if you wish to add a bit of heat, retrieve the chiles and, under running water, rub off the skin, cut a slit along the length, remove the seeds and veins, and cut lengthwise into strips. Return the sliced chiles to the bowl with the onions.)

CHILE CON LIMÓN
FIERY HABANERO "CONFETTI" SAUCE

Several restaurants in Yucatán offer this quick salsa to their die-hard chile lovers. It is often what waiters bring you if you just ask for "chile"; sometimes it is known as Chile con limón, since most cooks use lime (*limón*) juice instead of sour orange (*naranja agria*, or Seville orange). I like to make it with an assortment of colors of habanero for a festive, confetti-like appearance on the table.

YIELD: 10–12 SERVINGS

FOR THE SALSA
15 medium chiles habaneros (3½ oz. / 100 g total), in assorted colors if desired
¾ cup (187.5 ml) lime juice
Pinch sea salt

PREPARE SALSA AND FINISH
While wearing gloves, cut off the stems of the habaneros then thinly slice them into julienne strips or rounds across the width, leaving the seeds intact. Transfer the chiles to a nonreactive mixing bowl and combine with the juice and salt. Allow them to stand at room temperature 30 minutes or until ready to serve.

SALPICÓN
CHOPPED VEGETABLE GARNISH

Many chopped salsas in Yucatán are called "*salpicón*," ranging from simple mixtures such as radishes and onions or cabbage and citrus juice, to this more inclusive version featuring all that and more. Yucatecan fish, poultry, and meat dishes are perfectly lightened and counterbalanced by this salad/salsa hybrid. Shredded cabbage, chopped radishes, onions, cilantro, and chile are lightly dressed with Seville orange juice, then heaped atop tacos or served on the plate like a simple salad. When mixed with shredded meats, it becomes rather like a Cobb salad, as in Tsi'ik de venado (p. 421) or Chicharra en salpicón (p. 212). Tsi'ik is a New World relative of *salmagundi*, a seventeenth-century English composed salad of meats and vegetables.

TO PREPARE AHEAD

Seville orange juice substitute (p. 514), unless fresh Seville oranges are available

YIELD: APPROXIMATELY 6 SERVINGS

FFOR THE *SALPICÓN*

1 cup (85 g) green cabbage, finely shredded
½ cup (60 g) radishes, diced or cut into julienne strips
½ cup (90 g) tomatoes (about 1 medium Roma), seeded and cut into medium dice
½ cup (85 g) red onion, cut into medium dice
¼ cup (20 g) chives, chopped
2 medium chiles habaneros (½ oz. / 14 g total), or to taste, stems removed, seeds intact, finely chopped
½ cup (125 ml) Seville orange juice, or substitute
¼ cup (15 g) cilantro, finely chopped
1 tsp. (6 g) sea salt, or to taste

ASSEMBLE *SALPICÓN*

Toss the first 6 ingredients together and refrigerate until ready to serve.

FINISH AND SERVE

Immediately before serving, add the remaining ingredients and toss to combine. Check the seasonings.

X'NIPEK / X'NI'PEEK'
ZESTY FRESH TOMATO TABLE SAUCE

"*X'nipek*" in Mayan means "nose of the dog"—a playful description of a sauce so hot it makes your nose sweat. You will recognize it: in other parts of Mexico or even north of the border, a version of is it called either *pico de gallo* or *salsa mexicana*. While similar, the Yucatecan recipe swaps out a couple of important ingredients: the relatively mild chile serrano is replaced by our fiery habanero. And the finishing splash of Seville orange juice instead of lime juice makes it truly Yucatecan.

TO PREPARE AHEAD

Seville orange juice substitute (p. 514), unless fresh Seville oranges are available

YIELD: 10–12 SERVINGS

FOR THE SALSA

6 medium Roma tomatoes (21 oz. / 600 g), seeded, cut into medium dice, drained in a sieve for 20 minutes
½ medium white onion (5 oz. / 137.5 g), finely chopped
1 medium chile habanero (¼ oz. / 7 g), charred, stem removed, seeds intact, and finely chopped
¼ cup (15 g) cilantro, finely chopped
¼ cup (62.5 ml) Seville orange juice, or substitute
Pinch sea salt

ASSEMBLE SAUCE AND FINISH

Combine the first 3 ingredients in a bowl and refrigerate until ready to serve. Immediately before serving, bring the sauce to room temperature, then add the remaining ingredients and toss to combine.

⚜ OTHER STAPLES ⚜

ABOUT LARD

I am particularly trenchant about lard. People gasp at the sometimes hefty quantities of lard used in my classes and in Mexican cooking in general, but there simply is no substitute for its flavor. For the fat-phobic, you may use Spanish olive oil instead, but I remind you that lard is high in polyunsaturated fats and omega-3 / omega-6 fatty acids and has 45 percent less cholesterol than butter, meaning it is not quite the demon many think it to be. And as for the real taste of Yucatán: stick to lard!

MANTECA
ENRICHED LARD

Sadly, the lard (*manteca*) available commercially outside Mexico is highly processed, purified, and, heaven forbid, sometimes even hydrogenated. (Check the label!) Commercial lard is white as snow, and about as flavorful. With just a bit of effort, you can render your own; there is ample instruction available for how to do so in other volumes or online. A simpler method, however, is to enrich commercial lard to approximate the qualities of lard from *chicharronerías*, which acquires its flavor from frequent boiling and from bits of burned meats that sink to the bottom of the frying vat. To achieve this end, I fry a bit of bacon in the pot as the lard melts and finish by boiling the lard for about 10 minutes more after removing the bacon, which may seem an agonizingly long time as your kitchen fills with smoke! (Be sure your kitchen is well ventilated or, better yet, prepare it on your outdoor cooker.) The fact is, even in Yucatán, lard bought at places other than *chicharronerías* may be insipid, such that many local cooks boil their lard for 10 or 15 minutes to darken it and concentrate the flavors.

Prepare ahead note: Enriched Lard will stay fresh for 2–3 weeks under refrigeration. It freezes well and will keep for several months. Make as large a quantity of this recipe as you have storage room for, then divide it into several separate freezer containers.

YIELD: APPROXIMATELY 2 LBS. (1 K)

FOR THE LARD
3½ oz. (100 g) smoked slab bacon, cut into 3–4 large chunks
2 lbs. (1 k) unhydrogenated lard

PREPARE LARD
Place the bacon and lard in a large, heavy pot, preferably cast iron, over medium heat. As the lard liquefies, continue cooking at a gentle boil until the bacon is thoroughly cooked and browned, about 10 minutes.

Remove the bacon and discard (or eat!). Raise the heat to high and boil the lard for an additional 8–10 minutes (see note above about smoke). Allow the lard to cool. Strain the cooled lard through a fine sieve into containers and cover. Refrigerate or freeze until ready to use.

MANTECA PARA TAMALES YUCATECOS
LARD FOR YUCATECAN-STYLE TAMALES

Lard for Yucatecan tamales is often stained a deep red-orange with *achiote*. So that you have both on hand, make the recipe for Enriched Lard above and divide it in half, reserving one portion for standard tamales and employing the rest to make this lard for Yucatecan tamales.

FOR THE LARD
½ recipe Enriched Lard (p. 513), about 1 lb. (500 g)
3 heaping Tbs. (36 g) whole *achiote* seeds

Place the lard in a large, heavy skillet, preferably cast iron, and heat it until shimmering. Add the *achiote* seeds and fry over high heat until the lard is stained orange from the seeds, about 1 minute. Allow the lard to cool, then strain it through a fine-mesh sieve into a container. Discard the seeds and refrigerate or freeze the lard until ready for use.

MOJO DE AJO
GARLIC AND CITRUS SAUCE

Straight from Cuba (with a couple of pit stops along the way), Mojo de ajo is by now thoroughly embraced in Yucatán, where it dresses many seafood dishes such as Camarón al mojo de ajo (p. 149) and Filete al mojo de ajo (p. 150). Sometimes blended with lime juice to provide its citrusy twang, in both Cuba and Yucatán the citrus is more commonly *naranja agria* (Seville orange, p. 46).

Prepare ahead note: Mojo de ajo keeps well in an airtight container under refrigeration for 1–2 weeks.

TO PREPARE AHEAD
Seville orange juice substitute (p. 514), unless fresh
   Seville oranges are available

YIELD: APPROXIMATELY 2 CUPS (500 ML)

FOR THE ROASTED GARLIC
6 medium heads garlic (approximately 1¾ oz. / 50 g each)
Spanish olive oil

FOR THE FLAVORED OIL AND FINISHING
1 cup (250ml) olive oil
4 medium cloves garlic (1 oz. / 24 g), peeled and
   thinly sliced
½ cup (125ml) Seville orange juice, or substitute
1 tsp. (6 g) sea salt
½ tsp. (2.5 g) freshly ground black pepper
½ tsp. (1 g) cuminseed, lightly toasted and ground

ROAST GARLIC
Preheat the oven to 350°F (176°C). Slice ⅛ inch (3 mm) off the top of each head of garlic and discard. Place the garlic in a shallow baking dish and drizzle with a bit of olive oil. Bake approximately 45 minutes, or until the garlic is just tender; remove it from oven and allow it to cool.

PREPARE FLAVORED OIL
Place the cup of olive oil in a medium skillet. Add the sliced garlic and cook over low heat until the garlic just begins to color; do not allow to brown. Remove the skillet from the heat and set aside.

PURÉE MOJO AND FINISH
When the baked garlic has cooled, squeeze the cloves out of the skins and discard the skins. Place the cloves in the jar of a blender, pour the sautéed garlic/olive oil mixture into the blender, and purée. Add the remaining ingredients and pulse to incorporate. Transfer to an airtight container and allow to rest at room temperature for 30 minutes to amalgamate flavors, then refrigerate until ready to use.

NARANJA AGRIA
SEVILLE ORANGE JUICE SUBSTITUTE

If you don't live in the tropics, you may be able to find fresh Seville oranges in January–February, when they tend to appear in certain places, in small quantities, and for a short period of time. Grab all you can find, juice them, and freeze the juice in ice cube trays. Pop the cubes into a resealable plastic bag and keep frozen until ready to use. You may do the same for this substitute. If you should find real Seville oranges, it is customary in Yucatán to peel them before juicing; folks say that reduces bitterness. Although some bottled "sour orange juice" products have entered the market, I don't recommend them: the ones I have tried are gelatinous in texture and leave an unpleasant detergent-like aftertaste. This recipe can be easily scaled up or down: the basic proportion is 2:1:1—lime juice:sweet orange juice:grapefruit juice.

YIELD: 2 CUPS (500 ML)

1 cup (250 ml) freshly squeezed lime juice
½ cup (125 ml) freshly squeezed sweet orange juice
½ cup (125 ml) freshly squeezed grapefruit juice
(preferably not pink)

PREPARE JUICE

Mix the juices together and strain into a nonreactive container or ice cube trays, as suggested above.

PAN MOLIDO PARA EMPANIZADO

SEASONED BREAD CRUMB MIXTURE FOR FRIED FOODS

This multipurpose bread crumb mixture can be used for any of Yucatán's breaded, fried meats or seafood.

TO PREPARE AHEAD

Recado para escabeche (p. 498)

YIELD: APPROXIMATELY 3 CUPS / 375 G

FOR THE BREADING

3 cups (365 g) bread crumbs
2 Tbs. (4 g) dried whole Mexican oregano, lightly toasted and finely ground
1 Tbs. (9 g) Recado para escabeche
1 tsp. (6g) sea salt
1 tsp. (6g) baking powder
1 tsp. (4g) garlic powder
¼ tsp. (0.75g) cayenne powder

PREPARE BREADING

Combine all ingredients in a resealable plastic bag and toss to mix. Seal and refrigerate or freeze until ready to use.

TOTOPOS

CRISPY FRIED TORTILLA CHIPS

Fresh tortillas have a very short life span: after only a couple of hours of being exposed to air, they become tough and leathery. In order not to waste them, cooks throughout Mexico allow the tortillas to dry, then fry them for a variety of uses. When tortillas are left whole and fried, they are known as Tostadas; when they are cut into triangles, they are known as Totopos para botanas—useful for dips. When cut into narrow strips, the Totopos para sopas are a frequent garnish for soups. Do yourself a favor: Try using lard for this recipe at least one time. You will not believe the difference in taste.

TO PREPARE AHEAD

Tortillas (p. 518)
Enriched Lard (p. 513)

YIELD: APPROXIMATELY 10 SERVINGS

FOR THE TOTOPOS

24 stale corn tortillas, sliced into quarters for Totopos para botanas, into ½ in. (1.25 cm) strips for Totopos para sopa, or left whole for Tostadas
Enriched Lard (Substitute: vegetable oil)
Sea salt to taste

FRY TOTOPOS AND FINISH

Add 2 inches (5 cm) lard or oil to a heavy skillet and heat until shimmering; a thermometer should read 375°F (190°C). Place 8–10 of the smaller tortilla pieces in the skillet at a time, or just 1 or 2 of the whole tortillas for Tostadas; avoid larger quantities or the tortillas will steam rather than brown. These cook quickly, so watch closely. After about 30 seconds, turn the tortilla pieces, using tongs or a spatula, to check for doneness. The pieces should be a pale golden brown. Fry for the same amount of time on the reverse side. When done, remove the Totopos to paper towels to drain. When all are fried and completely cool, sprinkle with salt to taste and store in an airtight container.

BASIC
TECHNIQUES

Many non-Mexican novice cooks suffer from the misconception that tortillas are made from finely ground cornmeal to which water and lard are added to create a dough. Not so. Hopefully, the following overview will help eliminate the confusion.

MAÍZ

The corn species broadly grown in Mexico is *maíz dentado* (*Zea mays* L. subs. *Mays indentata*), or "dent corn," named for the small impression marking each kernel. For millennia, the peoples of Mesoamerica have preserved this corn for long-term storage by drying it until rock hard. While dehydration is a good preservation strategy, these early peoples also learned that dried corn has at least two distinct disadvantages: it requires concerted effort to grind; and it is difficult to digest.

Nixtamal

To soften the corn, thereby reducing the labor required for grinding and easing its passage through the body, early Mesoamericans developed a method for rehydrating it. By boiling dried corn in water mixed with slaked lime (calcium hydroxide) or wood ashes or sometimes both, the corn softened, and the indigestible pericarp on each kernel dissolved and could be washed away. Unbeknownst to anyone until the advent of modern science, the process also greatly enhanced the nutritional value of the corn: calcium content soars a dramatic 750 percent; bound niacin is released; and proteins increase a percentage point or two over raw corn. This rehydrated corn is known as "*nixtamal*," a word from the Náhuatl compound "*nextli*," or "ashes," and "*tamalli*," "bread of maize dough."

Masa

"*Masa*" in Spanish means "dough." There are many kinds of *masa*, such as those of wheat flour and leavening for making bread, or pastry dough for piecrusts. But the most common use of the word in Mexico refers to dough made of corn. When the rehydrated corn known as *nixtamal* is ground, it becomes a thick, pliable dough: *masa*. Dough prepared in this way with no other ingredients is the stuff from which tortillas are made. Tamales and other maize breads are also made of this *masa*, although these will typically include lard, chicken stock, beans, or other enrichments.

Masa Harina

Masa harina—or *masa* flour—is a relative newcomer to Mexican gastronomy. The first successful mass-production of *masa harina* did not occur until one year after the end of World War II, and its sole purpose was for the industrialization of tortilla making in newfangled machines. *Masa harina* is made in almost the reverse process in which *masa* is made: *masa* made of ground rehydrated corn (*nixtamal*) is subsequently dehydrated and finely ground into flour. Cooks then add water or stock to convert it back into dough—*masa*. In spite of being industrially produced, *masa harina* does have its uses in the Yucatecan kitchen. It is not cornmeal, nor can the two be used interchangeably.

WHICH KIND OF *MASA* SHOULD YOU USE?

There are two basic methods for preparing corn *masa*: grinding nixtamalized corn into a stiff dough; or mixing *masa harina* with a liquid to create the dough.

To determine which *masa* to use, you must consider its end use. In Yucatán, *masa* is employed in four primary ways: to make tortillas; to make other maize breads (Pol'kanes, Pimitos, Tamales, etc.); to make beverages (Atole, Pozole); and to thicken stocks and sauces. While delicious tortillas warrant the labor involved in making real *nixtamal* or purchasing it at a *tortillería*, most recipes in this book work just as well with *masa* made from *masa harina*.

IF YOU WISH TO MAKE TORTILLAS

First choice: Use *masa* made from *nixtamal*. For best results, look for fresh *masa* in your area (see Resources, p. 540). Be certain to verify that it is made of real *nixtamal* instead of *masa harina*. You want the former. You also want to ask for "unprepared" *masa* ("prepared" *masa* will include other ingredients.) Alternatively, experiment and try making your own *nixtamal*: ample instruction for how to do so can be found in other publications or online.

Second choice: Tortillas made from *masa harina* are not only extremely challenging to make, but are also very disappointing taste-wise when you are familiar with the real thing. Even though I don't recommend it, if you wish to try your hand at it, just follow the recipe for Basic Masa from Masa Harina and the instructions for making tortillas (right).

IF YOU WISH TO MAKE TAMALES OR OTHER MAIZE BREADS, BEVERAGES, OR THICKENERS

For everything else in this book that posts *masa* in the recipe, the *masa* you will need can be made from either *nixtamal* or *masa harina*. Truthfully, with just a few adjustments, *masa harina* serves quite well for these uses.

First choice: *Masa* from *nixtamal*. Real *masa* made from *nixtamal* that you purchase at a *tortillería* or elsewhere requires no additional processing other than that described in the recipes for tamales and other foods found in this book. It should be used as soon as possible after purchase and kept tightly wrapped under refrigeration or frozen until needed.

Second choice: *Masa* from *masa harina*. *Masa harina* is widely available in the "ethnic" sections of most supermarkets with brand names like Maseca or Minsa (see Resources, p. 540). It will also say "*masa harina*" on the label and is packaged in small bags much like wheat flour. To prepare *masa* from *masa harina*, follow the instructions for Basic Masa from Masa Harina, following.

BASIC MASA FROM MASA HARINA

YIELD: 2 LBS. (1 K) OF *MASA*

FOR THE *MASA*
4 cups (540 g) *masa harina* (see Resources, p. 518)
2½ cups (625 ml) water

Mix the ingredients thoroughly and knead briefly to incorporate. Use the *masa* immediately or wrap it tightly in plastic wrap and refrigerate or freeze until ready to use.

MAKING TORTILLAS

Making a delicious tortilla is a routine chore for most Maya women but quite a challenge for first-timers. Practice makes perfect: statistically speaking, the average Maya woman prepares four meals a day for her extended family of fourteen, and at each meal she prepares ten to twenty tortillas per person. With so much experience, no wonder the Maya woman makes it look so easy!

In Yucatán, handmade tortillas are given shape on a flat surface, usually a squat wooden table; elsewhere in Mexico, they are patted out in the palms of the hands. Yucatán's tortillas are smaller than those in other regions, typically only about 4 inches (10 cm) in diameter, and very thin. If you opt to use commercial tortillas for the recipes in this book, they will usually be considerably larger—anywhere from 5½ to 8 inches (14 cm–20 cm) in diameter. Take this into account when calculating quantities for your meal.

TO PREPARE AHEAD
Masa prepared from either nixtamalized corn or from
   masa harina (p. 521)
2–3 plastic sandwich bags cut open along the 2 sides

FOR THE TORTILLAS
2 lbs. (1 k) *masa*
½ tsp. (3 g) sea salt (optional)

HAND METHOD
Preheat a comal or griddle on highest heat. Add salt, if using, to the *masa* and knead to combine. Form the *masa* into 20 individual balls weighing about 1¾ ounces (50 g) each. Keep the dough covered with a damp towel as you work.

Form the tortilla (see p. 519, steps 1–3).
Cook the tortilla (see pp. 519–520, steps 4–6).

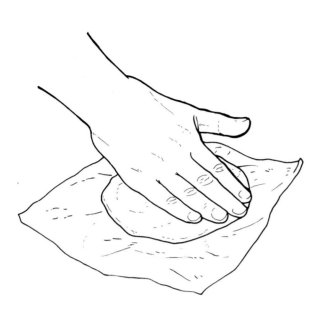

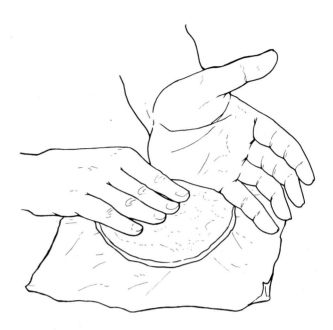

1. *Place the piece of plastic on a smooth work surface. Working with one of the balls of masa at a time, roughly flatten it into a round shape in the palms of your hands; it does not have to be perfectly round because you will finish it on the plastic. Center the round of masa on the plastic.* [AH]

2. *Flatten the tortilla with your dominant hand and cup the other hand around one side of the tortilla to help form the circular shape. As you press with one hand and round with the other, give the tortilla and plastic a 45° turn. Repeat until the tortilla reaches a diameter of about 4 inches (10 cm) and a thickness of 1/16 inch (1.5 mm).* [AH]

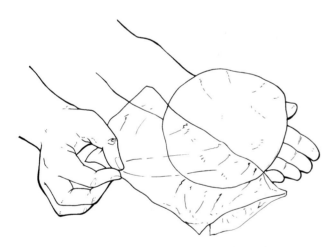

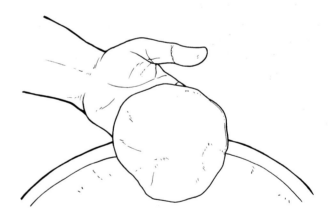

3. *Have the comal or griddle preheated and very hot. Lift the plastic and tortilla off the work surface, turn the tortilla with the plastic side up onto the palm of your hand, and gently peel away the plastic and set aside.* [AH]

4. *Transfer the tortilla to your dominant hand, making certain to leave about half of the tortilla hanging off the side of your palm opposite the thumb. Place the tortilla above the hottest part of the comal. Do not invert the tortilla; instead, lower the edge of the overhanging part of the tortilla onto the comal. Gently slide it off as you pull your hand away, allowing the tortilla to drape onto the surface of the comal. If the tortilla collapses, you probably will have to abandon it until it is fully cooked and can be scraped off with a spatula and discarded.* [AH]

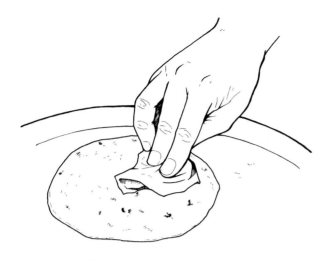

5. *Watch for signs that the tortilla is cooked: it will appear dry over the surface, with small cracks appearing around the edges. Once you have the technique down, you can flip the tortilla with your fingertips, but at first you may prefer to use a spatula. Gently lift up one edge of the tortilla, peel it away from the comal, and flip it to cook the other side. Assuming your comal is very hot, cooking the tortilla will take approximately 2 minutes per side.* [AH]

6. *A properly cooked tortilla will inflate when flipped to the other side; this is essential for making panuchos (p. 222). If it does not inflate automatically, wait a couple of seconds after flipping it and use a paper napkin or towel to press down firmly in the center of the tortilla. The pressure will cause the steam inside to expand and inflate the tortilla. Keep the tortillas warm in a basket lined with a towel as you finish the rest.* [AH]

TORTILLAS PARA PANUCHOS

The *panucho* is Yucatán's quintessential taco. The hollow inside a fresh tortilla is filled with strained beans before being topped with a range of meats and garnishes. If you wish to make *panuchos* (p. 434), make sure the tortilla inflates, remove it from the comal, and allow it to cool slightly. With a knife or your fingers, open a slit along one edge about 2 inches (5 cm) in length and set the tortilla aside until ready to fill.

PRESS METHOD

You may also use a tortilla press for forming tortillas. Presses are known in Spanish as "*aplastadoras*" and colloquially as "*mariconas*." While certainly easier and faster to make, tortillas made with a press do not have the same delicious flavor as those made by hand. One reason is that handmade tortillas have irregular bumps on the surface

from your fingertips; these bumps cook unevenly, allowing some light charring to occur, which dramatically enhances flavor due to the Maillard reaction. But if making tortillas by hand stymies you, a press will serve.

Begin as directed for the hand method, above.

Place the piece of plastic on the press, leaving half of it extended over one side. Place a ball of *masa* on the plastic on the press and fold the overhanging plastic over to cover. Now lower the top part of the press onto the *masa* and use the lever to press it firmly closed. It takes some practice to know exactly how much pressure to apply: the harder the pressure, the thinner the tortilla; the lighter the pressure, the thicker the tortilla. A pressed tortilla should be the same diameter and thickness as one made by hand (see above).

Cook the tortilla as directed in the hand method, above.

MAKING TAMALES

Whereas tortillas have no additions to the basic *masa* (except perhaps a pinch of salt), the *masa* for tamales includes fat, seasonings, and a few other ingredients to enhance flavor and lighten the texture.

As noted earlier, delicious tamales can be made with basic *masa* prepared from either *nixtamal* or *masa harina*, with inoffensive differences in taste and texture. I present here recipes for both. I also detail several options, including Yucatecan variants and vegetarian versions.

Masa for most traditional tamales in Yucatán comprises just three basics: *nixtamal*, lard, and salt. In colonial times, and possibly before (and still in some pueblos), the Mayas incorporated into their *masa* some stock from cooked game, skimming a bit of fat from the surface, too. Both stock and fat must have enriched the dough and dramatically improved the flavor. And throughout Mexico people added *tequesquite*—a mineral salt—as a leavening for the dough. The recipes here, then, reflect a few adjustments to the standard *tamal* recipe with the same lightening and flavor-enhancing goals in mind. I suggest the addition of baking powder (chemically similar to *tequesquite*) and recommend using stock or broth rather than water and salt. Finally, in a wanton departure from tradition, I suggest a smattering of roasted garlic for a more vibrant flavor, although I leave that as an option.

MASA PARA TAMALES I

MASA FOR TAMALES USING FRESH MASA FROM NIXTAMAL

Prepare ahead note: Basic Masa para tamales I made with fresh *masa* should be used immediately after preparing. Left at room temperature for any length of time, fresh *masa* tends to sour rather quickly. This natural fermentation is not a health hazard (in fact, fermented *masa* is specified for several Yucatecan dishes), but it gives an off taste to the tamales.

TO PREPARE AHEAD
Enriched Lard (p. 513)

YIELD: APPROXIMATELY 2½ LBS. (1.2 KG)

FOR THE *MASA*

½ cup (112 g) Enriched Lard, chilled

1 Tbs. (12 g) baking powder

2 lbs. (1 k) fresh *masa* from *nixtamal*

½ cup (67.5 g) *masa harina*

1 medium clove garlic (¼ oz. / 6 g), peeled, charred, and minced (optional)

3 Tbs. (36 g) powdered chicken bouillon, dissolved in ½ cup (125 ml) hot water

PREPARE *MASA*

Place the chilled lard and baking powder in the bowl of an electric mixer and beat on high speed until the lard turns fluffy and creamy, about 3 minutes.

Add the *masa* a bit at a time, beating after each addition until incorporated. Add the next 2 ingredients and beat on low to combine. With the mixer still running, slowly add the bouillon mixture. Add enough to create a moist but not soggy dough: it should be easily formed into a ball without sticking to your fingers. Beat the mixture on high speed until all ingredients are thoroughly incorporated and the dough has lightened, about 5 minutes. Wrap tightly in plastic wrap and refrigerate until ready to use.

MASA PARA TAMALES II

MASA FOR TAMALES USING MASA HARINA

The addition of fresh roasted corn makes this *masa* amazingly flavorful, considering it is made from *masa harina*. It tends to be a bit crumbly, however, but for tamales it doesn't matter since you can patch and plaster and mold everything back into place as you form them.

Prepare ahead note: The Masa para tamales II using *masa harina* must be made at least 30 minutes in advance and allowed to rest.

TO PREPARE AHEAD
Enriched Lard (p. 513)

YIELD: APPROXIMATELY 2½ LBS. (1.2 KG)

2 cups (350 g) fresh corn kernels (4–5 medium ears)

1 medium clove garlic (¼ oz. / 6 g), peeled and charred (optional)

1¾ cups (437.5 ml) chicken stock or bouillon

¾ cup (168 g) Enriched Lard, chilled

1 Tbs. (12 g) baking powder

3 cups (400 g) *masa harina*

1 tsp. (6 g) sea salt

PREPARE *MASA*

In a large, heavy, dry skillet, roast the corn kernels until pale golden and tender, stirring constantly, 3–4 minutes.

Place the garlic and stock in a blender jar and process until well blended. Add the corn and process 3–4 minutes, or until thoroughly liquefied; set aside.

Place the lard and baking powder in the bowl of a stand mixer and beat on high until the lard turns fluffy and creamy, about 3 minutes.

Add the *masa harina* and salt to the mixing bowl and beat for about 2 minutes, scraping down the bowl as needed, until the mixture turns into a crumbly mass resembling coarse cornmeal. Slowly add the liquid from the blender to the mixing bowl, beating constantly. Beat 2 minutes, scraping down the sides of the bowl as necessary. Form the *masa* into a ball, wrap tightly in plastic, and allow to rest at room temperature for 30 minutes to develop flavors.

MASA PARA TAMALES YUCATECOS

MASA FOR YUCATECAN-STYLE TAMALES, USING FRESH MASA OR MASA HARINA

Yucatecan tamales frequently feature unique tweaks not found outside the region. The dough for many Yucatecan tamales is tinged a deep yellow-orange color, achieved by frying *achiote* seeds in the lard, and it has a slight zing from chopped chile habanero.

- Ingredients for Masa para tamales I or II (pp. 521–522)
- Replace the Enriched Lard with the Lard for Yucatecan-Style Tamales (p. 513)

- 1 medium chile habanero (about ¼ oz. / 7 g), seeded and minced

Beat the Lard for Yucatecan-Style Tamales with the baking powder as specified in your recipe.

Add the remaining ingredients along with the minced chile and finish.

MASA PARA TAMALES VEGETARIANOS

MASA FOR VEGETARIAN TAMALES, USING FRESH MASA OR MASA HARINA

- Ingredients for Masa para tamales I or II (p. 521)
- Replace the Enriched Lard with the equivalent measure of Spanish olive oil, chilled until it solidifies (Note: Unlike the lard, the oil will liquefy rather than aerate as you beat it, but it does not affect the process. It will lighten somewhat in color)
- Replace the chicken stock with salted water or vegetable bouillon

Note: To make a vegetarian version of the orange-stained Masa para tamales yucatecos, fry the *achiote* seeds in the olive oil, strain, then chill as per the instructions in Lard for Yucatecan-Style Tamales (p. 513).

FORMING AND WRAPPING TAMALES

Whether small or large, wrapped in banana leaves or in corn husks, tamales in Yucatán share the nickname "*torteados*" because of the way in which they are formed. "*Tortear*" in Spanish means "to make tortillas" or, more generally, "to form into a tortilla shape." After shaping *masa* into a ball, cooks flatten it into a thick disk before filling and rolling it to make a *tamal*.

PREPARE LEAVES AND DIVIDE *MASA*

Select the size *tamal* you wish to make and cut banana leaves to the appropriate size (SM, M, L, or XL) as described on page 525 (or prepare the corn husks). Divide the *masa* into balls of equal weight as specified in the recipe. For variety, you may also make a lesser quantity of several different sizes and types of *tamal* with the same batch of *masa*.

FORM, FILL, AND WRAP TAMALES

Form balls of *masa* according to the size specified for the *tamal* (see measurements on p. 525). Finish and wrap as follows.

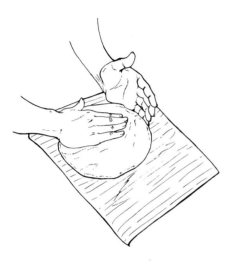

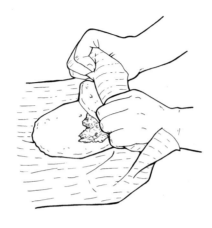

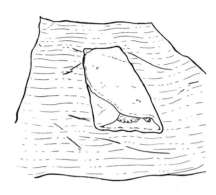

1. *Pat one of the balls into a small, thick tortilla in your palms and center the tortilla on the leaf. Flatten and shape it using the fingertips of one hand and the curved edge of the other, rotating the tortilla and leaf to give shape as you go.* [AH]

2. *Add the filling of choice in a strip down the middle of the tortilla. (Note: Avoid using too much filling, since this can break the tortilla and cause the filling to spill out the edges.) Using the edge of the leaf, lift the right side of the masa toward the left, folding the tortilla onto itself to the two-thirds point. Press down to seal the masa, then carefully peel open the leaf.* [AH]

3. *Repeat on the left side. Peel away the leaf to reveal a flattened cylinder and turn the sides of the banana leaf over the tamal and roll.* [AH]

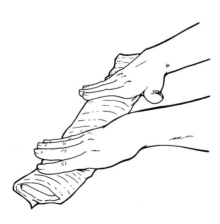
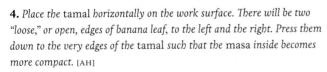

4. *Place the tamal horizontally on the work surface. There will be two "loose," or open, edges of banana leaf, to the left and the right. Press them down to the very edges of the tamal such that the masa inside becomes more compact.* [AH]

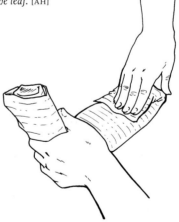

5. *Fold the edges up, then turn the tamal so the flap side is down on the work surface. Pat it firmly to seal. Use the reserved ribs to securely tie large or extra large tamales; there is no need to tie small or medium tamales. Leave the tamales positioned with the tucked edges under when you stack them in the steamer. Cook as instructed on page 526.* [AH]

IF YOU ARE USING CORN HUSKS

There are a couple of Yucatecan tamales that use the more "Mexican" corn husk wrapper. Dried husks are available in most Latin American groceries or online (see Resources, p. 539).

Place the husks in a large stockpot, cover with water, and bring to a boil. Keep the husks submerged with a heatproof plate or bowl. Reduce the heat and simmer for 10 minutes. Remove the pot from the heat and allow it to stand for 2 hours. Remove a few husks at a time only when you are ready to use them and pat dry with a towel.

Separate the largest and most pliable husks to use for tamales; cut the smaller ones lengthwise into ¼-inch (6 mm) strips to use as ties.

Fill and wrap as shown.

Arrange the tamales in a steamer and cook (p. 526). (Note: If tamales are well sealed at the base, you may lay them flat in the steamer; otherwise, position them upright.)

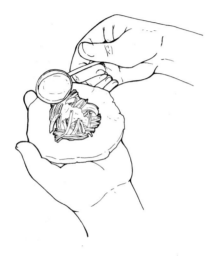

1. *Form a tortilla with the* masa *and top with fillings.* [AH]

2. *Fold the tortilla into an empanada shape and seal the edges closed to prevent leaks.* [AH]

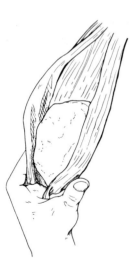

3. *Place the empanada inside the corn husk toward the base.* [AH]

4. *Fold and press the base closed and fold down the narrow pointed top.* [AH]

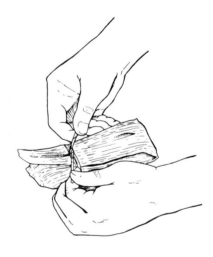

5. *Tie to secure.* [AH]

WORKING WITH BANANA LEAVES

Because banana leaves are used so frequently as wrappers in Yucatán—not only for tamales, but also for a range of dishes, from chicken and pork to seafood—you should learn the basic techniques for handling them. Banana leaves can be found in the freezer section of Asian or Mexican markets, or for online sources, see Resources, page 540.

Prepare the Banana Leaves

If you have access to fresh leaves, pass them briefly over an open flame to soften. If using fresh packaged leaves, gently wipe them with a damp towel. Frozen leaves are ready to use after thawing.

While there is no such thing as a standard size in nature, most of the packages of whole fresh leaves I purchase in Yucatán contain leaves that are on average 10 inches × 60 inches (25 cm × 150 cm). Frozen leaves are sized similarly. Due to tearing and deformities, you can rarely make use of the entire leaf, but save all but the smallest scraps to use as patches when you are wrapping something and the larger leaf tears.

Cut the sizes you will need all at the same time. Banana leaves are quite fragile, especially after being frozen and thawed, so you must work with them slowly and patiently. If you are not going to use the cut leaves immediately, place them in a resealable plastic bag, folding the largest leaves to fit, and freeze. The ribs also freeze well.

1. Unfold the leaves and place them flat on a work surface.
2. With scissors, cut off the central ribs (the thick "stem" that runs the length of the leaf). Cut or tear the ribs in half lengthwise and set them aside to use as ties.
3. Determine the size leaf you will need based on the kind of food you will be wrapping. Sizes that follow are approximate only, since you will have to conform to the natural contours of your leaves.

Choosing Banana Leaf Sizes / Dividing Masa

SM—Vaporcitos, Tamalitos, and other small Yucatecan Tamales

- Cut leaves to measure about 8 inches × 10 inches (20 cm × 25 cm).
- Divide the *masa* into 24 balls, each weighing about 1¾ ounces (50 g). (Note: Tamales wrapped in corn husks also require the weight of *masa* specified here. For *masa* that has beans in the dough, you will form approximately 30 balls.)
- Shape a tortilla on the leaf as described on page 523 (for corn husks, follow the instructions on page 524 and in the specific recipe). The tortilla should measure 5½ inches (14 cm) in diameter and ⅛-inch (0.125 cm) thick.
- Small tamales require about 2 teaspoons (10 g) of filling unless the recipe indicates otherwise.

M—Tamal redondo, Tamales campechanos

- Cut leaves to measure about 10 inches × 12 inches (25 cm × 30 cm).
- Divide the *masa* into 12 balls weighing about 3⅓ ounces (95 g) each. (Note: For *masa* that has beans in the dough, you will form approximately 14 balls.)
- Shape the tortilla on the leaf as described on page 523. The tortilla should measure 7½ inches (19 cm) in diameter and ⅛-inch (0.125 cm) thick.
- Medium tamales require about 1 rounded tablespoon (14 g) of filling unless the recipe indicates otherwise.

L—Tamal colado, Tamal de xmakulán, Horneados

- Cut leaves to measure about 10 inches × 16 inches (25 cm × 40 cm).
- Prepare *masa*, divide, form, and fill according to recipe instructions.

XL—Mucbilpollo, Brazo de reina, and other large tamales; also use for Cochinita pibil, Pescado en tikin xiik', or other large meat or seafood portions.

- Cut leaves to measure about 10 inches × 30 inches (25 cm × 75 cm).
- Finish according to recipe instructions.

COOKING TAMALES

Cooking methods for tamales are as varied as tamales themselves. Yucatán's most plentiful *tamal*—the Vaporcito—is steamed, as the name suggests. Larger tamales are often baked; still others may be cooked over hot coals. And for rituals or special occasions, tamales are "buried" and cooked in the underground oven known in Mayan as a *píib* (p. 418). Instructions for all methods follow.

Steaming

It is common throughout Mexico to see large aluminum pots percolating atop a fire and surrounded by crowds of people drooling over the precious contents. These are *vaporeras*—special *tamal* steamers. It's worth investigating your local Latin American market or online to see if you can find one (see Resources, p. 541). These special pots have several advantages:

- They are large. No one in Mexico makes four or five tamales at a time; rather, they are prepared by the dozen or even by the hundreds. *Vaporeras* come in a variety of sizes accommodating anywhere from thirty to eighty tamales or more. (If you are going to make tamales, remember: go for quantity. They freeze brilliantly and will make you the star of your next impromptu supper party.)
- They have a steam chamber. A convex groove running around the circumference of the interior toward the bottom of the pot provides a resting place for a removable perforated disk. A few inches of space separate the disk from the bottom of the pot; in this space goes the water that produces the steam. Wrapped tamales are stacked on top of the disk.
- They have tight-fitting lids. Actually, the structure of the pot/lid combination is such that the lid almost snaps or locks into place, trapping most of the steam inside. This aids even and thorough cooking.

The virtues of the special *vaporera* notwithstanding, it is easy enough to retrofit equipment you may already have. Use a large stockpot fitted with a lid and place a cake rack at the bottom: the rack should be spaced at least 2 inches (5 cm) from the bottom of the pot; if yours isn't that high, you can make simple "booties" of crumpled aluminum foil attached to the rack to create the extra space. Place a weight on the lid during cooking to hold in steam.

COOKING TIMES
- Vaporcitos, Tamalitos, and other small (SM) tamales steam for 1 hour.
- Cháamchamitos, Tamal de xmakulán, and other medium (M) to large (L) tamales steam for 1½ hours.

Baking

Extra large (XL) tamales, such as Brazo de reina or Mucbilpollo, are often baked. Preheat the oven to 350°F (176°C). Place the wrapped *tamal* on a baking sheet and bake for 45 minutes; flip it over and bake an additional 45 minutes, or until the *tamal* is firm when pressed. (Note: Depending on the size of the *tamal*, the moistness of the *masa*, and your particular oven, the *tamal* may take as long as 2 hours to bake. Remove it from the oven, open a bit of the leaf wrapper, and check to see if the *masa* is still soft and damp. If so, continue baking a bit longer until it is firm and dry.)

Smoking Methods

Foods cooked in the underground oven known as a *píib* acquire a marvelous smoky flavor. It is usually the largest tamales that are cooked this way, but it is not uncommon to mound dozens of smaller tamales in the *píib*, too, for special events. Without excavating your backyard, you can achieve the smoky taste in a couple of different ways:

- Charcoal or gas grill smoking method. Follow the grilling instructions on page 538. Wrap the *tamal* in a double layer of leaves to prevent scorching. Place it on the high rack inside the grill to one side, *not directly above the coals*, and proceed with wood chips as instructed. Depending on your grill, baking this way should take roughly the same time as oven baking, that is, 1–1½ hours. Test for doneness by opening the leaves at one corner to see if the *masa* is still moist or is cooked and firm.

- Stovetop smoking method. Follow the instructions on page 537. This method requires that you have a cast-iron Dutch oven in an adequate size to accommodate your *tamal*. After you add the wood chips and have the rack in place, place the *tamal* on the rack and cover the pot tightly. Smoke the *tamal* on highest heat for 15 minutes, then transfer it to a 350°F (176°C) oven to finish baking, another 1 hour and 15 minutes for medium and large tamales, and 1 hour for small tamales.

TAMAL TIPS

Although labor intensive, tamales are wonderful party treats, so be sure to make them in quantity.

Prepare tamales well in advance of your party. Form, wrap, and cook all the tamales when you have time, allow them to cool, then freeze. You may reheat in a steamer or oven prior to serving.

Tomate frito (p. 507) is invariably the primary accompaniment for tamales in Yucatán. Keep some in the freezer at all times to reheat immediately before serving.

❧ ARROZ / RICE ❧

Rice (*Oryza sativa*) has been an important feature of meals in Mexico since the Spanish first brought Asian rice to the New World in the 1520s. Along with the rice itself, early recipes for it arrived with the Spaniards, too, from Middle Eastern countries. Pilaf—derived from Turkish and Persian gastronomy and vocabulary—is still the cooking method of choice for rice throughout Mexico. Long-grain rice is sautéed in fat with onions and garlic, then a flavored liquid (saltwater or stock) is added, and the rice is left to steam and soften. Pilaf often features meats, as in the classic arroz con pollo.

PADDIES IN CAMPECHE

The warm, wet climate of the Gulf Coast proved to be a fertile growing ground for rice, and cultivation quickly spread from Veracruz, where it was first introduced, to the similar terrain and climate of the neighboring states of Tabasco and Campeche. In the eighteenth century, Campeche was the largest producer, and rice was introduced into the markets of Mérida as early as the 1720s.

Mexico produces two types of rice: Sinaloa (*largo*, or long grain) and Morelos (*grueso*, or fat). Both are classified as long-grain rice, although the Morelos variety is a bit shorter and wider than the Sinaloa. Look for long-grain rice for all pilaf recipes in this book.

There are a few easy tips for making pilaf, which I outline here and refer to again in the recipes:

- Remember, the standard pilaf formula is 1:2. Therefore, 1 cup rice requires 2 cups liquid; 2 cups rice needs 4 cups liquid, etc. For those recipes that include purées or flavored liquids, it is important to calculate the exact ratio, making adjustments so that you always arrive at exactly 1:2 rice to liquid.
- The goal for an excellent pilaf is light, fluffy, separate grains; it should not be gummy. While the latter texture is perfect for rice pudding or risotto, it is not desirable for pilaf. Gumminess is caused by the cooking

liquid's interactions with the starchy coating on the surface of the rice. Managing this interaction will keep your pilaf fluffy. Bear in mind that this starchy surface is soluble in water, not in fat.

- Rinse and wash the rice prior to cooking. This not only cleans it but also removes some of the starchy coating—a good thing for pilaf.
- Sauté the rice in fat before adding onions and garlic. Many recipes for pilaf instruct you to sauté or "sweat" the onions and garlic prior to adding the rice. To me, this is counterintuitive: the rice takes longer to cook and turn opaque than the onions and garlic take to cook and turn translucent.
- Add liquid in two stages. Add half the liquid after frying the rice, allow it to absorb, then add the rest. A brief rest between additions allows the rice to absorb the liquid more uniformly.
- Stirring is the enemy of pilaf! You should stir only when you are frying the rice. Because the starch is not soluble in fat, you can stir constantly during the frying process, which in fact is the right thing to do since you do not want the rice to brown. However, stirring once the liquid goes in will result in gummy rice. Since the starch is soluble in water, the stirring motion scrapes the starch off each individual grain. The moment you add liquids, remove your spoon and avoid the temptation to stir.
- Seal in steam. Covering the lid with a damp towel creates a seal around the edge of the skillet, which helps hold in the steam for more even cooking.
- Patience! So many novices are tempted to lift the lid to check how the rice is doing or, worse, to give it just a little stir to mix the ingredients. Don't do it! Trust me, after the 15–20 minute steeping period, you will finally lift the lid and discover that you have a pot of perfectly cooked rice. And you will have learned that this is probably the easiest way to prepare rice ever.

THE MANY COLORS OF RICE

Like Mexico itself, Mexican rice is a colorful thing. Even though recipes always begin with long-grain white rice, the vivid color and flavor at the end of cooking are determined by the ingredients of the cooking liquid:

- Arroz blanco (White Pilaf)—the most basic rice here, comforting, and served with almost every meal—features little more than salted water or chicken broth.
- Arroz amarillo (Yellow Pilaf) is tinged a pale golden color by what is sometimes known as "poor man's saffron": *achiote* (p. 63). Arroz amarillo is delicious with grilled meats or any dish featuring Mojo de ajo (p. 514).
- Arroz rojo (Red Pilaf) is both flavored and colored by tomato and occasionally *achiote*. Arroz rojo is an excellent base to use as a "dry soup" for chicken or seafood mixtures, such as Arroz con camarón (p. 528).
- Arroz verde (Green Pilaf) achieves its color thanks to a purée of fresh herbs and stock. Generally reserved for special occasions or family meals, Arroz verde makes only rare appearances in Yucatecan restaurants. Serve with grilled meats or fine cuts of steak.
- Arroz negro (Black Pilaf) in other parts of Mexico may be stained with squid or octopus ink, but Yucatecan cooks apply their infinite frugality by recycling the pitch-black cooking liquid from a pot of beans. Arroz negro always sidles up to Frijol con puerco.

Dry Soup?

A long-standing tradition in Mexico—alas, one that is slowly fading in Yucatán—is to serve something known as *sopa seca* (dry soup) as the second or third course during a meal. In contemporary cookbooks and restaurant menus you will still usually see rice dishes under the heading of Sopas rather than in a separate category. The equivalent of the pasta course in an Italian meal, *sopa seca* may indeed feature vermicelli or other noodles, but just as frequently, it is a simple pilaf, sometimes enhanced by the addition of some chicken, seafood, or vegetables.

A favorite *sopa seca* in Campeche is Arroz con camarón (Campeche-Style Shrimp with Red Pilaf): add 1 pound (500 g) peeled, deveined shrimp to Arroz rojo. Try strips of Pollo asado (p. 270) with the Arroz amarillo. Add mixed seafood to Arroz verde or cooked, cubed octopus to Arroz negro. Add these ingredients just before covering the skillet and allowing the rice to steam.

PILAF BASIC METHOD

Once you have mastered the basic pilaf theme, you can easily make any of the rice variations offered here. Follow the master recipe for Arroz blanco and add different ingredients as noted.

Prepare ahead note: Pilafs are best served immediately after preparing, although leftovers can be refrigerated 1–2 days, then steamed to reheat.

YIELD: 10–12 SERVINGS

ARROZ BLANCO

WHITE PILAF

TO PREPARE AHEAD
Enriched Lard (p. 513)

FOR SAUTÉING THE RICE
3 Tbs. (42 g) Enriched Lard

2 cups (400 g) long-grain white rice, rinsed, thoroughly drained, and air-dried

½ medium white onion (5 oz. / 137.5 g), finely chopped

2 medium cloves garlic (½ oz. / 12 g), peeled and minced

FOR SIMMERING AND STEAMING THE RICE
4 cups (1 L) hot water mixed with 1 tsp. (6 g) sea salt (Substitute: for a richer flavor, use chicken broth instead), divided

½ tsp. (2.5 ml) lemon juice (optional)

1 Tbs. (5 g) fresh cilantro or epazote leaves, chopped

SAUTÉ RICE

Choose a large skillet or saucepan with a tight-fitting lid. Heat the lard in the skillet until shimmering. Add the rice and cook over moderate heat, stirring constantly, until it begins to turn opaque, 2–3 minutes (individual grains will appear whiter than others). Add the onions and garlic and cook, stirring constantly, until the onions are translucent, 3–4 minutes. *Do not let the rice brown.*

SIMMER RICE

Add half the liquid to the skillet when the onions are trans-lucent. *Do not stir.* To incorporate the liquid, give the skillet a vigorous but brief shake. Cook uncovered over medium heat, *without stirring*, until the liquid is mostly absorbed, and you see small, percolating airholes over the surface.

STEAM RICE AND FINISH

Add the remaining 2 cups (500 ml) liquid, lemon juice, if using, and herbs to the rice and simmer until small airholes appear again. The rice should be quite dry, but there should still be a bit of liquid left. Wet a towel and wring it out. Spread it on a work surface and place the lid from your pot or skillet right side up in the center of the towel. Gather the corners of the towel up toward the knob of the lid. Place the wrapped lid on the skillet and simmer the rice on lowest heat for 3 minutes. Remove the skillet from the heat and allow the rice to steep, covered, for 20 minutes. Lift the lid, toss the rice lightly to incorporate all ingredients, and test for doneness; the rice should be slightly al dente. (Note: If you prefer softer rice, add a bit of water, cover, and simmer 2 minutes more. Remove the pan from the heat and steep the rice an additional 5 minutes.) Keep covered until serving.

ARROZ AMARILLO

YELLOW PILAF

Several vintage cookbooks specify using the stock of Puchero de tres carnes (p. 350) for this dish. The stock has a yellow-ish cast to it from the saffron, and the coriander seed that is the hallmark of Recado para puchero lends an aromatic freshness. Wanting the Puchero stock, however, you may instead add the *recado* to basic chicken stock to achieve the same flavor.

TO PREPARE AHEAD
Enriched Lard (p. 513)

Puchero de tres carnes (p. 350) or Recado para puchero (p. 499)

FOR SAUTÉING THE RICE
3 Tbs. (42 g) Enriched Lard

1 Tbs. (12 g) *achiote* seeds

2 cups (400 g) long-grain white rice, rinsed, thoroughly drained, and air-dried

½ medium red onion (5 oz. / 137.5 g), finely chopped

2 medium cloves garlic (½ oz. / 12 g), peeled and minced

2 medium chiles serranos (¾ oz. / 20 g), seeded and thinly sliced across the width

FOR SIMMERING AND STEAMING RICE

4 cups (1 L) stock from making Puchero de tres carnes (p. 350; substitute: chicken stock or bouillon mixed with ½ tsp. / 1.5 g Recado para puchero, divided)

1 medium Roma tomato (3½ oz. / 100 g), seeded and finely chopped

1 Tbs. (5 g) fresh cilantro or epazote leaves, chopped

SAUTÉ RICE

Heat the lard in a large skillet until melted. Add the *achiote* seeds and cook over medium heat 2–3 minutes, or until the fat is stained a deep red-orange color. Strain out the seeds and discard. Return the fat to the skillet and heat until shimmering. Add the rice and cook over moderate heat, stirring constantly, until it begins to turn opaque, 2–3 minutes. Add the next 3 ingredients and cook, stirring constantly, until the onions are translucent, 3–4 minutes. *Do not let the rice brown.*

SIMMER RICE

Immediately add half of the stock and all of the tomatoes to the rice mixture in the skillet. *Do not stir.* To incorporate the liquid into the rice, give the skillet a vigorous but brief shake. Cook uncovered over medium heat, *without stirring,* until the liquid is mostly absorbed and you see small, percolating airholes appearing over the surface.

STEAM RICE AND FINISH

Add the remaining liquid and herbs and simmer until small airholes appear again. The rice should be quite dry, but there should still be a bit of liquid left. Wrap the lid in a damp towel (see the instructions in Arroz blanco) and place on the skillet. Simmer on lowest heat for 3 minutes. Remove the skillet from the heat and allow the rice to steep, covered, for 20 minutes. Lift the lid, toss the rice lightly to incorporate the ingredients, and test for doneness; it should be slightly al dente. (Note: If you prefer softer rice, add a bit of water, cover, and simmer 2 minutes more. Remove the pan from the heat and steep the rice an additional 5 minutes.) Keep covered until serving.

ARROZ ROJO
RED PILAF

Sun-dried tomatoes are not a tradition of Yucatán, which surprises me somewhat, since we have a preponderance of tomatoes (not to mention sun!), and since one of the Mayas' favored preservation techniques was to sun dry. Nonetheless, *tomate deshidratado* is beginning to appear in more "upscale" cooking of the region, thanks to the proliferation of TV cooking shows, magazines, and increased imports. I have chosen to post the sun-dried tomatoes as an optional ingredient, but I do recommend them, since they accomplish what plain tomatoes simply cannot: delivering to the plate a deep and intense tomato flavor. If you are lucky, at the end of cooking time you should see a bit of crust forming at the bottom of the skillet. This is similar to the coveted *socarrat* of excellent Spanish paella. Fight for it!

TO PREPARE AHEAD

Recado rojo (p. 500)

Enriched Lard (p. 513)

FOR THE FLAVORED COOKING LIQUID

3 cups (750 ml) chicken stock or bouillon, divided

2 oz. (50 g) sun-dried tomatoes packed in oil, drained (optional)

1 Tbs. (15 g) Recado rojo

½ tsp. (2.5 g) freshly ground black pepper

1 tsp. (0.65 g) dried whole Mexican oregano, lightly toasted and ground

1 tsp. (6 g) sea salt

2 medium Roma tomatoes (7 oz. / 200 g), quartered

FOR SAUTÉING THE RICE

3 Tbs. (42 g) Enriched Lard

2 cups (400 g) long-grain white rice, rinsed, thoroughly drained, and air-dried

½ medium red onion (5 oz. / 137.5g), finely chopped

2 medium cloves garlic (½ oz. / 12 g), peeled and minced

2 medium chiles serranos (¾ oz. / 20 g), seeded and thinly sliced across the width

FOR STEAMING THE RICE

1 Tbs. (5 g) fresh cilantro or epazote leaves, chopped

Place 1 cup (250 ml) stock and the next 5 ingredients in the jar of a blender and liquefy thoroughly (the sun-dried tomatoes can be stubborn). Add the Roma tomatoes and process 10–15 seconds just to break them up but not totally liquefy them. You should have 2 cups (500 ml) liquid in the blender; if you have less, add a bit more stock; if you have too much, pour off any excess. Set aside.

SAUTÉ RICE

Heat the lard in a large skillet until shimmering. Add the rice and cook over moderate heat, stirring constantly, until it begins to turn opaque, 2–3 minutes. Add the next 3 ingredients and cook, stirring constantly, until the onions are translucent, 3–4 minutes. *Do not let the rice brown.*

STEAM RICE

Add the remaining 2 cups (500 ml) chicken stock to the rice mixture in the skillet. *Do not stir.* To incorporate the liquid into the rice, give the skillet a vigorous but brief shake. Cook, uncovered, over medium heat *without stirring* until the liquid is mostly absorbed and you see small, percolating airholes appearing over the surface. Pour the tomato liquid from the blender into the skillet. This is one situation in which I break my steadfast rule about stirring: the tomato liquid is quite thick, such that to incorporate it into the rice you need to give it one quick whirl with a wooden spoon until just blended. Don't overdo it! Add the cilantro or epazote.

Continue simmering until small airholes appear again. The rice should be quite dry, but there should still be a bit of liquid left. Wrap the lid in a damp towel (see instructions in Arroz blanco). Place the wrapped lid on the skillet and simmer on low heat for 3 minutes. Remove the skillet from the heat and allow the rice to steep, covered, for 20 minutes. Lift the lid, toss the rice lightly to incorporate ingredients, and test for doneness; it should be slightly al dente. (Note: If you prefer softer rice, add a bit of water, cover, and simmer 2 minutes more. Remove the skillet from the heat and steep the rice an additional 5 minutes.) Keep covered until serving.

VARIATION

Arroz con camarón (Campeche-Style Shrimp with Red Pilaf): To prepare this favorite, see "Dry Soup" (p. 528).

ARROZ VERDE
GREEN PILAF

The lime juice and zest are not traditional, but they do enhance the "green" note of the herb mixture and give the rice a bright, fresh taste.

TO PREPARE AHEAD
Enriched Lard (p. 513)

FOR THE FLAVORED COOKING LIQUID
3¾ cups (937.5 ml) chicken stock or bouillon, divided
¼ cup (15 g) *each* cilantro, epazote, and flat-leaf Italian parsley, coarsely chopped

FOR SAUTÉING THE RICE
3 Tbs. (42 g) Enriched Lard
2 cups (400 g) long-grain white rice, rinsed, thoroughly drained, and air-dried
½ medium white onion (5 oz. / 137.5 g), finely chopped
2 medium cloves garlic (½ oz. / 12g), peeled and minced
1 medium chile poblano (6 oz. / 150 g), charred, peeled, seeded, and cut into medium dice

FOR SIMMERING AND STEAMING THE RICE
¼ cup (62.5 ml) freshly squeezed lime juice
Zest of one lime, finely grated

PREPARE FLAVORED COOKING LIQUID
Place 1 cup (250 ml) of the stock and the herbs in the jar of a blender. Process for 30 seconds, or until the herbs are thoroughly liquefied. Set aside.

SAUTÉ RICE
Follow the master recipe for Arroz blanco, adding the diced chile to the sautéed rice at the same time you add the onions and garlic.

SIMMER AND STEAM RICE
Mix the lime juice with the remaining 2¾ cups (687.5 ml) stock and add to the rice, following the instructions for Arroz blanco.

Add the reserved flavored herb liquid from the blender and continue with the instructions for Arroz blanco. Sprinkle on the lime zest, cover as instructed, and allow to steam.

ARROZ NEGRO

BLACK PILAF

TO PREPARE AHEAD

Enriched Lard (p. 513)

4 cups (1 L) black bean liquid reserved from first cooking of Frijol k'abax (p. 504) or Frijole con puerco (p. 262)

FOR SAUTÉING THE RICE

3 Tbs. (42 g) Enriched Lard

2 cups (400 g) long-grain white rice, rinsed, thoroughly drained, and air-dried

½ medium white onion (5 oz. / 137.5 g), finely chopped

2 medium cloves garlic (½ oz. / 12 g), peeled and minced

2 medium chiles serranos (3/4 oz. / 20 g), seeded and thinly sliced across the width

FOR SIMMERING AND STEAMING THE RICE

¼ tsp. (0.5 g) cuminseed *and* ¼ tsp. (0.1625 g) dried whole Mexican oregano, lightly toasted and ground together

4 cups (1 L) cooking liquid from Frijol k'abax, divided

1 ½ tsp. (9 g) sea salt

1 Tbs. (5 g) fresh cilantro or epazote leaves, chopped

SAUTÉ RICE

Heat the lard in a large skillet until shimmering. Sauté the rice as in the master recipe for Arroz blanco, adding the chile at the same time you add the onions and garlic.

SIMMER AND STEAM RICE

Pass the ground spices through a fine-mesh sieve into the black bean liquid, add salt, and stir until dissolved. Pour half of the liquid into the skillet with the rice, then proceed with the instructions for Arroz blanco.

Add the remaining black bean cooking liquid followed by the cilantro or epazote and continue with the steps for Arroz blanco. Cover and allow to steam.

BASIC PREPARATION TECHNIQUES

Several simple preparation techniques give Yucatecan cuisine its unique flavor—even texture.

CHARRING VEGETABLES

Some cookbooks refer to this process as "toasting," others as "roasting." I call it what it is—charring—since in Yucatán the goal is thoroughly blackened, charred skin over at least 80 percent of the vegetable. The paper of garlic will have mostly burned away; tomatoes will be more black than red; all vegetables will be slightly softened from the cooking process.

Whichever the charring technique that is used, in Yucatán we never peel away the charred skin of a vegetable because it's the charred bits that add so much flavor. Peel onions before charring, then chop or use them as instructed in a recipe, leaving the charred bits intact. Whole heads of garlic are charred with the paper on; the paper is rubbed off afterward, but the separated cloves retain charring.

Individual cloves of garlic are peeled and then charred. Tomatoes are charred whole and never peeled.

On a gas stove: Place onions, tomatoes, and large chiles directly on gas burners and use tongs to turn. Whole heads of garlic, garlic cloves, and smaller chiles can be placed on metal skewers and held directly in the flame. (Note: If you prefer to keep the heat-producing capsaicin in chiles from leaching into the food you are preparing, do not place the chiles on a skewer and take care that they do not rupture as you char them.)

On an electric stove: Place a cast-iron skillet or griddle for 5 minutes on highest heat. Arrange the vegetables in one layer on the preheated pan and turn occasionally. (Charring will take a bit longer than directly over a flame.)

On an outdoor grill: Place the vegetables in a perforated grilling basket and locate it either directly on the hot coals of a charcoal fire or close to the flame of a gas grill.

On charring whole heads of garlic: Depending on the method you use, it can take 10–15 minutes to char a whole head. The ideal method is directly over a flame or on hot coals. The outer paper will catch fire; the garlic should display charring overall, and the paper should be mostly burned away. The head should be cooked and feel slightly soft when you squeeze it. Once the garlic has cooled, rub the black paper off between your palms, separate the head into sections, then into individual whole cloves, which will naturally pull away from any remaining paper. The cloves will have some charring still visible, which is important to the flavor.

TOASTING DRIED HERBS, SPICES, AND SEEDS

Use a small cast-iron skillet for this job; fine stainless steel will be destroyed since it must sit on highest heat with no contents for many minutes. Once the product is lightly browned, immediately transfer it to another container, or the residual heat of the skillet may burn it.

- *For dried herbs and spices:* Place herbs or spices in the skillet and turn the heat to highest. Watch the ingredients closely and move them frequently with a spoon or by shaking the skillet. As the ingredients turn fragrant, just begin to darken, and release a bit of smoke, immediately transfer them to a bowl until ready to use. The entire process usually takes 1–2 minutes.
- *For seeds:* This is the technique used for squash seeds and *cacao*. Place the empty, dry cast-iron skillet over highest heat for 10 minutes to preheat. Add the seeds and stir them or toss frequently to avoid scorching. As soon as you hear the seeds start to pop (the result of expanding steam from moisture inside), toss, stir, and shake to keep the seeds in constant movement. When golden brown or done as specified in your recipe, immediately remove the seeds from the heat and transfer to a colander to cool until ready for use.

CRUSHING AND GRINDING

- *Stone:* If you want to go traditional and end up with a coarsely textured product, grind on stone. The bowl-shaped *tamul* (*molcajete* in Mexico) is typically used for wet things like tomatoes, chiles, and onions. The *ka'* (metate in Mexico), or flat grinding stone, is usually used for dry foods like corn, roasted *cacao*, and seeds.
- *Coffee or spice mill:* This is extremely useful for grinding spices and dried herbs used in *recados*. Ideally, you will have one dedicated to that purpose, since the flavor of coffee can impact the flavor of the spices, and vice versa.
- *Food processor:* The food processor is useful for a variety of grinding chores. It works very well for dry seeds and grains as well as wet things like tomatoes.
- *Blender and immersion blender:* If a liquid or smooth purée is required, a blender works best.

PREPARING *MILANESA*-STYLE MEATS

In Yucatán, the term "*milanesa*" refers to any meat sliced thin, then pounded to be even thinner. The technique is used for pork, beef, and chicken and serves to tenderize meats and make them quick to cook.

- *For beef:* The beef usually used for *milanesa* in Yucatán is top round, but for better flavor and tenderness, you may use a more expensive cut such as tenderloin or top sirloin.
- *For pork:* Pork *milanesa* is generally from the leg or rump, but the more expensive loin will be leaner.
- *For chicken:* Chicken *milanesa* is always boneless, skinless breast.

Cutting across the grain, divide the beef top sirloin or tenderloin or the pork loin, leg, or rump into equal portions, each weighing about 4 ounces / 115 grams (or the size and quantity specified in your recipe). There is no need to cut the beef top round or chicken breasts. Place the pieces between two sheets of waxed paper and use a wooden mallet or rolling pin to pound and flatten to a thickness of about ⅛ inch (3 mm).

WORKING WITH CHILES

Chiles are the zest of life for most Yucatecans. Learning how to handle them can give you control over the heat of the dishes you prepare.

The chemical that makes chiles hot is called capsaicin. Although some capsaicin is found in the flesh of the chile, it is primarily located in the part of the chile known as the placenta—the network of veins and seeds that begins directly beneath the stem. Removing the placenta can greatly reduce the quantity of capsaicin in the chile.

Many salsas and other dishes achieve their character from the full heat of the chile; for these, the recipes in this book do not specify removing the seeds. For all others—or if you simply cannot tolerate the heat—follow the steps below.

Unless you have worked with chiles before and know your tolerance, you should wear gloves whenever you work with them. Even mild chiles can cause irritation to sensitive skin.

REMOVING SEEDS AND VEINS FROM A FRESH CHILE

1. *Cut or slice off the stem end. Cut the chile in half lengthwise and lay it flat.* [AH]

2. *Cut away the entire placenta with its veins and seeds and discard.* [AH]

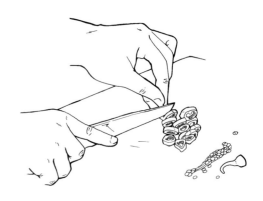

3. *Slice the chile across the width or as instructed in your recipe.* [AH]

REMOVING SEEDS AND VEINS FROM A DRIED CHILE

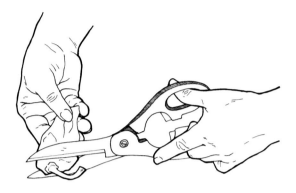

1. *Use scissors to cut off the stem end.* [AH]

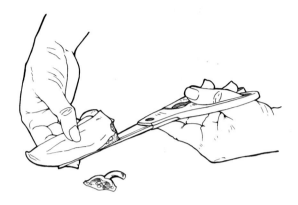

2. *Cut a slit up one side of the chile.* [AH]

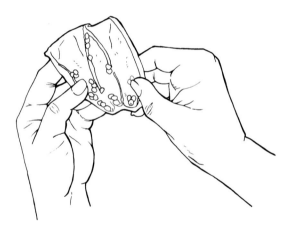

3. *Open the chile and flatten.* [AH]

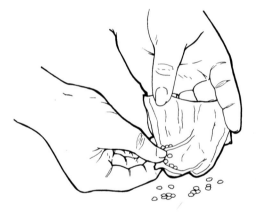

4. *Brush away the seeds and use your fingers to pull off the veins; discard.* [AH]

PEELING FRESH CHILES

In Yucatán, peeling is rarely done for habaneros, frequently done for serranos, and always done for poblanos:

• Char the chile first as instructed on page 532.

• Place the chile in a paper or resealable plastic bag, close, and leave for 10 minutes to soften.

• Remove the chile from the bag, hold it under running water, and gently rub away the burnt skin.

PREPARING MEATS FOR COOKING

All meats in Yucatán are given a refreshing bath in cold water prior to cooking. This may date from a time when most meats were preserved with salt and therefore had to be liberally soaked to make them edible. Further, it is typical nowadays for women to squeeze some Seville orange juice onto the meats during the bath, or to rub the meat with a half of the fruit. Not only does this aid in removing some of the gamey flavor, but it also adds a light citrus essence to finished dishes.

The act of soaking meats in salted water to improve flavor and tenderize them is not common in Yucatán, although on rare occasions, vintage regional cookbooks suggest a soak in *salmuera* (brine). The ancient Mayas frequently salted meat and fish to preserve it (p. 151), then refreshed it in water before cooking. For these reasons—not to mention the dramatic improvement in overall flavor and texture—I don't think brining is such a stretch from a historical perspective and warrants a little poetic license.

Avoid overbrining, since meat proteins that have broken down too much can become mushy. Because brining increases the saltiness of the finished product, all recipes in this book that specify brining have been adjusted for salt content to account for the brining step.

RECOMMENDED BRINING TIMES

Chicken, whole	4–8 hours
Chicken, breast or pieces	2–3 hours
Pork, butt, shoulder, roast	12–48 hours
Pork, loin, chops	4–6 hours
Quail, pheasant, game hens	1–2 hours
Rabbit, whole or pieces	2–3 hours
Turkey, whole	12–48 hours
Turkey, breast or pieces	6–8 hours
Venison, roast	12–36 hours
Venison, chops, pieces	6–8 hours

BRINE SOLUTION / SALMUERA

1 gallon (4 L) cold water
½ cup (145 g) sea salt
½ cup (100 g) sugar
2 tsp. (8 g) black peppercorns, coarsely crushed
10 allspice berries, coarsely crushed

Dissolve the salt and sugar in the water and add the crushed allspice and peppercorns. (I have good luck dissolving the salt and sugar in cold water. It takes a little longer, but I find it is still faster than dissolving it in hot water and then letting the water cool. The water must be cold before adding the meat.) Place the meat in the brine and refrigerate for the specified time. Drain the meat, rinse under cold water, and pat dry with paper towels. Discard the brining solution. (Note: For larger cuts such as a whole turkey, you will double or triple the brine solution recipe, making sure to maintain the exact proportions of water : salt : sugar. The solution should completely cover the meat.)

VARIATIONS

For other flavor enhancements, add 2–3 crushed cloves of garlic, a couple of bay leaves, a small stick of *canela* (Mexican cinnamon), and/or 6–8 whole cloves.

✺ THE ETHEREAL ESSENCE OF SMOKE ✺

Smoke is a key flavor essence of Yucatecan cuisine and is a prominent "ingredient" in many of the recipes in this book. A smoky quality can be imparted to foods by means of the stovetop smoking method, the charcoal grill smoking method, or the gas grill smoking method using wood smoking chips. In Yucatán, we use native hardwoods such as *boox káatsim* (*Acacia gaumeri* S. F. Blake), *sak káatsim* (*M. bahamensis* Benth.), *ja'abin* (*Piscidia communis* S. F. Blake), or several others, but you can achieve acceptable results with chips of another Fabaceae family member—mesquite (*Prosopis* spp.), which is more accessible and yields an appropriate "Mexican" flavor. Cured meats with a more intense flavor of smoke require slow cooking in a special cool smoker (see p. 477).

STOVETOP SMOKING METHOD

You will need the following:

- For large quantities of meat: a large cast-iron Dutch oven or roasting pan with a lid, approximately 9 quarts (9 L). For smaller quantities: a large cast-iron skillet at least 2½ inches (4 cm) deep, fitted with a lid. (Note: Because of the intense heat required for this method, enameled iron cookware is not recommended)
- Heavy-duty aluminum foil

- 10–12 inch (25 30 cm) diameter cooling rack, or one that fits comfortably in the bottom of your pot or skillet. The cooling rack needs to rest inside the pan or skillet about 1½ inches (4 cm) off the bottom of the pot; if your rack does not have legs, create them with balls of foil.
- 2 tablespoons (⅓ oz. / 10 g) wood smoking chips (see Resources, p. 537), preferably mesquite, dry, not soaked

1. *Line the sides and bottom of the interior of a Dutch oven, roasting pan, or skillet with large pieces of foil. Leave at least 6 inches (15.25 cm) of foil extending beyond the edge of the pot on all sides.* [AH]

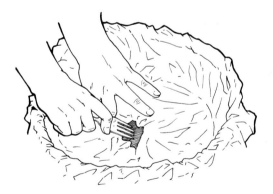

2. *Using a sharp object, cut and tear away a small hole in the foil at the center of the bottom about 3 inches (7.5 cm) in diameter to expose the pot's surface. Wrap the lid with aluminum foil and crimp tightly around the edges.* [AH]

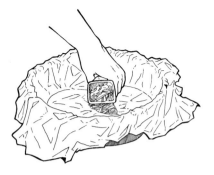  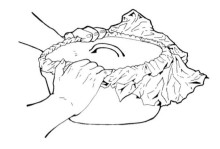

3. *Preheat the uncovered pot without the cake rack over highest heat for 10 minutes. Have food wrapped as per your recipe's instructions at hand. After preheating, place the smoking chips on the exposed surface where you cut away the foil.* [AH]

4. *Immediately place the rack at the bottom of the pot. Place the wrapped food on the rack, allowing space around packets so that steam and smoke can circulate. If you have an external-read thermometer, insert it into the meat, avoiding bone.* [AH]

5. *Put the lid in place and crimp the edges of the foil tightly all around to seal in the smoke and steam. When the food is done, remove the pot from the heat immediately and uncover to prevent overcooking.* [AH]

CHARCOAL GRILL SMOKING METHOD

You will need the following:

- Charcoal
- A shallow metal bowl or disposable aluminum roasting pan full of boiling water (only for meat or poultry)
- ½ cup (1½ oz. / 40 g) wood smoking chips, preferably mesquite, soaked in hot water for 30 minutes
- A grill or oven thermometer in the grill for an accurate heat reading
- An instant-read thermometer or standard meat thermometer

Preheat the grill, using plenty of charcoal. When the coals are red-hot, spread them to cover the bottom; they should extend from side to side. Place the pan full of water directly on top of the coals; replenish the water during cooking if necessary.

Arrange the prepared food in a grilling basket or tray. Drain the wood chips and spread half of them directly on the coals (add the remaining chips halfway through cooking time). Place the food on the lowest rack, directly above the pan of water. (Note: If you are charring vegetables, place them directly above or even on top of the hot coals, omitting the pan of water.)

Close the lid. For poultry, the internal temperature of the grill should be maintained at 350°F (176°C); you may also use this temperature for faster cooking of pork, beef, or venison. For slower roasting, maintain the grill temperature at 250°F (121°C). Cooking times will naturally vary according to your grill's condition, the cut of meat, and so on; use an instant-read thermometer from time to time to monitor the temperature. (Note: Resist the urge to open the lid for at least the first 30 minutes of cooking to avoid losing accumulated steam and smoke.)

GAS GRILL SMOKING METHOD

You will need the following:

- The same tools as for the charcoal grill smoking method, except charcoal
- ½ cup (1½ oz. / 40 g) wood smoking chips, preferably mesquite, dry, not soaked, loosely wrapped in aluminum foil to form a small pouch

Preheat the grill for 10 minutes. Place a metal pan full of water on the lowest grate, but *not* directly on the burners. Replenish the water during cooking if necessary.

Arrange the prepared food in a grilling basket or tray. Place the wood chip pouch under the grate, on top of a burner shield or as close to the flame as possible. Place the food on a grate directly above the pan of water. (Note: If you are charring vegetables, arrange them in a grilling basket and place it on the lowest rack, directly above the flame, omitting the pan of water.)

Refer to the temperatures in the instructions for the charcoal grill smoking method.

RESOURCES

Most of the items in this directory are now available in major supermarkets, greenmarkets, or Mexican markets in larger urban areas. This section will be useful for finding particularly unusual items and for cooks who live in smaller cities or towns.

CANNED FOODS

COCONUT CREAM / SWEETENED FOR USE IN COOKING AND COCKTAILS

- Amazon
  www.amazon.com
- Mexgrocer
  www.mexgrocer.com

GUAVA PASTE / THICK PURÉE OF GUAVA

- Mexgrocer
- Goya Foods
  www.goya.com

DRIED FOODS

CACAO / DRIED OR ROASTED BEANS AND NIBS

- Green Lifestyles
  on Planet Paradise
  www.gonegreenstore.com
- Loving Earth
  www.lovingearth.net
- New Leaf Chocolates
  www.newleafchocolates.com

CHILES / DRIED ANCHO, DE ÁRBOL, GUAJILLO, CHIPOTLE

- Frieda's Specialty Produce Co.
  www.friedas.com
- Grand Central Market
  www.grandcentralsquare.com
- Mexgrocer

- Pendery's
  www.penderys.com

CORN HUSKS / WRAPPERS FOR TAMALES

- Kalustyan's
  www.kalustyans.com
- Mexgrocer
- Pendery's

MASA HARINA / MAIZE MASA FLOUR

- Mexgrocer
- Pendery's

PEPITAS / SQUASH SEEDS, PEELED AND ROASTED

- Pendery's

PILONCILLO / UNREFINED BROWN SUGAR CONES

- Kalustyan's
- Mexgrocer
- Pendery's

FRESH FOODS

CHILES / FRESH BANANA, WAX, POBLANO, JALAPEÑO, HABANERO

- La Flor de Yucatán
  www.laflordeyucatan.net
- Mexgrocer

MASA / CORN DOUGH FROM NIXTAMAL

- Tortillería Nixtamal
  www.tortillerianixtamal.com
- El Rancho Tortillería & Market
  951.685.9484

FROZEN FOODS

BANANA LEAVES / FROZEN LEAVES FOR USE IN MANY YUCATECAN DISHES

- Temple of Thai
  www.templeofthai.com

FRUITS / GUANÁBANA PULP, GUAVA PULP, MAMEY, MARAÑÓN, NANCE, CIRUELA

- Amazonas Imports
  www.amazonasimports.com
- Goya Foods
- Quirch Foods
  www.quirchfoods.com
- Rio Grande Foods
  www.riograndefoods.com

HERBS, SPICES, AND CONDIMENTS

ACHIOTE / WHOLE SEEDS AND PASTE RECADO

- Kalustyan's
- Mexgrocer
- Pendery's

CALCIUM HYDROXIDE / "SLAKED" OR "PICKLING" LIME

- Amazon
- Canning Pantry
  www.canningpantry.com

CANELA (CEYLON CINNAMON OR MEXICAN CINNAMON) / STICK FORM AND GROUND

- Kalustyan's
- Mexgrocer
- Rancho Gordo
  www.ranchogordo.com

EPAZOTE / DRIED DYSPHANIA AMBROSIOIDES LEAVES

- Herbs of Mexico
  www.herbsofmexico.com
- Grand Central Market
- Latin Merchant
  www.latinmerchant.com
- El Mercado del Este de Los
  Angeles / 323.268.3451

HOJA SANTA / DRIED PIPER AURITUM LEAVES

- Grand Central Market
- El Mercado del Este de Los
  Angeles

MEXICAN HONEY / VARIOUS FLORAL FLAVORS

- Mexgrocer
- Amazon

- Harvey Nichols
  www.harveynichols.com
- Carrick's of Penreth
  www.carricksofpenrith.com

MEAT CURE POWDERS / PRAGUE POWDER CURE #1 / FOR SAUSAGES AND SMOKED MEATS

- The Great American Spice Co.
  www.americanspice.com
- Morton Salt
  www.mortonsalt.com
- My Spice Sage
  www.myspicesage.com

MEXICAN OREGANO / WHOLE AND FLAKES

- Mexgrocer
- Pendery's
- Rancho Gordo

MEXICAN VANILLA / EXTRACT AND PODS

- Gourmet Country
  www.gourmetcountry.com
- Kalustyan's
- Pendery's
- Rancho Gordo
- The Vanilla Co.
  www.vanilla.com
- Williams-Sonoma
  www.williams-sonoma.com

RECADOS / YUCATECAN SEASONING BLENDS

- Mexgrocer
- Pendery's
- La Perla Spice Co.
  www.delmayab.com

SEA SALT / "MAYA" OR YUCATECAN SEA SALT

- Rancho Gordo
- Mexgrocer
- The Salt Table
  www.salttable.com

SQUASH-SEED OIL / TYPICAL GARNISH FOR PAPADZULES (P. 280)

- Amazon
- Stony Brook Wholehearted Foods
  www.wholeheartedfoods.com

TOOLS AND UTENSILS

***APLASTADORA* / HAND PRESS FOR MAKING TORTILLAS**

- Mexgrocer
- Pendery's

COMAL / GRIDDLE

- Mexgrocer

***MOLINILLO* / HAND BEATER FOR FROTHING CHOCOLATE BEVERAGES**

- Amazon
- Mexgrocer

***MOLINO* / HAND GRINDER FOR CORN AND OTHER FOODS**

- Amazon
- Mexgrocer

***TAMUL (MOLCAJETE)* / STONE MORTAR AND PESTLE**

- Mexgrocer
- Pendery's

***VAPORERA* TAMAL STEAMERS**

- Mexgrocer

WOOD SMOKING CHIPS / MESQUITE

- Amazon
- Camarons Products
  www.camaronsproducts.com
- 4thegrill.com

BIBLIOGRAPHY

"About Sian Ka'an." Centro Ecológico Sian Ka'an. www.cesiak.org

Acevedo-Rodríguez, Pedro. "*Melicocceae (Sapindaceae) Milicoccus* and *Talisia.*" *Flora Neotrópica*, Vol. 87, 2003.

Administración Portuaria Integral de Progreso, S.A. de C.V. www .puertosyucatan.com

Aguilar Escalante, Sergio, and Alfonso Solís Pimentel. "Coastal Dune Stabilization using Geotextile Tubes at Las Coloradas." *Geosynthetics*, February 2008.

Aguirre, *dña.* María Ygnacia. *Prontuario de cocina para un diario regular.* Mérida: Imprenta de L. Seguí, 1832, and Lit. R. Caballero, 1896.

Alexander, Rani T. "Maya Settlement Shifts and Agrarian Ecology in Yucatán, 1800–2000." *Journal of Anthropological Research*, Vol. 62, 2006.

Alfaro-Velcamp, Theresa. *So Far from Allah, So Close to Mexico: Middle Eastern Immigrants in Modern Mexico.* Austin: University of Texas Press, 2007.

Almodóvar, Miguel Ángel. *La cocina del Cid: Historia de los yantares y banquetes de los caballeros medievales.* Madrid: Ediciones Nowtilus, 2007.

Amaro Gamboa, Jesús, and Miguel Güémez Pineda. *Vocabulario del uayeísmo en la cultura de Yucatán.* Mérida: Universidad Autónoma de Yucatán, 1999.

Andrews, Anthony P. "El comercio marítimo de los mayas del Posclásico." *Arqueología Mexicana*, Vol. 6, No. 33, 1998.

Angón Galván, Pedro. "Caracterización parcial del fruto de *Parmentiera edulis.*" MA thesis, Universidad Tecnológica de la Mixteca, Huajapan de León, Oaxaca, 2006.

Ávila Palafox, Ricardo. "Cantinas and Drinkers in Mexico." *Drinking: Anthropological Approaches*, Igor de Garine and Valerie de Gerine (eds.). Oxford: Berghahn Books, 2001.

Ayora-Díaz, Steffan Igor, and Gabriela Vargas-Cetina. "Romantic Moods: Food, Beer, Music and the Yucatecan Soul." *Drinking Cultures*, Thomas M. Wilson (ed.). London: Berg, 2005.

Barthélemy, Pascale, and Michel Boccara. *La cocina maya.* Paris: Ductus & "Psychanalyse et Pratiques Sociales," 2005.

Beard, James A. "Crème Brûlée Dessert: One of the Greatest." *Los Angeles Times*, 1970.

Bergmann, John F. "The Distribution of Cacao Cultivation in Pre-Columbian America." *Annals of the Association of American Geographers*, Vol. 59, No. 1, 1969.

Bojórquez Urzaiz, Carlos E. *La emigración cubana en Yucatán, 1868–1898.* Mérida: Imagen Contemporánea, 2000.

Braun, David (ed.). "Yucatan Biodiversity Assessed by Photography Expedition." *National Geographic News*, 2009. http:// blogs.nationalgeographic.com/blogs/news/chiefeditor/cultures /2009/11/

Bronson, Bennet. "Roots and the Subsistence of the Ancient Maya." *Southwestern Journal of Anthropology*, Vol. 22, 1966.

Caballero-Chávez, Vequí. "Pesquería de róbalo blanco en Ciudad del Carmen, Campeche." Mexico City: Instituto Nacional de Pesca, 2010.

Cabrera, Édgar, Carmen Salazar, and José Salvador Flores. "Anacardiaceae: Taxonomía florística y etnobotánica." *Etnoflora yucatanense*, fasc. 15, 2000.

Cabrera, Edgar, Evangelina Hernández, José Salvador Flores, and Carmen Salazar. "Annonaceae de la Península de Yucatán." *Etnoflora yucatanense*, fasc. 21, 2004.

Carreón, Gerardo. "Ría Lagartos Park Profile." ParksWatch Mexico. www.parkswatch.org

Casares G. Cantón, Raúl, Juan Duch Colell, Michel Antochiw Kolpa, Silvio Zavala Vallado, et al. *Yucatán en el tiempo.* Mérida, Yucatán, 1998.

Ceccarelli, Franca "¿Y dónde guardo las guayabas?" *El Periódico de Quintana Roo*, 2010. www.elperiodico.com.mx

Centurión Hidalgo, Dora, Jaime Cázares Camero, and Judith Espinosa Moreno. *Inventario de recursos fitogenéticos alimentarios de Tabasco.* Fundación Tabasco Produce, SIGOLFO. Villahermosa: Universidad Juárez Autónoma de Tabasco, 2004.

Cetina Sierra, José Adonay. "Apuntaciones para la historia legislativa del municipio de Mérida."

Chilam Balam de Chumayel. Princeton, N.J.: Princeton University Library, Digital Collections. Folio 36v.

Childs, Nathan. *Rice Situation and Outlook Yearbook*. Washington, D.C.: U.S. Department of Agriculture, 2009.

Coe, Michael D. *The Maya*. New York: Thames & Hudson, 1980.

Coe, Sophie D. *America's First Cuisines*. Austin: University of Texas Press, 1994.

Collette, B. B., and C. E. Nauen. "Scombrids of the World: An Annotated and Illustrated Catalogue of Tunas, Mackerels, Bonitos and Related Species Known to Date." Rome: *FAO Species Catalogue*, Vol. 2, 1983.

Colunga-García Marín, Patricia, and Daniel Zizumbo-Villarreal. "Domestication of Plants in Maya Lowlands." *Economic Botany*, Vol. 58, 2004.

Consejo Nacional para Cultura y las Artes. *La cocina familiar en el estado de Campeche*. Mexico City: Editorial Océano de México, 1988.

Corniola, Silvina. "Octopus Season in Campeche Ends on a High." Fish Information & Services/Mexico, 2010. www.fis.com

Covo Torres, Javier (ed.). *Bombas yucatecas: Las mejores bombas del folclor yucateco*. Mérida: Editorial Dante, 2008.

Cuanalo de la Cerda, Heriberto E., and Rogelio R. Guerra Mukul. *Homegarden Production and Productivity in a Mayan Community of Yucatán*. New York: Springer Science+Business Media, 2008.

Cuevas Seba, Teté. *Del líbano . . . lo que debemos recordar*. Mérida, 2009.

Dahlin, Bruce H., Daniel Bair, Tim Beach, Matthew Moriarty, and Richard Terry. "The Dirt on Food: Ancient Feasts and Markets among the Lowland Maya." *Pre-Columbian Foodways: Interdisciplinary Approaches to Food, Culture and Markets in Ancient Mesoamerica*, John Edward Staller and Michael Carrasco (eds.). New York: Springer Science+Business Media, 2010.

Davidson, Alan. *Oxford Companion to Food*. Oxford: Oxford University Press, 1999.

del Rocío Ruenes-Morales, María, Alejandro Casas, Juan José Jiménez-Osornio, and Javier Caballero. "Etnobotánica de *Spondias purpurea* L. (Anacardiaceae) en la península de Yucatán." *Interciencia*, Vol. 35, No. 4, 2010.

Demarest, Arthur. *Ancient Maya: The Rise and Fall of a Rainforest Civilization*. Cambridge: Cambridge University Press, 2004.

Diccionario de la lengua española. Madrid: Real Academia Española, 22nd edition, 2001.

Duke, James A. *Handbook of Energy Crops Online*, 1983. http://www.hort.purdue.edu/newcrop/duke_energy/Cocos_nucifera.html

Dunmire, William W. *Gardens of New Spain*. Austin: University of Texas Press, 2004.

Edwards Carter, Kaye. *Henry Perrine: Plant Pioneer of the Florida Frontier*. Lake Buena Vista, Fla.: Tailored Tours Publications, 1998.

Eiss, Paul K. "Hunting for the Virgin: Meat, Money, and Memory in Tetiz, Yucatán." *Cultural Anthropology*, Vol. 17, No. 3, 2002.

Emerson, R. A. "Preliminary Survey of the Milpa System of Maize Culture as Practiced by the Maya Indians of the Northern Part of the Yucatán Peninsula." *Annals of the Missouri Botanical Garden*, Vol. 40, No. 1, 1953.

Espuelas Barroso, Sergio, and Margarita Vilar Rodríguez. "The Determinants of Social Spending in Spain (1880–1960): Is Lindert Right?" Barcelona: Departament d'Història i Institucions Econòmiques, 2007.

Ferguson, M. E., P. J. Bramel, and S. Chandra. "Gene Diversity among Botanical Varieties in Peanut (*Arachis hypogaea* L.)." *Crop Science*, Vol. 44, 2004.

"FishWatch." NOAA National Marine Fisheries Service, 2010. www.nmfs.noaa.gov/fishwatch

"Flora digital del Centro de Investigación Científica de Yucatán." http://www.cicy.mx/sitios/flora%20digital/ficha_virtual.php?especie=1710

Flores, Alfredo. "Great Guava!" *Agricultural Research*, Vol. 55, No. 9, 2007.

Flores Guido, José Salvador, Gladiz Canto-Aviles, and Ana Flores Serrano. "Plantas de la flora yucatanense que provocan alguna toxicidad en el humano." *Revista Biomédica*, Vol. 12, 2001.

Fournier M., Michel André. "Mundo árabe." *Comida yucateca: Fusión de culturas gastronómicas*. Seville: Grupo Gastronautas, 2003.

Francis, John K. "*Bromelia pinguin*, Bromeliaceae." San Juan, P.R.: U.S. Department of Agriculture, Forest Service, International Institute of Tropical Forestry, 1998.

Gabriel, Jean-Pierre, and Dominique Persoone. *Cacao: The Roots of Chocolate*. Brussels: Editions Françoise Blouard, 2008.

Galindo-Tovar, María Elena, Nisao Ogata-Aguilar, and Amaury M. Arzate-Fernández. "Some Aspects of Avocado (*Persea americana* Mill.) Diversity and Domestication in Mesoamerica." *Genetic Resources and Crop Evolution*, Vol. 55, 2008.

García Quintanilla, Alejandra. "El dilema de *Ah Kimsah K'ax*: Él que mata al monte. Significados del monte entre los mayas milperos de Yucatán." *Revista Mesoamérica*, Vol. 21, No. 39, 2000. www.mayas.uady.mx/articulos/ahkimsah.html

Gómez-Pompa, Arturo, José Salvador Flores, and Mario Aliphat Fernández. "The Sacred Cacao Groves of the Maya." *Latin American Antiquity*, Vol. 1, No. 3, 1990.

Góngora, Miguel Ángel Moo, and Hipólito Pacheco Perera. "Su sabor es diferente de lo que parece." *Diario de Yucatán*, 14 May 2009.

Góngora Bianchi, Renán. "Historia de Yucatán: Valladolid, ciudad cuatro veces heroica." *Diario de Yucatán*, 1997.

Graham, Gladys R. *Tropical Cooking in Panama: A Handbook of Tropical Foods and How to Use Them*. Canal Zone, Republic of Panama: Canal Zone Experimental Gardens, 1947.

Hall, Grant D., Stanley M. Tarka, Jeffrey Hurst, David Stuart, and Richard E. Adams. "Cacao Residues in Ancient Maya Vessels from Rio Azul, Guatemala." *American Antiquity*, Vol. 55, No. 1, 1990.

Hammond, Norman. "New Light on the Most Ancient Maya." *Man*, New Series, Vol. 21, No. 3, 1986.

Hecht, Johanna. "The Manila Galleon Trade (1565–1815)." *Heilbrunn Timeline of Art History*. New York: Metropolitan Museum of Art, 2000– .

"Historia de Mérida." Mérida: Archivo Histórico del Ayuntamiento de Mérida, 2010.

Hixon, Raymond F., Roger T. Hanlon, Samuel M. Gillespie, and Wade L. Griffin. "Squid Fishery in Texas: Biological, Economic and Market Considerations." *Marine Fisheries Review*, 1980.

Houston, Stephen D., Oswaldo Fernando Chichilla Mazariegos, and

David Stuart (eds.). "The Fish as a Maya Symbol for Counting." *The Decipherment of Maya Writing.* Norman: University of Oklahoma Press, 2001.

Hull, K. "An Epigraphic Analysis of Classic-Period Maya Foodstuffs." *Pre-Columbian Foodways: Interdisciplinary Approaches to Food, Culture and Markets in Ancient Mesoamerica,* John E. Staller and Michael Carrasco (eds.). New York: Springer Science+Business Media, 2010.

Kane, G. C., and J. I. Lipsky. "Drug–Grapefruit Juice Interactions." *Mayo Clinic Proceedings,* Vol. 75, No. 9, 2000.

Karttunen, Frances. *An Analytical Dictionary of Nahuatl.* Norman: University of Oklahoma Press, 1992.

Landa, Fray Diego de. *Yucatán: Before and After the Conquest.* Translated and with notes by William Gates. Toronto: General Publishing Company, 1978.

Lange, Frederick W. "Marine Resources: A Viable Subsistence Alternative for the Prehistoric Lowland Maya." *American Anthropologist,* New Series, Vol. 73, No. 3, 1971.

Larousse gastronomique. New York: Clarkson Potter/Publishers, 2009.

Las Casas, Bartolomé de. *Historia de las Indias.* Biblioteca de Autores Españoles, Vol. 96. Madrid: Atlas, 1961.

León, Jorge. "Botánica de los cultivos tropicales." San José, C.R.: Agroamérica, 2000.

León, Perla, and Salvador Montiel. "Wild Meat Use and Traditional Hunting Practices in a Rural Mayan Community of the Yucatán Peninsula, Mexico." *Human Ecology,* Vol. 36, 2007.

Lillvik, Sonja. *The Painted Fish and Other Mayan Feasts.* Carrboro, NC: Cuzan Press, 2009.

Lira Saade, Rafael. "Cucurbitaceae de la Península de Yucatán." *Etnoflora yucatanense,* fasc. 22, 2004.

———, and S. Montes Hernández. "Cucurbits." *Neglected Crops, 1492: From a Different Perspective.* J. E. Hernández Bermejo and J. León (eds.). Plant Production and Protection Series No. 26. Rome: Food and Agriculture Organization, 1994.

Lockhart, James. *Nahuatl as Written: Lessons in Older Written Nahuatl, with Copious Examples and Texts.* Stanford: Stanford University Press and UCLA Latin American Studies, 2001.

Lovett, Richard A. "'Dinosaur Killer' Asteroid Only One Part of New Quadruple-Whammy Theory." *National Geographic News,* 2006. http://news.nationalgeographic.com/news/2006/10/061030-dinosaur-killer.html

Lubinsky, Pesach, Séverine Bory, Juan Hernández Hernández, Seung-Chul Kim, and Arturo Gómez-Pompa. "Origins and Dispersal of Cultivated Vanilla (*Vanilla planifolia* Jacks. Orchidaceae)." *Economic Botany,* Vol. 62, No. 2, 2008.

Madrigal, Alexis. "Yucatán Jungles Are Feral Maya Gardens." *Wired,* 2007. http://www.wired.com/wiredscience/2007/10/yucatan-jungles/

Mahdeem, Har. "Custard Apples." *Neglected Crops, 1492: From a Different Perspective.* J. E. Hernández Bermejo and J. León (eds.). Plant Production and Protection Series No. 26. Rome: Food and Agriculture Organization, 1994.

Manzur de Borge, María. *Lo mejor de la comida libanesa.* Mérida: Maldonado Editores del Mayab, 2007.

Martínez, Maximinio. *Catálogo de nombres vulgares y científicos de plantas mexicanas.* Mexico City: Fondo de Cultura Économica, 1979.

Martínez-Bustos, F., H. E. Martínez-Flores, E. Sanmartín-Martínez et al. "Effect of the Components of Maize on the Quality of *Masa* and *Tortillas* during the Traditional *Nixtamalization* Process." *Journal of the Science of Food and Agriculture,* Vol. 81, 2001.

Martínez-Castillo, Jaime, Daniel Zizumbo-Villarreal, Paul Gepts, and Patricia Colunga García Marín. "Gene Flow and Genetic Structure in the Wild–Weedy–Domesticated Complex of *Phaseolus lunatus* L. in Its Mesoamerican Center of Domestication and Diversity." *Crop Science,* Vol. 47, 2007.

Martyr, Peter. *De Orbe Novo.* 1530.

Mathews, Jennifer P. *Chicle: The Chewing Gum of the Americas: From the Ancient Maya to William Wrigley.* Tucson: University of Arizona Press, 2009.

McDonald, J. A., J. S. Flores, J. Morales, and A. N. García Argáez. "Convolvulaceae: Taxonomía y florística." *Etnoflora yucatanense,* fasc. 12, 1997.

McKillop, Heather. "Underwater Archaeology, Salt Production and Coastal Maya Trade at Stingray Lagoon, Belize." *Latin American Antiquity,* Vol. 6, No. 3, 1995.

Medellín, R. A., A. L. Gardner, and J. M. Aranda. "The Taxonomic Status of the Yucatán Brown Brocket, *Mazama pandora* (Mammalia:Cervidae)." *Proceedings of the Biological Society of Washington,* Vol. 111, 1998.

Mediz Bolio, Antonio (trans.). *Libro de Chilam Balam de Chumayel* (author's translation to English). Mérida: Dante, 2005.

Méndez Ramón, Mariaca, Alba González Jácome, and Luis Manuel Arias Reyes. "El huerto maya yucateco en el siglo XVI." Mexico City: ECOSUR, CINVESTAV, FOMIX, UIMQROO, CONCYTEY, 2010.

Menéndez Castillo, Rosa A., and Vania Pavón González. *Plectbranthus amboinicus* (Lour.) Spreng. *Revista Cubana de Plantas Medicinales,* Vol. 3, No. 3. 1999.

Mera Ovando, Luz María. "Aspectos socioeconómicos y culturales." *Origen y diversificación del maíz: Una revisión analítica,* Takeo Angel Kato Yamakake et al. (eds.). Mexico City: UNAM, UACM, CP. SEMARNAT, CONABIO, 2009.

"El mercado de bebidas alcohólicas en Yucatán." Mérida: Información Sistemática de la Península, 2010.

Merrick, Laura C. "Squashes, Pumpkins and Gourds." *Evolution of Crop Plants,* 2nd edition. London: Longman Scientific and Technical, 1995.

Miller, Allison, and Barbara Schaal. "Domestication of a Meso-american Cultivated Fruit Tree, *Spondias purpurea.*" *Proceedings of the National Academy of Sciences,* Vol. 102, No. 36, 2005.

Morales Ortiz, Edgar R., and Luis Gerardo Herrera Tuz. "Ciricote (*Cordia dodecandra* A. DC.): Protocolo para su colecta, beneficio y almacenaje." Mérida: Comisión Nacional Forestal, 2009.

Moreno, Nancy. "*Caricaceae.* Fasc. 10." *Flora de Veracruz.* Xalapa, Veracruz: Instituto Nacional de Investigaciones en Recursos Bióticos, 1980.

Morison, Samuel Eliot. *Admiral of the Ocean Sea.* New York: Little, Brown and Company, 1991.

Morton, Julia F. "Star Apple," "Canistel," "Cashew Apple," "Papaya,"

"Strawberry Pear," "Banana," "Sapodilla," and "Black Sapote." *Fruits of Warm Climates*. Miami: Julia F. Morton, 1987.

Murias, Analia. "Campeche, Yucatán Look to Consolidate Octopus Industry." Fish Information & Services/Mexico, 2009. www.fis.com

Navarrete A., Manuela. *La verdadera cocina regional*. Valladolid, Yucatán, 1910.

Navarrete Muñoz, Gonzalo. *Cocina maya*. Mérida: Líber, 2013.

Newstrom, Linda. "Evidence for the Origin of Chayote, *Sechium edule* (Cucurbitaceae)." *Economic Botany*, Vol. 45, No. 3, 1991.

Nola, Ruperto de. *Libre del Coch*. Lady Brighid ni Chiarain (trans.). Logroño, Spain, 1529.

Olver, Lynne (ed.). *The Food Timeline*. www.foodtimeline.org

"On Ramón." El Pilar Maya Forest Garden Network, 2009. http://mayaforestgardeners.org/about.php

Ott, Jonathan. "The Delphic Bee: Bees and Toxic Honeys as Pointers to Psychoactive and Other Medicinal Plants." *Economic Botany*, Vol. 52, No. 3, 1998.

Paris, Harry S. "History of the Cultivar-Groups of *Cucurbita pepo*." *Horticultural Reviews*, Vol. 25, 2001.

Parker, Ingrid M., Isis López, Jennifer J. Petersen, Natalia Anaya, Luis Cubilla-Ríos, and Daniel Potter. "Domestication Syndrome in *Caimito* (*Chrysophyllum cainito* l.): Fruit and Seed Characteristics." *Economic Botany*, Vol. 64, No. 2, 2010.

Pasztor, Suzanne B. "Campeche." *Mexico: An Encyclopedia of Contemporary Culture and History*. Don M. Coerver, Suzanne B. Pasztor, Robert Buffington (eds.). Santa Barbara, Calif.: abc-clio, 2004.

Peón Ancona, Juan Francisco. "Divulgaciones: El origen del pan francés." *Diario de Yucatán*, 3 October 2009.

———. "Panuchos, salbutes, tacos y horchata." Paper presented at "Los Cuatro Cronistas at the Olimpo Theater, Mérida, Yucatán," 19 January 2008.

Pickersgill, Barbara. "Migrations of Chili Peppers, *Capsicum* spp., in the Americas." *Pre-Columbian Plant Migration: Papers of the Peabody Museum of Archaeology and Ethnology*, Vol. 76. Doris Stone (ed.). Cambridge: Harvard University Press, 1984.

Pilcher, Jeffrey M. *¡Qué Vivan los Tamales! Food and the Making of Mexican Identity*. Albuquerque: University of New Mexico Press, 1998.

Pindell, James. "History of Tectonic Interactions between the Cuban Forearc Terrane and Mexico-Central America." Havana: unesco/igcp Project 433, V Cuban Geological Congress, 2005.

Piperno, Dolores R., and Deborah Pearsall. *The Origins of Agriculture in the Lowland Neotropics*. San Diego, Calif.: Academic Press, 1998.

Press, Michelle. "Ichthyology Biological Profiles: Common Snook." Florida Museum of Natural History. www.flmnh.ufl.edu/

Price, Douglas T., Vera Tiesler, and James H. Burton. "Early African Diaspora in Colonial Campeche, Mexico: Strontium Isotopic Evidence." *American Journal of Physical Anthropology*, Vol. 130, No. 4, 2006.

Productos de Harina S.A de C.V., Mérida. www.galletasdonde.com

Rain, Patricia. *Vanilla: The Cultural History of the World's Favorite Flavor and Fragrance*. New York: Penguin Group, 2004.

Recinos, Adrián. *Popol Vuh*. Mexico City: Fondo de Cultura Económica, Secretaría de Educación Pública, 1984.

Reed, Nelson A. *The Caste War of Yucatán*. Stanford, Calif.: Stanford University Press, 2001.

René Rivas, Luis. "The Origin, Relationships, and Geographical Distribution of the Marine Fishes of the Gulf of Mexico." *The Fishery Bulletin of the Fish and Wildlife Service*, Vol. 55, 1954.

Reyes Pavón, Leonor. "La educación feminina en Yucatán en la segunda mitad del siglo XIX." *Andanzas y tripulaciones*, Vol. 1, No. 3, 2004.

Rico-Gray, Víctor, José G. García-Franco, Alexandra Chemas, Armando Puch, and Paulino Simá. "Species Composition Similarity and Structure of Maya Homegardens in Tixpeual and Tixcacaltuyub, Yucatán, México." *Economic Botany*, Vol. 44, No. 4, 1990.

Rimas, Andrew, and Evan D. G. Fraser. *Beef: The Untold Story of How Milk, Meat and Muscle Shaped the World*. New York: HarperCollins, 2008.

Roach, John. "World's Longest Underground River Discovered in Mexico." *National Geographic News*, 2007. http://news.nationalgeographic.com/news/2007/03/070305-cave-river.html

Robelo, Cecilio. *Diccionario de aztequismos*. Cuernavaca, Mex.: Imprenta del Autor, 1904.

Robins, C. A., and G. C. Ray. *Mugil liza*. Valenciennes, 1986. www.fishbase.org

Romero R., María Eugenia. "La navegación maya." *Arqueología Mexicana*, Vol. 6, No. 33, 1998.

Rosado, Renán Irigoyen. *El comercio en Yucatán*. Mérida, 1951.

———. *Crónicas de Mérida*. Mérida, 1980.

Ross-Ibarra, Jeffrey. "Origen y domesticación de la chaya (Cnidoscolus aconitifolius Mill I.M. Johnst): La espinaca Maya." *Mexican Studies/Estudios Mexicanos*, Vol. 19, No. 3, 2003.

———, and Álvaro Molina-Cruz. "Ethnobotany of Chaya (*Cnidoscolus aconitifolius* spp. *aconitifolius* Breckon): A Nutritious Maya Vegetable." *Economic Botany*, Vol. 56, No. 4, 2002.

Rubial García, Antonio. *Historia de la vida cotidiana en México: La ciudad barroca*. Mexico City: Fondo de Cultura Económica, 2005.

Rubio Centeno, José. "Maestro e historiador de la Universidad Mesoamericana de San Agustín." Mérida.

Ruvalcaba, Mercado J. "Vida cotidiana y consumo de maíz en la huasteca veracruzana." *Cuadernos de la Casa Chata*, No. 134. Mexico City: Centro de Investigaciones y Estudios Superiores en Antropología Social, 1987.

Ruz *vda.* de Baqueiro, Lucrecia. *Cocina yucateca*. Havana: El Porvenir, 1944.

Sánchez G. J., M. M. Goodman, and C. W. Stuber. "Isozymatic and Morphological Diversity in the Races of Maize of Mexico." *Economic Botany*, Vol. 54, No. 1, 2000.

Secretaría de Desarrollo Urbano y Medio Ambiente del Gobierno del Estado de Yucatán. "Ciricote." http://www.seduma.yucatan.gob.mx/flora/fichas-tecnicas/Ciricote.pdf

Seijo, Juan Carlos. *The Spiny Lobster Fishery of Punta Allen, Mexico*. Rome: Fisheries and Aquaculture Department, Food and Agriculture Organization, 1989.

Sharer, Robert J. *The Ancient Maya*. 6th edition. Stanford, Calif.: Stanford University Press, 2006.

Smith, Cristina. "Our Debt to the Logwood Tree: The History of *Hematoxylin.*" *Medical Laboratory Observer*, Vol. 38, No. 5, June 2006.

Smyth, Michael P., Christopher D. Dore, and Nicholas P. Dunning. "Interpreting Prehistoric Settlement Patterns: Lessons from the Maya Center of Sayil, Yucatán." *Journal of Field Archaeology*, Vol. 22, No. 3, 1995.

Sohn López-Forment, Isabel. "Changes in Diversity in the Process of Milpa Intensification in the Henequen Zone in Yucatán, Mexico." Paper presented at Latin American Studies Association meeting, Chicago, September 24–26, 1998.

Solares-Leal, Ileana, and Óscar Álvarez-Gil. *Socioeconomic Assessment of Punta Allen: A Tool for the Management of a Coastal Community. Sian Ka'an Biosphere Reserve.* Cancún, 2003.

Sosa-Cordero, E., M.L.A. Liceaga-Correa, and J. C. Seijo. "The Punta Allen Lobster Fishery: Current Status and Recent Trends." *Case Studies on Fisheries Self-Governance*. Rome: Food and Agriculture Organization. www.fao.org

Species Fact Sheets: Penaeus Duorarum. Rome: Fisheries and Aquaculture Department, Food and Agriculture Organization, 2011. www.fao.org

Steinberg, Michael K. "Neotropical Kitchen Gardens as a Potential Research Landscape for Conservation Biologists." *Conservation Biology*, Vol. 12, No. 5, 1998.

Stephens, John Lloyd. *Incidents of Travel in Yucatán.* New York: Harper and Brothers, 1843.

Strupp Green, Judith. "Feasting with Foam: Ceremonial Drinks of Cacao, Maize and Pataxte Cacao." *Pre-Columbian Foodways: Interdisciplinary Approaches to Food, Culture and Markets in Ancient Mesoamerica.* John Edward Staller and Michael Carrasco (eds.). New York: Springer Science+Business Media, 2010.

Sweetser, Wendy. *The Connoisseur's Guide to Fish and Seafood.* New York: Sterling Publishing, 2009.

Taube, Karl A. "The Maize Tamale in Classic Maya Diet, Epigraphy and Art." *American Antiquity*, Vol. 54, No. 1, 1989.

Terán, Silvia, and Christian Rasmussen. *Xocén: El pueblo en el centro del mundo.* Mérida: Universidad Autónoma de Yucatán, 2005.

Thompson, J. Eric S. *Maya History and Religion.* Norman: University of Oklahoma Press, 1970.

Todd, Frank S. *Natural History of the Waterfowl.* Temecula, Calif.: Ibis Publishing, 1997.

Tokarz, Jessica. "Red Snapper Family: Lutjanidae." Ponce Inlet, Fla.: Marine Science Center. www.marinesciencecenter.com

Toriz, Carlos Ángeles, and Ana María Román de Carlos. *La producción apícola en México.* Mexico City: Universidad Autónoma de México, Seminario de Historia de la Medicina Veterinaria y Zootecnia, 2005.

Trutter, Marion (ed.). *Un paseo gastronómico por España.* Königswinter, Germany: Tandem Verlag GmbH, 2004.

Turner, Jack. *Spice: The History of a Temptation.* New York: Alfred A. Knopf, 2005.

Uhl, Susheela Raghavan. *Handbook of Spices, Seasonings and Flavorings.* Boca Raton, Fla.: CRC Press, 2000.

Valadez Azúa, Raúl. "Los animales domésticos." *Arqueología Mexicana*, Vol. 6, No. 35, 1999.

———, Raúl García Chávez, Bernardo Rodríguez Galicia, and Luis Gamboa Cabezas. "La alimentación prehispánica." *Ciencia y Desarrollo*, Vol. 157, 2001.

Valamoti, Soultana-María, Delwen Samuel, Mustafa Bayram, and Elena Marinova. "Prehistoric Cereal Foods from Greece and Bulgaria: Investigation of Starch Microstructure in Experimental and Archaeological Charred Remains." *Vegetation History and Archaeobotany*, Vol. 17, Supplement 1, 2008.

"Venta de bebidas alcohólicas." *Ley de Salud del Estado de Yucatán.* Congreso del Estado de Yucatán, Oficalía Mayor, Unidad de Servicios Técnico-Legislativos, 2007.

Victoria Ojeda, Jorge. *Piratas en Yucatán.* Mérida: Editorial Área Maya, 2007.

von Winning, Jean Bassford. "Forgotten Bastions along the Spanish Main: Campeche." *The Americas*, Vol. 6, No. 4, 1950.

Voss, Gilbert L., and Manuel Solís Ramírez. "*Octopus maya*, a New Species from the Bay of Campeche, Mexico." *Bulletin of Marine Science*, Vol. 16, No. 3, 1966.

Werner, Michael S. *Concise Encyclopedia of Mexico.* Chicago: Fitzroy Dearborn, 2001.

Wilken, Gene C. "Food-Producing Systems Available to the Ancient Maya." *American Antiquity*, Vol. 36, No. 4, 1974.

Williams, Eduardo. "Salt Production and Trade in Ancient Mesoamerica." *Pre-Columbian Foodways: Interdisciplinary Approaches to Food, Culture and Markets in Ancient Mesoamerica*, John Edward Staller and Michael Carrasco (eds.). New York: Springer Science+Business Media, 2010.

Wilson, Samuel M., Harry B. Iceland, and Thomas R. Hester. "Preceramic Connections between Yucatan and the Caribbean." *Latin American Antiquity*, Vol. 9, No. 4, 1998.

Xool, Mercedes, Isela Chan, Teresa Sandoval, María Valentina Ucan Montes, Celsa María Koyoc Chin, and María Canul Koyoc. *Recetario gastronómico: Cocina indígena.* Maxcanú, Yucatán: Comisión Nacional para el Desarrollo de los Pueblos Indígenas, 2004.

Yamakake, Takeo Angel Kato. "Teorías sobre el origen del maíz." *Origen y diversificación del maíz: Una revisión analítica*, Takeo Angel Kato Yamakake et al. (eds.). Mexico City: UNAM, UACM, CP. SEMARNAT, CONABIO, 2009.

Zavala y Alonso, Manuel (ed.). "Las vaquerías de la Península de Yucatán." Mexico City: Artes e Historia México, 2011.

INDEX TO RECIPES

BY CATEGORY

GENERAL INDEX